THE LOGIC OF LOVE IN
THE CANTERBURY TALES

MANISH SHARMA

The Logic of Love in
The Canterbury Tales

UNIVERSITY OF TORONTO PRESS
Toronto Buffalo London

Library and Archives Canada Cataloguing in Publication

Title: The logic of love in the Canterbury tales / Manish Sharma.
Names: Sharma, Manish, 1973– author.
Description: Includes bibliographical references and index.
Identifiers: Canadiana (print) 20210346809 | Canadiana (ebook) 20210346914 |
    ISBN 9781487509033 (hardcover) | ISBN 9781487539566 (EPUB) |
    ISBN 9781487539559 (PDF)
Subjects: LCSH: Chaucer, Geoffrey, –1400. Canterbury tales. |
    LCSH: Chaucer, Geoffrey, –1400 – Criticism and interpretation. |
    LCSH: Love in literature. | LCSH: Logic, Medieval, in literature.
Classification: LCC PR1875.L6 S53 2022 | DDC 821/.1–dc23

We wish to acknowledge the land on which the University of Toronto Press
operates. This land is the traditional territory of the Wendat, the Anishnaabeg, the
Haudenosaunee, the Métis, and the Mississaugas of the Credit First Nation.

University of Toronto Press acknowledges the financial support of the Government
of Canada, the Canada Council for the Arts, and the Ontario Arts Council, an agency
of the Government of Ontario, for its publishing activities.

For my mother and my father

Contents

Acknowledgments

The completion of a scholarly project evokes with special force the profound debt owed to one's teachers. In this regard, I have been particularly fortunate to benefit from the intellectual generosity and inestimable erudition of Dorothy Ann Bray, who was my first teacher of medieval literature, and E. Ruth Harvey, who was my first teacher of Chaucer.

The English department at Concordia University has provided an extraordinarily rich and supportive milieu for all my research endeavours. This book bears the deep impress of the wisdom, guidance, and learning of so many of my cherished colleagues, including Alan Bourassa, Nathan Brown, Marcie Frank, Andre Furlani, Judith Herz, Kevin Pask, Cynthia Quarrie, Eyvind Ronqvist, and Stephen Yeager. Outside of my home department, Michael Van Dussen (McGill University) has been a sagacious and scintillating interlocutor about Chaucer, especially matters related to medieval philosophy and theology. I have learned much from my students as well, and I wish to acknowledge here my debt to two keen interpreters of Chaucer's works: Yanina Chukhovich and Lawrence ("Larry") Capelovitch (1931–2017). I am grateful also to my research assistant, Ghislaine Comeau, for her aid with compiling the bibliography.

It has been a privilege to work with the University of Toronto Press. I am indebted to Suzanne Rancourt for so patiently shepherding my manuscript through to publication. My superb anonymous readers have been at once exacting and charitable. This book is immeasurably better on account of their meticulous assessments of its earlier versions.

Portions of Chapter 1 appeared previously in two journal articles: "Hylomorphic Recursion and Non-Decisional Poetics in the *Canterbury Tales*," *The Chaucer Review* 52, no. 3 (2017): 253–73 and "Chaucer, Kant, and Continental Materialism," *Diacritics* 45, no. 2 (2017): 54–83. I thank

Cornell University and the Pennsylvania State University Press for their permission to use the material contained therein.

My brothers, Manoj, Mandeep, and Shahram, have been constant in their support throughout the rigours of the writing process. It seems most fitting that a book about love should have been composed between the birth of my first child, Aalok, and my second, Eider. It is on their account that I have come to understand what it means to have a final cause. My partner, Gillian Sze, a prolific poet and children's author, is the rock upon which our family is founded. If I have said anything true about love in this book it is because of the example she has set.

Finally, I dedicate this book to my mother, Katy Sharma, and to the memory of my father, Dr. Manmohan Chandra Sharma (1947–2009) – a small token of recognition for the boundless effusion of their grace.

THE LOGIC OF LOVE IN
THE CANTERBURY TALES

Introduction: Flesh and Word in the *General Prologue*

The central argument of this book is that Geoffrey Chaucer is a logician of love. I am therefore proposing a new way to conjoin Chaucer's sophisticated engagement with philosophical thought and his obvious focus on amatory concerns.[1] While this effort has been made before, what distinguishes my study is the claim that Chaucer in the *Canterbury Tales* draws inventively on the resources of late medieval logic to conceive of love as paradox.[2] Chaucer's logical treatment of love in his *magnum opus* has so far escaped scholarly notice but, as I aim to show, it is fundamental to any understanding of his most famous work.

I can begin to formulate my position by reading against the scholarly grain an enigmatic passage from *the General Prologue* that characterizes *The Canterbury Tales* as extended reportage:

> But first I pray yow, of youre curteisye,
> That ye n'arette it nat my vileynye,
> Thogh that I pleynly speke in this mateere,
> To telle yow hir wordes and hir cheere,
> Ne thogh I speke hir wordes proprely.
> For this ye knowen al so wel as I:
> Whoso shal telle a tale after a man,
> He moot reherce as ny as evere he kan
> Everich a word, if it be in his charge,
> Al speke he never so rudeliche and large,
> Or ellis he moot telle his tale untrewe,
> Or feyne thyng, or fynde wordes newe.
> He may nat spare, althogh he were his brother;
> He moot as wel seye o word as another.
> Crist spak hymself ful brode in hooly writ,

> And wel ye woot no vileynye is it.
> Eek Plato seith, whoso kan hym rede,
> The wordes moote be cosyn to the dede.   (1.725–42)

Chaucer's pilgrim avatar here explains his intention to relate with complete fidelity the words of his companions. No matter how offensively or freely his fellow pilgrims speak, he will tell their tales with scrupulous accuracy and, in this way, follow the example of God, the preeminent Christian authority, and the teachings of Plato, a preeminent secular authority.

Critical scrutiny of this passage has focused particular attention on the concluding couplet, ultimately derived from Plato's *Timaeus* (29b) by way of Boethius's *Consolation of Philosophy*, as revelatory of Chaucer's own philosophical commitments.[3] Indeed, we find in Chaucer's *Boece* (Book 3, *prosa* 12, 205–7) Lady Philosophy informing her pupil that "thow hast lernyd by the sentence of Plato that nedes the wordis moot be cosynes to thinges of whiche thei speken." Jeffrey Alan Hirshberg thus suggests that "Chaucer's aphorism, and the context in which it is placed, are intended to evoke the recognition that both Christ and Plato employed human language as a sign of supramundane truths. That is the task of the poet as rhetorician: to create by words which must necessarily refer to the corporeal world, images of a higher, indeed of an eternal, Truth."[4] Paul Beekman Taylor likewise reads the above passage as evidence that "Chaucer's view of language is that of a Christian Platonist and that he aspires towards a linguistic realism in which intent informs deeds through the ministry of words."[5] Marc M. Pelen makes a nearly identical claim: "The 'cosyn' comments on the ultimate function of poetry, which is to speak of the eternity (cousin) beyond literal language (deed) that Plato's myths address, and adapts that concept to the Christian doctrines of God's eternity beyond time."[6] Chaucer's poetry directs us, then, away from the unstable and worldly domain of material particularity and towards the eternal and divine form of truth.

The argument that Platonism influences *The Canterbury Tales* through Chaucer's acquaintance with Boethius remains compelling.[7] Boethius was an important conduit for the transmission of Plato's thought into the medieval west, and his *Consolation* draws from the Greek philosopher's dialogues throughout.[8] Let us consider first his use in Book 3 of Plato's *Timaeus*. In the *Timaeus*, the Demiurge, a divine artisan, impresses upon the shapeless matter of the maternal *chora* ("receptacle") the eternal exemplars to populate the universe with copies of those ideas or forms. The *Consolation* clearly echoes this metaphysical arrangement as the words of Lady Philosophy demonstrate:

> [T]how that duellest thiselve ay steadfast and stable, and yevest alle othere thynges to ben meved, ne foreyne causes necesseden the nevere to compoune werk of floterynge matere, but oonly the forme of sovereyn good iset within the withoute envye, that moevede the freely. Thow, that art althir-fayrest, berynge the faire world in thy thought, formedest this world to the lyknesse semblable of that faire world in thy thought. Thou drawest alle thing of thy sovereyn ensaumpler and comaundest that this world, parfytely ymakid, have frely and absolut his parfyt parties.
>
> (Book 3, *metrum* 9, 5–17)

In recognizing the allusion to the *Timaeus* in these verses, John Marenbon comments that Boethius, "whose project of translating Aristotle and Plato had not gone beyond Aristotle's logic, obviously wished, through the poetry, to fill the *Consolation* with reminders of the Platonic positions and arguments that underlie the Neoplatonic arguments of the prose sections."[9] Boethius, as did Augustine, Plotinus, and Philo of Alexandria before him, situates the Platonic forms within the mind of God as divine ideas that impose order upon indeterminate and "floterynge matere." The Legend of Philomela from the *Legend of Good Women* reveals Chaucer's willingness to consider exactly this Neoplatonic conception elsewhere in his writing. Though questioning the rationale behind the creation of the monstrous Tereus, the narrator addresses God as the "yevere of the forms, that hast wrought/ This fayre world and bar it in thy thought/Eternally er thow thy werk began" (2328–9).[10] The *Consolation*, however, mobilizes the Platonic notion of a transcendent and ideal cause in the service of furthering Boethius's therapeutic account of a cosmos that is rational, just, and providentially ordered.

Later, in Book 3 of the *Consolation*, a book devoted to explicating the rationality and goodness of creation, Boethius echoes Plato's description of the highest reality from his *Republic* (508e), according to which all forms participate in the supreme form of the Good, the ultimate object of philosophical knowledge. Lady Philosophy thus seeks to direct the suffering prisoner away from the counterfeit goods of the world, as does Socrates for his interlocutor in the *Gorgias* (464b–466a), and orient his desire towards the ultimate good that is the highest *telos*, end, or aim of creation:

> "So as men trowen," quod sche, "and that rightfully, that God governeth alle thinges by the keye of his goodnesse, and alle thise same thinges, as

I have taught the, hasten hem by naturel entencioun to come to good, there may no man douten that thei ne ben governed voluntariely, and that they ne converten hem of here owene wil to the wil of here ordeynour, as thei that ben accordynge and enclynynge to here governour and here king." (Book 3, *prosa* 12, 86–96)

It is striking, then, that in the passage from *the General Prologue* that references Plato and even alludes to Book 3, *prosa* 12 of the *Consolation*, Chaucer the poet should so explicitly "abdicate" his own role as the transcendent cause or "governour" of the *Canterbury Tales*. The pilgrim Chaucer is merely a fellow traveller, immanent to the narrative universe of the *Tales* and concerned only to transcribe the words of his peers conscientiously. But the deposition of transcendent authority means that this narrative universe lacks an ordering principle. Without a governing intention or, to use scholastic-Aristotelian terminology, a "final cause" to order the material and orient the reader, the meaning of the tale collection becomes, arguably, chaotically dispersed and contingent. In her discussion of authorial *intentio* and *causa finalis* in medieval literature, Rosemarie P. McGerr avers that "[f]or many medieval readers and writers, authorial intent came to be of great concern because it served as one of the prime arguments in the defense of secular literature against criticism by some Christian authorities. Even poetry, though suspect because of its connection with the fabulous or the mixing of false with true, found in this defense the possibility of redemption: writers such as Augustine, Macrobius, Bernard Silvestris, and Thomas Aquinas argued that poetry could function as a means of ethical teaching, a tool of moral philosophy."[11] And yet, Chaucer refuses to impose an authoritative *causa finalis* upon *The Canterbury Tales*, making it difficult to ascribe at this stage a self-evident ethical purpose to his work. If Chaucer will not govern or *authorize* his work, instead situating himself on the same narrative plane as his characters, how can he orient his readers to the Good? Accordingly, it may be more convincing to locate Chaucer's philosophical sympathies elsewhere than Neoplatonism, despite his citation of Plato by way of the *Consolation*.

It could be instead that the passage I have cited from *the General Prologue* manifests the influence of late medieval nominalism. This philosophical position was famously championed by thinkers such as the Oxford Franciscan William of Ockham and the Parisian cleric John Buridan, though the basic contours of nominalism were available even in late antiquity in Boethius's *Second Commentary on Porphyry's Isagoge*. Nominalism opposes itself to "realism."[12] The realist philosopher asserts the extramental existence of essences, forms, or "universals" that may be predicated of many particular things: Universals include humanity, horseness, and whiteness, for instance. We can subdivide realism into two basic categories: An extreme realist, such as Plato, claims that universals exist independently of the particular things that receive their impress; a moderate realist, as Aristotle was usually understood to be, claims that universals only exist within and by virtue of particular things. For the extreme realist, forms are ontologically primary. For the moderate realist, particular things as composites of form and matter have a certain ontological primacy – though Aristotle does understand God, the unmoved mover, as pure actuality, or form, without matter. The majority of scholastic thinkers from the thirteenth and fourteenth centuries, including Duns Scotus and Thomas Aquinas, were guided by what they understood as Aristotle's moderate realism, though notable extreme realists include the Englishmen Walter Burley and John Wyclif. Ockham's critique of realist ontology stems from his conviction that Aristotle has been misunderstood on the extramental existence of universals. Ockham insists that it is incoherent to posit that a single universal is in any way identical to many individuals: A substance cannot be both one and many. If the unique universal form "humanity" is in many humans, how could God destroy just one human without destroying the universal "humanity" and therefore all humans? Moreover, if we predicate "humanity" of both Adam and Bill but Adam is tall and slim and Bill is short and round, then the universal "humanity" simultaneously possesses the contradictory attributes of shortness and tallness, svelteness and rotundity. Realism, according to Ockham, forces us into maintaining such untenable positions.[13] For Ockham's nominalism, therefore, universals are merely acts of the mind that collocate a plurality of similar individual entities but possess no extramental existence whatsoever. As a remarkable consequence of this ontological parsimony, only singular things exist, untethered from any relation to a common exemplar.

Ockham's critique of realism undermines the Neoplatonic stance that God creates the world by means of the exemplary forms that exist within the divine intellect. Ockham views God's putative reliance on eternal and immutable forms, whether within his mind or without, as an unacceptable impingement upon divine freedom. In this regard, Armand Maurer states that "No theologian in the Middle Ages was more concerned than Ockham to uphold the autonomy and liberty of God against all philosophical threats to these divine prerogatives."[14] God does not require ideas to create: His generation of the world is a radically contingent act of his omnipotent will that depends upon nothing but himself. Consequently, individual entities exist without the transcendent guarantee of eternal forms. Late medieval nominalism thus placed limits on the capacity of the mortal intellect to access divine truth and decoupled the synthesis of faith and reason that was central to Aquinas's legacy. For Ockham, everything that is currently ordained, including moral laws, depends solely on the arbitrary will of God and, as long as no contradiction is generated, could become otherwise at any moment. In establishing this contingency, Ockham draws on the distinction between God's absolute power (*potentia absoluta*) and his arbitrarily self-limited and ordained power (*potentia ordinata*).[15] The contingency of creation for the voluntarist Ockham, correlatively, must detach the human will from any divine predetermination.[16] Chaucer's resignation of his authority in the *General Prologue* may, therefore, reflect the influence of nominalist theology, generating a narrative universe that is unmoored from any transcendent authorial security and thus open to the contingencies of readerly reception.

It would seem that we find ourselves in an interpretive deadlock. Chaucer abandons transcendent causality to descend into the textual world he has created, but he does so by adducing the transcendent causality of Platonism.[17] This deadlock evokes a persistent interpretive crux in Chaucerian scholarship, neatly articulated by Geoffrey W. Gust: Chaucer "appears at one instant to be extremely authoritative, self-assured, and even confrontational, while immediately thereafter he may be construed as submissive and subordinate to his characters and literary predecessors; he seems both confident in his abilities as an *auctor*, and resigned to the influence other authorities and narrative constructs have over him."[18] I will propose a new way to consider the oft-remarked instability of Chaucer's authority by returning to the function of Christ and Plato in lines 1.739–42.[19] The author of *The Canterbury Tales* invokes the towering authority of these two figures to legitimate the abdication of his own authority. He may relinquish his own authority by claiming to be a mere reporter, subordinate to his own fictive constructions, but he does so *authoritatively*. Emily Steiner's account of the nature of medieval authority is relevant here: "Medieval theories of authorship, found largely in academic glosses on canonical works, consistently identify authorship with authority, situating both in established traditions, with ultimate reference, at least in the case of biblical texts, to the supreme author, God."[20] What better way to authorize an authorial position than to bring to bear the supreme Christian and secular authorities? Chaucer, in other words, authorizes his lack of authority; he *authoritatively abdicates authority* over his textual creation. But does he then remain an authority?

A Chaucerian Insoluble

I wish to contend that what I understand as Chaucer's authoritative abdication of authority in the *General Prologue* generates a semantic paradox: By imposing his authority, Chaucer deposes it; by deposing his authority, he imposes it. This paradox exhibits a structure similar to paradoxes called *insolubilia* that fascinated and exercised medieval logicians, particularly in the late medieval period at Oxford. The most famous of these *insolubilia* is the Liar paradox, of which the basic form is the following: "This statement is false," where "This statement" refers to "This statement is false." If we analyse the truth values of this locution, it becomes apparent that, in violation of the principle of non-contradiction, its veracity entails its falsity, and its falsity entails its veracity. Truth and falsity, to use a term I will deploy frequently in this study, are somehow *entangled*. The Liar paradox is (not) true. It is the case for the Liar paradox and for Chaucer's authoritative abdication of authority that both generate "biconditional" but contradictory propositions of the form: A if and only if not-A (A ⇔ ~A). In the former case, "this statement is false" is true if and only if "this statement is false" is false. Likewise, in the latter case, Chaucer is an authority if and only if Chaucer has no authority.

The study of insolubles has a long history and the status of these paradoxical statements continues to be debated by contemporary philosophers and logicians.[21] In the Middle Ages, insolubles such as the Liar paradox were understood as a sub-category of *sophismata*, sentences that pose some challenge to ordinary understandings of grammar or logic. The source of medieval interest in insolubles in particular and *sophismata* in general remains obscure but could be linked to twelfth-century translations of Aristotle's *Organon*. Paul Vincent Spade and Stephen Read note that "the earliest known medieval statement of the Liar occurs in 1132, around the time the *Sophistical Refutations* first began to circulate in Western Europe in Latin translation."[22] Aristotle does ask in this text if "the same man can at the same time say what is both false and true" (180b2–4), but whether it was the *logica nova* that generated intense fascination in such paradoxes is impossible to conclude with any certainty. Prior to the fourteenth century, medieval approaches to resolving the Liar paradox invariably relied upon the semiotic theories of Aristotle and, especially, Augustine.[23] Augustine understands a sign as a thing that signifies some *other* thing. Self-reference, therefore, was deemed an aberrant mode of signification. In this early period, the principles of "cassation" and "restriction," were the most common means employed to resolve paradoxes of self-reference, including the

Liar paradox. Cassation, or "annulment," is simply the theory that in uttering an insoluble, a speaker says nothing whatsoever. The theory of restriction, by contrast, insists that "the part cannot supposit for the whole"; a term within a proposition cannot refer to the entire proposition, thus blocking the self-referentiality that generates the paradox in the case of the Liar. Closely related to *restrictio* is the use of the distinction *secundum quid et simpliciter* derived from Aristotle's approach to resolving fallacies in his *Sophistical Refutations*. In the self-referential case of "this statement is false," for instance, its "truth" is merely *secundum quid* and not *simpliciter*. The Liar paradox refers to itself as "false" and *truly* is indeed so. The insoluble is thus not true "absolutely" but only in a certain respect; the paradox is thereby resolved.[24]

The sophistication with which insolubles were treated advanced considerably in the early fourteenth century with the developments in logic associated with the *via moderna*, a product largely of the technical innovations of Ockham in the philosophy of language. Owing to the importance of *sophismata* as pedagogical instruments in the Arts curriculum of fourteenth-century universities, a great deal of energy was devoted to using these technical innovations to focus not only on logical puzzles but also on *obligationes* – games in which opponents attempted to trick each other into contradictions by accepting faulty, but seemingly reasonable, premises. Thomas Bradwardine's treatise on insolubles, titled *De insolubilibus*, published while he was Regent Master in Arts at Oxford in the early 1320s, was a signal development in the field. Francesco Bottino shows how Bradwardine and his fellow Mertonian calculators developed a "metalinguistic" strategy for dealing with *insolubilia* that distinguished between primary and secondary levels of signification instead of merely rejecting self-reference as illegitimate: "Above all, we find in this mode the distinction between a *significatio primario* or *principalis* and a secondary way of signifying."[25] In fact, Catarina Dutilh Novaes and Stephen Read regard Bradwardine's solution to the Liar paradox as a more nuanced version of Aristotle's "undeveloped hunch" regarding *secundum quid et simpliciter*.[26] The key to Bradwardine's innovative resolution of the Liar is the manner with which he "blocks" its truth and so interrupts its circularity. He does not agree with the *restringentes* and the *cassantes* that self-reference is simply impossible or meaningless. Bradwardine asserts first of all that a proposition signifies that a certain state of affairs is the case. He then invents a powerful closure principle: a proposition also signifies *everything* that follows from it. For Bradwardine, a proposition is true if and only if everything that it signifies is the case; it is false if it signifies anything other than what is the case. Propositions are either true or false – or "bivalent." In the case of the Liar paradox, Bradwardine establishes that it must signify *more* than just its falsity. If the Liar paradox only signified its falsity, we would remain trapped within a vicious circle of logical entailment (A ⇔ ~A). However, if "This statement is false" is indeed false, then it cannot signify *only* as is the case. Bradwardine demonstrates that the Liar paradox, whatever else it signifies, must also signify that it is true. The Liar paradox signifies primarily that it is false and, consequently, signifies secondarily that it is true. But such a conjunction is impossible. There must be something signified by the Liar paradox, therefore, that is not the case and so it fails Bradwardine's strict truth condition. Bradwardine thus concludes that the Liar is just false. In his words, "si aliqua propositio significet se non esse veram vel se esse falsam, ipsa significat se esse veram et est falsa."[27]

Bradwardine's approach to the Liar was highly influential and celebrated. Among the Mertonian calculators, perhaps only the solution proposed by William Heytesbury in his *Regulae solvendi sophismata*, composed around 1335, was as famous.[28] Later in the fourteenth century, another Mertonian logician and friend to Chaucer, Ralph Strode, praises Bradwardine in his own treatise on *insolubilia* as "the prince of modern philosophers of nature" and remarks that "He was the first one who discovered something worthwhile about insolubles."[29] Notably, Chaucer mentions the predestinarian Bradwardine in the *Nun's Priest's Tale* (7.3242) in the course of the Nun's Priest's précis of the clerical "disputisoun" (7.3238) around free will and divine prescience. The *Nun's Priest's Tale*, as I will show in Chapter 1, is a particularly clear example of Chaucer's idiosyncratic use of insoluble logic.[30] Of course, "philosophical" Strode, along with "moral" Gower, is also one of the dedicatees of *Troilus and Criseyde* (5.1857).[31]

Kathryn Lynch provides the most extended argument for the direct impact on Chaucer's poetry of the *insolubilia* literature produced by the Oxford logicians, focusing her argument mainly on *The Legend of Good Women*. Lynch finds in Chaucer's classical legendary a profound reflection on the unstable relationship between poetry and truth: "Just as the liar paradox offered the philosopher a chance to exercise his powers of thought upon a logical problem, so the narrative of impossibility permitted Chaucer to explore and display the anatomy of his art, to reveal and revel in the paradoxes of fiction that point toward truth but never arrive there." In the same way that the Liar paradox suspends us between truth and falsity, Chaucer asks us "to stand back, to think critically, and to recognize the betrayals of language that reside at the center of all story-telling and all truth-telling, indeed to understand how fiction and testament, a lie and the truth (like Tarquinius and Lucrece) inevitably testify against each other."[32] I am sympathetic to Lynch's claim that the *Legend* is an "extended exploration of an 'impossible,'" and I will argue that *The Canterbury Tales* may be characterized in much the same way.[33] I also agree with Lynch that Chaucer has no interest in resolving paradoxes but encourages us to linger in the state of undecidability that they engender. Where we differ first of all is in my claim that Chaucer does not merely borrow the Liar paradox to contemplate his art; he *invents* an insoluble: the authoritative abdication of authority. Secondly, whereas Lynch argues that in *The Legend of Good Women* the logic of the insoluble allows Chaucer to meditate on the relationship between fiction and truth, I will argue that the logic of the insoluble in *The Canterbury Tales* reveals exactly what Chaucer means by love.

Love and Judgment

The philosophers of the fourteenth-century approach the Liar paradox as an intriguing problem to be solved. As Ockham himself states in his *Summa Logicae*, insolubles are not so called "because they cannot be solved in any way, but because they are solved with difficulty."[34] Logicians confronted with the maddening undecidability of the Liar paradox, its entanglement of truth and falsehood, thus seek a way to block its self-referential circularity so as to decide upon it. For Chaucer, by contrast, the lover *does not decide* upon the undecidable. Love, in other words, entails the suspension of decision. To formulate this connection between logic and love, it is necessary to appeal to Christ's Sermon on the Mount, specifically Matthew 7:1–5:

> Judge not that ye be not judged, for with what measure ye mete, it shall be measured to you again, and with what judgment you judge, ye shall be judged. And how sayst thou to thy brother, Brother, let me draw out the mote which is in thy eye and behold a beam is in thy own eye? Thou hypocrite, cast out first the beam in thy own eye, and then shalt thou see to cast out the mote out of thy brother's eye.[35]

This scriptural passage, paraphrased by the Reeve in his prologue (1.3918–20), is in my view crucial to our understanding of the paradigm of love expressed by *The Canterbury Tales*. Accordingly, to say that the lover does not decide is also to say that that the lover does not judge. Chaucer reads Christ's admonition from the Sermon on the Mount as both an ethical and a logical prescription.

We find the most obvious example of this non-judgmental posture in the pilgrim Chaucer's own comportment towards his peers. As has long been noted, no matter how depraved appear his fellow pilgrims, the narrator in the *General Prologue* consistently avoids explicit criticism or censure, often praising those who least deserve it, usually for achievements of dubious merit. The Friar is a case in point: "Ther nas no man nowher so vertuous./He was the beste beggere in his hous" (1.251–2). In her foundational analysis of the *General Prologue*, Jill Mann observes of Chaucer's treatment of the pilgrims "that all these ambiguities, together with the 'omission of the victim' and the confusion of moral and emotional reactions, add up to Chaucer's *consistent removal of the possibility of moral judgement.*"[36] I agree with Mann's assessment of Chaucer's strategy in the presentation of his pilgrims. Chaucer inverts the usual function of the estate satire, which is moral castigation. I disagree, however, with Mann's account of Chaucer's purpose in removing avenues for moral judgment:

> To say that the ethic of the *General Prologue* is based on an ethic of this world is not to adopt the older critical position that Chaucer is unconcerned with morality. The adoption of this ethic at this particular point does not constitute a definitive attitude but a piece of observation – and the comic irony ensures that the reader does not identify with this ethic. Chaucer's inquiry is epistemological as well as moral. This is how the world operates, and as the world, it can operate no other way. The contrast with heavenly values is made at the end of the *Canterbury Tales*, as critics have noted, but it is made in such a way that it cannot affect the validity of the initial statement – the world can only operate by the world's values.[37]

Rather than merely observing the necessary values of this world and implicitly contrasting them to the values of the next, I propose that the narrator's non-judgmental comportment towards the pilgrims should be read not as ironic but instead as indicating his love for all of them. Chaucer is certainly not suggesting that we adopt the ethic of the world, but he is encouraging us to emulate his own attitude towards its denizens – one of love and forgiveness, devoid of censoriousness and judgment.

The lack of overt criticism in the *General Prologue* prompts J. Stephen Russell, for instance, to state that "The portraits of the pilgrims in the *General Prologue* thus require Chaucer's readers to make drastic decisions about them."[38] I think the opposite is the case: We should resist the urge to decide. It is no wonder, then, that Chaucer seems to suspend his pilgrims between formal types and particular individuals, between realist universality and nominalist singularity.[39] The pilgrims each embody an insoluble structure. I can provide a more specific example of this undecidability in the portrait of an individual who seems to be Chaucer's most corrupt pilgrim: the Pardoner. Perhaps the most discussed line of his description is the following: "I trowe he were a gelding or a mare" (1.691). I will have occasion to treat this line in more detail in Chapter 5. For now, it suffices to say that this description has long generated and continues to generate speculation as to how to delimit the Pardoner's gender and sexuality. In my view, however, line 1.691 tells us far more about the pilgrim Chaucer than it does about the Pardoner. We should note that the narrator refuses to decide between two mutually exclusive possibilities: neutered male or female. Unlike Bradwardine's approach to the Liar paradox, say, Chaucer makes no effort to block one of two contradictory interpretive avenues but permits both to exist in suspension. Chaucer the pilgrim will not decide upon – he will not judge – his most vicious companion on the way to Canterbury. He insists, therefore, on *loving*, not on *solving*, the Pardoner. This book will attempt to demonstrate that in order to further our understanding of *The Canterbury Tales*, we must develop a charitable hermeneutic consistent with this non-judgmental stance.

The Kenotic Analogue

To make more persuasive the pilgrim Chaucer's embodiment of non-judgmental charity, it is necessary to clarify further the association of paradox and love. Let us return, then, to the Chaucerian insoluble I locate in lines 1.725–42: Chaucer authoritatively abdicates his authority to descend into the textual universe he has authored and subordinate himself to his literary creations as a mere reporter of their speech. This insoluble construction entangles author and authored such that we cannot decide on Chaucer's authoritative transcendence of *The Canterbury Tales* or on his non-authoritative immanence within them. Thus, in contrast to E. Talbot Donaldson, I do not attempt to secure an ironic authorial presence "above" a fictive counterpart, implicitly postulating a moral ideal with which the pilgrims may or may not accord.[40] But neither do I disperse Chaucerian authority into polyvocality,[41] differential traces,[42] author functions,[43] or textual networks.[44] Chaucer's self-fictionalizing gesture, in my view, serves as an analogue of Christ's *kenosis*, or "self-emptying." St. Paul thus writes in Philippians 2:5–7, Christ "who being in the form of God, thought it not robbery to be equal with God: But emptied himself, taking the form of a servant, being made in the likeness of men, and in habit found as a man." Nicholas Watson locates in late medieval England a correlation between the empowerment of vernacular writers vis-à-vis the institutional authority of Latin and the increased attention to a particular model of kenotic theology: "In this model, developed most fully in vernacular texts, Christ is not veiled by the flesh, nor is his manifestation in the flesh the mere preliminary to his textualization in Scripture it sometimes is in Lollard thinking. Rather, the act of kenosis itself, Christ's extravagant gift of his divinity in humility and love, is seen as a revelation of God's essential nature, which is *more fully* understood through Christ's incarnation than by any other means."[45] I consider *The Canterbury Tales* to be participating, however idiosyncratically, in the nexus Watson identifies, along with texts such as William Langland's *Piers Plowman* and Julian of Norwich's *Revelation of Love*.[46] With his contemporaries in the late fourteenth century, Chaucer draws on the resources of the vernacular to contemplate the divine gift of charity via the incarnation.

As a consequence of his authoritative abdication of authority, therefore, Chaucer "incarnates" himself within *The Canterbury Tales* as a figure who is *at once* creator and created, author and authored. Flesh becomes word in an artful inversion of the Johannine gospel (1.14). Chaucer thus suspends himself between authorial transcendence and fictive immanence, an otherworldly and "elvyssh" (7.703) presence who is simultaneously within and without his narrative creation. In the Thopas-Melibee link, for instance, Chaucer says of *The Tale of Melibee* that it is a "murye tale I *write*," as if addressing the reader of the entire *Canterbury Tales*; in the next line, he asks his audience to "*herkneth* what that I shal *seye*/And lat me *tellen* al my tale" (7.964–5), as if delivering the tale extemporaneously to his fellow pilgrims. The first line of the *Retraction*, where Chaucer again seems to speak on his own behalf, echoes the *Melibee* in this regard: "Now preye I to hem alle that *herkne* this litel tretys or *rede* ..." (10.1081). By authoritatively abdicating his authority, Chaucer *entangles* authorial transcendence and fictive immanence, comprehending and imitating the incarnation of Christ, the most profound manifestation of divine charity, by means of the insoluble logic of love.

The metaphysics of the incarnation in the medieval period relied, either directly or indirectly, upon the orthodox position supplied by the Chalcedonian decree of 451 AD: Christ is *one* person with *two* natures, fully divine and fully human "without confusion, change, division or separation."[47] One important purpose of the Council of Chalcedon was to defend the orthodoxy against the heretical position of the Monophysites. The Chalcedonian Council occurred only twenty years after the Council of Ephesus, in which the heresy of Nestorianism was condemned. The Monophysites asserted that Christ had only one divine nature in one person. Inversely, the Nestorians claimed that Christ existed as two persons with two natures, divine and human. The positions espoused by the great range of Christological heresies in antiquity and the Middle Ages (Apollinarism, Arianism, Docetism, Miaphysitism, Monothelitism, etc.) testify to the ontological challenges spawned by maintaining the orthodox formulation of the incarnation. Thomas V. Morris summarizes the problem: "In the Judeo-Christian vision of reality, no beings could be more divergent from each other than God the creator of all and any kind of creature. And even granting the *Imago Dei*, the doctrine that human beings are created in the image of God, humanity and divinity can certainly seem to be so divergent as to render it metaphysically and even logically impossible for any single individual to be both human and divine, truly God and truly man."[48] Along with the trinity, the incarnation is a fundamental mystery of the Christian faith and Aquinas, a passionate advocate for the Chalcedonian orthodoxy and the humanity of Christ, makes clear that it is not wholly given to rational demonstration.[49] In his *Summa contra gentiles*, for instance, Aquinas suggests that the union of God and man in Christ is analogous to the union of soul and body, form and matter, insofar as the body is the instrument of the soul; but he admits that humans cannot perfectly explain exactly how this mysterious convergence operates in the hypostatic union.[50] Chaucer's emulation of Christ's incarnation by means of a paradox thus acknowledges its fundamentally inexplicable quality. The logic of the insoluble allows Chaucer to stage the mystery of the incarnation: the simultaneous divinity and humanity of Christ such that he both is and is not the supreme authority. Just as Christ assumes the "form of a servant" in his *kenosis*, Chaucer subordinates himself to his creations as their *amanuensis*. Understanding the pilgrim Chaucer's role in *The Canterbury Tales* as an imitation of Christ, moreover, not only gives me a way to account for his non-judgmental attitude in the *General Prologue* (not to mention his omniscience), it also permits me to read his humiliation in the Thopas-Melibee link as a passionate self-sacrifice on behalf of his most judgmental creation, the Prioress. Finally, this reading will allow me to interpret Chaucer's *Retraction* as a paradoxical response to the doctrine of the Last Judgment whereby Chaucer entangles without synthesis his role as judgmental Father, separating virtuous works from vain, and his role as non-judgmental Son, loving all of them.

Methodology and Scope

The Liar paradox entangles two mutually exclusive interpretive decisions: It is true if and only if it is false. The Chaucerian paradox I have identified also entangles two mutually exclusive interpretive decisions:

There is authority if and only if there is no authority. In the subsequent chapters of this book, I will demonstrate that the entire *Canterbury Tales* can be read according to the terms supplied by this insoluble. Simply put, judgmental characters will disentangle the Chaucerian insoluble and decide either *for* or *against* authority. Non-judgmental characters will emulate the pilgrim Chaucer and *refuse* to decide either for or against authority. If love is an insoluble, then the lover does not decide on love. It will become apparent in the course of my analysis, particularly in the cases of the Wife of Bath, the Pardoner, and Chaucer himself, that the readers of *The Canterbury Tales* are not exempted from this precept.

"Authority" in *The Canterbury Tales* comprehends, though not exclusively: order, universality, mastery, morality, spirituality, *sentence*, purity, philosophy, and masculinity. The absence of authority encompasses: chaos, particularity, freedom, carnality, literality, *solas*, impurity, poetry, and femininity. I will use concepts from Chaucer's Neoplatonic and scholastic inheritance to designate these two series. The term "form" will refer to elements from the authoritative series, and the term "matter" will refer to elements from the non-authoritative series. I regard form in its classical and medieval acceptations as the principle that gives definition and purpose to matter in its indeterminate potentiality.[51] Aristotle presents the case in gendered terms in Book 1 of his *Physics*, "what desires the form is matter, as the female desires the male and the ugly the beautiful."[52] Form provides to matter a final cause, just as authorial *intentio* provides a final cause to the matter of the literary work.[53] In *The Canterbury Tales*, if the formal term imposes itself upon the corresponding material term, we witness the *formalist* relation: Form is related to matter. As we have seen, this is the basic structure of medieval realism, whether moderate or extreme. Contrariwise, if the material term does not receive the ordering influence of the correlative formal term, we observe the *materialist* non-relation: Form is not related to matter. This, as we have also seen, is the basic structure of medieval nominalism. Finally, the philosophical meta-language I propose gives me a way to express compactly the undecidable logic of love in *The Canterbury Tales*: Form is (not) related to matter. Love, we could say, is a (non-)synthesis of formalism and materialism. Love entangles, but does not synthesize, form and matter.

My use of the concepts "form" and "matter" is not merely heuristic but grounded in an acknowledgment by medievalists that with the emergence of scholasticism these correlative terms were intimately linked to literary praxis. D. Vance Smith thus observes that "[i]n the thirteenth century, a highly abstract conception of literary form organized along numerical relationships started to yield to shaping by the four Aristotelian causes: the material cause (the plot, narrative, topic), the final cause (its purpose), the efficient cause (the author), and the formal cause. The formal cause is divided into two parts: the *forma tractatus* (*ordinatio*: chapters, prologue, and so forth), and the *forma tractandi*, its mode of proceeding (*modus procedendi*)."[54] Kellie Robertson likewise maintains that "[w]hat may appear to modern eyes as 'academic' natural philosophical debates about how to represent the world – what is the relation of matter to form? is matter prior to or simultaneous with form? – helped to produce the culturally specific relationships that existed between poets and their literary subject matter and, subsequently, between readers and the textual matter they encountered."[55] Chaucer conceives of authority, whether his own or that of his characters, as a *formative* principle in *The Canterbury Tales*, just as Boethius considers God in the *Consolation of Philosophy*. As the formative principle impresses itself upon formless matter, so authority impresses itself upon that which is otherwise unauthorized. Chaucer therefore imagines three possible interactions between form and matter: either 1) matter submits to form; 2) matter resists submission to form; or 3) it is undecidable whether matter submits to form. Chaucer's conception of love derives from the coincidence of three domains: *insolubilia*, Christology, and the philosophical antinomy of realism and nominalism. Scholars have drawn singly on these domains to contextualize *The Canterbury Tales* but have not yet considered the possibility of their mutual implication. I express this implicative structure as the (non-)relation of form and matter.

To elucidate further my approach to *The Canterbury Tales* it will help to contrast it with the approaches of other scholars who also have concerned themselves with Chaucer's contemplation of philosophy, theology, and love. I will begin with D. W. Robertson Jr.'s critical method from his *Preface to Chaucer*. Robertson's exegetical approach to medieval literature in general and Chaucer in particular, as is well known, relies upon the Augustinian distinction between charity and cupidity from the latter's *De doctrina Christiana*.[56] Augustine states therein: "By love I mean the impulse of one's mind to enjoy God on his own account and to enjoy oneself and one's neighbour on account of God; and by lust I mean the impulse of one's mind to enjoy oneself and one's neighbour and any corporeal thing not on account of God."[57] Simply put, charity aims at God while cupidity does not. The principle of charity subtends biblical exegesis, which must seek a spiritual meaning that is consonant with divine love when the literal meaning of Scripture appears to contradict it: "We must first explain the way to discover whether an expression is literal or figurative. Generally speaking, it is this: Anything in the divine discourse that cannot be related either to good morals or to the true faith should be taken as figurative. Good morals have to do with our love of God and our neighbour, the true faith with our understanding of God and our neighbour."[58] As Brian Stock explains Augustine's hermeneutic programme, "To understand a statement literally that is intended figuratively is to substitute flesh for spirit and to eliminate signification from the doctrine of signs. The result is a Pauline death or slavery of the soul, whereas reading spiritually is a 'liberation' (3.8.1–4)."[59] Instead of delighting in the lethal carnality of the letter, therefore, we must access the elevated enjoyment of spiritual truth that orients us towards God. But, in contrast to Robertsonian exegetics, the charitable hermeneutic that I propose does not decide between the letter and the spirit, the material and the immaterial. Love for Chaucer, as we will see, entangles material carnality and formal spirituality in a manner that is suggested by the immediate juxtaposition in the *General Prologue* of the instinctual bodily compulsions of birds during mating season and the spiritual longing of Christians "to goon on pilgrimages" (1.12). The Chaucerian lover, as my reading of *The Clerk's Tale* will indicate, suspends any decision between elevated spiritual enjoyment and carnal delectation. Chaucer does not oppose charity to cupidity; he opposes charity to *judgment*.

My reading of love as paradox has certain affinities with Mark Miller's analysis in his *Philosophical Chaucer: Love, Sex, and Agency in the* Canterbury Tales. Miller derives a non-psychoanalytical model of desire from an original reading of *The Consolation of Philosophy* and argues that Chaucer adopts this model in *The Canterbury Tales*. For Miller, the subject is always caught within a libidinal antinomy: The subject desires absolute autonomy from a restrictive embeddedness within socio-historical particularity; the very condition of its desire, however, just is this embeddedness. Miller describes the situation as follows:

> On the one hand, in wanting to follow "its own self," to heed the call of the reflective drive, the human desires its death as the particular one it is, for that existence seems like an impediment to its autonomy; and since it still desires and wills that existence, it feels marked as guilty, unworthy of freedom. On the other, in wanting to maintain the particularity of its attachments and the solidity of its sense of itself, the human desires the death of its autonomy, and in so doing embraces the unworthiness that marks it.[60]

The subject is thus caught between the drive towards "self-dissolution" and the desire for "abject particularity" – a situation that Miller describes as "constitutively masochistic."[61] Miller then demonstrates how this antinomy structures the discourse of the Knight, the Miller, the Wife of Bath, and the Clerk.

Miller's focus on the masochistic antinomy of desire certainly resonates with my focus on the undecidability of love. But I wish to insist on a sharp distinction here, one that also distinguishes my reading of *The Canterbury Tales* from psychoanalytical interpretations. Miller assumes that Chaucer's intention is to represent *subjects* with conflicted interiorities and complex desires, produced by the complex dialectic of agency and politico-historical emplacement. In H. Marshall Leicester's influential reading of *The Canterbury Tales*, comparably, the subject "is the continually shifting vector product of all the forces in play at the subject site, including unconscious desire, concealed or mystified material and social power, the structures of language, whose relation to consciousness is perhaps less clear, and of course consciousness itself."[62] But I would go so far as to say that Chaucer makes *no attempt* to represent subjectivity in *The Canterbury Tales*.[63] In place of a psychological reading, therefore, I am proposing a *logical* reading. What Chaucer is doing with *The Canterbury Tales* is narrativizing an insoluble structure and the chasms opened by its contradictions have provided a capacious space for interpretive activity. As I will attempt to show, scholars have perceived the vacillations of inconsistent subjectivity where there are, in fact, only the contradictions engendered by undecidability. The subject has functioned in Chaucerian criticism to suture incompatible determinations. I can state the case in Kantian terms: if the logic of love – form is (not) related to matter – is Chaucer's "(non-)synthetic *a priori*" then the subject is a "transcendental illusion."[64] The Wife of Bath's or the Pardoner's occasionally self-contradictory discourse, for instance, does not provide evidence of a sophisticated psychic economy, but expresses precisely the same logic as inheres in *The Physician's Tale* or *The Summoner's Tale*. The tendency to isolate individual tales or groups of tales is inevitably distortive, leading us often to "invent" a subject where there is only the logical structure of love. My analysis will therefore consider every tale in the sequence to bring to light the extraordinary logical consistency of the *Canterbury Tales*.

In its deployment of Lacanian psychoanalysis, Jessica Rosenfeld's *Ethics and Enjoyment in Late Medieval Poetry: Love after Aristotle* also supplies an instructive contrast to my reading of *The Canterbury Tales*. Rosenfeld examines the reception of Aristotelian ethics within medieval moral thought, noting that "Many late medieval poets recognized that what was most radical in Aristotle was not only that happiness is worth striving for on earth rather than being deferred to the afterlife, but also the corollary insistence on contingency as a component of love and happiness – what the Middle Ages refer to as fortune, and often personify and deify as Lady Fortuna."[65] Rosenfeld thus locates a telling intersection between the Lacanian conception of love as feminine *jouissance* and the Aristotelian notion of love as *philia*. She argues that both Lacan and Aristotle insist that it is the sheer contingency of love between finite beings that makes it valuable and ethical – a position at odds with Lady Philosophy's claim in *The Consolation of Philosophy* that the only proper object of love is a necessary and eternal being. In *The Book of the Duchess, Troilus and Criseyde*, and *The Franklin's Tale*, Rosenfeld finds that Chaucer represents earthly love in ways that underscore its exposure to chance, fortune, and contingency while according it the ethical dignity that is its due.

I will return to Rosenfeld's analysis in the course of reading *The Franklin's Tale*. For now, it suffices to say that I agree with Rosenfeld that Chaucer does not understand love as necessity, though he certainly draws on this idea for Theseus's speech from *The Knight's Tale* on the "Firste Moevere" and his "faire cheine of love" (1.2986–7). The source for this passage is the *Boece*, Book 2, *metrum* 8, 13–25:

> al this accordaunce [and] ordenaunce of thynges is bounde with love, that governeth erthe and see, and hath also comandement to the hevene. And yif this love slaked the bridelis, alle thynges that now loven hem togidres wolden make batayle contynuely, and striven to fordo the fassoun of this world, the which they now leden in accordable feith by fayre moevynges. This love halt togidres peples joyned with an holy boond, and knytteth sacrement of mariages of chaste loves; and love enditeth lawes to trewe felawes.

As opposed to a terrestrial love that is vulnerable to the contingent depredations of fortune, the bond of divine love knits together into a necessary unity all the elements of the cosmos. But the notion that love is a necessary bond guaranteed by a supreme phallic authority is exactly what Lacan terms "fantasy." Instead, for Lacan, the sexual relation does not exist: there can be no *necessary* relation between speaking beings – between subjects of the signifier.[66] I will argue in my first chapter via a reading of *The Nun's Priest's Tale* and *The Franklin's Tale* that Chaucerian love must be distinguished both from the Boethian position and the Lacanian position. Love for Chaucer is neither necessary relation nor contingent non-relation; love in *The Canterbury Tales*, accordingly, is best understood as (non-)relation. Lovers together constitute an insoluble: It is *undecidable* whether or not a necessary relation fuses them into union. Chaucerian lovers, as we will see, are entangled but not synthesized – neither decidedly one nor decidedly two. In Lacanian terms: "the sexual relation does (not) exist."

It remains to consider, in a necessarily preliminary fashion, how my reading of *The Canterbury Tales* resituates this text within the broader ambit of Ricardian literary production. I will focus particular attention on Langland's *Piers Plowman* and John Gower's *Confessio Amantis*, two poetic texts that also draw deeply on philosophical and theological resources to contemplate the nature of love. Nevertheless, the erudite Langland's relationship to academic learning is complicated, as exemplified, for instance, by Clergy's comment that Piers Plowman himself supersedes the learning of his seven sons, the liberal arts, by means of his knowledge of love:

> "For one Pieres the Ploughman hath inpugned us alle
> And sette all sciences at a soppe save love one,
> And no tixte ne taketh to meyntene his cause."   (B.13.124–6)

James Simpson remarks that "to call love itself a 'science' in this context is to insist that, paradoxically, the essential knowledge is not academic, but moral: the poem's narrative is being propelled beyond academic learning precisely by an academic figure, who expresses the proper humility of the learned before the biggest questions."[67] Indeed, in the C-text, the excessive and misdirected learning of friars is condemned by *Liberum Arbitrium* in a passage that explicitly mentions *insolubilia*:

> "And riht as hony is euel to defie,
> Riht so sothly sciences swelleth a mannes soule
> And doth hym to be deynous and deme that beth nat lered.
> '*Non plus sapere*,' saide the wyse, '*quam oportet sapere*,
> Laste synne of pruyde wexe.'
> Freres fele tymes to the folk ther they prechen
> Mouen motyues, mony tymes insolibles and falaes,
> That bothe lewed and lered of ere beleue douten.   (C.16.226–32)

The elite learning of the arrogant friars, devoted as it is to specious arguments and logical dilemmas, can only sow doubt instead of strengthening the faith. For David Aers, this passage points to "Langland's suspicion that the church now legitimizes a version of Christian theology in which the narratives and histories through which God is revealed are subordinated to modern forms of Aristotelian logic."[68] Here we witness a stark divergence between the characterization of love in *Piers Plowman* and what I regard as its expression *The Canterbury Tales*. Love for Chaucer just *is* an insoluble, while for Langland *insolubilia* are the province of the antichrist's agents – the opponents of charity.

In a recent monograph, Curtis Gruenler provides a compelling account of Langland's ambivalence towards the philosophical and theological innovations of the fourteenth century, especially the nominalist *via moderna* that was flourishing in the university milieu. Gruenler locates in *Piers Plowman* a "poetics of enigma" ultimately derived from Augustine's reading of St. Paul and 1 Corinthians 13:12: "We see now through a mirror in an enigma, then face to face." For Gruenler, "the enigmatic might best be defined as a style or practice of language that intensifies spiritual meaning by generating a metaphorical surplus while drawing attention to its inadequacy in the face of what it points to."[69] A "theology of participation," which has its roots in a Christianized Platonism, corresponds to and nourishes an enigmatic poetics insofar as it directs the self towards a loving knowledge of God that will never be complete during this life but is deepened and enriched by the sustained, playful, and communal contemplation of divine mysteries. According to Gruenler, Langland's enigmatic poetics is in tension with the logic and metaphysics emergent in the early fourteenth century, instead "preserving an old theological vision of participation that both new theology and strong assertions of church authority in his time were making harder to imagine."[70] We have already observed this tension between fourteenth-century university masters and their precursors in the logical innovations of the Mertonian calculators. Early fourteenth-century English thinkers, Ockham and Bradwardine chief among them, championed a highly technical approach to logic, theology, and metaphysics, and, for Gruenler, their reliance on "the language of disambiguation, exclusive categories, and logical demonstration contributed to dismantling the participatory imagination of human freedom and salvation that had been cultivated through other forms of writing."[71] Ockham, as we have seen, critiques the realist claim that universals exist in the mind of God so as to insist on the arbitrariness of his will and a resultant chasm between the natural and the supernatural. A participatory theology depends, by contrast, upon an enigmatic coincidence between immanence and transcendence.

Gruenler argues that Chaucer in the *House of Fame* and *The Canterbury Tales* secularizes the enigmatic mode and thus recovers "a poetics of enigma in the absence of a Christian Platonic vision of participation."[72] Hence, "Chaucer can be seen as more committed even than Dante or Langland to a sacramental understanding of art that finds the transcendent in the immanent, divinity in the particular. As in nominalism, focus shifts from the universal to the species, and risks disconnection, but it also retains at least the possibility of participation in the divine through the infinite mystery of human experience."[73] Norm Klassen goes even further, insisting on Chaucer's unequivocal embrace of an Augustinian participatory theology: "Chaucer's rhetorical handling of the pilgrimage motif ultimately reflects his theology of the Word. His own considerable theological performance amounts to a vivid interpretation of Augustine, for whom language and participation are inextricably bound together."[74] I wish to contest the assessment of *The Canterbury Tales* as operating in an "enigmatic" mode, whether secularized or theological. Chaucer, in my view, does not at all share Langland's disdain for the abstruse logical puzzles that so exercised fourteenth-century logicians, but instead relies upon insoluble logic as the primary structural principle of his text. However, there is an important distinction to be made here: Chaucer does not align with the concern of his philosophical contemporaries to *solve* the insoluble. Rather, the refusal to decide on the undecidable is for Chaucer the very essence of love, charity, and forgiveness. It is only by repudiating decision and judgment that we emulate Christ's loving comportment towards creation. Therefore, love does indeed permit an avenue towards participation in the divine, in contrast to the tendency of the fourteenth-century *moderni* to disconnect the natural from the supernatural. Perhaps, then, I can adjust Gruenler's terms and describe the literary mode of *The Canterbury Tales* as "non-enigmatic" participation. In place of the enigma, Chaucer substitutes the insoluble. In place of either Platonic correspondence or nominalist disconnection between immanence and transcendence, Chaucer substitutes *entanglement*. And while the interpretation of enigmas for Gruenler is infinite, open-ended, and playful, we will see in the *Retraction* that Chaucer renders it undecidable whether *The Canterbury Tales* are in fact interpretively open or interpretively closed.

Indeed, Chaucer's writings invariably have been understood by modern scholars as eschewing didactic and moral closure, and his open poetics has often been contrasted to that of his contemporary and acquaintance, John Gower – or "moral Gower" as Chaucer calls him in the dedication of *Troilus and Criseyde*. While I have no desire to insist on any stark opposition between Chaucer as ludic ironist and Gower as didactic moralist, I do wish to sketch here some significant points of diffraction between Gower's major vernacular achievement, the *Confessio Amantis*, and Chaucer's *Canterbury Tales* when both are regarded as sustained meditations on the nature of love.[75] My reading of these two poems will attempt to complicate Paul Strohm's influential claim that Chaucer and Gower "may be seen as offering us, at the level of form, a mediated version of the pervasive fourteenth-century social conflict between hierarchical and anti-hierarchical, 'vertical' and 'horizontal' conceptions of reality and of the state."[76] Let us begin with Gower's Prologue and the narrator's wistful recollection of a golden age, characterized by a socio-political harmony assured by stable governance:[77]

> The citees knewen no debat,
> The poeple stod in obeissance
> Under the reule of governance,
> And pes, which ryhtwisnesse keste,
> With charité tho stod in reste.　　　　　　　　　(Prologue 106–10)

The present age, by contrast, is riven by dissension and disorder, a consequence primarily of an absence of the ideal love that informed the golden age:

> But now men tellen natheles
> That love is fro the world departed,
> So stant the pes unevene parted.　　　　　　　　(Prologue 168–70)

Gower's tendency to correlate the macrocosm and the microcosm expresses itself in the disordered and troubled state of Amans, who is of course also suffering from the "departure" of love. In his complaint to Cupid and Venus, accordingly, he forlornly observes that he is farther from his beloved "Than erthe is fro the hevene above" (1.106). Amans here suggests that to attain his love is to bridge the gulf between the disorder of the world and the divine order of the heavens.

We would expect, then, that the lessons of Genius, the Priest of Venus, would serve to instruct Amans as to how to impose a rule upon himself so that his psychological state can mirror that of the harmonious golden age polity. Thus, Amans, when asking Genius about jealousy, utters the following request:

> Wherfore I wolde you beseche,
> That ye me wolde enforme and teche
> What maner thing it mihte be.　　　　　　　　　(5.449–51)

Simpson comments on this passage that "To 'enforme,' however, is not simply to teach, but to teach according to an ideal pattern, with the aim of forming the recipient of the teaching."[78] The recipient, in this case Amans, must learn to "formalize" his unruly desires by means of the governance of reason so that his psychological state may be inoculated against material disruption. Genius ultimately counsels Amans to abandon love unless "love and reson wole acorde" (8.2023).[79] The alternative is to become another Nero, described in Book 6 as completely lawless, rejecting any governance of his bestial appetites.

In its rationally formative operation, the instruction of Genius, himself a figure of the poet, is analogous to the creative activity of God, as evidenced by Genius's Aristotelian account in Book 7:

> Tofore the creacion
> Of eny worldes stacion,
> Of hevene, of erthe, or eke of helle,
> So as these olde bokes telle,
> As soun tofore the song is set
> And yit thei ben togedre knet,
> Riht so the hihe pourveance
> Tho hadde under his ordinance
> A gret substance, a gret matiere,
> Of which he wolde in his manere
> These othre thinges make and forme.
> For yit withouten eny forme
> Was that matiere universal,
> Which hihte ylem in special.   (7.203–16)

The *formative* activity of God as "ferste cause" (7.86) imposes a strict order upon the shapeless matter of the universe, and Book 7 of the *Confessio* details the organization of God's creation. Significantly, this organization subordinates the planetary aspect of Venus herself, whose constellation "Governeth alle the nacion/Of lovers, wher thei spiede or not" (7.774–5). Peter Nicholson remarks that Venus in Book 7 "is just one part, and not even the most important part, in a vast pattern of causes originating in the Creator."[80] But whereas God can subordinate Venus within the formal scheme of his providence, human beings, no matter how disciplined, are always subject to the exigencies of love. The narrator thus tells us in the Incipit to Book 1:

> And that is love, of which I mene
> To trete, as after schal be sene.
> In which ther can no man him reule,
> For loves lawe is out of reule,
> That of to moche or of to lite
> Wel nyh is every man to wyte,
> And natheles ther is no man

> In al this world so wys, that can
> Of love tempre the mesure,
> Bot as it falth in aventure.   (1.15–24)

But if human beings are incapable of regulating love, then the lengthy instruction of Amans by Genius is somewhat quixotic. Genius exhorts Amans to moderate desire with reason, but such an ordered state, the reader has been informed, is always susceptible to contingent disruptions. For this reason, the *Confessio* cannot end with Amans in a state of harmonious self-regulation, as existed in the mythical golden age. Instead, after receiving the teachings of Genius, Amans questions the instruction of his mentor: "Mi wo to you is bot a game,/That fielen noght of that I fiele" (8.2153–4). Amans goes on to say that for Genius "It is riht esi to comaunde" (8.2159), but for him to apply the lesson of rigorous self-discipline is an entirely different matter. The resolution to Amans' amatory distress, therefore, can occur only by *external*, supernatural means, through the ministrations of the very agents responsible for it. First Cupid removes the fiery dart of love from Amans, now "John Gower"; then Venus applies a healing ointment, after which she shows Gower in a mirror his aged, withered face, disqualifying him from the pursuit of love. The regulation of "the lawe of kynde" (8.3146) proceeds in Gower's case only because of the arbitrary debarment of Venus. This secular intercession anticipates the poet's final prayer that God through his grace supplant otherwise *incurable* "kyndely" love, "whiche no phisicien can hele" (8.3156), with the "charité" (8.3164) that orients the lover towards heaven.

The *Confessio Amantis* supplies us with a double perspective on love: On the one hand, *sub specie aeternitatis*, love is an element subordinated within God's providential regulation of the cosmos; on the other hand, for mortals, love is a force that can never be internally regulated. Love may submit to the authority of divine reason, but it rebels against the authority of human reason. Human existence in the *Confessio*, at least after a fantasmatic golden age, is thus inherently disordered, a situation that prompts Diane Watt to claim that Gower's poem "is not ethical, because, while it may warn against unreasonable conduct, it fails to give straightforward and coherent guidance about either how to govern or how to live one's life … While on many levels appearing to stand for truth and order, the poem partakes of the world's inevitable disorder."[81] J. Allan Mitchell accounts for this lack of "consistent guidance" by arguing that Gower supplies a "casuistic" morality founded on exemplarity and responsive to the unpredictability of the world: "The contingency of the ethical requires that for moral wisdom to be useful, it must adapt to changing circumstance ... the inexactitude of the ethics of exemplarity has a useful place insofar as it furnishes individuals with a flexible and adaptable means for deliberating upon and responding to the contingencies of circumstance."[82] Mitchell's justification of Gower's casuistic pragmatism only underscores the opposition in the *Confessio* of divine necessity and human contingency, and suggests the absence of any obvious way to bridge this metaphysical abyss.

Chaucer finds a radically different way to articulate order, disorder, and love in *The Canterbury Tales*. In *The Knight's Tale*, for instance, the Boethian "fair chain of love" does not straightforwardly subordinate the chaos and disorder represented by Venus. Instead, as I will show, Chaucer's disruption of chronology in the temple of Diana paradoxically entangles these two mutually exclusive conceptions of love. We cannot decide, consequently, whether love orders or disorders the narrative universe of *The Knight's Tale* and whether, relatedly, this universe is governed by *ad hoc* and amoral Saturnine pragmatism or a benevolent, providential design. Chaucer replaces the non-relation between heavenly order and earthly chaos that Gower institutes in the *Confessio Amantis* with a paradoxical (non-)relation. An analogous narrative situation holds in *The Franklin's Tale*, which is curiously suspended between the Boethian monotheism of Dorigen's prayer to God and the classicism of Aurelius's prayer to Apollo, an incongruity reinforced by the Franklin's own simultaneous abjuration and embrace of classical learning, whether rhetorical or astrological. Chaucer, as we will see, implies thereby that God manifests his love for humanity by at once imposing and deposing his own authority; *pace* Strohm, *The Canterbury Tales* describe a reality that is hierarchical and anti-hierarchical at the same time. Thus, *The Knight's Tale* and *The Franklin's Tale* both portray worlds at once authorized *and* unauthorized by God – simultaneously Christian and classical, simultaneously ordered and disordered. I can express this paradox otherwise: God strictly determines us to be absolutely free. Are we then subordinated to his authority or liberated from it? The paradigmatic instance of this insoluble logic may be found in the concluding stanza of *The Nun's Priest's Tale*: "Taketh the fruyt, and lat the chaff be stille" (7.3443). I argue in Chapter 1 that the Nun's Priest *frees* his fellow pilgrims to read his tale as they see fit; but he uses the *imperative* mood to do so. He commands his interpreters to be free. The Nun's Priest thus authoritatively abdicates his authority over his tale and his readers, in so doing escaping the binary of necessity and free will and emulating Christ's own non-judgmental love for creation.

Plan of the Book

I will begin my analysis of *The Canterbury Tales* with *The Nun's Priest's Tale* and *The Franklin's Tale*, as I regard these texts as particularly instructive expressions of Chaucerian undecidability. By treating the former as Chaucer's "Logic" and the latter as his "Ethics," I will refine the charitable hermeneutic that I believe adequate to the task of reading *The Canterbury Tales* without judgment. In subsequent chapters, I will read the remaining tales in order of fragment to demonstrate that each is structured according to the same insoluble logic. In Fragments 1–7, we will discover both judgmental and non-judgmental pilgrims. While the Knight, the Franklin, and the Nun's Priest are excellent examples of non-judgmental pilgrims, the Reeve is an excellent example of a judgmental pilgrim. We will also find that Chaucer's judgmental and *decisive* pilgrims narrate tales that implicate themselves, and thus simultaneously impose and depose their authority. For instance, *both* the libidinous, legalistic, and northern students, Aleyn and John, *and* Symkyn, the irascible, aged, bald, and sexually impotent miller, reflect the libidinous, legalistic, northern, irascible, aged, bald, and impotent Reeve within his tale. Oswald's humiliation of Robyn, achieved by the ignominious defeat of Symkyn, is also his own humiliation. The Reeve's authorial design paradoxically succeeds and fails at once. To paraphrase the Sermon on the Mount, to which the Reeve hypocritically alludes in his prologue, the judgmental are themselves judged by their own judgment. In Chapter 2, this is what I call Chaucer's "law of unintended consequences" and it expresses perfectly his logic of love: Authorial form does (not) relate to textual matter. In this way, therefore, even the judgmental pilgrims, the Prioress foremost among them, are aligned with the undecidability of love. Chaucer's law resembles Dante's *contrapasso*, whereby sin in the *Inferno* rebounds on the sinner.[83] But, instead of demonstrating the perfection of divine judgment and the self-destructiveness of sin, Chaucer's law of unintended consequences urges us to *avoid* judging any of his pilgrims so as to adopt a forgiving posture towards all of them. The inspiration Chaucer receives from Dante comes most profoundly not from the *Inferno* but from the *Paradiso*, as I will suggest in my reading of the *Retraction* in the final chapter.

Fragments 8–10 are organized according to a different scheme than Fragments 1–7. I argue in the final chapter of this book that Chaucer by means of the Second Nun, Canon's Yeoman, Manciple, and Parson contemplates his own literary authority. He therefore organizes the final movement of *The Canterbury Tales* using only four coordinates: Christian and secular; sentence and solace. The first term of each binary is "authoritative" and the second term is "non-authoritative." The hagiographical poetry of *The Second Nun's Tale* and its musical heroine represent "Christian solace" or "authorized poetry." In *The Canon's Yeoman's Prologue* and *Tale*, alchemical philosophy, that impenetrable and "slydynge science" (8.732), represents "secular sentence" or "unauthorized philosophy." The Manciple's chaotic tale and his erratic classical protagonist, the god of poetry, represent "secular solace" or "unauthorized poetry." Lastly, the orthodox Christian learning of the Parson, who eschews poetry and fabulation, represents "Christian sentence" or "authorized prose." In the final analysis, as my reading of the *Retraction* will suggest, it is impossible to judge whether Chaucer decides between Christian and secular, philosophy and poetry, poetry and prose, morality and pleasure. And it is in this way, paradoxically, that he identifies himself not as a Christian but instead as a lover of Christ.

1 Judge Not: The Nun's Priest on Logic, the Franklin on Love

I begin my analysis of *The Canterbury Tales* with *The Nun's Priest's Tale*, often regarded as Chaucer's *chef d'oeuvre*.[1] This is a tale that has received an intensive combination of critical acclaim and scholarly bafflement and, in a recent book-length analysis of the tale to which I will return below, Peter Travis wittily distils the prevailing sentiment: "since Chaucer's poem seems to have so brilliantly anticipated, parodied, and deconstructed the extrapolative importunities of our critical profession, sheer admiration might be our wisest option: dwarfling scholar had best retire and leave the field free and clear to Chaucer's gigantic genius."[2] Now "criticism," from the Greek verb *krinein*, just means the action of judgment or decision. I suggest, therefore, that literary criticism in its zeal to decide, in its zeal to judge, tends to obscure what Chaucer accomplishes with *The Nun's Priest's Tale*. My aim is not to submit this tale to further *critical* importunities but to reveal the interpretive consequences of reading it *uncritically*, or without decision. I will proceed by extracting a hitherto unremarked logic from *The Nun's Priest's Tale* and then deploying that logic to re-read *The Franklin's Tale*. What I will attempt to demonstrate is that once we have grasped the operation of this logic, we will be equipped to read *The Canterbury Tales* in a way that is "non-judgmental" and thus, in a Chaucerian sense, *loving*.

The Nun's Priest's Tale begins with an account of a perfectly ordered existence.[3] The widow in whose barnyard the action of the tale will take place is a model of self-regulation. She thus leads "a ful symple lyf" (7.2826), devoid of any superfluity or insalubrious luxury:

> No deyntee morsel passed thurgh hir throte;
> Hir diete was accordant to hir cote.
> Repleccioun ne made hire nevere sike;

> Attempreee diete was al hir phisik,
> And exercise, and hertes suffisaunce.   (7.2835–9)

The events of *The Nun's Priest's Tale*, however, lead us from the widow's carefully regulated and humble existence to the explosive anarchy of the narrative's conclusion. Chauntecleer's abduction by the fox and its consequences evoke comparisons to epic catastrophes, including the fall of Troy, the destruction of Carthage, and the burning of Rome by Nero (7.3355–73). The rooster's misadventure produces an explosion of activity that violently disrupts the bucolic tranquility of the barnyard:

> Ran Colle oure dogge, and Talbot and Gerland,
> And Malkyn, with a dystaf in hir hand;
> Ran cow and calf, and eek the verray hogges,
> So fered for the berkyng of the dogges
> And shoutyng of the men and wommen eeke
> They ronne so hem thoughte hir herte breeke.
> They yolleden as feendes doon in helle;
> The dokes cryden as 'men wolde hem quelle;
> The gees for feere flowen over the trees;
> Out of the hyve cam the swarm of bees.
> So hydous was the noyse – a, benedicitee! –
> Certes, he Jakke Straw and his meynee
> Ne made nevere shoutes half so shrille
> Whan that they wolden any Flemyng kille,
> As thilke day was maad upon the fox.
> Of bras they broghten bemes, and of box,
> Of horn, of boon, in whiche they blewe and powped,
> And therwithal they skriked and they howped.
> It semed as that hevene sholde falle.   (7.3383–401)

While the Nun's Priest first considers the upheavals of classical antiquity as appropriate *comparanda* for Chauntecleer's fate, he then shifts to near contemporaneity with the Peasants' Revolt and the indiscriminate slaughter of the Flemish. Finally, he aligns the cacophony generated by the fox's pursuers with the very end of the world, implicitly associating their horns with Gabriel's Last Trump.[4] Chauntecleer's kidnapping is thus akin to the abject collapse of all order. The judiciously measured life of the widow with which the tale began is dramatically inverted in this scene of utter chaos. Even the narrator has lost all sense of formal decorum. Despite the nod to Geoffrey of Vinsauf's *Poetria nova*, the Nun's Priest deploys an absurdly elevated register to describe a barnyard commonplace – a rhetorical *faux pas* that blatantly defies his "maister soverayn" (7.3347), exactly as the peasants revolting in 1381 blatantly defy theirs. The rhetorical disorder that the narrator exemplifies by means of his rejection of poetic decorum correlates to the bestial incomprehensibility of peasant "noyse" (7.3393). Instead of meaningful language, there is only meaningless shrieking and whooping: "And therwithal they skriked and howped" (7.3400). In each case, the principle of order, or form, no longer governs chaotic matter.

We careen in *The Nun's Priest's Tale* from order to chaos. The measured existence of the widow gives way to an explosive revolt against all measure. It is striking that literary criticism on the tale hews closely to these alternatives. There exists a well-attested scholarly consensus, referenced by Travis above, that the tale utterly subverts the function of the Aesopic beast fable by rendering it impossible to derive any particular moral whatsoever. Derek Pearsall, for instance, claims, "the fact that the tale has no point is the point of the tale."[5] Ann Astell likewise argues that the tale only "pretends to teach and thus precipitates learning – without, however, exercising any real control over what people learn. It panders to the audience, presenting a multitude of possible *sententiae*, expecting us to hear what we want to hear."[6] For Pearsall and Astell, therefore, the tale possesses no inherent order whatsoever. It is as chaotic as the barnyard calamity. Onno Oerlemans goes even further. Not only is it impossible for the reader to grasp the ultimate import of *The Nun's Priest's Tale*, the Nun's Priest himself has lost all control over his narrative: "the narrator is not supremely in control of the tale's complexity, or its delicious subversiveness; he has not carefully fractured or chipped away at the mirror, but has rather dropped and shattered it in his haste and anxiety, and is, perhaps, as amazed as anyone to see his tale in the end reflecting such a diversity of light."[7] In its chaotic openness, then, *The Nun's Priest's Tale* certainly delights, but it does not at all instruct. As Donaldson concludes, "The 'fruyt' of the tale is its chaff."[8]

But it is possible to insist on the opposite emphasis. According to exegetical critics of the Robertsonian school, we have but to read the tale as allegory to perceive its instructive univocality. Mortimer Donovan thus argues that "the key to the *moralite* is hidden in the identification of Chauntecleer as any holy man and Daun Russell as heretic and devil."[9] For Charles Dahlberg, similarly, "the cock-priest, whose duty it is to awaken himself and others, may be in a state of sloth where he is susceptible to the blandishments of the fox-friar and likely to lose his existence. Doctrinally speaking, a state like this amounts to the loss of free will and can be overcome only by awakening."[10] Once we have pierced the literal (or material) exterior of the poem, as do Donovan and Dahlberg, we access the spiritual (or formal) truth that is contained within. What initially appears equivocal then becomes univocal in the furtherance of Christian instruction. Now that medievalists have less confidence in such exegetical readings, however, scholars deploy other means to enclose the text's meaning. The new historicist critic could limit the significance of *The Nun's Priest's Tale* by arguing that the references to peasant quietism, in the shape of the widow, and peasant revolt, in the shape of Jack Straw, indicate that the tale should be understood as an attempt to contain the subversive import of the traumatic events of 1381.[11] Richard Fehrenbacher thus asserts of the Nun's Priest's reference to Romans 15:4 in the tale's closing lines that "Faced with the realization that literature cannot escape history, the narrator grafts on a conservative, culturally sanctioned mode of transcendent interpretation, through which both literature and history may be interpreted according to a Christian charity unsullied by temporal concerns."[12] But the responsible reader is not free to delight in the endless interpretive possibilities of *The Nun's Priest's Tale* and ignore its historical conditioning. Rather, the tale has a necessary relation to its sociopolitical circumstances, one that renders its signifying potential immanent to a specific discursive arena.

By contrast, Travis finds an ingenious way to synthesize the claims of historicism with the longstanding conviction that *The Nun's Priest's Tale* rejects any attempt to limit its meaning. For Travis, the absolute interpretive openness of the tale, a "disseminal text," is a consequence of its engagement with a *historically circumscribed* problematic:[13] "Unlike polysemy (favored by humanists in celebration of a text's plurality of meanings), in the disseminal text 'no series of semantic valences can any longer be closed or reassembled … The lack and the surplus can never be stabilized in the plenitude of a form.' Derrida's 'anti-idea' of dissemination provides surprisingly coherent depth to a central topos in the Middle Ages wherein language, especially poetic language, was seen as a form of problematic sexual emission." Travis thus historicizes the tale's disseminal quality: *The Nun's Priest's Tale* may be interpretively open, impossible to stabilize "in the plenitude of a *form*," but this openness is necessarily relative to a historically specific intellectual context.

I have sketched in broad strokes three different ways to consider the significance of *The Nun's Priest's Tale*. The tale's meaning is either necessarily immanent to a given politico-discursive conjuncture, or its meaning is freely open to the unpredictable vagaries of audience reception, or this interpretive openness is necessarily subordinate to the cultural and historical conditions of its production. What I want now to illustrate is that these literary critical approaches to *The Nun's Priest's Tale* just repeat its own reflection on necessity, freedom, and necessary freedom – or order, chaos, and ordered chaos. We must turn our attention, therefore, to the tale's notorious philosophical digression. In this passage, the narrator is so perturbed by the dire fate that awaits his rooster protagonist that he is moved to consider God's role in the conduct of worldly affairs:

> But I ne kan nat bulte it to the bren
> As kan the hooly doctour Augustyn,
> Or Boece, or the Bisshop Bradwardyn,
> Wheither that Goddes worthy forwityng
> Streyneth me nedely for to doon a thyng –
> "Nedely" clepe I symple necessitee –
> Or elles, if free choys be graunted me
> To do that same thyng, or do it noght,
> Though God forwoot it er that I was wroght;
> Or if his wityng streyneth never a deel
> But by necessitee condicioneel. (7.3240–50)

The Nun's Priest presents us here with some familiar alternatives. Either 1) God's foreknowledge of events predetermines all of our actions according to "symple necessitee" (7.3245) and all of our choices are governed by providential design. Or 2) our "free choys" (7.3246) is entirely unconstrained by divine prescience and final causality. Or 3) God does not have foreknowledge of our actions because he is outside of temporality, grasping all of time in an eternal present. This is the doctrine of "necessitee condicioneel" (7.3250) derived from Boethius's *Consolation of Philosophy*. As Lady Philosophy explains in Chaucer's translation of the *Consolation*: "But certes the futures that bytiden by fredom of arbitrie, God seth hem alle togidre presentz" (Book 5, *prosa* 6, 197–8). It is the case that we are free, because we are not predetermined, but this freedom remains relative to a providential order because God's superintendence is not eliminated. Human freedom, for Boethius, is a river rushing between the banks of divine order.[14]

According to the Nun's Priest's philosophical digression, therefore, human actions are either necessary, free, or necessarily free. The first alternative corresponds to the formalist relation: form or necessity dominates matter or freedom. The second alternative corresponds to the materialist non-relation: matter or freedom evades form or necessity. The third alternative synthesizes the formalist relation and the materialist non-relation: instead of strict predestination (absolute order) or wild anarchy (absolute freedom), there is ordered liberty (or relative freedom). I will call this synthesis a "meta-formalist" relation, by means of which the *relations*, formalism and materialism, are themselves treated as the *elements*, form and matter.

Let us now consider the relationship between the rarefied philosophical debate staged in the Nun's Priest's excursus and the narrative action of the humble barnyard. The narrator – disingenuously – asserts the irrelevance of his digression: "I wol nat han to do of swich mateere" (7.3251), he says of its esoteric content. But William H. Watts's claim that the Nun's Priest is "bewildered" by the divergent opinions on free will and predestination is belied by the carefully wrought thesis-antithesis-synthesis structure of the passage, however disguised by its asyndetic grammar.[15] What we encounter instead, as Grover C. Furr has observed, is a deliberate and precise parallelism between the metaphysical positions above and the positions taken up by the chickens below.[16] Chauntecleer is convinced that his terrifying dream is prophetic and that his fate is sealed, whatever his actions. He is thus implicitly a proponent of predestination – according to the parlance I have adopted, a formalist. The universe has no place for contingent events untethered to the divine plan. Pertelote, by contrast, has no truck with Chauntecleer's fatalism. She avers that Chauntecleer's disturbing vision is merely the product of a bodily imbalance that can be rectified by the appropriate pharmacological regimen. Pertelote is thus implicitly a proponent of free will, unconvinced that Chauntecleer's fate has been determined in advance: "Dredeth no dreem; I kan sey yow namoore" (7.2969). Even though her aim is to re-order Chauntecleer's humoral system, she is a materialist, rejecting the notion of transcendent causality. Just as form in the Western philosophical tradition tends to be gendered masculine and matter tends to be gendered feminine, so the rooster espouses the formalist position and the hen adopts the materialist position.

But now we come to the crux of the matter: Does the Nun's Priest himself privilege necessity over freedom, as would the predestinarian and the Boethian, or does he privilege freedom over necessity, as would the partisan of free will? On the one hand, Chauntecleer's dream indeed proves divinatory, supporting the formalist position. He does, after all, face calamity, as his dream foretold: The fox kidnaps Chauntecleer after lulling him into a false sense of security by flattering his considerable vanity. The Nun's Priest in fact bemoans the inexorability of fate after the kidnapping: "O destinee, that mayst nat been eschewed!" (7.3338). Surely, then, the Nun's Priest is a partisan of order and predestination. But, on the other hand, the Nun's Priest ratifies Pertelote's materialist

insistence that our actions are not constrained by a final cause by means
of an abbreviated citation of Saint Paul's Letter to the Romans 15:4:

> But ye that holden this tale a folye,
> As of a fox, or of a cok and hen,
> Taketh the moralite, goode men.
> For Seint Paul seith that al that writen is,
> To oure doctrine it is ywrite, ywis;
> Taketh the fruyt, and lat the chaf be stille.   (7.3438–43)

By taking Paul completely out of context, the narrator manages to abdicate any authority he may possess over the meaning of his tale. Paul
in his letter refers, after all, only to Scripture as a source of doctrine.
However, as Alastair Minnis states of the reception of Romans 15:4 in
the Middle Ages, "the 'all' came to mean 'almost anything,' writings of
all kinds … The onus is therefore placed on the discriminating reader."[17]
The Nun's Priest's deployment of Romans 15:4 thus *frees* us to read *The
Nun's Priest's Tale* as we see appropriate, our interpretive liberty unconstrained by an authorial imposition of morality and meaning. We can
take the doctrinal "fruit," without any indication by the Nun's Priest of
what that fruit may be. His Pauline interpretive pluralism entails the
rejection of an authorial cause. And if the reader can interpret the action
of the narrative without authoritative guidance, as do Chauntecleer and
the fox at the conclusion to the tale, it has no inherent order whatsoever.

It would be possible to conclude at this juncture that the Nun's Priest
should be understood as an unreliable narrator, oscillating confusedly
between the mutually exclusive alternatives of formalist necessity and
materialist freedom. But I will argue that his position is in fact rigorous and lucid, once we understand the logic that informs his address
to his audience. By citing Paul's claim that "al that writen is,/To oure
doctrine it is ywrite, ywis," the Nun's Priest no doubt encourages us
to read what has preceded this line freely, assigning his tale whatever
moral we deem appropriate. But our interpretive freedom then derives
from the Nun's Priest's imposition of the formidable authority of the
Pauline epistle and the patristic hermeneutic it implies.[18] Larry Scanlon
observes that these lines "do not offer an explicitly doctrinal moral –
some unitary formula to which the tale might be reduced." Rather,
"they simply invite the reader to submit the tale to the procedures of
Christian exegesis. The authority they offer is a mode of producing
authority."[19] I agree with this assessment but disagree with Scanlon that
the Nun's Priest's appropriation of Paul's authority without providing
a Christian moral "establishes the adequacy of the secular text" thereby

transferring legitimacy from ecclesiastical to secular authority.[20] I read this passage in the terms provided by the Nun's Priest's philosophical digression: contingency and necessity; human freedom and divine order. Thus, instead of limiting our interpretive freedom, the Nun's Priest's appropriation of Paul's fundamental authority unleashes it. The Nun's Priest *authoritatively* relinquishes authority over the meaning and morality of his tale, exactly the insoluble logic I located in lines 1.725–42 of the *General Prologue*.[21] As does the pilgrim Chaucer, the Nun's Priest imposes and deposes authorial order with one gesture, which makes him at once a formalist and a materialist. His tale is at once authorized and unauthorized.

Analogously, when the Nun's Priest invites us to "Taketh the fruyt, and lat the chaf be stille" what has he accomplished? With the verbs in the imperative mood, he has, in effect, *commanded* us to read his composition with total freedom. So, if we then proceed to interpret his narrative with untrammeled and unpredictable licence, has the Nun's Priest imposed his formal intention upon us or not? Are we, his readers, free or not? This is strictly undecidable. The Nun's Priest has *authoritatively* revoked his authority; we readers have *freely* abandoned our freedom. Instead of the formalist position (form is related to matter) or the materialist position (form is not related to matter) the Nun's Priest proposes an alternative that entangles these options: form is (not) related to matter.

When we reconsider the philosophical digression in light of this alternative, the logic of *The Nun's Priest's Tale* implies that it is undecidable whether God's formal authority determines the world (matter) or whether the world is free to go its own way. What holds for God also holds for the author's guiding intention: It is undecidable whether the author has imposed a final cause on the text (formalism) or whether the text is totally open to the unpredictable vicissitudes of audience reception (materialism). It is impossible to decide, in other words, between order and chaos. This means that the Nun's Priest's closural intention is simply to eliminate intentional closure. Formal closure, or authorial necessity, is simultaneously material openness, or readerly freedom. The text is authoritatively contained *because* it escapes all authoritative containment. The text escapes all authoritative containment *because* it is authoritatively contained. To impose order is to depose any order, and vice versa. The Nun's Priest, we could say, turns conditional necessity "inside out." For Boethius, necessity and freedom are synthesized – he gives us *both* order and freedom. There is freedom, but it is enclosed within the eternal present of God's vista. For Chaucer, by contrast, necessity and freedom are (non-)synthesized – he gives us *neither* order nor freedom in the same way the Liar paradox gives us neither truth nor falsity. The imposition of authorial form, instead of enclosing readerly freedom, *opens* an anarchic space of compossibility for infinite and unpredictable interpretive decisions and antagonisms into the future. Formalism and materialism, as I put it in my introduction, are entangled but not synthesized. This reading of *The Nun's Priest's Tale* allows me to put pressure on the current materialist consensus that "the resistance to form is at the heart of Chaucer's poetry."[22] Materialist readings of *The Canterbury Tales* are, in fact, too *decisive*.[23]

If we cannot decide whether the Nun's Priest is a formalist or a materialist, then we cannot decide if he is on the side of univocal truth or equivocal fiction. His tale is at once interpretively constrained by a serious moral cause *and* playfully free of any morality – open to the interpretive caprice of its audience. Chaucer, as I will now show, reflects upon this ambivalence by aligning the Nun's Priest with his avian hero. In *The Nun's Priest's Prologue*, the Nun's Priest responds to the Host's demands to "Telle us swich thyng as may oure hertes glade" (7.2811) and to "Looke that thyn herte be murie everemo" (7.2815) by promising to "be myrie" (7.2816). The Host in the epilogue to the tale validates the Nun's Priest's promise, calling his story a "murie tale" (7.3449). Harry then goes on to compare him at length to a brawny and hyper-potent "trede-foul" (7.3451), suggesting the affiliation of the narrator to his rooster protagonist. Now the narrator describes Chauntecleer's song on two occasions related by the use of the comparative adjective "murier." The first instance describes the accuracy of his time keeping:

> *His voys was murier than the murie orgon*
> On messe-dayes that in the chirche gon.
> Wel sikerer was his crowing in his logge
> Than is a clokke or an abbey orlogge.   (7.2851–4)

Chauntecleer's crowing, the Nun's Priest tells us, is more reliable than any clock or timepiece; this is on account of his instinctual attunement to the "ascension / Of the equynoxial in thilke toun" (7.2855–6). The second time Chauntecleer's singing is described as "murier" occurs as he regales his sunbathing sister-wives:

> Faire in the soon, to bathe hire myrily,
> Lith Pertelote, and alle hire sustres by,
> Agayn the sonne, and Chauntecleer so free
> *Soong murier than the mermayde in the see*

> (For Phisiologus seith sikerly
> How that they syngen wel and myrily).   (7.3267–71)

The Nun's Priest compares Chauntecleer's "murier" singing here to the sweet, treacherous, and feminine song of the sirens from the *Physiologus*, who sing "myrily." He then associates the sirens themselves with the irresistible object of Chauntecleer's lust, who bathes herself "myrily."[24] If Chauntecleer is indeed the Nun's Priest's representative in his tale, as suggested by the repetition of "murie" and the Host's jesting in the epilogue, should we then associate *The Nun's Priest's Tale* with the rooster's virile and truthful crowing or to his effeminate and seductive siren song?[25] If the former, the tale is formally truthful. If the latter, the tale is materially deceptive.

Exactly the same ambivalence, in fact, informs the Nun's Priest's own consideration of the truth of his tale, in a passage that occurs right after the narrator observes that a downturn in fortune awaits Chauntecleer:

> Now every wys man, lat him herkne me;
> This storie is also trewe, I undertake,
> As is the book of Launcelot de Lake,
> That wommen holde in ful greet reverence.   (7.3210–13)

Even as he asserts the truth of his story to a community of "wise men," the Nun's Priest associates his tale with feminized fiction – the kind of perilous fiction, moreover, that seduces Paolo and Francesca to adultery and damnation according to canto 5 of the *Inferno*.[26] But both the tale and the *Prose Lancelot* feature aristocratic males dangerously besotted with their lovers. Perhaps, then, these texts can serve a moral purpose, warning the wise man against the dangers of unregulated desire: "I am so ful of joye and solas, / That I diffye bothe sweven and dreem" (7.3170–1), exclaims the concupiscent rooster, recalling the inextinguishable ardour of Lancelot for his Queen. Does the tale then provide moral and instructive truth or is it just immoral and deceptive fiction?

Travis cites lines 7.3210–13, quoted above, as evidence that *The Nun's Priest's Tale* is an intellectual exercise for the reader, comparable to a scholastic *insolubilium* in its "self-referential parody instantiating a series of paradoxes and focusing especially on the thoughts of its own inscribed reader who is invited, indeed challenged, to rearticulate and refine his or her own understanding of the meanings of truth-in-fiction."[27] I read *The Nun's Priest's Tale*, and indeed *The Canterbury Tales*, *not* as an intellectual exercise that "affirmatively celebrates our critical ability to discover meanings in a text – even if the text itself is a congeries of resistant, logic-chopping, paradoxical, and disseminal signs."[28] Travis assumes that the insoluble structure of *The Nun's Priest's Tale* renders it interpretively *open* or "disseminal," thereby soliciting and refining our ability to criticize, or decide upon, the text. For Travis, the tale therefore draws on a major component of the fourteenth-century university Arts curriculum, which aimed to sharpen the logical abilities of students by training them in the analysis of *sophismata*. My position, by contrast, is that the insoluble structure of the tale renders it undecidable whether it is interpretively open *or* interpretively closed – authorized or unauthorized. Instead of soliciting and refining our *critical* abilities, as if we were Oxford undergraduates enrolled in the Faculty of Arts, the Nun's Priest urges us to become *uncritical* readers.

In the passage Travis considers, the Nun's Priest dramatically mobilizes his formal authority, demanding the attention and recognition of every wise *man*: "lat *hym* herkne me." But he assumes this magisterial and commanding stance only in order to undercut it, equating his tale to a seductive and dangerous fiction reverenced by *women*. The Nun's Priest once again authoritatively surrenders his authority. Likewise, his assertion that his story is "also trewe" as the *Lancelot* simultaneously affirms and denies the tale's veracity. *The Nun's Priest's Tale* is true, yes, but it is true only insofar as it is fictive. Truth and fiction are thereby entangled without synthesis. Exactly as is the case with the merry crowing of Chauntecleer, we cannot decide whether the Nun's Priest is an authoritative guide or an unreliable fraud. *The Nun's Priest's Tale* could provide moral instruction, but it could also be a dangerous siren song – one that, like the fox's treacherous words to the vain rooster, holds up a *speculum stultorum* to its audience. Are we, like Chauntecleer, being deceived by a story about talking chickens?[29] To cite the alternatives presented in the concluding stanza, the tale could provide instructive and masculine "moralite" (formalism), or it could provide only deceptive and feminine "folye" (materialism). These alternatives are ineluctably entangled in *The Nun's Priest's Tale* and, as we will see, in *The Canterbury Tales*.

I believe my reading of *The Nun's Priest's Tale* accounts for the ambivalence with which Chaucer represents the philosophical positions of both chickens. Let us begin with Chauntecleer. The rooster's explicitly formalist discourse is implicitly *materialist*. First of all, even though Chauntecleer is arguing on the side of predestined order, his speech on dreams is thoroughly disordered. As opposed to Pertelote's relatively cogent presentation of her case, Chauntecleer rambles on for 200 lines and midway proffers an emphatically irrelevant summation of his argument, suggesting that he has completely lost the thread of his long-winded discourse: "Mordre wol out, this my conclusioun" (7.3057). Second, many of the examples Chauntecleer provides can also support his intellectual adversary's position. Both Croesus (7.3138–40) and Hector (7.3141–8) have prophetic dreams, true, but both also ignore the admonitions of their wives and come to grief as a result. Third, it is entirely possible that Chauntecleer's apparently rational conviction that dreams are prophetic merely disguises an irrational aversion to taking his medicine:

> Shortly I seye, as for conclusioun,
> That I shal han of this avisioun
> Adversitee; and I seye forthermoor
> That I ne telle of laxatyves no stoor,
> For they been venymes, I woot it weel;
> I hem diffye, I love hem never a deel! (7.3151–6)

This latter interpretation of Chauntecleer's argument is rendered more compelling by the fact that he completely ignores the "sentence" (form) of his dream, acting instead to satisfy with Pertelote his carnal (material) urges. Chauntecleer's entire speech, therefore, has been a bombastic exercise in *pointless* erudition. An argument on behalf of a final cause is itself absolutely lacking a final cause.[30]

The ambivalence that characterizes Chauntecleer's discourse mirrors the ambivalence with which the Nun's Priest himself regards Pertelote's counsel. I will thus consider both the narrator's and Chauntecleer's antifeminism, which apparently serves in the tale to undermine Pertelote's position. Antifeminism, we should first observe, is a species of formalism: it demands the strict control of feminine disorder and is appalled by the dangers of unrestricted feminine chaos. In terms of its logic, therefore, antifeminism corresponds exactly to the doctrine of predestination, which rejects the inherence of undisciplined and "feminine" contingency or disorder (matter) in the cosmos. Now, in order to seduce his wife, Chauntecleer, an advocate of predestination, cites some stock antifeminist dogma that, predictably, aligns woman with disorder (*confusio*):

> "For al so siker as *In principio,*
> *Mulier est hominis confusio –*
> Madame, the sentence of this Latyn is,
> 'Womman is mannes joye and al his blis.'" (7.3163–6)

Sheila Delany observes the ambiguity that arises on account of Chauntecleer's mistranslation: "In Chauntecleer's mistranslation we may see either ignorance masquerading as erudition, or deliberate condescension intended to placate a mistaken but beloved spouse."[31] It may be the case that Chauntecleer is attempting to placate or flatter his wife, but an imperfect grasp of Latin impedes his objective. He does not know, according to this reading, that he has flagrantly mistranslated the antifeminist passage and is really insulting Pertelote.[32] It may also be the case, alternatively, that he is further undermining her medical advice by means of a dismissive, if veiled, appeal to antifeminism.[33] But I wish to propose another reading of this passage, one that brings it into line with my analysis of the rest of *The Nun's Priest's Tale*. Let us say the rooster does have expertise in Latin, as the broad scope of his reading strongly implies. By mistranslating *Mulier est hominis confusio*, he *deceptively* camouflages the antifeminist claim that men *cannot trust* women. Chauntecleer deceptively associates women with deception. He thus associates himself with the "feminine" position *and* the antifeminist position simultaneously. It is impossible to say for certain, accordingly, whether he is an antifeminist. I will now demonstrate that the ambivalence of Chauntecleer's misogyny aligns him even more closely with the narrator himself.

On the one hand, the Nun's Priest's misogyny seems clear, and he, like Chauntecleer, parrots some perfectly conventional antifeminist accusations:

> Wommennes conseils been ful ofte colde;
> Wommennes conseil broghte us first to wo
> And made Adam fro Paradys to go
> There as he was ful myrie and wel at ese.   (7.3256–9)

These lines appear decisively to identify the narrator's position regarding women. How could we possibly trust Pertelote's materialist argument about the vanity of dreams when the Nun's Priest himself, the author of the tale within which she features, is unambiguously telling us that women are not to be trusted? The Nun's Priest's apparent misogyny *ratifies*, surely, Chauntecleer's formalist position. But, on the other hand, the Nun's Priest issues a retraction of his hackneyed antifeminism:

> But for I noot to whom it myght displease,
> If I conseil of wommen wolde blame,
> Passe over, for I seyde it in my game.
> Rede auctors, where they trete of swich mateere,

> And what they seyn of wommen ye may heere.
> Thise been the cokkes words, and nat myne;
> I kan noon harm of no womman divyne.   (7.3260–6)

This passage injects some uncertainty into our understanding of the Nun's Priest's position with regard to Pertelote. Is his misogyny really to be dismissed as mere "game"? Or is his antifeminism actually a sincerely held position that he is just "retracting" to avoid giving offense to certain members of his audience, including his superior, the Prioress? The final line of the passage only intensifies the uncertainties in this passage, as Muscatine has shown.[34] The "delicious ambiguity" of line 7.3266 makes it impossible to know for certain whether women are in fact "divine" and thus insulated from any antifeminist criticism.

But the key to understanding the Nun's Priest's position on antifeminism occurs earlier in this section of the tale. We should note that the narrator patently misrepresents the conclusion to the debate between the chickens to blame Pertelote for the fate that awaits her husband. Chauntecleer, the Nun's Priest tells us, "tok his conseil of his wyf, with sorwe,/To walken in the yerd upon that morwe" (7.3253–4). But Chauntecleer does nothing of the sort; this is the opposite of what actually happens. He totally ignores his wife's counsel and follows instead his sexual urges. The Nun's Priest is stating: "Women's counsel cannot be trusted." But he has made it very clear that his own counsel is not to be trusted. He is thus confuting the veracity of women but only by "feminizing" himself. Like Chauntecleer, he deceptively asserts female deceptiveness – this is, in other words, a materialist rejection of materialism. Just as it is undecidable whether or not the Nun's Priest is an antifeminist, it is undecidable whether or not he is ratifying or invalidating Pertelote's materialist position on dreams. I can now elucidate the extraordinary logical consistency of *The Nun's Priest's Tale*: 1) we cannot decide whether the narrator is a formalist or a materialist; 2) we cannot decide whether Chauntecleer is a formalist or a materialist; thus 3) we cannot decide whether they misogynistically dismiss Pertelote's "feminine" materialism.

Following the lead of the Nun's Priest, I want now to digress somewhat to consider some of the philosophical implications of my reading of his tale.[35] I believe this tale supplies us with a powerful logic, one that has priority over the late medieval alternatives of realism (universal form is related to material particular) and nominalism (universal form is not related to material particular). Furr states that "Chaucer's indeterminate position on this philosophic dispute is mirrored in the fact that neither Pertelote, Chauntecleer, nor the Nun's Priest are shown to explain Chauntecleer's dream in a satisfactory manner."[36] What I have tried to show is that Chaucer's position, at least in *The Nun's Priest's Tale*, is perfectly determinate – so determinate, in fact, that I can write it here: form is (not) related to matter. Realism and nominalism are *decisions*; the Nun's Priest entangles these philosophical alternatives without deciding between them. What, then, would be the Nun's Priest's position on the related debate between determinism, advocated by Augustine and Bradwardine, and free will, advocated by Ockham and his Dominican disciple Robert Holcot?[37] Does God necessitate our actions, or are we entirely free to conduct ourselves as we will? Neither: God deterministically predestines us to be non-deterministically free. This is exactly what the Nun's Priest achieves when he directs us to "Take the fruit and leave the chaff." The author *commands* our absolute *liberty*. Likewise, the universe of *The Nun's Priest's Tale* possesses an insoluble structure: It is at the same time ordered and chaotic, authorized and unauthorized.

An equally striking consequence of the Nun's Priest's logic is that it allows us to revisit some of the foundational assumptions of modern literary criticism. Let us begin with Foucauldian archaeology and Derridean deconstruction, two philosophical methodologies that have had a significant impact on the way we analyse literary texts today. Michel Foucault, a formalist like Chauntecleer, is a rigorous thinker of final causality. The only distinction is that, for Foucault, final causality is historically contingent rather than divinely necessary. An *a priori* episteme (form) is thus the organizing principle for the discursive practices (matter) of a given epoch. Derrida, a materialist like Pertelote, is, as indicated above, a rigorous thinker of freedom. Whether spoken or written, linguistic signs (matter) are infinitely and unpredictably repeatable and thus can always break free from the wholly *contingent* imposition of meaning (form), by author, reader, or cultural situation.[38] Derrida is a brilliant and voluminous writer, but his basic insight is readily apprehensible: a text, like the "bad woman" of Western misogyny, has no final cause. Whether philosophical or literary, a text cannot come to rest in the *presence* and *purity* of formal necessity – it is aimless, oriented neither by *arche* or *telos*. Foucault crushes the text into its historicity, rendering it immanent to a determinate epistemic arrangement.[39] Derrida liberates the text from any contextual enclosure, precipitating it into unforeseeable futures. Foucault decides unilaterally on formal closure, Derrida decides unilaterally on material openness. But Chaucer refuses to decide: *The Nun's Priest's Tale* is radically closed to the future *because* it is absolutely open to the future; *The Nun's Priest's Tale* is absolutely open to the future *because* it is radically closed to the future.

Chaucerian undecidability is also more radical than G.W.F. Hegel's dialectic, though it emerges centuries before the culmination of spirit's itinerary. With regard to the becoming of Hegel's absolute idea, the *material* contingency of thought both is and is not the *formal* necessity of being. This means that matter is the negation of form: Necessity is related to contingency but related to contingency as its dialectical contradiction. As Hegel puts it in the Doctrine of Essence from his *Science of Logic*: "It is necessity itself, therefore, that determines itself as *contingency*: in its being it repels itself from itself, in this very repelling has only returned to itself, and in this turning back which is its being has repelled itself from itself."[40] On account of this negative relation, formal necessity is contingent (materialism) *and* material contingency is necessary (formalism). Hegel thus synthesizes necessity and freedom in "the speculative identity of identity and non-identity."[41] Hegel, like Boethius, synthesizes formalism and materialism by means of a meta-formalist decision. But Chaucerian logic, in contrast to Hegelian self-relating negation, is the refusal of a unilateral decision for *either* formalism or materialism: (non-)relation rather than negative relation. Again, formalism and materialism are entangled but not synthesized.

For philosophers, either order is absolute and chaos is relative (formalism) or chaos is absolute and order is relative (materialism). But, for Chaucer in *The Nun's Priest's Tale*, chaos is absolute *because* order is absolute; order is absolute *because* chaos is absolute. Strictly speaking, therefore, the deceptively simple Chaucerian principle – form is (not) related to matter – is not a philosophical thesis; but neither is it a poetics. According to Plato's *Republic* (10.604e–605e), philosophy regulates the mind by orienting thought towards the eternal truth of forms, while the aimless fabrications of poetry depose reason and generate psychic disorder. Thus, Lady Philosophy, with a gesture that echoes Book 10 of the *Republic*, curtly dismisses the classical Muses from the presence of Boethius early in the *Consolation*: "But ye withdrawen me this man, that hath ben noryssed in the studies or scoles of Eleatics and Achademycis in Grece. But goth now rather awey, ye mermaydenes, whiche that ben swete til it be at the laste, and suffreth this man to ben cured and heeled by myne muses (that is to seyn, by noteful sciences)" (Book 1, *prosa* 1, 66–73).[42] The import of the beguiling mermaids is the same for both the Nun's Priest and Boethius, associated as they are with the deceptions of feminine pleasure. But to align Chaucer with aimless and seductive poetry *or* truthful and restorative philosophy is to make a decision. Plato, therefore, could neither welcome Chaucer within the light of his republic of order nor could he expel him into the outer darkness of chaos. I will return to this claim in my final chapter, in which I will argue that Chaucer insolubly entangles purposeless solace and purposeful sentence.

My reading of *The Nun's Priest's Tale* suggests that it may be undecidable whether *The Canterbury Tales* themselves have an authorial final cause. If, for Chaucer, the imposition of authority is simultaneously the deposition of authority and vice versa, then we can never complacently decide that we have mastered this text, even if that is to decide that it eludes all mastery. I will go further still: By the time we reach Chaucer's *Retraction*, it will be impossible even to decide whether or not *The Canterbury Tales* are undecidable, lest undecidability itself collapse into a decision. These implications all follow rigorously from the logical principle that I have derived from *The Nun's Priest's Tale* and that I will deploy to read all the tales – form is (not) related to matter.

But, as my introduction anticipated, Chaucer is no mere logician, inviting us to ponder *insolubilia* for their own sake. Undecidability has a powerfully ethical valence in *The Canterbury Tales*. I turn now to Fragment 5 to demonstrate that, for Chaucer, it is only when we refuse to judge, only when we refuse to decide, that we love.

Fragment 5: The Squire and The Franklin

I will now attempt to demonstrate that the undecidable logic of *The Nun's Priest's Tale* is the key to the ethical problematic inscribed in *The Franklin's Tale*. The concern with ethics in Fragment 5 is made evident in its opening lines: The fragment begins with the Host requesting that the Squire "sey somewhat of love" (5.2). But the Squire's grandiose narrative most resembles the compassionate Canacee's elaborate preparations to catch the swooning falcon, who is wounding herself out of frenzied grief:

> And wel neigh for the routhe almost she deyde.
> And to the tree she gooth hastily,
> And on this faucon looketh pitously,
> And heeld hir lappe abroad, for wel she wiste
> The faukon moste fallen fro the twiste,
> Whan that it swowned next, for lak of blood.
> A longe whil to wayten hire she stood.   (5.438–44)

Canacee, wearing a magical ring that allows her to understand the language of birds, then addresses the falcon directly. She inquires after the cause of the bird's distress, promising to heal her wounds and amend her sorrow if she can. The result is incongruously comical:

> Tho shrighte this faucon yet moore pitously
> Than evere she dide, and fil to the grounde anon,
> And lith aswowne, deed and lyk a stoon,
> Til Canacee hath in hire lappe hire take
> Unto the tyme she gan of swough awake.　　　　　　　(5.472–6)

Despite Canacee's intention, and the amount of time she has to prepare, the grieving falcon tumbles off the tree and misses her lap, hitting the ground instead. Chaucer seems to suggest here a parallel between Canacee and the Squire himself. We can read *The Squire's Tale* in its surviving form as an elaborate, if unsuccessful, prelude. Brian Lee thus notes that the "speeches in the *Squire's Tale* are the speeches of those who would conclude if they could, but who end up saying more than they intend and less than they wish."[43] In fact, after Canacee and her attendants minister to the wounded falcon, the Squire shifts his narrative focus, promising "To speken of aventures and of batailles/That nevere yet was herd so grete mervailles" (5.659–60):

> First wol I telle yow of Cambyuskan,
> That in his tyme many a citee wan;
> And after wol I speke of Algarsif,
> How that he wan Theodora to his wif,
> For whom ful ofte in greet peril he was,
> Ne hadde he ben holpen by the steede of bras;
> And after wol I speke of Cambalo,
> That faught in lystes with the brethren two
> For Canace er that he myghte hire wynne.
> And ther I lefte I wol ayeyn bigynne.　　　　　　　(5.661–70)

Just as Canacee elaborately prepares to catch the falcon, the Squire elaborately prepares to extend his narration, giving us a detailed account of its form in anticipation of filling in its matter. Canacee's formal design does not succeed. Does the Squire's?

I would suggest that it is impossible to answer this question with absolute certainty, as scholarly consideration of the relationship of the Franklin to *The Squire's Tale* reflects.[44] The Franklin's address to the Squire at 5.673 *seems* to interrupt the latter's tale. But the Franklin's words to the Squire are so genteel that it is impossible to decide unequivocally whether he is curtailing an ungainly narrative or praising an unexpectedly bravura performance:

> "In feith, Squier, thow hast thee wel acquit
> And gentilly. I preise wel thy wit,"
> Quod the Frankeleyn, "considerynge thy yowthe,
> So feelyngly thou spekest, sire, I allow the!
> As to my doom, there is noon that is heere
> Of eloquence that shal be thy peere,
> If that thou lyve."   (5.673–9)

Perhaps the Squire has superbly executed his ambitious design, but the remainder of *The Squire's Tale* has been lost on account of the exigencies of revision or transmission. Or, as is the case for Canacee, his formal intention has come to naught because the Franklin has mercifully arrested an aimless narrative that is a product of youthful and undisciplined exuberance. Unless a missing piece of *The Squire's Tale* somehow comes to light, it is impossible to decide between these alternatives.

The Franklin goes on to compare the Squire to his son and the terms of his comparison reprise the distinction between purposefulness and aimlessness that arise on account of the ambiguous end to *The Squire's Tale*. The Squire he commends as virtuous: "God yeve thee good chaunce,/And in vertu sende thee continuance" (5.679–80). But the Franklin's son possesses no such "discrecioun" (5.685), and "to vertu listeth nat entende" (5.689). According to the Franklin, therefore, the Squire is oriented towards morality; the Franklin's son, by contrast, wastes his money on games of chance and wastes his time socializing with those who are unable to teach him gentility. The Squire's life is governed by the necessity of virtue (formalism), while the Franklin's son is chaotic, free of any higher purpose (materialism).

Finally, while the Franklin's putative interruption of the Squire is so courteous as to be undecidable whether it is even an interruption, the Host rudely and masterfully interrupts the Franklin's discourse on gentility: "Straw for youre gentillesse!" (5.695), he exclaims. The Host then commands the Franklin to "Telle on thy tale withouten wordes mo" (5.702). The refined Franklin takes no offense at Harry's high-handed speech and instead, without any rancour, *freely* relinquishes his freedom to the Host: "'Gladly, sire Hoost,' quod he, 'I wol obeye/Unto your wyl" (5.703–4). The Franklin willingly – *gladly* – surrenders to the Host's will. We cannot say that the Host has coercively mastered the Franklin, nor can we say that the Franklin has insubordinately rejected his governance.[45]

What I wish to suggest is that the Franklin's gentility in this linking passage exhibits an undecidable logic: First, we cannot decide whether he has mastered the Squire; second, we cannot decide whether the Host has mastered him. We will see that the Franklin's courteous words to the Squire and his exchange with the Host supply us with the terms we need to understand the former's tale and its relationship to the Nun's Priest's.

The Franklin's Prologue and Tale

The Squire's grandiose plan for his romance is in contrast to the Franklin's intention, expressed in the opening lines of his prologue (5.709–15), to narrate a Breton *lai*, usually a short romance that focuses on a single, emotionally charged episode. My interest, however, is in the succeeding lines of *The Franklin's Prologue*, which present us with a baffling contradiction:

> But, sires, by cause I am a burel man,
> At my bigynnyng first I yow biseche,
> Have me excused of my rude speche.
> I lerned nevere rethorik, certeyn;
> Thyng that I speke, it moot be bare and pleyn.
> I sleep nevere on the Mount of Pernaso,
> Ne lerned Marcus Tullius Scithero.
> Colours ne knowe I none, withouten drede,
> But swiche colours as growen in the mede,
> Or elles swiche as men dye or peynte.
> Colours of rethoryk been to me queynte;
> My spirit feeleth noght of swich mateere.   (5.716–27)

The Franklin's claim that he is a plain speaker entirely unlearned in classical rhetoric is made by means of a highly rhetorical flourish. Benjamin Harrison noted this discrepancy more than ninety years ago: "Here we observe that in the very act of admitting his shortcomings, the Franklin betrays an acquaintance with rhetorical custom."[46] In a recent study of the Franklin's use of figurative language, Joseph Turner argues that the prologue indicates a rejection of the artificiality of academic rhetoric.[47] Turner's larger argument is that the Franklin "provides a critique of the unrestrained power of poetic license to obscure truth."[48] I wish to contest both Turner's argument that the Franklin privileges truth over illusion and the frequent claim that the Franklin is an inconsistent, or even incompetent, rhetorician.[49] To do so, it is necessary to read *The Franklin's Prologue* in a manner suggested by my interpretation of *The*

Nun's Priest's Tale. What the Franklin accomplishes is a *rhetorical* denial of rhetoric: He rhetorically abandons rhetoric in favour of plain and bare speech in a manner that recalls Chauntecleer's *deceptive* assertion of feminine deceptiveness. But this means we cannot decide whether the Franklin is on the side of unadorned literal language or ornamental figurative language.

The Franklin's undecidable stance towards rhetoric is also his undecidable stance towards classical learning. He states that he has never slept on "the Mount of Pernaso" nor learned "Marcus Tullius Scithero." He uses classical learning to declare his ignorance of classical learning. As I will show, *The Franklin's Prologue* precisely anticipates his narrative. *The Franklin's Tale* entangles without synthesis the terms adduced by the prologue: literal language and figurative language; truth and fiction; Christian doctrine and pagan lore. But it is the opposition between form and matter that governs all these binaries. Rhetorical language is on the side of playful and equivocal matter as opposed to truthful and univocal form. Classical learning, likewise, is knowledge that is not subordinate to the authority of Christian truth. What *The Franklin's Prologue* reveals, therefore, is that the Franklin, like the Nun's Priest, will not decide on formalism or materialism. And, as we will see, it is only possible to understand the ethical dilemma that confronts Dorigen and Arveragus by acknowledging this undecidability.

The Franklin's Prologue thus makes it impossible to accept at face value the Franklin's statements regarding pagan illusion in his tale. After mentioning a book of "magyk natureel" (5.1125) spotted by Aurelius's brother on the desk of the Orleans clerk, the Franklin provides his opinion of the learning contained therein:

> Which book spak muchel of the operaciouns
> Touchynge the eighte and twenty mansiouns
> That longen to the moone, and swich folye
> As in oure dayes is nat worth a flye –
> For hooly chirches feith in oure bileve
> Ne suffreth noon illusioun us to greve.   (5.1129–34)

It is entirely understandable that critics, whether or not of the exegetical school, have understood *The Franklin's Tale* as conveying an unequivocal rejection of heathen practices and learning.[50] We are presented in this passage with an apparently unambiguous rejection of pagan illusion, deemed by the Franklin as mere folly not worth a fly. But it is possible to insert some doubt into the Franklin's blunt rejection of pagan astrology. To do so, I turn to a passage that describes the

season in which the clerk begins the astrological preparations necessary to effectuate his illusion:

> Phebus wax old, and hewed lyk laton,
> That in his hoote declynacion
> Shoon as the burned gold with stremes brighte;
> But now in Capricorn adoun he lighte,
> Where as he shoon ful pale, I dar wel seyn.
> The bittre frostes, with the sleet and reyn,
> Destroyed hath the grene in every yerd.
> Janus sit by the fyr, with double berd,
> And drynketh of his bugle horn the wyn;
> Biforn hym stant brawen of the tusked swyn,
> And 'Nowel' crieth every lusty man.   (5.1245–55)

Despite the Franklin's disavowal of pagan teaching, he cheerfully
demonstrates his own knowledge of classical astrology by means of
an elaborate description of winter that cites Phoebus, Capricorn, and
Janus. Even more striking is the rustic scene depicted in the final four
lines of the passage. Janus, the classical Roman god, presides over a
Christian feast, wherein the participants cry out "Noel" – a word of
Old French origin that refers to the Christmas season. Is this scene
classical, then, or is it Christian? Chaucer renders it impossible to
decide.[51] In the same way that Janus "with double berd" looks in two
directions at once, the Franklin simultaneously rejects and embraces
pagan illusions.

The Franklin's Tale supplies further support for this reading within six
lines of the above passage. The Franklin goes on to describe in detail the
work that the clerk does for the suffering Aurelius:

> This subtil clerk swich routhe had of this man
> That nyght and day he spedde hym that he kan
> To wayten a tyme of his conclusioun;
> This is to seye, to maken illusioun,
> By swich an apparence or jogelrye –
> I ne kan no termes of astrologye –
> That she and every wight sholde wene and seye
> That of Britaigne the rokkes were aweye,
> Or ellis they were sonken under grounde.
> So atte laste he hath his tyme yfounde
> To maken his japes and his wrecchednesse
> Of swich a supersticious cursednesse.   (5.1261–72)

Once more, the Franklin seems unambiguously to condemn the "wrec-chedenesse" and "supersticious cursednesse" of pagan illusions. But his admission that he "ne kan no termes of astrologye" should recall for us his prologue: "I lerned nevere rhetoric, certeyn" (5.719). Indeed, the logic of the above passage corresponds to the logic that inheres in the prologue. Thus, even though he claims not to know the terms of astrology, in the following twenty-three lines (5.1273–96) the Franklin with reasonable accuracy deploys astrological jargon to report the clerk's arcane calculations. I will cite a representative extract:

> His tables Tolletanes forth he brought,
> Ful wel corrected, ne ther lakked nought,
> Neither his collect ne his expans yeeris,
> Ne his rootes, ne his othere geris,
> As been his centris and his argumentz
> And his proporcioneles convenientz
> For his equacions in every thyng.
> And by his eighte speere in his wirkyng
> He knew ful wel how fer Alnath was shove
> Fro the heed of thilke fixe Aries above,
> That in the ninthe speere considered is.   (5.1273–83)

At the very least, this passage must be deemed inconsistent with the Franklin's assertion that he knows *no* astrological terminology. Critics, in fact, have been puzzled by this apparent contradiction. J.C. Eade remarks that "we cannot help seeing" the Franklin's claim of ignorance "more as an ironic disclaimer than as an apologetic aside, when such a welter of terms follows upon it."[52] Angela Lucas suggests a parallel between the Franklin's use of rhetoric and his use of astrology: "The various descriptions of astrology which the Franklin uses display not an *attitude* towards astrology, but conflicting *attitudes* towards it. He uses astrological jargon as a means of impressing his listeners, just as he uses rhetorical devices for the same purpose. Since the crux of his Tale depends upon the use of astrology, it must be worth more than a *flye* to him. His denouncing of it may be seen as an attempt to conform to whatever he thinks is the accepted attitude, but he is not absolutely clear what he is condemning."[53] Unlike Eade and Lucas, I do not believe that we need to appeal to irony or confusion to explain the evident contradiction in the Franklin's commentary on astrology. The Franklin's undecidable attitude towards the *matter* of pagan rhetoric in his prologue anticipates his undecidable attitude towards the *matter* of pagan illusion in his tale. He entangles without synthesis formal truth and material illusion in the same way that the Nun's Priest entangles without synthesis formal predestination and material free will. The Franklin's discourse, therefore, is neither oriented towards nor unmoored from the final authority of Christian truth.

Now that I have considered the Franklin's treatment of matter, I turn to his treatment of form. I can begin to do so by focusing on Dorigen's address to God, in which she questions the divine rationale behind the existence of those black rocks along the coast of Brittany that threaten her husband's homecoming. This address concerns itself, we should note, with the possibility that there is a disturbing and meaningless contingency in the universe:

> Eterne God, that thurgh thy purveiaunce
> Ledest the world by certein governaunce,
> In ydel, as men seyn, ye no thyng make.
> But, Lord, thise grisly feendly rokkes blake,
> That semen rather a foul confusion
> Of werk than any fair creacion
> Of swich a parfit wys God and a stable,
> Why han ye wroght this werk unresonable?
> For by this werk, south, north, ne west, ne eest,
> Ther nys yfostred man, ne bryd, ne beest;
> It dooth no good, to my wit, but anoyeth.
> Se ye nat, Lord, how mankynde it destroyeth?
> An hundred thousand bodyes of mankynde
> Han rokkes slayn, al be they nat in mynde,
> Which mankynde is so fair part of thy werk
> That thou it madest lyk to thyn owene merk.
> Thanne semed it ye hadde a greet chiertee
> Toward mankynde; but how thanne may it bee
> That ye swiche meenes make it to destroyen,
> Whiche meenes do no good, but evere anoyen?
> I woot wel clerkes wol seyn as hem leste,
> By argumentz, that al is for the beste,
> Though I ne kan the causes nat yknowe.
> But thilke God that made wynd to blowe
> As kepe my lord! This my conclusion.
> To clerkes lete I al disputison.   (5.865–90)

Critics have long observed the influence of Boethius's *Consolation of Philosophy* on Dorigen's complaint about the grisly black rocks.[54]

Her monotheistic prayer to God to protect her lord thus relies on a text absorbed into medieval Christianity, while Aurelius's prayer that the rocks around Brittany be covered with a flood appeals to members of the classical pantheon, primarily Apollo. *The Franklin's Tale* presents us with a world that is neither quite Christian nor quite pagan – exactly as the Franklin neither disavows nor avows pagan illusion.[55] In keeping with the Boethian themes it evokes, Dorigen's speech asserts above all a desire that the universe be strictly *ordered*. What disturbs her so deeply is the impossibility of assigning any meaning to the black rocks that populate the coast of Brittany, making it extremely dangerous to seafarers. Why, she ponders, would a just and reasonable God create anything unreasonable? Humankind is, after all, created in the divine image, God's "owene merk." But this divine "chiertee," or *love*, seems contradicted by those artefacts that "do no good, but evere anoyen." The black rocks cannot possibly accord with the divine plan of a loving creator. Even if clerks insist that everything is designed for the best, the rocks appear *free* of any meaning whatsoever. Dorigen's ruminations are not mere presumption, though many scholars have criticized what they perceive as her impertinent interrogation of providence.[56] Instead, Chaucer uses her complaint to identify Dorigen as a strict formalist: She finds intolerable the mere possibility of contingency in the universe, represented as it is by the black rocks. The appearance of contingent matter untethered to formal authority contradicts her notion of a loving God who leads the world "by certein governaunce."

Dorigen's *formal* conception of divine love corresponds precisely to her *formal* conception of marital love. To be untethered from Arveragus is as intolerable to her as the notion of matter untethered from a providential cause. It is for this reason that her reaction to her husband's absence is so overwhelming. Even the narrator seems to find her grief excessive:

> For his absence wepeth she and siketh,
> As doon thise noble wyves whan hem liketh.
> She moorneth, waketh, wayleth, fasteth, pleyneth;
> Desire of his presence hire so destreyneth
> That al this wyde world she sette at noght.   (5.817–21)

Arveragus is an ordering principle for Dorigen in the same way that God, ideally, serves as an ordering principle for the cosmos. Her need for Arveragus's stabilizing "presence" aligns exactly with her need for a God who stabilizes the cosmos by means of his "certein governance."

When she faces dishonour on account of her promise to Aurelius, therefore, she does not act independently but only contemplates suicide until her husband returns:

> Thus pleyned Dorigen a day or tweye,
> Purposynge evere that she wolde dye.
> But nathelees, upon the thridde nyght,
> Hoom cam Arveragus, this worthy knyght,
> And asked hire why that she weep so soore.   (5.1457–61)

Rosenfeld suggests that "Dorigen, by continuing to complain, survives and continues to live her story, accepting the world as it is."[57] I see little evidence in *The Franklin's Tale* that Dorigen accepts the status quo. If this were the case, why would she respond to Arveragus's query "Is there oght elles, Dorigen, but this?" with an agonized exclamation: "Nay, nay … God helpe me so as wys!/This is to muche, and it were Goddes wille" (5.1469–71). Dorigen does not accept the world as it is; it is too much for her. I am instead in complete agreement with Anne Lee's assessment of Dorigen's character:

> Despite the fact that the Franklin tells us that women desire liberty, I find no evidence for this in the character of Dorigen herself. Throughout the tale every thought, every action, every speech is motivated by her love for Arveragus, her desire to be his loving and beloved wife. Her extravagant grief in the wake of his departure for England (where he is going in order to maintain his reputation as a doughty knight) bears this out: she has no desire for mastery, or even for freedom. What she wants is to have her husband at her side, and without him she is lost.[58]

The most important element of Lee's analysis is her observation that Dorigen's attitude towards love is at odds with the Franklin's, who insists that "Love wol nat been constreyned by maistrye" (5.764). Dorigen may not desire to master Arveragus, but she certainly desires to be mastered *by* him. Love for Dorigen means constraint, whether this is the superintendence of a husband over his wife or the superintendence of God over his creation.

To refine our understanding of the Franklin's own position on love, we must consider Dorigen's promise to Aurelius and its consequences, which constitute the signal crux of the tale. Aurelius has been as devoted to Dorigen as Dorigen has been to Arveragus. In his abject state, the squire pleads to his beloved for some compassion: "Have mercy, sweete,

or ye wol do me deye!" (5.978). Dorigen's response makes it clear that
she will never entertain this possibility:

> "Is this youre wyl," quod she, "and sey ye thus?
> Nevere erst," quod she, "ne wiste I what ye mente.
> But now, Aurelie, I knowe youre entente,
> By thilke God that yaf me soule and lyf,
> Ne shal I nevere been untrewe wyf
> In word ne werk, as fer as I have wit;
> I wol been his to whom that I am knyt.
> Taak this for fynal answere as of me."
> But after that in pley thus seyde she:
> "Aurelie," quod she, "by heighe God above,
> Yet wolde I graunte yow to been youre love,
> Syn I yow se so pitously complayne.
> Looke what day that endelong Britayne
> Ye remoeve alle the rokkes, stoon by stoon,
> That they ne lette ship ne boot to goon –
> I seye, whan ye han maad the coost so clene
> Of rokkes that ther nys no stoon ysene,
> Thanne wol I love yow best of any man;
> Have heer my trouthe, in al that evere I kan."   (5.980–98)

Despite her "playful" oath, there can be no doubt that Dorigen's rejection of Aurelius's suit is unequivocal. When he asks if there is any possibility of her grace, Dorigen's response emphasizes the absurdity of his
attachment to her, reasserting Arveragus's total authority over her body:

> "What deyntee sholde a man han in his lyf
> For to go love another mannes wyf,
> That hath hir body what so that hym liketh?"   (5.1003–5)

While Dorigen has made her intent clear beyond doubt, there is still
the complication of her play. Play, like rhetoric and illusion, is at odds
with truth. Dorigen's nonsensical promise makes this clear: She is stating that she will *truly love* Aurelius only if he somehow removes that
which threatens her *true love's* homecoming. As Aurelius himself puts
it, "this were an inpossible" (5.1009). We should understand Dorigen's
meaningless playfulness, therefore, as *matter*. Dorigen unexpectedly
inserts some material equivocality into her otherwise formally univocal speech. But this is exactly how she understands the grisly black
rocks: As I argued above, the rocks appear to Dorigen as inexplicable

and gratuitous matter compromising the formal perfection of God's "purveiaunce" (5.865). Dorigen's inexplicable and gratuitous promise to Aurelius serves an identical function; it compromises the otherwise unequivocal clarity of her formal intention – her "fynal answere."[59]

The Franklin's Tale stages two responses to Dorigen's material playfulness: that of Aurelius and that of Arveragus. Let us consider Aurelius first. He takes Dorigen's gratuitous playfulness *seriously* – so seriously that he is willing to spend a vast sum to make the black rocks disappear. Aurelius thus imposes his own meaning on what is radically meaningless. According to Sandra McEntire, "from her playful words which he initially understood perfectly, Aurelius has constructed a new meaning from which he derives a new interpretation."[60] There is another way to say this: Aurelius imposes univocal form on equivocal matter. He accomplishes with Dorigen's promise, therefore, precisely what Dorigen wants God to do with the black rocks – he informs with meaning that which is meaningless. In doing so, however, he *decisively* masters Dorigen, explicitly contradicting the Franklin's assertion that love has nothing to do with mastery.

I now turn to Arveragus's treatment of Dorigen's playful promise, contained in lines that have earned as much critical scrutiny as any passage in *The Canterbury Tales*:

> "Ye shul youre trouthe holden, by my fay!
> For God so wisly have mercy upon me,
> I hadde wel levere ystiked for to be
> For verray love which that I to yow have,
> But if ye sholde youre trouthe kepe and save.
> Trouthe is the hyeste thyng that man may kepe" –
> But with that word he brast anon to wepe,
> And seyde, "I yow forbede, up peyne of deeth,
> That nevere, whil thee lasteth lyf ne breeth,
> To no wight telle thou of this aventure –
> As I may best, I wol my wo endure –
> Ne make no contenance of hevynesse,
> That folk of yow may demen harm or gesse."　　　　　(5.1474–86)

Influential readers of this passage have puzzled over the moral absurdity of holding a wife to a whimsical vow that violates a marital covenant: "Sire, I wol be youre humble trewe wyf – /Have heer my trouthe – til that myn herte breste" (5.758–9). Alan Gaylord thus concludes "that Chaucer, expecting his audience to recognize the ludicrous ethical acrobatics the Franklin makes his characters perform, has honed upon that expectation a cutting edge of irony, one which lays open the affectedly *gentil* values of the teller of the Tale."[61] Perhaps, then, the Franklin, a representative of a middling social rank, simply cannot comprehend the refined morality of the aristocratic elite and his tale devolves into moral inanity.[62] Nevertheless, Arveragus's comportment towards Dorigen has also earned praise from scholars who see Arveragus as respecting Dorigen's independent capacity to make binding oaths.[63] I also believe that Arveragus's conduct is exemplary, but not just within the narrative universe of *The Franklin's Tale*. Chaucer, by means of Arveragus's response to Dorigen's predicament, is teaching us exactly what he means by love.

Three key oppositions central to *The Franklin's Tale* structure Arveragus's speech: 1) formal truth versus material falsehood, 2) formal mastery versus material freedom, and 3) masculine form and feminine matter. First, Arveragus *masters* Dorigen by commanding her to stay *true* to her promise to Aurelius. But this means that he *frees* her from staying *true* to him. Arveragus thus masters Dorigen by freeing her; he frees her by mastering her. Accordingly, Dorigen must be true by being false; she must be false by being true.[64] Second, Arveragus asserts that there is nothing higher than *truth*. He then demands on pain of death that Dorigen keep up a deceptive *illusion* of marital fidelity. Dorigen must be truthful and deceptive at the same time, exactly as the Franklin entangles Christian truth and pagan illusion in his tale.[65] Third, Arveragus begins this scene with his emotions completely *mastered*, in a stereotypically "masculine" fashion. Once he has heard Dorigen's account of her predicament, he responds to her "with glad chiere, in freendly wyse" (5.1467). However, in the middle of his response, his feelings suddenly and violently break *free* of his control, in a stereotypically "feminine" fashion: "But with that word he brast anon to wepe" (5.1480). He goes so far as to threaten his beloved wife with death. With remarkable condensation, Arveragus's speech entangles formal truth and material untruth, formal mastery and material freedom. He neither masters nor frees Dorigen; he is on the side both of truth and of deception; and as "truth" is traditionally gendered masculine and "deception" traditionally gendered feminine, so Arveragus is an example of "masculine" self-control and "feminine" loss of control.

In Arveragus's comportment towards Dorigen, we witness exactly the (non-)relation that the Nun's Priest indicates that a text has to its authorial cause, or creation to its divine cause. In the same way that it is undecidable whether or not the Nun's Priest has mastered or freed his tale, it is undecidable whether or not Arveragus has mastered or freed his wife. To understand what Chaucer is doing in *The Franklin's*

Tale we need to appreciate the non-decisional structure of Arveragus's love. He has *authoritatively* relinquished his authority over Dorigen. Just as the Nun's Priest ("Take the fruit") commands his interpreters to be free, Arveragus commands his wife to be free. In this way, Arveragus precisely satisfies the Franklin's conditions regarding love. Arveragus avoids constraining his wife with a masterful decision by refusing to decide. Moreover, he maintains the "humble, wys accord" (5.791) that initially characterized their marriage: By *commanding* Dorigen to be *free*, he is "bothe in lordshipe and servage" (5.794). She is simultaneously his mastered subordinate and his free superior.[66] Likewise, when the Franklin insists earlier in the tale "That freendes everych oother moot obeye" (5.762), he is not merely expressing an ideal of mutuality, he is also implicitly generating the insoluble logic of love. If two friends submit to each other, each at once possesses and does not possess authority over the other. Each simultaneously masters and frees the other just as Arveragus simultaneously masters and frees Dorigen. But even though it gives direct expression to the paradoxical nature of love, this does not mean that we should view *The Franklin's Tale* as the culmination of the "marriage debate," a heuristic term initially associated with the gender politics of the Wife of Bath, Clerk, Merchant, and Franklin.[67] As I will show in the forthcoming chapters, the Franklin's logic is the logic of all *The Canterbury Tales*, not just one group.

For Chaucer, we only love or are ethical when it is undecidable whether we have mastered the beloved (formalism) or let the beloved go free (materialism). We can, therefore, see that even if Aurelius's masterful treatment of Dorigen is initially uncharitable, he does learn from Arveragus's example. After Dorigen has reluctantly left Arveragus and is making her way to the garden to convene with Aurelius, she meets with the squire "of aventure or grace" (5.1508). Tellingly, the Franklin will not decide whether their meeting is materially contingent ("aventure") or formally necessary ("grace"). The Franklin's comment anticipates the shift in Aurelius's comportment towards Dorigen. He moves away from decisive mastery and towards undecidable love:

> "Madame, seyth to youre lord Arveragus
> That sith I se his grete gentillesse
> To yow, and eek I se wel youre distresse,
> That him were levere han shame (and that were routhe)
> Than ye to me sholde breke thus youre trouthe,
> I have wel levere evere to suffre wo
> Than I departe the love bitwix yow two.

I yow relesse, madame, into youre hond
Quyt every serement and every bond
That ye han maad to me as heerbiforn,
Sith thilke tyme which that ye were born.
My trouthe I plighte, I shal yow never repreve
Of no biheste, and heere I take my leve,
As of the treweste and the beste wyf
That evere yet I knew in al my lyf."   (5.1526–40)

Aurelius employs a highly legalistic register in this passage. I propose that this is done to indicate the formally *binding* manner with which the squire materially *frees* Dorigen. As in *The Nun's Priest's Tale*, the formal imposition of order is at once the material deposition of any order. Aurelius, following Arveragus's lead, authoritatively revokes his authority over Dorigen, legalistically freeing her from every promise she has made to him since the time she was born. He formally constrains and materially frees her at the same time.

The illusionist clerk to whom Aurelius still owes a massive sum echoes this legalistic register:

"Sire, I releesse thee thy thousand pound,
As thou right now were cropen out of the ground,
Ne nevere er now ne haddest knowen me."   (5.1613–15)

The clerk formally "resets" his relationship to Aurelius in the same way that Aurelius formally "resets" his relationship to Dorigen. In a manner that is *binding*, he formally and legalistically *frees* Aurelius from the debt of a thousand pounds so that it is as if the two had never met. In both cases, it is a figure possessing the authority in the relationship that exercises this authority to revoke it completely. The author of *The Franklin's Tale* does not exclude himself from this logic. At the conclusion of the narrative, the Franklin addresses his audience directly:

"Lordynges, this question, thanne, wol I aske now,
Which was the mooste fre, as thynketh yow?
Now telleth me, er that ye ferther wende."   (5.1621–3)

Here Chaucer diverges significantly from his source, Menedon's story from Book 4 of Boccaccio's *Il Filocolo*, which contains a sequence of Love Questions.[68] At the conclusion of his narrative, Menedon poses a question to his audience regarding the conduct of the wife, her husband, the magician, Tebano, and the wife's lover, Tarolfo: "which of them showed the greater generosity?"[69] Fiammeta, who oversees the proceedings as queen, debates the case with Menedon, but her judgment in favour of the husband, who is willing to send his wife to Tarolfo on account of her promise, provides an authoritative conclusion to the deliberation: Fiammeta thus peremptorily states, "Let this be enough said about your question."[70] By contrast, instead of decisively imposing a final meaning upon his tale, the Franklin provides his audience with the interpretive *freedom* to debate its representation of "freedom."[71] But he does so by means of an imperative: "Now *telleth* me." The Franklin authoritatively abdicates his authorial prerogative to close off his narrative. This is a loving gesture, one that echoes the Nun's Priest's authoritative abdication of his own authority. In both cases, the interpreter is commanded to be free.

Chaucer's conception of love should return us to Dorigen's contemplation of divine "chiertee" (5.881). As we saw, Dorigen finds incompatible with her conception of divine love the presence of brute contingency, imaged for her in the "grisly black rocks." For Dorigen, a loving creator would ensure that everything in the universe *makes sense*: Love is order, necessity, or sufficient reason. Needless to say, this is an argument that is fundamental to every theology and every theodicy. The manifestation of brute contingency is a traumatic blot that can shake confidence in a just providential design. But Chaucer's understanding of God's "charity" is radically different, and he illustrates this understanding by means of Arvaragus's love for Dorigen. God demonstrates his love for us not by *masterfully* imposing an unassailable providential order but by authoritatively revoking his authority. God commands us to be free, which means that it is undecidable whether the cosmos is ordered or chaotic, necessary or contingent, serious or playful. We can now understand why Christian truth and pagan illusion are so inextricably entangled in *The Franklin's Tale*. For the Franklin, it is impossible to say with certainty whether the world is oriented towards a univocal divine truth or whether humans exist within the material confusion of equivocal illusions, disconnected from any final authority. But Chaucer's undecidable logic – form is (not) related to matter – is the logic of love. Indeed, as I will show later in this book, it is by refusing to decide on the formal closure or material openness of *The Canterbury Tales* that we manifest our love for him.

I will conclude this opening chapter by demonstrating how Chaucer's understanding of love evades the conceptual grasp of the Lacanian and Augustinian acceptations. For Lacan, there are two kinds of love that correspond to two modes of enjoyment: phallic *jouissance* and feminine *jouissance*. When we love according to the phallic mode, the Symbolic Father or Big Other *masters* us and the paternal interdict (*non du père*) organizes the coordinates of our enjoyment by means of the fantasmatic object *a* – the final cause of desire. When we love according to the feminine mode, we confront our abyssal *freedom* and are able to acknowledge that the Big Other does not exist to superintend and regulate our enjoyment. Love, in this case, cannot rely upon any transcendent guarantee. Masculine love, associated by Lacan with fantasy, is oriented by the *necessity* of a final cause; feminine love, associated by Lacan with truth, hinges on the *contingency* of the encounter.[72] Thus, a charitable reading for an Augustinian, for instance, is definitively closural, orienting our enjoyment towards a final authority: God himself. A charitable reading for a Lacanian is resolutely non-closural, insisting on the non-existence of any final authority.[73]

While both Lacan and Augustine decisively sequester a domain of necessity or form from a domain of freedom or matter, Lacan is a strict materialist and Augustine is a strict formalist. Lacan understands "phallic jouissance" as *authorized* enjoyment; Augustine calls authorized enjoyment "charity." Lacan understands "feminine jouissance" as *unauthorized* enjoyment; Augustine calls unauthorized enjoyment "cupidity." As we have seen, however, according to the Chaucerian configuration of love, formalism and materialism are entangled but not synthesized: Love for Chaucer is neither masculine form nor feminine matter – neither authorized nor unauthorized. For the remainder of this book, therefore, "form is (not) related to matter" will serve as my principle of charity. I will deploy this (non-)synthetic *a priori* to demonstrate that *The Canterbury Tales*, from Fragment 1 to Fragment 10, provide an extraordinarily sustained contemplation of love. Accordingly, with the interpretive tools acquired from the Franklin and the Nun's Priest, I return now to Fragment 1 of *The Canterbury Tales* to consider *The Knight's Tale* and its complex representation of formal order and material chaos.

2 Lest Ye Be Judged: Fragment 1 and the Law of Unintended Consequences

The Knight's Tale

According to Charles Muscatine's influential reading of *The Knight's Tale*, the "history of Thebes had perpetual interest for Chaucer as an example of the struggle between noble designs and chaos." Even though chaos is always encroaching on the dignified and "patterned edifice" of chivalric existence, the Knight through his spokesman, Theseus, insists that "true nobility is faith in the ultimate order of all things." Helen Cooper, writing twenty-five years later, echoes Muscatine's reading: "The *Knight's Tale* is not a Christian allegory; it is, consciously, a Christian analogy, in which the affirmation of continuing life after Arcite's death is seen as a reflection of the ultimate providential ordering of the universe."[1] Though it established the terrain for modern encounters with the tale, Muscatine's optimistic interpretation has not gone uncontested. Robert W. Hanning detects the hardened attitude of a professional soldier in "the Knight's vision of life as a deadly, and arbitrary, business."[2] What Hanning sees as the tale's ambivalent oscillation from philosophical optimism to stoic pessimism reflects "the real paradox of chivalry – its imposition of moral idealism on a deadly, and therefore potentially nihilistic, profession."[3] Thus, while Muscatine perceives chivalry in *The Knight's Tale* as a meaningful pursuit that corresponds to a divine order, Hanning suggests that the tale reveals the tensions inherent to the ideology of late medieval chivalry, which sought with difficulty to idealize and exalt its brutality.[4]

Scholars such as David Aers and Lee Patterson share Hanning's concern to complicate the tale's moral idealism, but they focus more explicitly on class, arguing that the tale undercuts the metaphysical sublimation of aristocratic power. Aers thus concludes: "Chaucer's work is an outstanding poetic inquiry into problems of order in cultural and metaphysical dimensions, one which includes especial attention to the uses of metaphysical language by those in power, the transformations of metaphysics into an ideology of unreflexive secular domination."[5] Patterson also argues that *The Knight's Tale* points to the radical inflexibility of chivalric ideology in its confrontation with historical contingency, citing in particular its "inability to come to self-consciousness, to rewrite its own ideology in relation to socioeconomic change."[6] Leicester's extended reading of *The Knight's Tale* likewise observes the suspicion of the narrative towards chivalric institutions. But he ascribes this ambivalence to the critical attitude of the Knight himself towards the structures he is describing: "Like so many other Canterbury pilgrims – such as the Wife of Bath and the Pardoner – the Knight is a critic of his own tale, commenting on and questioning the traditional styles and values of a story he did not make up himself in the very act of passing it on. He is also the first critic to notice the discrepancy between the ideal order Theseus's speech proposes and the reality of the world of the tale."[7] Fundamental scholarship on *The Knight's Tale* tends to revolve around the correspondence, or lack thereof, between ideal and real that it proposes. I will express the basic problematic using the terms I introduced in the previous chapter. Is *The Knight's Tale* an exercise in formalism, as Muscatine would have it, insisting that the coercive application of aristocratic desire finds an analogy and ultimate justification in a transcendent cause? Or does *The Knight's Tale* undermine the pertinence of any transcendent form, as Aers, Leicester, and Patterson argue, articulating the historically contingent and arbitrary quality of aristocratic culture – a culture that can only fantasize about timeless ethical and metaphysical legitimation?

As anticipated by my interpretation of *The Nun's Priest's Tale* and *The Franklin's Tale*, my reading of *The Knight's Tale* will argue that both formalist and materialist decisions about its representation of chivalric culture are not only inevitable but compossible. Formalism and materialism are as entangled in *The Knight's Tale* as they are in the Nun's Priest's and the Franklin's tales. This means, as we will see, that it is undecidable whether order in the tale is necessary or provisional. I will anticipate this interpretation by citing the prelude to the tale in the *General Prologue*. When the pilgrims draw lots to determine who will tell the first story, the cut falls to the Knight. But the narrator will not tell us whether this outcome came about "by aventure, or sort, or cas" (1.844). It is not possible for us to decide, in other words, whether the Knight's draw is a result of chance (materialism) or destiny (formalism). We now possess an important clue as to the tale's representation of chivalric order.

Nevertheless, there is no question that the Knight initially represents himself as a strict formalist. In this way, he recalls the Franklin, who seems in his prologue to reject material deception, or rhetoric, in favour of formal truth. The Knight characterizes himself as intensely concerned, therefore, with a well-ordered universe, as indicated in a passage inspired by Boethius's *Consolation*:

> The destinee, ministre general,
> That executeth in the world over al
> The purveiaunce that God hath seyn biforn,
> So strong it is that, though the world had sworn
> The contrarie of a thyng by ye or nay,
> Yet sometyme it shall fallen on a day
> That falleth nat eft withinne a thousand yeer.
> For certainly, oure appetites heer,
> Be it of were, or pees, or hate or love,
> Al is this reuled by the sighte above.   (1.1663–72)

In the same way that the Knight seems to regard destiny as an ineluctable order imposed from above, his tale seems to provide evidence of superb narrative control through its elaborate design, nested structure, and careful parallelism. The Knight states confidently that everything in the universe is in its appropriate place and at least appears to situate every narrative element in its appropriate place.[8] The Knight's representative within his tale, Theseus, is equally concerned with this kind of formal hygiene. The tale begins, therefore, with Theseus's imposition of masculine Athenian order on two realms that display an inability to govern themselves appropriately: Amazonia and Thebes. Amazonia is characterized by the brazen rejection of normative gender relations, and Thebes is characterized by an equally brazen disregard for both normative familial relations and the normative treatment of the dead.[9] Likewise, Theseus's intervention into the private feud between the Theban cousins transforms a deadly and secret combat between two outlaws into a socially sanctioned and *regulated* public spectacle, limited in its violence.

Theseus's martial rectification of the disorder that inheres in Amazonia and Thebes finds a precise reflex in his conception of love as an ordering principle:

> "The Firste Moevere of the cause above,
> Whan he first made the faire cheyne of love,
> Greet was th'effect, and heigh was his entente.

Wel wiste he why, and what thereof he mente,
For with that faire cheyne of love he bond
The fyr, the eyr, the water, and the lond
In certeyn boundes, that they may nat flee.
That same Prince and that Moevere," quod he,
"Hath stablissed in this wrecched world adoun
Certeyne dayes and duracioun
To al that is engendred in this place,
Over the whiche day they may nat pace,
Al mowe they yet tho dayes wel abregge.
Ther nedeth noght noon auctoritee t'allegge,
For it is preeved by experience,
But that me list declaren my sentence.
Thanne may men by this ordre wel discerne
That thilke Moevere stable is and eterne."   (1.2987–3004)

In another Boethian echo, the "First Mover," according to Theseus, binds together all the elements of the universe with an unbreakable chain of love. It is no coincidence that this speech on the cosmic bonds of love is intended to convince Emelye and Palamon (mainly Emelye) to accept "the *bond*/That highte matrimoigne or marriage" (1.3094–5). Their marriage will synchronize with the divine ordination of the cosmos. Furthermore, by means of this marital arrangement, Theseus can ensure that Thebes remains bound to Athens in "obeisaunce" (1.2974) by means of a political relationship that was threatened by Arcite's unforeseen demise. The tale then concludes with the submission of Amazonia (Emelye) to Thebes (Palamon), and the submission of Thebes (Palamon) to Athens (Theseus). According to this reading, *The Knight's Tale* indicates that love and war are both *formal* principles, functioning together to hold in check the chaos represented by these disordered nations. As the First Mover links fire, air, water, and land by means of his chain of love, so Theseus manages to link Athens, Thebes, and Amazonia by means of his wise governance.[10]

The Knight's Tale, however, complicates this formalist reading, making it difficult to conclude with any confidence that love and war operate on behalf of order rather than on behalf chaos. The disruption of the tale's formal conception of love and war occurs primarily in Part Three, with the description of the three temples commissioned by Theseus and the entreaties to Venus, Diana, and Mars by Palamon, Emelye, and Arcite, respectively. It is remarkable how poorly the depiction of love in the temple of Venus accords with Theseus's conception of love as an ordering principle. Thus, painted on the walls are allegorical representations of:

> Plesaunce and Hope, Desir, Foolhardynesse,
> Beautee and Youthe, Bauderie, Richesse,
> Charmes and Force, Lesynges, Flaterye,
> Despense, Bisynesse, and Jalousye,
> That wered of yelewe gooldes a gerland,
> And a cokkow sittynge on hir hand.   (1.1925–30)

Instead of bringing harmony, love as it is portrayed in Venus's temple brings torment, foolishness, falsehood, infidelity, and jealousy. Nor does the list of Venus's devotees inspire confidence that she is a rational overlord:

> Nat was foryeten the porter, Ydelnesse,
> Ne Narcisus the faire of yore agon,
> Ne yet the folye of kyng Salomon,
> Ne yet the grete strengthe of Ercules –
> Th' enchauntementz of Medea and Circes –
> Ne of Turnus, with the hardy fiers corage,
> The riche Cresus, kaytyf in servage.
> Thus may ye seen that wysdom ne richesse,
> Beautee ne sleighte, strengthe ne hardynesse,
> Ne may with Venus holde champartie.   (1.1940–9)

As these examples indicate, whether one is a mighty warrior, handsome youth, wealthy lord, powerful king, or seductive enchantress, it is impossible to match Venus in power. And because she is impossible to control, as the examples in this passage attest, she leaves in her wake obsession, vengeance, devastation, and death. Theseus's *formal* conception of love as a Boethian "fair chain" of order has as its counterpart a *material* conception of love as a venereal force of disruption and chaos. As Arcite says to Palamon after they both fall in love with Emelye, "Wostow nat wel the olde clerkes sawe,/That 'who shal yeve a lovere any lawe?'" (1.1163–4).[11] In the tale, love is both the divine law and rebellious against any law – shattering even the bonds of kinship and loyalty that join the Theban cousins.

The Knight's Tale treats war in exactly the same way as it treats love. On the one hand, Theseus is a crusader on behalf of Athenian order, forcefully bringing regulation and measure to the chaotic states of Amazonia and Thebes. On the other hand, he rides under the banner of Mars

(1.975–6), and the imagery depicted in the latter's temple is even more disturbing than that adorning Venus's temple:

> Yet saugh I Woodnesse, laughynge in his rage,
> Armed Compleint, Outhees, and fiers Outrage;
> The careyne in the busk, with throte ycorve;
> A thousand slayn, and nat of qualm ystorve;
> The tiraunt, with the pray by force yraft;
> The toun destroyed, ther was no thyng laft.
> Yet saugh I brent the shippes hoppesteres;
> The hunte strangled with the wilde beres;
> The sowe freten the child right in the cradel;
> The cook yscalded, for al his longe ladel.
> Noght was foryeten by the infortune of Marte.   (1.2011–21)

The images in the temple of Mars convey with horrifying force the notion that the god of war kills absolutely indiscriminately. Even the innocent child in the cradle, we are told, cannot avoid his baleful "infortune." Neither are his devotees, such as Theseus, the honoured "conquerour" (1.981), insulated from his malign influence:

> And al above, depeynted in a tour,
> Saugh I Conquest, sittynge in greet honour,
> With the sharpe swerd over his heed
> Hangynge by a soutil twynes threed.   (1.2027–30)

The temple of Mars represents the god as an agent of purposeless carnage, menacing the conquered as much as the conqueror. There is no warlord who can master Mars, just as there is no lover who can "holde champartie" (1.1949) with Venus. Thus, as with love, *The Knight's Tale* offers two fundamentally incompatible conceptions of war, one formalist and the other materialist. *The Knight's Tale* does not flinch, therefore, from showing us the devastation left in the wake of Theseus's martial exploits, particularly in the shape of thieves ransacking the bodies of dead soldiers after the defeat of Creon and the sack of Thebes (lines 1.1005–8). War and love both impose order and depose order; war and love are both forms of control *and* completely out of any control.

As is borne out by its critical history, it is tempting to interpret *The Knight's Tale* unilaterally as representing either the success or failure of the formal protocols that seek to contain material chaos. Perhaps the Knight understands Theseus's martial and political exploits as analogous to Boethian providence – by giving purpose and meaning to sheer contingency, he successfully makes "vertu of necessitee" (1.3042).[12] Or perhaps Theseus's ostensible inhibition of disorder just veils the opportunistic and arbitrary execution of Athenian power for its own sake, detached from any higher ideal.[13] I wish to argue that either interpretive decision would contravene what I understand as the *charitable*, and thus insoluble, structure of *The Knight's Tale*. Accordingly, it now becomes necessary to revise our conception of the Knight himself as an advocate of Boethian formalism, just as we did with the Nun's Priest and the Franklin. To do so, we must investigate whether the logic of his tale accords with his insistence on absolute providential order. The relevant question is the following: Is the Knight himself an agent of narrative order, or is he actually an agent of narrative chaos?[14] If the former, there is an ideal standard in the tale to which Theseus's conduct could conceivably correspond; if the latter, there is no such standard.

I will anticipate my treatment of this problem by attention to the Knight's description of Emelye bathing in the temple of Diana in advance of her petition to the goddess:

> This Emelye, with herte debonaire,
> Hir body wessh with water of a welle.
> But hou she dide hir ryte I dar nat telle,
> But it be any thing in general;   .
> And yet it were a game to heeren al.
> To hym that meneth wel it were no charge;
> But it is good a man been at his large.   (1.2282–8)

This passage, a notable expansion of the *Teseida*, is usually understood as indicating the Knight's masculine scopic enjoyment of Emelye's objectified and vulnerable body, in this way elucidating the tale's conservative gender politics.[15] My interest in this passage, by contrast, is the manner with which the Knight occupies two opposed positions simultaneously. He at once observes the *necessity* of a prohibition ("I dar nat telle") and claims the appropriateness of *freedom* ("But it is *good* a man to been *at his large*"). In other words, the Knight indicates the fitness of both lawful and lawless conduct – just as he portrays love and war as forces of order and chaos, he both respects and rejects the order of the law. I will read the account of Emelye's prayer to Diana according to this ambivalence.

Now, even though he appears to impose an extraordinary symmetry upon his tale, critics have discerned that the Knight is responsible for some radical departures from narrative continuity. The first of these logical problems occurs in the description of the temple of Diana and requires some comparison with the *Teseida* to elucidate. In Book 7 of Boccaccio's *Teseida*, as in *The Knight's Tale*, Palamone's prayer to Venus conflicts with Arcita's prayer to Mars. As the two deities have already acquiesced to their petitioners, an accord must be fashioned:[16]

> 67. Therefore, when she had heard [these] words from Palamone, the goddess went at once to the place where she was summoned. As a result unusual things were then heard in the famed house, and so a new dispute between Venus and Mars was born in the heavens. But a way was found by them and a masterful skill to satisfy the prayers of each faction.

In Boccaccio's poem, Emilia's entreaty to Diana follows the accord between Venus and Mars, and Diana thus informs Emilia that her destiny has already been fixed:[17]

> 89. The gods in the heavens have already determined that you will be the spouse of one of them – and Diana is already content with this – but which one of them it must be will be hidden from you for a while. What will occur outside of this company may rather be observed by you within the temple. Therefore gaze intently at the altar and you will see what your heart desires.

But Chaucer inserts a complication into the chronology of Boccaccio's narrative. In *The Knight's Tale*, Emelye's supplication to Diana at her temple and the goddess's prophetic response occur between Arcite's and Palamon's prayers, and therefore *before* the accord between Venus and Mars, orchestrated in the tale by Saturn. This narrative rearrangement disrupts the chronology of the tale, as Diana claims that the high gods have *already* predestined Emelye's fate:

> And therwithal Dyane gan appeere,
> With bowe in honde, right as an hunteresse,
> And seyde, "Doghter, stynt thyn hevynesse.
> Among the goddes hye it is affermed,
> And by eterne word writen and confermed,
> Thou shalt ben wedded unto oon of tho
> That han for thee so muchel care and wo,
> But unto which of hem I may nat telle.

> Farwel, for I ne may no lenger dwelle.
> The fires which that on myn auter brenne
> Shulle thee declaren, er that thou go henne,
> Thyn aventure of love, as in this cas."
> (1.2346–57)

The concord orchestrated by Saturn to satisfy both Venus and Mars will not happen for another hundred lines. Not only is it the case that the "goddes hye" have not yet "affermed" Emelye's fate, Diana tells her supplicant that the fires on her alter *shall* declare her adventure in love before she leaves the temple. But this augury has already occurred, terrifying Emelye well before Diana tells her to consult it:

> For which so soore agast was Emelye
> That she was wel ny mad and gan to crie,
> For she ne wiste what it signyfied.
> (1.2341–3)

In a tale that is otherwise exceedingly well ordered, the *disorder* of narrative chronology in the temple of Diana is remarkable. We can perceive a similar effect in the temple of Mars, also not in the *Teseida*, where the murders of Julius, Nero, and Antonius are depicted "Al be that thilke tyme they were unborn" (1.2033).

Susan Crane accounts for this narrative disruption by contrasting the aimlessness of romance to the purposiveness of other genres: "Adventure is the critical term most specific to romance, indicating the arbitrary, the random, and the unmotivated that divide the experience of romance from the clear necessities of epic struggle, the transcendent assurance of hagiography, and the instructive designs of chronicle."[18] For Crane, Chaucer's accommodation of Boccaccio's classical narrative to the romance genre injects a measure of disorder and irrationality into *The Knight's Tale*. Crane aligns the irrationality of romance with feminine difference, suggesting that Chaucer generates an absolutely traditional distinction between feminine aimlessness and masculine purpose: "It is particularly Chaucer's identification of feminine positions located outside the masculine designs of courtship and social order that connects the *Knight's Tale* to an idea of romance."[19] While I agree with Crane, and others, that Chaucer's manipulation of narrative chronology in the temple of Diana deserves careful scrutiny, I do not agree that this manipulation indicates a decisive separation of formal (and masculine) purposefulness from material (and feminine) aimlessness. I will argue, by contrast, that it is more persuasive to read Chaucer's disruption of narrative logic in *The Knight's Tale* in line with the insoluble logic proposed by the Nun's Priest's and Franklin's tales, whereby formalism and materialism are entangled without synthesis.

While it is true, as Crane remarks, that the timing of Diana's prophecy "does not submit to rational explanation," this eruption of feminine chaos simultaneously undermines *and* furthers masculine order.[20] That is, Diana's prophecy reinforces the Knight's statement that everything in the universe is perfectly ordered in advance. The goddess's assertion that Emelye's fate is already "by eterne word writen and confermed" (1.1250) corresponds exactly to the Knight's earlier contention that destiny executes in the world "The purveiaunce that God hath seyn biforn" (1.1665). Chaucer's manipulation of the *Teseida* thus gives Diana prophetic abilities not possessed by her fellow classical deities.[21] She knows what will happen next in the tale just as much as does the Knight, or God himself for that matter. However, her divination sharply contradicts the tale's narrative logic, affirming that the high gods have decided Emelye's fate when no such thing has yet occurred.

Likewise, the "sighte queynte" (1.2333) that Emelye perceives on Diana's altar indicates that the goddess's prescience is absolute, down to the specific details of the combat between Arcite's and Palamon's forces in Theseus's tournament.[22] Diana knows in advance that Arcite's forces will defeat Palamon's, and that Arcite will suffer a fatal accident. But even though her knowledge of future time seems perfect, Diana somehow does not see that Emelye has already witnessed her terrifying oracle; she informs her adherent that the fires on her altar "*shall declare*" her future "before she goes hence." But Emelye's frightened weeping after the augury was the cause of the goddess's appearance in the first place: "But oonly for the *feere* thus hath she cried" (1.2344), the Knight specifies. And it is because Diana believes the omen has not yet happened that she mistakenly concludes that Emelye is sad at this point rather than scared: "'Doghter, stynt thyn *hevynesse*'" (1.2348). The Knight could have situated Diana's speech right before Emelye sees the omen, as does Boccaccio, when Emelye does in fact weep "bittre teeris" (1.2327) of sadness. Instead, he makes Diana "right" and "wrong" *at the same time*. She says all the right things, but from the wrong narrative position: Diana simultaneously can and cannot see the future. She is at once on the side of formal order, forecasting events to come with flawless clarity, *and* on the side of material disorder, utterly confusing the tale's temporal organization. Here again we encounter the fundamental principle of Chaucerian logic: The imposition of (chronological) order is also the deposition of (chronological) order, and vice versa. *The Knight's Tale* is simultaneously perfectly ordered and chaotic; the Knight's Boethian formalism, however emphatically expressed, both does and does not hold.

Let us now consider Saturn, who effectuates a resolution between Venus and Mars in a passage that has no correlate in the *Teseida*.[23] The quarrel between Venus and Mars begins as soon as Arcite leaves the temple of Mars, having been granted victory by the god: "And right anon swich strif there is bigonne,/For thilke grauntyng, in the hevene above" (1.2438–9). By finding a resolution to this strife, Saturn certainly fulfils Diana's prophecy but, as we have seen, his actions on behalf of the quarreling gods starkly contradict her claim that such a resolution has already been "affermed" by the high gods in advance by "eterne word." How could the gods collectively affirm something eternally and also spontaneously erupt into dissent? Chronos, like Diana, both does and does not disrupt the narrative's chronology. His function in *The Knight's Tale* makes it impossible to decide between the formalism of predestination and the materialism of *ad hoc* pragmatics. It is impossible to say with any assurance, in other words, whether the accord Saturn achieves between Mars and Venus is necessary (i.e., eternally affirmed) or contingent (i.e., constituted spontaneously). Chaucer's modifications to the *Teseida* result in the insoluble entanglement of necessity and contingency.

It seems relevant also that the figure responsible for re-establishing order among the gods should explicitly associate himself with disorder:

> Myn is the drenchyng in the see so wan;
> Myn is the prison in the derke cote;
> Myn is the stranglyng and hangyng by the throte,
> The murmure and the cherles rebellyng,
> The groynynge, and the pryvee empoisoning.   (1.2456–60)

Saturn's speech claiming as his own domain "the cherles rebellyng" is sharply at odds with Theseus's Boethian conviction that anyone who complains about the established order of things "*rebel* is to hym that al may gye" (1.3046). Saturn's function in the narrative is identical to Diana's: that is, he works simultaneously for *and* against the tale's formalist logic. By proving Diana right and wrong, he both confirms and rebels against the Knight's professed faith in predestination and Theseus's conception of the binding chain of love. I would further suggest that Saturn's double function also refutes Crane's alignment of romance irrationality with the feminine gender: According to the terms of Crane's own analysis, chaotic rebellion against rational order,

Saturn's bailiwick, is the *feminine* prerogative. As in *The Nun's Priest's Tale*, therefore, the Knight makes it impossible in the case of both Diana and Saturn to disentangle masculine form (or order) from feminine matter (or disorder). Thus, we cannot pronounce whether the Knight is a Boethian narrator any more than we can pronounce whether the Nun's Priest is an advocate for predestination. The Knight disorders his tale by means of order; he orders his tale by means of disorder. The world he creates insolubly entangles the necessity of providential order and the contingency of Saturnine rebellion.[24] This world is at once Christian *and* classical.

We should consider another, related departure from narrative logic in *The Knight's Tale* upon which several scholars have remarked. The grove within which Arcite and Palamon initially fight over their love for Emelye and the city of Thebes itself seem to possess a bizarre ontological inconsistency. That is, both the grove and Thebes miraculously come back into existence after their destruction, a situation that has no precedent in the *Teseida*. In a recent study, Robert Emmett Finnegan summarizes the enigmatic situation: "The citizens of Chaucer's *Knight's Tale* – divine, semi-divine, human – occupy a curious universe. It is a place where the principle of contradiction does not hold: Thebes is demolished by line 900 but is somehow reconstituted by line 1283; the grove is razed to make room for the amphitheater and razed again to provide place and material for Arcite's funeral."[25] For Finnegan, the volatility of the Knight's narrative universe suggests that a golden age has been lost, replaced by a time that lacks its "primal innocence" and atemporal stability. No doubt, the preparation of Arcite's funeral site does violently displace the peaceful indigenous inhabitants, prompting V.A. Kolve to remark that Athenian order "is created by means of an appalling disorder."[26] The Knight thus describes at length how the mythical creatures who once dwelled in the grove "in reste and pees" (1.2927) then "Fledden forfered whan the wode was falle" (1.2930). Even the denuded landscape "agast was of the light" (1.2931) after the abrupt clearance.

The grove is a highly charged site in *The Knight's Tale*. It is initially the locus of Palamon and Arcite's savage and unregulated combat. Theseus then constructs his vast arena, a mile in circumference, on this spot specifically to constrain this unlicenced violence. Finally, the miraculously reconstituted grove is cleared again, with "appalling disorder" according to Kolve, to accommodate Arcite's funeral services. But Theseus's eulogy for Arcite provides the opportunity, as we have seen, to unite Palamon and Emelye, thereby ensuring for him the alliance and subservience of Thebes.

The city of Thebes, as Finnegan observes, is exactly like the grove in that the city destroyed by Theseus somehow returns to existence, contrary to the *Teseida*, in which Thebes, once destroyed, remains so. Both Palamon (1.1328–31) and Arcite (1.1543–6; 1559–61) mention the destruction of their city and the eradication of the line of Cadmus. But Palamon earlier in the same speech, in which he bemoans the loss of his city, worries about Arcite walking at large *in Thebes* (1.1283) and assembling an army of his Theban kin to make war on Athens (1.1285–9). Likewise, before Arcite tells us that only he and Palamon survive from the line of Cadmus, we are informed that after his release from Theseus's prison he remained for a year or two ... in Thebes (1.1381). Palamon, moreover, as he hides after his escape from Theseus's prison in the same grove where he will soon meet Arcite, plans to go back ... to Thebes, to marshal his friends for an attack on Athens (1.1481–6). In sum, the grove is both destroyed for the amphitheatre and remains in existence until Arcite's funeral, only to be destroyed again; Thebes is both destroyed by Theseus and remains in existence to consolidate Athenian imperium, at that very funeral.

We can now see how closely the Knight resembles his protagonist. As I argued, it is undecidable whether the former is an agent of narrative order or an agent of narrative disorder. Analogously, Theseus first ruthlessly devastates the city of Thebes and then incorporates its recreated version into the order of Athenian polity in the name of love. He is, impossibly, *both* the city's savage destroyer and its benevolent preserver. The grove, moreover, is the site of Theseus's grand amphitheatre, designed to contain the unruly passions of the Theban cousins and situated on the very spot where they first do unlawful battle. The grove is then recreated only so that we can witness how mercilessly Theseus demolishes it and scatters its peaceable inhabitants in preparation for Arcite's obsequies. Theseus violently displaces the grove's mythical inhabitants in the same way as he violently displaces the survivors of Thebes's fall. But Arcite's funeral also provides Theseus with the opportunity to guarantee peacefully the obeisance of Thebes through Palamon's marriage to Emelye. The grove and Thebes are thus entwined spaces, demonstrating by their ontological inconsistency Theseus's and the Knight's simultaneous commitment to formal order and material chaos.

Following Muscatine and Cooper, therefore, we are free to decide that the Knight is a proponent of chivalric order and view Theseus's effort to master the contingencies of existence as analogous to the operation of providence. Following Aers and Patterson, we are also free to decide that his tale undermines any faith in the divinely ordained necessity of aristocratic power, leaving us with a Theseus who is a shrewd and ruthless political operator. Correlatively, it is possible to understand love and war in *The Knight's Tale* as instruments working on behalf of a harmonious comity, whether cosmic or political. It is also possible to understand love and war as radically disintegrative forces, in the service only of chaotic upheaval. Though we may decide on either of these interpretive extremes, the Knight does not. The world of *The Knight's Tale* is neither Boethian nor Venusian, neither Christian nor classical. The Knight himself ultimately endorses neither order nor chaos. His tale therefore will supply no decisive response to Palamon's agonized query: "What governance is in this prescience/That giltelees tormenteth innocence?" (1.1313–14). The Knight, as we have seen, seems to assert his faith in the just disposition of the universe according to the "purveiaunce" (1.1665) of God; but his response to Arcite's catastrophic injury is strikingly flippant, evoking not supernatural, but only *natural* causality: "And certeinly, ther Nature wol nat worche/Fare wel phisik! Go ber the man to chirche!" (1.2759–60). In contrast to this glib treatment, Boccaccio's Arcita is received into the eighth heaven after his death and from the elevated vantage he is afforded can rain down laughter on the vanity of the world he left behind. The Knight will not permit us the assurance of such a transcendent metaphysical perspective.[27] Nor will the Franklin, for that matter, who removes Fiammeta's transcendent authority. Is human suffering then a component of a meaningful and benevolent providential design? Or is the universe as capriciously indifferent to our calamities as are the Knight and Saturn to Arcite's? Exactly as in *The Nun's Priest's Tale*, it is undecidable whether the Knight's world is governed by a stable authorial purpose or unleashed from all control. Exactly as in *The Franklin's Tale*, this insoluble structure is the supreme expression of Chaucerian love.

The Miller's Prologue and Tale

Obviously, my reading of *The Knight's Tale* has significant interpretive repercussions for the remainder of Fragment 1. The Miller's response to the Knight, in particular, must be read with the undecidability of the latter's tale firmly in mind. Indeed, once we acknowledge that it is impossible to characterize the Knight unequivocally as a proponent of Boethian order, the meaning of the first fragment of *The Canterbury Tales* changes dramatically. But let us first consider how the Miller is introduced in his prologue. As opposed to the strict self-control of the Knight, the Miller is described as so inebriated that he can barely stay on his horse. He himself admits that his drunkenness may cause him to "mysspeke or seye" (1.3139), washing his hands of responsibility for his discourse in "Pilates voys" (1.3124). The absence of sober purposiveness and dignified self-governance anticipates the Miller's rejection of the Host's leadership, as he threatens to leave the fellowship if he is not permitted to tell his tale next. The Miller dismisses the hierarchical order that the Host attempts to impose on the sequence of taletellers. The latter, rather insultingly, insists that "Som bettre man shal telle us first another" (1.3130); but the Miller resists Harry's attempt to assert his authority: "For I wol speke or elles go my wey" (1.3133). Nor will he respect any religious authority, promising blasphemously to relate "a legende and a lyf/Both of a carpenter and of his wyf" (1.3141–2).[28] The Miller is a material element that simply will not obey the governance of formal authority. His rebellion against secular and religious authority, I suggest, parallels his abdication of authorial responsibility for his tale.

The Miller's Tale, his prologue implies, will be as ungoverned as its inebriated narrator. And yet, though we are justified in expecting a chaotic tale, this expectation is sensationally disappointed. *The Miller's Tale* has instead long been admired for its mathematical precision, especially the *contrapasso* endured by Alisoun's suitors. For Patterson, accordingly, the tale "displays everywhere an apparent flawless orderliness: not only does the apparently random aimlessness of the plot reveal itself to be ordered by an exquisite logic, but the unthinkable hedonism of the action leads to judgments of impeccable exactness."[29] Notwithstanding the technical virtuosity of the Miller, his tale has been understood as a rejection of the kind of rhetorical and metaphysical order that animates *The Knight's Tale*. Again, it is Muscatine who has been responsible for the key terms of scholarly responses. He contrasts the formal "conventionalism" and artifice of the philosophical Knight to the liberated "naturalism" and pragmatism of the earthy Miller: "In this remarkable self-contained world of facts, no room is left for abstract, *a priori* formulations."[30] Morton Bloomfield likewise opposes the Knight's Boethianism to the Miller's "unBoethian universe, a world which seems rational but is not really so. We are far away from a world which seems irrational but is really rational."[31] For Kolve, in this sequel to *The Knight's Tale* "Chaucer sought a perfectly antithetical vision, a look at life through eyes uncomplicated by transcendent idea or ideal."[32] Though Patterson shifts the focus of analysis away from the tension between abstraction and pragmatism, transcendence and immanence, and towards the class antagonism characteristic of late medieval England, he still understands *The Miller's Tale* as a revolt against established systems of order. The Miller's representation of peasant identity thus allows it "both to counter the hegemonic culture of the aristocracy and to subvert the language of class hatred promoted by certain forms of clerical discourse."[33] This review of foundational treatments of the Miller indicates the critical tendency to understand him as a materialist, in some way or the other revolting against institutions of philosophical, ideological, and social regulation.[34] This revolt touches also the genre that the Miller selects. According to Cooper, the point of the fabliau "is its amorality: the fabliau is the expression of the non-official culture of carnal irreverence, of all those feeling suppressed by courtly politeness or religious asceticism that break into joyous burlesque."[35] I wish to complicate this longstanding reading of the Miller as the materialist antithesis of the formalist Knight. In so doing, I will provide an account of why an apparent rebel against order should relate such a superbly ordered narrative.

No doubt, the Miller explicitly revolts against the social hierarchy of the pilgrimage. He seeks, moreover, to "quite" a socially elite adversary by overturning what he takes as the Knight's vision of the cosmos. The Miller's rejection of the established social order suggests to us exactly how he has read *The Knight's Tale*. He has read it as a formalist narrative – an aristocratic testament to the unyielding chains that install necessary social and metaphysical hierarchies. The Miller's objective, therefore, is to respond to the vision of order the Knight has supplied with its opposite – a materialist narrative. He will tell a tale not about necessity, but about *contingency*. The Miller has interpreted *The Knight's Tale* as a story about absolute prescience and rigid hierarchization. *The Miller's Tale*, by contrast, will be a story about the impossibility of *knowing*, and thus *controlling*, everything in advance. As the Miller so famously tells the Reeve:

"An housbonde shal nat been inquisityf
Of Goddes pryvetee, nor of his wyf.
So he may fynde Goddes foyson there,
Of the remenant nedeth nat enquire."   (1.3163–6)

There is a limit, Robyn tells Oswald, to how much we can know about the secret designs (or genitals) of God and the secret designs (or genitals) of a woman. According to Frederick Biggs and Laura Howes, "the juxtaposition suggests that both ends of the spectrum – both theologically significant and mundane matters – defy human understanding."[36] To attempt to master, or *formalize*, the secrets of either woman or God is to court disaster; we must resist the temptation to inquire about the mysterious "remenant" so as to enjoy God's bounty. There will always be a material element in the cosmos that resists the decisive imposition of epistemological closure, in exactly the same way as the Miller resists decisive social emplacement by the Host. As matter is invariably gendered feminine in

The Canterbury Tales, we can readily guess who in *The Miller's Tale* symbolizes this irrepressible element.[37] And yet, the Miller's conviction that man must eschew epistemological mastery is *masterfully* conveyed: A husband *"shall not be* inquisitive." The Miller communicates his anti-authoritarian stance authoritatively – almost as a Mosaic commandment. He is a master of non-mastery; he teaches us to remain ignorant.

The logical structure of the Miller's speech to the Reeve anticipates Chaucer's own words in *The Miller's Prologue*. Like Pilate, to whom the Miller has been compared, Chaucer also washes his hands of any responsibility for the offensive "cherles tale" (1.3169) he is about to relate:

> And therfore every gentil wight I preye,
> For Goddes love, demeth nat that I seye
> Of yvel entente, but for I moot reherce
> Hir tales alle, be they bettre or werse,
> Or elles falsen som of my mateere.   (1.3171–5)

I agree that what Cooper calls a "dangerously bland Chaucerian innocence" is, as she suspects, highly relevant to any understanding of *The Miller's Tale*.[38] Echoing his words from the *General Prologue* (1.725–42), the narrator assures us that he is merely reporting what he has heard on the pilgrimage accurately and therefore deserves no judgment for material that may offend a genteel audience. The abdication of authorial responsibility, as we have seen in the *General Prologue* and *The Nun's Priest's Tale*, is a materialist gesture, one that eliminates a final authorial cause towards which a reader may be oriented. Chaucer's "entente," evil or otherwise, will not govern *The Miller's Tale*. But, as with the Nun's Priest and the corresponding passage from the *General Prologue*, Chaucer's renunciation of authorial intentionality is not as straightforward as it seems. For Michael Kuczynski, Chaucer here becomes "a cartoon moral teacher, flouting the very normative moral discourse he invokes, in order to suggest the difficulties of placing or even defining the crucial ethical concept of blaming."[39] I agree that this passage is paradoxical, though not exactly in the way that Kuczynski asserts. Again, we must be alert to Chaucer's use of the imperative mood. He *commands* his genteel readers not to "<u>demeth</u>" that he speaks from evil intent, but instead to "<u>Turne</u> over the leef and <u>chese</u> another tale" (1.3177) should they desire to read something more virtuous. He instructs a potentially outraged audience that it should "<u>Blameth</u> <u>nat</u> me" if it does in fact "chese amys" (1.3181). The prologue concludes with a final directive: "<u>Avyseth</u> yow, and <u>put</u> me out of blame;/And eek men shal nat maken ernest of game" (1.3185–6). Chaucer does indeed absolve himself of authorial control over, and thus culpability for, *The Miller's Tale*, but he only does so *authoritatively*. What appears to be a materialist gesture is in fact more complicated: Chaucer asserts his authority by repealing his authority; he repeals his authority by asserting it. And he uses the same authoritative words as the Miller ("An housbonde *shal nat* been inquisityf") to register this earnest rejection of earnestness: "And eek men *shal nat* maken ernest of game" (1.3186). Chaucer's words in *The Miller's Prologue* give us a new way to understand the Miller's response to the Knight. I will argue that the Miller too can only rebel against authority *authoritatively*, which makes it undecidable whether or not he is, in fact, a rebel.

We should therefore observe that the success of the Miller's materialist riposte to the Knight depends entirely on the validity of an interpretive decision: The Miller has *decided* that the Knight is a formalist. The Miller *judges* the Knight to be a proponent of order. As I have attempted to demonstrate, however, it is undecidable whether this is indeed the case. We cannot say for certain whether the Knight is insisting on Boethian order (formalism) or on the radical *absence* of any transcendent order (materialism); as with *The Nun's Priest's Tale*, it is impossible to decide one way or the other. But this means that the Miller has masterfully collapsed the interpretive ambivalence of *The Knight's Tale*. What is more, the Miller wishes to *overcome* what he sees as this vision of formal necessity by means of a competing vision of material contingency. The result is that it is undecidable whether the Miller is a materialist (he rebels against formal mastery) or a formalist (he formally masters the Knight by abusively misreading his tale and authoritatively substituting his own vision). The Miller revolts *masterfully* against mastery. Though he identifies himself as an anti-authoritarian, the Miller ends up imposing his own authority, precisely what Chaucer does in the *General Prologue* and *The Miller's Prologue*.

On account of the Miller's masterful relationship to the Knight, therefore, it is possible to read *The Miller's Tale* in two opposed ways:

1) The Knight = John, Absolon, and Nicholas; the Miller = Alisoun.
2) The Miller = John, Absolon, and Nicholas; the Knight = Alisoun.

I will begin with the first option. According to this reading, the Miller himself is represented in his tale by a material element that escapes formal capture. Just as the Miller revolts against the order the Host attempts to impose, Alisoun refuses to serve as a passive object for the designs of Nicholas, Absolon, and her husband, John.[40] Both she and the Miller, then, are comparable to the colt rejecting the "trave" (1.3282) in Chaucer's vivid simile. Instead of a quiescent cog in Nicholas's elaborate machination to dupe John, Alisoun usurps Nicholas's role as arch-trickster, seizing *ad hoc* upon an opportunity to humiliate her annoying suitor, Absolon, and setting into motion a chain of events that will bring both Nicholas and John to grief. Alisoun thus refuses containment within Nicholas's formal design, just as Arcite's death undermines Theseus's attempt to bring order to chaos. As an instance of pure contingency, her hilarious intrusion into the proceedings could not have been predicted. Indeed, the Miller has already informed us that Alisoun has her own desires to which we, and the characters in the tale, may not be privy: "And sikerly she hadde a likerous ye" (1.3244). But the manipulative Nicholas, a resolute formalist whose astrological expertise suggests insight into the divine plan, simply cannot tolerate any material contamination of his carefully plotted scheme. He seeks instead to re-assert his absolute mastery of the situation: "he wolde amenden al the jape" (1.3799). Of course, Absolon will not be duped twice and has returned to the window armed with a blistering "kultour." Consequently, the master of revels is himself mastered, finding himself impaled by the "iren hoot" (1.3809) that he could not foresee. Nicholas's bid to re-establish control over the night's events, echoing Theseus's bid to marry Palamon and Emelye after Arcite's death, leads instead to a most painful loss of all control.

Now let us consider how Absolon's absurd fantasy, within which he styles himself as an aristocratic lover and Alisoun as the courtly object of his passion, is dramatically ventilated. Absalon, like "hende" Nicholas, wishes intensely to handle the attractive wife: "I dar wel seyn, if she hadde been a mous/And he a cat, he wolde hire *hente* anon." (1.3346–7). But physical or sexual mastery is for both men a secondary objective. Nicholas, the master puppeteer, derives the greatest pleasure from engineering his hyperbolic stratagem. Absolon, the enthusiastic thespian, derives his greatest pleasure from manufacturing a hyperbolic fantasy structure within which he can play the lovesick page and install Alisoun, contrary to her desire, as his courtly beloved:[41]

> Fro day to day this joly Absolon
> So woweth hire that hym is wo bigon.
> He waketh al the nyght and al the day;
> He kembeth his lokkes brode, and made hym gay;
> He woweth hire by meenes and brocage,
> And swoor he wolde been hir owene page;

He syngeth, brokkynge as a nyghtyngale;
He sente hire pyment, meeth, and spiced ale,
And wafres, pipyng hoot out of the gleede;
And, for she was of town, he profred meede;
For som folk wol ben wonnen for richesse,
And somme for strokes, and somme for gentillesse.
Somtyme, to shewe his lightnesse and maistrye,
He pleyeth Herodes upon a scaffold hye.
But what availleth hym as in this cas?   (1.3371–85)

Though Alisoun is totally uninterested in Absolon's suit, the aloofness of the beloved just serves the courtly fantasy. The beloved, like Guinevere with Lancelot, is *supposed* to be reserved and capricious with her affections: "Wel litel thynken ye upon my wo,/That for youre love I swete ther I go" (1.3701–2), says Absolon before Alisoun's window.[42] Alisoun's disdain and distance only serves his desire for a gratification that is both childlike and absolutely *clean*: "I moorne as dooth a lamb after the tete" (1.3704). Though we may be tempted to consider Absolon's simile perverse, nothing could be farther from the case. The fastidious Absolon wants innocent, hygienic pleasure, such as that provided to an infant by a mother's breast. No wonder, then, that he echoes the biblical Song of Songs in his entreaty to Alisoun: "What do ye, hony-comb, sweete Alisoun,/My faire bryd, my sweete cynamome?" (1.3698–9). He formalizes his beloved in the same way that Christian exegetes improbably gloss, and thus sanitize, the carnality of the original.[43] Indeed, what Absolon's libidinal formation cannot tolerate is carnality in its filthy and *material* manifestation, liberated from any fantasmatic distortion or gloss: "Derk was the night as pich, or as the cole,/And at the wyndow out she putte hir hole (1.3731–2). It is the unpredictable, contingent, intrusion of a material contaminant, the secret "remenant," that disrupts both Absolon's extravagant fantasy and Nicholas's equally extravagant plot. These formal structures just cannot accommodate dirt any more than a Boethian could accept anarchy. Nicholas's disastrous attempt to re-assert his mastery after Alisoun's intrusion into his design should be read as an attempt to sanitize his plan of any trace of matter. Likewise, after Absolon kisses Alisoun's ass, the narrator asks rhetorically: "Who rubbeth now, who froteth now his lippes/With dust, with sond, with straw, with clooth, with chippes" (1.3747–8). The "squaymous" (1.3337) Absolon's comically desperate attempt to cleanse his mouth after its contact with unclean matter anticipates his more disturbing attempt to sanitize Alisoun's "dirty" region with the cleansing heat of a plowing implement.[44] But the Miller removes Alisoun from harm, and Nicholas is injured, quite literally, by the intrusion of contingency into his plan. Both Absolon and Nicholas seek to reinstate their formal mastery and put matter in its appropriate place. In both cases, however, Alisoun, the unruly material element, eludes formal decontamination.

I turn now to John, the carpenter, an artisan who imposes form on the raw matter with which he works. John's absurd fantasy that the eighteen-year-old Alisoun will return his love and serve as a faithful wife, a prospect as likely as a second Flood, is also detonated by the end of the tale. Alisoun and Nicholas openly collaborate to convince his neighbours that he is insane: "For whan he spak, he was anon bore doun/With hende Nicholas and Alisoun" (1.3831–2). John unexpectedly becomes the passive object of ridicule instead of another Noah, privy to the designs of God and master of his own destiny. His foolish conviction that Nicholas has given him insight into the highest rationality results in his being held as totally without reason: "For every clerk anonright heeld with oother./They seyde, 'The man is wood, my leeve brother'" (1.3847–8). The carpenter, instead of possessing divine intelligence, is appropriately judged "wood." What is more, the young wife he supposedly holds "narwe in cage" (1.3224) has flown the coop; rebellious matter has escaped formal containment. Nicholas, Absolon, and John each in a different way become the butt of a joke, unexpectedly mastered by what they wished to master. Nevertheless, John's apparently sincere love for Alisoun makes him a special case, to which I will return later in this chapter.

Read this way, *The Miller's Tale* is without doubt a superb refutation of the Knight's. The Miller brilliantly burlesques what he sees as the latter's formalist insistence on the containment of chaos within the scheme of predestination and containment of the feminine within the confines of masculine desire. By the end of the tale, the Miller's representative, Alisoun, stands unscathed and victorious – demonstrating the triumph of material freedom over the constraint of formal necessity. The men who would dominate feminine matter are instead dominated: Rather than mastering the future, they become victims of its unpredictability. *The Miller's Tale* precisely mirrors the action of his prologue, wherein the Miller frees himself from the hierarchical expectations of the Host and the decorous expectations of the Reeve, imposing his own desires on the fellowship of pilgrims.

But, as stated above, we can read *The Miller's Tale* in an inverse fashion. Let us now consider the second interpretive option with which the tale presents us. *The Miller's Tale* is intended, after all, to overcome, or "quite" (1.3127) the Knight's. The Miller wants to *master* the Knight, to subordinate him by indicating the absurdity of his formalist philosophy and the hierarchical order it maintains. But this only means that he seeks to replace one hierarchical order by another – one in which the Miller is on top. We can, therefore, against the Miller's intentions, identify him with the other formalists in his tale: John, Nicholas, and Absolon. Indeed, his tale is as spectacularly constructed as Nicholas's elaborate ruse or Absolon's hermetic fantasy structure. But, in this case, Alisoun unexpectedly becomes a representative of the Knight himself. It is for this reason, I propose, that Absolon wishes to "quyte" (1.3746) Alisoun just as the Miller wishes to "quite" (1.3127) the Knight – the only two times the Miller uses this term in his prologue and tale. But the men in *The Miller's Tale* disastrously misread Alisoun, considering her as a placid and plastic element suitable only for their desires and designs. Likewise, the Miller misreads *The Knight's Tale*, collapsing its insoluble entanglement of necessity and contingency by masterfully *deciding* that the narrative proposes only a vision of suffocating order – a reading that serves his anti-authoritarian posture. What the Miller does to *The Knight's Tale* is akin to what Aurelius does to Dorigen's promise: To further his designs, Aurelius decides that her pledge is formally serious rather than materially playful; for the same reason, the Miller decides that *The Knight's Tale* is about formal order rather than material chaos.

Now, if Alisoun may be read as the Knight's representative, we can understand why the Miller, as much as Nicholas, Absolon, and John, seeks to contain, or formalize, Alisoun. How does he do this? First, he itemizes in detail her physical charms, scrutinizing her at his leisure as a passive object for scopic, tactile, olfactory, and gustatory delectation. Though he tells us that she has a "likerous ye," Alisoun for the Miller is also a "popelote" (1.3254), a little doll to enjoy unilaterally, without any concern for her autonomy. Second, the Miller concludes Alisoun's *effictio* by abruptly constraining her socio-sexual opportunities:

> She was a prymerole, a piggesnye,
> For any lord to leggen in his bedde,
> Or yet for any good yeman to wedde.   (1.3268–70)

The Miller, at least in this passage, is as convinced as Alisoun's lovers that he knows exactly where she belongs and exactly what she is good for: Alisoun, according to the narrator, is a suitable plaything for the passing fancy of a lord or a suitable wife for a good yeoman. With blatant inconsistency, the rebellious peasant provides an extremely *conservative* range of social possibilities for another peasant. He even reinstates the class hierarchies that he rejected in his prologue by claiming that an aristocrat could use this under-class "wenche" (1.3254) as he sees fit. And in both of the hypothetical cases the Miller provides, Alisoun is the object of a verb: "leggen" or "wedde." Chaucer therefore aligns the Miller with the other men in the tale who desire to master, or objectify, feminine matter and fail. He wants to keep her "narwe in a cage" (1.3224) as much as her husband. But the Miller's desire to contain Alisoun does not come from his misogyny, as scholars such as Karma Lochrie have argued. For Lochrie, the Miller's "triumphant conclusion, that [Alisoun] is a good lay for a lord and wife for a yeoman, completes her conversion into the 'femme privee,' if you will, placed at masculine disposal both within the tale and between teller and reader."[45] But, as *The Miller's Prologue* makes clear, the unruly Miller *identifies* with uncontainable feminine matter. He is, as we have seen, a self-professed materialist. Rather than evidence of the Miller's misogyny, then, the desire to contain Alisoun comes from his desire to master (or "quite") a *masculine* adversary, the Knight. The Miller, just like Nicholas, is far more interested in conquering a middle-aged man than he is in conquering a young woman.[46]

The Miller's highly conservative estimation of Alisoun's social prospects matches his assessment of John's choice to marry a much younger woman:

> He knew nat Catoun, for his wit was rude,
> That bad man sholde wedde his simylitude.
> Men sholde wedden after hire estaat,
> For youthe and elde is often at debaat. (1.3227–30)

While the old husband with a youthful and sexually unsatisfied wife is a stock character in the fabliau, it is still very curious that an anti-authoritarian like the Miller should utter these lines. Here we have a drunken peasant, who rudely defies the authority of the Host, reproaching a fellow peasant for rudely defying the authority of Cato. Moreover, just as the Miller criticizes the carpenter for his lack of wit, the Host had criticized the Miller for his lack of wit when he refused to respect the social hierarchy of the pilgrimage: "Thou art a fool; thy *wit* is overcome" (1.3135). In his tale, the Miller echoes the socially conservative Host: he elevates himself over the rude carpenter in the same way that the Host elevated the Monk over the rude Miller. After rebelling against the class hierarchy of the pilgrimage, he reinstates a class hierarchy in his tale: He is refined and John, who knows no Cato, is rude. The Miller even insists that men should live their lives according to the wisdom of Cato's authority. But this means that the unruly Miller thumbs his nose at secular and ecclesiastical authority in his prologue while mobilizing the force of classical authority in his tale. Finally, the carpenter, according to the Miller, has foolishly married someone who is not of his "estaat" ("condition," "rank," or "degree"). He not only marries outside the appropriate age bracket, he is also a "riche gnof" (1.3188), a peasant who is upwardly mobile. But shouldn't the rebellious Miller applaud, not censure, John's defiance of social gradations, whether related to class or age? The Miller of course demonstrates no respect whatsoever for his own "estaat" when he demands to tell a tale in the Monk's place. Though he is rebellious according to one perspective, he is conservative according to another. With respect to one reading of the tale (Miller = Alisoun), the Miller is on the side of material freedom; with respect to another (Knight = Alisoun), he is on the side of formal order. John's brutal comeuppance thus possesses a double valence: On the one hand, it represents the carpenter's incapacity to *order* Alisoun, the material element in the tale, "for al his kepyng and his jalousie" (1.3851); on the other hand, it represents the humbling of someone who himself will not respect the *order* of things. For this reason, he is literally brought down in his falling tub, a movement precisely matched by his social humiliation at the hands of his wife and her lover.

Thus, the rebellious Miller simultaneously rejects and imposes order. But *The Knight's Tale* eludes the Miller's attempt to formalize it as much as Alisoun eludes the attempt of her three lovers to master her. *The Miller's Tale* has been so difficult to interpret because the same character, Alisoun, represents both the Miller *and* his philosophical adversary.[47] The Miller must collapse the undecidability of *The Knight's Tale*; he imperiously judges that the Knight is a proponent of formal order. The Miller's "masterful" misreading makes his tale at once a brilliant success and a spectacular failure: the Miller's revolt against mastery relies on his masterful treatment of the Knight. He limits the signifying potential of *The Knight's Tale* in the same way that he limits the social potential of Alisoun. And if, according to this second reading, Absolon and Nicholas are both representatives of the Miller, then the hot coulter is the equivalent of *The Miller's Tale*.[48] The Miller, in the very process of requiting the Knight, ends up screwing himself. His weapon hits the wrong target, just as Absolon misses Alisoun and sears his counterpart, Nicholas, instead. *The Miller's Tale* implicitly aligns its narrator with exactly the position he intends to confute: formalism. By formally mastering *The Knight's Tale*, the Miller at the same time realizes and contradicts his intention; he succeeds even as he is undone. How else could we read such a magnificently *ordered* assault on order?

In sum, it is impossible to decide whether the Miller is a formalist or a materialist. He revolts masterfully against any attempt to master him; he hierarchically rejects all hierarchy. We must be alert throughout *The Canterbury Tales* to this kind of recursive logic. It is as if the Miller revolts against revolution; is he then a revolutionary or a reactionary? Chaucer in *The Miller's Prologue* conforms to the same recursive structure: He *authoritatively* abandons his authority over his readers, demanding imperiously that they not blame him if they choose amiss what they will read. It is thus undecidable whether *The Miller's Tale* fulfils or contradicts its teller's intentions, which may account for the variance in the audience's response: "Diverse folk diversely they seyde" (1.3857). The pilgrims could be laughing at the superb requital of the Knight, or they could be laughing at the Miller's self-humiliation. His virtuosic critique of authority relies on his authoritative treatment of the Knight. It is this duplicity that gives the tale its insoluble structure. The Liar paradox is true because it is false; it is false because it is true. Analogously, the Miller succeeds because he fails; he fails because he succeeds. To put it otherwise, authorial intention, or form, does (not) govern his tale. But this, for Chaucer, is the logical structure of love. As we saw in *The Franklin's Tale*, we love when it is undecidable whether we have mastered the beloved. This is exactly the (non-)relation that holds between the Miller and the Knight. The latter is mastered (Miller = Alisoun) and unmastered (Knight = Alisoun) *at the same time*. The undecidability of *The Knight's Tale* ensures that the Miller simultaneously hits and misses his target. The Miller's response to the Knight is highly instructive for our reading of *The Canterbury Tales*. Time and again we will witness the same scenario: The attempt to dominate the adversary, even in the case of the most virulent animosity, is miraculously transmuted into love by Chaucer's logic. In Fragment 1, therefore, the interplay between the Knight and the Miller prepares us well to interpret *The Reeve's Tale* and its *ad hominem* spleen.

The Reeve's Prologue and Tale

The Reeve's response to the Miller and the Knight transforms the class disparity between "genteel" formalism and "churlish" materialism into the scholastic disparity between "learned" formalism and "lewd" materialism. The tale, therefore, has two components. In the first half, the unlearned Symkyn gets the better of the Cambridge students despite their elite university education; in the second half, order is restored as the learned, if randy, students humiliate the drunken miller and, what is more, damage his cherished prospects for social climbing. The first half of the tale thus aims to supply a materialist narrative: The unruly and uneducated social climber prevails. The second half aims to supply a formalist counter-narrative: The learned students put the status-seeking thug in his proper place. For Patterson, therefore, the Reeve disarms the "peasant class consciousness" generated by *The Miller's Tale*, containing the rebellious energies the Miller conjures.[49] This is in keeping with what we know of the Reeve from the *General Prologue*. The narrator tells us that he keeps a careful account of his lord's possessions and income such that everything "was hoolly in this Reves governynge" (1.599). As opposed to the rebellious Miller, the Reeve is a tyrannical middle manager, dreaded by the peasants on his lord's estate: "They were adrad of hym as of the deeth" (1.605). Alcuin Blamires effectively sums up the Reeve's management style: "His supervision of grain and livestock is not so much admirable in its efficiency as awesome in the rigorousness of its scrutiny."[50] The Reeve governs strictly; the Miller rejects all governance. The opposition of the materialist Miller and formalist Reeve, however, is deceptive. Despite the Reeve's formal intentions, *The Reeve's Tale*, exactly as the Miller's, simultaneously will and will not fulfil its author's purpose. The Miller implicitly becomes that which he wishes to humiliate. The Reeve, as we will see, endures the same fate.

As with both the Knight and the Miller, Chaucer again subtly indicates the undecidability of *The Reeve's Tale* even before it begins. The irritated Reeve in his prologue insists that he will *not* "quite" (1.3864) the Miller because he has no desire to "speke of ribaudye" (1.3865). By the end of the prologue, however, he has come to the opposite position: "I shal hym quite anon;/Right in his cherles termes wol I speke" (1.3916–17). The Reeve's discourse denies what it asserts and asserts what it denies. We should also note that the Reeve promises to comport himself towards the Miller in exactly the same way as the Miller has behaved towards him. He will use the Miller's own churlish "termes" against the Miller. The Reeve even borrows the Miller's own word from the latter's prologue, "quite," to indicate his oppositional strategy. To humiliate the Miller, therefore, the Reeve will *become* the Miller. This means, of course, that by humiliating the Miller the Reeve is also humiliating himself. His tale will thus succeed by failing and fail by succeeding, as does the Miller's own tale.

The Reeve's grotesque metaphors for his aging sexuality further emphasize the duplicity of his position. He is like an "open-ers" (1.3871), a fruit that is simultaneously rotten and ripe (1.3875), or a leek, that has "a hoor heed and a grene tayl" (1.3878). As will his tale, the Reeve embodies the contradiction of youth and age, decay and vitality; he is neither alive nor dead, but always dying: "For sikerly, whan I was bore, anon/Deeth drough the tappe of lyf and leet it gon" (1.3892–3).[51] The Reeve thus travesties Christ's admonition to Peter to avoid temptation from Matthew 26:41 ("the spirit is willing but the body is weak") by interpreting "spirit" as sexual desire: "Oure olde lemes mowe wel been unwelde,/But wyl ne shal nat faillen, that is sooth" (1.3886–7). In the process of remarking upon his spiritual potency and carnal impotency, the Reeve simultaneously espouses and perverts Christ's teaching by reading it carnally and not spiritually: He carnally claims that he can no longer be carnal. Indeed, the Host sharply rebukes this torsion of Scripture: "What shul we speke alday of hooly writ?/The devel made a reve for to preche" (1.3902–3).[52] But the Reeve's devilish preaching continues to the end of his prologue, with another travesty of Matthew:

> "This dronke Millere hath ytoold us heer
> How that bigyled was a carpenteer,
> Peraventure in scorn, for I am oon.
> And, by youre leve, I shal hym quite anoon;
> Right in his cherles termes wol I speke.
> I pray to God his nekke mote to-breke;
> He kan wel in myn eye seen a stalke,
> But in his owene he kan not seen a balke."   (1.3913–20)

The Reeve's citation of Matthew 7:1–4 reiterates his ambivalent treatment of Scripture: "Judge not that ye be not judged, for with what measure ye mete, it shall be measured to you again, and with what judgment you judge, ye shall be judged. And why sayst thou to thy brother, Brother, let me draw out the mote which is in thy eye and behold a beam is in thy own eye?" The Reeve uses Christ's Sermon on the Mount to condemn the Miller as a hypocrite. But he has just admitted that he will conduct himself in exactly the same way as the Miller. In his prologue, therefore, the Reeve *hypocritically* condemns the Miller's hypocrisy.[53] Paul Olson detects the same structure in the Reeve's speech: He "judges his rival for having made a judgment and so violates his premise in the asserting."[54] *The Reeve's Tale* will function analogously, condemning its narrator even as it condemns his adversary.

On a preliminary reading, *The Reeve's Tale* is a mere instrument for Oswald's vengeance on Robyn, who is caricatured in the tale by means of the drunken, thieving, murderous, and *arriviste* Symkyn. Symkyn is not only a brute; he is a brute who does not accept his place in the social pecking order, just as the Miller refuses to respect the social hierarchy on the pilgrimage. But a more circumspect reading of the tale reveals Chaucer's artistry. The tale is less about the obvious equation of the two millers, Robyn and Symkyn, and more about the Reeve's identification *both* with the Cambridge students and with Symkyn himself. The structure of double identification precisely reflects *The Miller's Tale*, in which we witnessed the narrator's identification both with Alison and her lovers.

We should consider first the most prominent parallels between the Reeve and the Cambridge students. Joseph Taylor states that "In the climactic scene of *The Reeve's Tale*, the clerks are not merely antagonists to Symkyn but his unwieldy doubles."[55] I agree but would argue that this doubling occurs much earlier. While the Reeve, according to the *General Prologue*, hails from Baldeswelle, in "Northfolk" (1.620), John and Aleyn are from Strother (1.4014–15), also northern, but much farther, perhaps as far Northumbria.[56] The Cambridge students, as the Reeve's representatives, are thus exaggerated versions of the pilgrim. Furthermore, as we have seen, the Reeve spends much of his prologue describing the challenging predicament of having a "coltes tooth" (1.3888) in an old man's failing body. He may be old, but he still burns with a young man's sexual desires and envies their physical capacities. Nevertheless, his sexual desires do find a convenient vehicle in the vengeance that Aleyn and John, his proxies, enact on Symkyn via his daughter and wife. But the parallels between the Reeve and the students are not only geographical and temperamental; they are also ethical. In blatant contradiction of the Sermon on the Mount, from which he cites, the Reeve is a proponent of talionic justice.[57] He justifies his counterattack on the Miller in exactly those terms: "For leveful is with force force of-showve" (1.3912). But Aleyn, plotting his vengeance on Symkyn, espouses a nearly identical principle:

> For, John, ther is a lawe that says thus:
> That gif a man in a point be agreved,
> That in another he sal be releved.   (1.4180–2)

The students and the Reeve share a legalistic standard of conduct that provides no space for forgiveness, but instead insists upon the precise repayment of words and deeds. In this regard, it is telling that Symkyn sarcastically invites Aleyn and John by means of their learned arguments to make his narrow house "A myle brood of twenty foot of space" (1.4123). The students give the miller precisely what he asks for when they deploy their legalistic training to claim an "esement" (1.4186), thereby affording Aleyn and John the freedom to move to spaces otherwise restricted to them. Indeed, this measure-for-measure economy governs the very structure of *The Reeve's Tale*. The first half of the tale, which relates the victory of the miller over the students, is a version of *The Miller's Tale*, in which the Reeve's representative, John the carpenter, receives a severe comeuppance after being tricked by Nicholas and Alisoun. Likewise, Symkyn tricks Aleyn and John, also the Reeve's representatives, by releasing their horse while he swindles them. The second half of the tale, which relates the triumph of the students over the miller, represents Oswald's balancing of the scales of justice. He appropriately closes the tale with a settling of accounts: "Thus have I quyt the Millere in my tale" (1.4324).

Unfortunately for the Reeve, his own tale requites him in kind as well.[58] We should also observe, therefore, the close parallels between the Reeve and Symkyn.[59] These parallels generate an alternative reading of *The Reeve's Tale* that contradicts the first. Above all, both Oswald ("colerik," 1.587) and the *"hoote*, deynous Symkyn" (1.3941) are explicitly characterized as choleric men. In line with their bilious temperaments, the Reeve carries a rusty blade by his side while the miller is heavily armed with edged weapons (1.3929–33). Just as the Cambridge students exaggerate aspects of the Reeve (e.g., his northerness and his horniness), so does Symkyn. Despite their hot dispositions, moreover, neither Symkyn nor the Reeve is in the vigour of youth or at the height of sexual potency. The Reeve reveals in his prologue that his will "desireth folie evere in oon" (1.3880) but bemoans that his "myght" (1.3879) is gone. Likewise, when describing John's exertions with Symkyn's wife, the Reeve slyly informs us that "So myrie a fit ne hadde she nat ful yoore" (1.4230). It has been a long time since Symkyn's wife has enjoyed herself in bed as she does with the youthful and vigorous clerk.

The first half of *The Reeve's Tale*, by contrast, relates the victory of wily age over spirited youth.[60] Apart from their physical characteristics, Symkyn and the Reeve share a predilection for theft and both steal from younger men. Symkyn cheats Aleyn and John at his mill, and Oswald, it is implied in the *General Prologue*, steals from his own lord, for whom the Reeve has been working since the latter was "twenty yeer of age" (1.601): "His lord wel koude he plesen subtilly,/To yeve and lene hym of his owene good" (1.610–11). Just as he amplifies the Reeve's choleric tendencies, Symkyn amplifies the former's penchant for fraud: "For therbiforn he stal but curteisly/But now he was a theef outrageously" (1.3997–8). As a result of Reeve's craftiness, we are told, his wealth may even exceed that of his superior: "He koude bettre than his lord purchace./Ful riche he was astored pryvely" (1.608–9). Though he mocks Symkyn's social ambitions, the Reeve himself is a social climber, as Murray Copland suggests by way of his priestly tendencies: "he has left his perfectly 'good' mystery for a quick step up the social scale."[61]

Certainly, the Reeve's proclivity for stealing from, and outdoing, his social superior anticipates Symkyn's delight at duping those who consider themselves his intellectual superiors. After they travel to the mill from their college, John and Aleyn pretend to be ignorant of the milling process so as to watch Symkyn carefully and ensure his honesty. But Symkyn is contemptuous of the obviousness of their scheme, stating:

> They wene that no man may hem bigyle,
> But by my thrift, yet shal I blere hir ye,
> For al the sleighte in hir philosophye.
> The moore queynte crekes that they make,
> The moore wol I stele whan I take.   (1.4048–52)

The superior learning of the young students has given them a confidence they do not merit, according to Symkyn. He will beguile them despite all the subtlety of their erudition. The final two lines of this passage, moreover, return us once again to the *lex talionis*, whereby the miller will pay back the students' clever tricks with proportionate theft ("The moore … The moore"). This is a logic of exchange to which the Reeve would certainly grant his approval, as the proverb he quotes at the close of his narrative indicates: "'Hym thar nat wene wel that yvele dooth.'/A gylour shal hymself bigyled be" (1.4320–1).

Thus, both the libidinous, legalistic, and northern students, Aleyn and John, *and* Symkyn, the choleric, armed, aged, dishonest, and sexually impotent miller, reflect the libidinous, northern, legalistic, choleric, armed, aged, dishonest, and impotent Reeve within his tale. Even the Reeve's tonsured pate (1.589) prefigures Symkyn's bald head: "As piled as an ape was his skulle" (1.3935). I suggest that the necessity of identifying the Reeve with the protagonists of his tale *and* Symkyn, the primary antagonist, means that, exactly like the Miller's narrative, *The Reeve's Tale* fails because it succeeds and succeeds because it fails. In fulfilling its author's intention (formalism) it escapes this intention (materialism), and vice versa. Even as he avenges himself upon the Miller, the Reeve unknowingly *becomes* him. It is fitting, therefore, that the miller's wife is unable during the climactic nighttime brawl to distinguish John from Symkyn: "But sikerly she nyste who was who" (1.4300).[62] The double identification of the Reeve has completely elided the difference between the combatants, for the reader as much as for Symkyn's wife.[63] The Reeve, therefore, is not only beating the Miller; he is also beating himself. Even more strikingly, *The Reeve's Tale* represents *itself* within itself. Symkyn, after all, is injured by precisely those figures who are supposed to advance his social and economic prospects: Malyne, who directs Aleyn to the missing cake of meal; his infant son, whose misplaced cradle leads Symkyn's wife to John's bed; and his "high-born" wife, who mistakenly beds a clerk and "mills" the miller's gleaming skull. Likewise, Oswald's tale, with which he expects to avenge himself upon the Miller, is simultaneously an instrument that turns back against him. *The Reeve's Tale* thus resembles the hot coulter of Absolon that causes Nicholas such grief: Both the Miller and the Reeve injure themselves with their own implements.

The "white thyng in hir ye" (1.4301) that distorts the wife's perception and leads her to club Symkyn at the climax of the tale is meant by Chaucer, I believe, to echo the Reeve's paraphrase of Matthew 7:1–4 in the final lines of his prologue: "He kan wel in myn eye seen a stalke,/ But in his owene he kan nat seen a balke" (1.3919–20). What *The Reeve's Tale* demonstrates above all is that judgment is *misjudgment*. The overconfident Cambridge students misjudge Symkyn, who overconfidently misjudges them in turn. Aleyn misjudges Symkyn for John when he boasts of his conquest of Malyne. The wife misjudges John for Symkyn during their nighttime tryst. The wife misjudges Symkyn for Aleyn when she brains the former. But Christ's caution from his Sermon on the Mount, "Judge not, lest ye be judged," has both an ethical and a hermeneutic significance for *The Canterbury Tales*. The Miller and the Reeve unequivocally judge the tellers and the tales that confront them. It should be no surprise, then, that the version of God that the Reeve favours is the supreme Judge, "that sitteth heighe in magestee" (1.4322). But Christ's teaching insists that judgment will only rebound upon the judgmental; indeed, this is exactly what happens to the Miller and the Reeve. The attempt by these pilgrims to master their adversaries only recoils upon them. Both the Miller and the Reeve thus exemplify what I call Chaucer's "law of unintended consequences": form is (not) related to matter. The realization of authorial intention is simultaneously the failure of authorial intention. This principle of charity, as I aim to prove, governs all the adversarial and vengeful pilgrims we will encounter in *The Canterbury Tales*. Chaucer is trying to teach us not to judge – not to *decide* – but instead to love. For this reason, even his judgmental pilgrims will deliver tales that are logically insoluble.

This interpretation of Fragment 1 allows me to provide an account of the most disturbing feature of *The Reeve's Tale*: the depiction of Malyne.[64] We should first consider the way that the Reeve depicts Symkyn's daughter. His perfunctory description focuses mainly on her body, which is represented in crude terms equally suitable to livestock: "This wenche thikke and wel ygrowen was/... With buttokes brode and brestes rounde and hye" (1.3973–5). These rough details are juxtaposed incongruously to Malyne's more delicate, even aristocratic, features: Like Guinevere, she possesses "eyen greye as glas" (1.3974); and "right fair was hire heer; I wol nay lye" (1.3976) the Reeve informs us. Tamarah Kohanski thus determines that Malyne does not provide "a uniform picture of lowness" but "a far more complex character, a subtle mixture of low and high traits."[65] Nevertheless, according to the narrative structure of the tale and in line with his crude assessment of her body, the Reeve equates Malyne to John's horse. Both are made to work against, rather than for, their masters. The students spend their time chasing their steed through the fens instead of forestalling Symkyn's shenanigans at the mill, and Malyne tells Aleyn exactly where her father has hidden the ill-gotten cake of meal. But, as her ambiguous portrait suggests, there is far more to Malyne than this.

As Symkyn also intends to arrange a noble marriage for her to advance his family's standing, Malyne's clear affection for Aleyn, along with the loss to him of her virginity, contributes to the ruin of his designs and his humiliation. Aleyn, by contrast, regards Malyne as mere property, to which he has been granted a legal right, or "esement" (1.4179 and 4186) by Symkyn's thieving. Aleyn makes his approach while she sleeps, "Til he so ny was, er she myghte espie,/That it had been to late for to crie" (1.4196). There is no possibility here of consent; Malyne is a passive object for the satisfaction of Aleyn's vengeance and lust. And yet, incongruously, Malyne shows considerable tenderness at their parting.[66] She sincerely commends Aleyn to God and, as he departs, we are told, "almoost she gan to wepe" (1.4248). The depth of emotion that this description reveals is unsettling and must complicate our response to a figure whom the Reeve regards as a mere fabliau "wenche" (1.3973) with a narrowly circumscribed role. Malyne seems to have fallen in love with her rapist.

Aleyn's own feelings for Malyne, and the improbability that he will reciprocate her affection, are conveyed by the triumphantly crude words that he intends to direct to his associate, but mistakenly speaks to Symkyn: "I have thries in this shorte nyght/Swyved the milleres doghter bolt upright" (1.4265–6). Malyne's desires simply do not matter in this tale, not to Aleyn, to the Reeve, or to Symkyn, for whom she is just an instrument for his social ambitions. The pathos of her fondness for Aleyn is a detail within the narrative that is, therefore, as incongruous as her strangely refined features. I agree with the assessment of W.W. Allman and D. Thomas Hanks Jr.: "The appearance of a woman as a speaking subject can never be assumed or taken as a given in medieval literature. Malyne's speech, we claim, is a narrative moment that has escaped not Chaucer's, but Oswald's control; the very least that can be made of the speech is that it is deeply ambiguous."[67] Malyne is intended only as a means, whether of sexual pleasure, of vengeance, of social advancement, or of plot. But beyond these crass functions imposed upon her, she also reveals her desire, at once hopeless and dignified, to be loved.

There are two other characters in Fragment 1 who function in the same way as Malyne within their respective tales: John and Emelye. As absurd and ill-advised as John's love for the teen-aged Alison may be, we cannot doubt it. The Miller tells us that the carpenter loves her "moore than his lyf" (1.3222), and, indeed, upon hearing of the impending apocalypse, his thoughts turn immediately to Alisoun: "Allas, my wyf!/And shal she drenche? Allas, myn Alisoun!" (1.3522–3). Even though the Miller informs us that "Jalous he was, and heeld hire narwe in cage" (1.3224), an opinion seconded by Alisoun (1.3294), John is relatively unperturbed by Absolon's nighttime wooing, has no problem lodging a virile young clerk, and leaves Alisoun to her own devices when he leaves for work in Oseney. As Miller observes, "we never see John as the jealously restrictive husband, despite the opportunities the Miller has to cast him in such a light."[68] But the carpenter's apparently sincere love, just as Malyne's, is irrelevant beyond its instrumentality to the Miller's plot. John's devotion to his young wife just works to make him more likely to accept Nicholas's hugely improbable fabrication. Alisoun herself is so unaffected by her husband's affection that she will betray him to his face. John's love for his wife simply does not matter to anyone – not to Nicholas, not to Absolon, not to Alisoun, and certainly not to the Miller. The carpenter's love is just a means in the service of a narrative final cause. The chain reaction of humiliations initiated by Alisoun's "nether eye" thus culminates with the broken-armed and, presumably, broken-hearted John as the focal point of communal mockery. But this punishment seems utterly disproportionate, especially as John is no more the stock fabliau type of the jealous husband than Malyne is the stock fabliau type of the lusty wench.

Is it not also the case that Emelye's prayer to Diana is above all an entreaty for love? The Amazon indicates to the goddess that she "love[s] huntynge and venerye/And for to walken in the wodes wilde" (1.2308–9), rather than to be a wife with a child. She then prays for Diana to "sende love and pees" between Palamon and Arcite (1.2316). Finally, she asks that, if she must be with one of her suitors, she be sent the lover that *most* desires her (1.2325). Jamie Friedman thus asserts that while "men engage its central ideologies, the *Knight's Tale* simultaneously tells the story of one woman's desire to live outside the regimes of male control and objectification produced and legitimated by that romance."[69] But the visit to the temple of Diana only serves to confirm Emelye's future: The narrative trajectory of the tale has already been *decided*. Even after Arcite's death, Theseus ensures a politically advantageous marriage to the surviving Theban prince and, in the final lines of the tale, Emelye is given no space either to concur with or gainsay Theseus's plan: "Lene me youre hond, for this is oure accord" (1.3082), he imperiously informs the speechless Amazon. Emelye's desire for what she loves, along with John's and Malyne's, has always already been overridden by an authorial cause.

But that incongruous element irrelevant to the narrative form of the Knight's, Miller's, and Reeve's tales suggests the only way to read them correctly or, better, *charitably*. Chaucer, in the same way as his own representatives in Fragment 1, Emelye, John, and Malyne, is pleading for a loving response. And if we are moved by the plight of these characters, as most if not all readers are, then we implicitly reject the violent, masterful, and judgmental manner with which they are treated in their tales. But the rejection of judgment, the rejection of decision, is exactly what Chaucer understands as love.

The Cook's Prologue and Tale

Now, I believe, we have a new way to read the truncated tale with which Fragment 1 concludes. Scholars have pondered two possible interpretations: perhaps 1) Chaucer intended to leave *The Cook's Tale* unfinished, or 2) some unforeseen event, such as Chaucer's death, prevented the fulfilment of his authorial design.[70] It is true that *The Cook's Tale* seems to extend the degenerative trajectory of Fragment 1, as Donald Howard suggests.[71] We begin with the elegant symmetries of the aristocratic Knight. The bawdy precision of the drunken Miller follows, and then the irascible Reeve ends his tale with a chaotic brawl. The hard-drinking Cook seems an excellent candidate to prolong this downward arc, and indeed offers to tell a "litel jape" (1.4343), rather than a moral (i.e., formal) tale. The exchange between Harry and Roger seems to emphasize the latter's materialist orientation. After teasing the Cook about the quality of his food, the Host concludes that "A man may seye ful sooth in game and pleye" (1.4355), suggesting that some synthesis of truth (form) and play (matter) is possible. The Cook's response is telling; he agrees that truth and game may be synthesized but that the result is infelicitous: "Thou seist ful sooth .../But 'sooth pley, quaad pley,' as the Flemyng seith" (1.4356–7). He will instead supply playful matter liberated from any relation to truthful form.

Harry, therefore, has no reason to take offense, even though the tale will be about an innkeeper (1.4360).

The Cook's materialism is emphatically reflected in his tale. The hero of his story, Perkyn Revelour, is represented as utterly purposeless and, as the Flemish proverb adumbrates, is *free* of any relation whatsoever to truth: "Revel and trouthe, as in a lowe degree,/They been ful wrothe al day as men may see" (1.4397–8). His master quickly fires him, leaving him jobless and homeless. Appropriately, Perkyn's counterpart is a prostitute, a female whose body escapes any masculine, or formal, containment. It is with mention of her that the tale prematurely concludes. A narrative, introduced as purposeless and populated by purposeless characters, ends before revealing any purpose. *The Cook's Tale* seems to be the perfect exemplification of matter without any relation to form.

But, unlike in the case of *The Tale of Sir Thopas* or *The Monk's Tale*, a character in the frame narrative does not interrupt *The Cook's Tale*.[72] So did Chaucer *intend* to abbreviate the tale (formalism) to indicate the aimlessness of Fragment 1? Or is the tale truncated on account of some *material* exigency beyond the author's control (materialism), such as his death? The note in the Hengwrt manuscript ("Of this Cokes tale maked Chaucer na moore"), identified by Linne R. Mooney as in the hand of Chaucer's acquaintance, professional scribe Adam Pinkhurst, does not eliminate this ambivalence.[73] *The Cook's Tale* raises the same problem as does the universe of *The Knight's Tale*. Is this tale evidence of the "noble design" of Fragment 1 or instead its exposure to the unpredictable "chaos" of historicity? I suggest that the way to read Chaucer lovingly, and in doing so redeem the otherwise meaningless suffering of Emelye, John, and Malyne, is to suspend any final judgment. The "fragmentary" state of *The Cook's Tale* insolubly entangles necessity and contingency in the same way as does Diana's speech to Emelye in the goddess's temple or the Nun's Priest's words to his audience at the close of his tale. What is said of *The Cook's Tale* could be said of the entire sequence of extant tales, which, of course, number far fewer than we would expect from the terms the Host establishes for the pilgrims in the *General Prologue* (1.791–5). Robert J. Meyer-Lee's scrutiny of the manuscript evidence leads him to conclude that we should not reflexively assume that the lacunary and disjunctive state of *The Canterbury Tales* is unintentional. We should instead acknowledge that its disjunctions and gaps produce "thematically rich tensions between design and contingency, order and spontaneity, eternity and history, life and death" that call for interpretation.[74] In line with Meyer-Lee's claim, it is my view that in order to bear witness to Chaucer's logic of love, *The Canterbury Tales* simply could not appear finished. An ostensibly complete work would possess an obvious *form*.[75]

In conclusion, Fragment 1 has equipped us with an additional interpretive implement, which I have called Chaucer's law of unintended consequences. According to this principle, the judgmental pilgrims of *The Canterbury Tales* will see their intentions thwarted even as they succeed. By contrast, the charitable pilgrims, in line with Christ's admonition from the Sermon on the Mount, refuse to judge. In the following chapter, dealing with the Man of Law and the Wife of Bath, we will encounter a radically judgmental narrator and one who may very well be Chaucer's most virtuosic teacher of love.

3 Vengeance and Forgiveness in Fragments 2 and 3

The Man of Law's Introduction, Prologue, and Tale

The Man of Law's introduction, prologue, and tale, I will argue in this chapter, reflect on the concerns of Fragment 1 and anticipate the Wife of Bath's confrontation with masculine authority. The impossible love of Emelye, John, and Malyne, callously disregarded within the first three tales of Fragment 1, finds an apt reflex in the Man of Law's treatment of Custance, especially her function within his tale as a pawn in the service of God, her father, and the Man of Law himself.

The Man of Law's Introduction is complex and elusive. Nevertheless, I believe our reading of Fragment 1 has given us the tools by means of which to resolve some of its interpretive challenges. It is crucial to determine above all whether the Man of Law may be characterized as *charitable* or *judgmental*. Does he attempt to master an opponent and impose his own authority? I propose that the Man of Law, just as the Miller and the Reeve, does, in fact, aim to outdo an adversary; the meta-fictional complication, in this case, is that the adversary is Chaucer himself. The adversarial tales of Fragment 1, as we saw, recoil upon their tellers in accordance with Chaucer's law of unintended consequences: The fulfilment of authorial intention is simultaneously the failure of authorial intention. To put it in terms borrowed from Matthew 7, terms particularly suitable to a lawyer, the judge is judged by his own judgment. Thus, the Miller and the Reeve, in humiliating their adversaries, also *become* their adversaries. The Man of Law finds himself in exactly the same predicament with Chaucer.

The apparent theme of the Man of Law's introduction and prologue is dearth: a dearth of time, a dearth of virgins, a dearth of stories, a dearth of money, and a dearth of poetic talent. The Host thus remarks upon the quickly fading day: "Lordynges, the tyme wasteth nyght and day"

(2.20). He notes that time, once lost, may never be retrieved "Namoore than wole Malkynes maydenhede/Whan she hath lost it in hir wantownesse" (2.30–1). The Man of Law, after observing that his obligation to tell a tale is a "dette" (2.41), remarks upon the lack of stories available to him in English. Chaucer, despite his dearth of technical refinement, has told them all:

> I kan right now no thrifty tale seyn
> That Chaucer, thogh he kan but lewedly
> On metres and on ryming craftily,
> Hath seyd hem in swich Englissh as he kan
> Of olde tyme, as knoweth many a man.   (2.46–50)

The only texts by Chaucer that the Man of Law mentions, however, are those that feature wives and faithful lovers from classical sources. The Man of Law thus calls attention to the Ovidian narrative of Ceyx and his devoted wife, Alcione, retold in Chaucer's early poem, *The Book of the Duchess*: "In youthe he made of Ceys and Alcione" (2.57). But he singles out for special mention the *Legend of Good Women* ("the Seintes Legende of Cupide" [2.61]) and provides a long list of the pagan women featured therein, including some who do not appear in extant versions of Chaucer's classical "hagiography." The Man of Law's inaccurate and incomplete account of the Chaucerian oeuvre prompts Rodney Delasanta to argue that "the Man of Law's introduction, prologue, and Tale are quietly networked with an interstitial patter of errors about things literary – like this erroneous catalogue of good women – that cannot be attributed to ignorance or planned revisions on Chaucer's part."[1] The Man of Law, I suggest, attempts here to formalize Chaucer's literary achievements. With a gesture at once masterful and distortive, analogous to the Miller's framing of the Knight or Absolon's framing of Alisoun, he identifies his competitor as a lacklustre prosodist who composes poems *only* about classical wives and lovers. The Man of Law's abusive framing of Chaucer's corpus gives him an avenue by means of which he can outdo his competitor: He will tell a story about a virtuous Christian wife instead of a virtuous classical wife.

The Man of Law imposes a further constraint upon himself, only intensifying the scarcity of tales available. He emphatically rejects all narratives that contain the motif of incest, regarding such acts as "unkynde abhomynaciouns" (2.88). In this, he says, he is following Chaucer's example, a poet who likewise avoids what the Man of Law deems an unpalatable topic. But the first example of an incestuous figure he mentions is "Canacee" (2.78), the heroine of Chaucer's own *Squire's Tale*. As Elizabeth Scala notes, "Not only does he praise Chaucer for his most inelegant poetry – forgetting the later dream-visions and *Troilus and Criseyde* – the Man of Law announces Chaucer's reluctance to tell a tale which he seems to be telling elsewhere."[2] How do we make sense of this? The incongruous mention of Canacee, I wish to argue, is an element of a pattern in the Man of Law's introduction and prologue, one that anticipates the structure of his tale. The Man of Law, as we will see, imitates Chaucer, but in precisely the opposite way that he intends. He *intends* to follow Chaucer by *not* telling of incest (such as between Canacee and her brother). He will indeed follow Chaucer, and thus realize his intention, but, as we will see, only by *telling* a tale of incest: *The Man of Law's Tale* will thus simultaneously accomplish and contradict its narrator's intention – a neat exemplification, as I aim to demonstrate, of the principle of unintended consequences.[3]

The Man of Law's disgust towards incest is directed most forcefully towards a father's sexual conquest of, and violence towards, his daughter, as occurs in the Greek romance of Apollonius of Tyre. According to the Man of Law, this narrative relates:

> How that the cursed kyng Antiochus
> Birafte his doghter of hir maydenhede
> That is so horrible a tale for to rede,
> Whan he hir threw upon the pavement.
>
> (2.82–5)

The rape of Antiochus's daughter and her loss of "maydenhede" echo what the Host says in passing about the proverbial "Malkyne." Furthermore, "Malkyne" is only one letter away from "Malyne," the innocent victim of sexual assault in *The Reeve's Tale*. I believe Chaucer's evocation of the violent abuse of innocence anticipates *The Man of Law's Tale* and the misfortunes his own heroine endures. The Man of Law, despite his protestations to the contrary, is going to tell a version of the story of Antiochus and his daughter, paralleled in his tale by the Emperor and Custance. I will go further: *The Man of Law's Tale* is also a version of the stories Chaucer tells in his *Legend of Good Women*. In the prologue to *The Legend of Good Women*, Cupid and Alceste command Chaucer to do penance for his slander of women "goode and trewe" (G 272). He is to accomplish this penance by composing hagiographical accounts of classical women, forcing characters such as Cleopatra and Medea into an artificially contracted and warped generic frame. Chaucer's treatment of these classical narratives is as distortive and abusive as the Man of Law's treatment of Chaucer's own literary achievements. In his tale, the Man of Law does not tell about a "good and true" pagan woman; he tells of a good and true Christian wife. But *The Man of Law's Tale* is also secular hagiography, forcing a worldly and often reluctant wife into the role of saint.[4] The Man of Law will do to Custance, therefore, exactly what Chaucer does to the heroines of his classical legendary. In this way, the Man of Law just becomes his poetic competitor.

The Man of Law's reference to Ovid's *Metamorphoses* bolsters my reading of the mirror relation between the pilgrim and Chaucer: "But of my tale how shal I doon this day?/Me were looth be likned, doutelees,/To Muses that men clepe Pierides" (2.91–2). Ovid denominates both the Muses, born in Pieria, *and* their ill-fated competitors, the daughters of Pierus, "the Pierides."[5] In Book 5 of the *Metamorphoses*, the nine daughters of Pierus engage in a singing competition with the nine Muses, and are metamorphosed into chattering magpies, renowned for their mimicry, after they refuse to accept graciously their defeat. The Man of Law's wish to avoid comparison to "Muses that men clepe Pierides" can be read as communicating that he does not wish to tell classical stories, as do Chaucer and the Pierian Muses. But this Ovidian reference also conjures the singing competition, in which both the winners and the losers are the Pierides. Analogously, the Man of Law will *become* his rival, Chaucer, so that victory in his own "singing competition" *is* defeat and defeat *is* victory. It is thus striking that the Man of Law spuriously claims that he will "speke in prose" (2.96), leaving rhymes to his competitor. This comment has encouraged scholars to believe that a prose tale was meant to come next, perhaps *Melibee*.[6] Of course, when it is time to tell his prologue and tale, the Man of Law selects rhyme royal, a *signature* Chaucerian rhyme scheme – one that he uses, and perhaps invents, for *Troilus and Criseyde*, *The Parliament of Fowls*, and three other *Canterbury Tales*. The adversarial Man of Law just becomes his competitor in the same way that the adversarial Reeve just becomes the Miller.[7]

It has long been surmised, relatedly, that the Man of Law is meant to represent Chaucer's friend, the lawyer Gower.[8] That the Man of Law is attempting to outdo Chaucer's *Legend of Good Women* by relating the story of Custance, which also appears in Book 2 of the *Confessio*, lends credence to Lynn Staley's suggestion that the *Legend* and the *Confessio* were written "possibly in a spirit of collaborative competition."[9] Lindeboom also sees in the Man of Law's discourse evidence that points to "a battle of writing wits which required [Chaucer and Gower] to be engaged in a mock duel."[10] But if *The Man of Law's Introduction* does indeed set the stage for a poetry competition between the two friends, we must take into consideration Chaucer's law of unintended consequences. If the Man of Law becomes Chaucer, so does Gower. And if Gower is Chaucer and Chaucer is Gower, it simply does not matter who outdoes whom: Victory is immediately defeat and defeat is immediately victory. Furthermore, as we have seen, we love when it is undecidable whether we have mastered the beloved. If we cannot decide whether Chaucer masters Gower or whether Gower masters Chaucer, then Chaucer transmutes any adversarial competition between the two into love.

I suggested above that *The Man of Law's Introduction* looks forward to a tale about the abuse, sexual and otherwise, of innocence. The allusion to the competition between the Muses and the Pierides in *Metamorphoses* 5 reinforces this reading, as Calliope's winning performance opens with Pluto's rape of Proserpina. The suffering that the Christian Custance endures should be understood through the lens of a classical narrative about innocence ravished. Along these lines, we should consider also the Man of Law's otherwise puzzling use of the *De Miseria Condicionis Humane* in his prologue. This is one of the works Chaucer is said to have translated in *The Legend of Good Women* (*Prologue* G 414–15) and he makes use of it throughout *The Man of Law's Tale*. Chaucer draws on an early passage in the *De Miseria* (I.14.1–14) for *The Man of Law's Prologue*, in which the ills that are attendant on poverty are condemned. The author of the *De Miseria*, Pope Innocent III, concludes, however, by denouncing wealth and the moral dangers it brings, insisting instead that virtue, rather than prosperity, should be admired. The Man of Law's borrowing from Innocent concludes in a very different fashion, praising the nobility and prudence of wealthy merchants:

> O riche marchauntz, full of wele been yee,
> O noble, o prudent folk, as in this cas!
> Youre bagges been nat fild with ambes as,
> But with sys cynk, that rennet for youre chaunce;
> At Cristemasse myrie may ye daunce!   (2.122–6)

The prologue's paean to merchants segues neatly into the account of the Syrian "chapmen" with which the tale begins, as W.W. Skeat noticed in his edition of *The Canterbury Tales*.[11] The Man of Law's departure from his source and the relevance of his strange adaptation of Innocent's text has occasioned a great deal of scholarly comment, especially in terms of its relevance for understanding the Man of Law's character. Thus, Robert Lewis asserts that "The Man of Law's speeches on poverty and wealth are similar in tone to the Reeve's discourse on old age in his own prologue, and I would suggest that, just as the Reeve's words help to characterize the Reeve, so the Man of Law's words serve to characterize further a side of his own character that has already been mentioned in the General Prologue: his concern is wealth."[12] More than three decades later, Graham Caie comes to an identical conclusion: "the Man of Law is incapable of concealing his concern for worldly possessions and his fear of poverty."[13] But the Man of Law's patently abusive reading of Pope Innocent's text need not motivate any contemplation of his psychology, something I will try to avoid throughout my analysis. I agree with A.C. Spearing that it is futile to locate a unified narrative "voice" in *The Man of Law's Tale*, or anywhere in *The Canterbury Tales*.[14] Rather than seeking a consistent voice, we must seek a consistent logic. In other words, does the Man of Law decide on formal mastery or material freedom? His adaptation of the *De Miseria* provides the answer. I propose that the Man of Law's abusive and masterful treatment of Pope Innocent's text ingeniously anticipates his narrative. His tale will also be about the abusive and masterful treatment of an "innocent."

In my view, this reading of *The Man of Law's Prologue* accounts for both the Man of Law's reference to *The Legend of Good Women* and his reference to the disturbing incest narrative from the romance of Apollonius of Tyre. In sum, the Man of Law's introduction and prologue present us with a series of structurally identical relationships: 1) the Man of Law abusively masters the Chaucerian corpus; 2) Chaucer abusively masters his classical heroines in *The Legend of Good Women*; 3) Antiochus abusively masters his own innocent daughter; 4) Pluto abusively masters the innocent Proserpina in Calliope's victorious performance against the Pierides; 5) the Man of Law abusively masters Innocent's *De Miseria* in anticipation of 6) his abusive mastery over the innocent Custance. We can now perceive how incest in *The Man of Law's Tale* has a double significance: On the one hand, it involves the *lawful* submission of feminine materiality to masculine form; on the other hand, it is an *unlawful* sexual practice, an "unkynde abhominacioun," that rebels against formal standards of conduct. The Man of Law's formalism, his intention to impose masculine form on feminine matter, puts him in a paradoxical situation: He must at once reject and condone non-normative desire.

Let us turn now to *The Man of Law's Tale* to support my reading of his introduction and prologue. I will begin by demonstrating how the narrator's formalism aligns him with both God and Custance's father.

As does the Knight, the Man of Law characterizes God as entirely in control of human destiny:

> For in the sterres, clerer than is glas,
> Is writen, God woot, whoso koude it rede,
> The deeth of every man, withouten drede.   (2.194–6)

The implacable formal discipline God imposes on the universe is described once again, when the Man of Law bemoans the cruelty of the *primum mobile*:

> O firste moevyng! Crueel firmament,
> With thy diurnal sweigh that crowdest ay
> And hurlest al from est til occident
> That naturelly wolde holde another way.   (2.295–8)

Though the stars are naturally inclined to move from west to east, we are told, the outermost sphere will brook no rebellion, hurling them in the opposite direction.[15] Mention of the Ptolemaic "firste moevyng" allows the narrator to evoke the utter relentlessness of fate. But it would be absurd to assume that the *primum mobile* is somehow independent of God in *The Man of Law's Tale*. I concur, therefore, with Helen Cooney's assessment: "this extraordinary apostrophe seems to me to be a deliberate manoeuvre on the Man of Law's part, another attempt to avoid attributing 'cruelty' directly to God or the workings of his providence."[16] Throughout the tale, in fact, God's omnipotence and omniscience are oppressively in evidence, ensuring that there is not a trace of material contingency in the unfolding of his design – however difficult it is for humans to perceive a final cause in the course of events. Indeed, in his consideration of Chaucer's departures from Nicholas Trevet's *Chronicles*, Edward Block notes that the Man of Law's rhetorical questions and biblical allusions have the "functional significance of emphasizing the fact that Constance's life was saved only by God's miraculous intervention."[17] Thus, when the Sultaness exiles Custance from Syria, God safeguards her survival on the rudderless boat; we are told:

> God liste to shewe his wonderful myracle
> In hire, for we sholde seen his myghty werkis;
> Crist, which that is to every harm triacle,
> By certeine meenes ofte, as knowen clerkis,
> Dooth thyng for certein ende that ful derk is

> To mannes wit, that for oure ignorance
> Ne konne noght knowe his prudent purveiance.   (2.477–83)

God intervenes miraculously on behalf of Custance, protecting her from the murderous designs of the Sultaness and preserving her for years on the sea of Greece. Christ, we are told, often intervenes in ways that are obscure, but always to further his "prudent purveiance."

The intrusive God of *The Man of Law's Tale* intervenes dramatically again when Custance is accused of the murder of Hermengyld. When the murderous knight perjures himself on the Bible, he is struck so violently by the hand of God that his eyes burst out of his head. God then speaks to him directly: "Thou has desclaundered, giltelees,/The doghter of hooly chirche in heigh presence" (2.674–5). Custaunce faces a similar situation when a heathen steward comes aboard her boat with lecherous intent. God once more ensures her safety by means of his direct interference:

> For with hir struglyng wel and myghtily
> The theef fil over bord al sodeynly,
> And in the see he dreynte for vengeance;
> And thus hath Crist unwemmed kept Custance.   (2.922–4)

While this passage initially raises the possibility of Custance's independence in pitching her assailant overboard, the Man of Law must contain immediately the prospect of feminine autonomy. It is Christ who keeps Custance "unwemmed," avenging himself on the steward as God avenged himself on the perjured knight. God is a highly physical, even brutal, presence in *The Man of Law's Tale* – an omnipotent agent who hovers watchfully and protectively around Custance at all times, ensuring that she fulfil the purpose he has appointed for her. Tellingly, the Man of Law's Christ does not represent charity and forgiveness; he represents judgment and vengeance. For the Man of Law, fittingly, God is, above all, *lawful* and brooks no contravention of his edicts. The tale concludes, therefore, with a prayer to Christ that imagines him not as merciful, but as powerful:

> Now Jhesu Crist, that of his myght may sende
> Joye after wo, governe us in his grace,
> And kepe us alle that been in this place! Amen.   (2.1160–2)

The "mighty" Christ of the Man of Law is, above all, a governor, rather than a self-sacrificing redeemer, and in this guise serves to counterpoint the actions of the other secular governors in the tale, especially Custance's father.

In this regard, it is significant that the Man of Law aligns the providence of God with the fate that the Emperor of Rome shapes for his daughter:

> Now wolde som men waiten, as I gesse,
> That I sholde tellen al the purveiance
> That th'Emperour, of his grete noblesse,
> Hath shapen for his doghter, dame Custance.
> Wel may men knowen that so greet ordinance
> May no man tellen in a litel clause
> As was arrayed for so high a cause.   (2.246–52)

The term, "purveiance," occurs only twice in *The Man of Law's Tale*, once to describe God's design and once to describe the Emperor's. The Emperor considers Custance an ideal emissary on behalf of "Cristes lawe deere" (2.237) and thus agrees to send her as a bride to the Sultan of Syria, contrary to her fervent wish. The Sultan has fallen in love with her on the basis of the Syrian merchants' description and is willing to convert to Christianity to wed her. The implacability of the Emperor mirrors the implacability of the "firste moevyng": neither bothers with the natural desires of those entities under their sway. The Man of Law, in contrast to Gower's account in the *Confessio*, repeatedly describes Custance as a profoundly unwilling confederate in her father's plan:

> Allas, what wonder is it thogh she wepte,
> That shal be sent to strange nacioun
> Fro freendes that so tendrely hire kepte,
> And to be bounden under subjeccion
> Of oon, she knoweth nat his condicioun?   (2.267–71)

Custance's parting speech to her father reiterates this sentiment, resigning herself to the punishing and ineluctable dominion of men:

> "Allas, unto the Barbre nacioun
> I moste anoon, syn that it is youre wille;
> But Crist, that starf for our redempcioun
> So yeve me grace his heestes to fulfille!
> I, wrecche womman, no fors though I spille!
> Wommen are born to thraldom and penance,
> And to been under mannes governance."   (2.281–7)

Custance in this passage identifies herself with the suffering Christ, who dies to redeem humankind, rather than the governing Christ, to whom the Man of Law prays at the close of his tale. Custance's identification with Christ aligns her father with God, whose inexorable will she is compelled to obey, as are the pagan characters in the tale. Sheila Delany understands Custance as a "humble woman who seeks no influence, who does not complain about her role but submits willingly to the authority of father, husband and God."[18] But Custance's speech arguably is not just willingly compliant, it is also bitterly resigned, remarking that her life is totally irrelevant to those with power over her: "no fors though I spille!" Robert Dawson thus argues that "Custance clarifies for her parents their heartlessness without openly challenging the validity of their actions or motives."[19] Custance understands very well, it seems, that forces beyond her control trap her ruthlessly. There is a sharp distinction between Custance's unwilling submission to her father and the *willing* submission of the pilgrims to the Host's authority. As the latter says to the Man of Law, "Ye been submytted, thurgh youre *free assent*,/To stonden in this cas at my juggement" (2.35–7). Contrastingly, the final two lines of Custance's speech communicate precisely the Man of Law's philosophy: Feminine matter in his tale must comply with masculine form ("mannes governance"), whether that is represented by the will of God, of the Emperor, or of the Man of Law himself. Custance can no more rebel against her inexorable father than the stars can rebel against the inexorable outermost sphere. Likewise, the suffocating authority of God and the Emperor in the tale corresponds to the suffocating authority of the Man of Law. Just as God intervenes constantly in the narrative by means of his ostentatious miracles, the Man of Law intervenes constantly into his narrative by means of his ostentatious rhetoric. Morton Bloomfield rightly observes that throughout his tale "he interrupts with apostrophes, similes and comparisons, apologies and defenses, rhetorical quotations and forward-pointing paragraphs."[20] God's formal control over the cosmos matches the Emperor's formal control over his daughter and the Man of Law's formal control over his narrative. Both God and the Emperor serve as the narrator's proxies within his tale.

As I argued above, Chaucer anticipates the forced subjection of Custance in *The Man of Law's Tale* through reference both to Antiochus and his daughter and Pluto and Proserpina. According to this network of allusions, it is difficult to avoid the conclusion that we are to understand as *rape* the Emperor's pitiless exploitation of his daughter for the purposes of extending Christian hegemony. This point has been made before. Both Margaret Schlauch and F.N. Robinson cite the Middle

English romance *Emaré* as an analogue for *The Man of Law's Tale*, while Thomas Hanks insists on the basis of manuscript evidence and verbal parallels that it is a source.[21] As Hanks observes, father–daughter incest is a component of *Emaré*, so that "the Man of Law's assurance in his head-link that he will tell no 'cursed stories' like the tale of Canacee's incest or that of Appollonius of Tyre becomes a less gratuitous fling at Gower, who had told both tales in the *Confessio Amantis*, for it is more integrally related to the tale Chaucer is about to tell."[22] Elizabeth Archibald notes that *The Man of Law's Tale* belongs to a group of medieval literary texts that regularly feature the motif of a flight from an incestuous father. She concludes: "Chaucer may have deliberately chosen a non-incestuous version of the Constance story for the *Man of Law's Tale*, but by the reference to Apollonius in the Introduction he made sure that his audience did not forget the ancient and widespread alternative plot of the flight from incest."[23] I concur, moreover, with Yvette Kisor's assessment of the relationship between Custance and the Emperor: "Chaucer's treatment of the story calls to light the connection between patriarchal society's insistence on paternal disposition of daughters in marriage – the accepted exercise of a father's control over his daughter's body – and what is its ultimate extension: incest."[24] The Man of Law has composed, therefore, exactly the kind of tale he earlier disavowed. He thought to imitate Chaucer by avoiding tales of incest, ignoring the incestuous subtext of Canacee's story from *The Squire's Tale*. Instead, he ends up imitating Chaucer by *composing* a tale of incest – a tale in which a father, whether the Emperor or God, can do as he likes with his daughter, no matter what her desires. In his introduction, incest for the Man of Law is an "*unkynde* abhomynacion." It is thus remarkable that God himself operates in a manner contrary to nature, or "kynde." The "firste moevying" or *primum mobile*, an extension of God's power, "hurlest al from est til occident/that *naturelly* wolde holde another way" (2.297–8). *The Man of Law's Tale* exemplifies the Chaucerian principle of unintended consequences: The narrator's formal intention is simultaneously realized and contradicted.

The Emperor's quasi-incestuous control over his daughter's body finds a reflex in the Man of Law's formalism, which insists above all on the strict regulation of feminine materiality. To demonstrate this point, we should consider his representation of the primary villains of his tale: the Sultaness of Syria and Donegild. As opposed to Custance, the Sultaness of Syria, is not so resigned to "mannes governance." She thus echoes Custance's speech to the Emperor while rejecting conversion to Christianity: "What sholde us tyden of this newe lawe/But thraldom to oure bodies and penance?" (2.337–8).[25] The opposition is stark: Custance is feminine matter subject, however unwillingly, to formal dominance; the Sultaness is feminine matter that rejects formal dominance – in the shape here of the "newe lawe" of Christianity as opposed to "Makometes law" (2.336).[26] The Man of Law is outraged by the rebellion against masculine authority enacted by both the Sultaness and Donegild, transforming them consequently into mere simulacra of femininity. After he relates the Sultaness's refusal to convert to Christianity and her scheme to revenge herself on Custance's betrothed, the Man of Law describes her as a "Virago" (2.359), a "Semyrame the secounde" (2.359), a "serpent under femynynytee" (2.360), and a "feyned womman" (2.362). Similarly, after telling of her treachery, the Man of Law calls Donegild "mannysh" (2.782) and a "feendlych spirit" (2.783), insisting that though her body is on earth, her soul is already in hell (2.784). Much like Dante's Satan, for the Man of Law, Donegild is merely animated matter, devoid of spiritual form. The Man of Law simply cannot tolerate unlawful femininity in revolt against a masculine final cause, whether that cause be a son, a sovereign, or God himself. The unacceptable nature of matter liberated from any relation to form echoes the description of Jason from *The Legend of Good Women*. Chaucer modifies the scholastic antifeminism of Guido delle Colonne to describe Jason in *The Legend of Medea* as profligate matter without a final cause: "As mater apetiteth forme alwey / And from forme into forme it passen may, / Or as a welle that were botomles, / Ryght so can false Jason have no pes" (*LGW*, 1582–5). Jason is a "false" man on account of his formlessness; according to the Man of Law, the Sultaness and Donegild are "false" women for exactly the same reason: their refusal of formal discipline.

Rebellious femininity is false femininity, and the Man of Law ensures that rebellious agents are vengefully extirpated from the narrative. Alla kills his own mother, "For that she traitour was to hire ligeance" (2.895). While relating this execution, Man of Law adverts to his source: "that may men pleynly rede" (2.894). In Trevet's version, in fact, Donegild begs her son for mercy, which is curtly refused.[27] Likewise, when the Emperor learns that the Sultaness is a "traytour" (2.957), he ordains an imperial force "On Surreyens to taken heigh vengeance" (2.963), which it does with extreme prejudice: "They brennen, sleen, and brynge hem to mischance / Ful many a day" (2.964–5). If a woman will not submit to the law voluntarily, she will be submitted mercilessly. The same goes for the non-Christian characters in the tale. This lawful formalism, it should be emphasized, has little to do with charity. But the Man of Law's merciless legalism aligns him, paradoxically, with the merciless Sultaness, who professes her devotion to "The hooly lawes of oure Alkaron" (2.332) and "Makometes lawe" (2.336). The Sultaness is, from the Christian perspective, a lawbreaker and, from the Muslim perspective, a law-keeper.[28] The same paradox, as we will see, structures the Prioress's attitude towards the Jews. *The Man of Law's Tale* represents Islam just as it represents incest. Incestuous fathers and Muslim believers are at once materially deviant *and* formally lawful. *The Man of Law's Tale* thus achieves and contradicts its narrator's intention to condemn these two "perversions."

Despite the formal control to which God, her father, and the Man of Law subject her, Custance struggles for liberation. It is remarkable, therefore, that she attempts to elude the fate for which she has been divinely appointed. She tries, in a most unsaintly fashion, to convince the Northumbrian constable to kill her after her tortuous seaborne exile and shipwreck:

> In hir langage mercy she bisoghte,
> The lyf out of hir body for to twynne,
> Hire to delivere of wo that she was inne.   (2.516–18)

In describing Custance's desire for death, Chaucer departs from both Trevet and Gower. Unfortunately for Custance, she must put herself in a man's governance to escape the thraldom of man's governance. The constable does not acquiesce to her wish for a merciful death, as the "wyl of Crist was that she sholde abyde" (2.511). As long as she functions as an instrument of God, she will be kept alive, regardless of how she suffers. In exactly the same way as God ignores Custance's suffering, so does the Man of Law. Custance's weeping, he admits, only serves to exhaust him. After the tearful reunion of Alla and Custance, he tells us:

> Greet was the pitee for to here hem pleyne,
> Thurgh whiche pleintes gan hir wo encresse.
> I pray yow alle my labour to relesse;
> I may nat telle hir wo until to-morwe,
> I am so wery for to speke of sorwe.   (2.1067–71)

The sorrow of his heroine is as uninteresting and irrelevant to the Man of Law as it is to the Emperor and God, who view Custance only as a cog in their larger machinations. Gower in the *Confessio Amantis*, by contrast, has no such diffidence and describes the grief of the Emperor himself as overwhelming when he is reunited with his daughter at Rome: "Wepende he keste hire ofte sithe,/So was his herte al overcome" (2.1523–4).

I can push this reading farther. It is not enough to say that the Man of Law ignores Custance's suffering; he actually seems to *enjoy* the oppressions she must endure. The description of Custance's wedding night is telling in this regard:

> They goon to bedde, as it was skile and right;
> For thogh that wyves be ful hooly thynges,
> They moste take in pacience at nyght
> Swiche manere necessaries as been plesynges
> To folk that han ywedded hem with rynges,
> And leye a lite hir hoolynesse aside,
> As for the tyme – it may no bet betide.   (2.708–14)

The virgin Custance, the Man of Law tells us, has no choice but to submit to whatever gives her new husband sexual pleasure. It is both "skile and right" that Custance's body now serve as an object of masculine lust, the Man of Law comments with obvious relish. Sexual submission is an extension of the "thraldom and penance" to which women are consigned and expected to endure with "pacience." The esteem in which the Man of Law holds this missionary and servant of God is revealed by the sneering comment that Custance must "leye a lite hir hoolynesse aside" to accept what is necessary to please her husband.[29] I suggested earlier that the Man of Law's formalist orientation towards Custance corresponds both to that of God and, more to the point, Custance's high-handed father. If we accept this equation, the Man of Law's evident satisfaction at the necessity that Custance fulfil her sexual obligations acquires a disturbingly incestuous dimension. Once again, a Chaucerian narrator *becomes* what he intends emphatically to reject. As his introduction suggests, just as the Pierides *are* their opponents, the Man of Law *is* Antiochus, who coercively "Birafte his doghter hir maydenhede" (2.83). The Man of Law does not only compose a tale that is implicitly about incest, in his insistence on and enjoyment of Custance's sexual submission, he resembles an incestuous father.

I will conclude this section by considering how *The Man of Law's Tale* looks forward to the Wife of Bath. To do so, it is necessary to observe how Custance eludes the crushing grip of Man of Law, even if just for an instant. I thus concur with Dinshaw that Custance possesses "a certain power of determining her narrative kinesis."[30] After a Roman senator rescues her and her son from their sea-borne exile, Custance is reunited in Rome with her husband, Alla. She requests that her husband seek an audience with the Emperor but insists that he not inform him of her presence. Alla and Custance encounter the Emperor in the street, and Custance submissively prostrates herself before him, uttering the following words:

> "Father," quod she, "youre yonge child Custance
> Is now ful clene out of youre remembrance."
>
> "I am youre doghter Custance," quod she,
> "That whilom ye han sent unto Surrye.
> It am I, fader, that in the salte see
> Was put allone and dampned for to dye.
> Now, goode fader, mercy I yow crye!
> Sende me namoore unto noon hethenesse,
> But thonketh my lord here of his kyndenesse."   (2.1105–13)

Custance's remonstrative tone comes through very clearly in this passage, especially in comparison to Trevet: "My lord and fair father Tiberius, I, your daughter Constance, thank God, who has granted me life even to this day, that I see you in health."[31] Nor is there any reproach in Gower's Constance when she meets her father (2.1514–18). Dawson calls Custance's speech from *The Man of Law's Tale* "something of a masterpiece of implied slander."[32] She begins by accusing her father of forgetting his child completely. She then reminds him of the missionary vocation he imposed upon her and insinuates that she blames him for her long suffering on the seas. She elides her voyage to Syria enjoined by her father with the two exiles commanded by the Sultaness and Donegild, suggesting each was a death sentence. Custance concludes by theatrically begging him for mercy while unequivocally rejecting the role of missionary both God and the Emperor unilaterally enforced, even though her marriage to Alla eliminates the authority her father once possessed over her. Furthermore, in Custance's reproachful words to the Emperor, she implicitly contrasts her father's conduct to the "kyndenesse" of her husband: "Sende me namoore unto noon hethenesse,/But thonketh my lord here of his kyndenesse" (2.1112–13). The Emperor is as "unkynde," the tale suggests, as the abominable and incestuous Antiochus. Custance's reproach is directed not only at her unkind father but also at his counterparts within *The Man of Law's Tale*: an unkind God and an unkind narrator.[33] I, therefore, disagree with Jill Mann's reading of this passage. She argues that "the division between cruel Father and suffering Son is, once again, an illusion; the Father *is* the Son who suffers, united in singleness of godhead. The Father's cruelty is the vehicle for the Son's love."[34] For Chaucer, however, as we

have seen, the decisive subjugation of matter by form, divine or authorial, is *never* love. The Man of Law's concern is not divine charity; it is
divine order – even if that order is achieved only by coercion, violence,
and vengeance.

Thus, when Custance's own child is frightened prior to their exile
from Northumbria, she explicitly tells him, "I wol do thee noon harm"
(2.836), distinguishing herself from the masculine figures in the tale who
are far less solicitous towards the suffering of their innocent children.
On behalf of her child, Custance prays instead to Mary, a mother who
surely can sympathize with her plight: "Thou sawe thy child yslayn
bifore thyne yen, / And yet now lyveth my litel child, parfay!" (2.848–9).
William Johnson observes that "Beneath the rudiments of conventional
hagiographic sentiment appears suggestions of the heroine's wilful-
ness and incipient autonomy." Her prayers "generate anxiety amidst
the external constraints of imposed marriage and banishment and the
internal constraint of feminine self caught in a typal role."[35] Baffled at
the injustice that threatens her guiltless son, Custance exclaims: "Why
wil thyn harde fader han thee spilt?" (2.857). The referent of "harde
fader" is, I believe, ambiguous here: it could be Alla, or it could be God
himself. The agonized query resonates also with the reproof Custance
directs towards her own father at their reunion: "Now, goode fader,
mercy I yow crye!" (2.1112). Custance again suggests that the parents
in the tale, God included, while certainly *lawful*, are devoid of charity.

Nevertheless, the Man of Law ensures that Custance's "incipient
autonomy," exemplified by the reproof she directs against the omnipotent masculine figures in his tale, is short lived. In Trevet's *Chronicles*,
after the death of her husband, Constance returns to Rome from England because she hears that her father is ill. In both Trevet's and Gower's
versions, the Emperor dies in her arms ten days after her arrival, and
Constance lives on independently for a year more. In *The Man of Law's
Tale*, Custance also returns to Rome after Alla's premature death, but
her father is not ill, as in Trevet's version. The Man of Law also departs
from his sources in his description of the reunion of father and daughter: "Doun on hir knees falleth she to grounde" (2.1153). Her abject posture, nowhere mentioned in Trevet's or Gower's versions, does not this
time precede another rebuke; rather, we are told that Custance weeps
"for tendrenesse in herte blithe" (2.1154). Her abjection before her father
matches her abjection before God the Father: "She heryeth God an hundred thousand sithe" (2.1155). Furthermore, there is no reprieve for
Custance from the authority of her father. The Man of Law goes on to
inform us that until death separates father and daughter, they "nevere
asunder wende" (2.1157). It is impossible to say who dies first, which

generates the unpleasant possibility that Custance spends the rest of her life in constant contact with her pitiless father. The Man of Law could have extended Alla's life, a man in the tale who actually loves Custance; he chooses instead to extend the Emperor's. Indeed, it is an implicit indictment of the implacable Christian authorities in the tale that the men who love Custance, Alla and the Sultan, figures linked by the name of the Islamic deity, do so initially as non-Christians, converting for the sake of marriage to her. The narrative begins and ends, therefore, with Custance's absolute submission to her father and to God – the Man of Law's proxies. When we consider the parallel narratives of Antiochus and his daughter or Pluto and Proserpina, it is apparent that the Man of Law has fashioned a conclusion that is at once lawful, consistent with his intention, and perverse, contrary to his intention.

The Man of Law's introduction, prologue, and tale represent masculine power at its most cavalier and authoritarian. Nevertheless, in her attempted suicide, her prayer to Mary, and her reproaches to her father, we briefly witness Custance's *material* resistance to the suffocating closure of *formal* authority. I will consider in the next section what it means for a woman, who rejects the formalism of masculine *auctoritas*, to occupy a position of dominance over husbands and clerks. Will she, like her masculine predecessors, become her adversary? Or is there an alternative to this oppositional determination?

The Wife of Bath's Prologue

Fragments 1 and 2 have prepared us to consider the formidable intricacies of the Wife of Bath's prologue and tale. What we will find, however, is that it is not simply the case that her tale both does and does not fulfil the intentions expressed in her prologue – as was the case most clearly with the Miller, the Reeve, and the Man of Law. Alisoun is not caught by the law of unintended consequences. Rather, Chaucer ups the ante with the Wife of Bath so that her discourse entangles a judgmental posture *and* a non-judgmental posture. What we will find in the last chapter of this book is that Chaucer proceeds in the same way with his *Retraction*.

In the famous first line of the Wife's prologue, she explicitly identifies herself as a materialist: "Experience, though noon auctoritee/Were in this world is right ynogh for me" (3.1–2). The Wife's rejection of authority corresponds precisely to the Miller's self-positioning after *The Knight's Tale*. Both speak from the position of feminine matter, revolting against the constraint of masculine form. Just as does the Miller, accordingly, the Wife will represent herself as irreverent towards the hierarchies that pretend to divine ordination. But, as we saw, the Miller, to assert his materialist vision against what he perceives as the formalism of the Knight, ultimately adopts the formalist position. The Miller becomes what he opposes and his tale, therefore, simultaneously succeeds and fails. At least on first reading, it seems that the Wife, to assert her materialist stance against what she perceives as the formalism of clerical authority, also ends up adopting the formalist position.

Alisoun thus accuses the clerical estate of tendentious interpretation of Scripture: "Men may devyne and glosen, up and down" (3.26), she confidently asserts. Of course, as has often been rehearsed in scholarship on the prologue, the Wife does the same thing. She *formally* glosses Scripture to defend her *materialist* position, i.e., that her carnality is perfectly acceptable, even welcome, in the eyes of God. I will supply one particularly apposite example:

> I nyl envye no virginitee.
> Lat hem be breed of pured whete-seed,
> And lat us wyves hoten barly-breed;
> And yet with barly-breed, Mark telle kan,
> Oure Lord Jhesu refresshed many a man.   (3.142–6)

The argument Alisoun forwards here is certainly more ingenious than it is convincing, playing on a possible double sense of "refresshed" (i.e., "restored" and "sexually satisfied"). She can thereby reject the ascetic standard of Jerome, who prescribes virginity as the ideal state for women, by appealing to a scriptural precedent. Jerome desires formalist containment of unruly femininity; the Wife desires materialist liberty on behalf of her irrepressible libido.[36] But the Wife of Bath is asserting her sexual freedom by using the tool of the clerk, the ingenious interpretation of Scripture, against the clerk.[37] It could then be argued that the Wife of Bath just becomes her adversary, exactly as do the Miller, the Reeve, and the Man of Law; her strategy simultaneously succeeds and fails.[38] As Catherine Cox puts it: "Hence the ambivalence of her narrative: her ostensibly profeminist arguments are betrayed by an articulation that supports what it professes to subvert. The Wife's narrative thus comes across as an anti-antifeminist (rather than 'feminist') misogamous discourse that may be read as a kind of antifeminist feminism."[39] Alisoun can only defeat a clerk like Jerome by becoming a clerk like Jerome. Her materialist "feminism," therefore, cannot disentangle itself from formalist antifeminism.[40] Alisoun's feminine experience has transformed her into a masculine authority, and in fact she is metaleptically cited as such by Justinus in *The Merchant's Tale* (4.1685).

The Wife's treatment of her first three husbands parallels what seems to be her approach to the interpretation of Scripture. She deploys the tools invented by men to dominate women in order to dominate men. From lines 3.335 to 3.378, therefore, Alisoun demonstrates how expertly she is able to embody the antifeminist stereotype of the shrewish wife in order to bludgeon her husbands into submission. The result is that she achieves absolute supremacy:

> And thus of o thyng I avaunte me:
> Atte ende I hadde the bettre in ech degree,
> By sleighte, or force, or by som maner thyng,
> As by continueel murmur or grucchyng.   (3.403–6)

The means by which Alisoun achieves victory over her "good" husbands corresponds to the strategy she deploys against the clerical estate. She uses the tools of the patriarchal establishment against the patriarchal establishment. Antifeminism glosses woman as matter lacking any form or higher purpose: Woman, the antifeminist will insist, is obsessed with carnality, wealth, petty trifles, gossip, and needless chiding. Two points need to be made here. First, to elude the domination of her husbands, Alisoun, at lines 3.335–78, *becomes* this misogynistic caricature of woman as sheer materiality. Second, she incarnates this feminine, or material, caricature to occupy the masculine, or formal position, and *master* her husbands, transforming them into plastic matter subservient to her will. Mann describes this predicament succinctly: "Chaucer's master-stroke in demonstrating the absoluteness of this confinement is his dramatization of the fact that the more vigorously the Wife asserts herself in opposition to traditional antifeminism, the more she conforms to its stereotyped image of her. As she gleefully uses it to berate her old husbands, she appears before us as its typical representative: rebellious, nagging, domineering."[41] The Wife of Bath can only conquer her masculine opponents by *accepting* and *assuming* the masculine position. She will recompense men in their own currency. The Reeve has already demonstrated this vengeful logic with his words about the Miller: "And, by youre leve, I shal hym quite anoon;/Right in his cherles termes wol I speke" (1.3917–18). The talionic principle of the Reeve relies on generating a formal equivalence between his terms and the Miller's. Similarly, just as she repays men in their own terms, the Wife demands repayment according to her own terms; she will not endure her elderly husbands' lust, Alisoun tells us, until they have made their "raunsom" (3.411) to her. In keeping with her mercantile profession, everything is fungible, "for al is to selle" (3.414).

I could accept this standard interpretation of the Wife of Bath's discourse and move on to the next chapter, content that I have demonstrated my central thesis. In realizing her intention to refute the clerical position, Alisoun must occupy the clerical position and thus contradict her intention. She succeeds and fails simultaneously, becoming what she masters. Again, intentional form is (not) related to textual matter. But such a reading of the prologue would ignore, I will argue, several complications. There is a long-established tradition of scholarship on the Wife that finds in her prologue and tale an alternative to a merely polemical stance. Leicester, in a characteristically sensitive reading, locates in her discourse "a deeper and more responsible feminism and a more searching critique of masculine domination."[42] Mann discovers in the Wife's prologue an "alternation of assertiveness and conciliation" that looks forward to "a visionary glimpse of *mutuality* in male-female relationships" in her tale.[43] Thomas A. Van maintains that "[t]he pairing of *Prologue* and *Tale* allows Chaucer to move us beyond gender antagonism to the theme of how to love well, for both *Prologue* and *Tale* close with hints about the need for an accommodation in human love strong enough to overrule the claims of eros and dominance."[44] I agree with Mann, Leicester, and Van that the Wife of Bath's prologue and tale suggest an alternative to a merely oppositional discursive programme. But to understand these texts, we have to find a way to sidestep the alternatives of antifeminist oppression (or formalism) and feminist liberation (or materialism) that have informed most scholarly analyses of Alisoun. The relevant question, therefore, is not: Does the Wife free herself from what Patterson calls "the masculine prison house of language"?[45] We should ask instead: Is the Wife a lover?

We can begin contemplating this question by considering the dialogue between Alisoun and the Pardoner that begins at line 3.163. The Pardoner, himself a rhetorically slippery character, ascribes to the Wife the authority of a clerk: "Ye been a noble prechour in this cas" (3.165). Alisoun's response indicates that she acknowledges her authoritative status, at least where tribulation in marriage is concerned: "I am an expert in al myn age" (3.174). Indeed, she seems to buttress her claim to authority by *citing* an ancient authority: Ptolemy, from his *Almageste*, at lines 3.180–1.[46] In this way, the Wife of Bath places herself in the strange position of simultaneously assuming and disavowing authority. She claims an authoritative status for her discourse even though she had rejected authority with the first line of her prologue. Moreover, the Wife of Bath's citation of Ptolemy, while it ostensibly authorizes her speech, is also ambivalent. Recall that to demonstrate how she deceived her first three husbands ("And al was fals," 3.382), she quotes herself berating them at length. In the course of this reported speech, Alisoun also cites from Ptolemy's *Almageste* (lines 3.324–7), just as she does when speaking to the pilgrims – the only other reference to Ptolemy in the prologue. Accordingly, she borrows Ptolemy's authority to *lie* to her first three husbands. She *could* be doing the same to her pilgrim audience and to us. Again, and in a way that recalls *The Nun's Priest's Tale*, we cannot quite decide whether her discourse is authorized or unauthorized, truthful or deceptive.

Furthermore, a commendation for preaching is somewhat dubious coming from the Pardoner – someone who in his own prologue will gleefully admit that he is a false preacher. It is impossible to say, therefore, whether or not he is telling the truth when he calls the Wife a "noble preacher," or what he even means by the phrase. Is Alisoun a noble preacher because she tells the truth, coded masculine, or because of her tricky rhetorical abilities, coded feminine? For John Alford, the answer is self-evident: As opposed to the logical Clerk, "[t]he Wife is not only one of the most rhetorical of the storytellers; she is Dame Rhetoric herself."[47] But this interpretation ignores the nuances of the Wife's own reflection on her discourse. Resuming her speech after the Pardoner's interruption, she states:

> But yet I praye to al this compaignye,
> If that I speke after my fantasye,
> As taketh not agrief of that I seye,
> For myn entente nys but for to pleye.   (3.189–92)

The term "fantasye" can mean, "desire," but also "delusion," just as John has a "fantasie" of a second flood in *The Miller's Tale* (1.3835). Is the Wife's preaching then merely fantastical? Even more telling is the final line of this passage. Alisoun claims that it is her *intent* only to *play*. If a discourse is intentional, it has an authorial purpose, a final cause, and is univocal (formalism). If a discourse is playful, it has no ultimate purpose and is equivocal (materialism). Thus, the intentional form the Wife imposes on her discourse is the absence of any intentional form.[48] This is exactly what the Nun's Priest accomplishes when he instructs his audience to "Take the fruit and leave the chaff." He authoritatively relinquishes his authority. Likewise, the Wife renders it undecidable whether her prologue is formally authorized or materially unauthorized. We are precluded from deciding whether she ends up occupying the "intentional" masculine position (formalism) or the "playful" feminine position (materialism). It is thus suggestive that Alisoun associates herself both with the masculine Mars and the feminine Venus: "Venus me yaf my lust, my likerousnesse, / and Mars yaf me my sturdy hardynesse" (3.611–12). Much like the Franklin, Alisoun's speech *entangles* authoritative truth and playful fiction; she is neither simply a reliable, truthful narrator nor is she simply an unreliable, false narrator.

I can elucidate this point by noting that the term "fantasye" occurs again in the Wife's prologue, in a context that signals the complications attendant upon Alisoun's account of her desire for Jankyn, the clerk. Jankyn perfectly embodies all the negative traits of clerical antifeminism: He is abusive and masterful to Alisoun; he skilfully glosses, or formalizes, feminine matter; and he merrily launches misogynistic barbs at her from his book of wicked wives. So why does Alisoun love best of all her husbands an eminent representative of the estate to which she appears dialectically opposed? I will cite in full her explanation:

> I trowe I loved hym best, for that he
> Was of his love daungerous to me.
> We wommen han, if that I shal nat lye,
> In this matere a queynte fantasye:
> Wayte what thyng we may nat lightly have,
> Thereafter wol we crie al day and crave.
> Forbede us thyng, and that desiren we;
> Presse on us faste, and thanne wol we flee.
> With daunger oute we al oure chaffare;
> Greet prees at market maketh deere ware,
> And to greet cheep is holde at litel prys:
> This knoweth every womman that is wys.   (3.513–24)

According to the Wife, the "queynte fantasye" of women is that they are prone to desiring that which is prohibited to them. The "daungerous" Jankyn is irresistible to the Wife because he represents this "forbidden fruit." Women, the Wife seems to insist, *require* an authoritative and forbidding agency against which they can then rebel. Her account of feminine desire explains her hostility to authoritative clerical prescriptions. What the clerics prohibit, Alisoun desires. But since she is constrained to desire only what is prohibited, clerical authority determines her even as she revolts. She implicitly *conforms* to masculine authority to formulate her explicit revolt *against* masculine authority. Precisely the same logic holds when she uses the tools of the patriarchal establishment against the patriarchal establishment. Her rebellion thus fails by succeeding and succeeds by failing; her intentions are at once realized and disappointed. More to the point, if the Wife really needs clerical antagonists to arouse, orient, and advance her desires, it should be no wonder that she is so enamoured of Jankyn, a prime representative of their estate.

But can we trust the Wife when she so willingly expresses to us the quaint secret of feminine desire? As in the case of her dialogue with the Pardoner and her double citation of Ptolemy, it is impossible to secure unequivocally the veracity (or falsity) of her discourse. I believe this is so for a number of reasons: 1) The phrase, "queynte fantasye" could be translated as a "tricky" or "ingenious delusion." 2) The Wife rhymes "fantasye" with "lye" (3.515–16). 3) Just fifty lines after testifying to the nature of feminine desire, Alisoun tells us that she *deceived* Jankyn as to the nature of *her* desire: "I bar hym on honde he hadde enchanted me – /My dame taughte me that soutiltee" (3.575–6). She even invents another fantasy, a dream of a bloody bed, to convince Jankyn of her desire for him: "And *al was fals*; I dremed of it right naught" (3.582). 4) Finally, the description of Alisoun's quaint fantasy concludes with a maxim borrowed from the commercial sphere to buttress and naturalize her claims: "Greet prees at market maketh deere ware,/And to greet cheep is holde at litel prys" (3.522–3).[49] The Wife uses exactly the same rhetorical tool to persuade Jankyn that she has been enchanted by him: "'But yet I hope that ye shal do me good,/For blood bitokeneth gold, as me was taught'" (3.581). Alisoun *could* be deceiving us just as she says she deceived Jankyn. The tactics she uses to lie to Jankyn are the same tactics she uses to convince her pilgrim audience; the same goes, as we have seen, for the tactics she uses to lie to her first three husbands. But, once again, we decide that Alisoun is telling the truth or lying about her desire at our interpretive peril. Leicester's deconstructive reading of the prologue supplies an instructive contrast. As a skilled Derridean, he regards the prologue as a web of indeterminacies that, while productive of determinate effects, remains beyond any ultimate determination.[50] Deconstruction always insists on the impossibility of textual *closure*. But this is to decide on the feminine openness of the Wife's discourse – an interpretive manoeuvre that just repeats Alford's association of the Wife with feminine rhetoric or Robertson's association of the Wife with feminine carnality. My point is that we cannot decide for certain whether the Wife's discourse is closed or open – "intentionally" truthful (formalism) or "playfully" deceptive (materialism). Her *intent* is not but for to *play*. Consequently, it is impossible to know for certain whether Alisoun is being truthful when she suggests that prohibitive authority determines feminine desire. Perhaps it is the case that Alisoun has revealed to us the secret of her desire and her discourse: She wants only what the clerks forbid, at once rejecting and relying upon their authority by conforming to antifeminist stereotypes. Or, perhaps, what she wants is something else altogether.

I can further this interpretation of *The Wife of Bath's Prologue* by considering her relationship to her shadowy fourth husband. This marriage appears adversarial from beginning to end. Alisoun is so enraged by his infidelity, she tells us, that she requites him in kind:

> I seye, I hadde in herte greet despit
> That he of any oother had delit.
> But he was quit, by God and by Seint Joce!
> I made hym of the same wode a croce;
> Nat of my body, in no foul manere,
> But certainly, I made folk swich cheere
> That in his ownene grece I made hym frye
> For anger, and for verray jalousie.   (3.481–8)

The Wife appears to "quite" her fourth husband in the same way as the Miller "quites" the Knight, the Reeve "quites" the Miller, and the Man of Law "quites" Chaucer himself. But the attempt to master the other vengefully in Fragments 1 and 2 consistently rebounded on the avenger. What distinguishes *The Wife of Bath's Prologue* is that Alisoun appears cognizant of the futility and self-destructiveness of vengeance, as is implied by her comment on the death of her fourth husband:

> He deyde whan I cam fro Jerusalem,
> And lith ygrave under the roode beem,
> Al is his tombe noght so curyus
> As was the sepulcre of hym Daryus,
> Which that Appelles wroghte subtilly;
> It nys but wast to burye hym preciously.
> Lat hym fare wel; God yeve his soule reste!
> He is now in his grave and in his cheste.   (3.495–502)

The allusion to Darius and Appelles seems to be mean-spirited. Such a scoundrel as was her fourth husband did not deserve such a fine tomb as Appelles crafted for Darius. His thrifty grave is a last humiliation inflicted by a long-suffering wife. But the Wife's apparent spite is complicated by the fact that her husband is buried *within* a church, in a space usually reserved for the wealthy. Moreover, when we examine the allusion more carefully, we learn that Appelles designs a sepulchre not only for Darius; he also crafts one for Darius's wife, Satira. If a marriage is infiltrated by the desire to requite the partner, the Wife may be suggesting, both parties will need tombs – both parties will be destroyed. Indeed, immediately after claiming peevishly that an expensive tomb for her husband would have been a waste, her tone abruptly shifts; Alisoun abandons any rancour and graciously commends her husband's soul to God's care to find the repose he clearly did not locate during his marriage: "God yeve his soule reste!"

Thus, the account of Alisoun's fourth husband is beautifully ambivalent. The allusion to Darius's sepulchre works in opposite ways simultaneously: 1) It suggests a final satisfying vengeance inflicted by a wife on her husband, and 2) it suggests the futility and self-destructiveness of vengeful marital strife. Similarly, it is difficult to conclude whether Alisoun is exultant or regretful about the tribulations she fashioned for her husband as requital for his infidelity: "I made hym of the same wode a croce" (3.484). Is he a criminal suffering for his crimes, or is he Christ suffering for her sins? And despite the appearance of talionic equivalence here, the Wife insists that she does not repay infidelity with infidelity: "Nat of my body, in no foule manere" (3.485).[51] She may flirt with other men, but she says that she remained sexually faithful to her husband, making it more difficult for us to align Alisoun with her marital "adversary." The Wife, we are also told, *hopes* that the purgatorial anguish she inflicted on him during his life has led him straight to bliss: "By God, in erthe I was his purgatorie,/For which I hope his soule be in glorie" (3.489–90). By "hope" does the Wife mean that she affectionately "wishes" that her husband has found glory, or does she just "expect" it, because of the severity of the purgatorial anguish she inflicted? We cannot exclude the possibility that Alisoun has forgiven her fourth husband.

Even the oath the Wife swears at line 3.483 is ambivalent in a related fashion. The Breton Saint Joce is the patron saint of pilgrims, so this is an appropriate oath for her to utter while on a pilgrimage to Canterbury.[52] She also mentions her pilgrimage to Jerusalem at line 3.495, making the oath even more pertinent. But Saint Joce was once a prince; he renounced his temporal power when he abdicated. The Wife of Bath may very well be suggesting in this passage that spouses should also give up their masterful ways. So, does she regret or revel in the torment she inflicted upon her fourth husband? Is she an advocate for vengeful mastery or gracious forgiveness? The careful ambivalence of this section of her prologue makes it impossible to decide for certain. But that is the point. To understand *The Wife of Bath's Prologue*, we just cannot decide whether she conforms to the shrewish and vindictive antifeminist caricature.

I will conclude my reading of the prologue with a consideration of its final section: the violent fisticuffs and eventual rapprochement between Alisoun and Jankyn. The scene begins with each party taking vengeance upon the other. Agonized by his incessant recitation of misogynistic *aperçus*, the Wife tears three pages from his book of wicked wives and punches him in the face so that he falls backwards into the fire. Enraged, Jankyn strikes his wife in the head with such force that she falls unconscious.[53] When she comes back to consciousness, she accuses the terrified Jankyn of murdering her for her property. Nevertheless, she asks for a final kiss. Aghast, Jankyn kneels beside her and utters the following words:

> "Deere suster Alisoun,
> As help me God, I shal thee nevere smyte!
> That I have doon, it is thyself to wyte.
> Foryeve it me, and that I biseke!"   (3.804–7)

Jankyn promises never to strike Alisoun again, and though he initially absolves himself for his actions by blaming her, he ends this brief speech with a plea for forgiveness. Jankyn thus places himself entirely at her mercy. Alisoun's initial response is, understandably, less than gracious; she strikes him again on the cheek in vengeance, saying: "Theef, thus muchel I am wreke;/Now wol I dye, I may no longer speke" (3.809–10). But at last husband and wife are accorded, and Jankyn, we are told, gives his wife absolute sovereignty over "hous and lond,/And of his tonge, and of his hond also" (3.814–15). Once he burns his antifeminist literature, the Wife seems to have won a total victory over her husband and the chief representative of clerical misogyny in the prologue:

> And whan that I hadde geten unto me,
> By maistrie, al the soveraynetee,
> And that he seyde, "Myn owene trewe wyf,
> Do as thee lust the terme of al thy lyf;
> Keep thyn honour, and keep eek myn estaat" –
> After that day we hadden nevere debaat.   (3.817–22)

On first reading, it appears that Alisoun has achieved everything she desires. The battle, physical and ideological, between the estate of wife and the estate of clerk has been decided unequivocally. The former has won mastery over the latter. However, the Wife, as we have seen, is never so straightforward about her aspirations. And so, as with the account of her fourth husband, the question arises: Is Alisoun here really an advocate of feminine "maistrie" in marriage or not?

To respond to this question, we need to consider Jankyn's position more carefully. Rather than perpetuating the futile cycle of vengeance, he says to his wife at line 3.807, "Forgive me." But what is the logical structure of this apparently simple utterance? On the one hand, of course, Jankyn has submitted to Alisoun, placing himself completely at her mercy. On the other hand, he uses the imperative mood to formulate his plea. In other words, Jankyn *imperatively submits*; the representative of clerical authority authoritatively relinquishes his authority to his wife. To reinforce this point, the same logic informs line 3.820. When Jankyn says to Alisoun, "*do* as you desire," he is, once again, commanding her to be absolutely free with him. It is thus undecidable whether he imposes (formalism) or deposes (materialism) his own authority. No wonder the locution "Forgive me" possesses such a strange dignity: It is not the utterance of the master, but neither is it the utterance of the slave. Correlatively, when we can respond graciously to the demand for forgiveness, it is undecidable whether we are obeying an imperative or whether we act freely. We have seen this kind of undecidable utterance before, in *The Franklin's Tale*. Jankyn's comportment towards Alisoun is structurally identical to Arveragus's towards Dorigen. Both command the beloved to be free. Jankyn loves Alisoun in the same way Arveragus loves Dorigen. Love and forgiveness – *caritas* – operate according to the same undecidable logic. To love is to forgive; to forgive is to love.

It is tempting to decide that Jankyn serves as a mouthpiece for the Wife's own convictions. Perhaps, considering the evidence adduced from her prologue, I should now conclude that Alisoun is not a proponent of matrimonial mastery, but rather of matrimonial charity. But if I then determine that Alisoun is being deceptive in the conclusion to her prologue, ascribing to Jankyn her own position, I will have made a decision: The Wife of Bath is a *liar* (materialist), not a truth-teller (formalist). Indeed, the charge of deceptiveness is, perhaps, the oldest weapon in the antifeminist battery. But if I conclude that the Wife is a truth-teller and thus a proponent of mastery in marriage, I decisively reject the ambivalence of her discourse and make her into another version of the Miller, the Reeve, and the Man of Law. She has just become her antifeminist adversary: the masterful clerk and domineering spouse who has strict "governance of hous and lond, / And of [Jankyn's] tonge, and of his hond also" (3.814–15). It seems that we have only two options, equally unpalatable: either we decide that the Wife is lying, and thus confirm fundamental antifeminist allegations; or we decide that the Wife is telling the truth, and thus make her the equivalent of a masterful antifeminist intent on subordinating the opposite gender. Does misogyny really come out on top?

There is an alternative: Instead of judging the Wife of Bath, instead of deciding on her, we love her. And, as adumbrated by my reading of her citations of Ptolemy and her "quaint fantasy," the only way to love Alisoun is not to judge whether she is formally truthful or materially deceptive. It is only via *charity*, not dialectical opposition, the Wife's prologue implies, that antifeminism will dissolve. In order to love Alisoun, therefore, I cannot masterfully decide whether she is masterful or loving. It is time to apply this lesson to her tale.

The Wife of Bath's Tale

Having established how elusive feminine desire is in her prologue, the Wife proceeds to tell a tale that is organized around the secret of feminine desire. The tale begins, however, with an act of brutal mastery that utterly ignores feminine autonomy. A rapist knight violently imposes himself upon an innocent maiden: "maugree hir heed/By verray force, he rafte hire maydenhed" (3.887–9). Chaucer here echoes the language he used to describe the violence of Antiochus upon his daughter in *The Man of Law's Introduction*: the king "Birafte his doghter of hir maydenhede" (2.83). As retribution for his crime of rape, Arthur sentences the protagonist of the tale to death. Queen Guinevere intercedes, saying that she will spare the knight if within a space of a year he can tell her: "What thyng is it that wommen moost desiren" (3.905). The knight is woefully unsuccessful in his quest for this precious secret, unable to find even two people who agree:

> He seketh every hous and every place
> Where as he hopeth for to fynde grace
> To lerne what thyng wommen loven moost,
> But he ne koude arryven in no coost
> Wher as he myghte fynde in this mateere
> Two creatures accordynge in-feere.   (3.919–25)

The Wife reviews the opinions on female desire that the knight collects, adding some of her own in a lengthy survey of the contenders (3.925–50). The final opinion in the Wife's list is that women desire to be held discreet, able to keep a secret (3.946–9). But she dismisses this possibility as ridiculous and demonstrates its implausibility by recounting the story of King Midas's ass's ears from Ovid's

Metamorphoses. According to Book 11 of the *Metamorphoses*, Apollo curses Midas for his poor taste in music, as the latter judges the rustic pipes of Pan to be superior to Apollo's sublime lyre during a competition held on the slopes of Mount Tmolus. Only Midas's barber is aware of his disfigurement, and he is unable to keep the secret, whispering it into a hole he digs in the ground. The hole is filled and, sometime later, reeds grow on the spot. When the wind blows, the hollow reeds speak Midas's shame. As is readily apparent, the Wife modifies this narrative, metamorphosing Midas's barber into his wife. In Alisoun's version, Midas's wife is incapable of keeping the secret of his deformity and whispers it into a brook. We are then instructed to read the remainder of the story in Ovid: "The remenant of the tale if ye wol here,/Redeth Ovyde, and ther ye may it leere" (3.981–2). How are we to understand this intertext?

Scholars have long assumed that the Wife's version of the Ovidian narrative reveals something crucial about her own secret intention, and this, of course, makes sense. Why else would the Wife so abruptly intercalate a lengthy allusion to Ovid that tantalizingly alters its source? Why else would she insist before the digression that women are incapable of keeping secrets? Patterson's influential analysis of the Midas digression supplies an edifying example. He is certain that the "tale of Midas is a digression that exemplifies the characteristic method of the Wife's rhetoric." Understanding the digression means comprehending both the Wife of Bath's desire and her discourse: "The initial image of feminine speaking appears now to have been only an enticement, the deferral a test of the reader's patience: if men are really committed to a disinterested quest for truth they will avoid a surface antifeminism in favor of the wisdom offered by the full story."[54] For Patterson, the enlightened masculine reader will not accept the Wife of Bath's version of the story, with its stereotypical depiction of a garrulous and indiscreet wife. If he has ears to hear, he will instead accept the Wife's invitation ("Redeth Ovyde") and return to the source to discover a tale of masculine deficiency: "her telling argues that men, their listening obstructed by the carnality symbolized by their ass's ears, will naturally prefer the immediate self-gratifications of antifeminism to the severer pleasures of self-knowledge."[55] Patterson insists that his way of reading the Midas digression avoids the impulsive mastery associated with antifeminism: "We can either master the text with the *auctoritee* of preemptive interpretations, or we can *acorden* with it through the negotiations of experience; we can display its carnality by hastily ripping off the *curtyn* of its rhetorical strategies, or we can patiently allow it to reveal itself to us."[56] As we detour through "solace" before we encounter the final "sentence," so we detour through the preceding *Canterbury Tales* before we encounter the Parson's absolutist morality.[57] But, as we have seen, the Wife of Bath refuses to disentangle sentence and solace, truth and deception, form and matter in the way Patterson suggests. It is not the case that we tarry pleasurably with the inessential matter of the digression *before* we reach its essential form. What I will attempt to show, rather, is that Alisoun's Midas digression simultaneously does *and* does not supply the truth of her desire. To do so, I must turn to Midas's earlier misadventure in *Metamorphoses* 11.

Let us consider, then, Midas's other foolish decision. Bacchus, Ovid informs us, promises the king a boon because he has returned to the god his tutor, Silenus. Famously, Midas asks that he be granted the gift of the golden touch. Bacchus reluctantly agrees to the imprudent request. Though initially delighted by his new power, Midas soon finds it a curse, as he is unable even to eat and drink. In torment, he prays to Bacchus for release:

> Ad caelumque manus et splendida bracchia tollens
> "Da veniam, Lenaee pater! Peccavimus," inquit,
> "Sed miserere, precor, speciosoque eripe damno!"
> Mite deum numen: Bacchus peccasse fatentem
> Restituit pactique fide data munera solvit.   (XI.131–5)

> He raised his hands and gleaming arms to heaven: "O Father Bacchus, give pardon! I have sinned," he said, but I beg you, forgive me, and rescue me from this costly curse!" The gods are kind: Bacchus, when the king confessed his fault, restored him, and took back what he had given in fulfilment of his promise.

In this scene, Midas begs forgiveness from Bacchus, but he uses three verbs in the imperative mood to do so: "da," "miserere," and "eripe." He commands Bacchus to free him from the awful gift for which he had earlier asked, *imperatively submitting* himself to the god's mercy. Midas thus echoes what Jankyn utters after he brutally strikes his wife at the conclusion to Alisoun's prologue. We should recall also that forgiveness and love for the Wife are structurally identical, as they are for Chaucer. Midas's imperative submission to Bacchus is thus a loving utterance: He authoritatively surrenders all authority to Bacchus in the same way Jankyn authoritatively surrenders all authority to Alisoun. The plea for forgiveness is command (formalism) and capitulation (materialism) *simultaneously*. In turn, Bacchus exercises his divine authority over Midas, but only by *withdrawing* his power, mercifully freeing the king from the torment inflicted by the cursed gift. He authoritatively withdraws his authority over his supplicant. Between Bacchus and Midas, therefore, there is love. If we accept that this is the significance of the Wife's allusion to Ovid, then she has indeed given away the secret to her tale and, by extension, the secret of feminine desire. Women, quite simply, desire loving, forgiving, charitable partners. And so it is that Midas lovingly demands grace from Bacchus and Bacchus forgivingly bestows it.

But, once again, we cannot *decide* that the Wife is misleading us with the allusion to Midas's donkey ears any more than we could decide that Jankyn was serving as her mouthpiece at the conclusion to her prologue. Truth and falsehood are inextricably entangled in her discourse. The Wife's version of the story of Midas is deceptive, yes; but it is also truthful. The adaptation of the Ovidian narrative is truthful insofar as it reveals that a wife is bursting to tell a secret; the adaptation is deceptive insofar as the secret has nothing to do with the story of Midas's ears. Instead, I propose, Alisoun wishes to reveal the secret of love that inheres in Ovid's narrative about Midas's golden touch. But she will only disclose the mystery of feminine desire to a lover – that is, one who refuses to decide unilaterally whether she is telling the truth or lying.

Once we have passed the Wife's Ovidian love test, we are in a position to gauge the knight's success or failure in his own quest to find the secret of feminine desire. The answer provided by the magical fairy to the knight also echoes the end of the prologue and the description of Jankyn's submission. After she tells him the answer to Guinevere's riddle, the knight announces the solution to Arthur's court:

> "My lige lady, generally," quod he,
> "Wommen desiren to have sovereynetee
> As wel over hir housbond as hir love,
> And for to been in maistrie hym above.
> This is youre mooste desir, thogh ye me kille.   (3.1037–41)

By this point, we have reason to be suspicious that the solution provided to the knight, that women desire mastery over their lovers and husbands, tells the whole story. The response of the assembled women is significant in this regard: "In al the court ne was ther wyf, ne mayde,/ Ne wydwe that contraried that he sayde" (3.1043–4). No one agrees with the knight; they just do not contradict his answer to Guinevere's riddle. It is crucial, therefore, to examine closely the conclusion to the tale, and the love test to which the rapist is submitted.

We should note first that the old wife enlists masculine authorities to refute the position of her husband, himself a representative of masculine authority. On their wedding night, the husband casts aspersions on his new wife's age, appearance, poverty, and gentility; she is beneath him, he insists – in no way his equal. His wife responds by citing Dante, Seneca, Boethius, and Valerius Maximus to undermine the grounds of his claim to superiority. As does Alisoun in the prologue, the aged wife in the tale deploys the tools of the patriarchal establishment against that establishment. The wife thereby *becomes* a masculine authority by means of her opposition *to* masculine authority. But there is a further complication here that we must consider. At the conclusion of her learned speech to her husband, in which she systematically rebuts his insults, the aged wife, unsatisfied with her intellectual victory, offers her uncivil spouse a famous choice:

> "Chese now," quod she, "oon of thise thynges tweye:
> To han me foul and old til that I deye,
> And be to yow a trewe, humble wyf,
> And nevere yow displease in al my lyf,
> Or elles ye wol han me yong and fair,
> And take youre aventure of the repair
> That shal be to youre hous by cause of me
> Or in som oother place, may wel be.
> Now chese yourselves, wheither that yow liketh.   (3.1219–27)

It is important to keep in mind that the wife is completely in control of the situation at this point. She has established her lawful right to her husband's body and authoritatively destroyed all of his claims to superiority. The knight is as much at her mercy as was the innocent maiden at the knight's mercy at the beginning of the tale or Midas at Bacchus's mercy in *Metamorphoses* 11.[58] But what does the aged wife do with her liberty? She *freely* relinquishes her freedom, allowing her husband to choose her destiny. I cannot say that she is free; I cannot say that she is not free. It is undecidable, therefore, whether her husband is now in a position of mastery over her – her loss of freedom, after all, is freely assumed. We should consider also the manner with which the wife presents the choice of risky beauty or homely faithfulness to her husband. She uses the same imperative twice: "choose now"; "now choose yourself." The old wife *authoritatively* relinquishes her authority to her husband. It is strictly undecidable, therefore, whether she is in a position of mastery over *him*.

The knight's response precisely mirrors his wife's:

> "My lady and my love, and wyf so deere,
> I put me in youre wise governance;
> Cheseth yourself which may be moost pleasance
> And moost honour to yow and me also.
> I do no fors the wheither of the two,
> For as you liketh, it suffiseth me.   (3.1230–5)

Now he has control over the situation, with the power to decide the future of his marriage and his wife. But, like his wife, the knight freely relinquishes his freedom, giving over "mastery" to her, as she acknowledges: "'Thanne have I gete of yow maistrie," quod she, /'Syn I may chese and governe as me lest?" (3.1236–7). To reinforce this point, the knight uses the same imperative his spouse had earlier deployed: "choose yourself." The knight refuses to decide on his wife in two ways simultaneously. First, he commands her (formalism) to be free (materialism) with him. Second, he refuses to decide whether his wife will be old and *submissive* or young and *capricious*. The knight refuses to decide, in other words, between mastering an old wife (formalism) and freeing a young one (materialism). Kathryn McKinley observes that the knight's imperative utterance has a performative force that makes his marriage to the wife consensual, rather than enforced: "When the knight's statements to the hag are understood in the context of his consent to her, they become, in so many words, the performative marriage statement 'I do.'"[59] McKinley does not note, however, that the knight's imperative utterances just echo his wife's, for whom consent is obviously not an issue. What is at issue here is not just consent and reciprocity in marriage; it is charity in *any* context.

In response to the knight's charitable gesture, the old wife renounces the mastery she has gained over the knight. Instead, she *freely* promises to *obey* him "in every thyng/That myghte doon hym plesance or likyng" (3.1255–6). Susanne Sara Thomas rightly argues that "the *wyf*'s promise of obedience arises from a position of independence and self-government, not from submission to the knight's authority."[60] I would modify this claim by suggesting that it is *undecidable* whether the wife submits to the knight's authority; she freely gives up her freedom to him. The final scene of the tale just doubles Jankyn's imperative submission to Alisoun. Chaucer emphasizes this parallel by having the rejuvenated wife echo Jankyn's words from the end of the prologue ("*Do* as thee *lust* the terme of al thy *lyf*"): "*Dooth* with my *lyf* and deth right as yow *lest*" (3.1248). At the conclusion of the tale, each party behaves as Jankyn ultimately does – that is, lovingly and forgivingly. I do not agree, therefore, with Lynne Dickson that "[i]n a strange affirmation of masculine desire, the Tale ultimately rewards the concession of masculine 'maistrie' with the very thing patriarchy wants to begin with: a passive, nonthreatening female who obeys."[61] The wife *freely* gives up her freedom to her partner. So does the knight. The wife commands her partner to be free. So does the knight. Between husband and wife there is now a reciprocal (non-)relation. It is undecidable whether the wife has mastered or freed her husband. It is undecidable whether the knight has mastered or freed his wife. Precisely the same insoluble logic is expressed when the Franklin tells us that friends must obey each other (5.762). We cannot decide who masters and who submits, who holds authority and who holds no authority.

The Wife of Bath's Tale concludes with the husband's heart "bathed in a bath of blisse" (3.1253). The imagery of liquid in the Wife's discourse is always charged, and Timothy O'Brien understands the ambivalence of water in Alisoun's prologue and tale both "as a sign of *luxuria* and feminine seductiveness, and as the element of baptism and renewal."[62] The conclusion of her tale thus recalls the opening of her prologue and the allusions to the Samaritan Woman and the Marriage at Cana from the Gospel of John. Christ promises the Samaritan Woman an unquenchable spring of eternal life and miraculously transforms water into wine for the celebrants at the wedding feast. The love and forgiveness of the wife for her husband in the tale images, therefore, the eternal font of divine charity, effectuating a miraculous transformation in lover and beloved. It is no coincidence, moreover, that Bacchus instructs the contrite Midas to bathe at the source of the river Patoclus to cleanse himself of his aureate curse – a classical reflex, perhaps, of the rejuvenating shrine towards which the Canterbury pilgrimage itself advances.[63]

This reading seems to have uncovered definitively the secret of the Wife of Bath's desire and collapses the ambivalence of her depiction. Surely, we know her intention by this point: She *must* be an advocate for love in marriage, not for sovereignty, whatever she says in her prologue. The Wife's epilogue, however, generates a further complication:

> And thus they lyve unto hir lyves ende
> In parfit joye; and Jhesu Crist us sende
> Housbondes meeke, yonge, and fressh abedde,
> And grace t'overbyde hem that we wedde;
> And eek I praye Jhesu shorte hir lyves

> That noght wol be governed by hir wyves;
> And olde and angry nygardes of dispence,
> God sende hem soone verray pestilence!   (3.1257–64)

Alisoun in this passage becomes once again a judgmental advocate for mastery and vengeance, praying for sexy, submissive young husbands and savage retribution on the miserly old bacon that will not obey her unconstrained will. Again, she embodies the antifeminist stereotype. Elizabeth Scala thus states: "As with many of the digressions, illogicalities, and falsehoods used locally and to comic effect in her Prologue, this obstreperous and abrupt ending characterizes her discourse as stereotypically 'feminine' precisely because self-contradictory and thus works in accord with what we see elsewhere in her Prologue and Tale. It makes her sound like 'herself,' a characterization that may, in fact, obscure our realization of how much like every self she sounds, since desire is located and revealed, precisely, at such points of discontinuity and contradiction."[64] I agree with Scala that the Wife has assumed a stereotyped discursive position here, but I disagree that the self-contradictory quality of the epilogue should be explained by any "subjective" vacillation. The reader's situation at this point is, in fact, identical to the knight's in the Wife's tale. Alisoun has been instructing us from her prologue onwards and now *we* are presented with two choices: either 1) the Wife of Bath is a judgmental advocate for marital mastery, dividing good, submissive husbands from bad, refractory husbands as God will divide the saints and sinners at the Last Judgment; or 2) the Wife of Bath is an advocate for marital charity, transcending this judgmental and critical attitude towards men. As tempting as it is by this point to align the Wife with charity, this would entail *deciding* on love – a gesture that is its very opposite. We would have to decide that the Wife is lying in her epilogue and telling the truth at the end of her tale. An identical choice, as we saw, presented itself at the end of her prologue.[65] But to decide masterfully on the Wife of Bath, whether to align her with judgment *or* with charity, is just to replicate Jankyn's glossatorial violence from the prologue and its literalized equivalent in the tale. We should follow instead the example of the reformed knight and refuse to choose between two mutually exclusive alternatives. In this way, we acknowledge that Alisoun's discourse insolubly entangles love and that which love excludes – judgment. Only in this way do we love her.

The classic interpretive manoeuvre is to associate Alisoun's tale with sentimental playfulness and her epilogue with a return to seriousness. Tison Pugh, for instance, comments on the Wife's tale that "it is a romance with all of the trappings of the genre, but she switches from the play of fantasy to the utter seriousness of her curse both against husbands who would control the lives of their wives and against male pilgrims who are complicit in the privileges of patriarchy."[66] In other words, the tale is *playful* fantasy, but the curse is *intentional* truth. But, if we have understood her teaching ("myn *entente* nys but for to *pleye*"), we will refuse to decide between the two options proffered. As in the Wife's digression on Midas, at the conclusion of her tale, truth and deception are entangled without any possible synthesis. To respond lovingly to her desire for love, expressed so poignantly by Midas's plea to Bacchus, we simply cannot decide whether Alisoun loves or judges. This is the fundamental lesson of the Wife of Bath and, indeed, *The Canterbury Tales*: The lover does not decide on love. As will become apparent, it is only by absorbing this lesson that we will be able to understand Chaucer's *Retraction*.

4 Reading Griselda Charitably in Fragment 4

The Friar's and the Summoner's Tales

The Friar's mocking comment on the length of the Wife of Bath's "preamble" to her tale initiates a feud with the Summoner that plays itself out before the Clerk has an opportunity to respond to Alisoun. The vengeful hatred between Summoner and Friar follows directly upon the Wife of Bath's illustration of love, indicating how easy it is to misunderstand or ignore this lesson. In this chapter, I will consider briefly the antagonism between the Friar and Summoner before turning to the Clerk and the Merchant. I will demonstrate thereby that only one of these pilgrims has been instructed by the Wife's lesson on love.

Indeed, the Wife does attempt to teach the Friar by means of her response to him at the beginning of her tale. While her tale is set long ago, when the land was "fulfild of fayerye" (3.859), in contemporary times, she tells us, friars have chased all the elves away with their charity, blessings, and prayers. Where the elves once walked, now go the friars. As a consequence:

> Wommen may go saufly up and doun.
> In every bussh or under every tree
> There is noon oother incubus but he,
> And he ne wol doon hem but dishonour.　　　　　　　　(3.877–80)

The great number of friars, "[a]s thikke as motes in the sonne-beam" (3.868), ensures that women are now safe, at least from supernatural despoliation. The final two lines of this passage, however, have been difficult to interpret. Dorothy Yamamoto notes that F.N. Robinson articulates the conventional meaning long accorded these lines: "The friar brought only dishonour upon the woman; the incubus always caused conception."[1] Yamamoto argues, by contrast, that the Wife means to evoke "a tradition in which the assault of the incubus was associated not simply – or even necessarily – with pregnancy but with appalling violence towards the victim and sometimes, too, towards the victim's family."[2] A friar, comparatively, is a trivial nuisance. Thus, on the one hand, friars are holy exorcists equipped with "grete charitee and prayers" (3.865) who have, Christ-like, saved women from the very considerable threat of demonic assaults. On the other hand, friars pose a new, if diminished, threat to the honour of women by taking the place of the incubi. Friars, therefore, are at once salvific and sinister, loving and lascivious. By substituting themselves for supernatural and lecherous predators they simultaneously rescue women and menace them anew. We have seen this situation before in *The Canterbury Tales*: The Wife is obliquely informing the Friar that his attempt to master his opponent, the lecherous (1.626) Summoner, will only lead to exchanging places with him. She is teaching the Friar the law of unintended consequences; he will switch places with his adversary, just as the friars in the Wife's anecdote switch places with the incubi. The Friar, however, is incapable of hearing this lesson, as his dismissive words to the Wife indicate (3.1270–7), and this is exactly what happens to him – he becomes the Summoner.

I turn, then, to the unambiguously vengeful exchange between the Friar and the Summoner. And, as with Fragments 1 and 2, vengeance in both cases rebounds upon the avenger. Each succeeds in masterfully humiliating the other, but in doing so humiliates himself, exemplifying Chaucer's law of unintended consequences. The Friar tells a tale about an urbane and learned devil who accompanies an avaricious and obtuse summoner hurtling recklessly towards damnation. As his portrait in the *General Prologue* attests, the Friar closely resembles both figures, hardly to the credit of one supposed to be a Master of Divinity. He is "the best beggere in his hous" (1.252) and rather than clothing appropriate to a mendicant scholar, he arrays himself "lyk a maister or a pope" (1.261).[3] His contempt for those he views as beneath his station, like the Summoner, is further conveyed by his unwillingness to associate with the poor: "It is nat honest; it may nat avaunce,/For to deelen with no swich poraille" (1.246–7). The reckless summoner and the condescending yeoman devil, sworn brothers in his tale (3.1450), together precisely diffract the Friar's

unpleasant synthesis of extreme venality and erudite supercilious-
ness. A brief passage from the *General Prologue* that anticipates *The
Friar's Tale* elegantly distils his character:

> For thogh a wydwe hadde noght a sho,
> So plesaunt was his *"In principio,"*
> Yet wolde he have a ferthyng, er he wente.   (1.253–5)

In three lines, the narrator condenses the Friar's contempt for the under-
class, his learning, his avarice, and his ersatz courtesy. This description
of Huberd serves also to associate him with the extortionate summoner
of his tale, who will not leave the poor widow, Mabely, until he has
squeezed her for twelve pence.

Scholars, such as Katie Homar, R.T. Lenaghan, and Leicester, have
noted the manner with which *The Friar's Tale* rebounds upon its teller.[4]
More specifically relevant to my purpose is how closely the Friar mirrors his summoner's reading practices. Upon witnessing a frustrated
carter consigning horses, cart, and hay to the devil, the summoner
turns to his companion and whispers in his ear: "Herestow nat how
that the cartere seith?/Hent it anon, for he hath yeve it thee" (3.1552–
3). The honest devil refuses to claim what the carter seems to have
committed to him: "'Nay,' quod the devel, 'God woot, never a deel!/
It is nat his entente, trust me weel" (3.1555–6). The devil is a formalist; the carter's intention must fix the meaning of his utterance. The
summoner, by contrast, is a materialist; the meaning of the carter's
utterance is detached from any intentional causality and can be interpreted willy-nilly. The contrasting interpretive tendencies of the bai-
liffs match their differing comportments towards authority. The devil
is loyal to his demanding master: "My wages been ful streite and ful
smale./My lord is hard to me and daungerous" (3.1426–7). What is
more, the devil admits that he can do nothing against God's knowledge or will: "Withouten hym we have no myght, certayn" (3.1487).
The summoner, however, has no problem operating beyond the cogni-
zance and authority of his master, the archdeacon: "His maister knew
nat alwey what he wan" (3.1345); "His maister hadde but half his
duetee" (3.1352). The devil orients himself towards a final authority;
the summoner does not.

The Friar himself must appear to be a holy and charitable man, one
who serves God rather than his personal animosities. The Host knows
this very well, as his warning in *The Friar's Prologue* attests: "A, sire, ye
sholde be hende/And curteys, as a man of youre estaat" (3.1286–7).

As a consequence, when it comes to interpreting his own tale, he must obscure its vengeful intent and make it appear as if it is designed to edify and improve spiritually its audience, the pilgrim Summoner included:

Herketh this word! Beth war, as in this cas:
"The leoun sit in his awayt alway
To sle the innocent, if that he may."
Disposeth ay youre hertes to withstonde
The feend, that yow wolde make thral and bonde.
He may nat tempte yow over youre myght,
For Crist wol be youre champion and knyght.
And prayeth that thise somonours hem repente
Of hir mysdedes, er that the feend hem hente!   (3.1656–64)

To maintain appearances, the Friar disingenuously interprets his own tale as a moral lesson, not as an instrument of vengeance. Obviously, however, the moral he provides has nothing whatsoever to do with a tale designed only to insult the Summoner. The imperceptive summoner in the tale is in no way whatsoever an innocent and has not been tempted at all by the devil. The summoner has instead done the devil's work for him, damning himself with his own words (especially at lines 3.1630–3). But this means that the Friar ignores the "entente" of his own tale in exactly the same way as the summoner ignores the "entente" of the exasperated carter. The Friar identifies with the formalist devil (who serves God) but becomes the materialist summoner (who serves only himself). The Friar's fate is thus that of the summoner: His own words turn against him. By identifying the author with his target, his tale succeeds and fails simultaneously.

The polished and courteous Friar, who maintains a sense of formal decorum, meets his match in the vulgar and bawdy Summoner, for whom formalities matter not at all. The Friar wishes to appear holy; the Summoner revels in blasphemy. The Friar contains himself; the Summoner does not, his very skin erupting with pustules. Nevertheless, the Summoner's brilliant riposte to the Friar reveals that the latter has clearly underestimated his adversary, exactly as the friar in *The Summoner's Tale* underestimates Thomas. The pilgrim Summoner resembles not at all his dim-witted counterpart in *The Friar's Tale* and is, in fact, capable of a devastating caricature of Friar Huberd in *The Summoner's Tale*. However successful is the tale in humiliating the Summoner's adversary, we should nevertheless observe that it is a story told by an angry vengeful man (the Summoner) to take vengeance on another angry vengeful man (Friar Huberd). What is more, it is a story *about* an angry vengeful man (Thomas) who takes vengeance on another angry vengeful man (Friar John) who is then *unable* to take vengeance on an angry vengeful man (Thomas). The recursive complexity of the tale is intensified by the fact that Friar John delivers an impromptu sermon to Thomas against anger that only serves to enrage Thomas, motivating the vengeful fart that in turn angers the hypocritical friar.

Thus, *The Summoner's Tale*, just as Friar John's sermon on anger, also rebounds on its speaker. Friar John and Thomas *both* reflect the angry and vengeful Summoner within his tale. The Summoner is described as "wood" in his prologue (3.166), as are both Thomas (3.2121) and Friar John (3.2153) in his tale. The antagonists, Thomas (3.1829) and Friar John (3.2161), moreover, are both described as angry "boors." Friar John and Thomas also both reflect the angry and vengeful Friar Huberd from the frame narrative. This double identification is made more likely by the fact that Thomas, the Summoner's surrogate in the tale, doubts the sincerity of the friar in the same way that Thomas the Apostle, who is mentioned by the friar at line 3.1980, doubts the truth of Christ's resurrection.[5] The fraternal orders located their origin narrative, of course, in the mission of Christ's apostles. The Summoner at once identifies with an apostolic figure *and* travesties the Pentecostal descent of the Holy Spirit upon the Apostles in the solution the squire provides to the problem of the subdivided fart.[6] *The Summoner's Tale* is thus about retributive attempts that succeed and fail: Thomas is successful and Friar John fails, due to the unexpected precision of Thomas's "ars-metrike." In fact, it should be no surprise that the vengeful Summoner should conclude his tale with a humiliating solution to a problem initially deemed *insoluble*, or "impossible" (3.2231), by the confounded lord. The judgmental pilgrims always decide on the undecidable. Nevertheless, Chaucer's law of unintended consequences ensures that judgment rebounds on the judgmental. Just as his tale describes successful and failed retributions, Chaucer's identification of the Summoner with both Thomas and Friar John means that the pilgrim's own vengeance succeeds and fails simultaneously. The Summoner at once humiliates and *becomes* his fraternal adversary. Once again, vengeance for Chaucer just means occupying the place of the target.

The Clerk's Prologue and Tale

Fragment 4 begins with the Clerk, whose prologue identifies the narrator's relationship to his precursor, Petrarch. The situation here is analogous to that in *The Man of Law's Introduction*, in which the Man of Law also identifies a literary precursor: Chaucer himself. We must consider first whether the Clerk's comportment towards Petrarch will be as adversarial as the one between the Man of Law and Chaucer, implicitly likened to the singing competition between the Muses and Pierides. Will the Clerk likewise attempt to outdo his precursor, thereby subjecting himself to the law of unintended consequences? I begin, then, by focusing attention on the logic that structures the Clerk's attitude towards Petrarch. Once we have grasped this logic, we will be better placed to analyse *The Clerk's Tale*.

While the Man of Law wishes to tell a tale outside the ambit of the Chaucerian oeuvre, *The Clerk's Tale* is one the narrator has learned from Petrarch.[7] But although Petrarch is in this way his acknowledged master, the Clerk makes it clear that his relationship to the humanist poet is vexed. The Clerk does not straightforwardly capitulate to any authority. He grants, for instance, that he is under the Host's "yerde" (4.22) and that the latter has "governance" (4.23) over the assembled pilgrims; but the Clerk's "obeisance" (4.24) will extend, as is appropriate for a philosopher, only "As fer as resoun axeth, hardily" (4.25). Despite his submission to the Host's authority, the Clerk remains entirely free to determine its limits. The Host both does and does not master the Clerk.

The Clerk's relationship to Petrarch is analogous. The Clerk signals its complications by echoing the Wife of Bath's description of her fourth husband's death. The Wife says of her late husband: "Lat hym fare wel; God yeve his soule reste!/He is now in his grave and in his cheste" (3.501–2). Likewise, the Clerk says of his late precursor: "He is now deed and nayled in his cheste;/I prey to God so yeve his soule reste!" (4.29–30). The Clerk's praise for Petrarch, which follows these lines, is as ambivalent as Alisoun's attitude towards her dead husband:

> Fraunceys Petrak, the lauriat poete,
> Highte this clerk, whos rethorike sweete
> Enlumyned al Ytaille of poetrie,
> As Lynyan dide of philosophie,
> Or lawe, or oother art particuler;
> But Deeth, that wol nat suffre us dwellen heer,
> But as it were a twynklyng of an ye,
> Hem bothe hath slayn, and alle shul we dye.   (4.31–8)

While noting that Petrarch is a celebrated poet, the Clerk tempers the honour he has received by juxtaposing poetry and philosophy. Petrarch may have illuminated Italy with his "rethorike sweete," but Giovanni da Lignano did the same with philosophy and law, the more "serious" domains of accomplishment.[8] We could expect that the Clerk, himself an Aristotelian logician given to pondering *sophismata*, would admire the formal discipline of philosophy and law at least as much as the material sweetness of poetry and rhetoric. Nevertheless, the accomplishments of both Italian masters cannot allow them to avoid humanity's ultimate fate, as Death is master over all.

This circumscription of Petrarch's stature anticipates the Clerk's critical assessment of the former's proem to the *Tale of Griselda*: "And trewely, as to my juggement,/Me thynketh it a thyng impertinent" (4.53–4). Nevertheless, the "impertinence" of Petrarch's proem does not stop the Clerk from impertinently translating most of it from lines 4.42–51. It is again unclear whether the Clerk submits to Petrarch's authority – he is simultaneously faithful and unfaithful to Petrarch in a way that echoes the Franklin's rhetorical disavowal of rhetoric. But the problem of mastery advances to another level of complexity. Petrarch's version of the Griselda story is itself a translation of Dioneo's narrative from Day 10 of Boccaccio's *Decameron*. Petrarch condescendingly remarks upon some of the deficiencies of the *Decameron* in a prefatory letter to Boccaccio: "I was delighted with my browsing, and as for the rather frankly uninhibited events that cropped up, your age when you wrote it is enough excuse, as are the style and the idiom, for levity is suitable in the stories and in those who would read them."[9] Petrarch's judgment on Boccaccio's *Decameron* calls attention to its flaws, though it excuses these as products of the author's immaturity.[10] When speaking of the final story in the collection, however, Petrarch is more laudatory: "But at the other end you have placed last – *and in great contrast to much of what precedes it* – a story that so pleased and engaged me that, amid enough duties to make me almost forget myself, I wanted to memorize it, so that I might recall its pleasures as often as I wished and retell it in conversation with my friends, as the opportunity might arise."[11] Petrarch accordingly translates Boccaccio's story of Griselda, while dismissing what precedes it. So, when the Clerk says he will translate Petrarch's story of Griselda, *while dismissing what precedes it* (the "prohemye"), is he not just imitating Petrarch? The Clerk, according to this reading, is following Petrarch faithfully by not following him faithfully; he is not following him faithfully by following him faithfully. It is thus undecidable whether Petrarch is his master. My reading is clearly at odds with the influential interpretation of David Wallace, who understands *The Clerk's Tale* "as an explicit critique of its Petrarchan source."[12] But I also do not agree with the opposite reading, supplied by Kathryn Lynch, that Chaucer demonstrates "a basic constancy or fidelity to the spirit of his [Petrarchan] source."[13] As I will attempt to demonstrate, we cannot quite decide whether the tale is a faithful imitation of or an unfaithful departure from its Latin antecedent.

The Host's description of the Clerk as a maid "newe spoused" (4.3) suggests, moreover, that the uncertain relation that holds between the Clerk and Petrarch anticipates the matrimonial arrangement that holds between Griselda and Walter.[14] Before we consider this marriage, however, we should read the dialogue with which *The Clerk's Tale* begins, alert to its logical structure.[15] Terrified that the Marquis will leave them without an heir, his subjects conscript the wisest of their number to approach Walter and beg him to take a wife. Though the spokesman is appropriately deferential in his comportment towards the Marquis, his speech of forty-nine lines contains no fewer than seven imperatives: "accepteth" (4.96), "boweth" (4.113), "thenketh" (4.116), "accepteth" (4.127), "chese" (4.130), "delivere" (4.134), and "taak" (4.135). On behalf of his anxious people, the spokesman *submissively commands* Walter to take a wife. He speaks commandingly from a position of utter powerlessness, much like Midas to Bacchus in *Metamorphoses* 11.

Chaucer emphasizes a logical structure he finds in his Petrarchan source, which accounts, I suggest, for his interest in the latter's version of the Griselda story. Walter's subject in the Latin source thus states: "I mean that you should turn your mind [applices] to marriage and lay [subicias] your neck (not merely free but imperial) under that lawful yoke, and do so [facias] before all else."[16] Petrarch uses the jussive subjunctive mood in three successive verbs to convey the authority with which Walter's subject speaks, despite his subordinate position. Chaucer's translation of this passage reveals his interest in stressing the undecidable entanglement of mastery and submission:

> "Boweth youre nekke under that blisful yok
> Of soveraynetee, noght of servyse,
> Which that men clepe spousaille or wedlock."   (4.113–15)

According to the spokesman, to *submit* to the yoke of marriage is to acquire *sovereignty* – submission is mastery and mastery is submission. In the Clerk's version of this passage from Petrarch, total surrender *is* mastery and mastery *is* total surrender. Critics, such as Rodney Delasanta, who see in Walter's arbitrary exercise of power the nominalist God's *potentia absoluta* must ignore the power exerted by submission in *The Clerk's Tale* – first by Walter's subjects and then by Griselda herself.[17] We cannot decide whether the wedded man, according to Walter's subject, is in a position of mastery or subjection. Exactly the same is true of the spokesman himself, who powerlessly exerts power over the sovereign.

Walter is moved to pity by his subjects' plea, even if he insists on characterizing marriage as constraint: "Ther I was free, I moot been in servage" (4.147). Nevertheless, he acquiesces to the demand of his subjects:

> But nathelees I se youre trewe entente,
> And truste upon youre wit, and have doon ay;
> Wherefore of my free wyl I wole assente
> To wedde me, as soone as evere I may.   (4.148–51)

Walter makes it clear that his assent to marriage is not merely compelled. His assent derives from an act of free will. He thus gives up his freedom, and accepts "servage," but he does so *freely*. Chaucer follows Petrarch closely here; Walter states in the source text: "I *submit myself freely* to the will of my subjects, confident in your prudence and faith."[18] In Petrarch, I would suggest, Chaucer found a source for his version of the ideal polity. The sovereign is neither free nor mastered. The subject is neither mastered nor free. Not only does the sovereign freely submit to the subject, the subject submissively masters the sovereign. It is not quite the case, as Wallace argues, that *The Clerk's Tale* critiques Petrarch's "tyrannic" humanism.[19] Chaucer instead keeps mastery (formalism) and freedom (materialism) in an insoluble suspension. Nor can I agree with Michaela Grodin's understanding of *The Clerk's Tale* as staging the irresolvable paradox of the need for political unity versus the Christian sanctity of the individual: "Given the nature of the unresolved conflict between the ideal of political absolutism and the needs of the individual, we are left to live with the poem's skeptical assessment of the general condition of mankind."[20] For Chaucer, what holds for ethics and love holds also for politics.[21] If the political agent, whether sovereign or subject, decides on mastery *or* freedom, the political (non-)relation has collapsed. *The Clerk's Tale* implicitly proposes, therefore, a charitable politics, one that avoids the decisiveness of formal absolutism or the material confusion imaged by a wavering rabble addicted to novelty: "O stormy peple! Unsad and evere untrewe! / Ay undiscreet and chaungynge as a fane!" (4.995–6).[22]

With this political structure in mind, we can now consider Griselda's response to Walter's marriage proposal, the central enigma of *The Clerk's Tale*:

> Wondrynge upon this word, quakynge for drede,
> She seyde, "Lord, undigne and unworthy
> Am I to thilke honour that ye me beede,
> But as ye wole youreself, right so wol I.

> And heere I swere that nevere willyngly,
> In werk ne thoght, I nyl yow disobeye,
> For to be deed, though me were looth to deye."   (4.358–64)

It is often and rightly noted that Griselda *freely* promises Walter more than what he had asked for. Walter had demanded obedience but not the total subjection of thought and deed. Chaucer is thus entirely faithful to Petrarch's account of Griselda's promise: "I know myself unworthy of such an honor, my lord. But if this is your will and my fate, I will never knowingly do – no, I will not even think anything contrary to your will."[23] Griselda's extreme and unmotivated devotion to Walter has been a subject of much scholarly interest. Critics tend to consider this devotion either as paradigmatic for the faithful Christian's comportment towards God or for the lover's comportment towards her human partner. John McCall argues that "the whole tradition of obedience declares that the free submission of one's will to a human superior is the normal means by which one submits to the will of God."[24] Linda Georgianna concurs: "Our experience of Griselda's mysterious assent forces us to confront the radical demands of faith, and our need to rationalize them."[25]

But this scene can also be given a secular inflection. Miller sees in Griselda's indissoluble attachment to Walter the fundamental antinomy of universality and particularity in love: "For in Grisilde's love of Walter's ugliness, just as much as in her unconditionality, the Clerk captures intuitions concerning love without which it becomes unrecognizable: that we love not just, as Plato would have it, the good in our beloved, but this particular person; that we love them not just in spite of, but because of, their embodiment in the desires, habits, history, and ideology that constitute their character."[26] Laura Ashe also comments on the unconditional nature of Griselda's love, seeing her infinite patience for Walter as indicative of a charitable hermeneutic: "Griselda pursues her own charitable reading of her husband and finds sense and justification in any and all of Walter's actions."[27] I agree with McCall and Georgianna that Griselda's obedience, unlike Custance's, indicates a radical autonomy. And I agree with Miller that Griselda's love for Walter is inherently antinomical. Finally, I agree with Ashe that Griselda's unconditional obedience should be considered in light of the hermeneutic of charity. But *The Clerk's Prologue*, as these scholars do not acknowledge, has already supplied the terms by means of which we can understand Griselda's obedience and love. Just as the Clerk asserts his autonomy from Petrarch even as he submits to the latter's authority, Griselda devotes herself absolutely to Walter as her final cause (formalism) and *for that reason* remains absolutely independent of Walter as her final cause (materialism). She freely promises to give up her freedom, ensuring that the more she submits to Walter's tyranny the more she asserts her radical autonomy.[28] Elizabeth Kirk likewise suggests that "[Griselda's] silence, her sealedness, and the price she is willing to pay to maintain them – not just her own life but the lives of those she loves and is responsible for – can also be seen as an affirmation of her autonomy, her selfhood, as an entity with the power of choice."[29] Though I do not agree that Griselda is a "self," the logical structure she instantiates is one we have witnessed from *The Nun's Priest's Tale* onwards: The imposition of Walter's formal authority is simultaneously the deposition of his formal authority.

It is for this reason that Griselda's powerlessness retains such extraordinary power. On account of her vow, Walter enjoys the total freedom to treat Griselda as he pleases; but, in his obsessive testing, he is absolutely mastered by her at the same time: "he ne myghte out of his herte throwe/This merveillous desir his wyf t'assaye" (4.453–4). The same is true of his eventual capitulation; it is Griselda's unwavering submission that masters Walter: "This sturdy markys gan his herte dresse/ To rewen upon hire wyfly stedfastnesse" (4.1049–50). As the people's spokesman says: Accepting the yoke of marriage is sovereignty, not service. Griselda is in the strange position of being freed by her submission. Walter is in the strange position of being mastered by his mastery. We cannot decide whether Griselda is mastered or free. We cannot decide whether Walter is mastered or free. The love between Walter and Griselda, therefore, is a narratively elongated version of the love between Walter and his subjects. The same logic holds in both cases: Walter is overcome by the power of the powerless.

When confronted with the undecidability of love, the temptation is always to decide. The conclusion to *The Clerk's Tale* presents us therefore with two possible ways of domesticating Griselda. Understandably, generations of scholars have read *The Clerk's Tale* in line with Petrarch's own interpretation of Griselda's story, which the Clerk both provides and seems to ratify. I will provide first Petrarch's concluding words to Boccaccio and then the Clerk's translation:[30]

> I thought it fitting to re-tell this story in a different style, not so much to urge the matrons of our time to imitate the patience of this wife (which seems to me almost unchanging) as to arouse readers to imitate her womanly constancy, so that they might dare to undertake for God what she undertook for her husband. God is the appropriate tester of evils, as the Apostle James said; but he tempts no one himself. Nevertheless he tests

us. Often he allows us to be belaboured with heavy stings, not so that he might know our spirit – he knew us before we were created – but so that our fragility might be shown to us by clear and familiar signs. I would have rated among the most steadfast of men one of whatever station who endured without complaint and for God what this little country wife endured for her mortal husband.

> This storie is seyd nat for that wyves sholde
> Folwen Grisilde as in humylitee,
> For it were inportable, though they wolde,
> But for that every wight, in his degree,
> Sholde be constant in adversitee
> As was Grisilde; therfore Petrak writeth
> This storie, which with heigh stile he enditeth.
>
> For sith a womman was so pacient
> Unto a mortal man, wel moore us oghte
> Receyven al in gree that God us sent;
> For greet skile is he preeve that he wroghte.
> But he ne tempteth no man that he boghte,
> As seith Seint Jame, if ye his pistel rede;
> He preeveth folk al day, it is no drede,
>
> And suffreth us for oure exercise,
> With sharp scourges of adversitee
> Ful ofte to be bete in sondry wise;
> Nat for to knowe oure wyl, for certes he,
> Er we were born, knew al oure freletee;
> And for oure beste is al his governance.
> Lat us thanne lyve in vertuous suffrance.   (4.1142–62)

All the difficulties of the narrative are smoothed away by Petrarch's univocal equation of Griselda with the ungendered human soul ("every wight"), suffering in patience whatever God sends in the way of adversity. Petrarch thus *masters* the legend of Griselda, imposing upon her problematic narrative a single comforting interpretation. And just as Petrarch imposes his authority on Griselda, the Petrarchan God imposes his authority upon us. He exercises his power unilaterally to test our devotion to him: "He preeveth folk al day, it is no drede," imposing upon us for our moral exercise the "sharp scourges of adversitee." Petrarch's God knows everything in advance, allowing little room for free will: "for certes he,/*Er we were born,* knew al oure freletee." According to

Petrarch's vision, everything is divinely ordered in advance. We reside within a moral and meaningful universe in which God governs everything "for oure best," without any possibility of brute contingency. Petrarch, much like the Man of Law, posits a formalist God who oversees a universe sanitized of material impurities – just as Petrarch himself glosses away Griselda's material femininity.

The question remains, however: Does the Clerk really endorse Petrarch's formalist interpretation of the Griselda narrative? We should recall once more *The Clerk's Prologue*; I argued above that the Clerk follows Petrarch by diverging from him, diverges from Petrarch by following him. Now, before turning to address the Wife of Bath and all her sect, the Clerk appears to subscribe faithfully to Petrarch's interpretation of the Griselda narrative: "Lat us thanne lyve in vertuous suffraunce," he says. The story of Griselda, the Clerk seems to be saying, teaches us all, women and men, to suffer adversity virtuously – exactly the moral Petrarch draws. At the same time, the Clerk makes a straightforward alignment between himself and Petrarch difficult to establish. Is he endorsing Petrarch's interpretation, or is he just citing it ("therfore Petrak writeth/This storie")? As numerous scholars have observed, furthermore, the Clerk throughout his tale seems bent on disabling the neat allegorical equations that Petrarch installs. He does this primarily by insisting on Griselda's gender, which Petrarch's allegorical interpretation seeks to efface. As Emma Campbell remarks, "Unlike Petrarch, the Clerk actively encourages the listener to respond to the text as a story about wives, and repeatedly suggests the social and political interactions of men and women as a means of identifying with and interpreting the story."[31] The Clerk repeatedly intervenes into his story, therefore, on behalf of women by criticizing their maltreatment by husbands: "But as for me, I seye that yvele it sit/To assaye a wyf whan that it is no need (4.460–1); "But wedded men ne knowe no mesure,/Whan that they fynde a pacient creature" (4.622–3); "But now of wommen wolde I axen fayn/If thise assayes myghte nat suffyse?" (4.696–7). The Clerk even asserts that women provide a superior example of "humblesse" (4.932) than Job himself. In a striking departure from the source, moreover, Walter, when revealing his subterfuge to his wife, says that the torments he inflicted were "But for t'assaye in thee thy *wommanheede*" (4.1075).[32] The Clerk cuts against the grain of Petrarchan formalism, insisting by contrast on the materiality of "womanhood."[33] The immaterial ideal of patience towards which we should incline competes, then, with Griselda's material embodiment: "It were ful hard to fynde now-a-dayes/In al a toun Grisildis thre or two" (4.1164–5), the Clerk observes.

The Clerk reinforces this emphasis on Griselda's wifehood by interfering with Petrarch's implicit equation of Walter and God. With his citation from James 1:13, Petrarch makes it clear that God does not tempt; he tests ("et ipse neminem temptet: *probat* tamen").[34] At the climax of Petrarch's Legend, when revealing his purpose to Griselda, Walter also uses the verb "probare": "*probasse* coniugem, non dampnasse" ("I have tested my wife, not condemned her").[35] In this way, he collapses the equivocality of the Latin "retemptare," which Petrarch uses twice to describe Walter's "testing" of Griselda. The Clerk follows Petrarch in stating that God "ne tempteth no man that he boghte" (4.1153). Rather, "He preeveth folk al day, it is no drede" (4.1155), a precise translation of Petrarch's "probat tamen." Nevertheless, Walter does "tempt" Griselda repeatedly, at lines 4.452, 4.458, 4.620, 4.621, 4.707, 4.735, and 4.786. Notably, Chaucer only deploys the negative sense of "tempte" elsewhere in *The Canterbury Tales*: seventeen times in *The Parson's Tale*, three times in *The Friar's Tale*, once in *The Man of Law's Tale*, and once in *The Tale of Melibee*. John McNamara comments on this interpretive difficulty: "Although some scholars interpret ['tempte'] as equivalent to our modern 'test,' Chaucer's repeated use of the term, especially in passages censuring Walter, cannot be explained so simply. 'Tempte' could mean 'test' in some places in the tale, but the fact that Chaucer also uses the term 'assaye' in conjunction with 'tempte' implies that 'tempte' carries connotations not usually associated with 'assaye,' or 'test.'"[36] In one of his many narrative interventions on her behalf, the Clerk says of Griselda, "O nedelees was she tempted in assay!" (4.621). Is Walter here testing or tempting? It is impossible to be sure. And if Walter's efforts are in fact "needless," how does this accord with the Clerk's statement that it is *reasonable* that God test us: "greet skile is he preeve that he wroghte" (4.1152)? By refusing to collapse decisively the semantic equivocality of "tempte" and by questioning the need for the marquis's attempts on Griselda's obedience, the Clerk further destabilizes Petrarch's allegorical formulation, ensuring that Walter's equivalence to God must remain uncertain.[37] *The Clerk's Tale* simultaneously asserts and denies the Petrarchan reading of Walter.

The Clerk renders it undecidable whether to read Walter as a testing God or as a tempting husband. Correlatively, he renders it undecidable whether to read Griselda as a patient Christian or as a patient wife. Nevertheless, formalist and materialist interpretive decisions are staged in *The Clerk's Tale* and what follows it. Petrarch formalizes the narrative while the Host and the Merchant materialize the narrative. The Host wishes earnestly that "My *wyf* at hoom had herd this legende ones!" (4.1215a). The Merchant in his prologue remarks bitterly on the large difference "Bitwix Grisildis grete pacience/And of my *wyf* the passyng crueltee" (4.1224–5). But a charitable reading of Griselda will not collapse her undecidability, either in the direction of form, like Petrarch, or in the direction of matter, like the Host and the Merchant.[38] *The Clerk's Tale* is neither formally closed by the Petrarchan moralization nor materially opened by a rejection of the same.[39] It is not exactly the case, as Dinshaw suggests, that the Clerk ultimately reads "like a woman," calling attention to the gendered possibilities that Petrarch's *translatio* obliterates.[40] The Clerk simply does not decide on masculine formalism or feminine materialism. My reading of *The Clerk's Tale* thus contradicts J. Allan Mitchell's argument that Griselda's unaccountable commitment to Walter, and her "monstrous" complicity with his infanticidal tendencies, makes us consider the nature of interpretive and ethical *decision*. For Mitchell, following Derrida and Lacan, such ethical decisions are both necessary and radically groundless: "Griselda thus survives the ordeal of undecidability not by tolerating or settling for some sort of indeterminacy (a contradiction in terms) but by acting on her convictions and surrendering the temporary comfort of never having to decide."[41] As I have argued from the outset, Chaucerian ethics cannot be encompassed by the materialism of deconstruction or psychoanalysis. Rather than arguing for a decisive ethics, the Clerk implicitly urges us *not* to decide, but instead to love. And we read lovingly when we refuse to materialize Griselda into her womanhood or formalize her into an androgynous ideal. We read Griselda lovingly when we refuse to solve her. In this way, moreover, we find a way to avoid already discredited and decisive hermeneutic practices contained in Fragment 3: namely, the literalist materialism of the obtuse summoner from *The Friar's Tale* and the spiritualist formalism of the smarmy friar from *The Summoner's Tale* ("Glosynge is a glorious thyng, certeyn" [3.1793]).[42]

Accordingly, the Clerk neither submissively follows nor masterfully dismisses Petrarch's version of the Griselda story. In his translation, he freely gives up his freedom to his precursor – precisely what Walter does for his subjects and Griselda does for Walter. Analogously, Griselda's "translation" (3.385) to the elite of Saluzzo, marked by her assumption of luxurious finery, does not mean that she has simply exchanged her lower-class origins for a higher caste, as Walter thinks to remind her: "I yow took out of youre povere array,/And putte yow in estaat of heigh noblesse" (4.467–8). Griselda *entangles* vulgarity and aristocracy; in the words of the Clerk, Walter has wedded "lowely – nay, but roially" (4.421). Griselda is somehow "low" and "high" at the same time, much as it is undecidable whether the Clerk follows or departs from Petrarch's narrative, "which with *heigh* stile he enditeth" (4.1148).

While a superbly effective ruler and tireless activist on behalf of the "commune profit" (4.431), she also retains her willingness and ability to perform humbly "al the feet of wyfly hoomliness" (4.429). Indeed, Griselda states bluntly that she could only withstand her "adversitee" (4.1042) while marchioness because she is "a povre fostred creature" (4.1043), unlike Walter's new "bride." Griselda both does and does not leave her poverty behind when Walter "translates" her to the aristocracy. Conversely, after Walter's "divorce," she wears on her way back to her rustic home an exquisite smock, which serves as compensation for her virginity (4.883–96).[43] *The Clerk's Tale* likewise entangles translated and translation in an act of love that recalls Petrarch's own words to Boccaccio: "I certainly hoped to make you glad by translating your work on my own initiative. Love of you and the story impelled me to what I would hardly have done for anyone else."[44] Despite the radical changes the Clerk makes to his source, at the conclusion to his prologue he humbly introduces the tale as Petrarch's, not his own: "But this *his tale*, which that ye may here" (4.56).

Furthermore, it is via the undecidable structure of love that the Clerk, just as the Nun's Priest, the Knight, and the Franklin, suggests an alternative model of the divine, one that contrasts with Petrarch's formalist God. Noting that the Clerk repeatedly associates Griselda with Christ, Jill Mann argues that "God is more truly imaged in Griselda's boundless suffering than in Walter's tyrannical cruelty."[45] The Clerk makes this association repeatedly: "But hye God somtyme senden kan/His grace into a litel oxes stalle" (4.206–7); Griselda's subjects believe "That she from hevene sent was, as men wende,/Peple to save and every wrong t'amende" (4.440–1). Christ's incarnation and redemptive self-sacrifice accord precisely with Griselda's free renunciation of freedom. God *freely* abandons his divine *freedom* in order to adopt our humanity, a gesture imitated by Chaucer in the *General Prologue* and, as we will observe, in the Thopas-Melibee link also.[46] This undecidable structure is the supreme testament to divine love, reflected in *The Clerk's Tale* by the insoluble logic of Griselda's love for Walter.

Can we make sense of *Lenvoy de Chaucer*, with which *The Clerk's Tale* concludes, in terms of Griselda's undecidability? I think this is possible. We should avoid the critical consensus that the Envoy is "ironic," somehow at odds with the Clerk's "true" feelings regarding women in general and the Wife of Bath in particular.[47] The Envoy just presents us with another example of Chaucer's insoluble logic. Most important to remark is that the Envoy, echoing the speech of Walter's subject, consists of an extended sequence of imperatives directed towards the Wife of Bath and her fellow arch-wives: "Lat noon ... Ne lat ... Folweth ...

But evere answereth … Beth nat … But sharply taak … Emprenteth wel … Ne suffreth … Beth egre … Ay clappeth … Ne dreed … Shewe thou … Be ay … And lat hym" (4.1184–1212). But the magisterial posture adopted by the Clerk accompanies only one message: "do not subordinate yourselves to men." The Clerk thus *authoritatively* instructs wives to revolt ferociously against the *authority* both of husbands and clerks. Wives should not have any "reverence" (4.1201) for the former and should ensure that the latter have no reason "To write of yow a storie of swich mervaille / As of Grisildis pacient and kynde" (4.1186–7). Instead of subordination, wives must "sharply taak on … the governaille" (4.1192). The Clerk is *commanding* wives to *free* themselves of any masculine authority, marital *or* clerical: "Be ay of chiere as light as leef on lynde" (4.1211). The Envoy to *The Clerk's Tale* simultaneously imposes itself upon and retracts itself from its female audience. The speaker neither formalizes nor materializes wives, exactly the charitable attitude we are to maintain towards Griselda. Thus, even though the Friar and the Summoner have ignored the import of the Wife of Bath's prologue and tale, the Clerk certainly was listening. This is in keeping with what we know of him: "And gladly wolde he lerne and gladly teche" (1.308).

It is tempting to conclude that the Clerk demonstrates his attentiveness to Alisoun in the best way possible, by loving her. But the Wife of Bath's fundamental lesson was that the lover does not decide on love. Her tale, therefore, concluded with a distinctly uncharitable epilogue that contradicted the loving reconciliation of the knight and his wife in her tale. Does the Envoy likewise undermine our interpretive security about the Clerk's love for Alisoun? In this regard, we should note the attribution of the Envoy to Chaucer in so many of the best manuscripts of *The Canterbury Tales*.[48] I propose that this attribution manifests an extension of the Wife of Bath's lesson. The charitable reader will not decide, ultimately, whether it is in fact Chaucer or the Clerk who is expressing his love for the Wife of Bath.

The Merchant's Prologue and Tale

The vengeful dispute between the Friar and the Summoner follows the Wife of Bath's lesson on charity. Likewise, the Merchant's vengeful assault on women and marriage follows the Clerk's loving response to the Wife of Bath. As is so often the case in *The Canterbury Tales*, we must be alert to the clues supplied in the prologue to *The Merchant's Tale* in order to establish the narrator's orientation towards form and matter. Accordingly, there are two elements in *The Merchant's Prologue* that will inform my reading of the tale that follows. I will consider first the Merchant's response to the representation of Griselda in *The Clerk's Tale*; I will consider second the logical consequences of his claim that his wife is so bad that were she "ycoupled" (4.1219) to the devil himself, "She wolde hym overmacche, I dar wel swere" (4.1220). There can be little doubt that the Merchant identifies himself as one of the adversarial pilgrims. The final section of this chapter will be devoted, therefore, to establishing precisely how his tale enacts, as it must, Chaucer's law of unintended consequences.

The Merchant's response to Griselda is illuminating. Bemoaning a marriage that has disappointed his expectations after only two months, he says:

> There is a long and large difference
> Bitwix Grisildis grete pacience
> And of my wyf the passyng crueltee.　　　　　　　　　　(4.1223–5)

Clearly, the Merchant has not understood the legend of Griselda in a Petrarchan fashion, and he has ignored the Clerk's admonition that the example she sets is "inportable" (4.1144). Wallace understands the Merchant's response to the Clerk as analogous to the Miller's response to the Knight: "the second tale, through judicious use of structural parallelism and grotesque realism, performs a humorous critique of the first."[49] I agree that the two situations are analogous, but I disagree on the nature of the analogy: the Miller and the Merchant both *misread* the Knight and the Clerk, respectively, by deciding on the undecidable.[50] The Merchant thus decides not on the formalist and Petrarchan interpretation, but follows the Host with a materialist reading: Griselda is a *woman* of exemplary patience, not an androgynously formal ideal towards which women *and* men should aspire. The Merchant's inability to see anything but dark matter untethered from illuminating form characterizes his orientation throughout his tale. I thus side with an older tradition of reading *The Merchant's Tale* that argues for the appropriateness of teller to tale on the basis of the prologue. This interpretive tradition tends to rely on claims about the effect that an unsuccessful marriage has had on the Merchant's now jaundiced and bitter personality. Kittredge thus feels the story is loaded with "savage and cynical satire";[51] Tatlock compares the acidity of the speaker to "a volcanic crater, the black rough floor burst now and again by a spurt of white-hot lava";[52] and C.H. Holman describes the Merchant's narrative as "one of the most savagely obscene, angrily embittered, pessimistic, and unsmiling tales in our language."[53] The tale, therefore, is an opportunity for a profoundly disappointed husband to assert vengefully his malice against women in general and wives in particular.

The "bitterness tradition" has been challenged by Chaucerians keen to insulate interpretations of the tale from the unverifiable assumption that its narrator was once like January but is now disaffected and cynical on account of the trials of matrimony. So, for instance, Martin Stevens argues that the "bitterness tradition" derives more from unwarranted speculation about the correlation of January's experience to the Merchant's life than any evidence provided by the prologue. Thus, "Amidst the derision and contempt that so many critics are wont to find in the tone of the *Merchant's Tale*, we are likely to forget that much of it is gay and laughable."[54] The basic point of the "anti-bitterness" camp is that speculation about the Merchant's psychology can distort our reception of his tale. In line with opponents of the "bitterness tradition," my concern is not with the interiority of the Merchant and its effect on the tale he tells. Contrariwise, in line with advocates of the "bitterness tradition," I will argue that the Merchant's prologue and tale are consistent, but only in terms of their logic.

Let us now recall the Merchant's materialist interpretation of *The Clerk's Tale* and consider how it anticipates several elements of his narration. After listing the aphrodisiacs that January imbibes in preparation for his sexual endeavours with his new wife, the Merchant notes the source of this medical lore along with a telling comment:

> He drynketh ypocras, clarree, and vernage
> Of spices hoote t'encreessen his corage;
> And many a letuarie hath he ful fyn,
> Swiche as the cursed monk, daun Constantyn,
> Hath writen in his book *De Coitu*.   (4.1807–11)

Constantinus Africanus is a "cursed monk" because of his focus on the physiology of sex in his *De Coitu*. Paul Delany notes that this text "is in no sense an erotic handbook like *Kama Sutra* or the Arabic love-manuals; it totally lacks frivolity, and it explains, in the medieval encyclopedic tradition, the function of coitus in the divine scheme."[55] But the Merchant disentangles the matter of carnality from any divine cause towards which it may intend. His reading of the *De Coitu* corresponds to his reading of *The Clerk's Tale*: In both cases, he eschews the formalist reading in favour of the materialist.

The Merchant's assessment of the *De Coitu* and its "cursed" author anticipates his response to January's paraphrase of Solomon's Song of Songs to seduce May into his garden of carnal delight: "Swiche olde lewed wordes used he" (4.2149). Once again, we witness the Merchant's materialist reading strategy. Just as he does with Griselda in *The Clerk's Tale*, he interprets the Song of Songs not allegorically and spiritually, as the marriage of Christ and Church, but literally and carnally, consonant with both Solomon's and January's erotic designs.[56] Likewise, when the Merchant describes the marriage of January and May, he deploys only Old Testament and secular references: Sarah and Rebecca (4.1704); Orpheus and Amphion (4.1716); Joab (4.1719); Theodamus (4.1720); Thebes (4.1721); Bacchus (4.1722); Venus (4.1723); Hymen (4.1730); Martianus Capella and the wedding of Mercury and Philology (4.1732–4); the Muses (4.1735); Esther and Ahasuerus (4.1744–5); Paris and Helen (4.1754). The Merchant cannot perceive the Christian and spiritual meaning of the marital sacrament but focuses instead on the literal, the secular, and the carnal.[57]

Indeed, both January and the Merchant staunchly refuse to perceive anything beyond matter. January thus expresses his desire for a young wife by means of a suggestive analogy: "But certeynly, a yong thyng may men gye,/Right as men may warm wex with handes plye" (4.1429–30). January sees a young bride as formless wax, awaiting his carnal manipulation. Whether they regard the feminine with disgust or delectation is irrelevant;[58] *matter* is all that January and the Merchant can perceive.[59] The former, fittingly, becomes "as blynd as is a *stoon*" (4.2156). The latter apologizes to the ladies in his audience before describing Damian's unerring thrust: "I kàn nat glose, I am a rude man" (4.2351). Given a second opportunity to describe the scene, he refuses altogether, lest he "speke uncurteisly" (4.2363). The Merchant's reticence recalls his account of January and May's wedding night: "But lest that precious folk be with me wroth,/How that he wroghte, I dar nat to yow telle" (4.1962–3). The self-described "rude" Merchant is incapable of formally decorous "preciousness"; hence, he can no more gloss, or formalize, the carnality of May's dalliance with Damian than he can gloss, or formalize, the carnality of Solomon's old, lewd words.

Now that we have identified the consistency of the Merchant's materialist vision across both prologue and tale, let us turn to the debate between Pluto and Proserpina that arises when the former regards May's adulterous intent in her husband's *locus amoenus*. The king and queen of "Fairye" function in multiple ways in the tale. First, Pluto and Proserpina evoke via Claudian's *De raptu Proserpinae*, cited at line 4.2232, the violent lust of an elderly man, such as January, for a young innocent, such as May.[60] *The Merchant's Tale* thus parallels the hastily arranged marriage of January and May to Pluto's abduction of Proserpina – the classical rape narrative that served, I suggested, as a subtext for the Man of Law's account of Custance, another unfortunate wife. Second,

Pluto, just like January, finds Solomon to be a useful authority. But whereas January borrows from the Song of Songs to seduce his wife, Pluto marshals the antifeminist material from Ecclesiastes 7:28 to annoy his. He thus quotes Solomon speaking of the upright individuals he has encountered on his travels: "Amonges a thousand men yet foond I oon,/But of wommen alle foond I noon" (4.2247–8). Third, while January (4.1247) and Solomon (4.2242) are both wealthy men, Pluto is, of course, the god of wealth. Finally, Pluto, an excellent surrogate for a merchant striving for prosperity, serves as a mouthpiece for the narrator's misogynistic convictions. Having witnessed the exchange of signals between Damian and May, the god turns in disgust to Proserpina:

> "My wyf," quod he, "ther may no wight seye nay;
> Th'experience so preveth every day
> The tresons which that womman doon to man.
> Ten hondred thousand [tales] tellen I kan
> Notable of youre untrouthe and brotilnesse."   (4.2237–41)

The Merchant thus amplifies his wife's betrayal of his marital expectations by having Pluto bemoan the endless treasons performed by women against men. Pluto shares the Merchant's materialist orientation: Woman is rebellious and "untruthful" matter that will not allow itself to be constrained by masculine form. But Pluto's and Solomon's antifeminism is just the obverse of January and the Merchant's carnal obsession, as Proserpina makes clear. She remarks, therefore, that despite his great authority, Solomon also "was a lecchour and an ydolastre" (4.2298). Proserpina formulates a devastating link between Solomon's antifeminism, his lecherous carnality, and his inability to see beyond idolatrous matter.[61] Relatedly, she undermines the authority of this Old Testament figure by implying an alignment with the materiality of the letter rather than the formality of the spirit: "this Jew, this Solomon" (4.2277). Solomon, just as Pluto, January, and the Merchant, fetishizes feminine matter, radically disentangling it from form. Each of these men, therefore, can only perceive woman as carnal, and this fetishism defines the limits of their vision.

Proserpina's astute rebuttal of her husband's facile misogyny is so effective that he is forced to concede the case: "'Dame,' quod this Pluto, "be no lenger wroth; I yeve it up!" (4.2311–12). Patterson reads Pluto's concession as indicative of the compromises and negotiations necessary in a fallen and historical world that no longer possesses the unshakeable assurances of an ahistorical paradise: "the uniformity of monolithic ideologies yields to a differential reality, in which negotiation and exchange are the governing practices. We have entered, almost without noticing, the realm in which a merchant will be most at home."[62] But Patterson's zeal to historicize *The Merchant's Tale* in terms of the bourgeois "market-based ethic" that emerged in the late fourteenth century leads him to ignore a crucial link between Pluto's concession and *The Merchant's Prologue*. Proserpina's ability to defeat Pluto in their debate in fact reveals the logical contortions of *The Merchant's Tale*. On the one hand, the Merchant in his prologue *expresses* his misogyny by insisting that bad wives, such as the one with which he has been saddled, can overmatch the devil himself. Women are worse than Satan! He demonstrates this claim by having Proserpina, the devil's wife, overmatch Pluto in their argument about the falsity of women. But, on the other hand, within his tale "overmatching the fiend" means *refuting* Pluto's, Solomon's, and the Merchant's trite misogyny. The Merchant's antifeminism is advanced (women can overmatch the devil) and undermined (a woman overmatches the devil's antifeminism) simultaneously. It is undecidable, therefore, whether the Merchant's discourse is misogynistic. His tale expresses his misogyny by refuting it; it refutes his misogyny by expressing it. Yet again in *The Canterbury Tales*, a vengeful pilgrim falls into the snare of Chaucer's law of unintended consequences. The Merchant's antifeminism fails and succeeds at the same time, at once realizing and contradicting his formal intention.

We now have a way to understand a major crux that has long exercised scholars writing on *The Merchant's Tale*. The lengthy passage at the beginning of the tale, extending from line 4.1267 to line 4.1392, seems at once to be a sincere encomium of wives and marriage and a sneering dissuasion against marriage.[63] The Merchant's discourse veers precipitously from the former to the latter, prompting critics, such as Robert Edwards, to observe: "The pious statements praising marriage obviously invite an ironic reading, but none of the voices in the tale, not even the Merchant's, is strong enough to claim the final authorial power to determine or limit the meaning."[64] It is difficult to take the following passage, for instance, as merely ironic:

> I warne thee, if wisely thou wolt wirche,
> Love wel thy wyf, as Crist loved his chirche.
> If thou lovest thyself, thou lovest thy wyf;
> No man hateth his flessh, but in his lyf
> He fostreth it, therefore I bidde thee
> Cherisse thy wyf, or thou shalt nevere thee.
> Housbonde and wyf, what so men jape or pleye,
> Of worldly folk holden the siker weye.
>
> (4.1383–90)

Just as earlier the Merchant instructs his audience to defy the "vanytee" of Theophrastus (4.1309–10), in this passage he condemns as mere "japery and play" the anti-matrimonial dogma of his ilk. The Merchant insists instead that the relationship between man and wife is akin to the sacred love between Christ and church, echoing the orthodoxy of the Parson himself: "Man sholde bere hym to his wyf in feith, in trouthe, and in love, as seith Seint Paul, that a man sholde loven his wyf as Crist loved hooly chirche, that loved it so wel that he deyde for it" (10.929). This is precisely the allegorical (or formal) meaning assigned to the Song of Songs, to which the Merchant is blind when he condemns January's old, lewd words.

But, if the Merchant indeed views matrimony as sacred love, it is on the surface confusing that he would utter the following snide remark: "A wyf wol laste, and in thyn hous endure,/Wel lenger than thee list, paraventure" (4.1317–18). It is surely sarcastic, moreover, that the Merchant cites the example of Eve in support of the claim "That wyf is mannes helpe and his confort" (4.1331). The same sardonic tone animates a later comment: "Suffre thy wyves tonge, as Catoun bit;/She shal commande, and thou shal suffren it" (4.1377–8). The Merchant's discourse is simultaneously cynical *and* sincere, which may account as well for the overblown rhetoric of his various apostrophes: "O perilous fyr, that in the bedstraw breadth!" (4.1783 ff.); "O sodeyn hap! O thou Fortune unstable!" (4.2057 ff.); "O Januarie, what myghte it thee availle…" (4.2107 ff.); "O noble Ovyde, ful sooth seystou, God woot…" (4.2125 ff.). The extreme rhetorical inflation of the Merchant's authorial presence only undermines its authenticity. Too much earnestness is none at all.

The entanglement of cynicism and sincerity, furthermore, may explain why the list of exemplary Old Testament women that the Merchant supplies at lines 4.1366–74 is ambivalent.[65] Rebekah assists Jacob in the deception of his father and her husband; Judith uses her sexuality to deceive and then assassinate the Assyrian general, Holofernes, and save the Israelites; Esther uses her influence as queen to beguile her gentile husband Ahasuerus (for whom she has considerable contempt), plot against Haman to save her uncle, and preserve the Israelites from genocide; finally, Abigail tricks her old and foolish husband, Nabal, to save him from the wrath of David, whom she marries after Nabal's death "with a haste," according to Emerson Brown, "that might redden the cheeks of Queen Gertrude."[66] Each of these women is both faithful *and* deceptive to the men in their lives. As Brown points out, "For all their obvious virtues, they do exhibit deceitful, treacherous, unfaithful, or even murderous behaviour."[67] But Prudence in *The Tale of Melibee* uses exactly the same list of women, apparently without irony, to buttress her claim that women provide good counsel: "yet han men founde ful many a good womman, and ful discret and wis in conseillynge" (7.1097).[68] The context of the list in *The Merchant's Tale* compels a more equivocal response. We can read these women as deceptive or true – as proving antifeminism or refuting it. The ambivalence of Rebekah, Judith, Abigail, and Esther is instructive for our reading of the Merchant's encomium of marriage. The temptation is to decide between cynicism or sincerity in the Merchant's discourse or to find some agreeable synthesis of the alternatives. But that is to misunderstand what Chaucer is doing throughout *The Canterbury Tales*. Instead, the Merchant's prologue and Tale function together to confute misogyny *misogynistically*. The Merchant's vengeful and *fiendish* antifeminism, thanks to the devil's wife, is its own refutation. Proserpina, a classical reflex of the Old Testament wives listed in the marriage encomium, at once advances the Merchant's misogyny and demolishes it.[69]

This reading of Proserpina and her Old Testament equivalents suggests how we are to understand May's role at the conclusion to *The Merchant's Tale*. Caught *in flagrante* with Damian in January's tree, May is nevertheless able to convince January that the sudden return of sight can generate phantasms. She concludes her speech with an exquisite double entendre implanted within a proverbial admonition:

> Beth war, I prey yow, for by hevene kyng,
> Ful many a man weneth to seen a thyng,
> And it is al another than it semeth.
> He that mysconceyveth, he misdemeth.   (4.2407–10)

There is an obvious pun here on the threat posed to the legitimacy of January's putative heirs.[70] But the artistry of May's speech goes beyond the double meaning of "misconceyveth." What I wish to argue is that she manages here to tell the truth and lie at the same time.[71] While *deceiving* January about her adultery, she tells him the *truth* about the dangers of his faulty vision. He misconceives May as pliable wax, and therefore misjudges her as submissive to his desires. However, rather than indeterminate matter receiving the form January impresses upon her, she acquires the *form* of the key to his garden by impressing it into indeterminate matter (4.2117) so that Damian can copy it (4.2121).[72] The Merchant, as I have argued above, shares January's carnal fetishism – along with Solomon and Pluto. In this connection, we already know that the Merchant "kan not glose" (4.2351); consequently, it is left to May to provide the formal truth of his tale even as she materially deceives January.[73]

May lies with the truth. Her final words thus serve as a fitting moral, one applicable not only to January's blindness but to the defective carnal vision of the Merchant and the men in his audience. The entanglement of truth and untruth in May's speech ensures that she, like Proserpina and her biblical analogues, only furthers the Merchant's antifeminism by undermining it.

In the final passage of the tale, the Merchant reveals that January has retreated complacently to the delightful garden of his carnal fantasy: "This Januarie, who is *glad* but he?" (4.2412). We should observe that four lines later the Merchant enjoins the men in his audience to do the same: "Now, goode men, I pray yow to be *glad*" (4.2416). As the Merchant states earlier, "Passe over is an ese" (4.2115). It is telling, therefore, that the Host in the epilogue to *The Merchant's Tale* does as he is instructed, complacently aligning women with deceptive matter:

> Lo, whiche sleightes and subtilitees
> In wommen been! For ay as bisy as bees
> Been they, us sely men for to deceyve,
> And from the soothe evere wol they weyve.   (4.2421–4)

And yet, despite the narrator's misogynistic advocacy, Chaucer's law of unintended consequences ensures that *The Merchant's Tale* becomes a testament to charity. The tale concludes, therefore, with reference to the sublimity of maternal love: "God blesse us, and his mooder Seinte Marie!" (4.2418).[74] It is the love of Mary for Christ and Ceres for Proserpina that is evoked when January looks up into the tree and perceives with agony May's infidelity: "And up he yaf a roryng and a cry, / As dooth the mooder whan that the child shal dye" (4.2364–5). We should compare the maternal grief described in this passage to the obscenely carnal lullaby that January sings to his new bride: "He lulleth hire; he kisseth hire ful ofte" (4.1823). In *The Merchant's Tale*, the divine compassion of maternal love serves to counterpoint the blind violence of plutonic carnality, and it is, fittingly, what January encounters when his eyes, ever so briefly, are opened.[75]

5 Governance and Rebellion in Fragment 6

Fragments 3 and 4 each feature the alternation of charitable pilgrims and vengeful pilgrims. The quarrel between the Friar and the Summoner follows the Wife of Bath's elaboration of her loving doctrine. The Merchant's blinkered assault on matrimony follows the Clerk's loving response to the Wife. While the Host identifies the theme of Fragment 5 as love (5.2), Fragment 6 contains two tales whose tellers, I will argue, emphatically reject love. The juxtaposition of Fragments 5 and 6 in the Ellesmere arrangement is therefore tantalizing, if not conclusively demonstrable, due to the self-enclosed nature of Fragment 6. As we have seen so far, those pilgrims who turn away from love in favour of mastery or vengeance are invariably subject to the law of unintended consequences. The Physician and the Pardoner are no exception: both may not be lovers, but each exemplifies the Chaucerian principle of love nonetheless. What we will see, however, is that the two pilgrims decide on love in opposite ways: The Physician privileges order over chaos; the Pardoner privileges chaos over order.

The Physician's Tale

It is almost expected now that one begins an analysis of *The Physician's Tale* by remarking on its lack of appeal. This is unsurprising, given that its subject matter is grotesque. Originally recounted in Livy's *Ab Urbe Condita* and retold in *The Romance of the Rose* and the *Confessio Amantis*, the Physician's version is faithful to its sources in recounting a story of a father who murders his own daughter to preserve her purity and their honour.[1] While many critics simply conclude that *The Physician's Tale* is the least successful of *The Canterbury Tales*,[2] others argue that its ineptitude is deliberate, serving to ridicule the teller.[3] Both scholarly parties observe the difficulty in deriving any instructive morality from the tale. Cooper's assessment reflects this critical bewilderment: "The tale seems to offer, and require, admiration both for inward virtue and for an outward honour that can express itself in murder."[4] My approach to the tale does not consider whether it is an artistic or moral success. I am concerned only with how *The Physician's Tale* exemplifies the insoluble structure of love, as every one of *The Canterbury Tales* does. In this regard, it is important to observe that *The Physician's Tale* is a text on formal authority: namely, the authority of the creator, the parent, the governor, and the judge. Jerome Mandel also notes this emphasis: "In this tale alone of Chaucer's tales, all the characters are defined in terms of the governor-governed relationship. Chaucer discusses matters of appearance and reality, fraud and honesty at levels of governance of increasing significance: in the individual, the family, the body politic, and the cosmos."[5] While I agree with Mandel that the tale represents both "good" authorities and "bad" authorities, my reading will reformulate this opposition using the terms of my analysis throughout: "masterful" governors and "loving" governors. I will conclude my analysis by considering whether the Physician himself falls into the former category or the latter. In doing so, I believe we can resolve some of the interpretive difficulties the tale has posed to its modern readers.

To accomplish this objective, it is necessary to consider methodically the series of hierarchical relationships that the tale presents: 1) God and Nature; 2) Nature and Virginia; 3) Apius and Claudius; 4) Apius and Virginia; 5) Virginius and Virginia; and 6) Jephthah and his daughter. We begin with God and Nature. The Physician describes the relationship of Nature to her governor in a speech that he hypothetically accords to the former:

> For he that is the formere principal
> Hath maked me his vicaire general,
> To forme and peynten erthely creaturis
> *Right as me list*, and ech thyng in my cure is
> Under the moone, that may wane and waxe,
> And for my werk right no thyng wol I axe;
> My lord and I been ful of oon accord.   (6.19–25)

Though Nature is the subordinate of God, who is the "formere principal," she remains *free* to "forme and peynten" earthly creatures as she desires. Nature is formed to be free. God exercises his formal authority only by revoking it, and the consequence is that he and Nature are of "one accord." Nature thus submits to the will of God by means of her absolute freedom. The God of *The Physician's Tale* loves Nature; accordingly, she is neither free of his authority nor mastered by it.

An identical relationship holds between Nature and Virginia. According to the Physician, Virginia is Nature's masterpiece: "For Nature hath with sovereyn diligence/Yformed hire in so greet excellence" (6.9–10). The perfection of God's authority over Nature results in the freedom of his chief deputy. Likewise, the perfection of Nature's authority over Virginia results in Virginia's freedom from external authority:

> Bacus hadde of hir mouth right no maistrie;
> For wyn and youthe dooth Venus encresse,
> As men in fyr wol casten oille or greesse.
> And of her owene vertu, unconstreyned,
> She hath ful ofte tyme syk hire feyned,
> For that she wolde fleen the compaignye
> Where likly was to treten of folye.   (6.58–64)

Virginia is not only free of the mastery of Bacchus, her virtue, we are told, requires no outside constraint whatsoever. Virginia governs herself just as Nature does. As the Physician later states: "This mayde, of which I wol this tale expresse,/So kepte hirself hir neded no maistresse" (6.105–6). The parallel between the two females is reinforced by Nature's insistence that no one can "countrefete" (6.13) her. The Physician likewise says of Virginia that "No countrefeted terms had she" (6.51).[6] Nature and Virginia are radically *original*. Nature cannot be copied and Virginia copies no one – neither slavishly conforms to a master. Both figures, in other words, are formed (formalism) to be free (materialism): Nature loves Virginia just as God loves Nature. Nature's allusion to the Ovidian narrative of Pygmalion (6.14), reprised in *The Romance of the Rose*, is thus doubly relevant. Pygmalion, like God and Nature, is a master artist who adores his creation; but there is also a darker resonance. Jean de Meun associates Pygmalion with Narcissus – both figures are infatuated with their own images in anticipation of Virginius's egoistical relationship with his namesake, Virginia.[7]

The ideal governance of God and Nature contrasts with the coercive and masterful relationship between the judge and "governour" (6.122), Apius, and his henchman, Claudius:

> This juge unto this cherl his tale hath toold
> In secree wise, and made hym to ensure
> He sholde telle it to no creature,
> And if he dide, he sholde lese his heed.

> Whan that assented was this cursed reed,
> Glad was this juge, and maked him greet cheere,
> And yaf him yiftes preciouse and deere.   (6.142–8)

Claudius's loyalty is guaranteed by means of threats and rewards. Nature, by contrast, neither asks nor requires any recompense for her work and nevertheless remains perfectly in accord with her governor: "And for my werk right no thyng wol I axe/My lord and I been ful of oon accord" (6.24–5). Moreover, Apius himself recognizes that with Virginia he cannot operate "by no force ne by no meede" (6.133). Unlike Claudius, her self-governance is so absolute as to be incorruptible. To satisfy his lust, therefore, Apius must pervert his judicial office and abuse the law. Once Claudius has made his fraudulent claim in court that Virginia is his servant and belongs in his house, Apius delivers his "sentence" (6.204). The consequence is that Virginius "Moste by force his deere doghter yiven/Unto the juge, in lecherie to liven" (6.205–6). There is an obvious contradiction here. The Physician has just told us that Apius knows he cannot operate by force on Virginia, yet Virginius is by force compelled to give Virginia to Apius. The contradiction suggests that Virginius has an alternative to murder, a possibility surely raised by the Physician's comment that both he and his daughter are "strong of freendes" (6.4 and 6.135) or that "a thousand peple in thraste" (6.260) to save Virginius himself from Apius's death sentence. As Sheila Delany asks, "How much does the father want his daughter to survive if he fails to consider these possibilities?"[8]

But, rather than consider alternatives to death, Virginius's response to the "sentence" of Apius on Virginia is to impose his own murderous "sentence" upon his daughter. Virginius at this point becomes, like Apius, a judge:

> O gemme of chastitee, in pacience
> Take thou thy deeth, for this is my *sentence*.
> For love, and nat for hate, thou most be deed;
> My pitous hand moot smyten of thyn heed.   (6.223–6)

Virginius's governance of his daughter radically contradicts the model supplied by God and by Nature. Instead of authoritatively withdrawing his authority, Virginius violently imposes it. Rather than giving his daughter freedom, he unequivocally collapses any space for her autonomy. Indeed, even when his daughter pleads for mercy and grace, he refuses stonily: "'No, certes, deere doghter myn'" (6.237).[9] In dramatic contrast, Virginius is able *spontaneously* to demonstrate "pitee" (6.272) towards Apius's confederate, Claudius, even though his "pitous" hand smote off Virginia's head.

Virginia's subsequent and anachronistic allusion to Jephthah's daughter, not coincidentally from the Book of Judges, reinforces the sense here that Virginius is acting as a bad judge. The allusion appears in the context of Virginia's request for time to grieve for her death:

> "Thanne yif me leyser, fader myn," quod she,
> "My deeth for to compleyne a litel space;
> For, pardee, Jepte yaf his doghter grace
> For to compleyne, er he hir slow, allas!
> And, God it woot, no thyng was hir trespas,
> But for she ran hir fader first to see,
> To welcome hym with greet solempnitee."   (6.238–44)

Jephthah, both a judge and a leader of the Israelites, foolishly vows to Jehovah that he will sacrifice the first creature that comes out of his home to greet him if he returns victorious over the Ammonites. He is victorious, but upon his return home it is his daughter who first greets him. Though he gives his daughter space to grieve her fate, Jephthah stays faithful to his rash promise.[10] It is notable that Virginius is not only unwilling to show mercy to Virginia, he also denies her the "grace" provided to Jephthah's daughter. Furthermore, Jepthah at least demonstrates Abrahamic obedience to God. *The Physician's Tale* is set in Roman antiquity, so Virginius's concern is entirely secular; he has no appeal to this mitigating factor, however slight. Virginius desires the avoidance of "shame" (6.214) for himself and his daughter within his community. Daniel Kline states the case bluntly: "Virginius's brutality stabilizes the father-daughter relationship, confirms his mastery of his daughter, and reinforces his control over access to her body. Virginius's reassertion of fatherly prerogative perversely costs his daughter's life, for in wake of the threat against his paternal claim on his daughter, Virginius shows that Virginia … is no more than an extension of himself and his own sociopolitical – and sociopathic – needs."[11] Virginius is, therefore, an even worse judge than Jephthah.

Although the violently unilateral and formalist "sentence" Virginius imposes on Virginia contradicts the model of love supplied by God and Nature, it appears very much in line with the Physician's model of governance. In the midst of a long digression on the governance of children (6.72–104), the Physician urges governesses to instruct their charges in "vertu" (6.82), exhorting them not to "assente" to any "vice" (6.87). The Physician also addresses parents directly:

> Ye fadres and ye moodres eek also,
> Though ye han children, be it oon or mo,
> Youre is the charge of al hir surveiaunce,
> Whil that they been under youre governaunce.
> Beth war, if by ensample of youre lyvynge,
> Or by youre necgligence in chastisynge,
> That they ne perisse; for I dar wel seye
> If that they doon, ye shul it deere abeye.
> Under a shepherde softe and necligent
> The wolf hath many a sheep and lamb torent.   (6.93–102)

The Physician encourages fathers and mothers to guard their children well and not to refrain from chastising them. This should, by now, be a familiar model of authority: The Physician is a formalist, eager to contain strictly any rebellious materiality. In accordance with the Physician's exhortation, Virginius clearly does not wish to be a negligent father or assent to any vice, lest his daughter's honour "perish." Neil Cartlidge reads the digression on parental governance as testifying to Chaucer's moralistic concern "to dramatize the weight of responsibility involved in protecting and educating the young."[12] It is, however, crucial to remark that the Physician has told us that Virginia knows perfectly well how to maintain her own virtue without external constraint. She does not need the surveillance and chastising of a zealous authority figure because, as the Physician repeatedly tells us, she is exquisitely *self-governed* – she "neded no maistresse" (6.106). According to this reading, then, Virginius's murderous intervention is entirely unnecessary. As Virginia does literally "perish" at Virginius's hands, it becomes possible that he is the wolf rending a lamb instead of the shepherd protecting one. The Physician also claims that "tresons *sovereyn pestilence*/Is whan a wight bitrayseth innocence" (6.91–2) echoing the "sovereyn diligence" (6.9) of Nature and the "sovereyn bountee" (6.136) of Virginia. While Apius is certainly a traitor to innocence, the label could apply to Virginius as well. While he successfully preserves Virginia's innocence from Apius's lechery, he only does so by betraying it himself. He traduces innocence by preserving it and vice versa; as Bloch puts it, "the maiden must lose her head in order to preserve her maidenhead."[13] Indeed, Patterson identifies an incestuous element in the father–daughter relationship: "That Virginius is here preempting Appius is made clear by his gesture of defiance: after severing the 'heed' (255) of this 'mayden' (132), he 'presente[s]' (256) it to the judge in place of the maidenhead that Appius had originally sought, a substitution that surreptitiously witnesses to the illicit ambiguity of the emotions that move him."[14] I

believe Patterson's reading strengthens my own: The fervidly overpro-
tective and controlling father is another version of the perverse Antiochus. Virginius's intention is to rescue Virginia's honour from Apius; he
does so, however, only by becoming Apius. Virginius's fate, as we will
see, anticipates the Physician's.

The Physician's Tale gives us two models of governance: loving, exemplified by God and Nature; and masterful, exemplified by Apius, Virginius, Jephthah, and the Physician himself. Aligning the Physician
with the other masterful governors in his tale also provides us with a
way to understand his otherwise incoherent conclusion. Angus Fletcher
sums up the critical consensus: "The fact that [the conclusion] makes
no mention of either Virginia or her virtue has led several critics to conclude that it is inappropriate, while even its defenders admit that it
seems only to offer a comment on the fate of Apius."[15] After informing us that Apius kills himself once he is imprisoned and that all his
confederates, save Claudius, are hanged, the Physician enacts his own
"sentence" upon his narrative:

> Heere may men seen how synne hath his merite.
> Beth war, for no man woot whom God wol smyte
> In no degree, ne in which manere wyse
> The worm of conscience may agryse
> Of wikked lyf, though it so pryvee be
> That no man woot therof but God and he.
> For be he lewed man, or ellis lered,
> He noot how soone that he shal been afered.
> Therfore I rede yow this conseil take:
> Forsaketh synne, er synne yow forsake.   (6.277–86)

I find it difficult to agree with Fletcher's reading of the Physician's
moral: "It is a final injunction to critics, warning them that when they
force text into simple divisions and didactic formulations, they abol-
ish the dimensions of meaning and character that compose text, that
compose Virginia."[16] I submit that it is the case, rather, that the Physician utterly disregards Virginia in the same way that her father does.
I am therefore more inclined to follow those critics, such as Emerson
Brown, who argue that Chaucer deliberately represents the Physician
as an incompetent narrator.[17]

Of particular interest in the passage above is the way the Physician
characterizes God. Instead of returning to the God who *lovingly* forms
Nature to be free, the Physician, as per his digression on governance,
elects in the final lines of his tale to represent God as a zealous and

controlling parental figure. We never know in advance whom God will "smyte," and his surveillance is so absolute that we are unable to keep any secrets from him. The God of the Physician's conclusion resembles most of all the obsessively controlling father, Virginius, who states, "My pitous hand moot *smyten* of thyn heed" (6.226). Later, we are told that Virginius "of *smoot*" (6.225) his daughter's head to keep her from shame. Tellingly, the Physician uses the same verb to describe Virginius's homicidal conduct and God's sudden vengeance on the sinful.[18]

For all its brevity, *The Physician's Tale* engages the profound metaphysical question that we have seen posed in *The Nun's Priest's Tale*, *The Franklin's Tale*, and *The Clerk's Tale*: Is God decisively masterful or undecidably loving? At the end of his tale, the Physician decides that God is a vengeful judge, and he emulates this formalist model in his imposition of a univocal verdict upon his tale: "Therfore I rede yow this conseil take:/Forsaketh synne, er synne yow forsake" (6.285–6). Obviously, this moral, while applicable to Apius, has nothing at all to do with the completely sinless Virginia. Without doubt, any number of stories could support the Physician's banal apothegm without necessitating the agonizingly protracted murder of a flawless child at the hands of her inexorable father.[19] In other words, the Physician kills Virginia *needlessly*. But so, as I have argued above, does Virginius, because the self-governed Virginia simply does not *need* him to oversee her virtue so fanatically. By this standard, the Physician and Virginius are both bad governors, unnecessarily destroying an innocent maiden in their charge. Contrary to their intentions, both the sentence that the Physician imposes and the sentence that Virginius executes effectuate the same outcome: the betrayal of innocence – what the Physician himself calls the "sovereign pestilence" (6.91).[20] In conclusion, even as the Physician's moral rightly castigates Apius, it wrongly disregards Virginia. As per the law of unintended consequences, the Physician becomes exactly what he condemns: a bad judge who betrays innocence. The Physician's moralizing insists on the inevitable recursion of sin on the sinner; his tale insists on the inevitable recursion of judgment on the judge.

I can further support this reading of *The Physician's Tale* by considering the words of the Host to the Physician in the introduction to *The Pardoner's Tale*. Chaucer here carefully aligns the Host's response to Virginia's fate with Virginius's. The Host is lacerated by how "*pitously* she was slayn" (6.298); he describes the story of her death as "*pitous*" (6.302), and he insists that "his herte is lost for *pitee* of this mayde" (6.317).[21] Similarly, Virginius approaches Virginia "With fadres *pitee* stikynge thurgh his herte" (6.211) and describes the hand that must decapitate her as "*pitous*" (6.226). The alignment between Virginius and the Host does not end there: It cannot be a coincidence that Harry states, "But wel I woot thou doost myn herte to erme/That I almoost have caught a *cardynacle*" (6.312–13). Virginia's plight has assailed the hearts of both men. Nevertheless, despite his sorrow at her death, the Host finds a way to blame the victim: "Allas, to deere boughte she beautee!" (6.293); "Hire beautee was hire deth, I dar wel seyn" (6.297). Does not Virginius do likewise? In a remarkable display of narcissism, he describes his daughter as the "endere of my lyf" (6.218), assigning the blameless Virginia culpability for his predicament. But the Host does not only echo Virginius's treatment of Virginia, he also echoes the Physician's. As I argued above, the Physician's final judgment on his tale betrays Virginia by rendering her death irrelevant – he kills her for no reason. And what is the Host's final judgment on her piteous death? "This is a pitous tale for to heere/But nathelees, passe over; is no fors" (6.302–3). Whatever pity she may evoke, ultimately Virginia's death does not matter. As the Host's reading emphasizes, Virginia's suffering is as irrelevant to the Physician's final intention for his tale as Malyne's is to the Reeve's or Custance's is to the Man of Law's.

The Pardoner's Introduction, Prologue, and Tale

My reading of *The Physician's Tale* suggests a new hypothesis regarding its link to the Pardoner's prologue and tale. The Physician imagines divine love in the speech of Nature and in the relationship between Nature and Virginia. But he rejects this charitable model in favour of one that posits the unilateral mastery of God as vengeful judge. The Pardoner's absolute embrace of *cupiditas* is an even more radical rejection of divine *caritas*. But while the Physician, as his judgmental posture indicates, decides to associate himself with formal order, the Pardoner decides to associate himself with material chaos – an alignment made explicitly by means of the base matter he sells as tokens of divinity.

The Pardoner is the latest in a line of self-professed materialists encountered in *The Canterbury Tales* so far. He resembles both the Miller and the Wife of Bath in his explicit rejection of formal standards of conduct. But while the Miller and the Wife seem to be opponents of the established order, in each case Chaucer complicates the materialist posture. The Miller, as we saw, ends up attempting to formalize the Knight, becoming what he wishes to reject. The Wife evades any oppositional determination and instead attempts to teach her audience about non-judgmental love. The Pardoner's case is unique in *The Canterbury Tales* for one reason: He is the most stalwart adversary of charity itself. The Pardoner does not merely oppose himself to another pilgrim; it is *love* that he emphatically rejects. I find Robert Miller's Robertsonian assessment compelling: "It is evident that by his act of will he has cut himself off from virtue and good works, and that this act has been performed, not 'amore Christi,' that is, through charity, but through its antithesis, *cupiditas*."[22] At the conclusion of Fragment 6, therefore, we find within *The Canterbury Tales* a threat to its guiding principle – divine love. It is for this reason that the Pardoner undermines the very *raison d'être* of the pilgrimage.[23] The pilgrims are on their way to the reliquary of Thomas Beckett, a site that promises spiritual and physical regeneration. Accompanying them is a charlatan who sells false relics and forged pardons.[24] Appropriately, his tale is set during the time of the plague, further emphasizing his association with spiritual and physical degradation. However, as we have seen, the Chaucerian principle of love – form is (not) related to matter – ensures that a speaker's formal intention succeeds only as it fails; it fails as it succeeds. According to the most extraordinary recursion in *The Canterbury Tales*, the Pardoner does not escape this logic. As I will demonstrate, therefore, the Pardoner, by means of his rejection of charity, *is aligned* with charity. The Pardoner embraces *cupiditas*, but in doing so also furthers *caritas*. The Pardoner exemplifies, therefore, a remarkable (non-)synthesis of cupidity and charity, suggested initially by the nourishment he requires before telling his tale: "'But first,' quod he, 'heere at this alestake/I wol bothe drynke and eten of a cake" (6.321–2). Is he consuming mere matter to satisfy his carnal urges, or is he symbolically partaking of the Eucharistic sacrament that signals divine charity?[25] This is a question, I will argue, that has no decisive answer.

My reading thus seeks to extend and complicate Alfred Kellogg's foundational Augustinian treatment of the Pardoner's prologue and tale, by means of which he analyses the always conflicted nature of sin: "In the teaching of Augustine, all sin is by the judgment of God punished, and if we look deeper, self-punished. Even the sin which to mortal eyes escapes punishment is overtaken by a secret penalty, and that penalty is the progressive mental deformity and suffering which sin itself inflicts upon its perpetrator – the 'secreta mentis poena.'"[26] According to Kellogg, the Pardoner's sin turns back on itself so that his triumphant perversity accompanies revulsion at his own depravity: "whatever be the impelling force, from the depths of his being comes revulsion, the voice of the created nature, the work of God within him which no evil can ever obliterate – which even in the midst of evil cannot lose its love of the good."[27] Instead of the complacency of absolute evil, therefore, within the Pardoner there remains an anguished sensitivity to the goodness of God and his creation.

The Augustinian notion of the inner torment of the sinner has been influential for scholarly considerations of the Pardoner. It is a commonplace of modern criticism on the latter's tale and prologue that he is not only depraved but also internally conflicted. Patterson, accordingly, understands the Pardoner as a man in despair. He is desperate for divine grace but finds it impossible to imagine that God's love could encompass him. His extravagant performance of evil, therefore, "conceals a motivational complexity that yearns for a redemption it simultaneously disdains."[28] For Leicester, similarly, the Pardoner demonstrates a "fundamental dialectical relation between presumption and despair."[29] He presumptuously cuts himself off from divine grace "and wills his own misery and evil as a protest against God."[30] The disenchanted Pardoner thus mocks the instruments of grace, implicitly asking: "what do you make of a church that licenses me, of a world in which I am possible, of a God that allows me to exist?"[31] And yet, "he is ultimately supportive of what he tries to undo because he has to constitute it in order to undo it." Both Leicester and Patterson depict the Pardoner as a subject simultaneously antagonistic to and implicated within the institutional and ideological apparatuses of orthodox medieval Christianity. Dinshaw's psychoanalytical approach, contrastingly, finds an explanation for the Pardoner's ambivalence not in disenchantment or despair, but in the Freudian acceptation of the fetish. The Pardoner's fake relics, fake documents, and fake words are partial objects representing his loss of plenitude while simultaneously compensating for his castration: "So the Pardoner believes in plenitude as fact while knowing it is a fiction, and he successfully plays on that belief held by the members of his audience as well. Cynical fraud and true believer at once, the Pardoner is a great success as a swindler – his promises of wholeness make him richer by far than any parish priest – precisely because he truly believes in his own false relics."[32] The Pardoner knows very well that he is irreparably fragmented but believes nevertheless that he can be made whole.

While I agree with Patterson, Leicester, and Dinshaw that the representation of the Pardoner's depravity is equivocal, I wish to approach his ambivalence towards Christian doctrine in a manner that avoids the ascription of subjectivity, whether historically or psychoanalytically determined. I do not believe that Chaucer represents the Pardoner as a *subject*, with all the motivational and psychological complexity this construct entails. As with the Wife of Bath, whom he closely resembles, we must resist grounding the inconsistencies and contradictions of his discourse in a putative interiority. In place of a conflicted subject,

I substitute, here as elsewhere, an insoluble structure.[33] My reading is not psychological, but logical. Following my argument throughout, I will elucidate how the Pardoner's prologue and tale reveal the operation of a logic that informs the entire *Canterbury Tales*. The Pardoner is clearly one of the adversarial pilgrims on the Canterbury pilgrimage: His formal intention is to reject love in favour of cupidity. According to Chaucer's logic, this intention can only realize itself by means of its failure: Form does (not) relate to matter. It is by means of Chaucer's law of unintended consequences, therefore, that I will explain the ambivalences and contradictions in the Pardoner's discourse.

From the outset of his prologue, the Pardoner informs his audience that the theme of his preaching is always the same:

> "Lordynges," quod he, "in chirches whan I preche,
> I peyne me to han an hauteyn speche,
> And rynge it out as round as gooth a belle,
> For I kan al by rote that I telle.
> My theme is alwey oon, and evere was –
> *Radix malorum est cupiditas.*"   (6.329–34)

The Pardoner's citation from Paul (1 Timothy 6:10) is obviously the core of his discourse. When in church, the Pardoner follows Pauline doctrine, preaching vigorously and brilliantly against cupidity and on behalf of charity – love in its highest expression. But the Pardoner repeatedly informs us that his preaching is only for profit: "But shortly myn entente I wol devyse:/I preche of no thyng but for coveityse" (6.423–4). Chaucer represents the Pardoner, therefore, as utterly bereft of any moral purpose, the perfect embodiment of causeless and degenerate freedom. In a particularly chilling passage, the Pardoner gives voice to his obsession with materiality and his concordant rejection of apostolic teaching:

> I wol noon of the apostles countrefete;
> I wol have moneie, wolle, chese, and whete,
> Al were it yeven of the povereste page,
> Or of the povereste wydwe in a village,
> Al sholde hir children sterve for famine.   (6.447–51)

Even in the starkest expression of the Pardoner's depravity and material rapacity, however, we can find an illuminating ambivalence. The Pardoner tells us that he will not "counterfeit" any of the apostles. The Middle English verb "countrefete" can mean "to imitate" but also, as in

Modern English, "to forge," or "to falsify." The Pardoner is stating that he will not *imitate* the apostles' example, but we can also understand this statement as indicating that he will not *falsify* the apostles' example. The Pardoner's language at once expresses his formal intention and contradicts it. If we just take this one line in isolation, it is undecidable whether the Pardoner is claiming to oppose the apostles or emulate them.

This line, I suggest, points to what Chaucer is doing with the entire *Pardoner's Prologue*. In fact, the insoluble entanglement of contradiction and emulation is visible earlier in the Pardoner's discourse. One of the Apostle Paul's lessons in 1 Timothy 6:1–11, the Pardoner's favourite scriptural passage, is to beware of hypocritical, false preachers who are only concerned with material gain and use Scripture perversely:

1. Whosoever are servants under the yoke, let them count their masters worthy of all honour; lest the name of the Lord and his doctrine be blasphemed. 2. But they that have believing masters, let them not despise them, because they are brethren; but serve them the rather, because they are faithful and beloved, who are partakers of the benefit. These things teach and exhort. 3. If any man teach otherwise, and consent not to the sound words of our Lord Jesus Christ, and to that doctrine which is according to godliness, 4. He is proud, knowing nothing, but sick about questions and strifes of words; from which arise envies, contentions, blasphemies, evil suspicions, 5. Conflicts of men corrupted in mind, and who are destitute of the truth, supposing gain to be godliness. 6. But godliness with contentment is great gain. 7. For we brought nothing into this world: and certainly we can carry nothing out. 8. But having food, and wherewith to be covered, with these we are content. 9. For they that will become rich, fall into temptation, and into the snare of the devil, and into many unprofitable and hurtful desires, which drown men into destruction and perdition. 10. For the desire of money is the root of all evils; which some coveting have erred from the faith, and have entangled themselves in many sorrows. 11. But thou, O man of God, fly these things: and pursue justice, godliness, faith, charity, patience, mildness.

The Pardoner perfectly embodies Paul's description of the false teacher here, but this is not at all something he is trying to hide. He cheerfully admits that he is a hypocritical preacher, only seeking material gain:

Of avarice and of swich cursednesse
Is al my prechyng, for to make hem free
To yeven hir pens, and namely unto me.
For myn entente is nat but for to wynne,

> And nothyng for correccioun of synne.
> I rekke nevere, whan that they been beryed,
> Though that hir soules goon a-blakeberyed!
>
> (6.400–6)

The Pardoner's radical self-exposure is, perhaps, the most remarkable aspect of his prologue, drawing comparisons to the allegorical figure, Fals-Semblant, from *The Romance of the Rose*.[34] It is, of course, irresistible to speculate about the motivation behind this gesture. Outside of allegory, why would anyone wish to exhibit such immorality so publicly? What could possibly be gained by this gleeful disclosure? This kind of speculation, while unavoidable, does not get us any closer to understanding what Chaucer is attempting to accomplish with the Pardoner. As A.J. Minnis asserts, "This *quaestor*'s professional offences, of which he makes no secret, may therefore be seen as far more important than any secret transgressions. Indeed, it could be said that the Pardoner's problem is not secrecy, but the *lack* of it."[35] Instead of indulging in *psychological* speculation, we should observe instead the precise *logical* relationship of the Pardoner's discourse to Pauline doctrine.[36] By admitting that he is a hypocritical preacher, avariciously preaching against avarice, is the Pardoner contradicting Paul, or is he emulating him? He is, after all, warning his audience, exactly as Paul does, against the hypocritical and avaricious preacher for whom gain is godliness – that preacher just happens to be *himself*. On this reading, the Pardoner is faithfully emulating Paul by contradicting him; he is contradicting Paul by faithfully emulating him. The Pardoner "counterfeits" Paul; his hypocrisy is itself hypocritical. Thus, he *follows* Pauline doctrine by *betraying* it. Janet Montelaro is certainly correct when she argues that "Paul's *fide non ficta* is precisely what the Pardoner abuses and contradicts, and his strategy for effectively undermining this Biblical text involves not only the use of fables and tales but a thematics of deviancy as well."[37] But the Pardoner is exposing his own contradiction of Paul, thereby ensuring that a deviant preacher does not remain hidden from his audience: As Paul says to Timothy, "But thou, O man of God, fly these things." Paul would have no choice but to (dis)approve of the Pardoner. Understood in this way, *The Pardoner's Prologue* is another version of 1 Timothy 6, which perhaps accounts for why "radix malorum est cupiditas" serves extradiegetically as Chaucer's epigraph for the Pardoner's discourse. We should recall that this is precisely how *The Clerk's Prologue* operates: The Clerk simultaneously emulates and departs from Petrarch in his criticism of the latter's proem. Analogously, the Man of Law's supersession of Chaucer is also his metamorphosis into his rival. In *The Pardoner's Prologue*, therefore, the Pardoner's radical materialism undermines itself, making it undecidable whether the Pardoner is in fact a cupidinous materialist or whether he is governed by an enlightened purpose. The insoluble logic that Chaucer derives from the Liar paradox structures each of these contradictions. The Pardoner is at once Paul's steadfast adversary (he is a false preacher) and his faithful disciple (he exposes a false preacher).

What is true of the Pardoner's relationship to Pauline doctrine is also true of his preaching. He therefore admits that his sermons are highly effective, even though this efficacy explicitly contravenes his intent:

> Of avarice and of swich cursednesse
> Is al my prechying, for to make hem free
> To yeven hir pens, and namely unto me.
> For myn entente is nat but for to wynne,
> And nothyng for correccioun of synne.   (6.400–4)

It is entirely within the Pardoner's mercenary interest to make his sermons as persuasive as possible. Even though he has no intention whatsoever to correct the members of his audience, the more likely it is that they reject the sin of avarice, the more likely he is to receive their "pens." But this means that he achieves his intention (winning profit) by contradicting his intention (correcting sin); he contradicts his intention (correcting sin) by achieving his intention (winning profit). His sermons at once conform to and betray his formal design, as he himself admits:

> But though myself be gilty in that synne,
> Yet kan I maken oother folk to twynne
> From avarice and soore to repente.
> But that is nat my principal entente;
> I preche nothyng but for coveitise.
> Of this mateere it oghte ynogh suffise.   (6.429–34)

The Pardoner is thus advancing the cause of *caritas* by embodying *cupiditas*. His brilliant sermons encourage his audience to abandon the latter for the former even though he preaches "*nothyng* but for coveitise." He thus furthers love by betraying love; he betrays love by furthering love. While critics have pondered the implications of an immoral man preaching a moral sermon, more recently in terms of Wycliffite norms, my focus is how precisely the Pardoner exemplifies Chaucer's law of unintended consequences.[38] While Miller associates the Pardoner solely with Paul's *vetus homo*, it is more accurate to say that he is both the Old Man and the New.[39] He entangles carnality and grace: He is on the side both of material letter and formal spirit.

I believe this reading of *The Pardoner's Prologue* permits me to resolve some of the cruces that have long exercised readers. Chief among them is the Pardoner's representation in the *General Prologue*:

> A voys he hadde as smal as hath a goot.
> No berd hadde he, ne nevere sholde have;
> As smothe it was as it were late shave;
> I trowe he were a geldyng or a mare.   (1.688–91)

Needless to say, the problem of the Pardoner's gender and sexuality has inspired much scholarship.[40] Once more, it is the urge to unveil a secret interiority that leads Chaucerians away from the logic of charity. Sexuality and gender in Chaucer studies, especially after the decline of exegetical interpretation, have become privileged tools for the investigation of subjectivity. But I agree with Derek Pearsall's assessment of interpretations that psychologize the Pardoner: "Psychologizing, that is, fantasizing about motives to be attributed to characters who appear to have none, is a sport that has no rules and is, therefore, in the end, not very satisfying."[41] We can debate endlessly about the hidden recesses of a pilgrim's interiority without ever grasping the logic that opens the space of compossibility for this debate. To say that the Pardoner's sexuality is normative (formalism) or non-normative (materialism) is to make a decision. But the Pardoner, as his prologue attests, is deviant because he is straight; he is straight because he is deviant. Chaucer's description of the Pardoner in the *General Prologue* is logically consonant with the latter's prologue and, as we will see, his tale. The narrator simply will not judge whether the Pardoner is a castrated male (gelding) or a female (mare).[42] In other words, he will not decide whether to align the Pardoner unilaterally with masculinity or femininity. This is a *lovingly* non-judgmental posture on the part of the pilgrim Chaucer. He treats the Pardoner as an insoluble without insisting on a solution.[43] We should follow the narrator's charitable example and refuse to decide whether the Pardoner in his prologue is a formalist, conforming to Pauline teaching, or a materialist, rejecting it entirely. It has always been an attractive interpretive option to crush the Pardoner into causeless materiality and thereby align him with the fraudulent artefacts in which he traffics. But once we suspend this decision, we have a way to understand his tale anew.[44]

The Host, still reeling from the pathetic fate of Virginia, asks the Pardoner to "Telle us som myrthe or japes right anon" (6.319). The assembled gentils immediately protest, deeply concerned about the kind of ribaldry of which the Pardoner is capable: "Nay let hym telle us of no ribaudye!/Telle us som moral thyng" (6.324–5). The Host wants a playful tale; the gentils demand something serious. Of course, the Pardoner satisfies neither entreaty. He does indeed tell his audience a "moral thing" (formalism), but one that is evacuated of any moral purpose (materialism). The tale is thus both morally purposeful and immorally purposeless – its morality serves the Pardoner's immorality; the Pardoner's immorality serves the cause of morality. Let us now turn to the tale proper and examine how it is structured by exactly this ambivalence.

The Pardoner's Tale is a story about self-destruction. The primary characters are three riotous compeers and an eerie old man: They all seek Death. It is difficult to contest that both parties represent the Pardoner himself; as is typical of *The Canterbury Tales*, narrators, in emulation of Chaucer himself, inhabit their own narratives.[45] The company of rioters, a perverse trinity directly opposed to divine charity, rejects all elevated purpose and indulges enthusiastically in the aimless, carnal pleasures that occupy the Pardoner: namely, eating, drinking, whoring, dancing, swearing, and gambling. The three young men focus obsessively on matter disconnected from form. Moreover, the rioters are as heedless of damnation as the Pardoner appears to be; instead, "ech of hem at otheres synne lough" (6.476). The old man whom the profligate company encounters in their quest for death leads them towards, rather than away from, annihilation. Both Pardoner and old man are, on the surface, false preachers: to follow the "crooked wey" (6.761) of the old man or the materialist Pardoner is to take a path that leads towards material gain and spiritual loss.

But such a reading does not exhaust the significance of this strange figure, the focal point of critical interest in *The Pardoner's Tale*. My interpretation will resist the temptation to collapse the old man into allegorical determinacy, whether the Wandering Jew,[46] Judas,[47] Noah,[48] Odin,[49] Death,[50] Dying,[51] Damnation,[52] Devil,[53] Old Age,[54] or the *vetus homo*.[55] I wish to argue instead that the same ambivalence that characterizes the Pardoner in his prologue characterizes the depiction of the old man in his tale. The old man points in two directions at once: towards the literality of matter and towards the spirituality of grace. It is according to these terms that we must read his address to Mother Earth:

Thus walk I, lyk a restelees kaityf,
And on the ground, which is my moodres gate,

> I knokke with my staf, bothe erly and late,
> And seye, "Leeve mooder, leet me in!
> Lo how I vanysshe, flessh, and blood, and skyn!
> Allas, whan shul my bones been at reste?
> Mooder, with yow wolde I chaunge my cheste
> That in my chamber longe tyme hath be,
> Ye, for an heyre clowt to wrappe me!"
> But yet to me she wol nat do that grace,
> For which ful pale and welked is my face.   (6.728–38)

This passage provides evidence of two contradictory orientations. First, the old man desires to collapse into feminine matter ("Leeve mooder, leet me in!"), a desire that corresponds to the abject materialism of the rioters. But, second, the old man's orientation towards causeless materiality is simultaneously an orientation towards a higher cause. The old man would prefer to *give up* ("chaunge") the material goods in his "cheste" for a penitential haircloth in which he may be wrapped and buried. The desire to collapse into sheer matter, to return to Mother Earth, is at once the desire for a penitential alignment with God, to wear the haircloth. Even as he seeks death, therefore, he asserts a wish for rejuvenation: As he states earlier in this passage, he tries fruitlessly to find someone who will "*chaunge* his youthe for myn age" (6.724). The old man's desperate quest to return to his mother's body is highly condensed; it registers both the desire for carnality associated with cupidity and the desire for rebirth associated with redemptive grace. But the old man can attain neither: We cannot collapse his ambivalence into matter or form – he is permanently suspended between material disintegration and spiritual rejuvenation.

Though both parties seek Death, therefore, it is crucial to distinguish the humble old man from his rash counterparts.[56] Notably, the former disapproves of the lawless conduct of the latter, even attempting to teach them a lesson from "Hooly Writ" to rectify their ignorant "vileynye":

> But, sires, to yow it is no curteisye
> To speken to an old man vileynye,
> But he trespasse in word or elles in dede.
> In Hooly Writ ye may yourself wel rede:
> "Agayns an oold man, hoor upon his heed,
> Ye sholde arise," wherefore I yeve yow reed,
> Ne dooth unto an oold man noon harm now,
> Namoore than that ye wolde men did to yow
> In age, if that ye so longe abyde.
> And God be with yow, where ye go or ryde!   (6.739–48)

Whereas the young rioters respect no law whatsoever, the old man instructs them in the law of God himself. He therefore cites from Leviticus 19 (according to marginal glosses in both Hengwrt and Ellesmere), which consists of a series of commandments, akin to the Decalogue, transmitted to Moses from Jehovah.[57] Even though the old man is a "restelees kaityf" (6.728) condemned to aimless wandering, he strives to correct the errant conduct of his interlocutors and direct them towards God's law, at least as instantiated in the Old Testament. The old man thus follows his account of seeking the mother (feminine matter) by encouraging the rioters to reverence the law of the father (masculine form) – a law, moreover, that insists that father figures should be reverenced.

When the rioters nevertheless demand *irreverently* that the old man show them the way to Death, his response is consistent with the ambivalence inherent to the Pardoner's representation:

> "Now, sires," quod he, "if that yow be so leef
> To fynde Deeth, turne up this croked way,
> For in that grove I lafte hym, by my fey,
> Under a tree, and there he wole abyde;
> Noght for youre boost he wole him no thyng hyde.
> See ye that ook? Right there ye shal hym fynde.
> God save yow, that boghte agayn mankynde,
> And yow amende!" Thus seyde this olde man.   (6.760–7)

On the one hand, the old man shows the way to destruction: He points the rioters to the gold florins under the oak tree that will be the cause of their death. On the other hand, the old man pointedly prays for their spiritual improvement and salvation, making reference to the death of death that is a consequence of Christ's self-sacrifice (and which the rioters literalize in their quest to kill Death): "God save yow, that boghte agayn mankynde."[58] The old man first appeals to the letter of Old Testament law and then to the spirit of New Testament grace in his entreaties for the rioters' "amendment." Analogously, the graceful act by means of which Christ "buys back" humankind from death counterpoints the base materiality of the gold florins that the rioters will find under the tree towards which the old man gestures.

It is crucial, therefore, that when interpreting the old man, we avoid the error of the rioters themselves – not the most reliable of readers as their materialist tendencies attest.[59] One of their number accordingly collapses the old man's ambivalence, associating him unequivocally with the "traytour Deeth" (6.753): "For soothly thou art oon of his assent/To sleen us yonge folk, thou false theef!" (6.758–9). No doubt, critics still level an identical judgment against the Pardoner.[60] But Chaucer's portrayal of the old man entangles without any synthesis a series of elements in a way that should be instructive for our response to the Pardoner: degeneration and rejuvenation; maternal matter and paternal form; Old Testament law and New Testament grace; death and the death of Death. And if, according to Paul, the letter (matter) kills and the spirit (form) gives life, it makes sense that the old man should be neither quite alive nor quite dead: "Lo, how I vanysshe, flesh, and blood, and skyn." He hovers between the two extremes, neither decisively one nor the other. The point, then, is not to *decide* upon the identity of the old man, however great the temptation to do so, but to acknowledge his insoluble status. In doing so, we emulate the pilgrim Chaucer's unwillingness to collapse the ambivalence of the Pardoner's gender status.

The entanglement of mutually exclusive terms in the figure of the old man suggests a new perspective on the Pardoner's baffling proposition to his audience at the conclusion to his tale and Harry's subsequent reaction. After demonstrating how he uses his tale to encourage members of his audience to buy his relics and pardons, he breaks character and turns to the assembled pilgrims:

> – And lo, sires, thus I preche.
> And Jhesu Crist, that is oure soules leche,
> So graunte yow his pardoun to receive,
> For that is best; I wol yow nat deceyve.   (6.915–18)

Here we have an apparently sincere benediction, one that explicitly contrasts the fake pardons in which the Pardoner traffics to the true pardon that is Christ's forgiveness – that which is "best," about which the Pardoner refuses to lie. However, the Pardoner abruptly follows this charitable admonition with an improbable attempt to sell the pilgrims his fake pardons and relics:

> But sires, o word forgat I in my tale:
> I have relikes and pardoun in my male,
> As faire as any man in Engelond,
> Whiche were me yeven by the popes hond.
> If any of yow wole, of devocion,
> Offren and han myn absolucion,
> Com forth anon, and kneleth here adoun,
> And mekely receyveth my pardoun.   (6.919–26)

The Pardoner oscillates from fraudulence to sincerity and then back to fraudulence. His final proposition makes no sense whatsoever, as John Halverson notes: "if the Pardoner is seriously attempting to play his confidence game with the pilgrims, he has chosen the worst possible method by insisting that it *is* a confidence game."[61] Any attempt to make the Pardoner's sales pitch meaningful is, I think, the wrong approach. As in his prologue, wherein he simultaneously betrays and furthers Christian doctrine, we should not decide here whether to align the Pardoner either with cupidity or charity. Thus, the Pardoner's charitable benediction is immediately and implausibly juxtaposed to his cupidinous offer. Analogously, the loving conclusion to *The Wife of Bath's Tale* is immediately and implausibly juxtaposed to its harshly judgmental epilogue. Chaucer is once again generating a logical structure, *not* a subject. He entangles without synthesis mutually exclusive determinations, generating a logical structure that ascriptions of subjectivity merely obfuscate. Recall that the old man in *The Pardoner's Tale* first points the rioters to their destruction and then prays for their salvation – an equally abrupt apposition. We should not decide to associate the Pardoner either with the sincere benediction *or* his fraudulent materialism.[62] Exactly as the Merchant in his marriage encomium, he must be understood as formally sincere and materially cynical at once. We do not witness here, as Dinshaw would have it, the fetishistic structure of disavowal – a psychological reading that *decisively* conceives of the Pardoner as matter lacking masculine (i.e., phallic) form; we witness instead the *undecidable* logic of love in which, as we will see, the reader is invited to participate.

The Host's response to the Pardoner's offer that for a groat he can "kisse the relikes everychon" (6.944) precisely mirrors this entanglement of earnestness and fraudulence:

> "Nay, nay!" quod he, "thanne have I Cristes curs!
> Lat be," quod he, "it shal nat be, so theech!
> Thou woldest make me kisse thyn olde breech,
> And swere it were a relyk of a seint,
> Though it were with thy fundement depeint!
> But, by the croys which that Seint Eleyne fond,
> I wolde I hadde thy coillons in myn hond
> In stide of relikes or of seintuarie.
> Lat kutte hem of, I wol thee helpe hem carie;
> They shul be shryned in an hogges toord!"   (6.946–55)

The tendency in contemporary criticism is to interpret Harry's response to the Pardoner as the vehement, if insecure, assertion of normative masculinity in the face of a queer challenge.[63] Thus, for Sturges, the Host "must reveal the unreal, simulated, imaginary status of the Pardoner's phallic authority … in order to maintain the illusion of a more important reality, or, better, the illusion of the real itself, guaranteed by the existence of God."[64] Burger likewise states that "[t]he Host's verbal abuse of the Pardoner has done little to reform the Pardoner either as man or as potent religious symbol: that the Pardoner constitutes a sexual, social, and moral solecism is now more immediately, even glaringly, evident than at any other time in his tale."[65] I will propose a different reading, one that does not regard Harry merely as Chaucer's standard-bearer for heteronormativity. But let us begin with his brutal rejoinder. While the Pardoner has aligned himself with causeless matter throughout his discourse, Harry emphatically reflects the orientation of his discourse back at him by means of his excremental imagery.[66] The Host is *decisive* here: The Pardoner is just filthy matter, *not* forgiveness. He thus opposes the Pardoner's fraudulent relics to the truest relic – the symbol of divine charity: "the croys which that Seint Eleyne fond."[67] His savage riposte thereby collapses the Pardoner's undecidability in a manner suggestively anticipated by the rioter's angry accusation against the old man, whom he associates unequivocally with Death: "For soothly thou art oon of his assent" (6.758). Just as the Host seems to perceive no ambivalence in the Pardoner, the rioter perceives no ambivalence in the Pardoner's narrative surrogate: each is a false thief for his accuser.[68] Moreover, the Host's decisive alignment of the Pardoner with excremental matter, answering the old man's desire to return to Mother Earth, corresponds to his threat to resolve decisively the enigma of the Pardoner's sex, something the pilgrim Chaucer charitably *refuses* to do. By characterizing him as a potential victim of castration, the Host unequivocally makes the Pardoner a man. He appears to solve the Pardoner.

The Host seems so thoroughly to have mastered the Pardoner with his blunt retort that the latter cannot utter a word in response: "So wroth he was, no word ne wolde he seye" (6.957). Harry certainly cuts off the Pardoner's best weapon. But this is not the end of the matter. It is important to observe that we cannot quite decide whether the Host's retort to the Pardoner is (formally) in earnest or (materially) in jest. Once Harry observes the Pardoner's wrath, he says "I wol no lenger *pleye*/With thee, ne with noon oother angry man" (6.958–9). However brutal are Harry's words to the Pardoner, Chaucer incorporates some uncertainty here. Chaucer achieves a similar effect when the Nun's Priest first asserts his misogyny and then immediately describes it as merely playful: "Passe over, for I seyde it in my game" (7.3262). We cannot be absolutely sure either of the righteous earnestness of the Host's potent insult or of its *playful* insincerity. But this uncertainty corresponds to the representation of the Pardoner: We cannot quite decide whether *he* is morally earnest, as indicated by his apparently sincere benediction, or immorally insincere, as indicated by the shockingly implausible offer of fake relics to his pilgrim audience. Harry ultimately refuses to decide on the Pardoner, declining to collapse his discursive ambivalence into excremental filth or to align it with sacramental charity. By suggesting that his retort may be "playful," the Host complicates his otherwise decisive association of the Pardoner with a false and filthy relic: the Pardoner's own shitty breeches. In the same way, the old man from the tale is suspended somewhere between material degradation and spiritual rejuvenation. The Pardoner's desire to return to matter, which Harry reflects in the Pardoner's enshrined testicles, is entangled with an orientation towards divine grace, which Harry figures by means of the cross. As we have seen, Chaucerian love is neither spiritual nor material; it manifests itself in the undecidable (non-)relation between these terms.

The Host, therefore, does not decide on the undecidable. His words to the Pardoner juxtapose savage earnestness (formalism) with playful jesting (materialism). We must learn from this example. There is, accordingly, one final interpretive challenge for the reader, posed by the tale's final lines:

> But right anon the worthy Knyght bigan,
> Whan that he saugh that al the peple lough,
> "Namoore of this, for it is right ynough!
> Sire Pardoner, be glad and myrie of cheere;
> And ye, sire Hoost, that been to me so deere,
> I prey yow that ye kisse the Pardoner.
> And Pardoner, I prey thee, drawe thee neer,
> And, as we diden, lat us laughe and pleye."
> Anon they kiste, and ryden forth hir weye.   (6.960–8)

The Knight intervenes upon hearing the judgmental and exclusive laughter of the assembled pilgrims to demand reconciliation and *forgiveness* between Harry and the Pardoner. I believe the question these lines pose is the following: Is the rapprochement between the Host and the Pardoner sincere, or is it as fraudulent as the latter's relics – merely a result of the Knight's authoritative intervention? In other words, can we be sure that the Pardoner has abandoned his rage in the name of charity, or does he remain furiously vengeful? "Thus quyte I folk that doon us displesances" (6.420), he tells us in his prologue. In contrast, Pugh sees no ambivalence here: "The final irony of the *Pardoner's Tale*, then, is the reinstitution of a homosocial bond that can never withstand the animosity that it cloaks. Any sort of friendship between Harry and the Pardoner carries a latent hint of forced queerness, in that they are compelled to unite with each other due to the commands of a powerful and aristocratic man, not in response to their own sense of homosocial affection."[69] Perhaps – but note that the Knight's speech corresponds logically to that of the Host's. He commandingly and *earnestly* insists on *play*: "Namoore of this, for it is right ynough! ... And, as we diden, lat us laughe and *pleye*." By entangling sincerity and play, just as the Liar paradox entangles truth and falsity, the Knight and the Host together suggest how we should understand the kiss of peace with which *The Pardoner's Tale* concludes. As with the epilogue to *The Wife of Bath's Tale*, there is a crucial reason why we should not judge whether the Pardoner is turning away from charity or towards it, whether the kiss he exchanges with the Host is in earnest or just an insincere token of forgiveness – an artefact as worthless as those he sells. I propose that Chaucer has given us the opportunity here to love the Pardoner, just as he does, and to respond with grace to the song he sings on the way to Canterbury: "Com hider, love, to me" (1.672).

6 Loving the Prioress in Fragment 7

Fragment 7 contains perhaps Chaucer's most notorious tale, told by the Prioress, and perhaps his *chef d'oeuvre*, told by the Nun's Priest, one of the Prioress's entourage. In this chapter, I will aim to demonstrate that the interpretive tools I have already derived from the latter can resolve some of the disturbing questions prompted by the former. Moreover, I will attempt to show that the pilgrim Chaucer's tales in Fragment 7 constitute *charitable* responses to the judgmental Prioress. *The Monk's Tale*, however, corresponds to the Prioress's in its *decisive* treatment of its subject matter.

The Shipman's Tale

To interpret perhaps the most problematic tale in the Canterbury sequence, *The Prioress's Tale*, I must investigate first how it is anticipated by the Shipman's. To do so, I will consider the latter's treatment of two themes: commerce and forgiveness. *The Shipman's Tale* is structured by means of the interrelation of two highly profitable exchanges – one conducted by a merchant and the other by his counterpart, a monk. The merchant purchases goods in Bruges but needs to obtain a loan of 20,000 shields from an Italian bank to cover the entire cost. He obtains a bill of exchange that obliges him to repay the amount at the Parisian branch of said bank. Upon his return to Paris, he borrows "A certeyn frankes" (7.334) from friends so that he can cover the loan he has pledged to repay. He then reimburses the loan, in franks rather than shields, at the Parisian branch, redeeming his "reconyssaunce" (7.330) and anticipating a profit of "A thousand frankes aboven al his costage" (7.372) thanks to a favourable rate of exchange.[1] Daun John is equally as felicitous in his dealings. Having agreed with the merchant's wife to pay one hundred franks for the pleasure of her body, he borrows exactly that sum from her husband, unbeknownst to her. Sometime after his night of pleasure, the monk returns the loan to a different "branch" of the same "bank," the merchant's wife, realizing a surplus sexual profit that is implicitly equated to the thousand franks the merchant has earned in his own transactions. Both the merchant and the monk are astute businessmen whose clever dealings allow them to earn a surplus yield well above their "costage" (7.45 and 7.372). Chaucer thus uses the same term to describe the initial outlay for the merchant's goods and the gratuities the monk distributes to the members of the merchant's household to ensure a warm welcome, "For which they were as glad of his comyng/ As fowel is fayn whan that the sonne up riseth" (7.50–1).

Now, since the monk tells the merchant that he has repaid the loan of one hundred franks to his wife, who has already spent the money paying off her debts, she finds herself beholden to her husband in the final scene of the tale. She thought she had received the franks in exchange for sex, but in fact she had only "borrowed" this sum from the merchant in a transaction brokered by Daun John. In the passage that follows, one that has no equivalent in the Italian analogues, she attempts to set the terms for repayment:[2]

> Ye han mo slakkere dettours than am I!
> For I wol paye yow wel and redily
> Fro day to day, and if so be I faille,
> I am your wyf; score it upon my taille,
> And I shal paye as soone as ever I may.
> For by my trouthe, I have on myn array,
> And nat on wast, bistowed every deel;
> And for I have bistowed it so weel
> For youre honour, for Goddes sake, I seye,
> As be nat wroth, but lat us laughe and pleye.
> Ye shal my joly body have to wedde;
> By God, I wol nat paye yow but abedde!
> Forgyve it me, myn owene spouse deere;
> Turne hiderward, and maketh bettre cheere.   (7.413–26)

Critical attention on *The Shipman's Tale* has focused overwhelmingly on the wife's willingness to commercialize her marital sex life, proposing first that her body serve as credit ("taille"), then as pledge ("wedde"), and finally as payment outright for the debt she has incurred.[3] Just as Daun John gets something for nothing, she expects payment for giving her husband what is already his. As Karla Taylor observes, "Since both money and conjugal sexuality ostensibly belong to the merchant in the first place – and since he has generously declared to the monk 'My gold is youres' (VII 284) – he winds up paying his own 'taille.'"[4] In a foundational interpretation, the influence of which still impacts contemporary responses, E. Talbot Donaldson perceives that in *The Shipman's Tale* a "reduction of all human values to commercial ones is accomplished with almost mathematical precision … Sensitivity to other values besides cash has been submitted to appraisal and, having been found nonconvertible, has been thrown away."[5] Scholars have differed as to whether the tale satirizes the moral deficiencies of mercantile ideology or whether, by contrast, the tale glibly naturalizes the commercialization of human relationships. An influential proponent of the former position is Janette Richardson, who argues that the merchant, though a man of "noble instincts," "has blindly accepted a worldly standard of values in place of spiritual truth; and, as everything in the tale, denouement included, shows, he is therefore doomed."[6] Patterson, contrariwise, sees no moral judgment in the tale, proposing instead that "in its unspoken but all the more profound generalization of the commercial condition beyond the confines of the merchant class, as in its implication of both poet and reader in this process, it manages to redefine a historically specific form of life as life per se."[7] Nevertheless, despite the critical tendency to view *The Shipman's Tale* as a uniform assertion of bourgeois mercantilism, whether this assertion is blameworthy or not, I will argue that it offers us an alternative interpretive avenue.

While noting that modern readings of *The Shipman's Tale* insist on its thoroughgoing commercialization of human relationships, Robert Epstein suggests on the basis of Maussian gift theory for the limitations of this approach: "in this most thoroughly economic and monetary tale, the characters themselves still have access to other measures of social worth and other modes of human interaction."[8] Rather than reducing all relationships to mercantile transactions, Epstein insists that "[t]here is something ultimately irreducible in the human connections in this tale – in the affection and attraction between merchant and wife, in the fondness of the merchant for friendship, and the pleasure he takes from companionship and generosity."[9] Epstein's salutary intervention into a long established scholarly consensus regarding mercantilism in *The Shipman's Tale* generates some important questions for my charitable approach to *The Canterbury Tales*. Does such a reading of *The Shipman's Tale* affirm that the human relationships therein are governed by a mercantile logic? Or does this reading lead to Epstein's conclusion, that human interactions can free themselves from the reductive calculus of the marketplace? To consider these questions and propose an alternative interpretation, we must reassess the dialogue between the merchant and his wife with which the tale concludes.

We should note that from lines 7.413 to 7.424, the wife assumes a highly imperious posture, demanding that her husband accord with her plan for repaying the hundred franks with her body: "By God, I wol not paye yow but abedde!" But the tone of the passage shifts abruptly at line 7.425. Instead of unilaterally and imperiously imposing her will upon her husband, the wife abandons her domineering tone. She humbly requests his forgiveness, imploring affectionately that he turn his face to her and "maketh bettre cheere." Scholars have either been too scandalized or too titillated by the hint of prostitution in the wife's earlier offer to consider this plea in isolation. It is invariably assumed that these lines are just contiguous with the wife's commercialization of her body. John Hermann, for instance, argues that this is "a payment of the marriage debt in the most literal and cupidinous way," insisting that "such forgiveness is merely monetary, and this confession is spectacularly deficient when set off against the confession and forgiveness proper to the discourse of penance."[10] But Hermann does not consider why there is any need for the wife to ask forgiveness once she has revealed her plan for reimbursing what she owes. A debtor with both the means and intent to pay does not have cause to apologize to a creditor. The wife is just seeking to reimburse her debt in a different currency – precisely what the merchant did earlier when he repaid his debt in franks rather than shields. He certainly does not feel the need to beg forgiveness from his creditors at the Parisian branch of the Italian bank! If forgiveness is called for here, this can only suggest that the tale's infamous equation of "franks" and "flanks" (7.200–1) may not be the only interpretive option conceivable in the final scene of the tale. The wife could be seeking merely monetary forgiveness, as Hermann claims, or her affectionate request could signify something more profound.

To understand this scene, we should observe first that the wife's request for forgiveness is framed as one of a series of imperatives: "<u>Forgyve</u> it me, myn owene spouse deere;/<u>Turne</u> hiderward, and <u>maketh</u> bettre cheere." The wife *imperatively submits* herself to the merchant's will. Exactly the same structure of imperative submission inheres in Jankyn's speech to the Wife of Bath after his physical assault: "<u>Foryeve</u> it me, and that I thee biseke" (3.818); "Myn owene trewe wyf,/<u>Do</u> as thee lust the terme of al thy lyf" (3.819–20). I have argued throughout my analysis that, for Chaucer, imperative submission is *love*. Both Jankyn and the merchant's wife command their spouses to be free – they authoritatively give up all authority. The link between the Wife of Bath and *The Shipman's Tale* has long been an interest of criticism on the latter.[11] Perhaps Chaucer did originally intend the tale for the Wife, as its opening nineteen lines and the correspondence between Jankyn and the merchant's wife suggests. Or perhaps Chaucer signals the interest of *The Shipman's Tale* in forgiveness by means of an ingenious misdirection. In either case, the wife's conceivably loving utterance to her husband stands in contrast both to the amoral equation of franks and flanks that precedes it and the fulsome performance she puts on for the monk: "'My deere love,' quod she, 'O my daun John'" (7.158). The situation in *The Shipman's Tale* is akin to what confronts us in *The Pardoner's Tale*. The Pardoner seems to make divine love something abjectly material; the wife seems to make marital love something abjectly material. The Pardoner's apparently sincere benediction immediately precedes his cynical offer to his audience; the wife's cynical offer to her husband immediately precedes her apparently sincere plea for forgiveness.

Nevertheless, the merchant's response to his wife's speech gives no clear indication that he has registered her vow to pay off her debt "abedde":

> This marchant saugh ther was no remedie,
> And for to chide it nere but folie,
> Sith that the thyng may nat amended be.
> "Now wyf," he seyde, "and I foryeve it thee;
> But, by thy lyf, ne be namoore so large.
> Keep bet thy good, this yeve I thee in charge."   (7.427–32)

Resigned to the fact that there is no remedy for the lost franks and unwilling to chide his wife bootlessly, the merchant instead forgives her, insisting only that she check somewhat her free-spending ways – a sensible business recommendation in keeping with the Merchant's prudent mien. But is the merchant willing to forgive his wife her monetary debt because she has promised another mode of compensation? Perhaps sex for money is the best he can hope for under these circumstances, "Sith that the thyng may nat amended be." Or is his forgiveness actually an expression of love responsive to his wife's affectionate plea, one that rejects the folly of vengeful chiding?[12] The Shipman's final lines only intensify this ambiguity: "Thus endeth my tale, and God us sende/ Taillynge ynough unto oure lyves ende" (7.433–4). On the one hand, the Shipman seems to establish a cheerfully amoral correspondence between sex and monetary credit with his pun on "taillynge."[13] This pun echoes the wife's own paronomastic alignment of sex and money. Should she fail to pay her husband back "wel and redily" (7.414), he is urged to "score it upon [her] taille" (7.416), an obvious double entendre.

On the other hand, the narrator's prayer to God for unlimited "tail-lynge" could be read as a plea for his infinite grace – the storehouse of "credit" available to the penitent sinner. Analogously, I suggest, we cannot be quite sure whether the merchant is reductively calculating or lovingly graceful in his answer to his wife.

Without unambiguous evidence that the merchant has accepted the wife's commodification of her body, it seems premature to decide that their marriage will move forward on these terms. And yet this is still the standard reading of the tale, as Cathy Hume's recent analysis attests: "At the end of the Shipman's Tale the merchant's wife is allowed to get away with paying him back in bed, and his slight annoyance with her abates. The wife succeeds in spending the money as she wanted and does no more than her marital duty to pacify her husband."[14] Epstein challenges this consensus by arguing that "marital sex in the Shipman's Tale is not a commodity at all. It is the gift that keeps on giving."[15] The structure of the tale, however, certainly aligns the wife's initial proposition with the merchant's commodity exchange: He converts shields into franks, and she converts franks into sex. But what I wish to propose is that the tale escapes the binary of commodity or gift. What we find instead is that the Shipman *entangles* commodification and grace, rendering it undecidable whether the relationship between husband and wife is reducible to a commercial transaction or whether it is indeed animated by love. To clarify this structure, I will have to reconsider the imbrication of sex and money in the tale.

The merchant's wife is obviously no Dorigen, but neither is she May. She deceives her husband and engages in a sleazy, adulterous liaison with his friend, the opportunistic Daun John. But she does so, she says, to earn the money to pay back a sum spent on making herself presentable for her husband; as she says to the monk: "For his honour, myself to *arraye*,/A Sonday next I moste nedes paye" (7.179–80). The narrator ratifies the wife's motivation: Husbands, the narrator states in the opening passage of the tale, "moot us clothe, and he moot us *arraye*,/Al for his owene worshipe richely" (7.12–13). However, the merchant himself seems confident that he has supplied her with enough to array herself appropriately. Before leaving for Bruges, he says to her: "Thee lakketh noon *array* ne no vitaille;/Of silver in thy purs shaltow nat faille" (7.247–8). In her final speech to her husband, however, the wife implicitly contests the husband's estimation of his monetary provision by justifying her extra expenditure: "For by my trouthe, I have on my *array*,/And nat on wast, bistowed every deel" (7.418–19).[16] Perhaps we are more inclined to believe the merchant rather than the wife, who is a proven liar. After all, he does demonstrate his generosity by readily loaning the hundred franks to the monk. But why, then, would the narrator anticipate the plot by suggesting that wives who have not received enough from their husbands are liable to look elsewhere for monetary support (7.15–19)? Here we find a neat ambivalence: Either the merchant has not provided his wife with the means to enhance his honour *or* she lacks nothing to maintain her array appropriately. If she does *not* have the requisite funds to advance her husband's interests, her prostitution with the monk is on the merchant's behalf. Accordingly, the implication would be that, despite her adultery, she loves him and wishes to honour him. However, if the wife *does* have the requisite funds to array herself, all she wishes is to realize a surplus profit. Accordingly, the implication would be that she is a self-interested entrepreneur, all too willing to commodify her marital relationship. And if we cannot decide, conversely, whether the merchant has provided sufficiently for his wife, it is difficult to say whether he loves his money more than her or her more than his money.

Curiously, the wife's arrangement with Daun John serves both to undermine and reinforce the likelihood that she loves her husband. Her affair is, of course, a flagrant betrayal of the merchant and a stark violation of her marriage vow, but it also serves to contrast the wife's contractual sex with her marital sex. The wife and the monk agree "That for thise hundred frankes he sholde *al nyght*/Have hire in his armes bolt upright" (7.315–16). This is exactly what happens: "In myrthe *al nyght* a bisy lyf they lede/Til it was day, that daun John wente his way" (7.318–19). The monk gets *exactly* what he paid for. Now let us consider the Shipman's account of the wife's lovemaking with her husband:

> His wyf ful redy mette hym atte gate,
> As she was wont of oold usage algate,
> And al that nyght in myrthe they bisette;
> For he was riche and cleerly out of dette.
> Whan it was day, this marchant gan embrace
> His wyf al newe, and kiste hire on hir face,
> And up he gooth and maketh it ful tough.
> "Namoore," quod she, "by God, ye have ynough!"
> And wantownly agayn with hym she pleyde.   (7.373–81)

It seems that the merchant's wife is long in the habit of greeting her husband at the front gate of their house after he has returned from his travels. This affectionate gesture is followed by a night of lovemaking that extends well into the next day. And even after she deems that he has had "ynough," the wife gives her husband still more pleasure. The Shipman makes it clear that she goes above and beyond her sexual debt to her husband. The night of revelry with Daun John is a perfunctory matter by comparison, only taking a single line to describe. John Finlayson also notes this contrast: "The actual cuckolding is hurried over as neutrally as the sexual relationship between them is presented and arranged – a not unpleasant but by no means emotionally engaged transaction, splendidly 'modern' and rhetorically non-judgmental. This contrasts with the 'myrthe' of the merchant's spousal relationship later."[17] As strange as it sounds, her adultery simultaneously counts for and against her love for her husband. The wife betrays her husband, but the manner of that betrayal demonstrates her fondness for him.

There are other interpretive ambiguities to consider. The passage above informs us that the married couple's extended bout of lovemaking occurs because the merchant is rich and clearly out of debt. This line is not as straightforward as it seems. The Shipman has told us that the merchant is willing to delay the satisfaction of his physical desires until after he tends to his business. Exasperated at his tardiness at dinner time and finding him anxiously preoccupied with his accounts, his wife asks him: "What, sire, how longe wol ye faste?" (7.215). Has the merchant, nervous about "the hap and fortune" of his "chapmanhede" (7.238), likewise *delayed* physical gratification with his wife until the successful completion of his business dealings or, as is usually supposed, is his ardour *aroused* by the successful completion of those dealings?[18] If the former is the case, we may assume that he loves his wife and can finally indulge his desire for her with an untroubled mind. If the latter is the case, we may assume that he just loves profit. Consider also that the merchant at the end of the tale instructs his wife to "Keep bet *thy* good" (7.432). But before leaving for Bruges, he had implored his wife "to kepe *oure* good" (7.243). Why does he switch from the first-person plural possessive to the second-person singular? It may be the case that "thy good" refers to his wife's body, implying that he has ascertained exactly what transpired between her and the monk. If this is indeed the case, then his forgiveness is truly an act of love. But it is impossible to be sure. Again, we see that the Shipman renders it impossible to decide whether the married couple is loving or just venal.

In this way, the Shipman renders the concluding scene of forgiveness precisely ambivalent: We cannot decide whether the merchant and his wife indeed end up exchanging franks for flanks or whether the merchant clears the ledger outright by means of an act of love. The entanglement of love and commerce, moreover, seems to account for the Host's mangled oath with which the Shipman–Prioress link begins: "Wel seyd, by *corpus dominus*" (7.436). Hermann reads this "barbarism" as "emblematic of the triumph of the flesh."[19] But this reading does not acknowledge the shared ambivalence of the tale's concluding scene and of Christ's sacrifice. On the one hand, the body of Christ represents God's unlimited capacity for forgiveness – his willingness to sacrifice himself for human failings. On the other hand, his body is a material element in a mercantile transaction. The speaker in the *Retraction* thus seeks "the benigne grace of hym that is kyng of kynges and preest over alle preestes, *that boghte us with the precious blood of his herte*:/so that I may been oon of hem at the day of doom that shulle be saved" (10.1091–2).[20] I do not believe it coincidental that *The Shipman's Tale* concludes with the wife's commercial offer followed by her husband's act of forgiveness. As we have seen, the Shipman throughout his tale insolubly entangles matter, whether in the shape of carnality or coin, and marital love, making it impossible to decide between sincere affection and crass mercantilism. This is precisely in keeping with the Chaucerian model of charity, which, as we have seen, suspends any judgment between the material and the immaterial. The Shipman's refusal to judge his characters for their brazen materialism does not signify fabliau amorality, therefore: It signifies love. I suggest that this is the rationale behind the juxtaposition of *The Shipman's Tale* and *The Prioress's Tale*. The Prioress is perhaps the most judgmental pilgrim in *The Canterbury Tales*. Her conception of love, as we will see, is radically formalist and simply cannot accommodate a material dimension.

The Prioress's Prologue and Tale

Heather Blurton and Hannah Johnson have done Chaucerians an important service by surveying and assessing the range of critical opinions on anti-Semitism in *The Prioress's Tale*. Postwar readings of the tale, they assert, "bifurcated into essentially two camps: scholars who believe that Chaucer intended the *Prioress's Tale* as a satire on antisemitism, and those who believe that the tale simply reflects the mores of its time."[21] I will begin my treatment of *The Prioress's Tale* by orienting it in terms of the bifurcation that Blurton and Johnson identify. My approach to *The Prioress's Tale* will not be historicist, whether 1) to argue that Chaucer's anti-Semitism is a product of his time[22] or 2) to argue that such a cosmopolitan writer would have had access to medieval views more tolerant of the Jews and could not have shared the simpleminded bigotry of the Prioress.[23] My reading of *The Prioress's Tale* will skirt these historicist arguments in favour of a strictly logical treatment, consistent with my approach to all the tales. Those scholars who believe that Chaucer is satirizing anti-Semitism tend to focus on the perceived childishness and shallow sentimentality of the Prioress, as indicated by her depiction in the *General Prologue*. I have argued throughout this monograph that "character" is secondary to, and derives from, Chaucer's logic, which is always primary. Thus, I also depart from those scholars who insist that Chaucer's intention is to satirize the Prioress because of her intellectual or temperamental deficiencies and thereby distance himself from her anti-Semitism.[24] But there is an even more compelling reason to reject the thesis that Chaucer is satirizing the Prioress: It simply would not be consistent with the Chaucerian conception of love to mock one of his pilgrims. The vengeful become what they despise in *The Canterbury Tales*. The oppositional strategy, as we have repeatedly seen, is ultimately self-defeating. No doubt, twenty-first-century readers of *The Canterbury Tales* would like to see the Prioress punished for her vengeful tale, whether by mockery or satire; but in keeping with his logic of charity and his *imitatio Christi*, Chaucer refuses to satisfy that desire. Chaucer does not satirize the Prioress; as we will see, he loves her and so forgives her.

Blurton and Johnson also identify a more recent scholarly tendency in readings of *The Prioress's Tale*: namely, the insistence that the professional literary critic assume ethical responsibility for reading and teaching a text that so effectively aestheticizes a horrific ideology.[25] I agree entirely. But I believe that Chaucer himself would expect us to submit the Prioress and her tale to an ethical, and therefore charitable, reading. He has given us all the tools we need to do so. Accordingly, my approach to the Prioress will be identical to my approach to the other pilgrims. I propose that she can only fall into one of three categories. Either 1) she is a materialist, like the Miller, the Cook, the Summoner, and the Pardoner; or 2) she is a formalist, like the Reeve, the Man of Law, the Friar, and the Physician; or 3) she does not decide between these alternatives, like the Knight, Wife of Bath, the Clerk, the Franklin, and the Nun's Priest. In short, either the Prioress *decides* on love or she does not. If she does decide, then she is subject to the law of unintended consequences, whereby her tale will contradict her intention even as it realizes it. In what follows, I will attempt to demonstrate that the Prioress is, in fact, one of the more extreme formalists on the Canterbury pilgrimage. According to the ineluctable logic of *The Canterbury Tales*, therefore, she will become exactly what she rejects. But *The Prioress's Tale* is too often read in isolation from *The Tale of Sir Thopas*, which directly follows it.[26] Only by reading the two tales together can we clarify how Chaucer ultimately comports himself towards his most vengeful creation.

I will begin my analysis of the Prioress by rehearsing what Chaucer understands by love. We love when it is undecidable whether we have formally mastered or materially freed the beloved. To recall my paradigmatic example: Arveragus loves Dorigen because he *commands* her to be *free*. Love entangles formal authority and the material absence of authority. But where can we find the Prioress's understanding of love? To consider this question, I will cite from the *General Prologue* perhaps the most famous lines of the Prioress's portrait:

> Of smal coral aboute hire arm she bar
> A peire of bedes, gauded al with grene,
> And thereon heng a brooch of gold ful sheene,
> On which ther was first write a crowned A,
> And after *Amor vincit omnia*.   (1.159–63)

On an elegant piece of forbidden jewellery is inscribed a Latin aphorism most likely derived from Virgil's *Eclogues* X.69: "omnia vincit Amor: et nos cedamus Amori." The classic reading of the adage, supplied a century ago by John Livingston Lowe, is that it generates two incompatible meanings:

> Now is it earthly love that conquers all, now heavenly; the phrase plays back and forth between the two. And it is precisely that happy ambiguity of the convention – itself the result of an earlier transfer – that makes Chaucer's use of it here, as a final summarizing touch, a master stroke. Which of the two loves does "amor" mean to the Prioress? I do not know; but I think she thought she meant love celestial.[27]

On the one hand, as Lowe's influential interpretation suggests, the brooch registers the undecidability of love. We cannot say whether "Amor" on the Prioress's brooch refers to the carnal and *material* variety of love or to the spiritual and *formal* kind. The inscription elegantly intimates, therefore, the conception of charity that informs the entire *Canterbury Tales*. However, in an amazing feat of condensation, "amor vincit Omnia" tells us something crucial about the Prioress also; it tells us exactly how she decides on love. Love for Madame Eglentyne is mastery. Love only conquers, it does not free; and we must accept without question its authority ("et nos cedamus Amori").[28] I will read the Prioress's prologue and tale as structured by this formalist posture.

Let us consider now her prologue, a text carefully attributed to the Prioress by Chaucer's deixis: "quod she" (7.454). This text has as its header a quotation from the opening of Psalm 8, "Domine Dominus noster," the first seven lines of which are paraphrased in the first stanza. Chaucer is here signalling again that for the Prioress the divine is associated with mastery – God is our *dominus*. This detail is entirely consistent with the inscription on the Prioress's brooch, associating love with mastery.[29] However *formally* exquisite the poetry of her prologue, moreover, the Prioress describes herself as completely lacking in autonomy, as helpless as a child and dependent on divine authority for the success of her endeavour:

> My konnyng is so wayk, O blisful Queene,
> For to declare thy grete worthynesse
> That I ne may the weighte nat susteene;
> But as a child of twelf month oold or lesse,
> That kan unnethes any word expresse,
> Right so fare I, and therefore I yow preye,
> Gydeth my song that I shal of yow seye.   (7.481–7)

The Prioress understands the human relationship to the divine as one of complete subjection; she is an infant before the Virgin Mother and prays as one barely capable of expressing herself. By way of contrast, we should recall the representation of Nature and Virginia from *The Physician's Tale*. Both, the Physician tells us, are formed to be perfectly free; neither requires any oversight whatsoever. Clearly, this is not the case for the Prioress. She simply cannot tolerate material freedom and the concern of her tale is, accordingly, the elimination of material pollutants – anything that resists orientation towards God as master (*Dominus*). We have seen this insistence on the absolute mastery of God before, in *The Man of Law's Tale*. There, Custance finds herself at the whim of an overpresent deity, father, and narrator. It is in keeping with the formalist stance that the Man of Law, just as the Prioress, should be horrified by matter unconstrained by form, whether that is in the shape non-normative sexual desires, rebellious femininity, or heathens who reject the true faith. The Man of Law and the Prioress share a legalistic orientation: both have no tolerance for the transgression of formal strictures.[30]

The Prioress's concern for order motivates her admiration for the spotless purity of the Virgin. Indeed, a number of scholars have detected the Prioress's staunch aversion to dirt; Patterson thus observes, "At virtually every level the *Prioress's Tale* witnesses to a drive toward the pure, the immaculate, and the unalloyed – toward, that is, the ahistorical."[31] The Prioress wishes to purge her world of the taint of material contingency. Merrall Llewelyn Price concurs: "the Prioress is a bastion of remarkable personal hygiene and decorum in an unsanitary world."[32] The Prioress's model, Mary, is thus the "white lylye flour" (7.461) and the "bush unbrent, brennynge in Moyses sighte" (7.468), wholly uncontaminated by her maternity. The formal cleanliness of the Virgin echoes precisely the Prioress's own concern with cleanliness in the *General Prologue*, wherein the narrator takes nine lines to describe her exquisite table manners (1.127–36) in a passage that has its source in the advice of an aged prostitute from *The Romance of the Rose*. The Prioress's greatest delight is in observing the formal codes that govern refined conduct: "In curteisie was set ful muchel hir lest" (1.132). The confrontation with brute matter is so disturbing for her that it takes an elaborate circumlocution to describe the Jewish latrine within which the schoolboy's body is deposited. Though she initially calls it a "pit," the Prioress requires two more lines to identify, with great delicacy, the site as a privy: "I seye that in a wardrobe they hym threwe / Where as thise Jewes purgen hire entraille" (7.572–3). Put bluntly, her objective throughout the tale is to contain shit with extreme fastidiousness.[33] The Prioress is thus the devotional equivalent of the equally fastidious Absolon. Though his squeamishness is highly comical, for Absolon too any affront to his obsession with cleanliness arouses a violent and vengeful reaction. The dirty region that Absolon kisses, therefore, must be exposed to a purifying fire. The Prioress deals in the same way with what she deems pollution. This includes the bawdy tale told before hers. In what seems to be a response to the decidedly unholy monk in *The Shipman's Tale*, she describes her abbot as "an hooly man, / As Monkes been – or elles oghte be" (7.642–3). With her abbot, the Prioress thus sanitizes the deceptive and libidinous Daun John.

It is telling, therefore, that *The Prioress's Tale* is set in an Asian city that scandalously contains a "Jewerye," one that is:

> Sustened by a lord of that contree
> For foule usure and lucre of vileynye,
> Hateful to Crist and to his compaignye;
> And thurgh the street men myghte ride or wende,
> For it was free and open at eyther ende.   (7.490–4)

The Jews and their usurious practices are characterized in terms that suggest the absence of physical and moral hygiene: "foul" and "villainous." The Jewish space therefore has no relationship whatsoever to divine causality. The Prioress, moreover, will not clarify whether it is usurious practices that are "Hateful to Christ" or, more disturbingly, the "Jewerye" and its inhabitants. Lacking a divine ordering principle, the Jewish space is "free and open," promiscuously accessible to all. Again, we witness the Prioress's suspicion towards the materiality of freedom. This is a space without clearly demarcated boundaries: it has no form whatsoever. John Archer calls it "a devouring monster" and an analogue of the Hell-Mouth from medieval pageants.[34] The tale begins, then, by undermining any neat segregation of Christian space and Jewish space; the Prioress situates the disordered "Jewerye" "Amonges Cristene folk" (7.489). From the outset, therefore, the Prioress represents the Jewish residence in the Asian city as pollution, anticipating its violent cleansing. The dirty has contaminated the clean, a situation that a formalist like the Prioress must find unacceptable.

The radical disorder of the Jewish residence, indicating matter without a final cause, is sharply opposed to the little schoolboy, whose only real character trait is his single-minded devotion to the Virgin Mary. Indeed, the schoolboy remains oriented towards, and subordinated to, the Virgin even after his death, compelled as he is to continue singing the *Alma redemptoris mater* even after his throat is cut: "Wherfore I synge, and synge *moot* certeyn" (7.663). The Prioress in this way generates a complex series of identifications by means of her prologue and tale. She identifies herself with the "litel clergeon" in their shared childlike fixation on the Virgin. The Prioress in her prologue thus begs for assistance in revering her patroness: "Help me to telle it in thy *reverence*" (7.473), she pleads. The clergeon, likewise, once he understands that the *Alma redemptoris mater* is a song "maked in *reverence* of Cristes mooder" (7.537–8), learns it by heart. But the Prioress also identifies, of course, with the Virgin herself on account of their shared concern with purity and maternity. And she identifies with the schoolboy's widowed mother, weeping over her small child, just as the Prioress weeps over her "smale houndes," whom she treats more like children than like pets (1.146–50).

At the same time, there exists a more problematic series of identifications between the Prioress and the characters within her tale. We are told that the provost of the city, who tortures and executes the Jews who knew of the murder of the schoolboy, hangs them "by the *lawe*" (7.634). The Prioress's reflexive observance of the codes of conduct that distinguish the mannerly and the unmannerly, the clean and the dirty, the ordered and the disordered, as witnessed in the *General Prologue*, is reflected in her tale by the provost's strict legalism. The imposition of the law brings formal order where there was once material chaos. Indeed, the provost and the Prioress are both utterly deferential to formal authority. But, as is often noted, the provost's application of the law precisely echoes Satan's exhortation to the Jews:

> O Hebrayk peple, allas!
> Is this to yow a thyng that is honest,
> That swich a boy shal walken as hym lest

> In youre despit, and synge of swych sentence,
> Which is agayn youre lawes reverence?   (7.560–4)

Mention of "the law" in this passage has encouraged modern scholars to provide a psychoanalytical interpretation of *The Prioress's Tale*,
according to which the Symbolic Law represents a superegoic paternal
order. Fradenburg's influential reading thus sees in the tale's demoni-
zation of Judaic law an attempt to find an external scapegoat for the
repressive violence internal to paternalistic Christian culture: "In short,
the violence done to children of 'Cristen blood' by 'Cristen folk' is being
attributed to the Jewish scapegoat, just as, in the doctrine of the New
Law versus the Old, the repressive authoritarianism of Christianity
is being attributed to Judaism so that new icons of belief – Mary, for
example, who is herself a libidinal threat to 'monotheism' and a champion of the abject – can be instituted with all the fervor of what Bataille
calls 'affective effervescence.'"[35] The Prioress projects the violence of
contingent alterity *and* the violence of repressive ipseity on to the alien
Judaic law. The tale thus indexes a desire for timeless infantile purity
even as it laments the "violent repression of change."[36] The Prioress's
fantasmatic projection vacillates, therefore, between the two modalities of death, immobile form, and material corruption: "the tale projects
both the disorder of violence *and* the violence of order onto the Jews.
It does so because the tale fears not only change, but the incapacity for
change – death in all its forms."[37] For Fradenburg, in short, the Jews
are the classic phobic object, made to absorb the contradictory desires
internal to Christian culture.

Patterson's Freudian reading of the Judaic law is close to Fradenburg's, despite their radical theoretical differences:[38]

> This narrative has a shape that to the post-Freudian reader is almost self-
> evidently Oedipal, with the Jews forced to play the role of the father who
> punishes with mutilation any transgression of the paternal law that for-
> bids the reunification of mother and child in order to impel the boy into
> the world of singular identity and social difference that constitutes history.
> In asserting the triumph of the maternal, the tale turns the harsh paternal
> law against itself: the Jews are executed according to their own "lawe"
> (hence the provost cites the Old Testament injunction, "Yvele shal have
> that yvele wol deserve" [632]), the provost and abbot join in the Marian
> celebration, and the clergeon is reunited with his heavenly Mother.

I agree with both Patterson and Fradenburg that *The Prioress's Tale* registers an "effort to escape into the absolutism of the eternal" to avoid

the fall into historical contingency.[39] The drive to escape the messiness of historicity by retreating to the tranquil realm of eternity corresponds precisely to what I describe as the Prioress's formalism. But whereas Patterson and Fradenburg treat the Prioress as a subject with an unconscious fantasy formation, I posit a logical structure that renders psychoanalytical speculation unnecessary: Form, or necessity, must relate to matter, or contingency. The Prioress, as much as the advocate of predestination, will not tolerate unruly matter. Her representative in the tale, the prefect, thus imposes formal order on material chaos, submitting the Jews to the order of the law. Accordingly, I read the Prioress's attitude towards the law in a way contrary to both Fradenburg and Patterson: Fradenburg understands the Prioress as distancing herself through projection from the law's "repressive authoritarianism"; Patterson reads the tale as turning "the harsh paternal law against itself" to assert "the triumph of the maternal." But, according to my reading, the Prioress does not at all seek to reject the law of the paternal regime. Both Patterson and Fradenburg impute to the Prioress a vacillating interiority that, as I will demonstrate, can better be explicated via Chaucer's law of unintended consequences. As a formalist, the Prioress is *decisively* on the side of a lawful paternal order that "conquers" (*vincit*) feminine and unclean matter. Her God can only be a *Dominus* and the utterly spotless Virgin Mary is merely an extension of his formal authority.

Now we can see exactly how the correspondence between the lawful prefect and the lawful Jews operates in *The Prioress's Tale*. It is crucial to observe that the Jews are as much formalists as the Prioress herself. Satan therefore urges them to apply their own law to eliminate a *material contaminant* from the precincts of their living space. Just as the Jewerye is described as "free and open" from the Christian perspective, the schoolboy walks *freely*, "as hym lest" (7.562), within the Jewish space. He pollutes this space with his singing, a singing that is "irreverent" to the Jewish law ("agayn youre lawes reverence" [7.564]). Strict adherence to the formalism of the law is the only way to contain polluting matter. *The Prioress's Tale* thus represents *both* the Jewish space within the Asian city *and* the Christian schoolboy within the Jewish space as matter out of place; the Jews who kill the schoolboy, therefore, are as committed to purity as is the Prioress – they are *also* formalists. As is the case with all the judgmental pilgrims in *The Canterbury Tales*, she becomes what she despises. Her tale imposes and defies her vengeful intention simultaneously; she switches places with her own target, as much as the Reeve or the Miller. The Prioress's reference in her prologue to the Old Testament Psalm 8 therefore makes perfect sense: She shares with the Jews in her tale a conception of God as lawful master – as *Dominus*. Both the Prioress and the Jews insist on *reverencing* authority.

The Jews deposit the clergeon's dirty body where they deposit shit. The Christians, by contrast, place his "sweete" body "in a tombe of marbul stones cleere" (7.681–2). The logic subtending both of these actions is identical: Christians and Jews in the tale extricate the clean from the dirty – the paradigmatic formalist procedure. Both sides in the tale are equally committed to order and form; both sides cannot tolerate the intrusion of matter. The tale simultaneously achieves and ruins the Prioress's hygienic programme: The clergeon is from one perspective reverently "clean" and from the other irreverently "dirty"; the Jews are from one perspective irreverently "dirty" and, from the other, reverently "clean." In *The Prioress's Tale*, we simply cannot disentangle what is formally clean, or lawfully ordered, and what is materially dirty, or lawlessly free. This ambivalence is consistent with the clergeon's earlier rule breaking. He learns the *Alma redemptoris mater* in defiance of his schoolteachers, who would beat him "thries in an houre" (7.542) if they were to learn of his misconduct. He is an unlawful miscreant because he is lawfully oriented towards Mary; he is lawfully oriented towards Mary because he is an unlawful miscreant. As he lies befouled in the Jewish privy, he is described as a "gemme of chastite, this emeraude,/And eek of martyrdom the ruby bright" (7.609–10). The clergeon is once again soiled matter and immaculate form simultaneously: Clean and dirty, in other words, are entangled but not synthesized. And there could be no more horrifying predicament for the Prioress than to be entangled with what she regards as filth. And yet, she too mirrors the clergeon's undecidable status. As devoted as she is to formal order and lawful cleanliness, her regard for the Benedictine Rule, as evidenced particularly by her jewellery, her pets, and her large retinue, is questionable at best.[40] It is for this reason, I believe, that the description of her exquisite cleanliness in the *General Prologue* comes from the advice of a prostitute. Her tale magnifies this entanglement of secular materialism and devotional formalism in its entanglement of dirty and clean. Those who *reverence* the law simultaneously break the law – the Jews, the clergeon, even the Prioress herself. This logical structure extends even to the Prioress's appearance. Consider the following description from the *General Prologue*: "For, hardily, she was nat undergrowe" (1.156). Does this line mean that the Prioress is overweight, or does it mean that the Prioress is just *well-formed*?

For Chaucer, it is only when we refuse to decide on formal cleanliness or material filth that we love. The beloved is neither decisively clean nor dirty, neither decisively lawful nor lawless, neither well-formed nor form-less. Emmy Stark Zitter is convinced of Chaucer's anti-Semitism because she believes that he subscribes to the Pauline doctrine of supersession, whereby new Christian grace leaves behind the old Judaic law.[41] The let-ter kills, and the spirit gives life. According to Zitter's reading, Chaucer criticizes the Prioress because she is unable to abandon the degraded legalism and literalism of the Jews: "The Prioress has not moved from the supposed Judaic state where the law prevails, to the Christian state of grace."[42] But this is not how the Chaucerian conception of love operates. Love, for Chaucer, emphatically does *not* supersede legalism. As we have seen from the outset, Chaucerian love entangles lawful order and chaotic disorder, just as it entangles lawful predestination and chaotic free will in *The Nun's Priest's Tale*. Chaucer does not reject the law; he just refuses to decide on it.

The implicit equation of the Prioress with the Jews that is produced by their shared concern for lawful hygiene accounts, I suggest, for the scripturally ambivalent treatment of the schoolboy's murder. The Jews are described as the "cursed folk of Herodes al newe" (7.574) and the grieving mother is described as "This newe Rachel" (7.627). Of course, the gentile Herod, king of Judea, slaughters innocent Jewish children, and Rachel is a Jewish mother lamenting her child. The massacred schoolboy could thus represent either an innocent Christian child *or* an innocent Jewish child. The Prioress's scriptural references here entan-gle incompatible Christian and Jewish references. But in the case both of Herod and Rachel, the adjective "new" indicates what is the Prior-ess's intention throughout her tale: to sanitize offending matter. What the Prioress does to the Jewish privy is exactly what she does to the Hebrew Bible. The narratives of Herod and Rachel are thus *formalized*, or glossed, according to the standard Pauline hermeneutic programme whereby the old letter is fulfilled in the new spirit.[43] The "formal" gloss of Herod and Rachel works to further the Prioress's intention, while the "material" letter undermines it.[44] But a charitable reading, as I have insisted from the outset, will always refuse to decide between formal-ism or materialism. We must read the references to Herod and Rachel in exactly the same way as we do the inscription of "Amor" on the Prioress's brooch, which could signify formally *or* materially. By decid-ing that the spirit must *conquer* the letter, therefore, the Prioress decides on the undecidable – she decides on love. For the charitable reader, by contrast, the literal ("dirty") meaning and the spiritual ("clean") mean-ing are always entangled without synthesis, as my reading of Griselda has already indicated. In the same way, the Jews in the tale are at once

lawful and lawless, clean and dirty. And if we can no more exclude the
literal meaning than the spiritual meaning, then *The Prioress's Tale* succeeds as it fails and fails as it succeeds.

The adjective "new" occurs in one more context that is pertinent to
my reading, celebrating the martyrs of the Book of Revelation:

> O cursed folk of Herodes al newe,
> What may youre yvel entente yow availle?
> Mordre wol out, certeyn it wol nat faille,
> And namely ther th'onour of God shal sprede;
> The blood out crieth on youre cursed dede.
>
> O martir, sowded to virginitee,
> Now maystow syngen, folwynge evere in oon
> The white Lamb celestial – quod she –
> Of which the grete evaungelist, Seint John,
> In Pathmos wroot, which seith that they that goon
> Biforn this Lamb and synge a song al newe,
> That nevere, flesshly, wommen they ne knewe.   (7.574–85)

This passage reiterates the Prioress's formal orientation, praising the
cleanliness of virginity, the whiteness of the Lamb, and the innocence
of the martyrs' song.[45] The lines clearly echo Revelation 14:1–5; indeed,
a marginal Latin gloss in the Hengwrt manuscript quotes Jerome's citation of the scriptural passage in his *Adversus Jovinianum*:

> Then I looked, and there before me was the Lamb, standing on Mount
> Zion, and with him 144,000 who had his name and his Father's name
> written on their foreheads. And I heard a sound from heaven like the
> roar of rushing waters and like a loud peal of thunder. The sound I
> heard was like that of harpists playing their harps. And they sang a
> new song before the throne and before the four living creatures and the
> elders. No one could learn the song except the 144,000 who had been
> redeemed from the earth. These are those who did not defile themselves
> with women, for they remained virgins. They follow the Lamb wher-
> ever he goes. They were purchased from among mankind and offered
> as first fruits to God and the Lamb. No lie was found in their mouths;
> they are blameless.

While the above passage accounts for the Prioress's mention of virgin
martyrs singing before the Lamb of Christ, it says nothing at all about

murder. I would, therefore, argue that Chaucer also draws on Revelation 6:9–11:

> And when he had opened the fifth seal, I saw under the altar the souls of them that were slain for the word of God, and for the testimony which they held. And they cried with a loud voice, saying: How long, O Lord (holy and true) dost thou not judge and revenge our blood on them that dwell on the earth? And white robes were given to every one of them one; and it was said to them, that they should rest for a little time, till their fellow servants, and their brethren, who are to be slain, even as they, should be filled up.

The parallels between this scriptural passage and the Prioress's apostrophe are, I believe, compelling. The Prioress is exclaiming on behalf of one "slain for the word of God." Her insistence that the schoolboy's "blood out crieth on youre cursed dede" echoes the martyrs' cry for vengeance on behalf of their own spilled blood. Furthermore, this passage from Revelation 6 anticipates what actually occurs in *The Prioress's Tale*, which is, after all, a narrative that recounts the vengeance taken on behalf of a martyr who cries out after death. The Jews are the targets of the narrator's avenging judgment, as if she herself is responding to the martyr's exclamation. She will thus vengefully master the offending actors, just as God will revenge the martyrs at the Last Judgment. But we have witnessed elsewhere in *The Canterbury Tales* what happens to judgmental pilgrims who wish to avenge themselves on those who have offended them. The Miller, the Reeve, the Friar, and the Summoner each *become* what they wish to master. This, as we have seen, is exactly what happens to the Prioress.

We perceived in *The Shipman's Tale* the entanglement of love and carnal matter figured by the *corpus Domini*. The opposition of the Shipman to the Prioress is exact. The emotional climax of *The Prioress's Tale* occurs when the abbot *removes* a kernel of matter from the dead clergeon's mouth to disencumber his spiritual form: "His tonge out caught, and took awey the greyn,/And he yaf up the goost ful softely" (7.671–2).[46] According to the moral calculus of the Prioress, and in contrast to *The Shipman's Tale*, love is without ambivalence. The dirty must be cleansed; the authority of law must be upheld; violence must be requited in kind; the debt must always be repaid: The law in its unilaterally formal operation leaves no space for the undecidability of charity. In place of the *corpus Domini*, therefore, the Prioress in her prologue decisively substitutes

God as *Dominus*. The Prioress's God only judges, he does not forgive: "'Yvele shal have that yvele wol deserve,'" the prefect intones, echoing the *lex talionis* from Exodus 21:23 before violently imposing the law on the Jewish offenders.[47]

The Prioress's incapacity to imagine forgiveness is precisely enacted by her tale.[48] In her prologue, she identifies herself with a child who is only beginning to grasp the rudiments of language. Likewise, the little clergeon of her tale does not yet understand the meaning of the *Alma redemptoris mater*: "Nought wiste he what this Latyn was to seye,/For he so yong and tender was of age" (7.523–4). He memorizes the antiphon, but only has a vague sense of its meaning, which he acquires by speaking with an older boy whose own knowledge is limited: "I kan namoore expounde in this mateere./I lerne song; I kan but small grammeere" (7.535–6). Let us now consider the words of the hymn with the benefit of a greater acquaintance with its "grammar":

Alma Redemptoris Mater, quae pervia caeli
Porta manes, et stella maris, succurre cadenti,
Surgere qui curat, populo: tu quae genuisti,
Natura mirante, tuum sanctum Genitorem
Virgo prius ac posterius, Gabrielis ab ore
Sumens illud Ave, peccatorum miserere.

Gentle Mother of the Redeemer, ever-open door of heaven and star of the sea, succour your fallen people who long to arise – you who gave birth, to Nature's wonderment, to your own holy Father, a virgin both before and afterwards, receiving that "Ave" from Gabriel's mouth – have mercy on [us] sinners.

For my purposes, the crucial part of the hymn is the two words with which it concludes: *peccatorum miserere*. We have already encountered a nearly identical construction, in Midas's prayer to Bacchus from *Metamorphoses* 11: "'Da veniam, Lenaee pater! *Peccavimus*,' inquit,/'Sed *miserere*, precor, speciosoque eripe damno!'" (132–3). As in Midas's plea, the supplicant from the *Alma redemptoris mater* uses the imperative mood to plead forgiveness for wrongs committed.[49] The same imperative verb, *miserere*, even appears in both contexts. I propose that this is the rationale for Chaucer's selection of the *Alma redemptoris mater* over the *Gaude Maria*, the latter a hymn far more frequently included in medieval analogues of *The Prioress's Tale*.[50] Midas imperatively submits to the mercy of Bacchus; the supplicant in the *Alma redemptoris mater* imperatively submits to the mercy of the Virgin. The locution, *miserere peccatorum*, is simultaneously a submissive plea and a strict command – authority is at once assumed and relinquished. The *Alma redemptoris mater*, just as does Midas's prayer, registers the paradox of love. But this means the Prioress's identification with the little clergeon is perfect. She cannot hear the lesson of the antiphon any more than he can.[51] After all, the Prioress has already decided: Love does not forgive; love only conquers.

I can further buttress the reading that the Prioress's formalism is incapable of encompassing forgiveness by considering the final stanza of the tale. In this passage, we find the notorious mention of little Hugh of Lincoln, alleged victim of a ritual murder by the Jews in 1255, which resulted after the intervention of Henry III in the execution of nineteen Jewish inhabitants of Lincoln on the basis of no evidence and a forced confession:[52]

> O yonge Hugh of Lincoln, slayn also
> With cursed Jewes, as it is notable,
> For it is but a litel while ago,
> Preye eek for us, we synful folk unstable,
> That of his mercy God so merciable
> On us his grete mercy multiplie,
> For reverence of his mooder Marie. Amen.   (7.684–91)

The final stanza of *The Prioress's Tale* seems to be a prayer for forgiveness, as suggested by the redundancy of "mercy … merciable … mercy." But this reading is complicated by the structure of the passage. We should note first the Prioress's reiteration of her identification with the Mary. Just as Mary in her tale demands that the little schoolboy keep praying after his death, so the Prioress demands that Hugh of Lincoln pray for "we synful folk" after his death. Mary and the Prioress both assume an authoritative posture over dead children in *The Prioress's Tale*. The Prioress's subordination of Hugh of Lincoln corresponds to the subordination of Christ himself in this stanza – another dead child.[53] Christ's mercy does not arise spontaneously according to the Prioress; rather, his mercy will only arise "For reverence of his mooder Marie." The Prioress expects Hugh of Lincoln to have reverence for her authority and, correspondingly, expects Christ to have reverence for Mary's authority. The Prioress establishes two parallel hierarchies in this stanza, constituting herself one final time as an analogue of the Virgin.

In Christ's "reverence" for his mother it is difficult to avoid hearing an echo of Satan's words to the Jews: He describes the clergeon's hymn as "agayn youre lawes *reverence*" (7.564). "Reverence" is one of the key words for the Prioress, and it always indicates a formal deference to authority.[54] So the Prioress has "reverence" (7.473) for the Virgin; she compares the clergeon's devotion to Mary to St. Nicholas's "reverence" (7.515) for Christ.[55] In the *General Prologue*, we see that she takes great pains to assume an authoritative posture and "to ben holden digne of reverence" (1.141). Even in the final lines of the tale, Chaucer makes it clear that for the Prioress, mercy only comes about via a *lawful reverence* for authority. This is in contrast to the *Alma redemptoris mater*, in which the speaker reverently submits to the mercy of the Virgin by irreverently commanding her (*miserere*).

The tale, therefore, ends where it began, if we recall the Host's exquisite deference to the Prioress when he requests a tale:

> My lady Prioresse, by youre leve,
> So that I wiste I sholde yow nat greve,
> I wolde demen that ye tellen sholde
> A tale next, if so were that ye wolde.
> Now wol ye vouche sauf, my lady deere?   (7.447–51)

The Host's address to the Prioress subtly anticipates the formalist logic by means of which the Prioress's discourse is organized from the outset. In sharp contrast to the jocular playfulness with which he addresses the Shipman, he speaks to the Prioress with the same formal delicacy with which she addresses the Virgin and with which she recites her tale. *The Prioress's Tale* does not just aestheticize brutality with its high stylistic register and decorous rhyme royal stanzas.[56] Its formalist aesthetic is entirely *consonant* with its brutality; unruly matter must always submit to conquering form. Compare *The Nun's Priest's Tale*, which at its explosive climax leaves behind all rhetorical decorum and restraint.

I will close this section on the Prioress by noting that the adjective "yonge" applied to Hugh of Lincoln, slain "but a *litel* while ago," corresponds to the adjective "new" applied to Herod and Rachel. The Prioress distinguishes the sanitized "new" versions of Herod and Rachel from the "old" versions, whose biblical narratives work against her intentions and must therefore be hermeneutically cleansed. In the case of Hugh of Lincoln, it is striking that the adjective "litel" was commonly used to distinguish the boy martyr from an eponymous archetype. As in the case of Herod and Rachel, therefore, a charitable reading would prompt us to seek an "old" Hugh of Lincoln who would counter the Prioress's intentions just as the "new" Hugh advances her intentions. There, of course, does exist such a personage: Bishop Hugh of Lincoln (d. 1200), a staunch defender of the Jews who risked his life to defend the local Jewish community against pogroms. Bishop Hugh exemplifies exactly the kind of charity of which the Prioress seems incapable.[57] This is more evidence that a charitable interpretation must be (ir)reverent to the Prioress's formalism: Such an interpretation will decide unilaterally neither for the new dispensation nor the old, neither for the spirit nor the letter, neither for the clean nor the dirty, neither for the Christian nor the Jew. Read in this way, even the vengeful *Prioress's Tale* furthers the cause of love.

The Tale of Sir Thopas

The narrator tells us that *The Prioress's Tale* has had a profound effect on its auditors: "Whan seid was al this miracle, every man/As sobre was that wonder was to se" (7.691–2). Are they moved by the Prioress's pious account of divine intervention, or are they astonished by the intensity of the Prioress's hatred for the "cursed Jewes" (7.675)?[58] Chaucer makes it impossible for us to decide. This interpretive deadlock prepares us to read *The Tale of Sir Thopas*. The Prioress has not been left behind with this thumping tale, even though it responds to Harry's call for the relief of "myrthe" (7.706). It is no wonder, then, that her use of rhyme royal leaks into *The Prologue of Sir Thopas*.[59] What I will argue in this section is that Chaucer the pilgrim responds to the Prioress in a manner precisely anticipated by his comportment in the *General Prologue* – that is, not with the judgment that most modern critics feel she richly deserves, but with a strict refusal of judgment that corresponds to the insoluble structure of love.

In a perceptive reading of *The Tale of Sir Thopas* from 1980, Mary Hamel makes an important contribution to scholarly comprehension of Fragment 7:[60]

> No one has yet suggested that there is any real relationship between the *Rime of Sir Thopas* itself and the preceding tale: only the *kind* of tale Chaucer tells is seen as a reaction to emotional intensity, as a response to the Host's challenge, or as a moment of comic relief between two serious stories. But *Sir Thopas* is related to the preceding tale as more than relief: it is a kind of parody. Along with Chaucer's burlesque of the popular romance, along with his satire of bourgeois knighthood, in a less obvious way he sends up the tale of the little clergeoun.

While I agree with Hamel that *Thopas* responds to *The Prioress's Tale*, I wish to complicate her argument that the "parodic ridicule" to which *Thopas* exposes the Prioress "awakens us from nightmare."[61] What

Hamel observes as parody is, according to the terms of my analysis, a dramatic reorientation. Whereas the Prioress orients herself towards the formal purity of divine authority, *Thopas* orients us towards the unclean materiality that the Prioress finds so intolerable. The Prioress only looks up, towards heaven and its spotless inhabitants, while Chaucer the pilgrim, according to the Host, looks only downward: "Thow lookest as thow woldest finde an hare/For evere upon the ground I see thee stare" (7.696–7). *The Tale of Sir Thopas* will thus respond to *The Prioress's Tale* in a way reminiscent of the Miller's response to the Knight. Chaucer's pilgrim avatar will retell *The Prioress's Tale*, but by substituting materialist aimlessness for her formalist purposiveness. This reorientation is adumbrated by the Host's peremptory demand for useless pleasure in place of useful instruction: "Telle us a tale of mirthe, and that anon!" (7.706). However, unlike the Miller's attempt to requite the Knight, I will argue that Chaucer's first contribution to the tale-telling contest avoids mockery in a proleptic exemplification of the doctrine of *The Tale of Melibee*.

Let us begin with the genre of *Thopas*: the tale rhyme romance.[62] Instead of inspiring reverence for the divine, as would a Miracle of the Virgin, Chaucer selects a genre more suitable for popular entertainment. In the same way that the exotic oriental locale gives way to the more prosaic setting of Flanders, the decorousness of rhyme royal gives way to the rollicking jauntiness and formulaic constructions of vulgar minstrelsy. We saw above how both the *General Prologue* and *The Prioress's Prologue* serve to establish a series of correspondences between the narrator and the figures that populate her tale. *The Prologue to Sir Thopas* operates in the same way, generating a series of correspondences between *The Tale of Sir Thopas* and its teller. Accordingly, the Host describes Chaucer as an adorable puppet instead of an accomplished poet: "This were a popet in an arm t'enbrace" (7.701). Thopas, likewise, is more a cuddly toy fit for a child than a fearsome knight: "Whit was his face as paindemain,/ Hise lippes rede as rose" (7.725–6).[63] The Prioress identifies herself both with her little schoolboy and Mary, the object of the clergeon's devotion; likewise, Chaucer is identified both with his diminutive knight and the object of Thopas's devotion: the elf queen. The Host thus notes of Chaucer that "He semeth *elvyssh* by his contenance" (7.703). In a typically Chaucerian feat of condensation, this description identifies the author as an otherworldly figure within a narrative of his creation (*The Canterbury Tales*) *and* links him to an otherworldly figure within another narrative of his creation (*The Tale of Sir Thopas*).[64]

Just as Chaucer's relationship to his tale doubles the Prioress's, his own hero doubles the Prioress's little clergeon. Both the Prioress and Chaucer tell stories about infantilized protagonists: The appellation

"Child Thopas" (7.830), while typical of popular romance vocabulary, also serves to reinforce the little knight's innocent puerility.[65] The Prioress calls her clergeon "This gemme of chastitee, this emeraude, / And eek of martyrdom the ruby bright" (7.609–10). Thopas is also a little gem, though not quite as precious as an emerald or a ruby. He is, nevertheless, "chaast and no lechour" (7.745). Thopas's coat of arms is "whit as is a lilye flour" (7.867) and he bears a "lilie flour" (7.907) on his helmet, evoking the spotless purity of Mary in *The Prioress's Prologue*, who also bears "the white lylye flour" (7.461).[66] The pious schoolboy's intense reverence for the Virgin anticipates, of course, Thopas's affection for the elf queen, as the fairy otherworld correlates to the otherworld of heaven. But while the Prioress's schoolboy is utterly purposeful in his irrevocable devotion to the heavenly Mary, Thopas is represented as comically purposeless as far as his beloved is concerned:

> Sire Thopas fil in love-longynge,
> Al whan he herde the thrustel synge,
> And pryked as he were wood.
> His faire steede in his prykinge
> So swatte that men myghte him wrynge;
> His sydes were al blood.   (7.772–7)

Instead of a love inspired by the divine, Thopas experiences a love inspired by bird-song – a love, moreover, that does not yet have an object upon which to settle. This aimless love then motivates the hero to "pryk" madly through the forests surrounding Poperyng in no particular direction until he exhausts himself; as Gaylord puts it, "*Sir Thopas* is a tale that gallops about without really arriving":[67]

> Sire Thopas eek so wery was
> For pryking on the softe gras,
> So fiers was his corage,
> That doun he leyde him in that plas.   (7.778–81)

The clergeon's devotion to Mary persists single-mindedly even after his death; by contrast, Thopas needs a restorative nap before he has even located the object of his fierce "corage."

Thopas's aimless love does belatedly discover an orientation in the shape of an elf queen about whom he has recently had a dream. As we saw in the previous section, love for the Prioress is a principle of order: Love conquers chaos. Thopas's love for the elf queen, by contrast, generates a metaleptic *disruption* of narrative order, whereby effect precedes cause. A stanza that names Mary, the figure from *The Prioress's Tale* to which the elf queen implicitly corresponds, introduces this inversion of cause and effect:

> O Seinte Marie, benedicite!
> What eyleth this love at me
> To bynde me so soore?
> Me dremed al this nyght, pardee,
> An elf-queene shal my lemman be
> And slepe under my gore.
> (7.784–9)

After being in love for more than two stanzas, Thopas finally decides whom it is that he actually loves. In this passage, Thopas appears "bound" to his beloved elf queen just as the Prioress and the schoolboy are bound to Saint Mary. But the land of Fairy happens to be guarded by a giant, "Sir Olifaunt," who threatens Thopas with dire consequences if he does not give up his quest:

> He seyde, "Child, by Termagaunt,
> But if thou prike out of myn haunt,
> Anon I sle thy steede
> With mace."
> (7.810–13)

Thopas is sufficiently perturbed by the threat of equine martyrdom that he withdraws "ful faste" (7.827), as opposed to the Prioress's schoolboy, who sings blithely to Mary even as he ventures into the dangerous territory of the "Jewerye." Thopas's love emphatically does not conquer all. Thopas instead needs a day to arm himself more heavily (though he is carrying a lance and a sword) while listening to inspiring love stories and snacking on ginger and liquorice. Thopas's retreat from fairyland comments on the elf queen's own function in the narrative. Mary descends from heaven to intervene miraculously in *The Prioress's Tale* and communicate with her adherent: "Be nat agast; I wol thee nat forsake" (7.669), she tells the dying schoolboy. The elf queen, by contrast, has a merely notional presence in *The Tale of Sir Thopas*, offering her devotee no guidance whatsoever: Thopas has no supernatural cause to orient him.

As Thopas responds to the schoolboy in *The Prioress's Tale* and the elf queen responds to Mary, so Olifaunt responds to the Jews. The murderous villains of *The Prioress's Tale* thus become an even more exotic, fantastical, and racialized bogeyman: a Saracen giant, who swears "by Termagaunt."[68] While the Prioress locates a Christian community within the orient ("Asye"), Chaucer transports an orientalized enemy into the occident ("Poperyng").[69] Rather than casting the Jews as enemies of the protagonist, as in *The Prioress's Tale*, we are informed that the "fyn hawberk" (7.863) Thopas dons in preparation for his battle against Olifaunt is "al ywrought of Jewes werk,/Ful strong it was of plate" (7.864–5). As Miriamne Krummel observes, "Rather than offering destruction and death, as did the Jews in the Prioress's Tale who underwrote the lord's sinful appetites for financial gain ... the Jewish armorer offers a constructive and positive influence."[70] The Jews protect the body of the childlike protagonist instead of violating it. We should also be alert to the resonances of the modifier "fyn," meaning "fine" or "excellent." In a recent analysis of the phrase, "Jewes werk," Jerome Mandel states that "it is plausible that Chaucer could attribute to Thopas's armour the fine quality of Jewish workmanship which was reputed throughout Europe."[71] Notwithstanding their reputation for craftsmanship, the "fyn" work of the Jews in *The Tale of Sir Thopas* contrasts the "*foule* usure" (7.491) and the filthy privy with which they are associated in *The Prioress's Tale*.[72] The Prioress aligns the Jews with what is unclean, excremental, and villainous. Chaucer aligns the Jews with what is salubrious, pleasant, and refined: "ful fyn" preserved ginger (7.854); "fyn and cleere" linen (7.858); and the "fyne and goode" herbs with which Thopas feeds his charger (7.914). The fine craftsmanship of the Jews, moreover, comments obliquely on the literary craftsmanship behind *The Tale of Sir Thopas*. Recall that the Host expects "Som deyntee thyng" (7.711) from the pilgrim Chaucer – an expectation that is sorely disappointed: "Myne eres aken of thy drasty speche" (7.923). The adjectives "deyntee" and "fyn" are nearly synonymous in Middle English, suggesting that the Jews are superior craftsmen while the pilgrim Chaucer is inferior. The former produce something "fyn," while the latter produces something, at least according to Harry, quite "foule." The inversion of *The Prioress's Tale* is precise: The narrator of *Sir Thopas* is associated with dirt, while the Jews are associated with what is clean.

Nevertheless, however exquisitely fabricated is his armour, it does appear as though Thopas requires little protection from his Islamic foe.[73] Not only does Olifaunt merely threaten his horse, in Thopas's retrospective account of the giant, Olifaunt seems to grow a few extra heads: "For nedes moste he fighte/With a geaunt with hevedes three" (7.841–2). Even Thopas feels the need to aggrandize the threat posed by the guardian of Fairy Land, perhaps suggesting that the Prioress's account of her own bogeyman is equally hyperbolic. We should observe also that Olifaunt casts stones at Thopas from a "staf-slinge" (7.829) as the little knight retreats. The ramifications of Chaucer's allusion here to the biblical story of David and Goliath are significant. By equipping Olifaunt with a slingshot, Chaucer unexpectedly transforms the giant into David and the diminutive Thopas into Goliath.[74] In their encounter, therefore, the tiny Thopas is comically enlarged, and his gigantic foe is comically diminished – the "combatants" suddenly exchange places. As a result, we cannot decide unequivocally just who is supposed to be David and who is supposed to be Goliath. Thopas has the right size for David, but Olifaunt has the right equipment. We witness here another subtle parallel to *The Prioress's Tale*: Just as Christians and Jews are aligned by their shared observance of the law, Thopas and Olifaunt are aligned by means of allusion to an Old Testament narrative. We cannot disentangle Christian and Jew in *The Prioress's Tale* any more than we can disentangle Christian and Saracen in *The Tale of Sir Thopas*. This mirroring effect extends to a metatextual level: The reflection of Thopas by Olifaunt and the reflection of the Christians by the Jews is simultaneously the reflection of *The Prioress's Tale* by *The Tale of Sir Thopas*.

Chaucer's aimless narrative about an aimless child-knight goes nowhere. Each fit halves the size of the one prior, evoking the potential for an endless dwindling. The Host mercifully brings the tale to a premature close, recalling how the abbot's merciful removal of the "greyn" from the dead schoolboy's tongue halts his potentially interminable singing: "'By God,' quod he, 'for pleynly at a word,/Thy drasty rymyng is nat worth a toord!" (7.929–30). The Prioress tells a tale that insists on the absolute cleanliness of form; Chaucer's materialist retelling of her narrative is, according to Harry, lower than excrement. Chaucer thus transforms the decorousness of rhyme royal into mere "rym dogerel" (7.925). The Prioress concludes her narrative with the spirit of the clergeon ascending to heaven and a prayer to an angel; the Host brusquely consigns *The Tale of Sir Thopas* to hell and the devil: "'Now swich a rym the devel I biteche!'" (7.924). Chaucer thus transforms the formal purity of *The Prioress's Tale* into material filth – a fitting response to the most fastidious member of the company, and highly reminiscent of Alisoun's treatment of Absolon or Thomas's retort to the hypocritical friar from *The Summoner's Tale*.

It is tempting to conclude my reading of *The Tale of Sir Thopas* here, satisfied in the knowledge that the Prioress has received an appropriate comeuppance for her bigoted revenge fantasy. But, as I mentioned at the beginning of this section, such a reading would entrap Chaucer within his own logic: By mastering the Prioress, he would *become* the Prioress. Thus, unlike the Miller, who tells a tale explicitly designed to quite the Knight, the pilgrim Chaucer, as he says twice (7.708 and 7.928), only knows *one* rhyme. Chaucer's avatar, at least, cannot be accused of hypocritically seeking vengeance on the Prioress when his storehouse of material is so limited. It is significant, moreover, that scholars have long observed the superb structure of this "incompetent" tale. On the one hand, J.A. Burrow acknowledges that *Sir Thopas* "seems to narrow away, section by section, toward nothingness."[75] The gradual dwindling of the romance suggests its aimlessness. The tale, like its protagonist, is going nowhere. On the other hand, the second and third fits contain exactly half the number of stanzas of the fit previous (18:9:4.5 = 4:2:1). Burrow, therefore, remarks: "The basic ratio 2:1 is one of those singled out by Macrobius in his commentary on 'Tullyus of the Drem of Scipioun' as being productive of harmony ... Such mathematical harmony of form is quite uncharacteristic of the minstrel and ballad poetry which *Thopas* appears to represent."[76] E.A. Jones extends Burrow's argument, arguing on the basis of a numerological analysis of the total lines in the tale that "in his use of the Perfect number 28, and more especially in his reliance on the ratios 2:1 and π, in what is on the face of it his most chaotic work Chaucer, more completely than in any of his other compositions, mimics the divinely ordered act of creation."[77] We cannot decide, in contrast to the Host, whether *The Tale of Sir Thopas* is infernally chaotic (materialism) or divinely ordered (formalism). The tale is both at once; Harry's unpredictable interruption paradoxically makes of it an image of perfection. But this also means that Chaucer's attitude towards the Prioress is undecidable: We cannot say whether he masterfully requites the Prioress by upending her tale or deferentially imitates her reverence for order. Chaucer, in other words, refuses to judge her.

Finally, Chaucer's abasement at the hands of the Host has always been read as a moment of high comedy, but it is surely more than that.[78] In the *General Prologue*, Chaucer descends into the world he has authored; in the Thopas-Melibee link, he allows himself to be humiliated by his own creation. He humiliates *himself* instead of humiliating the one pilgrim who, perhaps, most deserves it. Chaucer freely relinquishes his authorial freedom in a poignant imitation of Christ's loving and redemptive gesture. The Thopas-Melibee link is the culminating moment of Chaucer's own *kenosis*, initiated in the *General Prologue* by means of his authoritative abdication of authority. It is not coincidental, in my view, that Christ's passion is referenced three times within a space of fourteen lines in these linking passages. When the Host gives Chaucer the opportunity to tell a second tale, he responds: "Gladly ... by Goddes sweete pyne!" (7.936). Chaucer then describes the theme of the Gospels as "the peyne of Jhesu Crist" (7.944) and Christ's "pitous passioun" (7.950). I suggest that, despite its comic register, we witness in the prologue to the *Melibee* the author's own passion, and his passionate devotion to his creation. And so, instead of mocking the Prioress, instead of judging her, he sacrifices himself for her and thus forgives her.

The Tale of Melibee

It has long been assumed that *The Tale of Melibee* serves as a formal and sententious counterpoint to the purely material solace of *Thopas*.[79] I believe this reading arises from an unwarranted isolation of the two tales told by the pilgrim Chaucer in Fragment 7. I wish to argue instead that the first four tales of the fragment supply a unified movement organized around *The Prioress's Tale*. We begin Fragment 7 with *The Shipman's Tale*, which concludes with a wife requesting her husband to forgive her. *The Prioress's Tale* follows, told by a singularly unforgiving pilgrim. As I have argued above, we should read *The Tale of Sir Thopas* as representing Chaucer's own forgiveness for the vengeful Prioress. Finally, *The Tale of Melibee* returns to the scenario depicted at the conclusion of *The Shipman's Tale*: A wife urges her husband to abandon vengeance and forgive.[80] In Fragment 7, therefore, Chaucer carefully surrounds the Prioress with tales that endorse exactly what she will not consider: charity.

According to my reading, *The Tale of Sir Thopas* is entirely consistent with the doctrine espoused by Prudence in *The Tale of Melibee*. But what is the relationship of the *Melibee*, an extended discourse on love and forgiveness, to the entire *Canterbury Tales*? The pilgrim Chaucer gives some indication in the Thopas-Melibee link, and I will quote his lengthy speech in full:

> I wol yow telle a litel thyng in prose
> That oghte liken yow, as I suppose,
> Or elles, certes, ye been to daungerous.
> It is a moral tale vertuous,
> Al be it told somtyme in sondry wyse
> Of sondry folk, as I shal yow devyse.
> As thus: ye woot that every Evaungelist
> That telleth us the peyne of Jhesu Crist
> Ne seith nat alle thyng as his felawe dooth;
> But nathelees hir sentence is al sooth,
> And alle acorden as in hire sentence,
> Al be ther in hir tellyng difference.
> For somme of hem seyn moore, and somme seyn lesse,

> Whan they his pitous passioun expresse –
> I meene of Mark, Mathew, Luc, and John –
> But doutelees hir sentence is al oon.
> *Therfore*, lordynges alle, I yow biseche,
> If that yow thynke I varie as in my speche,
> As thus, though that I telle somwhat moore
> Of proverbes than ye han herd bifoore
> Comprehended in this litel tretys heere,
> To enforce with th'effect of my mateere;
> And though I nat the same wordes seye
> As ye han herd, yet to yow alle I preye
> Blameth me nat; for, as in my sentence,
> Shul ye nowher fynden difference
> Fro the sentence of this tretys lyte
> After the which this murye tale I write.
> And therfore herkneth what that I shal seye,
> And lat me tellen al my tale, I preye.   (7.937–66)

Some critics have deemed this convoluted introduction to *The Tale of Melibee* part of an extended joke.[81] Others, such as D.W. Robertson Jr. and Bernard F. Huppé, take these lines extremely seriously, understanding them as revealing the ultimate meaning of the entire sequence of tales. Both Robertson and Huppé interpret "tretys" at lines 7.957 and 7.963 as referring to *The Canterbury Tales*. This interpretation assumes that at line 7.953, with "Therfore," Chaucer is turning to address the reader, not his fellow pilgrims, who would not have a completed version of *The Canterbury Tales* available to consult. There is evidence to support this position; Chaucer previously instructed his readers to "Blameth me not" in *The Miller's Prologue* (1.3181), just as he does at line 7.961. At line 7.964, Chaucer states that he has *written* the "murye tale" to come, though he follows this assertion by requesting that his audience "herkneth what that I shal *seye*" and "lat me *tellen* al my tale."[82] His address seems to oscillate between two frames of reference, intra- and extra-diegetic, concluding the prologue with a pointed request not to be interrupted, perhaps recalling the Host's abrupt foreclosure of *Thopas*. This oscillation between "creator" and "created," author and authored, should evoke the paradox of love I associated with Chaucer's emulation of Christ in the introduction: the authoritative abdication of authority that suspends him between authorial transcendence and fictive immanence. Chaucer, in the Thopas-Melibee link, accordingly, represents himself as simultaneously within and without his narrative creation: He is both the writer and the written, as Christ is both supreme authority and devoid of any authority. I now wish to argue that Chaucer's attitude towards the *Melibee* itself reflects his comportment towards all his literary creations in the *General Prologue*: that is, non-judgmental and loving.

Chaucer's statement that the "sentence" of *Melibee* is the "sentence" of "this tretys lyte" prompts Huppé, following Robertson, to argue that "the sentence of the *Tale of Melibeus* is the sentence of the *Canterbury Tales*."[83] Huppé decides that the sentence of the *Melibee* is that worldly vengeance should be abandoned in favour of divine forgiveness, which makes this an attractive reading for me.[84] But Huppé's interpretation of the Thopas-Melibee link has not gone uncontested. Most scholars identify the "tretys" in question with other versions of *The Tale of Melibee*, such as its French source: the *Livre de Mellibee*, adapted by the Dominican friar Renaud de Louens from Albertano of Brescia's *Liber consolationis et consilii*.[85] In this case, Chaucer would be asserting, blandly and at length, that his translation of the source text has not interfered with its meaning. Still others, such as Thomas Farrell, identify the *Melibee* itself as the "tretys" indicated.[86] Dominick Grace, however, perceptively notes the ambiguity of this passage. Though he deems it unlikely that the term refers to the entire *Canterbury Tales*, he states that "Chaucer's use of the word 'tretys' in the Thopas-Melibee link is emblematic of the way he undercuts the idea that meaning is fixed and invariable, not only within the link itself, but throughout his writing."[87] For Grace, therefore, Chaucer's ambiguous use of language in the Thopas-Melibee link implicitly denies the possibility that a single "sentence" for any text is possible, even as Geoffrey asserts it: "No comfortable, pre-existing sentence can be relied upon to explain the meaning of Chaucer's tale."[88] How, then, should we read this passage?

As I mentioned above, there is evidence to suggest that Chaucer is interrupting his address to his pilgrim audience at line 7.953 to speak directly to his readers. If so, the "tretys" he references could indeed be the entire *Canterbury Tales*. There is at least no way to exclude definitively this possibility, as the semantic range of the term is vague.[89] It must be acknowledged, moreover, that a very similar ambiguity of reference occurs with the appearance of "litel tretys" in Chaucer's *Retraction* (10.1081).[90] Scholars have questioned in this latter context also whether the phrase refers just to *The Parson's Tale* or to the entire *Canterbury Tales*. I will address this related ambiguity in the following chapter, but for now it suffices to say that it is doubtful that the echo is coincidental, especially as the *Melibee* and the *Retraction* are both texts concerned with love and forgiveness.

So let us entertain the possibility that the "sentence" of the *Melibee*, the "murye tale" Geoffrey is about to relate, is indeed the "sentence" of *The Canterbury Tales*, embellished with more proverbs than usual.[91] Now, while Chaucer assures us that the *Melibee* is a moral and sententious tale, he studiously avoids informing us of its moral or sentence, implicitly delegating that interpretive responsibility to the reader. Much like *The Nun's Priest's Tale*, therefore, the *Melibee* is authorized and unauthorized at the same time. Nevertheless, let us also assume, without unequivocally deciding, that the sentence of the *Melibee* is, in fact, that love and forgiveness should always trump violence and vengeance – a reasonable interpretation based on Prudence's advice to her husband, counsel which he eventually accepts.[92] Chaucer would then be comparing his individual tales implicitly to the different accounts of Christ's "pitous passioun" by Matthew, Mark, Luke, and John (7.950–1). The words may be different, but each is conveying the lesson of divine love inherent in Christ's redemptive self-sacrifice. This is very close to the central argument of this book: We must understand each tale in light of the Chaucerian conception of charity. *The Canterbury Tales* may very well be characterized as a "treatise" on love.

But we cannot move too quickly here, or we risk imposing a masterful interpretive decision. As the scholars cited above have noted, the referent of "tretys" in the Thopas-Melibee link is anything but certain. If Chaucer is still addressing his pilgrim audience after the "Therfore," it makes more sense that the treatise he is indicating is some other version of the *Melibee* rather than *The Canterbury Tales*. By means of this referential ambiguity, Chaucer renders his formal intention for *The Canterbury Tales* strictly undecidable; we cannot decide for certain whether its governing sentence is indeed love, although it could be. We return here to the crucial lesson of *The Canterbury Tales*: The lover does not decide on love. It is undecidable whether Chaucer masters *The Canterbury Tales* by authoritatively imposing upon his literary creation the sentence of love. *Perhaps* the sentence of the *Melibee* is charity and *perhaps* the sentence of the *Melibee* is the sentence of *The Canterbury Tales*. But the referential ambiguities of the elliptical Thopas-Melibee link ensure that Chaucer's intentions remain undecidable. He thereby reproduces the non-judgmental – charitable – attitude of the pilgrim Chaucer towards his fellow pilgrims in the *General Prologue*: he will not decide on the *Melibee* or on *The Canterbury Tales*. This reading of the Thopas-Melibee link, furthermore, will serve to explicate Chaucer's *Retraction*, where, as I will argue, Chaucer again appears in *imitatio Christi* both as extra-diegetic creator and intra-diegetic creation.[93]

The undecidable structure instantiated by Geoffrey's speech in the Thopas-Melibee link is reiterated in his tale. Let us consider what Patterson refers to as a "devastating moment" late in the narrative, when Melibee decides to disinherit and exile his adversaries even though they have humbly and freely submitted themselves to him.[94] Melibee's vengeful judgment therefore ignores the extended instruction of his wife, demonstrating how the lesson of charity is always threatened by the temptation to decide masterfully – a circumstance that I believe some critical interpretations of the "litel tretys" from the Thopas-Melibee link exemplify. Prudence must intervene again and, with the support of classical and scriptural authorities, urges Melibee "to lat mercy been in [his] herte" (7.1867).[95] Melibee once more considers his wife's teaching and is ultimately convinced, as communicated by a passage that has no equivalent in the French source: "Whanne Melibee hadde herd the grete skiles and resouns of dame Prudence, and hire wise informaciouns and techynges, his herte gan enclyne to the wil of his wif, considerynge her trewe entente,/and conformed hym anon and assented fully to werken after hir conseil" (7.1870–2).[96] On account of his wife's wise *information*, Melibee *freely* assents to *conform* to Prudence's counsel. Prudence neither masters Melibee nor is he free of her formative influence. By way of contrast, the schoolboy in *The Prioress's Tale* is entirely mastered by Mary's authority after his death: "Wherefore I synge, and synge *moot* certeyn" (7.663). He has no choice but to keep singing until the "greyn" is removed from his tongue. The peripatetic Thopas, of course, receives no direction whatsoever from his beloved elf queen. Thopas is vertiginously free, and the clergeon is totally mastered; Melibee is neither.

Melibee's comportment towards his adversaries has the same undecidable structure as that which holds between himself and his wife. He thus says to his erstwhile enemies, who have submitted themselves to him completely: "yet for as much as I see and biholde youre grete humylitee/and that ye been sory and repentant of youre giltes,/it constreyneth me to doon yow grace and mercy" (7.1878–80).[97] The *submission* of his enemies *constrains* him to free them of their guilt, echoing his free *conformance* to Prudence's will. This is a resonance that has no parallel in the source text and in both cases indicates the power of those who are ostensibly powerless, much like Griselda and the people's spokesman from *The Clerk's Tale*. Kimberly Keller thus argues that Prudence "has taken the dialectic of the learned elite, and has used the power of the discourse to persuade a figure who accepts the discourse, but who would traditionally denigrate the worth of women or other social inferiors. Prudence's successful use of this discourse represents a transfer of important discursive techniques to the hands of people who have not previously enjoyed such status or power."[98] Melibee's enemies have submitted to Melibee, which means that he is their master. But their submission, as he states, constrains him to forgive them, which means they are his masters. His adversaries imperatively submit to Melibee. Melibee, correspondingly, exerts his authority not to master but to free his adversaries. Love, accordingly, comes to displace violence and vengefulness. And just as Melibee's enemies imperatively submit to him, so the Nun's Priest imperatively submits to us, when he commands us to read his narrative as we will. The following tales in Fragment 7 will make more explicit this correlation between charity and hermeneutics.

The Monk's Prologue and Tale

The prologue to *The Monk's Tale* extends the pattern we have witnessed from *The Shipman's Tale* onwards, introducing us to yet another authoritative female: the Host's formidable wife. Goodelief, the Host tells us, is both domineering and vengeful, demanding that her husband avenge any slight committed against her: "'False coward, wrek thy wyf!'" (7.1905). He wishes, in fact, that his wife "hadde herd this tale" (7.1894) of Prudence. He has good reason. Harry is deeply worried lest he kill someone at his wife's urging, for he is "perilous with knyf in hond" (7.1919). The pairing of Prudence, who lovingly urges forgiveness, and Goodelief, who masterfully urges vengeance, thus repeats the initial pairing of Fragment 7 in which *The Shipman's Tale*, which ends with a wife requesting forgiveness, precedes *The Prioress's Tale*, in which the narrator relates with satisfaction the vengeance taken on behalf of the murdered chorister. The opposition of mastery and forgiveness should guide also our understanding of the final two tales of Fragment 7. I will thus argue that the Monk, like the Prioress, is a formalist; the Nun's Priest, like Prudence, urges love.[99]

Nevertheless, the evidence initially suggests that the Monk is not decisive, but extraordinarily indecisive. First, he cannot settle on the number of stories he will tell: "I wol doon al my diligence/.../To telle yow a tale or two, or three" (7.1966–8). Second, he has some difficulty selecting the genre of the tale he will narrate: "I wol yow seyn the lyf of Seint Edward;/Or ellis, tragedies wol I telle" (7.1970–1).[100] Third, we cannot tell in advance whether the tragedies he will relate will be in prose or poetry: "In prose eek been endited many oon,/And eek in meetre in many a sondry wyse" (7.1980–1). Finally, he apologizes to his audience if his selection of tragedies has no *predictable* order, as he can only relate them as they come to his memory: "Have me excused of myn ignoraunce" (7.1990), he pleads, "Though I by ordre telle nat thise thynges" (7.1985).[101] I suggest that the unpredictability of the Monk identifies him neatly with the tragic protagonists of his tale: Just as his protagonists cannot anticipate the future, the Monk finds it extremely difficult to plan ahead.

The Monk apologizes for his chaotic lack of organization but then informs us that he intends to relate a series of tragedies, each of which is intended to convey identically a rather dreary "sentence":

> I wol biwaille in manere of tragedie
> The harm of hem that stoode in heigh degree,
> And fillen so that ther nas no remedie
> To brynge hem out of hir adversitee.
> For certein, whan that Fortune list to flee,
> Ther may no man the cours of hire withhholde.
> Lat no man truste on blynd prosperitee;
> Be war by thise ensamples trewe and olde.   (7.1991–8)

The Monk finally decides in advance on the univocal *form* of his mini-narratives. According to this design, his *De Casibus Virorum Illustrium* will exemplify the irremediable fall through the untrustworthiness of Fortune of those that stand in high degree.[102] It is nevertheless important to note that the Monk's tragedies do not all conform to his professed intention.[103] In fact, he begins with Lucifer's fall, which occurs explicitly without Fortune's intervention: "Fortune may noon angel dere" (7.2001). Adam follows, whose own fall occurs on account of "mysgovernaunce" (7.2012). Sampson, the next tragic protagonist, experiences his reversal not because of Fortune but because he makes the mistake of telling his wife the secret of his hair: "Beth war by this ensample oold and playn/That no men telle hir conseil til hir wyves/Of swich thyng as they wolde han secree fayn" (7.2091–3). The tragedy of Hercules appears to conform to the Monk's design but is followed by the comedic narrative of Nabugodonosor, who is humbled by God but eventually rectifies his prideful ways: "And til that tyme he leyd was on his beere/He knew that God was ful of myght and grace" (7.2181–2).[104] So much for the Monk's claim that "there nas no remedie" for the falls he will describe. What should we make, then, of the tale's deviations from the Monk's formal design? Again, I propose that the Monk, just as much as his tragic protagonists, is incapable of predicting the future. A *casus* awaits all those who have too much faith in what is to come.[105] The deviations of *The Monk's Tale* from the narrative plan asserted at its outset once more align the Monk with his own protagonists.

I can extend this reading by considering the interruption of *The Monk's Tale* by the Knight. As is true of of all the decisive pilgrims in *The Canterbury Tales*, the Monk's formalism renders him subject to Chaucer's law of unintended consequences. His intention to reiterate the same tragic form must succeed and fail simultaneously. I, therefore, contest Richard Neuse's characterization of *The Monk's Tale*, indeed each tale, as "a unique event unassimilable to the others."[106] The charitable logic that informs *The Monk's Tale* is the charitable logic that informs all the *Canterbury Tales*. We must acknowledge, then, that the Knight's abrupt foreclosure of *The Monk's Tale* is not just the tale's failure; this premature ending is its brilliant success. *The Monk's Tale* succeeds because it exemplifies its own theme: A monotonous tale that is intended to demonstrate Fortune's unpredictable interruptions is itself unpredictably interrupted. And this interruption is so perfectly timed as to occur right after the Monk reiterates his theme for the last time: "For whan men trusteth [Fortune], thanne wol she faille,/And covere hire brighte face with a clowde" (7.2765–6). The Monk becomes the final tragic protagonist of his series of tragedies. The ignominious failure of his tale dramatically proves its central thesis: No one should trust in Fortune – including the Monk himself. The Monk thinks that he is the master of Fortune's arbitrary nature, that he can rely with certainty on her uncertainty: "Thus kan Fortune hir wheel governe and gye,/And out of joye bringe men to sorwe" (7.2397–8). (Un)fortunately, he too ends up underneath her wheel, as do all those who put their trust in Fortune. Hence, the failure of *The Monk's Tale* is its success; its success is its failure.[107]

The Knight's interruption of the Monk at the start of *The Nun's Priest's Prologue* should bring to mind the structure of the former's tale. Though the Miller misjudges it, *The Knight's Tale* is, as we saw, rigorously undecidable: We cannot say for certain whether it testifies to the predetermined order of the cosmos or to its complete lack of order.[108] The Monk, by contrast, *decides* on the formal order of his tragedies so that they may express the same monotonous theme. The Knight thus complains:

> I seye for me, it is a greet disese,
> Whereas men han been in greet welthe and ese,
> To heeren of hire sodeyn fal, allas!   (7.2771–3)

The Knight claims that a broader view is necessary, one that does not decisively exclude the intrusion of *matter*: The "contrarye" of the Monk's bleak vision is accordingly "joye and greet *solas*" (7.2774). The Knight is not merely expressing his desire for a comedic trajectory, as the standard reading of his interruption claims.[109] For the Knight, as his tale attests, sentence (form) and solace (matter) ought to be insolubly entangled. As opposed to the Monk, he decides neither on formal order nor on material chaos. That it should be the Knight who interrupts the Monk at this juncture makes perfect sense: The undecidable structure of his own tale anticipates *The Nun's Priest's Tale*, which concludes Fragment 7.[110] The Nun's Priest, as we have already seen, will also entangle necessity (form) and freedom (matter), rendering it impossible to decide between predestination and anarchy – exactly as is the case in *The Knight's Tale*. Both the Knight's and the Nun's Priest's tales possess an identical logical structure. But the Monk, just as the Prioress, cannot tolerate material contingency, even though he tells a tale about Fortune's unpredictability: His characters are doomed to the ineluctable *necessity* of a fall, and his tale is sanitized of any trace of solace. It is consistent with the Monk's formalism, invariably gendered masculine, that the Host should be so keen to emphasize at length his overwhelming virility in *The Monk's Prologue*: "Thou woldest han been a tredefowel aright" (7.1945). The Monk will have no truck with feminine materiality, feminine solace.

It is thus no surprise that Harry seems to have missed everything that has been said between the Monk's decision to tell tragedies and his words right before the interruption: "[The Monk] spak how Fortune covered with a clowde/I noot nevere what; and als of a tragedie" (7.2782–3). It is only the clinking of the bells on the Monk's bridle that has saved the Host from an unfortunate fall of his own:

> By hevene kyng that for us alle dyde,
> I sholde er this han fallen doun for sleep,
> Althogh the slough had never been so deep;
> Thanne hadde your tale al be toold in veyn.
> For certainly, as that thise clerkes seyn,
> Whereas a man may have noon audience,
> Nought helpeth it to tellen his sentence.   (7.2796–802)

The Host insists here that the Monk's fidelity to formal "sentence" in isolation from material "solas" ensures unintended consequences. The relentless commitment to *one* meaning is simultaneously the absence of *any* meaning, because a tale devoid of solace has "noon audience" and is for that reason "toold in veyn." What is intended to be formally purposeful becomes at the same time materially purposeless.

In conclusion, modern scholarly assessments of Fragment 7 have not diverged far from Alan Gaylord's influential consideration of the sequence as "the Literature Group."[111] This is understandable, as the group features six different genres and five different metres. But the concerns of the fragment, I suggest, extend far beyond an investigation of literature and language. Fragment 7 allows us to perceive the sophisticated manner with which Chaucerian love entwines aesthetics, ethics, theology, and hermeneutics. A charitable aesthetics will decide neither on formal sentence nor material solace; a charitable ethics will refuse either to master or to free the beloved; a charitable theology will decide neither on predestination nor free will; finally, a charitable hermeneutic will, in line with the Nun's Priest's imperative that we "Taketh the fruyt, and lat the chaf be stille" (7.3443), neither collapse the text into univocality nor render it equivocally open. At the other extreme, the Prioress and the Monk, ecclesiasts who share a vexed relationship to the Benedictine Rule, share also a unilaterally formalist orientation.[112] Whether by means of a grim revenge fantasy or a somnolent sequence of tragedies, they demonstrate, in a manner that is distinctly *uncharitable*, what it means to decide on love. While I hesitate to isolate Fragment 7 too dogmatically, it does seem to provide within *The Canterbury Tales* Chaucer's most sustained elaboration, across an array of rarefied domains, of a general "theory" of love. It is for this reason, perhaps, that the pilgrim Chaucer's integral contribution is the lengthy *Melibee*, a treatise about charity that Chaucer implicitly encourages us to read charitably. Chaucer's focus on charity in the *Melibee* is in keeping with the significance of the Thopas-Melibee link for his emulation of Christ. Fragment 7 includes Chaucer's *passio* at the hands of the Host, a loving self-abasement on behalf of the Prioress, thus constituting an intermediate stage between his incarnation in the *General Prologue* and the Final Judgment of his *Retraction*.

In the next chapter, I will consider together the final three fragments of *The Canterbury Tales*. What we will see in the concluding movement of the work is that Chaucer shifts the emphasis towards the problem of authorial self-definition. In the final analysis, does Chaucer understand himself as a poet or a philosopher? Is his writing secular or Christian? As we will see, we must suspend our judgment until we reach the *Retraction*.

7 Loving Chaucer: Judgment and Charity in Fragments 8–10

I will argue in my concluding chapter that Chaucer structures the final three fragments of *The Canterbury Tales* by means of exactly four coordinates: Christian and secular; sentence and solace. The first term of each binary is formal and authoritative; the second term is material and non-authoritative. There are only four possible combinations. I will aim to demonstrate that the Second Nun's prologue and tale represent "Christian solace" (formalized matter) in the shape of sacred poetry. This is verse that is oriented towards divine authority and is, therefore, purposeful. Inversely, the Canon's Yeoman's prologue and tale represent "secular sentence" (materialized form) in the shape of alchemical philosophy. Alchemy is an *unauthorized* philosophy that, as we will see, is radically purposeless – it can come to no "conclusioun" (8.672). The Manciple's prologue and tale represent "secular solace" (materialized matter) in the shape of classical poetry and Phebus, the classical god of poetry. As opposed to *The Second Nun's Tale*, this is poetry that rebels against all authority and is, therefore, vertiginously chaotic. Inversely, the Parson's prologue and tale represent "Christian sentence" (formalized form) as exemplified by the speaker's authoritative prose intended to orient its audience towards the highest purpose: salvation. The Parson's discourse is absolutely ordered, and the Manciple's discourse is absolutely disordered. The Second Nun's discourse is relatively ordered, and the Canon's Yeoman's discourse is relatively disordered. The final four tales of the sequence thus identify four distinct literary categories and ask us to reflect on their pertinence to Chaucer's own authority.[1] Two questions in particular come to the fore: 1) Is Chaucer, in the final analysis, a secular or a Christian writer? And 2) is he concerned, ultimately, with the univocal truth of prose and philosophy or with the equivocal and deceptive play of poetry and fabulation?[2] The closest we will approach to a response to these questions must await consideration of Chaucer's *Retraction*, with which I will conclude this book.

The Second Nun's Prologue and Tale

The Second Nun's prologue and tale initiate the final movement of *The Canterbury Tales*.[3] It is appropriate, therefore, that both concern themselves with the nature of ends. *The Second Nun's Prologue* begins by reiterating Chaucer's fundamental opposition: formal purposefulness and material purposelessness. The first stanza accordingly rejects the idle life, the life devoid of an aim or end, in favour of the "busy":

> The ministre and norice unto vices,
> Which that men clepe in Englissh Ydelnesse,
> That porter of the gate is of delices,
> To eschue, and by hire contrarie oppresse –
> That is to seyn, by leveful bisynesse –
> Wel oghten we to doon al oure entente,
> Lest that the feend thurgh ydelnesse us hente.   (8.1–7)

The Second Nun finds a model of purposeful activity in St. Cecilia, and the former's versified translation of the latter's *vita* will itself be, she says, an act of "faithful bisynesse" (8.24). The formal ideal supplied by Cecilia finds an apt reflection in the Virgin Mary, as the Second Nun indicates in her *Invocacio ad Mariam*.[4] Both Cecilia, "mayde and martyr" (8.28) and the Virgin, "Mayde and Mooder" (8.36), guide the aimless sinner from the darkness of ignorance to divine clarity. Addressing Mary, the Second Nun prays:

> And, for that feith is deed withouten werkis,
> So for to werken yif me wit and space,
> That I be quit fro thennes that most derk is!   (8.64–6)

The Second Nun's prayer to Mary for illumination supplies a motif that is elaborated in her description of Cecilia. The saint, who shares with the Virgin the emblem of the lily (8.91), is associated moreover with wisdom as opposed to folly (8.93), vision as opposed to blindness (8.100), chastity as opposed to pollution (8.88), enlightenment as opposed to darkness (8.111–12), and eternal life as opposed to eternal death (8.104).[5] *The Second Nun's Prologue* thus establishes both Cecilia and Mary as guides who can lead the fallen from material confusion to formal purposefulness.

The prologue's treatment of gender mirrors this movement from materiality to form. The Second Nun calls herself an "unworthy *sone* of Eve," aligning herself with formal and "masculine" purposefulness as opposed to material and "feminine" aimlessness.[6] The Second Nun's shift in gender neatly anticipates her tale, which, of course, features a highly purposeful and "masculinized" saint who is, in the words of Gail Ashton, "active, strident, an aggressive female martyr, a virago, publicly clashing with male pagan authority."[7] Though some scholars have regarded Cecilia's authority as subversive of traditional gender roles, I see little that is unorthodox here.[8] Cecilia's authoritative status is entirely consistent with the Second Nun's strict formalism. Just as she provides a formal model of "busyness" for the Second Nun, Cecilia is a leader and a teacher whose vocation is to guide her charges away from pagan falsehood and towards divine truth.[9] As Carolyn Collette observes, "In the marriage of Cecile and Valerian and in the conversion of Valerian and Tiburce, we see that, as St. Augustine says, before man can achieve grace, the eye of the soul must be purified to see Truth. We are reminded that to achieve this purity we must give up our reliance on the material and see that triune God whose being, comprising three persons in one Godhead, defies experiential explanation."[10] Cecilia's instruction gives her converts a singularity of purpose that leads without detour from the darkness and impurity of the material world to the clarity and purity of the immaterial.

The orientation of base matter towards elevated form serves as a capsule summary of the narrative's structure. The tale that begins the closing section of *The Canterbury Tales* is set in an eerie twilight between life and death. It will culminate, however, with Cecilia's attainment of martyrdom, a state of spiritual elevation that leaves behind all worldly materiality. Indeed, Cecilia, as the Latin sources and Chaucer's translation attest, has been programmed for this purpose from the time she was born to pagan Romans:

> This maiden bright Cecile, as hir lif seyth,
> Was come of Romains, and of noble kinde;
> And from hir cradle up fostered in the feith
> Of Crist, and bar his gospel in hir minde.   (8.120–3)

Cecilia's unwavering trajectory towards God and martyrdom implies a detachment from the materiality of life even before death. The marriage between Valerian and Cecilia, tellingly, is a purely spiritual union devoid of sensuality or earthly pleasure.[11] Cecilia demands of Valerian a "clean love"; speaking of her angelic lover, she says to her husband,

"And if that ye in clene love me gye,/He wol yow loven as me, for youre clennesse" (8.159–60). As it is for the Prioress, love for the Second Nun and Cecilia is untouched by material contamination. In Raybin's judgment, therefore, "the living Cecile is in a very basic respect dead to the world, as are those she saves *from* the world."[12] The description of Cecilia as "half dead" (8.533) for three days after she has been nearly beheaded by Almachius's henchman corresponds precisely to the saint's liminal position throughout the narrative. But Pope Urban finds himself in an identical locus. Living during the time of Roman persecution of Christians, Urban, as Cecilia's husband discovers, lurks among the crypts of the early adherents to the faith: "[Valerian] foond this holy olde Urban anon,/Among the seintes buriels lotinge" (8.185–6).[13] Urban resides among the saintly dead, in a necropolis that will soon welcome Valerian, Tiburce, Maximus, and finally Cecilia herself. The martyrs in this tale live only in anticipation of membership in this city of the dead.[14]

The Second Nun's Tale thus emphasizes the rapidity of Valerian's conversion, and the ease with which he leaves his old life behind to qualify for the martyr's palm. Sherry Reames remarks that the Latin sources for the tale (the *Legenda Aurea* and a Franciscan abbreviation of Cecilia's *vita*), which Chaucer closely follows, radically abridge the process of conversion. Conversion in *The Second Nun's Tale* does not engage the intellect or require extended deliberation; it is a precipitous event that seizes the convert: "the *Legenda* and the tale create the impression that Valerian's conversion is something that happens to him, from the outside, and that it is enough for him to submit to it; he need not understand."[15] Indeed, it is the rapidity of his conversion that is specifically rewarded. Cecilia's angel grants Valerian a boon because he assents to the faith "so soone" (8.232). Eileen Jankowski also notes the emphasis on the speed of conversion in the tale: "Valerian is granted a 'boone' not as a further reward for rejecting pagan ways and embracing Christ's, but precisely because his decision is made with such dispatch."[16] Once converted, Valerian requests that his brother, Tiburce, witness the truth as well. The angel responds that God approves of Valerian's entreaty, informing him also that "'bothe, with the palme of martyrdom,/Ye shullen come unto his blisful feste'" (8.240–1). Tiburce's promotion to the exalted ranks of the martyrs is thus extraordinarily accelerated. At this point in the narrative, of course, he has yet to be converted. I therefore disagree with Joseph Grossi's claim that "Tiburce, like most people, has to grope his way towards a faith that a saint, previously chosen instrument of God, can embody and spread with relative ease."[17] Tiburce is oriented inexorably towards a divine final cause even *before* he knows it – he too is "previously chosen." The angel's prophecy illustrates with particular clarity the Second Nun's concern that Christian purpose should come to order pagan aimlessness. As a result, according to Reames, "Even in martyrdom, the converts in the tale look more like victims than heroes."[18] The converted pagans in the tale appear just as helpless to resist the overwhelming force of divine truth as Custance is to resist her missionary vocation in *The Man of Law's Tale*.

The Canon's Yeoman's Prologue and Tale

Instead of being locked into a purposeful activity, by contrast, the hapless alchemists in the Canon Yeoman's prologue and tale quest fruitlessly for some culmination to their sooty exertions: "For alle oure sleightes we kan nat conclude" (8.773).[19] The inverted relationship between the two representatives of Fragment 8 has long been noted. From a survey of past scholarship up to the 1990s, Patterson provides an instructive summary of the oppositions between the tales; I will quote it in full:[20]

> [T]he fires of Christian suffering that prove Cecilia's purity versus the fires of alchemy that discolour the Yeoman; Cecilia's 'bisynesse' versus the obsessive 'werkynge' of alchemy; the odor of sanctity versus the goatish stink of brimstone; the clearsighted Cecilia versus the bleary-eyed alchemists; the good end achieved by Christian martyrs versus the inconclusiveness of the alchemical quest; the 'leveful bisyness' with which the Second Nun relieves her 'ydelness' versus the leaden despair from which the Yeoman cannot free himself; the rootedness of Cecilia in the faith versus the endless questing of the vagabond alchemists; the verbal simplicity of the *Second Nuns Tale* versus the knotty intricacy of the Yeoman's discourse; the clarity of Christian doctrine versus the 'elvyssh nice lore' of alchemy; the spiritual conversion of sinners versus the failed transmutation of fallen matter; Urban's salvific refuge in the suburbs versus the Canon's guilty lurking; the martyrdom of Valerian and Tiburce versus the 'mortification' of the 'brothers' mercury and sulfur; Almachius's idolatrous worship of a stone versus the alchemists' quest for the philosopher's stone; Christian sapience versus worldly science; saintly charity versus alchemical cupidity; revelation versus reason; divinity versus demonism; God's divine work versus the Canon's diabolical labor.

I wish to synthesize this account of Fragment 8 by suggesting that it corresponds to a pattern we have witnessed throughout *The Canterbury Tales*: the representation of alchemy and alchemists in the Canon's Yeoman's prologue and tale dramatically overturns the formalism of the Second Nun's prologue and tale. We should understand alchemy above all, therefore, as a materialist practice.[21] Joseph Grennen's classic study identifies "multiplication" as a key term in *The Canon's Yeoman's Tale*, to which he opposes the "the unity and integrity which the legend of St. Cecilia displays."[22] "Unity" and "multiplicity," however, are just alternative terms for "form" and "matter." If alchemists are, in Grennen's words, "multipliers of words, treatises, recipes, ingredients, anything, in short, but the gold, health, or virtue which they imagined themselves to be seeking," then alchemy is an *aimless* doctrine that endlessly proliferates vain knowledge and empty sentence: "That *slidynge science* hath me maad so bare/That I have no good, wher that evere I faire" (8.732–3).[23]

But matter unconstrained by form is not only multiplicity; it is also contingency and deviation. We now have a way, I believe, to resolve a significant crux regarding the position and appearance of the Canon's Yeoman's prologue and tale. The Canon's Yeoman is not a member of the company that leaves the Tabard Inn. His contribution to the tale-telling thus seems to be a deviation from Chaucer's narrative plan, prompting Thomas Tyrwhitt, Chaucer's eighteenth-century editor, to speculate that "some sudden resentment had determined Chaucer to interrupt the regular course of his work, in order to insert a satire against the alchemists."[24] Other scholars have raised the possibility that *The Canon's Yeoman's Tale* may, in fact, be an apocryphal interpolation.[25] But it should be no surprise that a tale about an aberrant discourse should follow an "unexpected" interruption of the Canterbury pilgrimage. If *The Second Nun's Tale* tells a story, in the well-attested mould of the *passio*, about Cecilia's *rectilinear* movement from birth to martyrdom, *The Canon's Yeoman's Prologue* advertises itself, and the tale that follows, as a narrative *deviation*:

> Whan ended was the lif of Seinte Cecilie,
> Er we hadde riden fully five mile,
> At Boughton under Blee us gan atake
> A man that was clothed in clothes blake.   (8.554–7)

The precipitous entrance of the Canon's Yeoman on the scene, and the contrast it provides to a *vita* in which there are few, if any, surprises, prepare us for a radical reversal of the Second Nun's formalist orientation. This point is only reinforced by the fact that *The Second Nun's Tale* so closely translates its source material, while the Canon's Yeoman's prologue and tale seem to be Chaucer's *free* invention. The direction Chaucer receives from antecedent texts for the former is thus lacking when he composes the latter. Chaucer has no authority to guide him; exactly the same is true of the disciples of alchemy:

> And every man that oght hath in his cofre,
> Lat hym appiere and wexe a philosophre.
> Ascaunce that craft is so light to leere?
> Nay, nay, God woot, al be he monk or frere,
> Preest or chanoun, or any other wight,
> Though he sitte at his booke bothe day and nyght
> In lernyng of this elvysshe nyce lore,
> Al is in veyn, and parde muchel moore.   (8.836–43)

The disciple of alchemical philosophy receives absolutely no guidance as to how to master this "elvysshe nyce lore," no matter how much he ponders authoritative texts. Alchemy is thus a radically *unauthorized* doctrine in the same way that the Canon's Yeoman's prologue and tale do not appear to rely on any previous authority.

But the guidance that Chaucer receives from his sources for *The Second Nun's Tale* is analogous to the guidance that Valerian and Tiburce receive from Cecilia. The saint is an impeccable teacher for her converts, providing for Valerian and Tiburce flawless instruction in the faith, just as she supplies an exquisite formal model for the Second Nun.[26] As the interpretation by Jacob of Genoa indicates: "Cecilie is to seye 'the wey to blinde,'/For she ensample was by good techynge" (8.92–3). We can oppose here the consequences of the Canon's Yeoman's labour: "And of my swynk blered is myn ye" (8.730). Cecilia's instruction is supremely effective even at a remove, as Valerian and Tiburce are, because of her pedagogy, able to convert their would-be executioners:

> Whan Maximus hadde herd the seintes loore,
> He gat him of the tormentoures leve,
> And ladde hem to his hous withoute moore;
> And with hir preching, er that it were eve,
> They gonnen fro the tormentours reve,
> And fro Maxime, and fro the folk echone,·
> The false feith, to trow in God alone.   (8.372–8)

Cecilia's exemplary instruction makes her pupils into exemplary instructors, converting the Roman executioners as swiftly as they themselves were converted.[27] Even after Almachius's henchman mortally wounds her, Cecilia continues for three days to teach her disciples: "And nevere cessed hem the feith to teche/That she hadde fostred" (8.538–9). Indeed, her teaching continues even after her death; her final act is to enjoin Urban to make of her house a church, where instruction in the faith continues, according to the narrator, "into this day" (8.552). Chaucer thus follows a tale about a divinely truthful master with two accounts of demonically deceptive masters: the Canon from *The Canon's Yeoman's Prologue* and the canon from the Yeoman's tale. Of the latter, the Canon's Yeoman states: "He seemed freendly to hem that knewe him noght,/But he was feendly bothe in werk and thoght" (8.1302–3). Simply put, the good teachers of *The Second Nun's Tale* orient their pupils towards divine order. The bad teachers whom the Canon's Yeoman describes lead their disciples only into hellish chaos.

Cecilia's conversions in *The Second Nun's Tale* purify base materiality, miraculously transmuting ignorant pagans into precious heroes of the Christian faith who are willing to die for the cause. The masters of alchemy about whom the Yeoman discloses so much do the opposite, transmuting the precious into the base – Christians into adversaries of God (8.1476). *The Second Nun's Tale* thus stages a movement from chaos to order, while the Canon Yeoman's prologue and tale stage a movement from order to chaos. Chaucer signals this inverted trajectory by associating the dwelling of the alchemists, who are "in the *suburbes* of a toun …/*Lurkinge*" (8.657) with the dwelling of Pope *Urban*, who is "[a]mong the seintes buriels *lotinge*" (8.186). Alchemists lurk among those subject to no order, "robbours" and "theves" (8.659). In contrast, Urban resides among the martyrs, who defy pagan law on behalf of the highest order. The disordered alchemists are as lawless as their criminal neighbours, while the faithful martyrs remain absolutely true to a divine cause.

As opposed to the positive transformation effectuated by Cecilia, all that results from discipleship to the Canon and his false science is that health is transformed into sickness (8.728), wealth is transformed into poverty (8.734–6), and intelligence is transformed into madness and folly (8.741–2). Alchemy does exactly the opposite of what it is intended to do. As we saw in the case of Valerian and Tiburce, moreover, Cecilia makes her students themselves into good teachers; the failed alchemist, on the contrary, transmutes his disciples into false teachers:

> And whan he, thurgh his madnesse and folye,
> Hath lost his owene good thurgh jupartye,
> Thanne he exciteth oother folk thereto,
> To lese hir good, as he himself hath do.   (8.742–5)

The alchemist is only successful insofar as he inspires his students to propagate his vain, if addictive, science once he has lost his own wits and goods. Alchemists, such as the Yeoman's Canon, spread thereby the delusion of alchemy as if it were contagious disease, much like the rapid spread of Christianity in *The Second Nun's Tale*. But the Yeoman's own devotion to his master has come to an end, though he begins his discourse praising the Canon's "heigh discrecioun" (8.613). On the one hand, Cecilia's virtuosic pedagogy and mastery of Christian doctrine inspire absolute *fidelity* in her followers. On the other, the Canon's "mastery" of alchemy ultimately inspires *rebellion* on the part of his follower:

> And whan this Chanoun saw it wolde not bee,
> But his Yeman wolde telle his privetee,
> He fledde awey, for verray sorwe and shame.   (8.700–2)

Both the Canon in the prologue and the canon in the tale are only capable of (materialist) "false governaunce" (8.989), not the (formalist) true governance of Cecilia. Thus, there can be no unified community of alchemists under the auspices of a master. No wonder that when their efforts inevitably fail, the Canon's Yeoman and his fellows devolve into bickering and mutual recrimination: "Whan that oure pot is broke, as I have sayd,/Every man chit and halt hym yvele apayd" (8.920–1). The masters of alchemy lead their followers away from truth and towards confusion, motivating these disciples either to betray others or, as in the case of the Canon's Yeoman, betray their leader. Again, *The Second Nun's Tale* depicts Cecilia as an illuminating authority for her adherents; *The Canon's Yeoman's Tale* depicts the adherents of alchemy as completely lacking authoritative guidance and, therefore, blind.

This materialist disorientation is true of the Canon's Yeoman's own speech. Scholars have noted the disorganized and highly repetitive nature of his discourse. Speaking of *pars secunda*, which he believes apocryphal, Peter Brown points to its "pointless repetition, almost as if it were written as an exercise in creating a Chaucerian tale out of the material available in the prologue and *prima pars*."[28] Patterson is more emphatic, detecting an aimlessness that runs through both prologue and tale: "The Prologue keeps promising to arrive at the Tale – 'Passe over this; I go my tale unto' (*CYT* 898) – but keeps inserting more alchemical lore. And the Tale is constantly derailed by exclamatory interruptions, and then when told turns out to be not a formally organized narrative, with beginning, middle, and end, but a paratactic concatenation of one virtually identical trick after another, a series that could go on forever."[29] The Canon's Yeoman's discourse is thus perfectly consonant with alchemy; what is true of his prologue and tale is also true of alchemists, "For evere we lakken oure conclusioun" (8.672). Both the Yeoman's speech on alchemy and alchemy itself are labyrinthine and inconclusive discourses.

Indeed, in the first part of his tale, when he attempts to describe alchemical science, the Yeoman admits as much:

> There is also ful many another thyng
> That is unto our craft apertenyng.
> Though I by ordre hem nat reherce kan,
> By cause that I am a lewed man,
> Yet wol I telle hem as they come to mynde,
> Thogh I ne kan nat sette hem in hir kynde.   (8.784–9)

The treatment of alchemy has no formal outline upon which he or his audience can rely. Rather than providing a meticulous analysis of his subject, the Canon's Yeoman will just address topics as they come to his mind. As a result of this aimless presentation, forgetting details is always possible: "Yet forgat I to maken rehersaille" (8.852). When it seems that his précis of alchemy is over ("Passe over this; I go my tale unto" [8.898]), seventy-four lines still separate us from *pars secunda* and introduction to the false "chanoun of religioun" (8.972). Just twenty lines into his tale, the Canon's Yeoman digresses for another twenty to reassure "worshipful chanons religious" (8.992) that he is not slandering all of them.

The juxtaposition of the Second Nun and the Canon's Yeoman in the final movement of *The Canterbury Tales* thus replays the formal order/material chaos binary that we have witnessed throughout the sequence, within and between individual tales. However, as proposed in the introduction to this chapter, Chaucer also intercalates a series of ramified terms in anticipation of the Manciple's and Parson's prologues and tales. It is, therefore, significant that Cecilia is associated with purposeful poetry while alchemy is associated with its precise opposite: aimless philosophy. The association of Cecilia and Christian poetry is established first in *The Second Nun's Prologue*. In her invocation to Mary, the Second Nun mentions the singing that fills heaven: "Be myn advocate in that heighe place/Thereas withouten ende is songe 'Osanne'" (8.68–9). Heaven for the Second Nun is a place of poetry. Cecilia herself, we are told, accompanies with song the music that is playing on her wedding day:

> And whil the organs maden melodie,
> To God alone in herte thus sang she:
> "O Lord, my soule and eek my body gye
> Unwemmed, lest that I confounded be."   (8.134–7)

The Second Nun's use of poetry to relate a narrative about a holy Christian martyr follows the example supplied by Cecilia's holy song: *The Second Nun's Tale* itself provides an instance of *sacred* verse that is immune to the charge that poetry is aimless matter, dealing merely in lies or pleasure without a higher purpose. Just as Cecilia formalizes her previously aimless pagan converts, orienting them towards God, the Second Nun formalizes the aimless matter of poetry, orienting it towards God. And yet, in the final movement of *The Canterbury Tales*, there still remains some tension between *The Second Nun's Tale* and the Parson's prologue and tale, despite the orientation of both towards the divine.[30] Though I will address the Parson in more detail below, it is important to keep in mind that the elevated rhyme royal stanzas of the Second Nun would still be degraded for the Parson, who eschews all "rym" in favour of a "mirye tale in prose" (10.44–6).[31] The shift from the Second Nun to the Parson is also a shift, I suggest, from the materiality of feminine poetry to the formality of masculine prose.

But even before we encounter the Parson's more radical formalism, *The Canon's Yeoman's Tale* transfers our focus from poetry to its traditional rival, philosophy. Alchemy is thus called "philosophy" or alchemists are called "philosophers" twelve times by the Canon's Yeoman, at lines 837, 862, 1058, 1122, 1139, 1373, 1394, 1427, 1434, 1444, 1464, and 1473. I disagree, therefore, with the interpretive tradition that understands alchemy in the tale as a figure for poetry, thereby sidestepping its clear association with philosophy and, in the concluding passages of the tale, with none other than the arch-philosopher, Plato himself.[32] The inversion of *The Second Nun's Tale* by *The Canon's Yeoman's Tale* includes the opposition of poetry and philosophy. But alchemical philosophy in *The Canon's Yeoman's Tale* is a resolutely worldly, not an otherworldly, pursuit, attractive to those who aspire to material, not spiritual, reward. Even the spiritual vocation of the priest in the tale is perverted by the temptations of this science: "O sely preest! O sely innocent!/With coveitise anon thou shalt be blent!" (8.1076–7). The would-be alchemist, according to the Canon's Yeoman, is not oriented towards God but instead risks making God "his adversarie" (8.1476). The shadowy "philosophres fader," as the Canon's Yeoman informs us at line 8.1434, is the legendary Hermes Trismegistus, of pre-Christian Egyptian and Greek origin. That Chaucer should relate secular philosophy to "Hermes" anticipates his association of secular poetry with "Phebus" in *The Manciple's Tale*, the former's older brother in the classical pantheon

We should also consider alchemy's association with Plato. Plato is notorious for denigrating poetry as a vain enterprise – a stance he shares with the Parson and one that is adopted, as we have seen, by Lady Philosophy in the *Boece*. In *The Canon's Yeoman's Tale*, however, it is philosophy that is denigrated as vain and, remarkably, Plato is represented as a master of this inane science. This reversal helps us make sense of his otherwise puzzling appearance towards the end of *The Canon's Yeoman's Tale*. The Canon's Yeoman tells of a disciple of Plato who, in a dialogue recorded in the "book Senior" (8.1450), requests that his master clarify his terms when identifying the alchemical "philosopher's stone":

> "Telle me the name of the privee stoon."
> And Plato answerde unto hym anoon,
> "Take the stoon that Titanos men name."
> "Which is that?" quod he. "Magnasia is the same,"
> Seyde Plato. "Ye, sire, and is it thus?
> This is *ignotum per ignocius*."   (8.1452–7)

Though she observes that Plato is often associated with alchemical teaching, Dorothee Finkelstein also notes that in the *Senior Zadith filius Hamuel*, it is Solomon and a sage who are the interlocutors.[33] Chaucer's substitution ensures that the classical philosopher who repudiates poetry because of its lack of truth is represented as a philosophical master entirely unwilling to reveal the truth. Plato, unlike Cecilia, refuses to enlighten his disciple, explaining obscure by more obscure, and is thus yet another bad teacher of alchemy in a tale that has "false governance" as its primary theme.[34] Indeed, the problematic and obscure instruction of alchemical philosophers, such as Plato, is referenced in an earlier passage:

> Philosophres speken so mystily
> In this craft that men kan nat come thereby,
> For any wit that men han now-a-dayes.   (8.1394–6)

Plato, likewise, will no more initiate his disciple into the "misty" secrets of alchemical philosophy, that "elvysshe craft" (8.751), than the elf queen will guide the aimless Thopas's approach to Fairy Land.[35]

There is more evidence that the preeminent alchemical authorities simply will not guide their adherents in *The Canon's Yeoman's Tale*. The Canon's Yeoman cites Arnaldus of Villanova, the author of the *Rosarium philosophorum*, who claims in an earlier passage:

> "Lat no man bisye hym this art for to seche,
> But if that he th'entencioun and speche
> Of philosophres understonde kan;
> And if he do, he is a lewed man.
> For this science and this konnyng," quod he,
> Is of the secree of secretes, pardee."   (8.1442–7)

Let us compare this passage to the original, which Edgar Duncan notes is not from the *Rosarium*, as the Yeoman claims at line 8.1429, but from Arnaldus's *De secretis nature*: "Let no one, therefore, come to this science until he first have heard logic, afterwards philosophy, and know causes and natures of things and of the elements. Otherwise he would fatigue his soul and body in vain."[36] The original version of Arnaldus's claim straightforwardly indicates that the disciple of alchemy requires preparatory knowledge of a scholastic type, starting with logic and moving to Aristotelian etiology. But the Canon's Yeoman's version of Arnaldus's statement appears circular, especially if we construe "philosophres" at line 8.1444 as "alchemists," the usual meaning of the term in this tale. Arnaldus is thus made to imply that the only ones who should pursue alchemical philosophy are those who *already know* the "intention and speech" of alchemical philosophers. But what else is required to be an alchemist?

The suggestion, once more, is that alchemy is a discipline that cannot be taught. According to Arnaldus in *The Canon's Yeoman's Tale*, one does not become an alchemist; either one knows this science or one does not. This fact utterly precludes the disciple of alchemy, such as the Yeoman, from receiving any positive guidance whatsoever: "Ye been as boold as is Bayard the blynde,/That blondreth forth and peril casteth noon" (8.1413–14), he admits. The student of alchemy is always blundering in the dark, unable to access an intrinsically hermetic doctrine. Unlike Christianity, which Cecilia so adroitly imparts, alchemy can have no true teachers. As the Canon's Yeoman's Plato concludes:

> The philosophres sworn were everychoon
> That they sholden discovere it unto noon
> Ne in no book it write in no manere.
> For unto Crist it is so lief and deere
> That he wol nat that it discovered bee,
> But where it liketh to his deitee
> Men for t'enspire, and eek for to deffende
> Whom that hym liketh; lo this is the ende.   (8.1464–71)

The alchemical philosophers have sworn not to reveal the secrets of their doctrine to anyone. Alchemy is thus a vain science, and the mystery of transmutation can only be revealed by divine *fiat*: According to Sisk, alchemy "is part of 'Goddes pryvetee' – it is one of the mysteries of the faith that modern practitioners must trust in but cannot understand without divine revelation."[37] One cannot *learn* alchemy from human authorities – it is only ever revealed. The Canon's Yeoman's chaotic presentation of his case ultimately reveals the point of his indictment of alchemy: Even if the science is theoretically valid, its masters are either fraudulent or unwilling to impart its secrets. And if Christ himself will supply no revelation, alchemical philosophy must remain, as I have argued from the outset, a worldly, vain, and unauthorized doctrine.

The Aristotelian Clerk, "That unto logyk hadde long ago" (1.286), supplies an edifying contrast to the Canon's Yeoman as he is also ostensibly a disciple of secular philosophy. Chaucer makes it clear, however, that the Clerk's devotion to philosophy has nothing to do with the vain pursuit of wealth: "But al be that he was a philosophre,/Yet hadde he but litel gold in cofre" (1.297–8). The Clerk is no alchemical philosopher eager for lucre; his concern, rather, is moral virtue: "Sownynge in moral vertu was his speche" (1.307). Instead of devoting himself to material acquisitiveness, the Clerk spends all the money he receives from friends on books, while praying for the souls of his benefactors: "And bisily gan for the soules preye/Of hem that yaf him wherewith to scoleye" (1.301–2). The Clerk is as "busy" in his service of others as is Cecilia. In another correspondence to Fragment 8, pedagogy is explicitly an element of the Clerk's portrait. Much like Valerian and Tiburce, therefore, he is both a devoted student and a master: "And gladly wolde he lerne and gladly teche" (1.308). Alchemy, recall, is neither successfully taught nor learned. And in contrast to the needless multiplication of terms so characteristic of alchemical philosophy, Chaucer says of the Clerk: "Noght o word spak he moore than was neede,/And that was seyd in *forme* and reverence/And short and quyk and ful of hy sentence" (1.304–5). Those who pursue alchemy are worldly philosophers whose discourse is materially chaotic and oriented to no higher purpose; the Clerk's philosophical discourse, contrariwise, is formally regulated and oriented towards a moral cause. The Clerk in the *General Prologue* does to secular philosophy, in other words, what the Second Nun does to secular poetry and what Cecilia does to secular Romans: He formalizes it. This is exactly what the alchemists of the Canon's Yeoman's prologue and tale cannot do either to worthless lead or to their worthless discourse.[38]

While *The Second Nun's Tale* represents poetry as sacred, *The Canon's Yeoman's Tale* represents philosophy, poetry's adversary in Book 10 of Plato's *Republic*, as involuted, misleading, and dangerous. Reversing the longstanding association of philosophy with formal purposefulness and poetry with material aimlessness, in Fragment 8, philosophy is associated with aimlessness and poetry with purposefulness. The former has no reliable authorities; the latter has the most reliable authorities. But the Second Nun's opposition to secular philosophy is in place even before the Canon's Yeoman reveals the futility of learning alchemical lore. In her debate with Almachius, Cecilia humiliates the Roman judge by exposing the falsity of his doctrine. Almachius, she asserts, thinks he perceives divine form where there is, in fact, only base matter: "That ilke stoon a god thow wolt it calle" (8.501). Almachius's earthbound materialism inverts Cecilia's formalism; the latter is able to look upward and observe "That mighty God is in hise hevenes hye" (8.508). Where Cecilia sees, Almachius is blind (8.501); where she is wise, he is foolish (8.495); where she is purposeful, he is vain (8.497); and where she shows the way to life, he can only bring death:

> "But thow mayst seyn thy princes han thee maked
> Ministre of deeth; for if thow speke of mo
> Thow liest, for thy power is ful naked."
> "Do wey thy boldnesse," seide Almachius tho,
> "And sacrifice to oure goddes, er thow go.
> I recche nat what wrong thow me profre,
> For I kan suffer it as a philosophre." (8.484–90)

The materialist Almachius identifies himself as a philosopher, anticipating the association of alchemy with materialist philosophy in *The Canon's Yeoman's Tale*. And if Cecilia's opponent is a secular philosopher, this means, of course, that the god that the Roman judge worships is nothing more than a philosopher's stone. Almachius's otiose devotion to his idol evokes the *ignis fatuus* of alchemical research. The philosopher's stone is, according to the Canon's Yeoman, also a fool's quest. Since God "wil nat that the philosophres nevene/How that a man shal come unto this stoon," he counsels his audience to "lete it goon" (8.1473–5). The antagonism of Cecilia towards Almachius simultaneously registers, I suggest, the opposition of *The Second Nun's Tale*, and the purposeful activity it represents, to the aimless materialism of secular philosophy.

But the materialism associated with alchemy can still be exacerbated. Chaucer will follow the Canon's Yeoman's account of unauthorized *philosophy* with the Manciple's account of unauthorized *poetry*. In short, the Second Nun orients poetry (solace) towards a transcendent cause, while alchemy is fundamentally *causeless* philosophy (sentence). The Manciple, as we will see, moves us to the very extreme of chaos by representing *poetry* (solace) without a final cause. It is thus fitting that the protagonist of his tale is a classical figure, Phoebus Apollo, the volatile god of music and the bow.

The Manciple's Prologue and Tale

We can grasp what Chaucer is doing with *The Manciple's Tale* by comparing it to the two previous tales. *The Second Nun's Tale* features an outstanding teacher who provides unswerving direction to her disciples. *The Canon's Yeoman's Tale*, by contrast, represents the disciples of alchemical philosophy as utterly directionless – blundering about in the dark. *The Manciple's Tale*, like the Canon's Yeoman's, is also directionless. But the tale evidences an even more radical materialism because it rebels against its own author. *The Manciple's Tale* is acephalic: The text (matter) consistently does the opposite of its author's intention (form).

I will now show that *The Manciple's Prologue* prepares us to read the forthcoming tale by establishing an absolute non-relation between form and matter – here denominated by their aliases, "earnest" and "game." The pilgrims have reached Harbledown, only two miles from their destination. At least one of their company, the inebriated Cook, sleeps on his horse, as the pace of the proceedings have slowed considerably. Harry thus strives to shake his charges out of their lethargy with a sharp exclamation: "Sires, what! Dun is in the myre!" (9.5). He turns to the somnolent Cook and demands a tale as "penaunce" (9.12). The Host then playfully inquires after the reasons for his lethargy:

> What eyleth thee to slepe by the morwe?
> Hastow had fleen al nyght, or artow dronke?
> Or hastow with some quene al nyght yswonke,
> So that thow mayst nat holden up thyn heed?   (9.16–19)

Perhaps, the Host suggests, the Cook has fleas or is drunk or is exhausted by nocturnal exertions with a woman of ill repute. The Cook begs pardon, asserting that he would "levere slepe/Than the beste galon wyn in Chepe" (9.23–4). The Manciple seconds the Cook's request but gratuitously supplies a blunt assessment of the latter's unfortunate condition:

> For in good feith, thy visage is ful pale,
> Thyne eyen daswen eek, as that me thynketh,
> And, wel I woot, thy breeth ful soure stynketh:
> That sheweth wel thou art nat wel disposed.
> Of me, certeyn, thou shal nat been yglosed.
> See how he ganeth, lo, this dronken wight,
> As though he wolde swolwe us anonright.
> Hold cloos thy mouth, man, by thy fader kyn!
> The devel of helle sette his foot therein!
> Thy cursed breeth infecte wole us alle.
> Fy, stynkyng swyn! Fy, foule moote thee falle!
> A, taketh heede, sires, of this lusty man.   (9.30–41)

While the Host had jestingly provided some alternatives besides inebriation to explain the Cook's condition, the Manciple refuses to equivocate. The Manciple's objective is to silence the Cook, whom he feels will not acquit himself well by his tale. Chaucer faces a similar challenge; he is bringing the Canterbury pilgrimage to a close and must find the appropriate way to end the tale-telling competition. The Manciple's different strategies to silence the Cook are illuminating in this regard. The Manciple's first attempt to halt the Cook's speech deploys the unvarnished truth. He will silence the Cook by providing an insultingly honest appraisal of his state: The Cook will not be "yglosed," the Manciple claims – he will eschew all fiction. The Manciple initially positions himself, therefore, as a Christian moralist, expanding on the penitential motif in the Host's playful address to the Cook.[39] In place of the bawdy jesting of the Host, the Manciple's speech about his fellow pilgrim amounts to a mini-homily that rails against drunkenness, and the account of the hapless Cook serves as a convenient *exemplum* for his congregation: "taketh heede, sires, of this lusty man." The Cook and, by extension, the sin of drunkenness threaten to swallow the congregation into the yawning maw of hell.[40] An infernal stench wafts out of his mouth and the devil, we are told, may set his foot therein. The Manciple transforms the Cook into a monstrous Leviathan, an image most appropriate for his sermon in miniature.

However truthful, the Manciple's words transform the *playful* teasing of the Host into *earnest* opprobrium. The sight of a grossly inebriated man would not overly trouble the proprietor of the Tabard Inn. The Manciple, however, appears outraged and excoriates the Cook: "Fy, stynkyng swyn!" Nevertheless, the Manciple does manage to silence the Cook, who is so enraged by the Manciple's words that he becomes incapable of speaking and falls off his horse: "he gan nodde faste/For lakke of speche, and doun the hors hym caste" (9.47). But his moralizing, however truthful and effective in the short term, is nevertheless dangerous for him, as the Host indicates:

> But yet, Manciple, in feith thou art to nyce,
> Thus openly to repreve hym of his vice.
> Another day he wole, peraventure,
> Reclayme thee and brynge thee to lure;
> I meene, he speke wol of smale thynges,
> As for to pynchen at thy rekenynges,
> That were nat honest, if it cam to preef.   (9.69–75)

The Host strongly implies that the moralistic tone that the Manciple has adopted makes him vulnerable to reprisals. The vicious should not reprove others for their vices, the Host says, echoing the Reeve's citation of Matthew 7:3. We have witnessed repeatedly the self-destructiveness of *ad hominem* rhetoric in *The Canterbury Tales,* and the Manciple rapidly absorbs the Host's admonition. Unlike Cecilia, who is willing to sacrifice her life for truth in her confrontation with Almachius, the Manciple fears the consequences of his veracity. He immediately revises his strategy for silencing the tottering Cook, giving him even more wine to drink. The *seriousness* of his moralizing is transformed into *playful* japing, as the Manciple describes his action to Harry: "And right anon ye shul seen a good jape" (9.84). Upon imbibing, the Cook is indeed appeased, and the Host celebrates the reversal of rancour "t'acord and love" (9.98) with an acerbic prayer to Bacchus:

> O Bacus, yblessed be thy name,
> That so kanst turnen ernest into game!
> Worshipe and thank be to thy deitee!   (9.99–101)

The Manciple does precisely the opposite of what his sermon on drunkenness asserted: He gives the Cook more alcohol to imbibe. It is typical in scholarship on the tale to ascribe this about-face to the Manciple's cynicism and pragmatism. Again, this psychological reading must be avoided if we are to understand his tale. Instead, we should consider this inconsistency according to the logical terms deployed throughout my analysis. The Manciple's *formally earnest* moralizing is totally detached from his *material game*: Form is not related to matter *or* earnest is not related to game. We must read *The Manciple's Tale* according to this materialist logic.

It is customary to view *The Manciple's Tale* as internally inconsistent and its narrator as cynically evasive. Jamie Fumo describes the modern scholarly consensus on the tale as follows: "Critics have observed that nihilistic self-contradiction is a literary technique peculiar to the *Manciple's Tale*, in its verbose counsel of silence, its shift from approval to condemnation of the crow, and its patent refutation (in the crow's experience) of the Manciple's claim that plain, blunt speech is best."[41] Its tendency towards self-contradiction has prompted scholars to view *The Manciple's Tale* as representing language in general and poetry in particular at its most degraded. In the influential assessment of Donald Howard, "the *Manciple's Tale* lets language itself fall beneath corrupt human nature."[42] According to Patterson, therefore, "the Manciple prepares for the Parson not just by rehearsing one of the fables the Parson is going to reject but by casting doubt upon the whole poetic enterprise."[43] With Phebus's destruction of his musical instruments, then, we are implicitly counseled by Chaucer to leave poetic language behind and embrace the penitential prose of the Parson.

However, the notion that Chaucer is inviting us to *decide* on the status of either poetry or prose is one that I must reject. Rather, the final four tales of the sequence identify four coordinates that are carefully interrelated according to a logic Chaucer has deployed throughout *The Canterbury Tales*. That the Host should comprehend the Manciple's palliative offering to the Cook according to the classical pantheon indicates precisely how the Manciple's prologue and tale are responding to the Second Nun and Canon's Yeoman and looking forward to the Parson. As I argued above, the Second Nun's sacred poetry is equivalent to "Christian solace" or authorized verse, while alchemy is equivalent to "secular sentence" or unauthorized philosophy. The Parson's Christian prose, as we will see, is language that is in a state of absolute submission to authority. But the Host codes as "secular solace" or "classical game" the Manciple's bacchanalian ploy to quiet the Cook: "O Bacus, yblessed be thy name,/That so kanst turnen ernest into game!" (9.99–100). *The Manciple's Tale*, as the prologue adumbrates, will represent secular poetry as language that consistently transforms earnest truth into playful fiction.[44]

The history of commentary on *The Manciple's Tale* bears out how tempting it is to decide in favour of the Parson's formalist order and reject the Manciple's materialist chaos.[45] But, as I have argued from the outset, this is exactly the kind of decision that we must forestall if we are to read *The Canterbury Tales* charitably. It is worthy of note, I think, that Phebus himself comes to grief because he rashly decides. Let us turn, then, to *The Manciple's Tale* and consider how, in line with the prologue, it stages the non-relation of material game to the stability of earnest form. We should begin with the central character: While the Second Nun, a devotee of Mary, represents her protagonist as a Christian poet, the Manciple, a devotee of Bacchus, makes his protagonist the classical god of poetry:

> Pleyen he koude on every mynstralcie,
> And syngen that it was a melodie
> To heeren of his cleere voys the soun.   (9.113–15)

Even Phebus's pet crow is an outstanding singer, able to "countrefete the speche of every man" (9.134); he is a better melodist than any nightingale "by an hundred thousand deel" (9.136). But Phebus and his crow, borrowed as they are from Ovid, are secular poets whose singing, unlike Cecilia's, is not oriented towards God – it is playful solace untrammelled by earnest sentence. The Manciple's Phebus, nevertheless, bears little resemblance to the classical prototype, and the distance between the two is registered by the suspiciously deflationary account with which the tale begins:

> Whan Phebus dwelled here in the erthe adoun,
> As olde books maken mencioun,
> He was the mooste lusty bachiler
> In al this world, and eek the beste archer.
> He slow Phitoun, the serpent, as he lay
> Slepynge agayn the sonne upon a day;
> And many another noble worthy dede
> He with his bowe wroghte, as men may rede.   (9.105–12)

It is, of course, ridiculous to transform divine Apollo into the "lustiest bachelor" in the world, as hackneyed a description of a young knight-errant as is possible.[46] The fact that Phebus is married makes the term "bachelor" doubly inappropriate. Nor is it particularly impressive that chief among his "noble deeds" is killing a snake during a halcyon and sun-kissed slumber, though this act does anticipate the murderous sneak attack on his wife during an ignoble fit of pique. *The Manciple's Tale*'s treatment of Phebus destabilizes his authority, nowhere more dramatically than when he destroys his musical instruments and his bow and arrows during a childish tantrum. The tale's depiction of Phebus makes perfect sense: Secular poetry is language that defies all formal constraint; the secular poet, accordingly, is a figure radically lacking in authority. In a caricature of the incarnation, the divine Apollo is therefore brought from the heights of sublimity to "erthe adoun" in order to become the ridiculous Phebus.

Chaucer further emphasizes the secular poet's abject lack of authority by means of a charged classical allusion:

> Certes the kyng of Thebes, Amphioun,
> That with his syngyng walled that citee,
> Koude nevere syngen half so wel as hee.   (9.116–18)

The Manciple's passing mention of Amphion's role in constructing the walls of Thebes with his song is, of course, highly ambivalent. Whatever Phebus's musical skill, his singing is here associated with a classical city invariably linked to sexual, familial, and political disorder. Indeed, Phebus's own household is a disordered Thebes in miniature; instead of respecting the authority of the sovereign, Phebus's subjects, his wife and his crow, are either unfaithful or insolent.[47] As is repeatedly stressed, Phebus's wife prefers the embrace of a worthless wretch to the "flour of bachilrie" (9.125). Both irreverent subjects are introduced into the narrative in the same way: "Now hadde this Phebus in his hous a crowe" (9.130); "Now hadde this Phebus in his hous a wyf" (9.139). Amphion and Phebus, both secular poets, govern polities that will eventually implode on account of betrayal and violence. For all his "manhede and his governance" (9.158), therefore, Phebus cannot override the innately uncontrollable nature of his wife's desires. Masculine form cannot contain feminine matter. Chaucer anticipates in this way the relationship between the Manciple's authority and his own poetry; the latter too will prove innately uncontrollable.

The disorder of Thebes and the disorder of Phebus's household thus correlate to the utter disorder of the Manciple's narration. Just as Phebus's wife rebels against Phebus's authority, *The Manciple's Tale* rebels against the Manciple's authority. This is a fitting consequence for one who, according to the *General Prologue*, deceives his own masters: "And yet this Manciple sette hir aller cappe" (1.586). The Manciple's poetry takes on the materialist tendencies of its author. He claims in his tale on two occasions, moreover, that he is not "textueel" (9.235 and 316), indicating his ignorance of authoritative texts. *The Manciple's Tale* also gives us matter totally unconstrained by a final cause – matter that is uninformed by *authority*. The tale's relationship to the prologue is, therefore, extremely precise. In the prologue, the Manciple first earnestly castigates the Cook for his inebriation and then playfully gives him more to drink. He does the opposite of what he says. Likewise, in his tale, the Manciple will earnestly formulate an array of authorial positions, which his tale will playfully betray. The key to understanding

The Manciple's Tale, then, is acknowledging that it is out of control, that it cannot be governed. In this way, my reading inverts that of Fradenburg, who reads the tale as an obsessional script that is unable to imagine freedom from mastery: "[*The Manciple's Tale*] is unable to imagine a solution, unable to imagine an alternative freedom, because it is unable to imagine itself without the master – without the sovereign."[48] I disagree: The tale destroys any semblance of authority, beginning with its caricature of Apollo. As we will see, the tale does not just imagine chaotic freedom; it *enacts* chaotic freedom by destroying any relationship to authoritative truth.

We can perceive this disjunction between form and matter by examining in more detail the Manciple's lengthy digressions. Observing that Phebus has done all he can to please his wife, the Manciple anticipates her infidelity by remarking:

> But God it woot, ther may no man embrace
> As to destreyne a thyng which that nature
> Hath natureelly set in a creature.   (9.160–2)

The lines that follow attempt to demonstrate this thesis by arguing that a bird will always desire liberty from its cage, no matter how luxurious its lifestyle or what "deyntees" (9.166) it is fed; that a cat will prefer a mouse to "every deyntee that is in that hous" (9.179); and that a she-wolf will desire the least reputable partner when it comes time to mate. But this last example is highly problematic:

> A she-wolf hath also a vileyns kynde.
> The lewedeste wolf that she may fynde,
> Or leest of reputacioun, wol she take,
> In tyme whan hir lust to han a make.
> Alle thise ensamples speke I by thise men
> That been untrewe, and nothyng by wommen.
> For men han evere a likerous appetit
> On lower thyng to parfourne hire delit
> Than on hire wyves, be they never so faire,
> Ne never so trewe, ne so debonaire.   (9.183–92)

We should recall that it was the inability of Phebus to constrain his wife's natural desires that inspired the entire digression on the irrepressibility of natural instincts in the first place. And yet the Manciple then insists that his examples of the irrepressibility of natural instincts have nothing to do with women but are only relevant to men. The

Manciple contradicts himself again when he informs us, in a clear echo of line 9.185, that Phebus's wife has fallen in with "a man of *litel reputacioun*/Nat worth to Phebus in comparisoun" (9.199–200). Phebus's wife thus conducts herself exactly as the she-wolf in the Manciple's example, despite his statement to the contrary.[49] As in the prologue, *The Manciple's Tale* earnestly posits the truth and then playfully betrays it.

The tale provides an even more striking instance of the transformation of earnest to game with the Manciple's digression on Plato and truthful speech, which contains a clear echo of the *General Prologue* (1.741–2):

> And so bifel, whan Phebus was absent,
> His wyf anon hath for hir lemman sent,
> Hir lemman? Certes, this is a knavyssh speche!
> Foryeveth it me, and that I yow biseche.
> The wise Plato seith, as ye may rede,
> The word moot need accorde with the dede.
> If men shal telle proprely a thyng,
> The word moot cosyn be to the werkyng.
> I am a boystous man, right thus seye I:
> Ther nys no difference, trewely,
> Bitwixe a wyf that is of heigh degree,
> If of hyr body dishonest she bee,
> And a povre wenche, oother than this –
> If it so be they werke bothe amys –
> But that the gentile, in estaat above,
> She shal be cleped his lady, as in love;
> And for that oother is a povre womman,
> She shal be cleped his wenche or his lemman.
> And God it woot, myn owene deere brother,
> Men leyn that oon as lowe as lith that oother.
> Right so bitwixe a titlelees tiraunt
> And an outlawe or a theef erraunt,
> The same I seye: there is no difference.   (9.203–25)

The Manciple here reveals what it means for him to tell a tale "proprely." The lengthy digression on Plato and plain speech (9.207–37) are the equivalent in *The Manciple's Tale* of his earnest sermon on drunkenness from his prologue. The reference to Plato, as in the *General Prologue*, asserts a commitment to truth without obfuscation: To be a Platonist is to be a formalist. The Manciple claims, therefore, to reject arbitrary verbal distinctions that in any way obscure their objective correlate. He will no more accept such linguistic proliferation than he will "gloss" (9.34) the drunken Cook in the prologue. In line with his Platonic commitments, the Manciple appears to dismiss here exactly the obfuscations generated by poetic equivocality – poetry has many, potentially deceptive, ways to say the same thing. Like Plato, he insists that he is a speaker concerned only with formal univocality, not material equivocality.

The Manciple's digression on plain-speaking finds its inspiration in his consideration of the arbitrariness of class markers.[50] Thus, when the Manciple describes the wife's lover as her "lemman," he immediately apologizes: "Certes, this is knavyssh speche!/Foryeveth it me, and that I yow b´seche" (9.205–6). The word, "lemman," is apparently too freighted with classist implications for the narrator. If there is no difference between a higher-class "lady" and a lower-class "lemman" when they conduct themselves identically, then both terms just distort their referents. The word must accord with the deed: There ought to be a necessary relation, rather than contingent non-relation, between language and reality. But here the Manciple's explicit disavowal of class difference implicitly *relies* on class difference, with his use of the adjective "knavyssh" – meaning "churlish" or "lowborn."[51] It is as if the Manciple is saying, "It is most churlish of me to identify someone as a churl!" But this means that the Manciple's commitment to truthful language devoid of class distinctions is betrayed as soon as it is expressed. *The Manciple's Tale* immediately transforms earnest truthfulness into playful deceptiveness. Analogously, in the very midst of his rejection of distortive class gradations, the Manciple justifies his Platonic attitude by referring to himself with an adjective inflected by class: "I am a *boystous* man" (9.211) – meaning "rude" or "unrefined." Since he is a "rude," and not "refined," man, the Manciple states, he will ignore arbitrary distinctions between "rude" and "refined"! If Platonic plain-speaking means rejecting the language of class difference, the Manciple avows plain-speaking in theory while disavowing it in practice. This point is reinforced by the fact that after begging forgiveness for his use of "lemman" and spending thirty lines on the contingency of class difference, the Manciple immediately uses the classist term *again* in an identical fashion: "Whan Phebus wyf had sent for hir lemman" (9.238). The earnest avowal of Platonic truth, which has as its corollary the rejection of arbitrary class gradations, is once more playfully betrayed by the Manciple's language.

Furthermore, it should not escape notice that the first digression on natural inclinations is incompatible with the second digression on class difference. The Manciple's point in his first digression is that it is impossible to constrain natural tendencies. But these natural tendencies lead us to prefer the *lower* to the *higher*. The bird would prefer to reside in a forest that is "rude and cold" (9.170) rather than in its gilded cage. It would prefer to eat "wormes and swich wrecchednesse" (9.171) to the "deyntees" (9.166) of captivity. The cat likewise will eschew "every deyntee" (9.179) of its house to go chase after a mouse. When it is time to mate, the she-wolf, on account of her "vileyns kynde" (9.183), will seek "The lewedeste wolf that she may fynde,/Or leest of reputacioun" (9.184–5). Finally, men prefer "On lower thyng to parfourne hire delit" (9.190), even though their lovers be "never so faire,/Ne never so trewe, ne so debonaire" (9.191–2) as their wives. It is clear that these descriptions are rife with class markers. Animals prefer what is rude, lewd, and wretched to what is refined, civilized, and dainty. For their sexual gratification, men prefer lower things to their debonair (literally "well-bred") wives. In contrast, as we see in the Manciple's second digression, the Platonist must avoid the ascription of class difference; class indicators are arbitrary and misrepresent the truth. If this is true of the human world, it must *a fortiori* be true of the animal world, where class gradations can only be a metaphorical importation. Are there really wolves of good reputation? Consequently, the Manciple's earnest rejection of class difference betrays his earnest insistence on the dominance of natural inclinations, and vice versa. In both cases, therefore, what is earnestly asserted becomes mere game.

It is in the crow's speech to Phebus that we see these contradictory positions represented simultaneously. At first blush, the crow seems to be the most radical Platonist in the tale. He reveals the infidelity of Phebus's wife to his master by singing with no equivocality whatsoever: "Cokkow, Cokkow, Cokkow!" (9.243). In the crow's song, then, it appears that we have finally located an absolute coincidence of word and deed. Indeed, a number of critics remark that the crow upholds the Manciple's ideal of speech. Richard Hazelton, for instance, states: "The plain-speaking, truth-telling narrator – 'if the sothe I shal sayn' (l. 143), 'if men shal telle proprely a thyng' (1. 209) – in a very real sense creates the plain-speaking, truth-telling crow in his own image."[52] The crow himself swears to Phebus that his insulting language is accurate: "By God ... I synge nat amys" (9.248). However, if plain speech indeed ignores class, as the Manciple asserts, it is surprising to witness the terms the crow uses to compare Phebus and his rival:

> "Phebus," quod he, "for al thy worthynesse,
> For al thy beautee and thy gentilesse,

> For al thy song and al thy mynstralcye,
> For al thy waityng, blered is thyn ye
> With oon of litel reputacioun,
> Noght worth to thee, as in comparisoun,
> The montance of a gnat, so moote I thryve!
> For on thy bed thy wyf I saugh hym swyve."   (9.249–56)

The crow remarks upon Phebus's great "worthynesse" and his "gentilesse," both clear indicators of his superior social status. By comparison, in an obvious echo of the Manciple's comments on the she-wolf's natural tendencies, the adulterous lover has but a "litel reputacioun" in comparison to Phebus. Consequently, it seems that the straight-talking crow does, in fact, rely on class difference to describe the vast social inferiority of the wife's lover, exactly what a Platonist is supposed to avoid. Nonetheless, the crow *refuses* to use honorifics when addressing Phebus, obviously a social superior. By using the familiar form of the second-person pronoun and brazenly inappropriate diction, the crow ignores linguistic markers of class difference in his speech to his master.[53] But he deploys precisely those markers to compare Phebus and the wife's lover. The crow thus earnestly affirms *both* the Manciple's position on natural inclinations *and* his position on the arbitrariness class distinctions. But these standpoints, as I have just argued, are contradictory. To affirm earnestly both positions, therefore, is also to betray playfully both positions. In this respect, it is pertinent that the crow is able to "countrefete the speche of every man" when "he sholde *telle a tale* (9.134–5). The only tale the crow tells is an analogue of *The Manciple's Tale*. Both the Manciple and the crow deny what they affirm and affirm what they deny.

Phebus's response to murdering his wife also demonstrates the conversion of earnest into game. Though the crow has demonstrated his wife's infidelity with the help of "sadde tokenes" (9.258), Phebus miraculously transforms her into a woman "so *sad* and eek so trewe" (9.275). The honest crow, by contrast, is transformed into a "traitour" (9.271) and a "false theef" (9.292); his enraged master goes on to assert: "'I wol thee quite anon thy false tale'" (9.293). The god, therefore, betrays his earlier position. Though he first believes his pet, Phebus ultimately transforms the crow's formal truth into material deception, transforming in turn the wife's material deception into formal truth. Phebus, exactly as the Manciple in the prologue, renders false what is true and renders true what is false. While the secular philosopher, like the alchemist, has no access to the truth, the secular poet, like Phebus, betrays the truth. Unauthorized philosophy is confused, blundering about in the dark; but unauthorized poetry is traitorous, rebelling against any stable truth. Secular philosophy has authorities, such as Plato, even if they refuse to provide any guidance. Secular poetry, however, doggedly undermines the very possibility of authority.

The conclusion to *The Manciple's Tale* furthers the project of dismantling the secular poet's formal authority. First, instead of insisting on plain-speaking, as before, the Manciple proposes a different moral:

> Lordynges, by this ensample I yow preye,
> Beth war, and taketh kep what that ye seye:
> Ne telleth nevere no man in youre lyf
> How that another man hath dight his wyf;
> He wol yow haten mortally, certeyn.
> Daun Salomon, as wise clerkes seyn,
> Techeth a man to kepen his tonge weel.   (9.309–15)

Obviously, the Manciple's second moral contradicts his earlier insistence on the correspondence of words and deeds. Instead, we are supposed to learn from the example of the crow that truthfulness is not the best policy; the best policy is verbal restraint, especially where adultery is concerned. Thus, just as the Manciple's Platonism betrays his insistence on the hegemony of natural inclinations, the Manciple's moralizing on verbal restraint betrays his Platonism. I can go further: The Manciple's advice to keep silent is betrayed by the first digression on the irrepressibility of natural desires. There we are told, recall, that a bird in a cage always desires freedom *above all else*. But Phebus's caged crow attains this coveted objective by *speaking*, and by speaking about adultery: that is, "How that another man hath dight his wyf." But the Manciple makes the crow serve as an example of the *dangers* of speaking: "Lordynges, by this ensample I yow preye,/Beth war, and taketh kep what that ye seye." According to the Manciple's first digression, however, the crow gets exactly what he wants, and he does so by refusing to keep silent.[54] The circuit of betrayals is complete: Every authorial position earnestly assumed by the Manciple is, therefore, betrayed by another authorial position earnestly assumed by the Manciple.[55] *The Manciple's Tale* is a serpent devouring its own tail.

It is also the case that every authorial position assumed by the Manciple betrays *itself*. Before his exposition has even concluded, the Manciple denies the relevance to women of his digression on natural inclinations even though it obviously applies to Phebus's wife: "Alle this ensamples speke I by thise men/That been untrewe, and nothyng by wommen" (9.187–8). The Manciple's second digression on the unreliability of linguistic class markers betrays itself, as discussed above, on account of his claim to be a "boystous man" (9.211). He rudely urges us to ignore class distinctions between rude and refined. Finally, the Manciple notoriously supports his moral about the need for verbal restraint by appealing to the authority of his mother. But his mother's exhortation to speak as little as possible is extraordinarily prolix, taking up forty-four lines (9.318–62) when only one is really needed.[56] Her entire speech merely varies a single commandment: "keep wel thy tonge" (9.319, 333, and 362), which itself only restates verbatim the Manciple's own advice: Daun Salomon, as wise clerkes seyn,/Techeth a man *to kepen his tonge weel* (9.314–15). Now the moral the Manciple posits is one that is most fitting for a tale in which no one can speak without betraying himself. But the Manciple's mother falls into a performative contradiction, verbosely advising that one should never be verbose – needlessly declaiming that one should never needlessly declaim. Not only does the Manciple's mother uselessly repeat the Manciple's moral, she cites the same authority: "Reed Salomon, so wys and honurable" (9.344).[57] The Manciple's citation of his mother's advice thus betrays its own intention, exactly as do his first two authorial interventions. No authoritative standpoint can survive the collapse of earnest into game, form into matter. For Peter Travis, "the tale is an utterance that cannot be trusted by any wary reader: whatever its narrator says is said only that it may be gainsaid."[58] But this is true of all the speakers in the tale: The Manciple, the crow, Phebus, and the Manciple's mother each somehow betray their own position.

Needless to say, needlessly citing one's own mother in support of any argument does not do much to advance anyone's authority. *The Manciple's Tale* begins by dismantling the authority of Phebus and concludes by dismantling what is left of the authority of the Manciple. The Manciple, therefore, is much like a king of Thebes, as the allusion to Amphion at the beginning of his tale implies. He oversees only chaos. But this, for Chaucer, is the condition of the secular poet, such as Ovid, who supplies Chaucer with the ultimate source of *The Manciple's Tale*. Secular poetry is a domain of bacchanalian play that betrays all formal authority, even that of its own author. When earnest becomes game, truth becomes falsehood, and order becomes chaos. But if poetry without an authoritative final cause is rebelliously open, then prose with an authoritative final cause is obediently closed. Following the Manciple, accordingly, we encounter a speaker whose control over his discourse is absolute.

The Parson's Prologue and Tale

The final sequence of *The Canterbury Tales* begins with Christian poetry and secular philosophy. It ends with secular poetry and Christian prose. We begin, therefore, with relative order followed by relative chaos. We conclude with absolute chaos followed by absolute order. In the place of the Manciple's anarchic materialism, the Parson will substitute a rigorous formalism. Two echoes in particular signal the close relationship between the two tales. The Manciple refuses to "yglose" the Cook's drunken state (9.34), and the Parson promises that he "wol nat glose" (10.45). The Manciple twice insists that he is not "textueel" (9.235 and 316). The Parson sincerely and humbly expresses an identical sentiment regarding his treatise on penitence:

> But nathelees, this meditacioun
> I putte it ay under correccioun
> Of clerkes, for I am nat textueel.   (10.55–7)

While the Manciple's ignorance of authority suggests the waywardness of his "boystous" poetics, the Parson's remark that his tale will supply only the "sentence" without ornamentation recalls Chaucer's words to the Host prior to *The Tale of Melibee*. Chaucer the pilgrim there promises to preserve the core "sentence" in his treatise on forgiveness, even if there are superficial differences between his version and its antecedents. The sententious prose of *Melibee,* therefore, follows the aimless poetry of *Thopas,* just as the sententious prose of *The Parson's Tale* follows the aimless poetry of *The Manciple's Tale.*

The dialogue between the Host and the Parson reiterates this distinction between formal earnestness and material game. I will begin by considering Harry's imperious speech:

> "Sire preest," quod he, "artow a vicary?
> Or arte a person? Sey sooth, by thy fey!
> Be what thou be, ne breke thou nat oure pley;
> For every man, save thou, hath told his tale.
> Unbokele and shewe us what is in thy male;
> For trewely, me thynketh by thy cheere
> Thou sholdest knytte up wel a greet mateere.
> Telle us a fable anon, for cokkes bones!"   (10.22–9)

Harry does not want the "play" of the pilgrims interrupted and, accordingly, demands "a fable" from the Parson in a manner that echoes the

Pardoner's seemingly obscene demand that the Host "Unbokele anon thy purs" (6.945). At the same time, he desires from the Parson something that will "knytte up" the "greet mateere" of the pilgrimage. The Host's directive to the Parson is thus highly ambivalent: The latter may continue the *play* (materialism) or impose a *closural* form on the matter of the tale telling (formalism). The alternatives the Host supplies to the Parson in fact resonate with the two basic ways that his tale has been understood by modern Chaucerian scholarship. Siegfried Wenzel's review of critical approaches to the tale at the turn of the millennium provides a sharp summary of the opposing camps:

> To explain the difference, to find a way that would place The Parson's Tale in a meaningful relation to *The Canterbury Tales* as a whole, has been a major task of Chaucer criticism over the last century, and all indications are that it will remain so. In the attempt to relate The Parson's Tale to the other tales and the pilgrimage framework and to reconcile its obvious differences in tone, style, and subject matter, the reader has, I think, two basic options: one is to read The Parson's Tale as one among twenty-four tales in which Chaucer has a wide variety of characters tell tales that, to say the least, fit their narrators' professions and personal characteristics, and may do so in an ironic vein; the other is to read The Parson's Tale as in some fashion set apart. I will call the former view *perspectivist* and the latter *teleological*, that is, having an orientation toward a goal.[59]

For proponents of the "perspectivist" view, *The Parson's Tale* is just one element in the "pley" that the Host has orchestrated and does not possess any transcendent authority. In the words of Laurie A. Finke, "Paradoxically, the open-ended nature of Chaucer's narrative underscores the significance of the tales' diversity. It reminds us that the ethical aesthetic, and rhetorical values of the whole work ought to determine the significance of the Parson's Tale, not the reverse."[60] But for proponents of the "teleological" view, *The Parson's Tale* is the ultimate orientation of the tale-telling competition, and it provides the authoritative standard of meaning by means of which the preceding tales should be judged. Patterson thus concludes, "In sum, while the Parson has the last word he must wait until last to say it, and although the transcendence of his message is never in doubt he must wait until the imperfect and even immoral expressions of merely verbal art have been passed in review."[61] For the perspectivist reading of *The Parson's Tale*, *The Canterbury Tales* are dialogically open (materialism); for the teleological reading, *The Canterbury Tales* are authoritatively closed (formalism). In the final section of this chapter, therefore, I will investigate whether with *The Parson's Tale* and Chaucer's *Retraction* 1) earnest intent authoritatively subordinates play; or 2) the game remains open – unauthorized; or 3) instead of earnest closure or playful openness, we encounter again the authoritative revocation of authority that, for Chaucer, signals love.

Whatever Chaucer's intentions for the final movement of *The Canterbury Tales*, which I will consider below, there can be no doubt that the Parson's response to the Host demonstrates his unequivocal formalism:

> Thou getest fable noon ytold for me,
> For Paul, that writeth unto Thymothee,
> Repreveth hem that weyven soothfastnesse
> And tellen fables and swich wrecchednesse.
> Why sholde I sowen draf out of my fest,
> Whan I may sowen whete, if that me lest?
> For which I seye, if that yow list to here
> Moralitee and vertuous mateere.   (10.31–8)

The citation of Paul's letter to Timothy recalls the Pardoner – both a preacher and a fabulist. But whereas the Pardoner has no problem alternating between sentence (form) and solace (matter), the Parson will have nothing to do with such "wrecchednesse." The above passage also echoes the Nun's Priest's instruction to his audience: take the fruit and leave the chaff. But while the Nun's Priest's frankly allocates space for radical interpretive freedom, the Parson narrows that avenue. The image of wheat and chaff within a clenched fist suggests the Parson's tight authorial control over his material. We will encounter nothing but morality and virtuous matter within his tale, purified of such equivocal pollutants as fables and poetry. The Parson's formal rigour corresponds to the upward trajectory he initiates. In *The Manciple's Tale*, language is purposeless; for the Parson, it has the highest possible purpose – the confession of our sins in preparation for salvation. We move, therefore, between two cities; instead of the Theban disorder encountered in *The Manciple's Tale*, the Parson will show the way to the source of all order: the "Jerusalem celestial" (10.51).

In accordance with the Host's directive to be "fructuous" (10.71), and as opposed to the barren Pardoner, the Parson lectures his audience on the tree of penitence (10.111), the fruit of which is salvation:

> Manye been the ways espirituels that leden folk to oure Lord Jhesu Crist
> and to the regne of glorie. Of which weyes there is a ful noble wey and a

> ful convenable which may nat fayle to man ne to womman that thurgh
> synne hath mysgoon from the righte wey of Jerusalem celestial; and this
> wey is cleped Penitence. (10.78–9)

The movement from sin to heaven via penitence is the movement from
the crooked path to the noble path and from chaos to order. This treatise on order, analogously, is itself exceedingly well ordered. The last
tale thus surpasses the first tale in terms of its architectonic regularity.
The structure of the tale perfectly mirrors its penitential doctrine: that
is, it imposes virtuous form upon delinquent matter. For the Parson, as
for the Knight's Boethian God, every detail is planned out in advance.
At the start of his treatise, the Parson provides the main sections of his
entire treatise, promising to inform his audience:

> [W]hat is Penitence, and whennes it is cleped Penitence, and in how
> manye maneres been the acciouns or werkynges of Penitence, and how
> manye speces ther been of Penitence, and whiche thynges apertenen
> and bihoven to Penitence, and whiche thynges destourben Penitence.
> (10.81–2)

The Canon's Yeoman's disquisition on alchemy, we should recall,
was unplanned. He spoke of the nature of his science extemporaneously in a prologue and tale that appear to be Chaucer's own inven-
tions. By contrast, the form of the Parson's discourse is wholly predetermined – there is hardly a trace of contingency in his tale. All
that remains to the Parson once the general form of his discourse
on penitence has been established is to fill in the particular matter.
This is true also of the subsections of *The Parson's Tale*; each sub-
section begins by exhaustively anticipating the matter it will treat.
Finally, unlike the extemporaneous and disordered composition of
The Canon's Yeoman's Tale, the Parson acknowledges that his "medi-
tacioun" (10.55) relies on well-known sources, from which he takes
the "sentence" (10.58). This is not a discourse generated *ex nihilo*, but
one, like *The Second Nun's Tale*, that is authorized by its influential
antecedents: namely, Raymund of Pennaforte's *Summa de paenitentia*
and William Peraldus's double *Summa de vitiis et virtutibus* – known
through the redactions "Primo" and "Quoniam." According to Richard Newhauser, "The basis for Chaucer's penitential and moral theology in the *Parson's Tale*, thus, has a conservative foundation, for it
is derived from contextual sources which were roughly 150 years old
by the time he adopted them for this treatise."[62] The Parson will not
deviate from the formal orthodoxies of Christian doctrine; and if he

does, he expects that he "wol stonde to correccioun" (10.60). In this way, Chaucer counterposes the authorized prose of the Parson to the unauthorized discourse of alchemy and the unauthorized poetry of *The Manciple's Tale*.

Throughout his treatise, the Parson proceeds by means of careful and scholastic division of genus into species. The tree of penitence is, therefore, composed of the root of contrition, the leaves of confession, and the fruit of satisfaction (10.111–14). Contrition itself is understood in four ways: "what is Contricioun, and whiche been the causes that moeven a man to Contricioun, and how he sholde be contrite, and what Contricioun availeth to the soule" (10.127). The causes of contrition are themselves subdivided into six. The Parson then turns to confession, which is addressed in three ways: "Now shul ye understonde what is Confessioun, and whether it oghte nedes be doon or noon, and whiche thynges been covenable to verray Confessioun" (10.316). Having defined confession as the showing of sins to a priest, the Parson considers the topic of sin according to three subdivisions: "And forther over, it is necessarie to understonde whennes that synnes spryngen, and how they encreessen, and whiche they been" (10.320). This final subdivision leads the Parson to treat the distinction between venial and deadly sins, and the middle of *The Parson's Tale* is taken up by analysis of the latter. Strikingly, the seven deadly sins also constitute a tree, the negative correlate of the penitential tree: "Of the roote of thise sevene synnes, thanne, is Pride the general roote of alle harmes. For of the roote spryngen certein braunches [which are the six remaining deadly sins]. And everich of thise chief synnes hath his braunches and his twigges" (10.388–9). The treatment of each deadly sin is accompanied by consideration of its remedy.

The Parson completes his treatise by focusing on the fruit of the tree of penitence, satisfaction, which is achieved in two basic ways: "almesse and in bodily peyne" (10.1028). Both alms-giving and bodily pain are further subdivided. In line with his introductory plan, the Parson moves to consider next those things that disturb penitence: "drede, shame, hope, and wanhope, that is desperacion" (10.1056). He concludes his treatise with an account of the reward, or "fruyt" of penitence, which is the endless bliss of heaven (10.1076).

In its methodical ordering of its subject, *The Parson's Tale* not only orients its audience towards the divine, it also emulates the divine:

> And eek Job seith that in helle is noon ordre of rule. And al be it so that God hath creat alle thynges in right ordre, and no thyng withouten ordre, but alle thynges been ordeyned and nombred; yet, nathelees, they that

been dampned been nothyng in ordre, ne holden noon ordre, for the erthe ne shal bere hem no fruyt. (10.217–18)

For the Parson, God imposes an absolute order on creation; hell, by contrast, is the absence of any possible order. The relationship between divine form and hellish matter is identical to the relationship between virtue and vice:

For it is sooth that God, and resoun, and sensualitee, and the body of man been so ordeyned that everich of thise foure thynges sholde have lordship over that oother, as thus: God sholde have lordshipe over resoun, and resoun over sensualitee, and sensualitee over the body of man. But soothly, when man synneth, al this ordre or ordinaunce is turned up-so-doun. (10.260–2)

Sin overturns the formal ordinance of God in a replication of the Fall. Thus, the victory of the flesh over the reason of Adam, symbolized by the consumption of the fruit, results for the Parson in the degradation of humanity into "vile and corrupt *mateere*" (10.332). Precisely the opposite trajectory results from penitence, which leads to the fruit of heavenly bliss and the purification of the corrupted mortal body:

[T]here as the body of man, that whilom was foul and derk, is moore cleer than the sonne; ther as the body, that whilom was syk, freele, and fieble, and mortal, is inmortal, and so strong and so hool that ther may no thyng apeyren it. (10.1088)

The Parson's fructuous discourse links the fruitful tree of penitence to the fruit of eternal reward. This is the fruit that is forbidden to the sinner, just as the fruit of the knowledge of good and evil was forbidden to Adam and Eve. The tree of deadly sins, which leads to hell, is a reflex of the tree of Eden; it also inverts the tree of penitence, which leads to heaven. The Parson's meticulously *formulated* treatise aims to purify sinners of the taint of foul matter and lead them to the source of all ordination, even as it emulates that ordination. It aims for absolute linguistic clarity, just as it aims to clarify the foul and dark bodies of sinful mortals.

Despite the nobility of this purpose and the sterling testimonial provided on his behalf in the *General Prologue*, the Parson shares a disturbing characteristic with another extreme formalist. *The Parson's Tale* and *The Prioress's Tale*, it must be admitted, are both anti-Semitic texts. In the context of a warning against taking Christ's name in vain, the Parson thus states: "For certes, it semeth that ye thynke that the cursede Jewes ne dismembred nat ynough the preciouse persone of Crist, but ye dismembre hym moore" (10.591). The Parson expresses a similar sentiment eight lines later: "Thanne semeth it that men that sweren so horribly by his blessed name, that they despise it moore booldely than dide the cursede Jewes or elles the devel, that trembleth whan he heereth his name" (10.598). In the phrase "cursede Jewes" and in the alignment of the Jews with the devil, the Parson clearly echoes the Prioress, Chaucer's most vengeful pilgrim. As a consequence of their *unforgiving* zeal to isolate formal purity from material filth, they associate the divine with the former and the Jews with the latter.[63] It is also notable that the Prioress, though committed to regulating disorder, seems to defy the Benedictine rule, as suggested by her description in the *General Prologue*. The Parson shares the Prioress's commitment to order, but the Host suggests in the epilogue to *The Man of Law's Tale* that he too defies orthodoxy: "I smelle a Lollere in the wynd … This Lollere heer wil prechen us somwhat" (2.1173–77). The Shipman reinforces the Host's suggestion of heresy: "He wolde sowen som difficulte, / Or springen cokkel in oure clene corn" (2.1183–4). As Minnis observes, "if the Parson continues to act like a Lollard they can expect the clean corn of orthodoxy to be infiltrated and sullied with the weeds of heresy."[64] The entanglement of lawfulness and lawlessness, clean and unclean, accompanies the formal decisiveness of both the Prioress and the Parson, only intensifying their proximity. My reading of the *Retraction* will, therefore, seek to determine whether in the final reckoning Chaucer decisively endorses the absolute priority of form over matter, as do the Prioress and the Parson, or whether the conception of charity for which I have argued throughout animates also his final estimation of his oeuvre.

Conclusion: Retracting the *Retraction*

Qual è 'l geomètra che tutto s'affige/per misurar lo cerchio, e non ritrova,/pensando, quel principio ond' elli indige:/tale era io a quella vista nuova;/veder voleva come si convenne/l'imago al cerchio, e come vi s'indova. (Paradiso 33.133–8)

Despite the Parson's formalist inclinations, his tale is a treatise above all on divine charity. God's love extends to us all, no matter how compromised by sin we may be. Thus, the sixth spur to contrition is the hope of "foryifnesse of synne, and the yifte of grace wel for to do, and the glorie of hevene" (10.283), which is the reward for good deeds. Forgiveness, as the Parson's gloss of Christ's name indicates, is the fruitfulness of Christ's love:

> *Nazarenus* is as muche for to seye as "florisshynge," in which a man shal hope that he that yeveth hym remissioun of synnes shal yeve hym eek grace wel for to do. For in the flour is hope of fruyt in tyme comynge, and in foryifnesse of synnes hope of grace wel for to do. (10.288)

Love is as bountiful as springtime, the season of the Canterbury pilgrimage, giving hope that the forgiven one may also forgive, that the beloved may also love – just as the model of love that Arveragus provides inspires Aurelius and the illusionist in *The Franklin's Tale*, just as the knight in *The Wife of Bath's Tale* reciprocates his spouse's charity. We have already encountered the undecidable structure of forgiveness in Fragment 7, in both *The Shipman's Tale* and *The Tale of Melibee*. I argued in the previous chapter that these tales prepare us for the Nun's Priest's loving commandment that we should "Take the *fruit* and leave the chaff." I believe that the complex association of love, forgiveness, and fructuousness in both *The Nun's Priest's Tale* and *The Parson's Tale* prepares us to read Chaucer's *Retraction*. In this regard, it is striking that Chaucer should depart from one of his main sources for *The Parson's Tale* just to interpolate the image of the fruitful tree of penance. Even Wenzel is surprised by this manoeuvre: "It is all the more startling that Chaucer, while following Pennaforte's procedure of illustrating the three parts of Penitence with an image, replaces Pennaforte's three day-journeys with the Tree of Penance, whose root is contrition, its branches and leaves confession, and its fruit satisfaction (112–14)."[65] The fruitful tree is a crucial metaphor for Chaucer. It is his hope, I suggest, that his love for us will engender a flourishing of charity in return. How, then, can we read his *Retraction* forgivingly?

We should remark first of all that it is difficult to say whether the *Retraction* is an extension of *The Parson's Tale* or an independent unit.[66] In fact, the Parson's voice blends seamlessly with Chaucer's for at least the first two lines of the *Retraction*:

> *Here taketh the makere of this book his leve.*
> Now preye I to hem alle that herkne this litel tretys or rede, that if ther be any thyng in it that liketh hem, that thereof they thanken oure lord Jhesu Crist of whom procedeth al wit and al goodnesse, And if ther be any thyng that displese hem, I preye hem also that they arrette it to the defaute of

myn unkonnynge and nat to my wyl, that wolde ful fayn have seyd bettre
if I had konnynge. (10.1081–2)

The Parson had informed his audience in his prologue that his tale
would "stonde to correccioun" (10.60) because he is "nat textueel"
(10.57), a sentiment echoed in the *Retraction* by the humble assertion that
mistakes in the preceding treatise are a result of the author's "defaute."
At the same time, the phrase "litel tretys" should recall for us *The Tale of
Melibee*, the prologue to which also includes the phrases, "a litel thyng
in prose" (7.937), "litel tretys" (7.957), and "tretys lyte" (7.963). In the
prologue to *Melibee*, as I argued, the referent of "tretys" is ambiguous,
and could be the entire *Canterbury Tales* or another version of *Melibee*.
This ambiguity precluded our deciding that the "sentence" of *Melibee*
is the "sentence" of *The Canterbury Tales*, however attractive this reading. Not coincidentally, "litel tretys" in the *Retraction*, another text that
concerns itself with forgiveness, is also referentially ambiguous. Is the
speaker referring, as Minnis argues, to *The Parson's Tale* or, as Robertson and Huppé again claim, to the entire *Canterbury Tales* as the "little
treatise"?[67] It is suggestive, moreover, that the speaker prays in the first
line of the *Retraction* to those who have "hearkened" or "read" his treatise. The same equivocation appears in the Thopas-Melibee link. There,
Chaucer claims to have *written* his "murye tale" (7.964). But he then
prays to his audience to *"herkneth* what that I shal *seye"* (7.965), implying that he is speaking to the pilgrims. Similarly, later in the *Retraction*, the speaker expresses the wish to have *"seyd* bettre" before citing
Paul's adage: "For oure booke *seith*, 'al that is *writen'"* (10.1082–3). The
citation from Paul, moreover, comes from "oure booke," which could
mean Scripture, if Chaucer is addressing the pilgrims, or *The Canterbury
Tales*, if he is addressing a reader of the volume, which, of course, contains Paul's words in *The Nun's Priest's Tale*. As in the Thopas-Melibee
link, Chaucer invites us to conceive of him simultaneously as transcendent creator, or "makere," and immanent created; as he first did in the
General Prologue, Chaucer insolubly entangles his transcendence to,
and his immanence within, his narrative creation. The first two lines of
the *Retraction* thus evoke both the discourse of the Parson and the discourse of Chaucer from the prologue to *Melibee*. Will Chaucer's attitude
towards his literary works reflect the Parson's judgmental formalism
by unequivocally rejecting sinful and vain fabulation? Or will Chaucer, following the ambivalent prologue to *Melibee*, refuse to impose any
such decisive judgment, or "sentence," on his works? Our task now,
therefore, is to consider whether the *Retraction* is a judgmental or a non-
judgmental text.

Extending the penitential theme of *The Parson's Tale*, the speaker in the *Retraction* not only submits himself to the judgment of his audience for any deficiency in his treatise, he also submits himself to the judgment of God for his sinful compositions:

> Wherefore I biseke yow mekely, for the mercy of God, that ye preye for me that Crist have mercy on me and foryeve me my giltes; and namely of my translacions and enditynges of worldly vanitees, the whiche I revoke in my retracciouns: as is the book of Troilus; the book also of Fame; the book of the XXV. Ladies; the book of the Duchesse; the book of Seint Valentynes day of the Parlement of Briddes; the tales of Caunterbury, thilke that sownen into synne; the book of the Leoun; and many another book, if they were in my remembrance, and many a song and many a leccherous lay, that Crist for his grete mercy foryeve me the synne. (10.1084–7)

But the speaker's humble submission to both God and his reader in his appeal for forgiveness imposes simultaneously an authorial "final judgment," or final *decision*, on his work. Chaucer, in confessing his "giltes" so as to cleanse himself from sinful contamination, separates virtuous from vain, worthy from unworthy, as will the ultimate Judge at the end of time. Deirdre Riley makes a similar point: "This act of categorization is in itself an examination, a self-autopsy/taxonomy: Chaucer is judging himself – he is both the judge and the judged."[68] Chaucer assumes a posture of judgmental mastery over his oeuvre as does God at the Day of Judgment. And here, as opposed to *The Nun's Priest's Tale*, the author decisively separates the "fruit" from the "chaff"; he does not leave this task to his audience. His procedure is analogous to that of the Wife of Bath in her epilogue, in which she decisively separates "good," obedient husbands from "bad," obdurate ones. Read in this way, lines 10.1084–7 of the *Retraction* appear entirely consonant with the formal orthodoxies of *The Parson's Tale*, according to which we submit ourselves to God's mercy by anatomizing and rejecting our sins. Chaucer, in the *Retraction*, judgmentally *orders* his accomplishments and clearly distinguishes what is formally purposeful from what is materially vain.[69]

There are, however, some complications as far as this formalist reading of the *Retraction* is concerned. Between the two passages cited above, acting as a kind of hinge, Chaucer echoes the conclusion to *The Nun's Priest's Tale* with another citation of Romans 15:4: "For oure book seith, 'Al that is writen is writen for oure doctrine,' and that is myn entente" (10.1083). What I can say for certain is that line 10.1083 has a curious, but by now not unfamiliar, logic. Let us consider this line in isolation. On the one hand, the citation of Paul, as in *The Nun's Priest's Tale*, indicates that the reader may find useful instruction in a work, notwithstanding the formal intention of the author. The priority of audience reception is the materialist position: The closural intention of the author does not govern the reception of the work, and we are free to interpret it as we see appropriate. On the other hand, Chaucer identifies this abdication of authorial intention *as his authorial intention*: "and that is myn entente."[70] For the last time in *The Canterbury Tales*, material openness is formal closure; formal closure is material openness. In this passage, Chaucer neither masters nor does he free his works; once more, he authoritatively revokes his authority. "'Al that is writen is writen for oure doctrine,' and that is myn entente" is logically equivalent to the Nun's Priest's imperative: "Taketh the fruyt, and lat the chaf be stille." Both lines simultaneously impose and depose the author's guiding intention; both lines refuse to decide between form or matter. This is a gesture we now can understand as loving – as forgiving. In an exemplary reading of the *Retraction*'s ambivalence, Travis notes that Chaucer composes in iambic pentameter a line from the passage cited above that condemns poetry: "many a song and many a leccherous lay."[71] The logic is identical: Chaucer poetically revokes poetry; he materially revokes matter. He is on the side of formalism and materialism simultaneously. According to this reading, Chaucer is expressing his love for *all* his literary creations, those that are formally virtuous and those that are materially vain.

The *Retraction* offers two mutually exclusive interpretive possibilities.[72] First, the *Retraction* enacts a formalist operation and follows the Parson in judgmentally separating the virtuous from the vain, the clean from the dirty, truth from fable, and the moral from the sinful. In this case, the teleological interpretation of *The Parson's Tale* holds. But second, Chaucer also tells us via his citation of Paul at line 10.1083 that he loves his virtuous (formalist) and his vain (materialist) writings, his sententious works and his fables. In this case, the perspectival interpretation of *The Parson's Tale* holds. According to this latter possibility, Chaucer loves the Manciple as much as the Parson, the Canon's Yeoman as much as the Second Nun. He decides neither for the secular (materialism) nor for the Christian (formalism), neither for sentence (formalism) nor for solace (materialism). He thereby assumes the non-judgmental attitude of the pilgrim Chaucer towards his companions. I argued in the introduction to this book that Chaucer's authoritative abdication of authority in the *General Prologue* should be understood as an analogue of Christ's incarnation. In the *General Prologue*, Chaucer descends into his own work and adopts a non-judgmental and thus loving comportment towards his creations, no matter how vicious. In the Thopas-Melibee link, Chaucer refuses to judge the Prioress, his most judgmental pilgrim, and instead humiliates himself, right before delivering a tale about forgiveness that we are implicitly urged to read forgivingly. Finally, in the *Retraction*, we find Chaucer again emulating Christ by adopting a charitably non-judgmental posture towards his literary works, whether virtuous or vain. What Chaucer is implying from the beginning to the end of *The Canterbury Tales* is that God loves, and thus forgives, all his creations – no matter what their failings.

But by offering us two mutually exclusive interpretive options – judgment and charity; decision and love – the *Retraction* presents *us* with the opportunity to love Chaucer. We witnessed an identical structure at the conclusion of *The Wife of Bath's Tale*, the harshly judgmental epilogue of which contradicts the loving and reciprocal submission of the knight and his wife. With the final instantiation of his insoluble logic, Chaucer is at once, impossibly, judgmental *and* non-judgmental – loving *and* decisive. What I wish now to propose is that this paradox replies to the final canto of Dante's *Paradiso* in providing to the reader a startling vision of God, but one that is translated into the logic of love.[73] To advance this claim, I must turn to the final passages of Chaucer's earlier masterpiece.

Let us recall first that the concluding stanza of *Troilus and Criseyde* includes a close paraphrase of canto 14.28–30 of the *Paradiso*:[74]

> Thow oon, and two, and thre, eterne on lyve,
> That regnest ay in thre, and two, and oon,
> Uncircumscript, and al maist circumscrive,
> Us from visible and invisible foon
> Defende, and to thy mercy, everichoon,
> So make us, Jesus, for thi mercy, digne,
> For love of mayde and moder thyn benigne.   (5.1863–9)

The corresponding passage from the *Comedy* describes the praise for the trinity of the philosophers and the theologians, each arranged in a circle in the sphere of the Sun.[75] As Dante ascends to the sphere of Mars, a third circle of souls forms a ring around the first two. This third circle represents the Holy Spirit and completes a searing image of the triune god (14.73–5), an image that the pilgrim can only perceive with Beatrice's assistance. The sphere of Mars perhaps suggests an appropriate final destination for the warrior Troilus after his sojourn in the "holughnesse of the eighthe spere" (5.1809). His own longing for Criseyde finds a reflex in Dante's description of the ardent yearning of the elect to be reunited with the flesh at the Day of Judgment (14.61–3). Appropriately, this yearning adumbrates in *Paradiso* 14 a vision of Christ on the cross (14.94–140), signifying the loving entanglement of immortal spirit and mortal carnality that Chaucer emulates at the beginning of *The Canterbury Tales*. However, after his death, Troilus leaves the material world behind with contemptuous judgment: We are told that he "dampned al oure werk that foloweth so / The blynde lust, the which that may nat laste, / And sholden al oure herte on heven caste" (5.1821–3). His formalist adherence to predestination, asserted at length in Book 4 (958–1078), precisely anticipates this formalist rejection of materiality. The narrator in Book 5 follows Troilus's lead:

> Lo here, of payens corsed olde rites!
> Lo here, what all hire goddes may availle!
> Lo here, thise wrecched worldes appetites!
> Lo here, the fyn and guerdoun for travaille
> Of Jove, Appollo, of Mars, of swich rascaille!
> Lo here, the forme of olde clerkis speche
> In poetrie, if ye hire bokes seche.   (5.1849–55)

Just as *Paradiso* 14 provides only a facsimile of the trinity, so Chaucer leaves us in *Troilus and Criseyde* with only a *partial* vision of love, one that judgmentally rejects the matter of the secular world – its rites, passions, idols, and poetry. He descends *back into* this world in the *General Prologue*, however, with a redemptive purpose: to entangle formal transcendence and material immanence via a charitable (non-)synthesis. In this way, I suggest, we can understand *Troilus and Criseyde* as Chaucer's Old Testament, and *The Canterbury Tales* as his New.

The pilgrim Dante's indirect vision of the trinity in *Paradiso* 14 anticipates the unmediated theophany that he experiences in *Paradiso* 33. Likewise, Chaucer tells us that *Troilus and Criseyde*, the "litel … tragedye" (5.1786), looks forward to "som comedye" (5.1788), implicitly proposing an alignment between Dante's *Comedy* and *The Canterbury Tales*.[76] I will thus seek to demonstrate that just as the conclusion to *Troilus and Criseyde* responds to *Paradiso* 14, the conclusion to *The Canterbury Tales* responds to *Paradiso* 33.[77] John M. Fyler nevertheless writes of Chaucer's anticipation of *The Canterbury Tales* in *Troilus and Criseyde* that "the promised comedy, though it does indeed offer a plentiful diversity of styles and voices, high style set against low and decorous against indecorous, does not … move to the Dantean transcendence of world and language at the end of *Paradiso* 33. The replication of terms conceals a world of difference: Chaucer's comedy, unlike Dante's *Commedia*, is earthbound."[78] William Franke formulates a similar claim by arguing that Dante's poetry was supported by the high medieval synthesis of faith and reason not available to Chaucer after Scotus and Ockham. Thus, while Dante aimed to express the highest truth, Chaucer "never demonstrated any confidence that poetry could in any way represent the reality of the divine."[79] In my view, however, Chaucer is not just an "earthbound" author; he devotes the whole of *The Canterbury Tales*, including the *Retraction*, to the comprehension of divine love – a love that insolubly entangles heaven and earth. In contrast to Fyler and Franke, therefore, I suggest that *The Canterbury Tales* culminates with a vision of God that precisely counterpoints Dante's own revelation. Chaucer reads Dante's *Paradiso* 33 in much the same way as the Clerk reads Petrarch's Legend of Griselda.

Near the conclusion of *Paradiso* 33, as his vision gradually sharpens, Dante perceives three rings of different colours emerging into focus from within "the universal form" (*La forma universal*) of the "knot" (*nodo*) that binds together the scattered pages of the universe into a single volume of love (33.86–7).[80] The second ring appears as a reflection of the first and in their reciprocal love conspire the third (33.115–20).[81] Dante raptly contemplates the second ring, which bears within it a human effigy he recognizes as his own image.[82] In the momentary refulgence of inspiration, as if "squaring the circle" (33.132–5), he comprehends the impossible union of creator and created, infinite and finite, divinity and humanity (33.139–41).[83] The *Paradiso* concludes with the pilgrim sensing his participation in the celestial love that perfectly revolves the cosmos (33.142–6). For Dante, as for the Parson, the Second Nun, the Prioress, and the Man of Law, this love decisively excludes any trace of disorder, dirt, or contingency.[84]

The geometrical impossibility of squaring the circle corresponds in the *Retraction* to the logical impossibility figured by the reciprocal exclusion of judgment and charity. Does Chaucer authoritatively impose order, or does he love unauthorized chaos? We cannot decide. Chaucer is *at once* the judgmental Father, the authoritative "makere" transcendent to his narrative creation, and the all-forgiving Son, who descends and is textualized within it.[85] Here, the principal lesson of *The Canterbury Tales* reasserts itself: The lover does not decide on love. If we are to love him, we can decide neither on Chaucer's judgmental mastery over his creations nor on his non-judgmental charity towards all of them. Only so do we participate in the love that insolubly entangles the Father and the Son. As the Liar paradox is (not) true, so the Father is (not) the Son. Loving Chaucer, then, means not judging whether Chaucer judges. Even to say that Chaucer is a lover is to make a judgment. I would then, much like Robertson and Huppé, uncharitably fix charity as the *form* of *The Canterbury Tales* – the Dantean *nodo* that synthesizes the entire volume.[86] Instead, all I can decide is that Chaucer's ultimate intention must be that we leave his ultimate intention undecidable. In this way, Chaucer boldly submits to his forgiving reader just what it could mean to love God.

Notes

Introduction: Flesh and Word in the *General Prologue*

1 Chaucer's status as both a "philosophical poet" and "love poet" was well established even among his contemporaries. In Thomas Usk's *Testament of Love*, for instance, Love herself describes Chaucer as "myne owne trewe servaunt, the noble philosophical poete in Englissh" (3.559–60). Quotation taken from Shoaf, ed., *The Testament of Love*.

2 See Hill, *Chaucer's Neoplatonism*; Rosenfeld, *Ethics and Enjoyment*; Miller, *Philosophical Chaucer*; Klassen, *Chaucer on Love*.

3 Citations from the Platonic dialogues are taken from Cooper and Hutchinson, eds., *Plato: Complete Works*.

4 Hirshberg, "'Cosyn to the Dede,'" 40.

5 Taylor, "Chaucer's *Cosyn to the Dede*," 315–27, at 325. Robert Myles also reads Chaucer's citation of Plato as demonstrating his "intentional realism" and concern with the appropriate and ethical use of language: "Words depend for their 'good entencioun' upon the 'good entencioun' or the good will of the human speaker. The Boethian emphasis is on the will of the speaker, not on the words themselves; this is also a late medieval emphasis; and Boethius's understanding of the function of the human will in directing the proper 'cosyning'/cousining or the improper 'cosyning'/duping of the relationship between the word and the thing, is also Chaucer's understanding. Implicit here, for Chaucer, is a linguistic intentionalist realism." See his *Chaucerian Realism*, 24.

6 Pelen, "Chaucer's *Cosyn to the dede*," 91–107, at 103.

7 See, most recently, Hill, *Chaucer's Neoplatonism*, who argues that "what Chaucer has especially and most comfortably extracted from its brief appearances in Boethius *Consolation*, where the perfect imbues the imperfect, down to which it flows, is a Platonic process of comparing similarities among related concepts and manifestations" (6).

8 On the transmission of Plato, see Gersh, "The Medieval Legacy from Ancient Platonism," 3–30.

9 Marenbon, *Boethius*, 152.

10 For a recent account of Chaucer's divergence from Boethian Neoplatonism in the Legend of Philomela, see Schrock, "Neoplatonic Theodicy," 27–43.

11 McGerr, *Chaucer's Open Books*, 25. See also Allen, *The Ethical Poetic of the Later Middle Ages*, who observes that medieval authors assimilated "literature" to the category of "ethics": "Poems, of course, insofar as they are objects, or instances of human behaviour, remained the same – all their decorum, virtuosity, textual richness, emotional power, remain. But under the definitions of the medieval critics, they enjoy a different status, they benefit from a different ideology. They are not literature, but ethics" (xvi). See further Johnson, *Practicing Literary Theory in the Middle Ages*.

12 On the late medieval context of nominalism, see Oberman, *Harvest*. On the influence of nominalism on Chaucer, see especially Utz, ed., *Literary Nominalism*; Keiper, Bode, and Utz, eds., *Nominalism and Literary Discourse*; Peck, "Chaucer and the Nominalist Questions," 745–60. For a thorough account of scholarship that considers Chaucer's relationship to fourteenth-century philosophy, see Hill, *"She, This in Blak,"* 1–21 and the corresponding notes on 101–13.

13 Loux, trans., *Ockham's Theory of Terms*, 79–82; 1.15.

14 Maurer, *The Philosophy of William Ockham*, 226.

15 On this distinction, see Gerber, *It Could Have Been Otherwise*, 309–49.

16 On the influence of Ockham's understanding of contingency on Chaucer, see the germinal analysis by Delany, "The Late Medieval Attack on Analogical Thought," 19–41; this essay was originally published in *Mosaic* 5, no. 4 (1972): 31–52. See further Clark, "Ockham on Human and Divine Freedom," 122–60.

17 Nolan makes a similar point; see "'A Poet Ther Was,'" 154–69, at 163: "What distinguishes Chaucer from earlier poets is that he refuses to give the Platonic doctrine to an authority figure. Instead of speaking it through Philosophia or Raison or Gracedieu, he presents it through his pilgrim voice. The pilgrim as historian proposes to use words not to represent things or truth or doctrine or ideas, as a clerk would have done, but to mimic the transient words and gestures of others."

18 Gust, *Constructing Chaucer*, 2. See also Miller's reading of the *House of Fame* in her *Poetic License*, 71: "Throughout the poem the narrator has alternately asserted his superiority to and attempted to disappear behind previously authorized versions of 'trouthe,' claiming and disclaiming his role as author as he tests and rejects all available authorities, including himself."

19 For a recent consideration of the ambivalence of Chaucer's authority, see Fumo, *The Legacy of Apollo*, who contends that Chaucer locates in

the figure of Apollo a model for "vatic" poetics, associated with "the perverse energies of fragmentation and ironic self-reflexivity" (17). But the final movement of *The Canterbury Tales* stages Phebus's destruction of his instruments in *The Manciple's Tale* – a gesture that looks forward to "the Parson's caustic medicines, which reject fable altogether" (203). On Chaucer's treatment of authority, see Seal, *Father Chaucer*; Galloway, *"Auctorite,"* 21–36; Wallace, *Chaucerian Polity*; Scanlon, *Narrative, Authority, and Power*; Lerer, *Chaucer and His Readers*.

20 Steiner, "Authority," 142–59, at 143.

21 See, for instance, Beall, ed., *Revenge of the Liar*; Rahman, Tulenheimo, and Genot, eds., *Unity, Truth, and the Liar*.

22 Spade and Read, "Insolubles."

23 See Bottin, "Metalinguistic Science, 235–48. See also Spade, "Five Early Theories," 24–46.

24 See Novaes and Read, *"Secundum Quid et Simpliciter,"* 175–91.

25 Bottin, "Metalinguistic Science," 241.

26 Novaes and Read, *"Secundum Quid et Simpliciter,"* 191.

27 Quoted in Novaes and Read, *"Secundum Quid et Simpliciter,"* 184. I am most grateful to Stephen Read for his assistance in clarifying the nuances of Bradwardine's argument.

28 Heytesbury treats paradoxical statements within the context of obligational disputations and the rules governing the participants in this game. Obligations depend upon a *casus*, or hypothetical situation: The meaning of "this statement is false," for instance, depends upon the referent of "this statement" and so a paradox is only generated by a particular *casus*. "This statement is false" can signify as it normally does or, in a *casus* where "this statement" supposits for the whole statement, it cannot signify as it normally does – it has a secondary signification. But how exactly the statement differs from its normal signification is the responsibility of the one who establishes the *casus* to identify, which "passes the buck" to the opponent in the *disputatio*. Even still, according to Heytesbury, in an insoluble *casus*, "this statement is false" must still be false because its total signification is a conjunction of its normal and secondary significations. Its normal signification is that it is false; if one element of a conjunction is false, the conjunction is false. For an analysis of Heytesbury's proof, see Pironet, "William Heytesbury," 255–334.

29 Quoted in Spade, "Bradwardine's Theory of Signification," 115–34, at 116.

30 My reading of *The Nun's Priest's Tale* will, therefore, engage with the work of two scholars who have made related claims: Travis, *Disseminal Chaucer*, and Baker, "Literature, Logic, and Mathematics."

31 Two manuscripts of *Troilus and Criseyde* preserve the alternative "sophistical" instead of "philosophical," a reading curiously in line with

Strode's interest in *sophismata* and *insolubilia* and, perhaps, the nature of his influence on Chaucer. Lynch makes this point in *Philosophical Visions*, 9. See also Reichl, "Chaucer's *Troilus*," 133–52, at 134, who also notes this variant but expresses doubt that Chaucer read Strode's technical treatises. By contrast, Olson makes a case for the influence of Strode's logical writings on Chaucer; see his "Snub and White," 185–211. See also Delasanta, "Chaucer and Strode," 205–18; Courtenay, *School and Scholars*; Bennett, *Chaucer at Oxford and Cambridge*.

32 Lynch, *Philosophical Visions*, 139.

33 Ibid., 113.

34 William of Ockham, *Summa Logicae*, 744–6; 3.3.46. Translation taken from Spade, *De insolubilibus*, 2.

35 Translations of the Vulgate taken from Kinney, ed., *The Vulgate Bible*. On Chaucer's use of the Sermon on the Mount in *The Canterbury Tales*, see Jeffrey, "Dante and Chaucer," 81–108.

36 Mann, *Estates Satire*, 197 (emphasis in original).

37 Ibid., 200–1.

38 Russell, *Chaucer and the Trivium*, 66.

39 Mann, *Estates Satire*, 187. But see Wimsatt, "Canterbury Pilgrims," 633–45, who finds in Chaucer's portraits evidence for Scotistic influence: "The multiple formalities of an entity are contracted in a process of individuation, which seals the *haeccitas* of the individual … It is no doubt obvious that if we see Chaucer's pilgrims as both types and individuals, then Scotus's common nature would be relevant to their types, and his process of contraction would account for their individuality" (636). Wimsatt counters the argument of Gerald Morgan, who sees the pilgrims only as "archetypes" and "concrete universals," not individuals. See Morgan, "The Universality of the Portraits," 481–93. At the other extreme, of course, is Manly, who argues that the pilgrims correspond to historical persons. See his *Some New Light on Chaucer*.

40 See Donaldson, "Chaucer the Pilgrim," 928–36, at 936: "In his poem the poet arranges for the moralist to define austerely what ought to be and for his fictional representative – who, as the representative of all mankind, is no mere fiction – to go on affirming affectionately what is."

41 See Lawton, *Chaucer's Narrators*.

42 See, for instance, Leicester Jr., "The Art of Impersonation," 213–24; *Disenchanted Self*.

43 See Trigg's discussion of Chaucerian authorship in *Congenial Souls*, 40–73.

44 See Mooney, "Chaucer's Scribe," 97–138; Stubbs and Mooney, *Scribes and the City*; Warner, *Chaucer's Scribes*.

45 Watson, "Conceptions of the Word," 85–124, at 101. See also Watson's "Censorship and Cultural Change," 822–64. On Chaucer's sophisticated use of theology, see Rhodes, *Poetry Does Theology*.

46 On the late medieval vernacular focus on the embodiment of Christ, see
   also Beckwith, *Christ's Body*. She argues that "The body of Christ is …
   where the local, minute realization of embodiment, the necessity of its
   specific and detailed placing, is blessed by the transcendent at the very
   same time as it compromises it. It is both an articulation, and a deep-rooted,
   structuring critique in symbolic terms of such idealism" (109). See further
   Bynum, *Holy Feast*.

47 See Price and Gaddis, trans., *Council of Chalcedon*. The relevant passage
   from the Council's accepted definition indicates that Christ must be
   "acknowledged in two natures without confusion, change, division, or
   separation (the difference of the natures being in no way destroyed by the
   union, but rather the distinctive character of each nature being preserved
   and coming together into one person and one hypostasis), not parted or
   divided into two persons, but one and the same Son, Only-begotten, God,
   Word, Lord, Jesus Christ" (2.204).

48 Morris, "Metaphysics," 211–24, at 213. See further Cross, *Metaphysics of the
   Incarnation*. On the influence of Chalcedon on scholastic Christology, see
   Oberman, *Harvest*, 249–80.

49 On Aquinas's treatment of incarnational metaphysics, see Stump,
   Aquinas, 407–26. On the challenges posed to Aristotelian logic in the late
   medieval period by the paradoxes entailed by the incarnational and
   trinitarian mysteries, see Ashe, "True Contradictions," 111–46. For Ashe,
   in accordance with my reading of Chaucer, moral existence demands the
   capacity to accept the irrevocability of "true contradictions."

50 See Chapter 41 of O'Neill, trans., *Summa Contra Gentiles*.

51 See further Pasnau, "Form and Matter," 635–46.

52 Aristotle, *Physics*, 1:328; 1.192a23–24. On the gendering of these
   fundamental philosophical terms, see Colebrook, *Gender*, 40–75. On the
   Aristotelian association of woman with matter in a medieval English
   context, see Robertson, "Practicing Women," 505–28.

53 See Peterson, *Aquinas*, 154–5: "form is the good of matter, and existence, the
   act of all acts, is the good of essence. So good is being as desirable, as the term,
   goal, or end of some activity, tendency, or appetite. It is actual fulfillment with
   respect to what has potentiality for, or is bent toward, that fulfillment. What
   good is is seen by contrasting it with its opposite, evil. As evil consists in a
   thing's being defective in some way, i.e. in its *lacking* a form it ought to have,
   so good consists in a thing's *having* the form it ought to have."

54 Smith, "Medieval Forma," 66–79, at 70. See also Minnis, *Medieval Theory of
   Authorship*, 118–59.

55 Robertson, "Medieval Materialism," 99–118, at 111–12. See also her *Nature
   Speaks*; Barker, "Matter and Form"; Cannon, "Form," 177–90; Simpson,
   Sciences and the Self, 1–21.

56 See Robertson Jr., *Preface to Chaucer*, 295. For a recent consideration of the continuing vitality of exegetical criticism, see Gaylord, "Reflections," 311–33.

57 Green, ed. and trans., *Augustine*, 149; 3.10.16.

58 Ibid., 148–9; 3.10.14.

59 Stock, *Augustine the Reader*, 204.

60 Miller, *Philosophical Chaucer*, 138–9.

61 Ibid., 139.

62 Leicester, *Disenchanted Self*, 14.

63 My "anti-subjective" reading is anticipated by Benson, "Trust the Tale," 22–33.

64 For Immanuel Kant, a "transcendental illusion" comes about when in pre-critical philosophy "the subjective necessity of a certain connection of our concepts on behalf of the understanding is taken for an objective necessity, the determination of things in themselves." See Kant, *Critique of Pure Reason*, 386; A297/B354.

65 Rosenfeld, *Ethics and Enjoyment*, 8.

66 See Lacan, "Knowledge and Truth," 90–103, at 94: "The 'doesn't stop not being written,' on the contrary, is the impossible, as I define it on the basis of the fact that it cannot in any case be written, and it is with this that I characterize the sexual relationship – the sexual relationship doesn't stop not being written. Because of this, the apparent necessity of the phallic function turns out to be mere contingency."

67 Simpson, "*Piers Plowman*," 97–114, at 108.

68 Aers, *Beyond Reformation?*, 4.

69 Gruenler, *Poetics of Enigma*, 71.

70 Ibid., 274.

71 Ibid., 277.

72 Ibid., 375.

73 Ibid., 378–9.

74 Klassen, *Beatific Vision*, 27. See further Johnson, *Staging Contemplation*.

75 According to my reading, it may even be the case that the *Confessio Amantis* quite precisely anticipates *The Canterbury Tales*: in the 1390 redaction of the *Confessio*, Venus urges Gower to request that Chaucer "make his testament of love" (VIII 2955*). Citation taken from Macaulay, *Complete Works of John Gower*. See further Lindeboom, *Venus' Owne Clerk*; Astell, *Universe of Learning*.

76 Strohm, "Form and Social Statement," 17–40, at 20.

77 All further quotations from the *Confessio Amantis* are taken from Peck, ed., *John Gower*.

78 Simpson, *Sciences and the Self*, 5.

79 On the opposition of love and reason, see Bakalian, *Aspects of Love*, 3–12.

80 Nicholson, *Love and Ethics*, 343.
81 Watt, *Amoral Gower*,xviii. On the moral uncertainty Gower generates in the
     Confessio, see also Olsson, *Structures of Conversion*.
82 Mitchell, *Ethics and Exemplarity*, 40.
83 See, for instance, Neuse, *Chaucer's Dante*, who claims of the Friar and the
     Summoner that "[e]ach in his way is a spectacular example of *contrapasso*, the
     concept that governs the representation of the damned in the *Inferno*. At the
     heart of this concept … is the idea that the sin is its own punishment and that
     the torments of the damned are therefore strictly self-inflicted" (201–2).

1. Judge Not: The Nun's Priest on Logic, the Franklin on Love

 1 See in this regard Frese, "Masterpiece?," 330–43, who argues that critical
     estimation of the tale as Chaucer's masterpiece is anticipated by Chaucer
     himself.
 2 Travis, *Disseminal Chaucer*, 3.
 3 See Finlayson, "The 'Povre Widwe,'" 269–73, who argues that the widow's
     ascetic existence serves to criticize the excesses of the clerical estate.
 4 On the pursuit of the fox as a parody of the aristocratic hunt, see Pattison,
     "Ironic Imitations," 141–61.
 5 Pearsall, *"Nun's Priest's Tale,"* 12. For similar opinions, see Manning,
     "Attitude Toward Fables," 403–16.
 6 Astell, "Causes of Books," 269–87, at 281. See also Narkiss, "Escape from
     Fable," 46–63, who claims that "Chaucer's use of the fable highlights
     interchangeability, a propensity for doubling repetition and substitutions.
     It is this ambiguating propensity that open the fable to interpretation, and
     casts doubt on the finality of fable as revealer of ultimate truths. This in
     turn foregrounds the notion of the audience, for whose benefit the truths
     are revealed, and in relation to whom the fable has an interpretative
     function. The fable changes from an authoritative rhetorical form into a
     form of dialogue between text and audience" (60).
 7 Oerlemans, "Seriousness," 317–28, at 319. That "the Priest has lost control
     of his argument" is also argued by Pelen, "Chaucer's Chauntecleer,"
     329–35, at 332. In the same vein, see Chapin, "Morality Ovidized," 7–33,
     at 25: "With Chaucer, modern authorship is born in the renunciation of
     (sententious) authority."
 8 Donaldson, "Patristic Exegesis," 1–26, at 20.
 9 Donovan, "'Moralite,'" 498–508, at 498.
10 Dahlberg, "Cock and Fox," 277–90, at 290. See also Levy and Adams,
     "Paradise Lost and Regained," 178–92.
11 See, for instance, Fehrenbacher, "Literature and History," 134–48; Justice,
     Writing and Rebellion, 207–13; Astell, "Peasants' Revolt," 53–60; Strohm,

Social Chaucer, 165–8; Knight, *Geoffrey Chaucer*, 141–5; Travis, "Fox Chase," 195–220; Ganim, *Chaucerian Theatricality*, 113–15; Warner, "Man's Babylon," 82–107.

12 Fehrenbacher, "Literature and History," 145.

13 See Travis, *Disseminal Chaucer*, 17; Travis is citing Derrida, *Dissemination*, 268.

14 On the satirical treatment of Boethius in the tale, see Payne, "Three Theories," 201–19.

15 Watts, "Clerks," 145–55, at 154.

16 See Furr, "Nominalism," 135–46, who identifies Chauntecleer as a realist partisan of determinism and Pertelote as a nominalist partisan of free will.

17 Minnis, *Medieval Theory of Authorship*, 205.

18 See Weele and Powell, "Chaucer's Kitchen," 39–50, who find in the Nun's Priest's admonition evidence that he seeks to orient his readers to the good: "Once we see that many of the elements, whether in the fable's structure and imagery or in its stylistic devices, work together effectively against the backdrop of Plato's contrast of true and false arts, then the priest's closing words also take on another, ethical significance. For wise persons will stand on the tradition of St. Paul and St. Augustine, which commands that one 'taketh the fruyt,' or moral of the tale, and 'lat the chaf be stille.' But, more important, they will heed the 'fruit' by understanding, like Plato, that a true rhetorician aims only at the good." This is an excellent example of a formalist reading of the tale.

19 Scanlon, "Authority of Fable," 43–68, at 49. See also Scanlon's *Narrative, Authority, and Power*, 229–44.

20 Scanlon, "Authority of Fable," 55.

21 The same logic is evident in the otherwise bewildering concluding prayer to the tale: "Now, goode god, if that it be thy wille,/As seith my lord, so make us alle goode men,/And brynge us to his heighe blisse. Amen" (7.3444–6). Who is the Nun's Priest's "lord" and what could possibly be his "heighe blisse" such that it may be distinguished from God's? The Nun's Priest authorizes his statement by appealing to his lord but renders it impossible to discern who that authority may be. His authorizing gesture simultaneously undermines itself. Chaucer arguably performs the same maneuver at the end of the House of Fame: "But he semed for to be/A man of gret auctorite" (3.2157–8). But see Field, "Ending," 302–6, who proposes "Christ" as the lord and Baker, "Bradwardinian Benediction," 236–43, who proposes Bradwardine.

22 Prendergast and Rosenfeld, eds., *Subversion of Form*, 11.

23 Turner's *Chaucerian Conflict* provides a book-length example of such a materialist reading: "Chaucer's poetry and prose are concerned with depicting the inevitably destructive nature of human fellowship and

desire" (2). For Turner, Chaucer represents "human fellowship and desire" as chaotic, lacking any final purpose.

24 On Chauntecleer's singing, see also Zeeman, "Gender of Song," 141–82; Friedman, "Mermaid's Song," 250–66; Schrader, "Daun Burnel," 284–90.

25 See further Camargo, "Rhetorical Ethos," 173–86, who argues that the Pardoner, the Parson, and the Nun's Priest each express different rhetorical modalities: the Pardoner wishes to move his audience with *pathos*, the Parson wishes to teach his audience with *logos*, and the Nun's Priest wishes only to delight his audience with his *ethos*.

26 Travis, *Disseminal Chaucer*, 307–14, also suggests that Chaucer is alluding to Dante with reference to the *Prose Lancelot*. See further Bovaird-Abbo, "Reading Lancelot," 84–97, who suggests that the Nun's Priest's "views the female gender as an obstacle to social advancement" and that his misogynistic reading of the *Lancelot* indicates his "failure to read fully the Arthurian legend becomes symptomatic of his narrow and illiterate worldview" (95).

27 Travis, *Disseminal Chaucer*, 312. See also Mcalpine, "The Triumph of Fiction," 81: the Nun's Priest "implies that his story is as meaningless, or at least that he intends to render it as meaningless, as certain romantic stories favored by women. The comparative structure, 'also trewe … As,' underpins this obvious irony, but Chaucer also uses this same structure to surface critical questions of his own. How true *is* the story of Lancelot? If it holds no truth, what makes it false? If it is true in some sense, what is the nature of that truth?"

28 Travis, *Disseminal Chaucer*, 334.

29 But see Mann, "*Speculum Stultorum*," 262–82, who argues that both texts satirize the urge to find morality within them: "Like the *Speculum Stultorum*, Chaucer's *Nun's Priest's Tale* teasingly encourages us to look for a serious moral at the base of an allegory" (271). See also Ziolkowski, "Humour," 1–26, at 25–6, who observes the playful use of formal logic in the *Speculum Stultorum*. See also Greene, *Logical Fictions*.

30 See Baker, "Literature, Logic, and Mathematics," 125, who formulates a related argument: "The irony is that while the narrator cites Bradwardine, the rooster silently constructs the arguments that lead him to his deterministic conclusion with material from the work of Bradwardine's 'Pelagian' adversary, Holcot."

31 Delany, "'Mulier est hominis confusio,'" 1–8, at 7.

32 Scholars who conclude that Chauntecleer's Latinity fails him include Manning, "Fabular Jangling," 3–16; Petty Jr., "Uncooperative Speech," 413–23. Scholars who conclude that Chauntecleer deliberately mistranslates the Latin include Wheeler, *Representations of the Feminine*, 15; Pizzorno, "Chauntecleer's Bad Latin," 387–409.

33 Pertelote's medical knowledge may indeed deserve disparagement. Kauffman, "Pertelote's Parlous Parle," 41–8, argues that the pharmacological regimen she prescribes "would, in fact, have hastened the departure of even the mightiest of epic heroes, either human or rooster" (47). On the philosophical resonances of Pertelote's attempt to balance her husband's humoral system, see Gallacher, "Food, Laxatives, and Catharsis," 49–68.

34 Muscatine, *French Tradition*, 239; See also Besserman, "Chaucerian Wordplay," 68–73.

35 See also Sharma, "Continental Materialism," 54–83.

36 Furr, "Nominalism," 143.

37 On the influence of Holcot's Wisdom commentary on the debate between Pertelote and Chauntecleer, see Pratt, "Some Latin Sources," 538–70.

38 Chaucer's insoluble logic is much closer to Paul de Man's conception of undecidability. For de Man, language is ultimately meaningless, functioning as the "material substrate" of meaning. He thus points to "the absolute randomness of language, prior to any figuration or meaning" (*Allegories of Reading*, 299). But we can only refer to the meaninglessness of language from *within* language. Thus, "the deconstruction states the fallacy of reference in a necessarily referential mode" (ibid., 125). Any possible statement can be ironized, a situation that de Man describes as a "permanent parabasis" (ibid., 301). While, for Derrida, a text is "undecidable" because we cannot decide on its ultimate meaning, for de Man, even to say that a text is "undecidable" is problematic. Hans Jost-Frey observes that "the undecidability of the referentiality of the statement does not establish control over it, but rather confers on undecidability, in its turn, the uncertain status of all statement, thereby preventing it from being turned into a truth" ("Undecidability," 124). Both Chaucer and de Man draw on the recursive structure of the Liar paradox to generate their own paradoxes: the "authoritative abdication of authority" in the former case and the "meaningless assertion of meaninglessness" in the latter.

39 See further Patterson's classic account of Foucault's influence on new historicism in *Negotiating the Past*, 41–74.

40 Hegel, *Science of Logic*, 486. On Hegel's relationship to medieval dialectics, see Cole, *The Birth of Theory*, 24–61.

41 Hegel, *Difference*, 156. Inversely, we could conceive of Theodor W. Adorno's negative dialectics as a "meta-materialist" decision for the non-synthesis of formalism and materialism, or the non-identity of identity and non-identity. See his *Negative Dialectics*, 143–61. For a recent Adornian reading of Chaucer, see Nolan, "Medieval Sensation," 145–58.

42 Plato in the *Republic* (10.606e–607a) also makes a relevant distinction between two kinds of poetry, one that anticipates, as we will see, the

distinction between *The Second Nun's Tale* and *The Manciple's Tale*.
Acceptable poetry, strictly limited to hymns to the gods and eulogies
for virtuous men, has been *formalized* and therefore orients its audience
towards the idea of the good. Bad poetry, by contrast, is *aimless*, not
related to any form, and can only engender in its audience contradictory
impressions and effeminate emotions that lead away from the regulation
of masculine reason.

43 Lee, "The Question of Closure," 190–200, at 193.

44 Those scholars who believe the Franklin interrupts the Squire include
Peterson, "The Finished Fragment," 62–74; Duncan, "'Straw for Your
Gentilesse,'" 161–4. Scholars who believe the Franklin does not interrupt
include Clark, "Does the Franklin Interrupt the Squire?," 160–1; Neville,
"Canterbury Scheme," 167–79; Seaman, "An Interruption?," 12–18. See
also Partridge, "Minding the Gaps," 51–85.

45 Pugh, "Mutual Masochism," 149–81, also notes the paradoxical quality of the
Franklin's response to the Host: "the Franklin promises fidelity to Harry's rule
while simultaneously excluding his full adherence to this authority" (178).

46 Harrison, "Rhetorical Inconsistency," 55–61, at 56.

47 Turner, "Speaking 'Amys,'" 217–36, at 224.

48 Ibid., 236. See also McEntire, "Illusions and Interpretation," 145–63.
McEntire argues that Chaucer implicitly claims that "Storytelling,
metaphors, are dangerous; they create appearances. And storytellers are
both creators and illusionists at one and the same time. In aligning the
magic of the magician with mere verbosity, Chaucer obliquely warns
about being too credulous a believer in the workings of magicians and
wordsmiths" (160).

49 On the Franklin's rhetorical inconsistency or incompetence, see, for
instance, Knight, "Rhetoric and Poetry," 14–30; Gaylord, "Promises,"
331–65; Camargo, "Oxford Renaissance," 173–207.

50 See, for instance, the exegetical reading of Joseph, "Chaucer's Theodicy,"
20–32, who argues that despite its pagan setting, the tale "treats the
virtues associated with *gentilesse* within the context of Christian theology.
Dorigen's complaint about the black rocks and her consequent error in
the garden may be seen as elements in a Christian *felix culpa*. The tale
reconciles the representative suffering of Dorigen with the omnipotence
of a benign God who can shed His grace upon the world at will" (32). See
more recently Lee, "Apollo's Chariot," 47–67. Lee insists that "Whereas
the *Squire's Tale* is pagan, incomplete, and magical, the Franklin's sequel
(and I use that word advisedly) is not merely complete in itself but a
completion of the unity called fragment 5; it repudiates magic by treating
it as mere illusion, and it contains a Christian subtext in its ostensibly
pagan setting" (47).

51 See also McEntire, "Illusions and Interpretation," 158: "That Chaucer inserts this explicitly evocative term [i.e., "Nowel"] into the context of his pagan cosmological schema, his singular use of the term, microcosmically mimics the story as a whole."

52 Eade, "Astronomy," 53–85, at 68.

53 Lucas, "Astronomy, Astrology and Magic," 5–16, at 16.

54 See, for instance, Jefferson, *Consolation of Philosophy*, 47–80; Hume, "The Pagan Setting," 289–94; Bachman Jr., "'To Maken Illusioun,'" 55–67;

55 On the juxtaposition of pagan and Christian frames of reference in the tale, see Hume, "The Pagan Setting," 289–94; Pearsall, *The Canterbury Tales*, 147. While Hume dismisses the Christian references in the Dorigen's prayer as "commonplaces," Pearsall regards her appeal to "Eterne God" as "highly ambiguous." See also Minnis, *Pagan Antiquity*, who observes "the currency, in the age of Chaucer, of a more liberal attitude to the pagan past than had existed hitherto" (59).

56 See Kearney, "Truth and Illusion," 245–53; Benjamin, "The Concept of Order," 119–24.

57 Rosenfeld, *Ethics and Enjoyment*, 169. On Dorigen's dilatory strategy, see also Kao, "Shameful and Unshameful," 99–139; Gaston, "The Poetics of Time Management," 227–56.

58 Lee, "'A Woman True and Fair,'" 169–78, at 170. See also Crane, "The Franklin as Dorigen," 236–52, who believes Dorigen's lengthy contemplation of suicide "makes a small place for self-assertion under the sign of acquiescence. That she preserves herself precisely in order to submit to Arveragus's command reaffirms her functional dependence" (249). See also Hansen, *Fictions of Gender*, on Dorigen's "excess of desire" (274) more characteristic of Chaucer's men. Dorigen's dependence on Arveragus has led scholars to consider her immature, overemotional, and silly. See in this regard Berger, "The F-Fragment," 135–56; Burlin, "Chaucer's Franklin," 55–73; Kaske, "Chaucer's Marriage Group," 45–65; Peck, "Sovereignty," 253–71. By way of contrast, see Raybin, "Rereading Dorigen, Rereading Marriage," 65–86, who focuses on Dorigen's radical freedom: "queenlike, she rises above the vulgarity of her lover and the pettiness of her husband to lift them with her to a higher moral level" (81).

59 See Battles, "Reconsidered," 38–59, who notes that "Dorigen exhibits, in the garden scene, behavior that we see neither before nor after this moment. In fact, up until this point, Dorigen seems incapable of jest. By making Dorigen's playful conduct towards Aurelius unprecedented, Chaucer introduces an erratic, perhaps impulsive, element into Dorigen" (53).

60 McEntire, "Illusions and Interpretations," 152.

61 Gaylord, "Promises," 331–65 at 365. Other scholars who believe the tale satirizes the teller are Spearing, ed., *The Franklin's Prologue and Tale*; Aers,

Creative Imagination, 160–9; Huppé, *A Reading*, 174. For a more recent consideration of gentility in the tale, see Lucas, "Aurelius," 181–200.

62 For harsh assessments of Arveragus's resolution to his wife's dilemma, see also Wurtele, "The Truth about 'Trouthe,'" 359–74; Frazier, "Digression on Marriage," 75–85; Blamires, *Chaucer, Ethics, and Gender*, 152–71. More recently, Pugh, "Mutual Masochism," 175, remarks on Arveragus's "capricious and arbitrary reaction to Dorigen's amatory suffering."

63 See Mann, *Geoffrey Chaucer*, 116; Lawler, *The One and the Many*, 79; Morgan, "Moral Argument," 285–306. See, more recently, McTaggart, *Shame and Guilt*, 74: "when we consider the cost to Arveragus in terms of shame, it becomes clear that it no way could this acceptance of cuckoldry amount to an exercise of *maistrie*."

64 Mathewson, "Illusion of Morality," 27–37, also observes this paradox: "this act of fidelity, if carried out, requires sexual infidelity to Arveragus" (31). Greene views this contradiction as indicating the limitations of a deontological ethics of "trouthe" in "Moral Obligations," 88–107.

65 See, by way of contrast, Hume, "Private and Public Faces of Marriage," 284–303: "Arveragus is trying to sustain a social image of a successful, faithful marriage that fits with society's expectations rather than his own principles" (299–300). See also Ganze, "Dorigen and Honor," 312–29.

66 In contrast, Frazier, "The Digression on Marriage," 75–85, argues that the Franklin's rumination on the ideal marriage is disconnected from his narrative, instead constituting a response to the Wife of Bath, Clerk, and Merchant.

67 See Kittredge, "Chaucer's Discussion of Marriage," 435–67. Although Kittredge is invariably credited with the idea of Chaucer's "Marriage Group," Scala, "The Women in Chaucer's 'Marriage Group,'" 50–6 and Pearsall, "Eleanor Prescott Hammond," 29–36, have shown that the scholar who invented the term was Eleanor Prescott Hammond. See her *Chaucer: A Bibliographic Manual*, 256.

68 The first to demonstrate Chaucer's indebtedness to the *Filocolo* for *The Franklin's Tale* was Rajna, "L'Episodio delle questioni," 40–3; "Le Origini della novella," 204–67.

69 Edwards, "The *Franklin's Tale*," 1.230–1.

70 Ibid., 238. For detailed considerations of the relationship between Menedon's story and *The Franklin's Tale*, see especially Pearcy, "Épreuves d'amour," 159–85; Burger, "*Cosa impossibile*," 165–78; Edwards, "Source, Context, and Cultural Translation," 141–62; Battles, "Reconsidered," 38–59; Rossi-Reder, "Male Movement and Female Fixity," 105–16.

71 On the conclusion to *The Franklin's Tale* and the interpretive openness it generates, see also Gravlee, "Presence, Absence, and Difference," 177–87.

72 See Lacan, *On Feminine Sexuality*, 145: "I incarnated contingency in the expression 'stops not being written.' For here there is nothing but encounter, the encounter in the partner of symptoms and affects, of everything that marks in each of us the trace of his exile – not as subject but as speaking – his exile from the sexual relationship."

73 On the debate between historicism and psychoanalysis in Chaucer studies, see Patterson, "Pardoner on the Couch," 638–80; Fradenburg, "Sacrifice your Love," 43–78; Scala, "Historicists and Their Discontents," 108–31; Sebastian, "Theory Wars," 767–77.

2. Lest Ye Be Judged: Fragment 1 and the Law of Unintended Consequences

1 Muscatine, *French Tradition*, 189–90; Cooper, *Structure*, 104. On the triumph of order over chaos in the tale, see also Frost, "Interpretation," 289–304. Fichte, "Man's Free Will," 335–60; Brewer, "Problem of Cultural Translatability," 103–12; Finlayson, "Dialogue of Romance, Epic, and Philosophy," 126–49.

2 Hanning, "'The Struggle," 519–41, at 537. Scholars who read the tale as stressing the incapacity of formal protocols for containing disorder include Salter, *Chaucer*; Neuse, "Chaucer's Human Comedy," 299–315; Foster, "Humor," 88–94; Blake, "Order and the Noble Life," 3–19; Scheps, "Chaucer's Theseus," 19–34.

3 Hanning, "Noble Designs," 540. On the related problem of whether the Knight's portrait in the *General Prologue* is straightforwardly laudatory or contains some implicit criticism, see Rigby, "The Knight," 42–62.

4 On the tension between history and the stasis of chivalric ideology, see also Shimomura, "The Walking Dead," 1–37.

5 Aers, *Creative Imagination*, 195.

6 Patterson, *Subject of History*, 230.

7 Leicester, *Disenchanted Self*, 362. See also Amtower, "Mimetic Desire," 125–44; Knapp, *Chaucer and the Social Contest*, 31: "The *Knight's Tale* is the product of a hope that there lives a benign stability at the center of the world … Yet such a vision is always fragile, vulnerable to the perils of its own retelling, which threaten to disclose the struggles raging just beneath the calm surface of a seemingly authorized text."

8 According to Spearing, *Medieval to Renaissance*, the tale is characterized by a "classical simplicity and rationality of structure" that permits "no narrative complications, no irrelevancies, none of the procedure by digression that is the typical method of medieval romance" (39). See the outline of the tale's intricately patterned structure provided by Cooper, *Oxford Guides to Chaucer*, 74.

9 On the resistance of the Amazons to submission, even after their defeat by Theseus, see Stein, "The Conquest of Femeneye," 188–205; J. Friedman, "Between Boccaccio and Chaucer," 203–22; Weisl, *Conquering the Reign of Femenye*.

10 For a recent reading that praises Theseus's humanity and zeal for justice, see Morgan, "Worthiness," 115–58. On Theseus as an ideal ruler, especially in comparison to Richard II, see also Rigby, *Wisdom and Chivalry*.

11 On the besotted Arcite's lack of respect for oaths, see "Forsworn and Fordone," 416–32; Stretter, "Rewriting Perfect Friendship," 234–52.

12 See, for instance, Minnis, *Pagan Antiquity*, 143: Theseus "imposes law and order on anarchy and potential chaos, brings reason to bear on destructive passions, reconciles warring factions, and in general makes a virtue of necessity. The state of Athens can be happy because its king is a philosopher, a *sapiens* in the subject-areas of ethics, politics, and even metaphysics."

13 See, for instance, Blake, "Order and the Noble Life," 18–19: "Theseus is deluded in believing in Jupiter – that is, the gracious Jupiter of the "cheyne of love" – and leaving Saturn – disorder, chance, the arbitrariness of Fortune – out of account. He is deluded in believing in the efficacy of his own will, with the implicit assumption that it is an instrument of the divine intention. The tale reveals, in fact, that the 'noble life' is like any made, artificial, human order: it offers aesthetic satisfaction, but it is not the earthly embodiment of God's scheme, nor a purposeful, effective agent in the working out of any "ultimate order of all things."

14 Blake also notes that the Knight "seems downright capricious sometimes." Ibid., 17.

15 See Friedman, "Limits of Female Interiority," 212–16; Johnston, "Keyhole Politics," 73–97; Spearing, *The Medieval Poet as Voyeur*, 22; O'Brien, "Fire and Blood:," 157–67; Sherman, "The Politics of Discourse," 87–114. See also Knapp, *Social Contest*, 24, who suggests that the Knight averts his eyes from Emelye so as not to make the same error as Actaeon.

16 I cite the translation of the *Teseida* provided by Coleman, "The *Knight's Tale*," 1.177.

17 Ibid., 1.182.

18 Crane, "Medieval Romance and Feminine Difference," 47–63, at 49.

19 Ibid., 62.

20 Ibid., 59.

21 The proleptic depictions on the walls of the temple of Mars parallel the suspension of temporal logic in the temple of Diana. We see represented there Caesar, Nero, and Antony, "Al be that thilke tyme they were unborn" (1.2033).

22 On the repetition of the word "queynte" in this passage as testifying to Emelye's submissiveness to Theseus's masculine and political designs, see

O'Brien, "Fire and Blood," 157–67. On the special status of Diana's temple as compared to the temples of Mars and Venus, see Harrison, "'Tears for Passing Things,'" 108–16.

23 On the function of Saturn in *The Knight's Tale*, see Gaylord, "The Role of Saturn," 171–90; Schweitzer, "Fate and Freedom," 13–45. While Gaylord and Schweitzer argue from a Boethian standpoint that Saturn represents misdirected desires, other scholars have detected a link between Saturnine influence and disease. See in this regard Smith, "Plague," 367–414; Fumo, "The Pestilential Gaze," 85–136.

24 See, by contrast, Cook, "Pagan Antiquity," 26–41: "the attraction that the pagan past potentially held for medieval Christians had to do with the eternal appeal of losable goods: Chaucer saw in his culture's fascination with the ill-fated Troy a fascination with obliteration and utter loss, and with the paradoxical pleasures that such losses bring" (39). On memory, mourning, and the pagan past, see also Edwards, "The Work of Mourning," 361–84; Hunter, "*Remenants* of Things Past," 126–46.

25 Finnegan, "A Curious Condition of Being," 285–98, at 285. On the reappearance of the grove, see also Eyler and Sexton, "Once More to the Grove," 433–9. On the grove as a location that reflects Chaucer's consideration of land use policies, see Grimes, "Arboreal Politics," 340–64.

26 Kolve, *Imagery of Narrative*, 131.

27 On the unwillingness of the Knight to decide on the final destination of Arcite's soul, see Rack, "Heterodoxy and Disjunction," 89–102.

28 On the Miller's blasphemy, see the classic treatment by Rowland, "Chaucer's Blasphemous Churl," 43–55.

29 Patterson, *Subject*, 259. See, more recently, Blamires, "Philosophical Sleaze?," 621–41, who sees the tale as structured by its interest in Boethian providence: "Chaucer's fabliaux, in short, stand informed by a Boethian structure. It is a structure that enables him to arrange for readers a moment of epiphany, holding the rest of the tale in one glance. It answered to – and continues to articulate – humans' enthusiasm for trying to understand their situation in a supposedly providential universe" (640). See also Bryan, "Poetics of the Pun," 1–37, who sees the contingent meanings produced by puns coalescing into a higher order: "Thus the strange accidents and chaotic dialects of English, exacerbated by the uncertain conditions of textual transmission, make it easier for intentions to go awry, just as Chaucer had always worried. But these accidents are here imagined as part of a pattern that is both artistic and philosophical. Here the Boethian universe reasserts itself, and the unpredictable power struggles between the intentions of virtuosic writers and refractory readers melt back into the problems of intentionality on a broader scale" (35). On the

contribution of Boethian musical theory to the structure of both tales, see Chapman, "Aesthetic of Musica," 633–55.

30 Muscatine, *French Tradition*, 226.

31 Bloomfield, "An UnBoethian Interpretation," 207.

32 Kolve, *Imagery*, 215. See also Jambeck, "Characterization and Syntax," 73–85, who argues that *The Miller's Tale* is "calculated to give the lie to the Knight's comic vision: the idealism of romance giving way to the profanity of fabliau, highcourt artifice to homely naturalism, elegant poetic to barnyard colloquialism, expressions of *fine amour* to the vulgarities of coltish appetite" (73).

33 Patterson, *Subject*, 274. See also Zieman, "Chaucer's Voys," 70–91, who argues that Chaucer in *The Miller's Tale* associates the peasant class with his project of generating a new vernacular poetics. On the Miller's inventive use of vernacularity, see Heyworth, "Ineloquent Ends," 956–83.

34 See also Knight's consideration of Miller as one of the "anti-hegemonic" figures in *The Canterbury Tales*, in "Sociology of Literature," 15–51.

35 Cooper, *The Canterbury Tales*, 96.

36 Biggs and Howes, "Theophany," 269–79, at 271. On the ineffability of the private parts of God and woman, see also Bishop, "Confusion of Orifices," 231–46.

37 See Woods, "Private and Public Space," 166–78, for whom Alisoun's body is "the most private space in the tale" (166). See also Fernández, "Private Practices," 141–74, who argues that "Alison recognizes the limits of her agency and, as it were, works with the limitations of any attempt to mark private spaces, that is, with the fact that private spaces are bound to be violated. The men in the tale, by contrast, do not recognize such limits and thus suffer the consequences" (166).

38 Cooper, *The Canterbury Tales*, 310.

39 Kuczynski, "Chaucerian Apology," 315–28, at 326. See also Hanna, "Pilate's Voice/Shirley's Case," 267–82, who argues that Chaucer is attempting with limited success to bracket the vulgar voice of the Miller so as to maintain a distinction between high and low culture.

40 Glenn Burger also observes the alignment of the Miller and Alisoun, asserting that "part of the project of the *Miller's Tale* – as a specific textual moment in the here and now – is to "open up" a hegemonic masculine identity supposedly securely anchored in transcendent notions of class and blood in order to admit 'new men' like Chaucer and his immediate audience. And such a move requires fantasizing the male body as abject, open, and effeminate" (*Chaucer's Queer Nation*, 32).

41 See, for instance, Donaldson, "Alisoun's Language," 139–53: "Absolon imposes courtly discourse upon Alisoun to make her conform to the image of the courtly lady. By making her the object of his 'love longyngs,' he

reinforces his own language self-image by reducing Alisoun to a reflection dependent on his flattery and discourse for her own identity. Absolon is the 'wiley glossator' whose desire to control Alisoun is exposed by the failure of his reading as he tries to define Alisoun's sexuality through the language of courtly love" (145). See also Tripp Jr., "The Darker Side," 207–12.

42 On Alisoun as the Virgin, especially in Absolon's discourse, see Beidler, "'Now, Deere Lady,'" 219–22; Fein, "Herb Paris," 302–17.

43 See the classic treatment by Kaske, "The *Cantica Canticorum*," 479–500.

44 On the therapeutic function of the medical procedure that Absolon's act mimes, see Williams, "Radical Therapy," 227–35; Walls, "Absolon as Barber-Surgeon," 391–8.

45 Lochrie, *Covert Operations*, 172. For a comparable reading of the Miller's implicit misogyny and the way it complicates his apparent "celebration of female desire," see also Hansen, *Fictions of Gender*, 223–40.

46 On masculine competition as the governing principle of Fragment 1, see Jensen, "Male Competition," 320–8.

47 Miller, *Philosophical Chaucer*, perceives a similar ambivalence in the character of Alisoun. He argues that Alisoun is at once attractive and aversive because she represents both a passive, feminine object of desire and the Miller's active, masculine subject position. Thus, the Miller "imagines that to be an object of desire is to be castrated, powerless, passive; that one cannot be both desired and active; that to be an object of desire is to be no more than an object, to be objectified. The scary side of the thought of touching Alisoun would then be the thought that she might be aroused by the touching, that she might desire you, so make of you an object, a castrate" (72–3). Miller's insistence that the Miller codes femininity as merely "passive" does not take into account the alignment of the feminine with rebellious and chaotic matter.

48 David Lorenzo Boyd follows Patterson in *Subject of History* by interpreting *The Miller's Tale* as a critique of aristocratic and clerical oppression of the peasant class. He understands sodomy in the tale as representative of abusive misinterpretation: "By first associating clerkly misinterpretation with the sodomitical and then illustrating how the brotherhood of clerks misinterprets John's predicament – saving one of its own while reinforcing the dominant social understanding of the peasants as stupid – does not the Miller imply with this clever juxtaposition that, in a metaphorical sense at least, the Church 'sodomizes' through (mis)interpretation the lowly third estate?" See his "Sodomy, Quitting, and Desire," 243–60, at 256.

49 Patterson, *Subject*, 274. On the relationship of *The Reeve's Tale* to the peasant uprising of 1381, see also Harwood, "Psychoanalytic Politics," 2–27.

50 Blamires, "Chaucer the Reactionary," 523–39, at 532.

51 On the imagery of aging in *The Reeve's Prologue*, see also Smith, "Chaucer's Reeve," 101–6; Harley, "Four Fires of the Afterlife," 85–9; MacLaine, "Chaucer's Wine-Cast Image," 129–31; Everest, "Sex and Old Age," 99–114.

52 On the satanic associations of the Reeve, see Ellis, "Chaucer's Devilish Reeve," 150–61; Vasta, "How Chaucer's Reeve Succeeds," 1–12; Friedman, "A Reading of Chaucer's *Reeve's Tale*," 8–19.

53 The cynical depiction of the simoniac parson in his tale seems to condense many elements of the Reeve's own portrait: his priestly appearance (1.589–90), his hypocritical preaching, his lechery, and his willingness to steal from his lord's estate. The parson, of course, wishes to marry his granddaughter into some "worthy blood of auncetrye" (1.3982) to pass on "hooly chirches good" (1.3983) even if "he hooly chirche sholde devoure" (1.3986). See further Plummer, "Simony and Patrimony," 49–60.

54 Olson, "*Reeve's Tale*," 1–17, at 14.

55 Taylor, "Uncanny Regionalism," 468–89, at 483.

56 The significance of the North, in terms of dialect and culture, has dominated consideration of *The Reeve's Tale*. See, for instance, Tolkien, "Chaucer as a Philologist," 1–70; Garbáty, "Satire and Regionalism," 1–8; Horobin, "Chaucer's Norfolk Reeve," 609–12; Taylor, "Chaucer's Uncanny Regionalism"; Epstein, "Dialect, Regionalism, and Philologism," 95–124.

57 See Baird, "The Law and the *Reeve's Tale*," 679–83, who argues that "what the leering Chaucer, who stands behind his ascetic and preaching Reeve of Prologue and Tale, succeeds so well at establishing, it seems to me, is a standard by which one law is measured by another – the old by the new, the Continental by the English, the private by the public, the Mosaic by the Christian" (680).

58 Olson, "*Reeve's Tale*," also sees the tale as rebounding upon its teller, but in terms of the divine judgment it calls forth: "And when, in the ending of the tale, [the Reeve] shows the merciless miller as, likewise, measured mercilessly, he sets forth the principles of his own doom by promising to himself as rigorous judge a judgment as merciless as that which he brings down on his victim" (16).

59 Other scholars have noted some of these parallels between the Reeve and Symkyn. See, for instance, Heffernan, "Reconsideration," 37–43, at 41–2.

60 See further Fein, "'Lat the children pleye,'" 73–104.

61 Copland, "*Reeve's Tale*," 14–32, at 26.

62 On the treatment of perception in the tale, see Brown, "Containment of Symkyn," 225–36; Grennen, "The Calculating Reeve," 245–59; Yager, "'A Whit Thyng in Hir Ye,'" 393–404.

63 Taylor, "Chaucer's Uncanny Regionalism," also notes this elision: "Before his own undoing, however, Symkyn quite literally reshapes Aleyn's visage

into his own image: 'And on the nose he smoot hym with his fest./Doun ran the blody streem upon his brest;/And in the floor, with nose and mouth tobroke,/They walwe as doon two pigges in a poke' (I.4275–78). Symkyn gives Aleyn the 'kamus nose' (I.3974) he and his daughter notably wear, and the miller and clerk then fall into a pile indistinguishable as 'two pigges in a poke'" (483–4).

64 My consideration of Malyne's rape will proceed within the context provided by Hansen, *Fictions of Gender*, 208–44; Kohanski, "In Search of Malyne," 228–38; Pigg, "Performing the Perverse," 53–62; Allman and Hanks Jr., "Rough Love," 36–65; Sidhu, "'To Late for to Crie,'" 3–23.

65 Kohanski, "In Search," 230.

66 In an influential reading, Robert E. Kaske is undisturbed by this scene, arguing that the tenderness between Aleyn and Malyne at their parting should be understood as a parody of the aubade tradition ("An Aube in the Reeve's Tale," 295–310).

67 Allman and Hanks, "Rough Love," 46.

68 Miller, *Philosophical Chaucer*, 64. For Miller, John is singled out for special punishment because he most radically contravenes the narrator's naturalistic philosophy: "The fact that John loves Alisoun more than he does his own life, that the end of the world for him means first of all her death, provides the wedge in his psyche that opens him to Nicholas's plot. It also provides the clearest case for his perversity on the Miller's account; for the Miller's carelessness, and his entire view of motivation, is predicated on nothing mattering more than one's own life. More pointedly, no one can matter that much. Other people are at most the objects or instruments of self-gratification: in the genesis of motivation, self-interest always comes first" (64–5).

69 Friedman, "Limits of Female Interiority," 215.

70 See Casey, "Unfinished Business," 185–96 for a recent and thorough account of this debate. Casey's conclusion, made on the basis of consideration of the manuscript evidence, anticipates my own reading: "So what are we to make of the *Cook's Tale*? How can it be complete and incomplete at the same time? The accumulation of sins within it and the startling vulgarity of the final line may cause one to suspect that Chaucer intended to interrupt the tale of Perkyn's misadventures, as he does the *Tale of Sir Thopas*, the *Squire's Tale*, and the *Monk's Tale*. Thus, the tale may be complete for Chaucer, although not completed by the Cook. Ultimately, we may never know what Chaucer had in mind for the *Cook's Tale*. Without new textual evidence, all speculation is suspect, and the commentary must remain, like many of Chaucer's stories, open" (191).

71 Howard, *Idea of the Canterbury Tales*, 245.

72 See further Partridge, "Minding the Gaps," 51–85.

73 On Chaucer's relationship to Adam Pinkhurst, see Mooney, "Chaucer's Scribe." On Pinkhurst's note, see also Horobin, "Adam Pinkhurst," 351–67, at 358–9.

74 Meyer-Lee, "Abandon the Fragments," 47–83, at 72–3. See also his "Fragments IV and V," 1–31.

75 A related point is made by Cohen, *Medieval Identity Machines*, 23: "The *Canterbury Tales* project could not be finished by Chaucer because it aspires to no totality." My claim, however, is that we cannot decide whether the *Tales* aspire to totality.

3. Vengeance and Forgiveness in Fragments 2 and 3

1 Delasanta, "And of Great Reverence," 288–310, at 291.

2 Scala, "Canacee and the Chaucer Canon," 15–39, at 25. On the suppression of incest in the prologue and tale, see also Dinshaw, *Sexual Poetics*, 88–112; Goodall, "'Unkynde abhomynaciouns,'" 94–102.

3 On the traces of incest in *The Man of Law's Tale*, to which I will return below, see also Kisor, "Moments of Silence, Acts of Speech," 141–62; Archibald, "The Flight from Incest," 259–72; Hanks Jr., "Emaré," 182–6; Benson, "Incest and Moral Poetry," 100–9; Ashton, "Her Father's Daughter," 416–27.

4 See, for instance, Furrow, "The Man of Law's St. Custance," 223–35: "What lingers in the mind is not just the holiness, but the life that comes with the holiness: the marriage, the sexual relationship, the virtuous and wealthy life in this world are the oddities that stand out against the backdrop of the saint's legend. It is these that are the important burden of the story, assertions made boldly if never altogether convincingly by the Man of Law that a holy woman need not be a virgin, an ascetic, or a martyr" (233). See also Brody, "Chaucer's Rhyme Royal Tales," 113–31.

5 See Ovid, *Tristia*, 5.3.10, and *Metamorphoses*, 5.293–678.

6 See the explanatory note in the *Riverside Chaucer*, 854.

7 But see Edwards, "'I speke in prose,'" 469–70, who claims, in what I believe is a strained reading, that "prose" in the *Man of Law's Introduction* signifies "verse dealing with religious and historical subject matter" (470).

8 See Fisher, *John Gower*; David, "The Man of Law vs. Chaucer," 217–25.

9 Staley, "Gower, Richard II, Henry of Derby," 68–96, at 70. Gower also deploys rhyme royal in the *Confessio*, perhaps in imitation of Chaucer. See Dean, "Gower, Chaucer, and Rhyme Royal," 251–75. Contrariwise, on Chaucer's debt to Gower for the tale of Custance, see Allen, "Chaucer Answers Gower," 627–55; Nicholson, "The *Man of Law's Tale*," 153–74.

10 Lindeboom, *Chaucer's Debt*, 123–46, at 146.

11 Skeat, ed., *The Complete Works of Geoffrey Chaucer*, 3.406.

12 Lewis, "Artistic Use," 485–92, at 487.
13 Caie, "Innocent III's *De Miseria*," 175–85, at 183. See also Cooney, "Immanent Justice," 264–87: "I would suggest that what we have in the Man of Law's Tale is an exposition of a doctrine which, while unimpeachably orthodox, nevertheless emerges as being – at best – facile, and – at worst – fraudulent. If Chaucer did indeed intend any irony in the relation between this Canterbury pilgrim and his tale, it must surely derive from the fact that prevailing medieval orthodoxy on matters of divine providence and justice is in the end seen to coincide so perfectly with the essentially worldly, acquisitive and of course, legalistic perspective of the Man of Law" (285).
14 See Spearing, "Narrative Voice," 715–46: "Manifestly, what we find in the *Man of Law's Tale*, as in most Chaucerian narratives, is not a fixed deictic center but one that is liberated from fixity and enables us to imagine narrative events in a whole variety of different emotional perspectives. The I implied by the tale's many deictics and quasi-deictics has not single position; it is not a point of origin from which a voice emerges, a point outside the story or outside language, as a speaker is outside what he says, but is merely a part of the process of narration" (734–5).
15 Graham D. Caie sees an inaccuracy in the Man of Law's understanding of the Ptolemaic universe: The heavens are *supposed* to move from east to west. Perhaps, then, as he does with incest, the Man of Law confuses what he sees as "natural" (the subjugation of females) and what is "unnatural" ("abominable" sexual relations). See "The Significance of Marginal Glosses," 75–88, at 86.
16 Cooney, "Immanent Justice," 275.
17 See Block, "Originality, Controlling Purpose, and Craftsmanship," 572–616, at 613. See also Farrell, "The Help of God," 239–43.
18 Delany, "Womanliness," 63–72, at 67. See also Yunck, "Religious Elements," 249–61, who states that Custance is "not a character in the modern sense: she is a vehicle for the providential theme and a vessel of divine grace" (257). For Dinshaw, *Sexual Poetics*, 139, she is "an essential blankness that will be inscribed by men."
19 Dawson, "Custance in Context," 293–308, at 296–7.
20 Bloomfield, "The *Man of Law's Tale*," 384–90, at 385. Astell, "Apostrophe, Prayer, and Structure," 81–97, also notes the Man of Law's overblown rhetoric, arguing that "By putting Custance's story on the lips of a sentimental (albeit sympathetic) narrator, Chaucer makes a powerful comment on the popular piety of his time that, with its misdirected veneration of the saints, threatened to obscure the true, exemplary power of their holy lives through 'golden legends' and sensational display" (96).
21 Schlauch, *Chaucer's Constance*; Robinson, ed., The *Works of Geoffrey Chaucer*, 6.

22 Hanks Jr., "Emaré," 182–6, at 185.

23 Archibald, "The Flight from Incest," 259–72, at 269. See also Ashton, "Her Father's Daughter," 416–27.

24 Kisor, "Moments of Silence," 141–62, at 157.

25 See Schibanoff, "Worlds Apart," 59–96, who finds in the tale an effort to contain the threat posed by "proximate Others," such as women, heretics, and the oriental. See also Dinshaw, "Pale Faces," 19–41; Lavezzo, "Beyond Rome," 149–80; Chapters 2 and 4 of Heng, *Empire of Magic*.

26 For a reading of Custance's mission to Syria in the context of crusading literature, see Lewis, "History, Mission, and Crusade," 353–82.

27 *Sources and Analogues*, 2.318: "And she, suddenly overcome with fear, and seeing the king like a man out of his mind, holding his naked sword over her, and fully aware she was guilty of such great treachery, begging for mercy, without more delay she confessed to all her crime. And the king with great fierceness told her she would have such mercy as her treason required. 'For you had no pity on me, nor on my wife, nor my child, neither will I have any pity on you!' And with that he struck off her head and [cut] her body to pieces as she lay naked in her bed." Also significant in this passage are the incestuous undertones generated by the "naked sword" of the son cutting into the naked body of the mother.

28 On the conflict and commerce between eastern and western laws in the tale, see also Lynch, "Storytelling, Exchange, and Constancy," 409–22.

29 Scholars have long been troubled by the tone of this passage. See, for instance, Robinson, *Chaucer and the English Tradition*, 156: "The final sign that Chaucer can't keep up the mysterious holiness comes in the occasional lapse into the manner of the Wife of Bath, which is, in this context, very much like giggling in church." Furrow, "Sex and Saeculum," concurs with Robinson: "I must agree that the tone of the passages is odd, the jocularity perhaps a little snickering" (224).

30 Dinshaw, *Sexual Poetics*, 112.

31 *Sources and Analogues*, 2.326.

32 Dawson, "Rethinking the Protagonist," 299.

33 But see Lynch, "'Diversitee bitwene hir bothe lawes,'" 74–92, who understands *The Man of Law's Tale* as demonstrating the limitations of human law as compared to divine law: "We live under a law that, even as it seeks accommodation, can never achieve perfect harmony with the laws of the Creator. Still, we have reason to hope for something better. The limitations in human justice that Chaucer explores in the *Man of Law's Tale* would lack full meaning if they were not also seen against the perfect, uncompromised justice that ultimately secures for the tale's heroine her

eternal, though elusive, 'reward'" (92). On the distinction between human and divine law, see also Grennen, "Chaucer's Man of Law," 498–514.

34 Mann, *Feminizing Chaucer*, 106.

35 W.C. Johnson Jr., "The Man of Law's Tale," 201–22, at 211. On Custance's resistance to the designs of the Man of Law, see also Hendrix, "'Tennance Profitable,'" 141–66, who reads Custance as resisting "the Man of Law's efforts to fix and commoditize her" (157).

36 See Tinkle, "Contested Authority," 268–93, at 269–70: "Jerome drafts the women to articulate a specific kind of resistance to his ascetic interpretive program; after alluding to the women's counterargument, he argues with it, and, not incidentally, marginalizes their 'carnal,' 'feminine' stance. Far from reproducing Jerome's agenda, Chaucer reverses the exegetical drama: in the *Wife of Bath's Prologue* Jerome's feminine interlocutors emerge from the wings and take the stage for a stunning soliloquy." For a similar account of the Wife's exegetical stratagem, see Longsworth, "The Wife of Bath," 372–87.

37 On the rhetorical character of Jerome's *Adversus Jovinianum*, see Smith, "The Wife of Bath Debates Jerome," 129–45, at 131, who argues that "Jerome summons up all his rhetorical skills, all his knowledge of the Greek, Latin, and Hebrew classics, and a biting wit in this ambitious if crude attack. There is never the slightest question of Jerome finding any common ground with this 'Epicurus of Christianity.' Jerome's is the all-out war of the diatribe satirist, out to combat his arch-enemy." On the association of Alisoun's literal counter-interpretation of scripture with Lollard heterodoxy, see Tinkle, "The Wife of Bath's Marginal Authority," 67–101; Blamires, "The Wife of Bath and Lollardy," 224–42; Besserman, *Chaucer's Biblical Poetics*, 138–59.

38 Dinshaw, *Sexual Poetics*, 115, by contrast, finds the Wife's mimetic strategy, following Irigaray, subversive of the dominant order: "Speaking as the excluded Other, she explicitly and affirmatively assumes the place that patriarchal discourse accords the feminine. Far from being trapped within the 'prison house' of antifeminist discourse, the Wife of Bath, I argue, 'convert[s] a form of subordination into an affirmation,' to adapt Luce Irigaray's words here; she *mimics* the operations of patriarchal discourse." See also Carruthers, "The Wife of Bath and the Painting of Lions," 209–22; Delany, "Strategies of Silence," 49–69; Schibanoff, "Taking the Gold out of Egypt," 83–110; Minnis, *Fallible Authors*, 253–64.

39 Cox, *Gender and Language in Chaucer*, 37. See also Hanning, "Roasting a Friar," 3–21: "Chaucer's Wife is thus an ironic representation of his awareness of how, by imposing identity on others by means of transmitted authorities, we give them only the options of conforming to or rebelling against stereotypes – and, in the latter case, of conforming to counterstereotypes" (19).

40 On the uncertainties engendered by the Wife's "feminism," see also
Hansen, "'Of his love daungerous to me,'" 273–89: "Despite their obvious
love of speaking and their fluency with words, both Chaucer and the Wife
also seem to share a fantasy of silent submission to higher forces. As we
have seen, the happy endings of the Wife's prologue and tale, however
undercut by their failure to seem fully consistent with other aspects of her
performance, reveal a romantic willingness to become what most men are
said to want women to be" (285). On the sadomasochism of the prologue
and tale, see Miller, *Philosophical Chaucer*, 191–215.

41 Mann, *Feminizing Chaucer*, 66. Likewise, Lindley, "'Vanysshed was this
Daunce, He Nyste Where,'" 1–21, sees the Wife of Bath's discourse as "an
authoritative warning about the dangers of authority" (18).

42 Leicester, "Of a Fire in the Dark," 174.

43 Mann, *Feminizing Chaucer*, 68 and 74. See also Knapp, *Social Contest*, 127–8:
"She has proved that *caritas*, the foundation stone of Christian ethics is
contradicted by anti-feminist discourse."

44 Van, "False Texts," 179–93, at 180.

45 Patterson, *Subject of History*, 313.

46 See Laird, "The Astronomer Ptolemy," 289–99, who argues that the Wife
degrades Ptolemy's moral wisdom.

47 Alford, "The Wife of Bath versus the Clerk of Oxford," 108–32, at 110.
Alford's interpretation of the Wife is in line with Robertson; the former
understands her as feminine rhetoric, the latter understands her as
feminine carnality. See Robertson, *Preface*, 330: "the wife represents
carnality, with reference both to the Scriptures and to life generally."

48 For a different approach to paradox in the Wife's discourse, see Masi,
"Boethius," 65–78.

49 For a recent discussion of the semantic range of "queynte," see Bjork, "The
Wife of Bath's *Bele Chose*," 336–49.

50 See Leicester, "'My bed was ful of verray blood,'" 234–54. In the conclusion
to his analysis of Alisoun's dream of Jankyn, he states: "I want to end by
suggesting that, far from always producing the same result in any text, a
deconstructive understanding of text itself as the space of indeterminacies
is more productive of different *determinate* effects in the same text and
outside it than any search for a final determinate meaning could provide"
(254). For a similar reading, see Straus, "The Subversive Discourse,"
527–54: "The Wife is the uncontrollable voice that eludes interpretative
truth. The ultimate secret she reveals is that all who think they can control,
penetrate and master such texts as she represents are deluded" (550).

51 See Burton, "The Wife of Bath's Fourth and Fifth Husbands," 34–50, who
also detects the ambivalence the Alisoun demonstrates towards her fourth
husband: "It would obviously have been a more complete revenge (in

her own judgment and in that of her listeners), as well as a more likely way to have fired her husband's jealousy, if she had indeed lit many candles at her lantern instead of merely pretending to have done so; she could then more justly have claimed that she had 'made hym of the same wode a croce'" (40). See also Palomo, "The Fate of the Wife of Bath's 'Bad Husbands,'" 303–19: "She 'made hym of the same wode a croce,' and yet the expression itself suggests a sorrow and injury that talionic justice could not completely alleviate" (308).

52 See Haskell, "The St. Joce Oath," 85–7.

53 For a recent consideration of the various modalities of masculine violence in the prologue, see Parsons, "Beaten for a Book," 163–94.

54 Patterson, "For the Wyves Love of Bathe," 658. See further Pelen, "Chaucer's Wife of Midas Reconsidered," 141–60, who also argues that the Midas digression reveals the secret of Alisoun's desire. He thus concludes: "Midas's Wife also represents in her confession by the marsh the secret longing of Alisoun herself to be judged as the instrument of Christ's sovereign authority in a poem about a timeless union beyond youth and age, or beyond the perils of the love chase." See more recently Pitcher, *Chaucer's Feminine Subjects*, 35: "The story of Midas suggests that the parable of feminine desire within which it appears be understood as the expression of Alison's own subjectivity."

55 Patterson, "For the Wyves Love of Bathe," 657–8.

56 Ibid., 694.

57 Ibid., 695: "The 'joly body' of the Wife's text is thus a paradigm for the *Canterbury Tales* as a whole: just as her speaking is a dilation that defers her conclusion, so too are the *Tales* as a whole a 'game' or 'pleye' that postpones the penance of Canterbury." See also Rigby, "The Wife of Bath," 133–65, who argues that the teachings of the Parson eventually correct the errors of the Wife of Bath: "Those critics who offer a didactic or moralistic reading of Chaucer are often seen by their opponents as offering an excessively serious interpretation of his work. In the case of the Wife of Bath, however, it is those who take Alisoun's words seriously, understanding literally a defence of women which was meant ironically, who, in this case at least, are guilty of the sin of making 'ernest of game'" (158).

58 On the manner in which this inversion undermines the juridical reification of gender difference, see Edwards, "The Rhetoric of Rape," 3–26.

59 McKinley, "The Silenced Knight," 359–78, at 366.

60 Thomas, "The Problem of Defining *Sovereyneytee*," 87–97, at 96. See, by contrast, Scala, "Desire in the *Canterbury Tales*," 91–108, whose Lacanian reading of the tale's conclusion posits the Wife's "fantasy of submission to a worthy man, a desire that positions her somewhat uncomfortably as

the silent maiden and accounts for the rape opening her unique version of this traditional tale" (107). See also Nakley, "'Rowned She a Pistel,'" 61–87, who argues that the Wife's reflection on sovereignty in marriage encodes a fantasy of national identity that can cross lines of class and gender.
61 Dickson, "Deflection in the Mirror," 61–90, at 89.
62 O'Brien, "Troubling Waters," 377–91, at 391. See also Normandin, "The Wife of Bath's Urinary Imagination," 244–63.
63 Robertson observes that Midas's bath in the fountain to wash away his curse is "a remedy that would have had rather obvious connotations to medieval readers" ("The Wife of Bath and Midas," 1–20, at 6).
64 Scala, *Desire in the* Canterbury Tales, 135–6.
65 By contrast, Meyer, "Chaucer's Tandem Romances," 221–38, understands the tale as reversing the emphasis of the prologue: "The shrill virago of the prologue really does want to dominate husbands like Jankyn. In the tale, however, the patient hag requires submission only to complete the moral re-education and renewal of the hero" (234).
66 Pugh, "Queering Genres," 115–42, at 134.

4. Reading Griselda Charitably in Fragment 4

1 Robinson, ed., *The Works of Geoffrey Chaucer*.
2 Yamamoto, "Noon Oother Incubus but He," 275–8.
3 For a detailed assessment of the Friar's clothing, see Hodges, "Chaucer's Friar," 317–43.
4 Homar, "Chaucer's Novelized, Carnivalized Exemplum," 85–105, argues that "the summoner's avarice and extortion echo the mendicant Friar's questionable acquisition of profits as described in the *General Prologue*. The similarities between the devil-yeoman, with his calm demeanor, fine clothes, and scholarly acumen, likewise invite a comparison with Huberd through the author's double-voiced intervention" (90). Lenaghan, "The Irony of the Friar's Tale," 281–94, states: "In confusing the narrative levels to enmesh his fellow pilgrim in the irony directed at the summoner in the tale, the Friar himself has slipped into his own net. When churchmen like these come together with a devil, the devil is the only one you can trust. It is surely Chaucer's final irony that the only major voice left uncompromised at the end of the tale is the fiend's" (293). Leicester, "'No Vileyns Word,'" 21–39, concludes: "Because he tries to have everything – 'vileynye' and 'worthynesse,' demonic hatred and Christian charity, insult and apology – he ends with nothing. The tale the Friar finally tells is a precise expression of his 'status' in the widest sense: it is too 'honeste' to let him express his anger in a satisfying way, and not honest enough to protect him. In the quarrel with the Summoner his responses have

rendered him both committed and condemned to that least satisfactory of gestures, the pulled punch" (37).

5 See Clark, "Doubting Thomas," 164–78. Clark notes that "the character of Chaucer's Thomas provides a mirror image of the dissembling friar. In terms of the St. Thomas parody, the old man assumes the symbolic role of 'doubting Thomas,' complementing the friar's parodic 'Thomas of India'" (169).

6 See further Levitan, "The Parody of Pentecost," 236–46; Szittya, "The Friar as False Apostle," 19–46; Finlayson, "Chaucer's *Summoner's Tale*," 455–70.

7 The classic treatment of the sources to *The Clerk's Tale*, Petrarch's version and the anonymous *Livre Griseldis*, is Severs, *The Literary Relationship of Chaucer's Clerkes Tale*. See also Kellogg, "The Evolution of the Clerk's Tale," 276–329; Kirkpatrick, "The Griselda Story," 231–47; Morse, "The Exemplary Griselda," 51–86.

8 On the contemporary meaning of this reference, see McCall, "Chaucer and John of Legnano," 484–9.

9 *Epistolae Seniles*, XVII.3. Quotation taken from *Sources and Analogues*, 1.108.

10 See also Schwebel, "Redressing Griselda," 274–99, who notes "Chaucer's characterization of the proem as too long may perhaps parody Petrarch's earlier assertion that he did not read all of the *Decameron* because it was 'very lengthy'" (292).

11 Ibid., 108–9; my emphasis. For a detailed account of the epistolary exchange between Petrarch and Boccaccio, see Middleton, "The Clerk and His Tale," 121–50.

12 Wallace, *Chaucerian Polity*, 286.

13 Lynch, "Despoiling Griselda," 41–70, at 44.

14 On this parallel, see Dinshaw, *Sexual Poetics*, 195.

15 The importance of political relationships to the tale has long been remarked. See Muscatine, *French Tradition*, 194–6. See also Grodin, "Chaucer's *Clerk's Tale*," 63–92.

16 *Sources and Analogues*, 1.112–13.

17 Delasanta, "Nominalism," 209–31. See also Stepsis, "*Potentia Absoluta*," 129–46; Steinmetz, "Late Medieval Nominalism," 38–54.

18 The Latin reads: "Ceterum subiectorum michi voluntatibus me sponte subicio, et prudencie vestre fisus et fidei" (*Sources and Analogues*, 1.112–13).

19 Wallace, *Chaucerian Polity*, 292.

20 Grodin, "Political Paradox," 91.

21 On the metaphor of the sovereign's marriage to the state, see Johnson, "The Prince and His People," 17–29.

22 Heffernan proposes a similar argument: "The Clerk's Tale shows, therefore, that while the masses may not be sources of authority, they have the power – and are obligated to use that power – to voice their

desire for needed reform. The lack of critical perspective in the 'unsad' multitude is as dangerous to the commonweal in permitting suffering to go unquestioned as is the blind obedience of Walter's henchman, the sergeant" ("Tyranny and Commune Profit," 332–40, at 339).

23 *Sources and Analogues*, 1.116. The Latin original reads: "Ego, mi domine, inquit, tanto honore me indignam scio; ac si voluntas tua, sique sors mea est, [nil] ego umquam sciens, ne dum faciam, sed [eciam] cogitabo, quod contra animum tuum sit" (1.117).

24 McCall, "The *Clerk's Tale*," 260–9, at 267.

25 Georgianna, "*The Clerk's Tale*," 793–821, at 818.

26 Miller, *Philosophical Chaucer*, 248.

27 Ashe, "Reading Like a Clerk," 935–44, at 939.

28 In a related argument, Ashton understands Griselda's conformity to Walter's will as simultaneously subversive: "Griselda's mimesis deflects Walter's cruelty, and is a means of survival in a world whose rules she knows inside out. It enables her to protect herself and resist appropriation. It also permits her to undermine subtly criticize that world, to turn back upon it all that it has imposed upon woman, and thus fracture its univocal assertion of power ("Patient Mimesis," 232–8, at 237). Ashton's focus on Griselda, however, means she does not detect similar patterns in the conduct of Walter's subjects or the Clerk himself.

29 Kirk, "Nominalism," 111–20, at 118.

30 *Sources and Analogues*, 1.128.

31 Campbell, "Sexual Politics," 191–216, at 209.

32 See further Williams, "'T'assaye in thee thy wommanheede,'" 93–127.

33 See Dinshaw, *Sexual Poetics*, 150: "This allegorization, in fact, precisely thematizes what Petrarch's *translatio* in general does: as interlingual substitution, it excludes women from the audience of the tale; as trope here, it eliminates the particular concerns of women and subsumes them into a larger vision of *man*kind." See also Van Dyke, "Subjected Subjects," 45–68.

34 The Vulgate reads: "nemo cum temptatur dicat quoniam a Deo temptor Deus enim intemptator malorum est ipse autem neminem temptat" ("When tempted, no one should say, 'God is tempting me.' For God cannot be tempted by evil, nor does he tempt anyone").

35 *Sources and Analogues*, 1.128–9.

36 McNamara, "Epistle of St. James," 184–93, at 188. See also Meyer-Lee, *Literary Value*, 50: "if the phrase 'tempted in assay' is meaningful beyond simple tautology (in contrast with the common emphatic redundancy of 'tempted and/or assayed'), 'tempted' here must carry some shadow of its malevolent meaning."

37 While Petrarch implicitly aligns Walter and God, Phillippe de Mézières in his *Le Miroir des Dames Mariées*, a version Chaucer likely knew, explicitly

rejects this alignment: "combien que Dieu ne tempte pas les hommes, selon ce que dit saint Jacques l'apostre, comme fist le marquis s'espouse" ("however, God does not tempt men, according to Saint James the apostle – as this husband did his spouse"). See Goodwin, "The Griselda Story in France," 1.132–3.

38 See, by contrast, Edwards, "'The Sclaundre of Walter,'" 15–41, at 18, who argues that Chaucer reconciles these interpretive extremes: "aesthetically Chaucer finds a middle ground between Boccaccio's hermeneutic multiplicity and Petrarch's closure."

39 Edden, "Sacred and Secular," 369–76, supplies an excellent example of a materialist reading of the tale: "The reader is disturbed because of an anxiety that the happy ending is not necessarily inevitable, that Griselda inhabits an arbitrary world in which she may suffer again. If she exemplifies anything, it is the human condition, viewed *not sub specie aeternitatis*, but from a this-worldly point of view. It is from this firm location in a bleak secular world, unrelieved by Christian consolation, that the tale derives its power to move rather than merely to teach" (376).

40 Dinshaw, *Sexual Poetics*, 154.

41 Mitchell, *Ethics and Exemplary Narrative*, 137. See also Mitchell's "Chaucer's *Clerk's Tale*," 1–26.

42 See, by way of contrast, Normandin, "'Non Intellegant,'" 189–223, at 208–9, who argues that the Clerk belongs to a "glossing group" consisting also of the Wife, the Friar, and the Summoner and that he finds a way to defend his glossatorial "vocation" against its denigration by the Wife and the Summoner.

43 On the moral valence of the dialectic between riches and rudeness in the tale, see Denny-Brown, "*Povre* Griselda," 77–115.

44 *Sources and Analogues*, 1.110.

45 Mann, *Feminizing Chaucer*, 125.

46 See also Condren, "The *Clerk's Tale*," 99–114: "Thus it is that Griselda embodies the medieval Christian's perception of the great irony of the Incarnation, the deliberate absence of all the symbols and demonstrations of worldly power. The Redemption called for Christ willingly to submit Himself to the temporal authority of man, to become subject to creatures who owe their very existence to Him" (111).

47 See, for instance, Morse, "Exemplary Griselda," 84: "as the Clerk's advice to women to practice the Wife's 'crabbed eloquence' becomes more and more outrageous, his sincerity becomes more and more doubtful. Chaucer's is a conventional Clerk, hostile to the antifeminist type of woman that clerks had developed to rail against. The Clerk is, however, a teacher: his irony makes the antifeminist type unattractive and thus presses the female audience to prefer Griselda's example." See also Ganim, "Carnival Voices," 112–27; Chickering, "Form and Interpretation," 352–72.

48 For an excellent assessment of the codicological and interpretive issues presented by this attribution, see Farrell, "The *Envoy de Chaucer*," 329–36.
49 Wallace, *Chaucerian Polity*, 294.
50 On the association of mercantilism and misinterpretation, see Ladd, "The Mercantile (Mis)Reader," 17–32.
51 Kittredge, *Chaucer and his Poetry*, 202.
52 Tatlock, "Chaucer's *Merchant's Tale*," 367–81, at 375.
53 Holman, "Courtly Love," 241–52, at 243. On the Merchant's "warped vision," see also David, *The Strumpet Muse*, 179; Harrington, "Chaucer's *Merchant's Tale*," 25–31; Sedgewick, "Structure," 337–45; Donaldson, *Speaking of Chaucer*, 30–45.
54 Stevens, "'And Venus Laugheth,'" 118–31, at 127. See also Burger, "Present Panic,"49–73; Crocker, "Performative Passivity," 178–98. Brown Jr. provides a survey of the debate in a two-part essay: "Chaucer, the Merchant, and Their Tale," 141–56 and 247–62.
55 Delany, "Constantinus Africanus," 560–6, at 564. See also his "Constantinus Africanus's *De Coitu*," 55–65: "The Creator, who wanted the race of animals to continue firmly and stably, planned for it to be renewed by intercourse and generation, so that by this complete renewal the race would not perish" (56).
56 See Neuse, "Marriage,"115–31, who observes the challenge posed to medieval exegetes by the eroticism of the *Song of Songs*: "In Augustine's formulation, whenever the literal reading of a biblical text does not promote charity, its meaning should be taken only in an allegorical sense. Now, the one biblical text most critically affected by this principle of selectivity is the Song of Songs, with the result that its status in the ecclesiastical tradition is a matter of some considerable uncertainty. In commenting on the Song of Songs, Augustine invoked Paul's dictum about the letter that kills and warned the read against taking in a 'carnal' sense 'much that is written in the Song of Songs,' because it will lead 'not to the fruit of luminous charity but to a disposition of libidinous cupidity'" (119).
57 For a recent reading of the Merchant's inveterate literality, see also Fyler, "Hateful Contraries," 15–45.
58 For a psychoanalytical approach to the ambivalence of the narrator's attitude towards sexuality, see Donie, "'Ye gete namoore of me,'" 313–41.
59 On the treatment of blindness in the tale, see Palmer, "Your Malady," 197–205; Kohler, "Vision," 137–50; Lucas, "The Mirror in the Marketplace,"123–45; Brown, "An Optical Theme," 231–43.
60 See Wentersdorf, "Imagery, Structure, and Theme," 35–62: The "allusion to rape in the *Merchant's Tale* makes it obvious that beneath the outward impression of a potentially happy marriage between an entranced groom

and his modestly silent bride, there is the harsh truth of an unnatural union between a naïve and libidinous dotard and a lusty wench who apparently has been pressured … into a marriage that disgusts her physically and in her eyes merits revenge" (42). See also Wentersdorf, "Theme and Structure," 522–7. See, by contrast, Dalbey, "The Devil in the Garden," 408–15, who reads the classical figures in line with Christian mythographers: "The lust for earthly pleasure which rules the actions of Pluto and Proserpine, the devil and his queen, also rules the lives of the human characters. January, May, and Damyan, blindly following the path of earthly lust, finally put themselves, both spiritually and physically, under the devil's control" (415).

61 On the effectiveness of Proserpina's anti-misogynistic rhetoric, see Turner, "Rhetoric and Performing Anger," 427–54; Pugh, "Gender," 473–96.

62 Patterson, *Subject of History*, 343–4.

63 See Benson, "The Marriage 'Encomium,'" 48–60; Edwards, "Narration and Doctrine," 342–67; Jordan, "The Non-Dramatic Disunity," 293–9; Neuse, "Marriage," 115–31; Stevens, "'And Venus Laugheth,'" 118–31.

64 Edwards, "Narration and Doctrine," 353.

65 On the ambivalence of these figures, see Brown Jr., "Biblical Women," 387–412.

66 Ibid., 395.

67 Ibid., 398. See also Benson, "Marriage 'Encomium,'" 36: "the mention of Rebecca, Judith, Abigail, and Esther raises as many questions as it answers: the advice of all four involved deceit, and in three cases the authority of a husband was subverted."

68 On the relation between these tales, see also Walling, "Placebo Effects," 1–24.

69 See Otten, "Proserpine," 277–87, who associates Proserpina with these biblical wives on the basis that all are Deliverers – Proserpina specifically of women.

70 See, for instance, Bleeth, "Joseph's Doubting," 58–66.

71 Seal, "Pregnant Desire," 284–306, detects a related ambivalence in May's putative reference to her pregnancy: "While January assumes that the female appetite about which she assures him denotes the culmination of his own successful virility and the triumph of his model of masculine-only arousal, the text seems to indicate that May's hunger is only peripherally tied to her pregnancy, a figurative marker of a much deeper and less reproductively centered insatiability that has now been stirred from dormancy" (306). On May's attempt to secure more desirable paternity for her offspring, see Blamires, "May in January's Tree," 106–17.

72 See further Zedolik, "'The Gardyn is Enclosed Al Aboute,'" 490–503.

73 Edwards also observes that the narrator refuses to provide a moral for his tale: "Chaucer's ending does not clarify the tale's effect by providing

a resolution that is tonally appropriate, one that permits us to align our experience with the narrator's final exhortation to be 'glad'" ("The *Merchant's Tale*," 409–26, at 417).

74 See, by way of contrast, Simmons-O'Neill, "Love in Hell," 389–407, who argues that the invocation of Mary "in the anti-feminist context, does not so much praise Mary as it reminds listeners that no other woman is any good" (406). For an early psychoanalytical interpretation of maternity in the tale, see Kloss, "Chaucer's the *Merchant's Tale*," 65–79.

75 For a related interpretation of January as *mater dolorosa*, see Neuse, "Marriage," 127: "The 'crucifixion' he-she witnesses – the sex-change he undergoes in the simile seems perfectly appropriate – signifies, I surmise, the potential death of his old self and its rebirth as able to see the great mystery of the other, of conception, birth, and death, in a way perhaps only the caring, grieving mother can." See also Fumo, "An Interpretive Crux," 1–37.

5. Governance and Rebellion in Fragment 6

1 On the treatment of sexual purity in the tale, see Bloch, "Poetics of Virginity," 113–34.

2 See, for instance, Muscatine, *Poetry and Crisis*, 138–9; Donaldson, ed., *Chaucer's Poetry*, 927; Pearsall, *The Canterbury Tales*, 277–9.

3 Gardner, *The Poetry of Chaucer*, 297; Robertson Jr., "The Physician's Comic Tale," 129–39; and Brown Jr., "What is Chaucer Doing," 129–49.

4 Cooper, *Canterbury Tales*, 253.

5 Mandel, "Governance," 316–32, at 317.

6 See further Collette, "'Peynting with Greet Cost,'" 49–62, who finds in Nature's language of counterfeiting and painting an echo of late medieval thinking on the power of images. See also Young, "The Maidenly Virtues," 340–9, who proposes as a source for the description of Virginia's virtues the *De erudition filiorum nobelium* of Vincent of Beauvais, especially a passage in which Vincent censures the use of makeup.

7 Pitcher, *Chaucer's Feminine Subjects*, 114–15, discusses the narcissistic dimension of the reference.

8 Delany, "Politics," 47–60, at 53.

9 I, therefore, find unlikely the argument of Lianna Farber that "Virginius's success at governance lies not in his ability to make judgments but in his ability to describe reality in such a way that others, most particularly his own daughter, come to agree with him" ("The Creation of Consent," 151–64, at 162). "Creating consent" is, in my view, an odd way to describe unilaterally eliminating the possibility of mercy.

10 See the outstanding analysis of the allusion to Jephthah's daughter by Kline, "Jephthah's Daughter," 77–103.

11 Ibid., 94. See also Middleton, "The *Physician's Tale*," 9–32, at 21: "Despite the passionate tone of these lines, their rhetorical posture is detached and self-regarding … The structure of her father's speech reveals that Virginia is seen as an object, not a person."

12 Cartlidge, "Wayward Sons," 134–60, at 160.

13 Bloch, "Poetics of Virginity," 113.

14 Patterson, *Subject of History*, 373. Lomperis also locates an incestuous dimension to the relationship between Virginius and Virginia in "Unruly Bodies," 21–37.

15 Fletcher, "Sentencing of Virginia," 300–8, at 306.

16 Ibid., 306.

17 Brown, "What is Chaucer Doing," 143.

18 The proximity of Virginius to the Physician's God renders problematic Seal's claim that Virginius's failure is his "Jewish literalism" ("Reading Like a Jew," 298–317).

19 Longsworth makes a similar point in "The Doctor's Dilemma," 223–33: "Just how the worm of conscience applies to Virginia is not very clear. It does apply to the villains, of course; but in bringing the villains front and center for his pious afterthoughts, the Physician has left his heroine stranded and has left his story, where it has been tending all along, in a structural shambles." For Lee, "The Position and Purpose," 141–60, "The Physician's last line … is a cue for the Pardoner's Tale rather a summing up of his own" (148).

20 See also Flannery, "A Bloody Shame," 337–57: "I would suggest that what we see in the Physician's tortuous moralisation is a repeated attempt to fit the story into an interpretive framework, to make it have meaning; in the eyes of its narrator, it is a story that *should* have lessons to bestow. But the fact that, as so many critics have noted, the climax of the story seems to be such a pointless destruction of an innocent life (a moment whose pathos is deliberately heightened by Chaucer) invites the reader, like Virginia, to ask for something beyond the framework of death-or-dishonour that shapes the tale" (352).

21 In a recent reading of the Host's words, Pugh argues that "Harry's masculinity is again revealed to be merely a facade, and the force of his emotional response to the *Physician's Tale* thus reveals another queer chink in the alpha-male masculinity depicted in the *General Prologue*." See "Queering Harry Bailly," 39–69, at 55.

22 Miller, "Chaucer's Pardoner," 180–99, at 186.

23 On the Pardoner's disruption of the pilgrimage's spiritual purpose, see Minnis, *Fallible Authors*, 165.

24 On the importance of relics to the Pardoner's depiction, see Leitch, "Locating Authorial Ethics," 403–18; Malo, "The Pardoner's Relics,"

82–102; Storm, "The Pardoner's Invitation," 810–18; Vance, "Chaucer's Pardoner," 723–45; Knapp, "The Relyk of a Seint," 1–26; Kamowski, "'Coillons,'" 1–8.

25 See Nichols Jr., "Ale and Cake," 498–504; Miller and Bosse, "Chaucer's Pardoner," 171–84, at 184; Minnis, *Fallible Authors*, 140–1; Stevens and Falvey, "Substance, Accident, and Transformations," 142–58; Bowers, "'Dronkenesse is Ful of Stryvyng,'" 757–84.

26 Kellogg, "An Augustinian Interpretation," 465–81, at 465. Kellogg draws on Kittredge's influential reading of the Pardoner, who finds in the apparently sincere *explicit* to his tale "an ejaculation profoundly affecting in its reminiscence of the Pardoner's better nature, which he had himself thought dead long ago" (*Chaucer*, 123). This reading is rejected by Pearsall, "Chaucer's Pardoner," 358–65, according to whom the Pardoner "is, both theologically and in ordinary human terms that need no gloss, dead" (362).

27 Kellogg, "Augustinian Interpretation," 474. See also Reiss, "Final Irony," 260–6, who states of the Pardoner: "evil and fraud are present in him, but they are blended with both good words – his sermon – and innocence of a type traditionally associated with those who are pure and above the worldly" (265).

28 Patterson, *Subject of History*, 401–2.

29 Leicester, *Disenchanted Self*, 61.

30 Ibid., 57.

31 Ibid., 186.

32 Dinshaw, *Sexual Poetics*, 180.

33 See also the brief but highly perceptive article by Scott, "Paradoxes of Dream and Fable," 25–32, who associates *The Nun's Priest's Tale* and *The Pardoner's Tale* through their shared exemplification of the Liar paradox. See further Pearcy, "Chaucer's Amphibologies," 1–10.

34 On the contemporary relevance of the Pardoner's hypocrisy, see Fletcher, "The Topical Hypocrisy," 110–26. On the perverse honesty of the Pardoner and how it relates him to Fals-Semblant from the *Romance of the Rose*, see Chance, "'Disfigured is thy face,'" 423–37; Morgan, "The Self-Revealing Tendencies," 241–55. On Fals-Semblant's use of the Liar paradox, see Greene, *Logical Fictions*, 118–42.

35 Minnis, "Reclaiming the Pardoners," 311–34, at 327.

36 On the Pardoner's relationship to the Pauline ideal of preaching, see also Cespedes, "Preaching," 1–18; Waters, "Holy Duplicity," 75–113.

37 Montelaro, "The Pardoner's Self-Reflexive *Peyne*," 6–16, at 10.

38 On the Pardoner's violation of Wycliffite norms for preaching, for instance, see Lavinsky, "Turned to Fables," 442–64. See also Minnis, *Fallible Authors*, 121–69.

39 See Miller, "Scriptural Eunuch," 188: "If the Pardoner may be analyzed in terms of the *eunuchus non Dei*, his nature and status among the pilgrims of the *Canterbury Tales* may be further clarified in terms of its equivalent – the *vetus homo*. The term 'Old Man' is Paul's (cf. Col. iii, 1–10; Eph. iv, 17–24; Rom. vi, 1 ff.), who also calls him the 'body of sin.' As an aspect of the nature of man, the *vetus homo* represents the flesh and its manifold lusts, opposed to the *novus homo*: that is, the spirit and reason, by which these are subdued."

40 The bibliography on this topic is vast and still growing at the time of this writing. A good place to begin is McAlpine, "The Pardoner's Homosexuality," 8–22. See further Benson, "Chaucer's Pardoner," 337–49; Kelly, "The Pardoner's Voice," 411–44; Meyers, "Chaucer's Pardoner," 54–62; Kruger, "Claiming the Pardoner," 115–39; Whitney, "What's Wrong with the Pardoner?," 357–89. See also Pugh, *Chaucer's (Anti-)Eroticisms*.

41 Pearsall, "Death of a Salesman," 360.

42 In line with my reading, Sturges has also observed that the Pardoner's sexuality and gender are "undecidable in ways similar to those described by Irigaray." See *Chaucer's Pardoner and Gender Theory*, 57.

43 See Horrox, "The Pardoner," 443–59, at 457: "The debate over the Pardoner's sexuality continues, although many of the protagonists would agree that it is impossible to arrive at a definitive verdict. Chaucer lays down too many contradictory 'clues' for them to all be fitted into one model."

44 See, by contrast, Ashe, "How to Read Both," who regards the contradictions of the Pardoner's discourse as evidence only of his absolute degeneracy: "He lives out an absolute contradiction. He is, in short, Satan" (139).

45 See Twombly, "The *Pardoner's Tale*," 250–69, at 250–1, who also notes this double identification.

46 See, for instance, Brink, *History of English Literature*, 171; Bushnell, "The Wandering Jew," 450–60.

47 See Braswell, "Chaucer's Palimpsest," 303–10.

48 See Beidler, "Noah and the Old Man," 250–4.

49 See Barakat, "Odin," 210–15; Harris, "Odin's Old Age," 24–38.

50 See Kittredge, *Chaucer and His Poetry*, 215; Robinson, *Complete Works*, 836; David, "Criticism and the Old Man," 39–44.

51 See Hatcher, "Life without Death," 246–52; Nitecki, "The Convention of the Old Man's Lament," 76–84.

52 See Purdon, "The Pardoner's Old Man," 334–49.

53 Olsen, "'They shul desiren to dye,'" 367–71.

54 See Hamilton, "Death and Old Age," 571–6.

55 See Miller, "Scriptural Eunuch," 197.

56 Astell, "The *Translatio*," 411–28, accounts for this discrepancy to insist
on the equation of the old man and the avaricious rioters. For Astell, the
old man is a sign of Avarice but disfigured because he is translated from
his appropriate place: "The semiotic clustering of old men with gold
as *signa* of Avarice thus defines the *locus proprius* of the Pardoner's Old
Man. As a figure of Avarice, however, the Old Man is clearly disfigured.
That is to say, he displays characteristics at odds with his apparent
allegorical reference; his portrait is, to use a term of Michael Riffaterre,
'ungrammatical.' Not only does the narrative separate the Old Man from
his emblematic *locus*, the gold hoard; it also displaces the attribute of
unkindness, which is conventionally associated with avaricious old men.
The youths are unkind, not the Old Man" (420).
57 On the Pardoner's use of Old Testament material, see Cox, "Water of
Bitterness," 131–64.
58 On the echo of Hosea 13:14 here, generally viewed as a prophecy of
Christ's redemption, see Shoaf, *Currency of the Word*, 220 and 274.
59 For a philosophical reading of the taverners' materialist reading practices,
see Smith, "Death and Texts," 131–44.
60 For instance, in a recent reading of the use of anti-Judaic tropes in the
Pardoner's prologue and tale, Lampert-Weissig states: "The Pardoner
is, then, a hollow man and Chaucer draws upon the perceived spiritual
emptiness of the Jews to amplify this portrayal. The Pardoner's sexuality,
even while its particulars may be subject to interpretation, is clearly
something debased, devoid of love, and even of reproductive purpose.
So too did medieval Christians portray the rituals and the faith of the
Jews as dead and pointless. The Pardoner's relics and even his sermon
require living faith in order to effect good. The Pardoner's faith is empty
and fruitless; Chaucer's references to the Jews evoke and reinforce that
depiction of the Pardoner's barren state. The Pardoner and his relics lay
bare the way that the relationship between the spiritual and material can
be twisted and perverted; invoking the anti-Judaism that animates relic
discourse deepens and reinforces this portrayal" ("Chaucer's Pardoner,"
337–60, at 354).
61 Halverson, "Chaucer's Pardoner," 184–202, at 187.
62 See, by contrast, Dinshaw, "Chaucer's Queer Touches," 75–92, at 89:
"Critics have hashed out these questions time and again: he's faking there,
he's being sincere here. But the queer, always playing a role (and thereby
revealing that everyone does), eliminating any idea of essence, obviates all
question of originality, sincerity, even truth."
63 See, for instance, Legassie, "Chaucer's Pardoner and Host," 183–223;
Dinshaw, "Queer Touches." A notable exception is Green, "The Pardoner's
Pants," 131–45: "'You are the kind of man,' the Host is in effect saying,

'who would not only cuckold me but add insult to injury by trying to get me to kiss your filthy pants'" (145). See also Copeland, "The Pardoner's Body," 138–59, who argues that the Host attempts in this passage to contain the Pardoner's rhetorical excesses.

64 Sturges, *Chaucer's Pardoner*, 76.

65 Burger, *Queer Nation*, 146. See also Bowers, "Queering the Summoner," 301–24, at 305–6.

66 On the correspondence of scatology and cynicism in the figure of the Pardoner, see Stockton, "Cynicism," 143–64.

67 See Storm, "The Pardoner's Invitation," 815: the Host "by juxtaposing the image of the true cross with that of the Pardoner's 'coillons,' reminds the pilgrims of 'relics' that are not only physically but spiritually impotent – relics that very nearly interposed themselves between the pilgrims and the real thing."

68 Howard, *Idea*, is also uncomfortable with the violence of the Host's words. His rejoinder "is not a virtuous act – it is 'quiting.' The Host is as much in the wrong as the Pardoner" (340).

69 Pugh, "'For to be Sworne Bretheren Til They Deye,'" 282–310, at 302.

6. Loving the Prioress in Fragment 7

1 On the technical background of the merchant's dealings, see Cahn, "Chaucer's Merchants," 81–119.

2 On the relationship of the tale to Boccaccio's *Decameron* 8.1 and 8.2 and Sercambi's *Novella* XXXII, see Guerin, "The *Shipman's Tale*," 412–19; Scattergood, "The *Shipman's Tale*," 2.565–81.

3 See Silverman, "Sex and Money," 329–36; Donaldson, *Chaucer's Poetry*, 931–2; Patterson, *Chaucer and the Subject of History*, 349–66; Fulton, "Mercantile Ideology," 311–28; Rogers and Dower, "Thinking about Money," 119–38.

4 Taylor, "Social Aesthetics," 298–322, at 303.

5 Donaldson, 931–2.

6 Richardson, "The Façade of Bawdry," 303–13, at 312. See also Keiser, "Language and Meaning," 147–61; Levy, "The Quaint World," 112–18; Winnick, "Luke 12," 164–90. See, more recently, Fulton, "Mercantile Ideology," 323, who argues that the tale forwards a critique of the merchant based not on Christian ethics but on the basis of his fitness for urban governance: "At a time of urban unrest, dissatisfaction with city governments and the growth of a powerful class of wealthy merchants negotiating with lower bourgeoisie and gentry, the tale interrogates the fitness of a mercantile ideology based on commodification to provide an ideology of urban government, and finds it wanting" (323).

7 Patterson, *Subject of History*, 365. Coley, "Money and the Plow," 449–73, reinforces Patterson's argument: "the *Shipman's Tale* functions within the *Canterbury Tales* not only to evince a recognition of the increasing role of international merchants in the later Middle Ages, but also, and more fundamentally, to naturalize and confirm their critical role within England's evolving economy" (473). On the lack of moral judgment in the tale, see also Nicholson, "The *Shipman's Tale*," 583–96: "from the opening statement of the marital dilemmas of the typical fabliau until the harmonious but ambivalent resolution, the narrator of the 'Shipman's Tale' must take no explicit position at the expense of any of the characters because it is his good-humored willingness to portray their way of life uncritically that allows the multiple incongruities of the poem to emerge" (594). Cooper, *Structure*, 163, makes a similar point: "Half the fun of the other fabliaux lies in their conscious breaking of moral and social norms; here, that the wife sells her favours and the monk cheats her of the price passes without causing a ripple on the surface. Of all the fabliaux in the *Canterbury Tales*, this is the only one to be totally amoral, for the contrasting moral context has disappeared."
8 Epstein, "The Lack of Interest," 27–48, at 48. See now his *Chaucer's Gifts*.
9 Ibid., 48. See also Kendall, "The Great Household in the City," 145–61, who suggests that dialectically entwined with the commercialism of the tale is an aristocratic social economy of largesse and gift.
10 Hermann, "Dismemberment, Dissemination, Discourse," 302–37, at 327.
11 For an account of the scholarly commentary on the relationship between the Wife and *The Shipman's Tale*, see Dane, "Invention of Chaucerian Fabliaux," 287–300. For an influential essay rejecting ascription of the tale to the Wife, see Copland, "The *Shipman's Tale*," 11–28.
12 Other scholars have detected the ambiguity in the merchant's response. See, for instance, Scattergood, "Originality," 210–31: "He forgives his wife; but it appears rather as if he was persuaded by her explanation of how the 'mistake' occurred and not distracted by her verbal virtuosity or by the fact that she is suggesting some sort of bargain. He ignores the dimensions she adds to his original rebuke, or perhaps he does not understand them. Perhaps the implication is that he cannot conceive meanings for the words 'dettour,' 'paye,' 'taille,' 'wedde,' other than mercantile ones" (225).
13 A major focus of criticism on *The Shipman's Tale* is the narrator's predilection for punning. See Abraham, "Cosyn and Cosynage," 319–27; Schneider, "'Taillynge Ynough,'" 201–9; Stock, "The Meaning of *Chevyssaunce*," 245–9; Hermann, "Sign and Symbol"; Joseph, "Chaucer's Coinage," 341–57; Rogers and Dower, "Thinking about Money," 119–38.
14 Hume, "Domestic Opportunities," 138–62, at 156.
15 Epstein, "Lack of Interest," 47.

16 See also Coletti, "The 'Mulier Fortis,'" 236–49, who sees in tale's focus on "array" an ironic allusion to the ideal wife described in Proverbs 31:10–31.

17 Finlayson, "Chaucer's *Shipman's Tale*," 336–51, at 345.

18 For instance, Finlayson, "Civilizing of Fabliau," 346, assumes that it is "money, which has bought his wife's 'virtue' and freed her from debt" that "confirms the merchant in the success of his profession, that is, his identity, and stimulates him to pay his marital 'debt' with vigour."

19 Hermann, "Sign and Symbol," 326.

20 On the commercial language Chaucer uses to characterize the Redemption in the *Canterbury Tales*, see Georgianna, "Love So Dearly Bought," 85–116.

21 Blurton and Johnson, *The Critics and the Prioress*, 16–17.

22 See Friedman, "The *Prioress's Tale*," 118–29; Zitter, "Anti-Semitism," 277–84; Ridley, *The Prioress and the Critics*; Frank, "Seeing the Prioress Whole," 229–37; Alexander, "Madame Eglentyne," 109–20; Dahood, "The Punishment of the Jews," 465–90; Lavezzo, "The Minster and the Privy," 363–82. Tomasch, "Postcolonial Chaucer," 243–60.

23 See Spector, "Empathy and Enmity," 211–28; Rex, *The Sins of Madame Eglentyne*; Kelly, "The *Prioress's Tale* in Context," 71–129; Besserman, "Ideology," 48–72.

24 See Blurton and Johnson, *The Critics and the Prioress*, 24.

25 See especially Fradenburg, "Criticism," 69–115; Patterson, "'The Living Witnesses,'" 507–60. For an essay on the dangers of allowing modern ethical judgments to inform our understanding of the Prioress, see Calabrese, "Performing the Prioress," 66–91.

26 Notable exceptions to this tendency include Hamel, "Something Completely Different," 250–9; Gaylord, "Miracle," 65–84; Besserman, "Ideology," 121–42.

27 Lowe, *Convention and Revolt in Poetry*, 66. See also Jacobs, "Further Biblical Allusions," 151–4, who traces the scriptural, and especially Pauline, resonances of the motto. On the relationship of the motto to its use in the *Romance of the Rose*, see Finlayson, "Chaucer's Prioress," 171–4. On the significance of the Virgilian origins of the motto, see McGowan, "*Et Nos Cedamus Amori*," 199–202.

28 See also O'Brien, "Seductive Violence," 178–96, who notes that in her tale, "the *vincit*, not the *amor*, begins to dominate" (190).

29 But see Murton, "The *Prioress's Prologue*," 318–40, who seeks to detach the prologue from debates around the tale to focus on Chaucer's reflection on the ability of language to access the transcendent.

30 It has been suggested that the narrator's observation that the Prioress's "gretteste ooth was but by Seinte Loy [Eligius]" (1.120) reinforces her legalistic orientation. Fleissner proposes that "loy" is a "subliminal play on words" reflecting the Old French word for "law" ("The Oath," 197–8, at 198).

31 Patterson "'Living Witnesses,'" 511. See also Fradenburg, "Anti-Semitism," who argues that the Prioress cannot tolerate the danger that contingency poses to the static purity of form: "The *Prioress's Tale* is a narrative in which all change can only be imagined as crisis" (108).

32 Price, "Sadism and Sentimentality," 197–214. On the tale's focus on establishing social purity, see also Despres, "Chaucer's Cultic Anti-Judaism," 413–27.

33 See Spector, "Enmity and Empathy," fn. 31. See also Lavezzo, "The Minster and the Privy," who argues that the "exposure of the privy registers how the space associated with oppressed groups are always susceptible to violation" (375). In the terms of my analysis, the Christian gaze formally masters the intimate Jewish space.

34 Archer, "Structure of Anti-Semitism," 46–54, at 50.

35 Fradenburg, "Criticism," 105.

36 Ibid., 110, fn. 28.

37 Ibid., 105.

38 Patterson, "Martyrdom and Imitation," 513.

39 Ibid., 512. For another psychoanalytical reading of the tale influenced, like Fradenburg's, by Julia Kristeva, see Marvin, "'I Will Thee Not Forsake,'" 35–58.

40 See Simons, "The Prioress's Disobedience," 77–83. See, more recently, the account supplied by Lewis, "The Prioress and the Second Nun," 94–113, who argues that the Prioress's "potential for authority remains enclosed and inhibited by her femininity" (110).

41 See, for instance, Hirsh, "Reopening the *Prioress's Tale*," 30–45: "Chaucer saw what many have since intuited reading the tale, that we are all 'synful folk,' and have listened to Satan, and have participated in Adam's sin and Christ's death. Finally we are all Jews, the tale, at its deepest reach, implies; but we are saved by Christ's ever reenacted action" (41).

42 Zitter, "Anti-Semitism," 277–84, at 279.

43 In this regard, see the exegetical reading of *The Prioress's Tale* by Hawkins, "Chaucer's Prioress," 599–624.

44 See Adams, "Chaucer's 'New Rachel,'" 9–18. Although Adams ultimately hesitates to claim that Chaucer has "put his axe to the whole exegetical tree" (18) of medieval anti-Semitism, he does state that the allusion to Rachel arguably "turns the Prioress's racially constituted universe topsy-turvy and makes hash of her anti-Semitism" (12).

45 On the Prioress's concern with martyrdom, see Pigg, "Refiguring Martyrdom," 65–73.

46 There has been a great deal of scholarly speculation on the precise identity of the "greyn" that Mary places in the schoolboy's mouth. See, for instance, Beichner, "The Grain of Paradise," 302–7; Bratcher,

"The 'Greyn,'" 444–5; Taylor, "Little Clergeon," 82–9; Friedman, "The Mysterious Greyn," 328–33; Maltman, "The Divine Granary," 163–70. Perhaps the most widely accepted interpretation has been provided by Oliver, "Singing Bread," 357–64. Oliver proposes that the "greyn" is a piece of manna or a Eucharistic wafer.

47 On this parallel, see Archer, "Structure of Anti-Semitism," 50.

48 Relatedly, many analogues of *The Prioress's Tale* supply an alternative to torture and execution, as the Jews therein convert upon witnessing the miracle of the singing child. See Broughton, "*Prioress's Prologue* and *Tale*," 587–9.

49 See also the Austinian analysis of the *Alma redemptoris mater* by Orth, "The Problem of the Performative," 196–210, wherein he argues that "the *Alma* is both an assertive and a directive. It praises and exerts. But the potent illocutionary force of the utterance obtains in its status as a directive. By overlooking that fact, by misapprehending the speech-act category into which the *Alma* falls, the child aggravates what the narrative has already suggested: the initial failure of his performative act" (204). On the performative force of aurality in the tale, see Albin, "*The Prioress's Tale*," 91–112.

50 See Boenig, "The *Alma Redemptoris Mater*," 321–6, who argues that the *Alma Redemptoris Mater* would be far easier for a "little" seven-year-old boy to learn and sing than the more challenging *Gaude Maria*. In some versions, moreover, the *Gaude Maria* has as its final line an anti-Semitic jibe: "erubescat Judaeus infelix, qui dicit Christum Joseph semine esse natum" (may the unhappy Jew blush in shame, who says that Christ was born of Joseph's seed). See Boyd, ed., *A Variorum Edition*, 15. Boyd argues elsewhere, however, that the *Gaude Maria* in its Sarum use did not include this line, rendering it less likely that Chaucer's audience would understand his choice of the *Alma redemptoris mater* as based on the *Gaude Maria*'s anti-Semitism "'Alma Redemptoris Mater,'" 277. On the sources of the prologue and tale, see also Broughton, "The *Prioress's Prologue* and *Tale*," 2.583–98.

51 On the disjunction of language and intention staged by recitation of the *Alma Redemptoris Mater*, see Russell, "Song," 176–89.

52 See the account in Langmuir, "The Knight's Tale," 459–82. On historical accounts of Jews murdering children in England, see Dahood, "English Historical Narratives," 125–40.

53 See also Ferster, "'Your Praise is Performed,'" 149–68, whose reading of the concluding stanza coincides with mine: "When the tale turns almost obsessively to God and his mercy, it seems to replace Mary's authority with His, but it turns out, in the last line, that He is to be merciful to us because of His respect for His mother. Even God is drawn into worship of His mother, who is here referred to not only by her relationship to

Him, but by her own name" (161). On the assertive feminine voice of the Prioress, see also Robertson, "Aspects of Female Piety," 145–60.

54 Barr, "Religious Practice," 39–65, also notes the importance of the term to the Prioress but associates "reverence" with "connotations of orchestrated veneration" (47) in a reading that focuses on affective devotion to the Virgin but does not address Jewish reverence for the law.

55 It should be noted, however, that St. Nicholas disdains an authoritative figure in a way reminiscent of the clergeon, the Jews, and the Prioress herself. As Osberg observes, "the infant Nicholas honored Christ by fasting, refusing his mother's breast on Wednesdays and Fridays ("A Voice for the Prioress," 25–54, at 27).

56 For an analysis of the critical tendency to admire the aesthetic quality of *The Prioress's Tale* while disavowing its repugnant content, see Wilsbacher, "Lumiansky's Paradox," 1–28.

57 This suggestion is made by Beach, "The Appearance of Pity, Love, and Reverence," 5–10. Critics have noted that the relevance of Hugh of Lincoln's appearance at the end of the tale is not immediately apparent. In an essay that argues that Chaucer is seeking to honour the city of Lincoln itself, Ferris, "Chaucer at Lincoln," 295–321, observes of the tale's final verse: "This stanza is so familiar to readers of Chaucer that most of us have probably assumed that the reference to little Hugh is not only appropriate in a general way but as it were inevitable, the most natural one that Chaucer could have made. But by Chaucer's day, Hugh was obscure and unhonored even in Lincoln. Instead, Chaucer might well have mentioned any one of a number of English boys reputed to have been killed by Jews" (300).

58 For a recent consideration of the pilgrims' response to *The Prioress's Tale*, see Gayk, "'To wondre upon this thing,'" 138–56.

59 It may also be the case that *The Prioress's Prologue* leaks backwards into *The Shipman's Tale*. We are told in the latter that a "mayde child" (7.95) is in the company of the wife during her negotiation with the monk, "Which as hir list she may governe and gye" (7.96). All these elements are present in *The Prioress's Prologue*, wherein the Prioress refers to Mary as "mooder Mayde" (7.467), describes herself as a "child" (7.484), and prays to the Virgin, "Gydeth my song" (7.487). For more on the "mayde child," see Beidler, "Medieval Children," 186–204.

60 Hamel, "Something Completely Different," 250–9, at 253. On *Thopas* as a parody of *The Prioress's Tale*, see also Boyarin, *Miracles of the Virgin*, 156–8.

61 Hamel, "Something Completely Different," 258.

62 For a recent consideration of the tale's genre, especially in connection to its *mise en page* in authoritative manuscripts, see Brantley, "Reading the Forms," 416–38. See also Cannon, "Auchinleck Manuscript," 131–46.

63 On the association of the tale with puppetry, see Haskell, "Sir Thopas," 253–61.

64 On the connotations of the term "elvyssh," see also Gaylord, "'Elvyssh' Prosody," 83–104; Green, "Changing Chaucer," 27–52; Hall, "Elves on the Brain," 225–43.

65 Raybin argues, in fact, that the tale is designed to amuse the young. See his "*Sir Thopas*," 225–48.

66 On Thopas's association with chastity, see Conley, "The Peculiar Name Thopas," 42–61.

67 Gaylord, "'Elvyssh' Prosody," 89.

68 Hamel, "Something Completely Different," thus states of the ridiculous Olifaunt: "By this means, then, the superstitious terror of the Satanic Jews that informs the Prioress's Tale is reduced to what it really is – a child's fear of the imagined unknown" (158).

69 On the associations that would have been generated by the Flemish setting of the tale, see Wallace, "In Flaundres," 63–91.

70 Krummel, "Jewish Geography," 129.

71 See Mandel, "'Jewes Werk,'" 59–68, at 65.

72 See, by contrast, Kao, "Cute Chaucer," 147–71, who argues that "the trauma of religious violence recounted by the Prioress ... is sublimated by Chaucer into a minor reference to Thopas's armor (*hawberk*) as a product of 'Jewes werk'" (166).

73 Whatever the quality of the armor, scholars have noted the absurdity of the arming scene. Mark Dicicco thus finds Thopas's gear to be "a hodgepodge collection of mismatched pieces displaying types and technologies of armour used in different centuries but never together" ("The Arming of Sir Thopas, 14–16, at 15).

74 See also Loomis, "Sir Thopas," 311–13.

75 Burrow, "*Sir Thopas*," 54–8, at 57.

76 Ibid., 57–8.

77 Jones, "'Lo, Lordes Myne, Heere is a Fit!,'" 248–52, at 252.

78 See, for instance, Mann's reading: Chaucer "does not remain external to his creation, the hidden puppet-master pulling the strings. Instead he enters it, placing himself on the same fictional level as the other pilgrims, and his authority on a level with theirs. And he enters it only to be hooted off the stage; his literary 'auctoritee' is rejected by his own literary creations" (*Geoffrey Chaucer*, 126).

79 See Olson, "'Thopas-Melibee' Link," 147–53 and Gaylord, "Sentence and Solaas," 226–35, who both understand *Thopas* as pure solace and *Melibee* as pure sentence. See also Benson, "Their Telling Difference," 61–76, who understands the juxtaposition of tales not as indicating "art versus meaning" but as an investigation of the "meaning of art." He thus asks,

"Can a poet delight without instructing or instruct without delight?"
(66). Patterson's historicized approach to *Thopas* and *Melibee* is related.
He regards the pairing as staging a conflict between different possibilities
of authorial self-definition available to the late fourteenth-century
English poet: "the juxtapositioning of the two tales, and the dramatic
context in which they are located, should lead us to the conclusion that
Chaucer is disowning not the childish frivolity of *Sir Thopas* but the
pragmatic didacticism of *Melibee* and that he is defining his authorial
identity not according to the decorous role of princely adviser but rather
in terms provided by the obsolete and disregarded tradition of minstrel
performance" ("'What Man Artow?,'" 117–75, at 123). Patterson explicitly
reverses the interpretation of Green, who suggests that Chaucer's
"position as court entertainer, successor to generations of professional
minstrels, is belittled in the self-mockery of Sir Thopas, but as the adviser
to kings the author of the Melibee writes essentially without irony" (*Poets
and Princepleasers*, 143).

80 See, by way of contrast, Taylor, "Social Aesthetics," 298–322, who
    argues that the Shipman's punning disrupts the possibility of linguistic
    community while *Melibee* reconstitutes civic discourse by means of its
    inclusively multilingual doublets. On the style of *Melibee*, see the classic
    treatment by Bornstein, "Chaucer's *Tale of Melibee*," 236–54.

81 See, for instance, Palomo, "What Chaucer Really Did," 304–20.

82 On the combination of oral and literate discursive modalities in prologue
    and tale, see Foster, "Echoes of Communal Response," 409–30.

83 See Robertson Jr., *A Preface to Chaucer*, 368–9; Huppé, *A Reading*, 236. For a
    more recent reading that suggests that *Melibee* provides the core doctrine
    of *The Canterbury Tales*, see Foster, "Has Anyone Here Read *Melibee*,"
    398–409. Foster argues that the "conjunction of 'commune profit' and
    personal salvation" contained in the *Melibee* "may be the fulcrum on which
    the moral edification of the whole of the *Canterbury Tales* depends." He
    goes on to state that "If this is so, then *Melibee* is very important indeed; it
    is conceptually central to the journey of life that the *Tales* represent" (402).

84 See Huppé, *A Reading*, 239: "In short, the *Tale of Melibeus* is an allegory of
    Penance, and of the inward meaning of the words of the Lord's Prayer:
    forgive us our sins as we forgive those who have sinned against us. To live
    for the world is to fall prey to the old foes of mankind; to triumph over
    them is to perceive the sin in one's own heart, to feel contrition for this sin,
    and through the Sacrament of Penance achieve God's cure."

85 See Clark "'This Litel Tretys,'" 152–6. Olson, "Thopas-Melibee Link,"
    147–53, believes that "tretys" does not refer to a specific antecedent to the
    Melibee, referring instead to the various materials out of which it has been
    composed.

86 See Farrell, "Chaucer's Little Treatise," 61–7.

87 Grace, "Chaucer's Little Treatises," 157–70, at 157–8.

88 Ibid., 169. On the indeterminacy and interpretive multiplicity of *Melibee*, see also Kempton, "Chaucer's *Tale of Melibee*," 263–78; Waterhouse and Griffiths, "'Sweete Wordes,'" 338–61; Grace, "Telling Differences," 367–400.

89 See Olson, "Thopas-Melibee Link," 150: "It appears, then, that on occasion Chaucer uses 'tretys' to refer to a discussion or document without entailing a specific literary sense of expository tract or a specific political sense of treaty. (*Pace* Robertson and Huppé, there is no evidence elsewhere in Chaucer that it might refer to a collection of fictions.)" Olson does not consider the referential ambiguity of "litel tretys" in Chaucer's *Retraction* (10.1081).

90 Chaucer's tendency to diminish his accomplishment appears also in *Troilus and Criseyde*, which the narrator describes as a "litel bok" (5.1786).

91 For a consideration of the precise meaning of "proverb" in the Thopas-Melibee link, see Hill, "Chaucer's Parabolic Narrative," 365–70, who argues that "proverb" means "parable," suggesting that *Melibee* should be read allegorically, not literally.

92 See Yeager, "Chaucer's Prudent Poetics," 307–21. Yeager argues that despite Chaucer's admission that his version of the *Melibee* may use proverbial wisdom in a way different than expected by his audience, "he asserts that nonetheless the moral content of the tale will be clear to its readers. And again, the moral of the tale is that retributive violence is always wrong, and any rhetorical method that may be used to justify retributive violence must be undermined and resisted" (320).

93 See, for instance, Howard, *Idea of the Canterbury Tales*, 315: "Only again in the *Retraction* does [Chaucer] appear before us without irony." On the relationship between *Melibee* and the *Retraction*, see also Yeager, "*Pax Poetica*," 97–121, who notes, "Forgiveness, certainly, is a theme central to both. In the *Melibee* it forms the core of Prudence's advice to her husband, providing the conclusion to her closely reasoned argument against both and the taking of revenge upon one's enemies. In the *Retraction* the forgiveness Chaucer seeks is his own, from God, despite his self-expressed unworthiness" (117–18). On Chaucer's pacifism in light of current events, see also Scattergood, "Chaucer and the French War," 287–96; Ferster, *Fictions of Advice*, 89–107.

94 Patterson, "'What Man Artow," 157.

95 On the consonance of Christian and secular ethics in the *Melibee*, see DeMarco, "Violence, Law, and Ciceronian Ethics," 125–69.

96 The *Livre de Mellibee* reads: "Quant Mellibee ot oÿ toutes les paroles Dame Prudence et ses sages enseignemens, si fut en grant paix de

cuer et loa Dieu, qui lui avoit donné si sage compagnie" (Askins, "The *Tale of Melibee*," 1.407). Johnson states of Chaucer's version that "The three clauses that Chaucer adds here are designed to emphasize the subtle hierarchical shift that has taken place in Melibeus and to do by suggesting a rational progression. Thus, Melibeus' heart inclines; he considers her intent; he finally conforms and assents to her counsel" ("Inverse Counsel," 137–55, at 144). My position aligns well with Johnson's: Melibee's acquiescence to Prudence is not emotional or coerced but rational and thus free. For an analysis of Prudence's discourse using the tools of historical pragmatics, see Pakkala-Weckström, "Prudence and the Power of Persuasion," 399–412. For a feminist reading of Prudence's persuasive discourse, see Daileader, "The 'Thopas-Melibee' Sequence," 26–39. On the *Melibee* as one of "several contemporary works intended to instruct women of the nobility and the aristocracy in how to govern themselves, their households, and their husbands" (419), see Collette, "Heeding the Counsel of Prudence," 416–33. Collette's argument is extended by Saraceni, "Chaucer's Feminine Pretexts," 403–35. Both productively complicate the generic affiliation of the *Melibee* with the *Fürstenspiegel*, or "mirror for princes," a thesis forwarded by scholars such as Green, Scattergood, Yeager, and Patterson. See also Wallace, *Chaucerian Polity*, who states that the "*Melibee* is not a *Fürstenspiegel*, but a handbook for go-betweens" (221), such as Chaucer.

97 Chaucer closely follows the *Livre de Mellibee* here: "toutevoie la grant humilité que je voy en vous me contraint a vous faire grace" (Askins, "The *Tale of Melibee*," 1.408).

98 Keller, "Prudence's Pedagogy," 415–26, at 424.

99 See further Ramazani, "Chaucer's Monk," 260–76, who also characterizes the Monk as a formalist: "Chaucer rejects not tragedy but the Monk's formulaic version of it. The Monk's formalism, stemming from his urge to collect and reduce, prevents him from seeing that the basis of tragedy is not an 'objective' structure but an affective and hermeneutic program, carrying us from comic hope to tragic grief" (274).

100 On the significance of the Monk's mention of Edward the Confessor, see Astell, "The Monk's Tragical 'Seint Edward,'" 399–405.

101 On the Monk's disruption of chronology, see Kelly, *Chaucerian Tragedy*, 67–8.

102 On the relationship of Chaucer's *De Casibus* to its Italian antecedents, see, for instance, Piero Boitani, "The *Monk's Tale*," 50–69; Haas, "Chaucer's *Monk's Tale*," 44–70; Pinti, "The 'Comedy,'" 277–97; Wallace, *Chaucerian Polity*, 299–336.

103 On inconsistency of the Monk's treatment of Fortune, see Strange, "The *Monk's Tale*," 167–80, who states: "No synthesis of doctrinal Fortune and

passional *Fortuna* is ever achieved in the *Monk's Tale*. Rather, the Monk veers from one to the other and back again for a multiplicity of reasons until the two collide in this one last tale, and the Monk reaches to the striking image of Fortune covering her bright face with a cloud just when men seem to know and to trust her" (176). Jensen seeks to account for this inconsistency in "'Winkers' and 'Janglers,'" 183–95: "In his tale the Monk is exploring the nature of tragedy in a Christian context by examining the way pagan Fortune applies to pagan figures and seeing the extent to which that concept may be applied to Christian stories" (185). On the Monk's use of Boethius for his portrayal of Fortune, see Lepley, "The Monk's Boethian Tale," 162–70.

104 See further Reed Jr., "Nebuchadnezzar and Chauntecleer," 44–56, who argues that the Nun's Priest is inspired by the tragi-comedy of Nabugodonosor to tell his tale of the fall and rise of Chauntecleer.

105 On the imagery of falling in *The Canterbury Tales*, see Allen, "Moral and Aesthetic Falls," 36–49.

106 Neuse, "They Had Their World," 415–23, at 423.

107 See, by contrast, Johnson, "Tragic Nihilism," 7–31, who argues that the Monk successfully "assaults tragedy as a literary category" by allowing us to "peer into the negative space surrounding the tragic, the lamentable, but also radiantly ecstatic truth of New Testament history" (24–5).

108 But see Fry, "The Ending of the *Monk's Tale*," 355–68, who accounts for the Knight's interruption by noting that it occurs when the Monk is relating "the tragedy of Pedro of Cyprus, [the Knight's] old commander" (366).

109 See, for instance, Kelly, "The Evolution of the *Monk's Tale*," 407–14. Kelly argues that "the Knight's reason for interrupting is … not because the tragedies have not held his attention, but rather because they have fulfilled their goal too well and have made him depressed. He prefers, at least in the context of travel entertainment, the pattern of comedy – that is, the unfunny medieval kind of comedy – with misfortune at the beginning and good fortune at the end. That is the way the Knight's own Tale works" (413). See also the classic treatment by Kaske, "The Knight's Interruption," 249–68.

110 For a different view, see Jones, "The *Monk's Tale*," 387–97, who argues that the Monk is responding directly to the Knight and critiquing the latter's mercenary appreciation for modern tyrants, such as Peter of Cyprus and Bernabò Visconti.

111 See Gaylord, "*Sentence* and *Solaas*, 226–35. Cooper argues that the Fragment explores "the status of language" (*Structure*, 162); Astell suggests that Chaucer is investigating "the problem of writing" ("Chaucer's 'Literature Group,'" 282); Travis understands the Fragment as "a metapoetic quest for a fully realized supreme fiction" (*Disseminal Chaucer*, 30).

112 On the relationship between the Prioress and the Monk, see also
Knight, "Colloquium on the *Monk's Tale*," 381–6: "Daun Piers, that
knightly kind of monk, is as much an estate transgressor as the
ladylike Prioress, and the often-noted barely Christian character of his
tales indicates that he, like her, is not aware of the role inherent to the
estate in which they are located, however much they might like to be
elsewhere" (386).

7. Loving Chaucer: Judgment and Charity in Fragments 8–10

 1 See, by way of contrast, Meyer-Lee, *Literary Value*, in which he argues
that Chaucer reflects on his authority and the value of his literary activity
through the Clerk, the Merchant, the Squire, and the Franklin, "the very
four pilgrims whose social identities most overlap with those several
identities that characterized his own social experience." Thus, Meyer-Lee
reads Fragments 4–5 "as a meditation on the conflict between writing and
Chaucer's day jobs, with the latter understood to encompass the nexus
of values associated with the specific normative masculine occupational
identities of clerk, merchant, squire, and franklin" (3).
 2 On the ethical significance of the prosimetrical arrangement of the final
fragments, see also Johnson, *Practicing Literary Theory*, 140–66.
 3 On the Second Nun's prologue and tale as initiating the closing movement
of *The Canterbury Tales*, see Benson, "The Order," 77–120; Howard, *Idea*,
288–306; Dean, "Dismantling," 746–62; Jankowski, "Chaucer's *Second
Nun's Tale*," 128–48.
 4 On the significance of Mary for understanding the tale, see Peck, "The
Ideas of 'Entente,'" 17–37.
 5 On the relationship of the prologue to the tale in terms of the polarities
I have enumerated, see also Clogan, "Figural Style," 213–40; Kolve,
"Chaucer's *Second Nun's Tale*," 137–76.
 6 See, by contrast, Dobbs, "The Canaanite Woman," 203–22, who regards the
ambiguity of gender in the prologue as reflective of the collapse of cultural
boundaries, reinforcing a theme of dissolving boundaries in the tale.
 7 Ashton, *The Generation of Identity*, 56–8. See also Winstead, *Virgin Martyrs*,
who calls Cecilia "shrewish" (64) and "aggressive" (83). On the preference of
male hagiographers for the "virago," see Schulenberg, "Saints' Lives," 300.
 8 On the subversiveness of Cecilia see, for instance, Arthur, "Equivocal
Subjectivity," 217–31.
 9 On the relevance of *The Second Nun's Tale* to the contemporary issue of
female preaching, see Blamires, "Women and Preaching," 135–52, at 151;
Reames, "Artistry, Decorum, and Purpose," 177–99, at 180–1.
10 Collette, "A Closer Look," 337–49, at 347–8.

11 On the marriage of Valerian and Cecilia as part of the Marriage Group,
see Hinckley, "The Debate on Marriage," 292–305, at 303. See also Reames,
"Mary, Sanctity and Prayers," 81–96; Howard, "The Conclusion of the
Marriage Group," 223–32.

12 Raybin, "Chaucer's Creation and Recreation," 196–212, at 203.

13 On the relevance of the tale's depiction of the *ecclesia primitiva* to
contemporary reformist thought, see Sisk, "Religion, Alchemy, and
Nostalgic Idealism," 151–77; Aers, *Faith, Ethics and Church*, 40; Johnson,
"Chaucer's Tale," 314–33.

14 See Summit, "History as Topography," 211–46, at 235, who describes
Cecilia's converts as devoid of subjectivity and programmed only for self-
destruction.

15 Reames, "The Cecilia Legend," 38–57, at 43. In light of the discovery of a
Franciscan abridgement of the Cecilia legend, Reames adjusts her view of
Chaucer's relationship to his sources in "A Recent Discovery," 337–61.

16 Jankowski, "Apocalyptic Imagination," 131.

17 Grossi Jr., "Unhidden Piety," 298–309, at 305.

18 Reames, "The Cecilia Legend," 53. See also Eggebroten, "Laughter
in the *Second Nun's Tale*," 55–61. While Reames argues that the lack
of intellectual engagement in the process of conversion reflects
Chaucer's "theological pessimism" (45–6), Eggebroten counters "that
Chaucer felt his fourteenth-century audience was not interested in
watching the growth of faith and in being persuaded of the truth of
Christianity (perhaps unlike a fourth- or twentieth-century audience).
He expected his readers, already persuaded, to view the whole story
as a series of skirmishes preceding a familiar conclusion – martyrdom"
(58). Jankowski, "Apocalyptic Imagination," understands the
clipped narrative as testifying to an apocalyptic imagination with an
eschatological focus. Robertson suggests that the lack of reasoning
associated with conversion in the tale indicates Chaucer's interest in
free will: "By redirecting the reader's attention away from cognitive
processes and towards those indiscernible processes of the will that
bodily sensation can trigger, Chaucer celebrates rather than denigrates
the human, for he brings to the fore that aspect of the human that even
more than reason defines human beings: free will." See "Apprehending
the Divine," 111–30, at 112.

19 On medieval and early modern alchemy, and the criticism engendered by
the practice, see Newman, *Promethean Ambitions*.

20 Patterson, "Perpetual Motion," 27. See further Gardner, "The *Canon's
Yeoman's Prologue* and *Tale*," 1–17; Grenberg, "The Canon's Yeoman's
Tale," 37–54; Olmert, "The *Canon's Yeoman's Tale*," 70–94; Olson, "Chaucer,
Dante, and the Structure of Fragment VIII," 222–36; Rosenberg, "Contrary

Tales," 278–91; Rosenberg, "Swindling Alchemist, Antichrist," 566–80; Scattergood, "Chaucer in the Suburbs," 145–62.

21 See also Muscatine, *French Tradition*, 217: "The extremely naturalistic characterization of the Yeoman serves the conception of alchemy as a blind materialism." My use of the term "materialism" is certainly related to Muscatine's, but broader in its comprehension.

22 Grennen, "Saint Cecilia's 'Chemical Wedding,'" 466–81, at 473.

23 Ibid., 472. For Patterson, by contrast, the linguistic chaos associated with alchemy anticipates considerations of the modern subject as a radical absence: "The more he talks about the self that so fascinates him, the more dispersed it becomes, leaving him a cipher, an absence, a desire – a being who seeks rather than an object sought" ("Perpetual Motion," 39). The notion that the prologue and tale are particularly charged anticipations of capitalistic modernity is also explored by Harwood, "Chaucer and the Silence of History," 338–50; Knapp, "The Work of Alchemy," 575–99. Epstein challenges this view in "Dismal Science," 209–48.

24 Quoted in Skeat, ed., *The Complete Works*, 3.493.

25 See, for instance, Brown, *"Canon's Yeoman's Tale,"* 481–90. See also Hartung, "Pars Secunda," 111–28, who argues that the tale of the fraudulent canon is an earlier work, authentic, but not composed for inclusion in *The Canterbury Tales*.

26 For a recent assessment of Cecilia's pastoral role, see Long, "'O sweete and wel beloved spouse deere,'" 159–90.

27 Sisk, "Nostalgic Idealism," also comments on the extreme efficacy of Cecilia's teaching: "Her 'wise loore' (414) is so persuasive, in fact, that the people she converts go on to become preachers in their own right, bringing still others to the faith in a blessed contagion of conversion" (154).

28 Brown, *"Canon's Yeoman's Tale,"* 487.

29 Patterson, "Technology of the Self," 34.

30 On the relationship between the Second Nun and the Parson, see also Kolve, "Chaucer's *Second Nun's Tale*, 137–74: "second only to *the Parson's Tale* ... *the Second Nun's Tale* is the most absolute of the Canterbury narratives – uncompromised by irony ... and uncolored by the idiosyncrasies of a personal narrative voice" (156–7).

31 On the use of rhyme royal in Chaucer's overtly Christian tales, see Nolan, "Chaucer's Tales of Transcendence," 21–38.

32 See Bruhn, "Art, Anxiety, and Alchemy," 288–315. For Bruhn, alchemy serves as a metaphor Chaucer's poetry. Both are failed discourses "which cannot come to any conclusion except one that runs counter to the 'sadde,' stable, and authorized truth of revealed religion" (312). See also Calabrese, "Meretricious Mixtures," 277–90, who argues that alchemy represents Chaucer's Ovidian poetics. Hilberry, "'And in Oure Madnesse

Everemoore We Rave,'" 435–43, concludes, "While Chaucer in the Canon's Yeoman's Tale confirms alchemy's failure to change base metals into gold, he succeeds in transmuting the language of alchemy into poetry" (442). These scholars do not mention the persistent association in the tale of alchemy with philosophy rather than poetry. In a related vein, see, more recently, Ingham, *The Medieval New*, who suggests that "Chaucer stages a competition between poetic and artisanal making" such that the "poet, himself an experimental fabulist, offers both a wider view and a deeper analysis of alchemy's promise and risk than the craft alchemist can" (164).

33 Finkelstein, "'Secree of Secrees,'" 260–76, at 268. On the sources for Chaucer's knowledge of alchemy, see also Duncan, "The Literature of Alchemy," 633–56. On the history of criticism on the concluding passages of the tale, see Keiser, "Conclusion," 1–21.

34 On the contrasting epistemologies of the two tales, especially their treatment of secret knowledge, see Longsworth, "Privileged Knowledge," 87–96.

35 Herz, "The *Canon's Yeoman's Prologue* and *Tale*," 231–7, makes a similar point: "The seeking after the 'slydynge science' is the one romance in the life of the Yeoman. And the traditional heroine of Romance, elusive, changing of face, a temptress, and a setter of impossible tasks is something like the mistress who has dominated the Yeoman's life" (235).

36 The passage is translated by Duncan, "'Arnald of the Newe Town,'" 7–11, at 9.

37 Sisk, "Religion, Alchemy, and Nostalgic Idealism," 166.

38 In his reading of *The Canon's Yeoman's Tale*, Muscatine, *French Tradition*, 215, also locates "a distinction between false alchemy and true, between men's alchemy and God's." Kensak, "What Ails Chaucer's Cook?," 213–31, likewise observes, "Unlike the alchemists who labor in vain, Saint Cecile effortlessly transforms leaden souls into spiritual gold" (216).

39 On the suggestions of penance in the prologue and tale, see Allen, "Penitential Sermons," 77–96, who argues that "they prepare us to accept the Parson's overt concern with the sacrament and draw us to pursue seriously the examination of conscience we undergo as we read the *Parson's Tale*" (92).

40 See further Pearcy, "Hell Mouth," 167–75.

41 Fumo, "Thinking upon the Crow," 355–75, at 369.

42 Howard, *Idea*, 304. On the Manciple's cynical degradation of language, see also Harwood, "Language and the Real," 268–79; Hazelton, "The *Manciple's Tale*," 1–31; Gruber, "The *Manciple's Tale*," 43–50; Scattergood, "The Manciple's Manner of Speaking," 124–46; Trask, "The Manciple's Problem," 109–16; Dean, "Dismantling the Canterbury Book," 746–62; Fradenburg, "The Manciple's Servant Tongue," 85–118; Patton, "False 'Rekenynges,'" 399–414.

43 Patterson, "The *Parson's Tale*," 331–80, at 377. See, more recently, Powell, "Game Over," 40–58, at 47: "the *Manciple's Tale* gives way to a form of language that surely seemed to Chaucer both more stable and more reliable: the sermon, or, more properly, the sermonic penitential manual, a genre that fits with the pilgrimage frame of the Tales far better than its storytelling frame. It is not just that the Manciple's words prepare us for the Parson's, but that the reversal ends the contest Harry Bailly had started, returning us to the longing for pilgrimages with which the *Canterbury Tales* begins. That reversal is cataclysmic. It signals the triumph of doctrine over worldly vanity, of true – the Parson would say the Father's – authority over the inherently misguided and misleading jangling of the Manciple's mother." Fumo's book-length consideration of Chaucer's Apolline mythography echoes this position in its concluding pages: "In silencing the crow and shattering his musical instruments, finally, Phebus not only negates the possibilities of poetry but, in effect, silences his own oracle, setting the stage for a contrast between the contingent nature of pagan truth and its Christian antithesis in the *Parson's Tale*" (*The Legacy of Apollo*, 225).

44 On Chaucer's sensitivity to the risks of poetic language, see Hanning, "Chaucer and the Dangers of Poetry," 17–26.

45 See, by way of contrast, Grudin, "Poetics of Guile," 329–42, who argues that the tale, instead of characterizing poetry as debased, suggests the manner with which the poet can convey truth while protecting himself: "The *Manciple's Prologue* and *Tale* would seem to suggest that if the poet is to speak and to survive in a world in which 'flessh is so newefangel, with meschaunce' (193) – the world not perceived by Phebus whose eye was 'blered' for all his 'worthynesse' (249–52) – his creations necessarily require artfulness, if not guile" (339). Hirsh applauds the Manciple's pragmatism in "The Politics of Spirituality," 129–46. Striar echoes Grudin in his argument that *The Manciple's Tale* reveals something fundamental about Chaucerian poetics; see "The *Manciple's Tale*," 173–204. According to Striar, Chaucer "redefines the conventional boundaries of the Christian-humanist dialectic … transfiguring that dialectic and himself through the one personage paradoxically common to both contexts: Phoebus Apollo, the figure for both Christ and poetry" (198).

46 On the deflation of the Ovidian Apollo in the tale, see further Kensak, "Apollo Exterminans," 143–57; On the domestic tyranny of Phebus, see Wallace, *Chaucerian Polity*, 247–60.

47 For an assessment of how the tale registers the threat posed to the social order by adultery, see Herman, "Treason," 318–28.

48 Fradenburg, "The Manciple's Servant Tongue," 109.

49 Cox understands the Manciple's retraction here as evidence of his antifeminism. See "The Jangler's 'Bourde,'" 1–21. For Cox, the danger of

"feminine speech, represented conventionally by prolixity, is the subject of the Manciple's narrative" (7).

50 On Chaucer's sensitivity to the nuances of class markers, see Brewer, "Class Distinction in Chaucer," 290–305. Harwood notes, in fact, that the representation of class is not present in the sources and analogues of *The Manciple's Tale*. See "Language and the Real," 269–70.

51 See Fulk, "Reinterpreting the *Manciple's Tale*," 485–93, who also makes a case for the "self-defeating logic of the [Manciple's] argument": "This is purportedly an apology for offending the sensibilities of refined listeners. Actually, it is no apology at all. Rather, it does away with the very refinements and social distinctions the Manciple claims to have violated" (487). Though he is correct in identifying the recursive logic of the passage, I do not agree that the Manciple is apologizing to refined listeners. As the following lines indicate, he is apologizing for his deployment of arbitrary distinctions between rude and refined.

52 Hazelton, "Parody and Critique," 28. See also McGavin, "How Nasty is Phebus's Crow?" 444–58, who defends the probity of the crow.

53 See, by contrast, Trigg, "Friendship, Association, and Service," 325–30, who has a very different understanding of these lines: "When challenged, the bird speaks to Phoebus directly, as an equal, even addressing him as 'thou,' the same form the god uses to him. In the pronominal forms of address, then, theirs is a friendship, a reciprocal relationship" (329).

54 That *The Manciple's Tale* is straightforwardly a warning against verbosity, with the crow as the chief example, is influentially proposed by Severs, "Is the *Manciple's Tale* a Success?" 1–16. In line with Severs's reading, there is a well-established tradition of scholarship that reads the tale as Chaucer's reflection on the dangerous role of the courtier-poet, who must speak with care to the sovereign. See, for instance, Grudin, "Poetics of Guile"; Storm, "Speech, Circumspection, and Orthodontics," 109–26; Bertolet, "The Anxiety of Exclusion," 183–218. But Raybin proposes that the crow gets what he wants all along. See "The Death of a Silent Woman," 19–37, where he argues that the crow "uses his knowledge, voice, and wit to gain freedom from a gilded cage" (31). It should also be noted that nowhere in the sources of *The Manciple's Tale* is Apollo's bird in a cage.

55 Scholars have long observed the Manciple's incompetent moralizing. See, for instance, Campbell, "Polonius among the Pilgrims," 140–6; Trask, "The Manciple's Problem," 109–16.

56 On the opposition between the profane silence at the end of *The Manciple's Tale* and the divine silence which *The Parson's Tale* anticipates, see Kensak, "Manciple's Tale," 190–206.

57 On the biblical sources for the mother's speech, see Delany, "Doer of the Word," 250–4. On maternal speech in *The Canterbury Tales* as a whole, see Sleeth, "'My Dames Loore,'" 174–84.

58 Travis, "The Manciple's Phallic Matrix," 317–24. Travis's Lacanian reading ascribes the contradictions of the narrative to the Manciple's simultaneous desire for, and hatred of, the maternal: "much of the Manciple's *agon* – consumption, self-castration, infantilization, fear of/desire for the feminine other – is an aspect of his fundamental life-and-death struggle with language itself as a surrogate replacement and displacement of what has been lost and is longed-for, desired and reviled" (322).

59 Wenzel, "The *Parson's Tale*," 1–10, at 5–6. In an earlier essay, Lawton, "Chaucer's Two Ways," 3–40, proposes to divide responses to *The Parson's Tale* into four categories: "absolute," "ironic," "dualistic," and "textual." The absolute reading unifies *The Parson's Tale* with everything that precedes it as the moral epitome of *The Canterbury Tales*. The ironic reading argues for limitations in the Parson's discourse that undermine its authoritative status. The dualistic approach locates an absolute disjunction between *The Parson's Tale* and the preceding tales, especially in its rejection of poetry and fabulation. Finally, the textual reading argues that *The Parson's Tale* and the *Retraction* were not intended by Chaucer to conclude *The Canterbury Tales* but are conceivably the appendices of a later compiler. Lawton's own position is both dualistic and textual.

60 Finke, "'To Knytte Up Al this Feeste,'" 95–107, at 104. See also Portnoy, "Beyond the Gothic Cathedral," 279–92; Mann, *Geoffrey Chaucer*, 121; Cooper, *The Structure of the Canterbury Tales* 200–7; Finlayson, "The Satiric Mode," 94–116; Sayce, "Chaucer's 'Retractions,'" 230–48; Allen, "The Old Way," 255–71. See, more recently, Pitard, "Sowing Difficulty," 299–330, who deploys the terms of Wenzel's analysis in his conclusion: "While Chaucer insists on a perspectivist vision, then, this perspectivism is clearly distinct from relativism. His submission of his text for correction in the Retractions does not mean that he could not care less; it means that he could not care more. It is a plea for engagement, consistent with the idea that submitting a text for a reader's correction is a strategy that imagines 'the search for truth as a collaborative project that does not end with the completion of the text'" (330). Pitard is citing Wogan-Brown, Watson, Taylor, and Evans, eds., *The Idea of the Vernacular*, 13.

61 Patterson, "The *Parson's Tale*," 331–80, at 380. See also Pearsall, "Chaucer's Religious Tales," 11–19; Dean, "Dismantling the Canterbury Book"; Knight, "Chaucer's Religious Canterbury Tales," 156–66; Lawler, *The One and the Many*, 147–72.

62 Newhauser, *Sources and Analogues*, 1.531–2. On Chaucer's treatment of his source material, see by Wenzel, "The Source for the 'Remedia,'" 433–53; "Seven Deadly Sins," 351–78; "Notes on the *Parson's Tale*," 237–56.

63 For a negative characterization of the Parson, see in particular Aers, *Creative Imagination*, who argues for "Chaucer's detachment from the Parson" (108), while describing the latter as characterized by "self-righteous masculine violence" (111). On the narrowness of the Parson's understanding of Christian doctrine, see Kaske, "Getting around the Parson's Tale, 147–77.

64 Minnis, *Fallible Authors*, 26. On the Parson's (and Chaucer's) relation to Lollard heterodoxy, see also Winstead, "Contours of Orthodoxy," 239–59; Cole, *Literature and Heresy*, 75–100; McCormack, *Chaucer and the Culture of Dissent*; Fletcher, "Chaucer the Heretic," 53–121; Little, "Chaucer's Parson," 3–25.

65 Wenzel, "Notes," 241. Wenzel finds a possible source for Chaucer's imagery in the second part of the Anglo-Norman *Compileison*, titled the *Compileison de seinte penance*. On the imagery of flowering and fruitfulness in the tale, see Raybin, "'Manye Been the Weyes,'" 11–43. Raybin finds the echo of the *General Prologue* especially pertinent: "Not only do the broadly encyclopedic scope and more narrow penitential focus of The Parson's Tale highlight the juxtaposition of myriad human behaviors and a common spiritual goal, but modified versions of the roots-flower and pilgrimage images appear in the opening passages of the tale, joining with the opening of the General Prologue to provide a frame of imagery within which Chaucer's book may be read." For Twu, "Chaucer's Vision of the Tree of Life," 341–78, "the domesticity of the vegetable images emphasizes the late fourteenth-century understanding of the process as 'the penitence of every day' (X 101) over the Fourth Lateran Council's more immediate concern of seeing it undertaken 'saltern semel in anno' (at least once a year), as reflected in Raymund's *Summa*" (346). See also Georgianna, "Love So Dearly Bought," 85–116, at 114; Taylor, "The Parson's Amyable Tongue," 401–9, at 401.

66 On the possibility that the *Retraction* contains multiple voices and is not a unified statement, see Wurtele, "Penitence," 335–60. First to pose this argument was Spies, "Chaucers Retractio," 383–94. For a more recent assessment of the manuscript evidence, see Wolfe, "Placing Chaucer's *Retraction*," 427–31.

67 See Robertson, *Preface to Chaucer*, 368–9; Huppé, *A Reading*, 237. Jordan also observes the ambiguous referent of "litel tretys" in the *Retraction*. See his *Chaucer's Poetics*, 170. Minnis, *Medieval Theory of Authorship*, 207, decides tentatively in favour of *The Parson's Tale* but does not eliminate the alternative: "The 'litel tretys' to which he refers must be the treatise

on penitence now known as the Parson's Tale, for the *Canterbury Tales* considered as a whole is not a treatise in the technical sense of the term, and it could hardly be called little (though it should be remembered that Chaucer calls his *Troilus and Criseyde* a 'litel bok' at v, line 1789)."

68 Riley, "Retraction and Re-Collection," 263–90, at 280.

69 This reading of the *Retraction* corresponds to Gascoigne's account of Chaucer's deathbed confession, whereby he contritely abjures all his sinful works. For recent considerations of the relevance of Gascoigne's *Dictionarum Theologicum* to our understanding of the *Retraction*, see Vaughan, "Personal Politics," 103–22; Cook, "'Here taketh the makere of this book his leve,'" 32–54.

70 See, by contrast, Ginsberg, "Chaucer's Canterbury Poetics," 55–89, who argues for the unifying function of Chaucer's intent in line 10.1083 but does not address his simultaneous assertion of readerly freedom: "In the *Retraction*, Chaucer defends his fiction and disowns it in the same breath; the structure of opposition, however, is not ironic, but allegorical, because the oppositions are resolved in the univocality of Chaucer's intention" (89). For Ginsberg, Chaucerian allegory in the *Retraction* permits *The Canterbury Tales* to coalesce into a univocal form that sublates the contradiction between divine truth and worldly fiction: "acts that undermine the social ideal are immoral because they undo the sanctioned material order, and commendable because they proclaim every earthly community the shadow of a different, higher sodality that will finally replace it" (61). Astell, "Sacrifice of Art," 323–40, also argues that Chaucer's sinful works are part of *The Canterbury Tales*' intentional unity: "Far from being necessarily harmful or useless, Chaucer's writing may indeed "sownen into sinne" (a sorrowful consequence for which Chaucer takes at least partial blame), but they also teach the avoidance of vice and the pursuit of virtue, depending on the reader's reception of them" (337).

71 Travis, "Deconstructing Chaucer's *Retraction*," 135–58. Travis, as a Derridean, must insist on the *Retraction*'s resistance to closure: "Chaucer places his readers, like his pilgrims, on the inside of the margin, giving them space for further dialogue and more time to live within the pilgrimage of his poems. Chaucer's poetry stops, but his pilgrim-readers in the impending darkness continue to bob up and down, wondering, possibly, how it will all end" (157–8). Burger also champions a "non-teleological" position, arguing that "the end-tales (Fragments VIII, IX, and X) continue to look 'forward' in the manner of the Canterbury project, that is, to a productive 'middle' state between London and Canterbury, between 'middle' class and clerical orthodoxy, between national and penitential body. Such a disjunct and displaced 'present' in the three fragments 'ending' the *Tales* thus continues to explore the torsions

produced in the *Tales'* attempts to map Chaucer's queer nation as it emerges into representability" (xxiii–xxiv). See also McGerr, *Open Books*, 131–57.

72 See also Sayce, "Chaucer's 'Retractions,'" 230–48, who identifies in the *Retraction* "the tension between traditional ecclesiastical teaching and the growing autonomy of secular literature" (245). See further, Obermeier, *History and Anatomy*, who argues that "the syntax of the retraction reinforces its relative indeterminacy even as it seems to affirm its penitent purpose" (218).

73 Citations from the original, along with translations, are taken from Durling, ed. and trans., *The Divine Comedy of Dante Alighieri*.

74 This paraphrase has long been recognized. See, for instance, Wheeler, "Ending of *Troilus and Criseyde*," 105–23; Wetherbee, *Chaucer and the Poets*, 224–44; Pulsiano, "Redeemed Language, 153–74; Ginsburg, "Aesthetics *Sine Nomine*," 234–40.

75 Quell' uno e due e tre che sempre/e regna sempre in tre e 'n due e 'n uno,/ non circunscritto, e tutto circunscrive ("That One and Two and Three that ever lives and always reigns in Three and Two and One, not circumscribed, but circumscribing all things").

76 On this alignment, see, for instance, Windeatt, *Troilus and Criseyde*, 210.

77 See also Fumo, "The God of Love," 157–75. Fumo also links the conclusion of *Troilus and Criseyde* to the *Retraction*. She reads both conclusions through the penance Cupid assigns to Chaucer, arguing that the *Retraction* reveals Chaucer's anxiety that God himself may not acknowledge his true intention.

78 Fyler, *Language and the Declining World*, 139.

79 Franke, "Enditynges of Worldly Vanitees," 87–106, at 89. On Chaucer's belated and "lapsarian poetics," as compared to his established precursors, including Dante, see Hanning, "Toward a Lapsarian Poetics," 29–58.

80 For a recent consideration of the image of the knotted rings, see Saiber and Mbirika, "The Three *Giri* of *Paradiso* XXXIII," 237–72.

81 See Augustine's account of the trinity in McKenna, trans., *Augustine*, 199; 15.17.27: "Now we are to speak about the Holy Spirit, insofar as God the Giver shall permit. According to the Sacred Scriptures, this Holy Spirit is neither the Spirit of the Father alone, nor of the Son alone, but the Spirit of both, and, therefore, He insinuates to us the common love by which the Father and the Son mutually love each other." For a recent explication of Augustine's account, see Thom, *The Logic of the Trinity*, 19–41; see also Coffey, "The Holy Spirit," 193–229.

82 See further Kay, "Dante's Empyrean," 37–65.

83 On Dante's geometrical simile, see Herzman and Towsley, "Squaring the Circle," 95–125.

84 See the words of St. Bernard from *Paradiso* 32.52–5: "Dentro a l'ampiezza di questo reame/casüal unto non puote aver sito,/se non come tristizia o sete o fame,/ché per etterna legge è stabilito/quantun que vedi" ("Within this ample kingdom no effect of chance can have a place, no more than sadness or thirst or hunger, for eternal law establishes whatever you see"). Both the Prioress and the Second Nun use *Paradiso* 33 in their prologues. See further Murton, "The *Prioress's Prologue*," 318–40. In line with the Prioress's and the Parson's anti-Semitism, Dante calls the lowest circle of the Inferno, "Judecca" and charges the Jews with deicide in *Paradiso* 7.47. In line with the Man of Law's anti-Islamic rhetoric, he relegates Mohammed to the eighth circle of hell, ninth *bolgia*, among others he views as schismatics. See further Barolini, "Dante's Sympathy," 177–204; Tomasch, "Judecca, Dante's Satan, and the *Dis*-placed Jew," 247–67.

85 On Chaucer's "authorial presence" in the *Retraction*, see Partridge, "'The Makere of this Boke,'" 106–53. Partridge argues that by referring to himself as a "makere," Chaucer "elides the scribe(s) and their production of the intermediary copies through which the work has in fact reached the reader. The *Retraction* with its rubrics asserts the author over the scribe, and creates a fiction of Chaucer's direct supervision and control over the text … One reason that readers are especially interested in the question of whether Chaucer 'meant' what he said here, and are likely to invoke the issue of sincerity, is that the *Retraction* so strongly creates a sense of presence – as if Chaucer is dropping his 'masks' and is 'speaking' more directly to the reader than he does elsewhere in his work" (130–1).

86 See Fyler, *Language*, 188, where he states of the *Retraction* in comparison to *Paradiso* 33 that Chaucer "prepares himself, with a gesture more of sybilline dispersion than of collection, more of expectant hope than of fading vision, for the refining purgatorial fire" (188).

Abbreviations

ChauR	*The Chaucer Review*
ELH	*English Literary History*
ELN	*English Language Notes*
ES	*English Studies*
JEGP	*Journal of English and Germanic Philology*
JMEMS	*Journal of Medieval and Early Modern Studies*
MÆ	*Medium Ævum*
MLN	*Modern Language Notes*
MLQ	*Modern Language Quarterly*
MLR	*Modern Language Review*
MP	*Modern Philology*
NM	*Neuphilologische Mitteilungen*
PMLA	*Publications of the Modern Language Association*
PQ	*Philological Quarterly*
RES	*Review of English Studies*
SAC	*Studies in the Age of Chaucer*
SFQ	*Southern Folklore Quarterly*
SP	*Studies in Philology*
TSLL	*Texas Studies in Literature and Language*
UTQ	*University of Toronto Quarterly*

Bibliography

Abraham, David H. "Cosyn and Cosynage: Pun and Structure in the *Shipman's Tale*." *ChauR* 11, no. 4 (1977): 319–27.

Adams, Robert. "Chaucer's 'New Rachel' and the Theological Roots of Medieval Anti-Semitism." *Bulletin of the John Rylands Library* 77 (1995): 9–18.

Adorno, Theodor W. *Negative Dialectics*. Translated by E.B. Ashton. New York: The Seabury Press, 1973.

Aers, David. *Beyond Reformation? An Essay on William Langland's Piers Plowman and the End of Constantinian Christianity*. Notre Dame, IN: University of Notre Dame Press, 2015.

– *Chaucer, Langland, and the Creative Imagination*. London: Routledge, 1980.

– *Faith, Ethics and Church: Writing in England, 1360–1409*. Cambridge: D.S. Brewer, 2000.

Albin, Andrew. "*The Prioress's Tale*, Sonorous and Silent." *ChauR* 48, no. 1 (2013): 91–112.

Alexander, Philip S. "Madame Eglentyne, Geoffrey Chaucer, and the Problem of Medieval Anti-Semitism." *Bulletin of the John Rylands Library* 74 (1992): 109–20.

Alford, John A. "The Wife of Bath versus the Clerk of Oxford: What Their Rivalry Means." *ChauR* 21, no. 2 (1986): 108–32.

Allen, Elizabeth. "Chaucer Answers Gower: Constance and the Trouble with Reading." *ELH* 64, no. 3 (1997): 627–55.

Allen, Judson Boyce. *The Ethical Poetic of the Later Middle Ages: A Decorum of Convenient Distinction*. Toronto: University of Toronto Press, 1982.

– "The Old Way and the Parson's Way: An Ironic Reading of the *Parson's Tale*." *Journal of Medieval and Renaissance Studies* 3 (1973): 255–71.

Allen, Mark. "Moral and Aesthetic Falls on the Canterbury Way." *South Central Review* 8, no. 2 (1991): 36–49.

– "Penitential Sermons, the Manciple, and the End of the *Canterbury Tales*." *SAC* 9 (1987): 77–96.

Allman, W.W., and D. Thomas Hanks Jr. "Rough Love: Notes toward and Erotics of the *Canterbury Tales*." *ChauR* 38, no. 1 (2003): 36–65.

Amtower, Laurel. "Mimetic Desire and the Misappropriation of the Ideal in the *Knight's Tale*." *Exemplaria* 8, no. 1 (1996): 125–44.

Aquinas, Thomas. *Summa Contra Gentiles, Book 4: Salvation*. Translated by Charles J. O'Neill. Notre Dame, IN: Notre Dame University Press, 1956.

Archer, John. "The Structure of Anti-Semitism in the *Prioress's Tale*." *ChauR* 19, no. 1 (1984): 46–54.

Archibald, Elizabeth. "The Flight from Incest: Two Late Classical Precursors of the Constance Theme." *ChauR* 20, no. 4 (1986): 259–72.

Arthur, Karen. "Equivocal Subjectivity in Chaucer's *Second Nun's Prologue* and *Tale*." *ChauR* 32, no. 3 (1998): 217–31.

Ashe, Laura. "Reading Like a Clerk in the *Clerk's Tale*." *MLR* 101, no. 4 (2006): 935–44.

Ashton, Gail. *The Generation of Identity in Late Medieval Hagiography: Speaking the Saint*. London and New York: Routledge, 2000.

– "Her Father's Daughter: The Realignment of Father-Daughter Kinship in Three Romance Tales." *ChauR* 34, no. 4 (2000): 416–27.

– "Patient Mimesis: Griselda and the *Clerk's Tale*," *ChauR* 32, no. 3 (1998): 232–38.

Astell, Ann W. "Apostrophe, Prayer, and the Structure of the *Man of Law's Tale*." *SAC* 13 (1991): 81–97.

– *Chaucer and the Universe of Learning*. Ithaca, NY: Cornell University Press, 1996.

– "Chaucer's 'Literature Group' and the Medieval Causes of Books." *ELH* 59, no. 2 (1992): 269–87.

– "The Monk's Tragical 'Seint Edward.'" *SAC* 22 (2000): 399–405.

– "Nietzsche, Chaucer, and the Sacrifice of Art." *ChauR* 39, no. 3 (2005): 323–40.

– "The Peasants' Revolt: Cock-Crow in Gower and Chaucer." *Essays in Medieval Studies* 10 (1993): 53–60.

– "The *Translatio* of Chaucer's Pardoner." *Exemplaria* 4, no. 2 (1992): 411–28.

Bachman, W Bryant, Jr. "'To Maken Illusioun': The Philosophy of Magic and the Magic of Philosophy." *ChauR* 12, no. 1 (1977): 55–67.

Baird, Joseph L. "The Law and the *Reeve's Tale*." *NM* 70, no. 4 (1969): 679–83.

Bakalian, Ellen Shaw. *Aspects of Love in John Gower's* Confessio Amantis. New York: Routledge, 2004.

Baker, David Philip. "A Bradwardinian Benediction: The Ending of the *Nun's Priest's Tale* Revisited." *MÆ* 82, no. 2 (2013): 236–43.

– "Literature, Logic, and Mathematics in the Fourteenth Century." PhD diss., Durham University, 2013.

Barakat, Robert A. "Odin: Old Man of the *Pardoner's Tale*." *SFQ* 28 (1964): 210–15.

Barker, Justin. "Matter and Form in Medieval English Literature." PhD diss., Purdue University, 2017.

Barnes, Jonathan, ed. *The Complete Works of Aristotle*. 2 volumes. Princeton, NJ: Princeton University Press, 1984.

Barolini, Teodolinda. "Dante's Sympathy for the Other or the Non-Stereotyping Imagination: Sexual and Racialized Others in the *Commedia*." *Critica del testo* 14 (2011): 177–204.

Barr, Helen. "Religious Practice in Chaucer's *Prioress's Tale*: Rabbit And/Or Duck?" *SAC* 32 (2010): 39–65.

Battles, Dominique. "Chaucer's *Franklin's Tale* and Boccaccio's *Filocolo* Reconsidered." *ChauR* 34, no. 1 (1999): 38–59.

Beach, Charles Franklyn. "The Appearance of Pity, Love, and Reverence: Chaucer's Prioress and Her Tale." In *Proceedings, Northeast Regional Meeting of the Conference on Christianity and Literature, 2003*, 5–10. Farmingdale, NY: Farmingdale State University, 2004.

Beall, J.C., ed. *Revenge of the Liar: New Essays on the Paradox*. Oxford: Oxford University Press, 2007.

Beckwith, Sarah. *Christ's Body: Identity, Culture, and Society in Late Medieval Writings*. London: Routledge, 1993.

Beichner, Paul E. "The Grain of Paradise." *Speculum* 36, no. 2 (1961): 302–7.

Beidler, Peter G. "Medieval Children Witness Their Mothers' Indiscretions: The Maid Child in Chaucer's *Shipman's Tale*." *ChauR* 44, no. 2 (2009): 186–204.

– "Noah and the Old Man in the *Pardoner's Tale*." *ChauR* 15, no. 3 (1981): 250–4.

– "'Now, Deere Lady': Absolon's Marian Couplet in the *Miller's Tale*." *ChauR* 39, no. 2 (2004): 219–22.

Benjamin, Edwin B. "The Concept of Order in the *Franklin's Tale*." *PQ* 38 (1959): 119–24.

Bennett, J.A.W. *Chaucer at Oxford and Cambridge*. Toronto: University of Toronto Press, 1974.

Benson, C. David. "Chaucer's Pardoner: His Sexuality and Modern Critics." *Mediaevalia* 8 (1982): 337–49.

– "Incest and Moral Poetry in Gower's *Confessio Amantis*." *ChauR* 19, no. 2 (1984): 100–9.

– "Their Telling Difference: Chaucer the Pilgrim and His Two Contrasting Tales." *ChauR* 18, no. 1 (1983): 61–76.

– "Trust the Tale, Not the Teller." In *Drama, Narrative and Poetry in the Canterbury Tales*, 22-33. Toulouse, France: Presses Universitaires du Mirail, 2003.

Benson, Donald R. "The Marriage 'Encomium' in the *Merchant's Tale*: A Chaucerian Crux." *ChauR* 14, no. 1 (1979–80): 48–60.

Benson, Larry D. "The Order of the *Canterbury Tales*." *SAC* 3 (1981): 77–120.

Berger, Harry. "The F-Fragment of the *Canterbury Tales*: Part II." *ChauR* 1, no. 3 (1966): 135–56.

Bertolet, Craig E. "The Anxiety of Exclusion: Speech, Power, and Chaucer's Manciple." *SAC* 33 (2011): 183–218.

Besserman, Lawrence. "Chaucerian Wordplay: The Nun's Priest and his 'Womman Divyne.'" *ChauR* 12, no. 1 (1977): 68–73.

– *Chaucer's Biblical Poetics*. Norman, OK: University of Oklahoma Press, 1998, 138–59.

– "Ideology, Antisemitism, and Chaucer's *Prioress's Tale*." *ChauR* 36, no. 1 (2001): 48–72.

Biggs, Frederick M., and Laura L. Howes. "Theophany in the *Miller's Tale*." *MÆ* 65, no. 2 (1996): 269–79.

Bishop, Louise M. "'Of Goddes pryvetee nor of his wyf': Confusion of Orifices in Chaucer's *Miller's Tale*." *TSLL* 44, no. 3 (2002): 231–46.

Bjork, Robert E. "The Wife of Bath's *Bele Chose*." *ChauR* 53, no. 3 (2018): 336–49.

Blake, Kathleen A. "Order and the Noble Life in Chaucer's *Knight's Tale*?" *MLQ* 34, no. 1 (1973): 3–19.

Blamires, Alcuin. *Chaucer, Ethics, and Gender*. Oxford: Oxford University Press, 2006.

– "Chaucer the Reactionary: Ideology and the *General Prologue* to the *Canterbury Tales*." *RES* 51, no. 204 (2000): 523–39.

– "May in January's Tree: Genealogical Configuration in the *Merchant's Tale*." *ChauR* 45, no. 1 (2010): 106–17.

– "Philosophical Sleaze? The 'strok of thought' in the *Miller's Tale* and Chaucerian Fabliaux." *MLR* 102, no. 3 (2007): 621–41.

– "The Wife of Bath and Lollardy." *MÆ* 58, no. 2 (1989): 224–42.

– "Women and Preaching in Medieval Orthodoxy, Heresy, and Saints' Lives." *Viator* 26 (1995): 135–52.

Bleeth, Kenneth. "Joseph's Doubting of Mary and the Conclusion of the Merchant's Tale." *ChauR* 21, no. 1 (1986): 58–66.

Bloch, R. Howard. "Chaucer's Maiden's Head: The *Physician's Tale* and the Poetics of Virginity." *Representations* 28 (1989): 113–34.

Block, Edward A. "Originality, Controlling Purpose, and Craftsmanship in Chaucer's *Man of Law's Tale*." *PMLA* 68, no. 3 (1953): 572–616.

Bloomfield, Morton W. "The *Man of Law's Tale*: A Tragedy of Victimization and a Christian Comedy." *PMLA* 87, no. 3 (1972): 384–90.

– "The *Miller's Tale* – An UnBoethian Interpretation." In *Medieval Literature and Folklore Studies: Essays in Honor of Francis Lee Utley*, edited Jerome Mandel and Bruce A. Rosenberg, 2015–11. New Brunswick, NJ: Rutgers University Press, 1971.

Blurton, Heather, and Hannah Johnson. *The Critics and the Prioress: Antisemitism, Criticism and Chaucer's* Prioress's Tale, Ann Arbor: University of Michigan Press, 2017.

Boenig, Robert. "The *Alma Redemptoris Mater, Gaude Maria,* and the *Prioress's Tale.*" *Notes and Queries* 46 (1999): 321–6.

Boitani, Piero. "The *Monk's Tale*: Dante and Boccaccio." *MÆ* 45, no. 1 (1976): 50–69.

Bornstein, Diane. "Chaucer's *Tale of Melibee* as an Example of the Style Clergial." *ChauR* 12, no. 4 (1978): 236–54.

Bottin, Francesco. "The Mertonians' Metalinguistic Science and the *Insolubilia.*" In *The Rise of British Logic*, Papers in Mediaeval Studies 7, edited by P. Osmund Lewry, 235–48. Toronto: PIMS, 1983.

Bovaird-Abbo, Kristin. "'Sire Nonnes Preest': Reading Lancelot in Geoffrey Chaucer's *Nun's Priest's Tale.*" *CEA Critic* 76, no. 1 (2014): 84–97.

Bowers, John M. "'Dronkenesse is Ful of Stryvyng': Alcoholism and Ritual Violence in Chaucer's *Pardoner's Tale.*" *ELH* 57, no. 4 (1990): 757–84.

– "Queering the Summoner." In *Speaking Images*, 301–24.

Boyarin, Adrienne Williams. *Miracles of the Virgin in Medieval England: Law and Jewishness in Marian Legends.* Cambridge: D.S. Brewer, 2010, 156–8.

Boyd, Beverly, ed. *A Variorum Edition of* The Works of Geoffrey Chaucer: *Volume II,* The Canterbury Tales, *Part Twenty:* The Prioress's Tale. Norman, OK: University of Oklahoma Press, 1987.

– "The Little Clergeon's 'Alma Redemptoris Mater.'" *Notes and Queries* 202 (1957): 277.

Boyd, David Lorenzo. "Seeking Goddes 'Pryvetee': Sodomy, Quitting, and Desire in the *Miller's Tale.*" In *Words and Works: Studies in Medieval Language and Literature in Honour of Fred C. Robinson*, edited by Peter S. Baker and Nicholas Howe, 243–60. Toronto: University of Toronto Press, 1998.

Brantley, Jessica. "Reading the Forms of *Sir Thopas.*" *ChauR* 47, no. 4 (2013): 416–38.

Braswell, Mary Flowers. "Chaucer's Palimpsest: Judas Iscariot and the *Pardoner's Tale.*" *ChauR* 29, no. 3 (1995): 303–10.

Bratcher, James T. "The 'Greyn' in the Prioress's Tale." *Notes and Queries* 208 (1963): 444–5.

Brewer, Derek. "Chaucer's Knight's Tale and the Problem of Cultural Translatability." In *Corresponding Powers: Studies in Honour of Professor Hisaaki Yamanouchi*, edited by George Hughes, 103–12. Cambridge: D.S. Brewer, 1997.

– "Class Distinction in Chaucer." *Speculum* 43, no. 2 (1968): 290–305.

Brody, Saul Nathaniel. "Chaucer's Rhyme Royal Tales and the Secularization of the Saint." *ChauR* 20, no. 2 (1985): 113–31.

Brown, Emerson, Jr. "Biblical Women in the *Merchant's Tale*: Feminism, Antifeminism, and Beyond." *Viator* 5 (1974): 387–412.
– "Chaucer, the Merchant, and Their Tale: Getting beyond Old Controversies." *ChauR* 13, no. 2 and 13, no. 3 (1978–9): 141–56 and 247–62.
– "What Is Chaucer Doing with the Physician and His Tale?" *PQ* 60, no. 2 (1981): 129–49.
Brown, Peter. "An Optical Theme in the *Merchant's Tale*." *SAC Proceedings* 1 (1984): 231–43.
– "Is the *Canon's Yeoman's Tale* Apocryphal?" *ES* 64, no. 6 (1983): 481–90.
– "The Containment of Symkyn: The Function of Space in the *Reeve's Tale*." *ChauR* 14, no. 3 (1980): 225–36.
Bruhn, Mark J. "Art, Anxiety, and Alchemy in the *Canon's Yeoman's Tale*." *ChauR* 33, no. 3 (1999): 288–315.
Bryan, Jennifer. "'A berd! A berd!': Chaucer's Miller and the Poetics of the Pun." *SAC* 38 (2016): 1–37.
Burger, Douglas A. "*The Cosa Impossibile* of *Il Filocolo* and the *Impossible* of the *Franklin's Tale*." In *Chaucer and the Craft of Fiction*, edited by Leigh A. Arrathoon, 165–78. Rochester, MI: Solaris Press, 1986.
Burger, Glenn. *Chaucer's Queer Nation*. Minneapolis, MN: University of Minnesota Press, 2003.
– "Present Panic in the *Merchant's Tale*." *SAC* 24 (2002): 49–73.
Burlin, Robert. "The Art of Chaucer's Franklin." *Neophilologus* 51, no. 1 (1967): 55–73.
Burrow, J.A. "*Sir Thopas*: An Agony in Three Fits." *RES* 22, no. 85 (1971): 54–58.
Burton, T.L. "The Wife of Bath's Fourth and Fifth Husbands and her Ideal Sixth: The Growth of Marital Philosophy." *ChauR* 13, no. 1 (1978): 34–50.
Bushnell, Nelson S. "The Wandering Jew and the *Pardoner's Tale*." *SP* 28, no. 3 (1931): 450–60.
Bynum, Caroline Walker. *Holy Feast and Holy Fast: The Religious Significance of Food to Medieval Women*. Berkeley: University of California Press, 1987.
Cahn, Kenneth S. "Chaucer's Merchants and the Foreign Exchange: An Introduction to Medieval Finance." *SAC* 2 (1980): 81–119.
Caie, Graham D. "Innocent III's *De Miseria* as a Gloss on the *Man of Law's Prologue* and *Tale*." *NM* 100, no. 2 (1999): 175–85.
– "The Significance of Marginal Glosses in the Earliest Manuscripts of the *Canterbury Tales*." In *Chaucer and the Scriptural Tradition*, edited by David Lyle Jeffrey, 75–88. Ottawa: University of Ottawa Press, 1984.
Calabrese, Michael A. "Meretricious Mixtures: Gold, Dung, and the *Canon's Yeoman's Prologue* and *Tale*." *ChauR* 27, no. 3 (1993): 277–90.
– "Performing the Prioress: 'Conscience' and Responsibility in Studies of Chaucer's *Prioress's Tale*." *TSLL* 44, no. 1 (2002): 66–91.

Camargo, Martin. "Chaucer and the Oxford Renaissance of Anglo-Latin Rhetoric." *SAC* 34 (2012): 173–207.

– "Rhetorical Ethos and the *Nun's Priest's Tale*." *Comparative Literature Studies* 33, no. 2 (1996): 173–86.

Campbell, Emma. "Sexual Politics and the Politics of Translation in the Tale of Griselda." *Comparative Literature* 55, no. 3 (2003): 191–216.

Campbell, Jackson J. "Polonius among the Pilgrims." *ChauR* 7, no. 2 (1972): 140–6.

Cannon, Christopher. "Chaucer and the Auchinleck Manuscript Reconsidered." *ChauR* 46, nos. 1–2 (2011): 131–46.

– "Form." In *Middle English*, edited by Paul Strohm, 177–90. Oxford: Oxford University Press, 2007.

Carruthers, Mary. "The Wife of Bath and the Painting of Lions." *PMLA* 94, no. 2 (1979): 209–22.

Cartlidge, Neil. "Wayward Sons and Failing Fathers: Chaucer's Moralistic Paternalism – and a Possible Source for the *Cook's Tale*." *ChauR* 47, no. 2 (2012): 134–60.

Casey, Jim. "Unfinished Business: The Termination of the *Cook's Tale*." *ChauR* 41, no. 2 (2006): 185–96.

Cespedes, Frank V. "Chaucer's Pardoner and Preaching." *ELH* 44, no. 1 (1977): 1–18.

Chance, Jane. "'Disfigured is thy face': Chaucer's Pardoner and the Protean Shape-Shifter Fals-Semblant (A Response to Britton Harwood)." *PQ* 67, no. 4 (1988): 423–37.

Chapin, Arthur. "Morality Ovidized: Sententiousness and the Aphoristic Moment in the *Nun's Priest's Tale*." *Yale Journal of Criticism* 8, no. 1 (1995): 7–33.

Chapman, Juliana. "Melodye and Noyse: An Aesthetic of Musica in the *Knight's Tale* and the *Miller's Tale*." *SP* 112, no. 4 (2015): 633–55.

Chaucer, Geoffrey. *The Riverside Chaucer*, 3rd ed. Edited by Larry D. Benson. Boston: Houghton Mifflin, 1987.

Chickering, Howell. "Form and Interpretation in the *Envoy* to the *Clerk's Tale*." *ChauR* 29, no. 4 (1995): 352–72.

Clark, David W. "Ockham on Human and Divine Freedom." *Franciscan Studies* 38 (1978): 122–60.

Clark, John W. "Does the Franklin Interrupt the Squire?" *ChauR* 7, no. 2 (1972–3), 160–1.

– "'This Litel Tretys' Again." *ChauR* 6, no. 2 (1971/2): 152–6.

Clark, Roy Peter. "Doubting Thomas in Chaucer's *Summoner's Tale*." *ChauR* 11, no. 2 (1976): 164–78.

Clogan, Paul M. "The Figural Style and Meaning of the *Second Nun's Prologue* and *Tale*." *Medievalia et Humanistica* 3 (1972): 213–40.

Coffey, David. "The Holy Spirit as the Mutual Love of the Father and the Son." *Theological Studies* 51, no. 2 (1990): 193–229.

Cohen, Jeffrey Jerome. *Medieval Identity Machines*. Minneapolis, MN: University of Minnesota Press, 2003.

Cole, Andrew. *Literature and Heresy in the Age of Chaucer*. Cambridge: Cambridge University Press, 2008.

– *The Birth of Theory*. Chicago: University of Chicago Press, 2014.

Colebrook, Claire. *Gender*. Houndmills, UK: Palgrave Macmillan, 2004.

Coletti, Theresa. "The 'Mulier Fortis' and Chaucer's *Shipman's Tale*." *ChauR* 15, no. 3 (1981): 236–49.

Coley, David K. "Money and the Plow, or the *Shipman's Tale* of Tithing." *ChauR* 49, no. 4 (2015): 449–73.

Collette, Carolyn P. "A Closer Look at Seinte Cecile's Special Vision." *ChauR* 10, no. 4 (1976): 337–49.

– "Heeding the Counsel of Prudence: A Context for the *Melibee*." *ChauR* 29, no. 4 (1995): 416–33.

– "'Peynting with Greet Cost': Virginia as Image in the *Physician's Tale*." *Chaucer Yearbook* 2 (1995): 49–62.

Condren, Edward I. "The *Clerk's Tale* of Man Tempting God." *Criticism* 26, no. 2 (1984): 99–114.

Conley, John. "The Peculiar Name Thopas." *SP* 73, no. 1 (1976): 42–61.

Cook, Alexandra. "'O sweete harm so queynte': Loving Pagan Antiquity in *Troilus and Criseyde* and the *Knight's Tale*." *ES* 91, no. 1 (2010): 26–41.

Cook, Megan L. "'Here taketh the makere of this book his leve': The *Retraction* and Chaucer's Works in Tudor England." *SP* 113, no. 1 (2016): 32–54.

Cooney, Helen. "Wonder and Immanent Justice in the *Man of Law's Tale*." *ChauR* 33, no. 3 (1999): 264–87.

Cooper, Helen. *Oxford Guides to Chaucer: The Canterbury Tales*, 2nd ed. Oxford: Oxford University Press, 1996.

– *The Structure of the Canterbury Tales*. Athens: University of Georgia Press, 1984.

Cooper, John M., and D.S. Hutchinson, eds. *Plato: Complete Works*. Indianapolis: Hackett Publishing, 1997.

Copeland, Rita. "The Pardoner's Body and the Disciplining of Rhetoric." In *Framing Medieval Bodies*, edited by Sarah Kay and Miri Rubin, 138–59. Manchester: Manchester University Press, 1994.

Copland, Murray. "The *Reeve's Tale*: Harlotrie or Sermonyng?" *MÆ* 31, no. 1 (1962): 14–32.

– "The *Shipman's Tale*: Chaucer and Boccaccio." *MÆ* 35, no. 1 (1966): 11–28.

Courtenay, William J. *School and Scholars in Fourteenth-Century England*. Princeton, NJ: Princeton University Press, 1987.

Cox, Catherine S. *Gender and Language in Chaucer*. Gainesville: University Press of Florida, 1997.

– "The Jangler's 'Bourde': Gender, Renunciation, and Chaucer's Manciple." *South Atlantic Review* 61, no. 4 (1996): 1–21.

– "Water of Bitterness: The Pardoner and/as the Sotah." *Exemplaria* 16, no. 1 (2004): 131–64.

Crane, Susan. "Medieval Romance and Feminine Difference in the *Knight's Tale*." *SAC* 12 (1990): 47–63.

– "The Franklin as Dorigen." *ChauR* 24, no. 3 (1990): 236–52.

Crocker, Holly A. "Performative Passivity and Fantasies of Masculinity in the *Merchant's Tale*." *ChauR* 38, no. 2 (2003): 178–98.

Cross, Richard. *The Metaphysics of the Incarnation: Thomas Aquinas to Duns Scotus*. Oxford: Oxford University Press, 2002.

Dahlberg, Charles. "Chaucer's Cock and Fox." *JEGP* 53, no. 3 (1954): 277–90.

Dahood, Roger. "English Historical Narratives of Jewish Child-Murder, Chaucer's *Prioress's Tale*, and the Date of Chaucer's Unknown Source." *SAC* 31 (2009): 125–40.

– "The Punishment of the Jews, Hugh of Lincoln, and the Question of Satire in Chaucer's *Prioress's Tale*." *Viator* 36 (2005): 465–90.

Daileader, Celia R. "The 'Thopas-Melibee' Sequence and the Defeat of Antifeminism." *ChauR* 29, no. 1 (1994): 26–39.

Dalbey, Marcia A. "The Devil in the Garden: Pluto and Proserpine in Chaucer's *Merchant's Tale*." *NM* 75, no. 3 (1974): 408–15.

Dane, Joseph A. "The Wife of Bath's *Shipman's Tale* and the Invention of Chaucerian Fabliaux." *MLR* 99, no. 2 (2004): 287–300.

David, Alfred. "Criticism and the Old Man in Chaucer's *Pardoner's Tale*." *College English* 27, no. 1 (1965): 39–44.

– "The Man of Law vs. Chaucer: A Case in Poetics." *PMLA* 82, no. 2 (1967): 217–25.

– *The Strumpet Muse: Art and Morals in Chaucer's Poetry*. Bloomington: University of Indiana Press, 1976.

Dawson, Robert B. "Custance in Context: Rethinking the Protagonist of the *Man of Law's Tale*." *ChauR* 26, no. 3 (1992): 293–308.

De Man, Paul. *Allegories of Reading: Figural Language in Nietzsche, Rilke, and Proust*. New Haven, CT: Yale University Press, 1979.

Dean, James. "Dismantling the Canterbury Book." *PMLA* 100, no. 5 (1985): 746–62.

– "Gower, Chaucer, and Rhyme Royal." *SP* 88, no. 3 (1991): 251–75.

Delany, Paul. "Constantinus Africanus and Chaucer's *Merchant's Tale*." *PQ* 46, no. 4 (1967): 560–66.

– "Constantinus Africanus's *De Coitu*: A Translation." *ChauR* 4, no. 1 (1969): 55–65.

Delany, Sheila. "Doer of the Word: The Epistle of St. James as a Source for Chaucer's *Manciple's Tale.*" *ChauR* 17, no. 3 (1983): 250–54.

– "The Late Medieval Attack on Analogical Thought: Undoing Substantial Connection." In *Medieval Literary Politics: Shapes of Ideology*, edited by Sheila Delany, 19–41. Manchester: Manchester University Press, 1990; originally published in *Mosaic* 5, no. 4 (1972): 31–52.

– "'Mulier est hominis confusio': Chaucer's Anti-popular *Nun's Priest's Tale.*" *Mosaic* 17, no. 1 (1984): 1–8.

– "Politics and the Paralysis of Poetic Imagination in the *Physician's Tale.*" *SAC* 3 (1981): 47–60.

– "Strategies of Silence in the Wife of Bath's Recital." *Exemplaria* 2, no. 1 (1990): 49–69.

– "Womanliness in the *Man of Law's Tale.*" *ChauR* 9, no. 1 (1974): 63–72.

Delasanta, Rodney. "And of Great Reverence: Chaucer's Man of Law." *ChauR* 5, no. 4 (1971): 288–310.

– "Chaucer and Strode." *ChauR* 26, no. 2 (1991): 205–18.

– "Nominalism and the *Clerk's Tale* Revisited." *ChauR* 31, no. 3 (1997): 209–31.

DeMarco, Patricia. "Violence, Law, and Ciceronian Ethics in Chaucer's *Tale of Melibee.*" *SAC* 30 (2008): 125–69.

Denny-Brown, Andrea. "*Povre* Griselda and the All-Consuming *Archewyves.*" *SAC* 28 (2006): 77–115.

Derrida, Jacques. *Dissemination.* Translated by Barbara Johnson. Chicago: University of Chicago Press, 1981.

Despres, Denise L. "Chaucer's Cultic Anti-Judaism and Chaucer's Litel Clergeon." *MP* 91, no. 4 (1994): 413–27.

Dicicco, Mark. "The Arming of Sir Thopas Reconsidered." *Notes and Queries* 46, no. 1 (1999): 14–16.

Dickson, Lynne. "Deflection in the Mirror: Feminine Discourse in the *Wife of Bath's Prologue* and *Tale.*" *SAC* 15 (1993): 61–90.

Dinshaw, Carolyn. "Chaucer's Queer Touches / A Queer Touches Chaucer." *Exemplaria* 7, no. 1 (1995): 75–92.

– *Chaucer's Sexual Poetics.* Madison: University of Wisconsin Press, 1989.

– "Pale Faces: Race, Religion, and Affect in Chaucer's Texts and Their Readers." *SAC* 23 (2001): 19–41.

Dobbs, Elizabeth A. "The Canaanite Woman, the Second Nun, and St. Cecilia." *Christianity and Literature* 62, no. 2 (2013): 203–22.

Donaldson, E. Talbot. "Chaucer the Pilgrim." *PMLA* 69, no. 4 (1954): 928–36.

– *Chaucer's Poetry: An Anthology for the Modern Reader.* New York: Ronald Press, 1958.

– "Patristic Exegesis: The Opposition." In *Critical Approaches to Medieval Literature: Selected Papers from the English Institute, 1958–1959*, edited by Dorothy Bethurum, 1–26. New York: Columbia University Press, 1960.

– *Speaking of Chaucer*. Durham, NC: Labyrinth Books, 1983.

Donaldson, Kara Virginia. "Alisoun's Language: Body, Text, and Glossing in Chaucer's The *Miller's Tale*." *PQ* 71, no. 2 (1992): 139–53.

Donie, R. Jacob. "'Ye gete namoore of me': Narrative, Textual, and Linguistic Desires in Chaucer's *Merchant's Tale*." *Exemplaria* 24, no. 4 (2012): 313–41.

Donovan, Mortimer J. "The 'Moralite' of the Nun's Priest's Sermon." *JEGP* 52, no. 4 (1953): 498–508.

Duncan, Charles F. "'Straw for Your Gentilesse': The Gentle Franklin's Interruption of the Squire." *ChauR* 5, no. 2 (1970–1): 161–4.

Duncan, Edgar H. "Chaucer and 'Arnald of the Newe Town': A Reprise." *Interpretations* 9, no. 1 (1977): 7–11.

– "The Literature of Alchemy and Chaucer's *Canon's Yeoman's Tale*: Framework, Theme, and Characters." *Speculum* 43, no. 4 (1968): 633–56.

Durling, Robert M., ed. and trans. *The Divine Comedy of Dante Alighieri*, 3 vols. Oxford: Oxford University Press, 2011.

Eade, J.C. "'We ben to lewed or to slowe': Chaucer's Astronomy and Audience Participation." *SAC* 4 (1982): 53–85.

Edden, Valerie. "Sacred and Secular in the *Clerk's Tale*." *ChauR* 26, no. 4 (1992): 369–76.

Edwards, A.S.G. "'I speke in prose': *Man of Law's Tale*, 96." *NM* 92, no. 4 (1991): 469–70.

– "The *Merchant's Tale* and Moral Chaucer." *MLQ* 51 (1990): 409–26.

Edwards, Elizabeth B. "The Work of Mourning in the *Knight's Tale*." *Exemplaria* 20, no. 4 (2008): 361–84.

Edwards, Robert R. "Narration and Doctrine in the *Merchant's Tale*." *Speculum* 66, no. 2 (1991): 342–67.

– "Source, Context, and Cultural Translation in the *Franklin's Tale*." *MP* 94, no. 2 (1996): 141–62.

– "The *Franklin's Tale*." In *Sources and Analogues of the* Canterbury Tales, 2 vols., edited by Robert M. Correale and Mary Hamel, 1:230–1. Cambridge: D.S. Brewer, 2002 and 2005.

– "'The Sclaundre of Walter': The *Clerk's Tale* and the Problem of Hermeneutics." In *Mediaevalitas: Reading the Middle Ages*, edited by Piero Boitani and Anna Torti, 15–41. Cambridge: D.S. Brewer, 1996.

Edwards, Suzanne. "The Rhetoric of Rape and the Politics of Gender in the *Wife of Bath's Tale* and the *1382 Statue of Rapes*." *Exemplaria* 23, no. 1 (2011): 3–26.

Eggebroten, Anne. "Laughter in the *Second Nun's Tale*: A Redefinition of Genre." *ChauR* 19, no. 1 (1984): 55–61.

Ellis, Deborah S. "Chaucer's Devilish Reeve." *ChauR* 27, no. 2 (1992): 150–61.

Epstein, Robert. "Dismal Science: Chaucer and Gower on Alchemy and Economy." *SAC* 36 (2014): 209–48.

– "'Fer in the north; I kan nat telle where': Dialect, Regionalism, and Philologism." *SAC* 30 (2008): 95–124.

– "The Lack of Interest in the *Shipman's Tale*: Chaucer and the Social Theory of the Gift." *MP* 113, no. 1 (2015): 27–48.

Everest, Carol A. "Sex and Old Age in Chaucer's *Reeve's Prologue*." *ChauR* 31, no. 2 (1996): 99–114.

Eyler, Joshua R., and John P. Sexton. "Once More to the Grove: A Note on Symbolic Space in the *Knight's Tale*." *ChauR* 40, no. 4 (2006): 433–9.

Farber, Lianna. "The Creation of Consent in the *Physician's Tale*." *ChauR* 39, no. 2 (2004): 151–64.

Farrell, Robert T. "Chaucer's Use of the Theme of the Help of God in the *Man of Law's Tale*." *NM* 71, no. 2 (1970): 239–43.

Farrell, Thomas J. "Chaucer's Little Treatise, the *Melibee*." *ChauR* 20, no. 1 (1985): 61–7.

– "The *Envoy de Chaucer* and the *Clerk's Tale*." *ChauR* 24, no. 4 (1990): 329–36.

Fehrenbacher, Richard. "'A Yeerd Enclosed Al Aboute': Literature and History in the *Nun's Priest's Tale*." *ChauR* 29, no. 2 (1994): 134–48.

Fein, Susanna G. "'Lat the children pleye,': the Game Betwixt the Ages in the *Reeve's Tale*." In *Rebels and Rivals: The Contestive Spirit in the Canterbury Tales*, edited by Susanna G. Fein, David Raybin, and Peter C. Braeger, 73–104. Kalamazoo, MI: Medieval Institute Publications, 2001.

– "Why Did Absolon Put a 'Trewelove' under His Tongue?: Herb Paris as a Healing 'Grace' in Middle English Literature." *ChauR* 25, no. 4 (1991): 302–17.

Fernández, Mariá Bullón. "Private Practices in Chaucer's *Miller's Tale*." *SAC* 28 (2006): 141–74.

Ferris, Sumner. "Chaucer at Lincoln (1387): The *Prioress's Tale* as a Political Poem." *ChauR* 15, no. 4 (1981): 295–321.

Ferster, Judith. *Fictions of Advice: The Literature and Politics of Counsel in Late Medieval England*. Philadelphia: University of Pennsylvania Press, 1996, 89–107.

– "'Your Praise is Performed by Men and Children': Language and Gender in the *Prioress's Prologue* and *Tale*." *Exemplaria* 2, no. 1 (1990): 149–68.

Fichte, Joerg O. "Man's Free Will and the Poet's Choice: The Creation of Artistic Order in the *Knight's Tale*." *Anglia* 93 (1975): 335–60.

Field, P.J.C. "The Ending of Chaucer's *Nun's Priest's Tale*." *MÆ* 71, no. 2 (2002): 302–6.

Finke, Laurie A. "'To Knytte Up Al this Feeste': The Parson's Rhetoric and the Ending of the *Canterbury Tales*." *Leeds Studies in English* 15 (1984): 95–107.

Finkelstein, Dorothee. "The Code of Chaucer's 'Secree of Secrees': Arabic Alchemical Terminology in the *Canon's Yeoman's Tale*." *Archiv für das Studium der neueren Sprachen und Literaturen* 207 (1970): 260–76.

Finlayson, John. "Chaucer's Prioress and *Amor Vincit Omnia*." *Studia Neophilologica* 60, no. 2 (1988): 171–4.
– "Chaucer's *Shipman's Tale*, Boccaccio, and the 'Civilizing' of Fabliau." *ChauR* 36, no. 4 (2002): 336–51.
– "Chaucer's *Summoner's Tale*: Flatulence, Blasphemy, and the Emperor's Clothes." *SP* 101, no. 4 (2007): 455–70.
– "The *Knight's Tale*: The Dialogue of Romance, Epic, and Philosophy." *ChauR* 27, no. 2 (1992): 126–49.
– "The 'Povre Widwe' in the *Nun's Priest's Tale* and Boccaccio's *Decameron*." *NM* 99, no. 3 (1998): 269–73.
– "The Satiric Mode and the *Parson's Tale*." *ChauR* 6, no. 2 (1971–2): 94–116.
Finnegan, Robert Emmett. "A Curious Condition of Being: The City and the Grove in Chaucer's *Knight's Tale*." *SP* 106, no. 3 (2009): 285–98.
Fisher, John H. *John Gower: Moral Philosopher and Friend of Chaucer*. New York: New York University Press, 1964.
Flannery, Mary C. "A Bloody Shame: Chaucer's Honourable Women." *RES* 62, no. 255 (2011): 337–57.
Fleissner, Robert F. "The Oath of the Prioress." *NM* 86, no. 2 (1985): 197–8.
Fletcher, Alan J. "Chaucer the Heretic." *SAC* 25 (2003): 53–121.
– "The Topical Hypocrisy of Chaucer's Pardoner." *ChauR* 25, no. 2 (1990): 110–26.
Fletcher, Angus. "The Sentencing of Virginia in the *Physician's Tale*." *ChauR* 34, no. 3 (2000): 300–8.
Foster, Edward E. "Has Anyone Here Read *Melibee*." *ChauR* 34, no. 4 (2000): 398–409.
– "Humor in the *Knight's Tale*." *ChauR* 3, no. 2 (1968), 88–94.
Foster, Michael. "Echoes of Communal Response in the *Tale of Melibee*." *ChauR* 42, no. 4 (2008): 409–30.
Fradenburg, Louise A.O. "Criticism, Anti-Semitism, and the *Prioress's Tale*." *Exemplaria* 1, no. 1 (1989): 69–115.
– "The Manciple's Servant Tongue: Politics and Poetry in the *Canterbury Tales*." *ELH* 52, no. 1 (1985): 85–118.
– *Sacrifice Your Love: Psychoanalysis, Historicism, Chaucer*. Minneapolis: University of Minnesota Press, 2002.
Frank, Hardy Long. "Seeing the Prioress Whole." *ChauR* 25, no. 3 (1991): 229–37.
Franke, William. "'Enditynges of Worldly Vanitees': Truth and Poetry in Chaucer as Compared with Dante." *ChauR* 34, no. 1 (1999): 87–106.
Frazier, Terry J. "The Digression on Marriage in the *Franklin's Tale*." *South Atlantic Bulletin* 43, no. 1 (1978): 75–85.
Frese, Dolores Warwick. "The *Nun's Priest's Tale*: Chaucer's Identified Masterpiece?" *ChauR* 16, no. 4 (1982): 330–43.

Friedman, Albert B. "The Mysterious Greyn in the *Prioress's Tale*." *ChauR* 11, no. 4 (1977): 328–33.

– "The *Prioress's Tale* and Chaucer's Anti-Semitism." *ChauR* 9, no. 2 (1974): 118–29.

Friedman, Jamie A. "Between Boccaccio and Chaucer: The Limits of Female Interiority in the Knight's *Tale*." In *The Inner Life of Women in Medieval Romance Literature: Grief, Guilt, and Hypocrisy*, edited by Jeff Rider and Jamie Friedman, 203–22. New York: Palgrave, 2011.

Friedman, John Block. "The *Nun's Priest's Tale*: The Preacher and the Mermaid's Song." *ChauR* 7, no. 4 (1973): 250–66.

– "A Reading of Chaucer's *Reeve's Tale*." *ChauR* 2 (1967): 8–19.

Frost, William. "An Interpretation of Chaucer's *Knight's Tale*." *RES* 25, no. 100 (1949): 289–304.

Fry, Donald K. "The Ending of the *Monk's Tale*." *JEGP* 71, no. 3 (1972): 355–68.

Fulk, R.D. "Reinterpreting the *Manciple's Tale*." *JEGP* 78, no. 4 (1979): 485–93.

Fulton, Helen. "Mercantile Ideology in Chaucer's *Shipman's Tale*." *ChauR* 36, no. 4 (2002): 311–28.

Fumo, Jamie C. "The God of Love and Love of God: Palinodic Exchange in the Prologue of the *Legend of Good Women* and the *Retraction*." In *The Legend of Good Women: Context and Reception*, edited by Carolyn P. Collett, 157–75. Cambridge: D.S. Brewer, 2006.

– "An Interpretive Crux in Januarie's Garden: Chaucer's *Merchant Tale* and the Crucifixion." *Mediaevalia* 23 (2002): 1–37.

– *The Legacy of Apollo: Antiquity, Authority, and Chaucerian Poetics*. Toronto: University of Toronto Press, 2010.

– "The Pestilential Gaze: From Epidemiology to Erotomania in the *Knight's Tale*." *SAC* 35 (2013): 85–136.

– "Thinking upon the Crow: The *Manciple's Tale* and Ovidian Mythography." *ChauR* 38, no. 4 (2004): 355–75.

Furr, Grover C. "Nominalism in the *Nun's Priest's Tale*: A Preliminary Study." In *Literary Nominalism and the Theory of Rereading Late Medieval Texts*, edited by Richard J. Utz, 135–46. Lewiston, NY: E. Mellen Press, 1995.

Furrow, Melissa M. "The Man of Law's St. Custance: Sex and the Saeculum." *ChauR* 24, no. 3 (1990): 223–35.

Fyler, John M. "Hateful Contraries in the *Merchant's Tale*." *Critical Survey* 30, no. 2 (2017): 15–45.

– *Language and the Declining World in Chaucer, Dante, and Jean de Meun*. Cambridge: Cambridge University Press, 2007.

Gallacher, Patrick. "Food, Laxatives, and Catharsis in Chaucer's *Nun's Priest's Tale*." *Speculum* 51, no. 1 (1976): 49–68.

Galloway, Andrew. "*Auctorite*." In *A New Companion to Chaucer*, edited by Peter Brown, 21–36. Hoboken, NJ: Wiley Blackwell, 2019.

Ganim, John M. "Carnival Voices and the *Envoy* to the *Clerk's Tale*." *ChauR* 22, no. 2 (1987): 112–27.

– *Chaucerian Theatricality*. Princeton, NJ: Princeton University Press, 1990.

Ganze, Alison. "'My Trouthe for to Holde: Allas, Allas!' Dorigen and Honor in the Franklin's Tale." *ChauR* 42, no. 3 (2008): 312–29.

Garbáty, Thomas J. "Satire and Regionalism: The Reeve and His Tale." *ChauR* 8, no. 1 (1973): 1–8.

Gardner, John. "The *Canon's Yeoman's Prologue* and *Tale*: An Interpretation." *PQ* 46, no. 1 (1967): 1–17.

– *The Poetry of Chaucer*. Carbondale: Southern Illinois University Press, 1977.

Gaston, Kara. "The Poetics of Time Management from the *Metamorphoses* to *Il Filocolo* and the *Franklin's Tale*." *SAC* 37 (2015): 227–56.

Gayk, Shannon. "'To wondre upon this thyng': Chaucer's *Prioress's Tale*." *Exemplaria* 22, no. 2 (2010): 138–56.

Gaylord, Alan T. "Chaucer's Dainty 'Dogerel': The 'Elvyssh' Prosody of *Sir Thopas*." *SAC* 1 (1979): 83–104.

– "The 'Miracle' of *Sir Thopas*." *SAC* 6 (1984): 65–84.

– "The Promises in the *Franklin's Tale*." *ELH* 31, no. 4 (1964): 331–65.

– "Reflections on D. W. Robertson Jr. and 'Exegetical Criticism." *ChauR* 40, no. 3 (2006): 311–33.

– "The Role of Saturn in the *Knight's Tale*." *ChauR* 8, no. 3 (1974): 171–90.

– "*Sentence* and *Solaas* in Fragment VII of the *Canterbury Tales*: Harry Bailly as Horseback Editor." *PMLA* 82, no. 2 (1967): 226–35.

Georgianna, Linda. "*The Clerk's Tale* and the Grammar of Assent." *Speculum* 70 (1995): 793–821.

– "Love So Dearly Bought: The Terms of Redemption in the *Canterbury Tales*." *SAC* 12 (1990): 85–116.

Gerber, Hester Goodenough. *It Could Have Been Otherwise*. Leiden, Netherlands: Brill, 2004.

Gersh, Stephen. "The Medieval Legacy from Ancient Platonism." In his *Reading Plato, Tracing Plato: From Ancient Commentary to Medieval Reception*, 3–30. Burlington, VT: Ashgate, 2005.

Ginsburg, Warren. "Aesthetics *Sine Nomine*." *ChauR* 39, no. 3 (2005): 234–40.

– "Chaucer's Canterbury Poetics: Irony, Allegory, and the *Prologue* to the *Manciple's Tale*." *SAC* 18 (1996): 55–89.

Goodall, Peter. "'Unkynde abhomynaciouns' in Chaucer and Gower." *Parergon* 5 (1987): 94–102.

Grace, Dominick M. "Chaucer's Little Treatises." *Florilegium* 14 (1995–6): 157–70.

– "Telling Differences: Chaucer's *Tale of Melibee* and Renaud de Louens' *Livre de Melibee et Prudence*." *PQ* 82, no. 4 (2003): 367–400.

Gravlee, Cynthia A. "Presence, Absence, and Difference: Reception and Deception in the *Franklin's Tale*." In *Desiring Discourse: The Literature of Love,*

Ovid Through Chaucer, edited by James J. Paxson and Cynthia A. Gravlee, 177–87. London: Associated University Presses, 1998.

Green, R.P.H., ed. and trans. *Augustine: De Doctrina Christiana*. Oxford: Clarendon Press, 1996.

Green, Richard Firth. "Changing Chaucer." *SAC* 25 (2003): 27–52.

– "The Pardoner's Pants (and Why They Matter)." *SAC* 15 (1993): 131–45.

– *Poets and Princepleasers: Literature and the English Court in the Late Middle Ages*. Toronto: University of Toronto Press, 1980.

Greene, Darragh. "Moral Obligations, Virtue Ethics, and *Gentil* Character in Chaucer's *Franklin's Tale*." *ChauR* 50, nos. 1/2 (2015): 88–107.

Greene, Virginie. *Logical Fictions in Medieval Literature and Philosophy*. Cambridge: Cambridge University Press, 2014.

Grenberg, Bruce L. "The Canon's Yeoman's Tale: Boethian Wisdom and the Alchemists." *ChauR* 1, no. 1 (1966): 37–54.

Grennen, Joseph E. "The Calculating Reeve and His Camera Obscura." *Journal of Medieval and Renaissance Studies* 14, no. 2 (1984): 245–59.

– "Chaucer's Man of Law and the Constancy of Justice." *JEGP* 84, no. 4 (1985): 498–514.

– "Saint Cecilia's 'Chemical Wedding': the Unity of the *Canterbury Tales*, Fragment VIII." *JEGP* 65, no. 3 (1966): 466–81.

Grimes, Jodi. "Arboreal Politics in the *Knight's Tale*." *ChauR* 46, no. 3 (2012): 340–64.

Grodin, Michaela Paasche. "Chaucer's *Clerk's Tale* as Political Paradox." *SAC* 11 (1989): 63–92.

– "Chaucer's *Manciple's Tale* and the Poetics of Guile." *ChauR* 25, no. 4 (1991): 329–42.

Grossi, Joseph L., Jr. "The Unhidden Piety of Chaucer's 'Seint Cecilie.'" *ChauR* 36, no. 3 (2002): 298–309.

Gruber, Loren C. "The *Manciple's Tale*: One Key to Chaucer's Language." In *New Views on Chaucer: Essays in Generative Criticism*, edited by Loren C. Gruber and William C. Johnson, 43–50. Denver: Society for New Language Study, 1973.

Gruenler, Curtis A. *Piers Plowman and the Poetics of Enigma: Riddles, Rhetoric, and Theology*. Notre Dame, IN: University of Notre Dame Press, 2017.

Guerin, Richard. "The *Shipman's Tale*: The Italian Analogues." *ES* 52, nos. 1–6 (1971): 412–19.

Gust, Geoffrey W. *Constructing Chaucer: Author and Autofiction in the Critical Tradition*. New York: Palgrave Macmillan, 2009.

Haas, Renate. "Chaucer's *Monk's Tale*: An Ingenious Criticism of Early Humanist Conceptions of Tragedy." *Humanistica Lovaniensia* 36 (1987): 44–70.

Hall, Alaric. "Elves on the Brain: Chaucer, Old English, and *Elvish*." *Anglia* 124, no. 2 (2006): 225–43.

Halverson, John. "Chaucer's Pardoner and the Progress of Criticism." *ChauR* 4, no. 3 (1970): 184–202.

Hamel, Mary. "And Now for Something Completely Different: The Relationship between the *Prioress's Tale* and the *Rime of Sir Thopas*." *ChauR* 14, no. 3 (1980): 250–9.

Hamilton, Marie P. "Death and Old Age in the *Pardoner's Tale*." *SP* 36, no. 4 (1939): 571–6.

Hammond, Eleanor Prescott. *Chaucer: A Bibliographic Manual*. New York: Macmillan, 1908.

Hanks, D. Thomas, Jr. "Emaré: An Influence on the *Man of Law's Tale*." *ChauR* 18, no. 2 (1983): 182–6.

Hanna, Ralph. "Pilate's Voice/Shirley's Case." In his *Pursuing History: Middle English Manuscripts and Their Texts*, 267–82. Stanford, CA: Stanford University Press, 1996.

Hanning, Robert W. "'And countrefete the speche of every man/He koude, whan he sholde telle a tale': Toward a Lapsarian Poetics for the *Canterbury Tales*." *SAC* 21 (1999): 29–58.

– "Chaucer and the Dangers of Poetry." *CEA Critic* 46, nos. 3/4 (1984): 17–26.

– "Roasting a Friar, Mis-taking a Wife, and Other Acts of Textual Harassment in the *Canterbury Tales*." *SAC* 7 (1985): 3–21.

– "'The Struggle between Noble Designs and Chaos': The Literary Tradition of Chaucer's *Knight's Tale*." *The Literary Review* 23, no. 4 (1980): 519–41.

Hansen, Elaine Tuttle. *Chaucer and the Fictions of Gender*. Berkeley: University of California Press, 1992.

– "'Of his love daungerous to me': Liberation, Subversion, and Domestic Violence in the *Wife of Bath's Prologue* and *Tale*." In *The Wife of Bath: Geoffrey Chaucer*, edited by Peter G. Beidler, 273–89. Boston: Bedford Books, 1996.

Harley, Marta. "The Reeve's 'Foure Gleedes' and St. Fursey's Vision of the Four Fires of the Afterlife." *MÆ* 56, no. 1 (1987): 85–9.

Harrington, Norman T. "Chaucer's *Merchant's Tale*: Another Swing of the Pendulum." *PMLA* 86, no. 1 (1971): 25–31.

Harris, Richard L. "Odin's Old Age: A Study of the Old Man in the *Pardoners Tale*." *SFQ* 33 (1969): 24–38.

Harrison, Benjamin S. "The Rhetorical Inconsistency of the Franklin." *SP* 32, no. 1 (1935): 55–61.

Harrison, Joseph. "'Tears for Passing Things': The Temple of Diana in the *Knight's Tale*." *PQ* 63, no. 1 (1984): 108–16.

Hartung, Albert E. "Pars Secunda and the Development of the *Canon's Yeoman's Tale*." *ChauR* 12 (1977): 111–28.

Harwood, Britton J. "Chaucer and the Silence of History: Situating the *Canon's Yeoman's Tale*." *PMLA* 102, no. 3 (1987): 338–50.

– "Language and the Real: Chaucer's Manciple." *ChauR* 6, no. 4 (1972): 268–79.

– "Psychoanalytic Politics: Chaucer and Two Peasants." *ELH* 68, no. 1 (2001): 2–27.

Haskell, Ann S. "Sir Thopas: The Puppet's Puppet." *ChauR* 9, no. 3 (1975): 253–61.

– "The St. Joce Oath in the *Wife of Bath's Prologue*." *ChauR* 1, no. 2 (1966): 85–7.

Hatcher, Elizabeth R. "Life without Death: The Old Man in Chaucer's *Pardoner's Tale*." *ChauR* 9, no. 3 (1975): 246–52.

Hawkins, Sherman. "Chaucer's Prioress and the Sacrifice of Praise." *JEGP* 63, no. 4 (1964): 599–624.

Hazelton, Richard. "The *Manciple's Tale*: Parody and Critique." *JEGP* 62, no. 1 (1963): 1–31.

Heffernan, Carol Falvo. "A Reconsideration of the Cask Figure in the *Reeve's Prologue*." *ChauR* 15, no. 1 (1980): 37–43.

– "Tyranny and Commune Profit in the *Clerk's Tale*." *ChauR* 17, no. 4 (1983): 332–40.

Hegel, G.W.F. *The Difference between Fichte's and Schelling's System of Philosophy*. Translated by Walter Cerf and H.S. Harris. Albany: State University of New York Press, 1977.

– *The Science of Logic*. Translated by George di Giovanni. Cambridge: Cambridge University Press, 2010.

Hendrix, Laurel L. "'Tennance Profitable': The Currency of Custance in Chaucer's *Man of Law's Tale*." *Exemplaria* 6, no. 1 (1994): 141–66.

Heng, Geraldine. *Empire of Magic: Medieval Romance and the Politics of Cultural Fantasy*. New York: Columbia University Press, 2003.

Herman, Peter C. "Treason in the *Manciple's Tale*." *ChauR* 25, no. 4 (1991): 318–28.

Hermann, John P. "Dismemberment, Dissemination, Discourse: Sign and Symbol in the *Shipman's Tale*." *ChauR* 19, no. 4 (1985): 302–37.

Herz, Judith Scherer. "The *Canon's Yeoman's Prologue* and *Tale*." *MP* 58, no. 4 (1961): 231–7.

Herzman, Ronald B., and Gary W. Towsley. "Squaring the Circle: *Paradiso* 33 and the Poetics of Geometry." *Traditio* 49 (1994): 95–125.

Heyworth, Gregory. "Ineloquent Ends: *Simplicitas*, Proctolalia, and the Profane Vernacular in the *Miller's Tale*." *Speculum* 84, no. 4 (2009): 956–83.

Hilberry, Jane. "'And in Oure Madnesse Everemoore We Rave': Technical Language in the *Canon's Yeoman's Tale*." *ChauR* 21, no. 4 (1987): 435–43.

Hill, John M. *Chaucer's Neoplatonism: Varieties of Love, Friendship, and Community*. London: Lexington Books, 2018.

Hill, T.E. *"She, This in Blak": Vision, Truth, and Will in Geoffrey Chaucer's Troilus and Criseyde*. New York and London: Routledge, 2006.

Hill, Thomas D. "Chaucer's Parabolic Narrative: The Prologue to the *Tale of Melibee*, Lines 953–58." *ChauR* 46, no. 3 (2012): 365–70.

Hinckley, Henry. "The Debate on Marriage in the *Canterbury Tales*." *PMLA* 32, no. 2 (1917): 292–305.

Hirsh, John C. "Reopening the *Prioress's Tale*." *ChauR* 10, no. 1 (1975): 30–45.

– "The Politics of Spirituality: The Second Nun and the Manciple." *ChauR* 12, no. 2 (1977): 129–46.

Hirshberg, Jeffrey A. "'Cosyn to the Dede': the *Canterbury Tales* and the Platonic Tradition in Medieval Rhetoric." PhD diss., University of Wisconsin, 1977.

Hodges, Laura F. "Chaucer's Friar: 'Typet' and 'Semycope.'" *ChauR* 34, no. 3 (2000): 317–43.

Holman, C. Hugh. "Courtly Love in the *Merchant's* and *Franklin's Tales*." *ELH* 18, no. 4 (1951): 241–52.

Homar, Katie. "Chaucer's Novelized, Carnivalized Exemplum: A Bakhtinian Reading of the *Friar's Tale*." *ChauR* 45, no. 1 (2010): 85–105.

Horobin, Simon. "Adam Pinkhurst, Geoffrey Chaucer, and the Hengwrt Manuscript of the *Canterbury Tales*." *ChauR* 44, no. 4 (2010): 351–67.

– "Chaucer's Norfolk Reeve." *Neophilologus* 86, no. 4 (2002): 609–12.

Horrox, Rosemary. "The Pardoner." In *Historians on Chaucer: The 'General Prologue' to the* Canterbury Tales, edited by Stephen H. Rigby, 443–59. Oxford: Oxford University Press, 2014.

Howard, Donald R. "The Conclusion of the Marriage Group: Chaucer and the Human Condition." *MP* 57, no. 4 (1960): 223–32.

– *The Idea of the Canterbury Tales*. Berkeley: University of California Press, 1976.

Hume, Cathy. "Domestic Opportunities: The Social Comedy of the *Shipman's Tale*." *ChauR* 41, no. 2 (2006): 138–62.

– "'The name of soveraynetee': The Private and Public Faces of Marriage in the *Franklin's Tale*." *SP* 105, no. 3 (2008): 284–303.

Hume, Kathryn. "The Pagan Setting of the *Franklin's Tale* and the Sources of Dorigen's Cosmology." *Studia Neophilologica* 44, no. 2 (1972): 289–94.

Hunter, Brooke. "*Remenants* of Things Past: Memory and the *Knight's Tale*." *Exemplaria* 23, no. 2 (2011): 126–46.

Huppé, Bernard F. *A Reading of the* Canterbury Tales. New York: SUNY Press, 1964.

Ingham, Patricia Clare. *The Medieval New: Ambivalence in an Age of Innovation*. Philadelphia: University of Pennsylvania Press, 2015.

Jacobs, Edward Craney. "Further Biblical Allusions for Chaucer's Prioress." *ChauR* 15, no. 2 (1980): 151–4.

Jambeck, Thomas J. "Characterization and Syntax in the *Miller's Tale*." *The Journal of Narrative Technique* 5, no. 2 (1975): 73–85.

Jankowski, Eileen S. "Chaucer's *Second Nun's Tale* and the Apocalyptic Imagination." *ChauR* 36, no. 2 (2001): 128–48.

Jefferson, Bernard L. *Chaucer and the Consolation of Philosophy of Boethius*. Princeton, NJ: Princeton University Press, 1917, reprinted 1968.

Jeffrey, David Lyle. "Dante and Chaucer." In *The Sermon on the Mount Through the Centuries*, edited by Jeffrey P. Greenman, Timothy Larsen, and Stephen R. Spencer, 81–108. Grand Rapids, MI: Brazos Press, 2007.

Jensen, Emily. "Male Competition as a Unifying Motif in Fragment A of the *Canterbury Tales*." *ChauR* 24, no. 4 (1990): 320–8.

– "'Winkers' and 'Janglers': Teller/Listener/Reader Response in the *Monk's Tale*, the Link, and the *Nun's Priest's Tale*." *ChauR* 32, no. 3 (1997): 183–95.

Johnson, Eleanor. *Practicing Literary Theory in the Middle Ages: Ethics and the Mixed Form in Chaucer, Gower, Usk, and Hoccleve*. Chicago: University of Chicago Press, 2013.

– *Staging Contemplation: Participatory Theology in Middle English Prose, Verse, and Drama*. Chicago: University of Chicago Press, 2018.

– "Tragic Nihilism in the *Canterbury Tales*." *JMEMS* 49, no. 1 (2019): 7–31.

Johnson, Lynn Staley. "Chaucer's Tale of the Second Nun and the Strategies of Dissent." *SP* 89, no. 3 (1992): 314–33.

– "Inverse Counsel: Contexts for the *Melibee*." *SP* 87, no. 2 (1990) 137–55.

– "The Prince and His People: A Study of the Two Covenants in the *Clerk's Tale*." *ChauR* 10, no. 1 (1975): 17–29.

Johnson, William C., Jr. "The Man of Law's Tale: Aesthetics and Christianity in Chaucer." *ChauR* 16, no. 3 (1982): 201–22.

Johnston, Andrew J. "The Keyhole Politics of Chaucerian Theatricality: Voyeurism in the *Knight's Tale*." *Poetica* 34, nos. 1/2 (2002): 73–97.

Jones, E.A. "'Lo, Lordes Myne, Heere is a Fit!': The Structure of Chaucer's *Sir Thopas*." *RES* 51, no. 202 (2000): 248–52.

Jones, Terry. "The *Monk's Tale*." *SAC* 22 (2000): 387–97.

Jordan, Robert M. *Chaucer's Poetics and the Modern Reader*. Berkeley: University of California Press, 1987.

– "The Non-Dramatic Disunity of the *Merchant's Tale*." *PMLA* 78, no. 4 (1963): 293–9.

Joseph, Gerhard. "Chaucer's Coinage: Foreign Exchange and the Puns of the *Shipman's Tale*." *ChauR* 17, no. 4 (1983): 341–57.

– "The *Franklin's Tale*: Chaucer's Theodicy." *ChauR* 1, no. 1 (1966): 20–32.

Jost-Frey, Hans. "Undecidability." In *The Lesson of Paul de Man*, edited by Peter Brooks, Shoshana Felman, and J. Hillis Miller, 124–33. New Haven, CT: Yale University Press, 1985.

Justice, Steven. *Writing and Rebellion: England in 1381*. Berkeley: University of California Press, 1994), 207–13.

Kamowski, William. "'Coillons,' Relics, Skepticism and Faith on Chaucer's Road to Canterbury: An Observation on the Pardoner's and the Host's Confrontation." *ELN* 28 (1991): 1–8.

Kant, Immanuel. *Critique of Pure Reason*. Edited and translated by Paul Guyer and Allen W. Wood. Cambridge: Cambridge University Press, 1998.

Kao, Wan-Chuan. "Conduct Shameful and Unshameful in the *Franklin's Tale*." *SAC* 34 (2012): 99–139.

– "Cute Chaucer." *Exemplaria* 30, no. 2 (2018): 147–71.

Kaske, Carol V. "Getting Around the Parson's Tale: An Alternative to Allegory and Irony." In *Chaucer at Albany*, edited by Rossell Hope Robbins, 147–77. New York: Burt Franklin, 1975.

Kaske, Robert E. "An Aube in the Reeve's Tale." *ELH* 26, no. 3 (1959): 295–310.

– "The *Cantica Canticorum* in the *Miller's Tale*." *SP* 59, no. 3 (1962): 479–500.

– "Chaucer's Marriage Group." In *Chaucer the Love Poet*, edited by Jerome Mitchell and William Provost, 45–65. Athens: University of Georgia Press, 1973.

– "The Knight's Interruption of the *Monk's Tale*." *ELH* 24, no. 4 (1957): 249–68.

Kauffman, Corinne E. "Pertelote's Parlous Parle." *ChauR* 4, no. 1 (1969): 41–8.

Kay, Richard. "Dante's Empyrean and the Eye of God." *Speculum* 78, no. 1 (2003): 37–65.

Kearney, A.M. "Truth and Illusion in the *Franklin's Tale*." *Essays in Criticism* 19, no. 3 (1969): 245–53.

Keiper, Hugo, Christoph Bode, and Richard Utz, eds. *Nominalism and Literary Discourse: New Perspectives*. Amsterdam: Rodopi, 1997.

Keiser, George R. "The Conclusion of the *Canon's Yeoman's Tale*: Readings and (Mis)Readings." *ChauR* 35, no. 1 (2000): 1–21.

– "Language and Meaning in Chaucer's *Shipman's Tale*." *ChauR* 12, no. 3 (1978): 147–61.

Keller, Kimberly. "Prudence's Pedagogy of the Oppressed." *NM* 98, no. 4 (1997): 415–26.

Kellogg, Alfred L. "An Augustinian Interpretation of Chaucer's Pardoner." *Speculum* 26, no. 3 (1951): 465–81.

– "The Evolution of the *Clerk's Tale*: A Study in Connotation." In his *Chaucer, Langland, Arthur: Essays in Middle English Literature*, 276–329. New Brunswick, NJ: Rutgers University Press, 1972.

Kelly, Henry Ansgar. *Chaucerian Tragedy*. Cambridge: D.S. Brewer, 2000.

– "The Evolution of the *Monk's Tale*: Tragical to Farcical." *SAC* 22 (2000): 407–14.

– "The Pardoner's Voice, Disjunctive Narrative, and Modes of Effemination." In *Speaking Images: Essays in Honor of V. A. Kolve*, edited by Robert F. Yeager and Charlotte C. Morse, 411–44. Asheville, NC: Pegasus Press, 2001.

– "The *Prioress's Tale* in Context: Good and Bad Reports of Non-Christians in Fourteenth-Century England." In *Studies in Medieval and Renaissance History: Nation, Ethnicity, and Identity in Medieval and Renaissance Europe*, edited by Philip Soergel, 71–129. New York: AMS Press, 2006.

Kempton, Daniel. "Chaucer's *Tale of Melibee*: 'A Litel Thyng in Prose.'" *Genre* 21, no. 3 (1988): 263–78.

Kendall, Elliot. "The Great Household in the City: The *Shipman's Tale*." In *Chaucer and the City*, edited by Ardis Butterfield, 145–61. Cambridge: D.S. Brewer, 2006.

Kensak, Michael. "Apollo Exterminans: The God of Poetry in Chaucer's *Manciple's Tale*." *SP* 98, no. 2 (2001): 143–57.

– "*Manciple's Tale*, Paradiso, Anticlaudianus." *ChauR* 34, no. 2 (1999): 190–206.

– "What Ails Chaucer's Cook? Spiritual Alchemy and the Ending of the *Canterbury Tales*." *PQ* 80, no. 3 (2001): 213–31.

Kinney, Angela M., ed. *The Vulgate Bible: Douay-Rheims Translation*, 6 vols. Cambridge, MA: Harvard University Press, 2010–13.

Kirk, Elizabeth D. "Nominalism and the Dynamics of the *Clerk's Tale*." In *Chaucer's Religious Tales*, edited by C. David Benson and Elizabeth Robertson, 111–20. Cambridge: D.S. Brewer, 1990.

Kirkpatrick, Robin. "The Griselda Story in Boccaccio, Petrarch and Chaucer." In *Chaucer and the Italian Trecento*, edited by Piero Boitani, 231–47. Cambridge: Cambridge University Press, 1983.

Kisor, Yvette. "Moments of Silence, Acts of Speech: Uncovering the Incest Motif in the *Man of Law's Tale*." *ChauR* 40, no. 2 (2005): 141–62.

Kittredge, George L. *Chaucer and his Poetry*. Cambridge, MA: Harvard University Press, 1915.

– *Chaucer: Modern Essays in Criticism*. Edited by E. Wagenknecht. Oxford: Oxford University Press, 1959.

– "Chaucer's Discussion of Marriage." *MP* 9 (1912): 435–67.

Klassen, Norman. *Chaucer on Love, Knowledge and Sight*. Rochester, NY: D.S. Brewer, 1995.

– *The Fellowship of the Beatific Vision: Chaucer on Overcoming Tyranny and Becoming Ourselves*. Eugene, OR: Cascade Books, 2016.

Kline, Daniel T. "Jephthah's Daughter and Chaucer's Virginia: The Critique of Sacrifice in the *Physician's Tale*." *JEGP* 107, no. 1 (2008): 77–103.

Kloss, Robert J. "Chaucer's the *Merchant's Tale*: Tender Youth and Stooping Age." *American Imago* 31, no. 1 (1974): 65–79.

Knapp, Daniel. "The Relyk of a Seint: A Gloss on Chaucer's Pilgrimage." *ELH* 39, no. 1 (1972): 1–26.

Knapp, Peggy. *Chaucer and the Social Contest*. New York: Routledge, 1990.

– "The Work of Alchemy." *JMEMS* 30 (2000): 575–99.

Knight, Stephen. "Chaucer and the Sociology of Literature." *SAC* 2 (1980): 15–51.

– "Chaucer's Religious Canterbury Tales." In *Medieval English Religious and Ethical Literature: Essays in Honour of G. H. Russell*, edited by Gregory Kratzmann and James Simpson, 156–66. Cambridge: D.S. Brewer, 1986.

– "Colloquium on the *Monk's Tale*: 'My lord, the Monk.'" *SAC* 22 (2000): 381–6.
– *Geoffrey Chaucer*. Oxford: Oxford University Press, 1986.
– "Rhetoric and Poetry in the *Franklin's Tale*." *ChauR* 4, no. 1 (1969): 14–30.
Kohanski, Tamarah. "In Search of Malyne." *ChauR* 27, no. 3 (1993): 228–38.
Kohler, Michelle. "Vision, Logic, and the Comic Production of Reality in the *Merchant's Tale* and French Fabliaux." *ChauR* 39, no. 2 (2004): 137–50.
Kolve, V.A. *Chaucer and the Imagery of Narrative: The First Five Canterbury Tales*. Stanford, CA: Stanford University Press, 1984.
– "Chaucer's *Second Nun's Tale* and the Iconography of Saint Cecilia." In *New Perspectives on Chaucer Criticism*, edited by Donald M. Rose, 137–76. Norman, OK: Pilgrim Books, 1981.
Kruger, Steven F. "Claiming the Pardoner: Toward a Gay Reading of Chaucer's *Pardoner's Tale*." *Exemplaria* 6, no. 1 (1994): 115–39.
Krummel, Miriamne Ara. "Globalizing Jewish Communities: Mapping a Jewish Geography in Fragment VII of the *Canterbury Tales*." *TSLL* 50, no. 2 (2008): 121–42.
Kuczynski, Michael P. "'Don't Blame Me': The Metaethics of a Chaucerian Apology." *ChauR* 37, no. 4 (2003): 315–28.
Lacan, Jacques. "Knowledge and Truth." In *On Feminine Sexuality: The Limits of Love and Knowledge*, translated by Bruce Fink, 90–103. New York: W. W. Norton, 1998.
Ladd, Roger A. "The Mercantile (Mis)Reader in the *Canterbury Tales*." *SP* 99, no. 1 (2002): 17–32.
Laird, Edgar. "The Astronomer Ptolemy and the Morality of the *Wife of Bath's Prologue*." *ChauR* 34, no. 3 (2000): 289–99.
Lampert-Weissig, Lisa. "Chaucer's Pardoner and the Jews." *Exemplaria* 28, no. 4 (2016): 337–60.
Langmuir, Gavin I. "The Knight's Tale of Young Hugh of Lincoln." *Speculum* 47, no. 3 (1972): 459–82.
Lavezzo, Kathy. "Beyond Rome: Mapping Gender and Justice in the *Man of Law's Tale*." *SAC* 24 (2002): 149–80.
– "The Minster and the Privy: Rereading the *Prioress's Tale*." *PMLA* 126, no. 2 (2011): 363–82.
Lavinsky, David. "Turned to Fables: Efficacy, Form, and Literary Making in the *Pardoner's Tale*." *ChauR* 50, nos. 3–4 (2015): 442–64.
Lawler, Traugott. *The One and the Many in the Canterbury Tales*. Hamden, CT: Archon Books, 1980.
Lawton, David. *Chaucer's Narrators*. Cambridge: D.S. Brewer, 1985.
– "Chaucer's Two Ways: The Pilgrimage Frame of the *Canterbury Tales*." *SAC* 9 (1987): 3–40.
Lee, Anne Thompson. "'A Woman True and Fair': Chaucer's Portrayal of Dorigen in the *Franklin's Tale*." *ChauR* 19, no. 2 (1984): 169–78.

Lee, Brian S. "Apollo's Chariot and the Christian Subtext of the *Franklin's Tale*." *Journal of Medieval Religious Cultures* 36, no. 1 (2010): 47–67.

– "The Position and Purpose of the *Physician's Tale*." *ChauR* 22, no. 2 (1987): 141–60.

– "The Question of Closure in Fragment V of the *Canterbury Tales*." *Yearbook of ES* 22 (1992): 190–200.

Legassie, Shayne Aaron. "Chaucer's Pardoner and Host – on the Road, in the Alehouse." *SAC* 29 (2007): 183–223.

Leicester, H. Marshall, Jr. "The Art of Impersonation: A General Prologue to the *Canterbury Tales*." *PMLA* 95, no. 2 (1980): 213–24.

– *The Disenchanted Self: Representing the Subject in the* Canterbury Tales. Berkeley: University of California Press, 1990.

– "'My bed was ful of verray blood': Subject, Dream and Rape in the *Wife of Bath's Prologue* and *Tale*." In *The Wife of Bath*, edited by Peter G. Beidler, 234–54. Boston: Bedford Books, 1996.

– "'No Vileyns Word': Social Context and Performance in Chaucer's *Friar's Tale*." *ChauR* 17, no. 1 (1982): 21–39.

– "Of a Fire in the Dark: Public and Private Feminism in the *Wife of Bath's Tale*." *Women's Studies* 11, nos. 1–2 (1984): 157–78.

Leitch, Megan G. "Locating Authorial Ethics: The Idea of the *Male* or Book-Bag in the Canterbury Tales and Other Middle English Poems." *ChauR* 46, no. 4 (2012): 403–18.

Lenaghan, R.T. "The Irony of the Friar's Tale." *ChauR* 7, no. 4 (1973): 281–94.

Lepley, Douglas L. "The Monk's Boethian Tale." *ChauR* 12, no. 3 (1978): 162–70.

Lerer, Seth. *Chaucer and His Readers: Imagining the Author in Late Medieval England*. Princeton, NJ: Princeton University Press, 1993.

Levitan, Alan. "The Parody of Pentecost in Chaucer's *Summoner's Tale*." *University of Toronto Quarterly* 40 (1971): 236–46.

Levy, Bernard S. "The Quaint World of the *Shipman's Tale*." *Studies in Short Fiction* 4, no. 2 (1967): 112–18.

Levy, Bernard S., and George R. Adams. "Chauntecleer's Paradise Lost and Regained." *Mediaeval Studies* 29 (1967): 178–92.

Lewis, Celia M. "History, Mission, and Crusade in the *Canterbury Tales*." *ChauR* 42, no. 4 (2008): 353–82.

Lewis, Katherine J. "The Prioress and the Second Nun." In *Historians on Chaucer: the 'General Prologue' to the Canterbury Tales*, edited by Stephen H. Rigby, 94–113. Oxford: Oxford University Press, 2014.

Lewis, Robert Enzer. "Chaucer's Artistic Use of Pope Innocent III's *De Miseria Humane Conditionis* in the *Man of Law's Prologue* and *Tale*." *PMLA* 81, no. 7 (1966): 485–92.

Lindeboom, B.W. *Venus' Owne Clerk: Chaucer's Debt to the* Confessio Amantis. Amsterdam and New York: Rodopi, 2007.

Lindley, Arthur. "'Vanysshed Was this Daunce, He Nyste Where': Alisoun's Absence in the *Wife of Bath's Prologue* and *Tale*." *ELH* 59, no. 1 (1992): 1–21.

Little, Katherine C. "Chaucer's Parson and the Specter of Wycliffism." *SAC* 25 (2003): 3–25.

Lochrie, Karma. *Covert Operations: The Medieval Uses of Secrecy*. Philadelphia: University of Pennsylvania Press, 1999.

Lomperis, Linda. "Unruly Bodies and Ruling Practices: Chaucer's *Physician's Tale* as Socially Symbolic Act." In *Feminist Approaches to the Body in Medieval Literature*, edited by Linda Lomperis and Sarah Stanbury, 21–37. Philadelphia: University of Pennsylvania Press, 1993.

Long, Mary Beth. "'O sweete and wel beloved spouse deere': A Pastoral Reading of Cecilia's Post-Nuptial Persuasion in the *Second Nun's Tale*." *SAC* 39 (2017): 159–90.

Longsworth, Robert M. "The Doctor's Dilemma: A Comic View of the *Physician's Tale*." *Criticism* 13, no. 3 (1971): 223–33.

– "Privileged Knowledge: St. Cecilia and the Alchemist in the *Canterbury Tales*." *ChauR* 27, no. 1 (1992): 87–96.

– "The Wife of Bath and the Samaritan Woman." *ChauR* 34, no. 4 (2000): 372–87.

Loomis, Laura Hibbard. "Sir Thopas and David and Goliath." *MLN* 51, no. 5 (1936): 311–13.

Loux, Michael J., trans. *Ockham's Theory of Terms: Part I of the* Summa Logicae. Notre Dame, IN: University of Notre Dame Press, 1974.

Lowe, John Livingston. *Convention and Revolt in Poetry*. Boston: Houghton Mifflin, 1919.

Lucas, Angela. "Astronomy, Astrology and Magic in Chaucer's *Franklin's Tale*." *The Maynooth Review* 8 (1983): 5–16.

– "'But if a man be virtuous withal': Has Aurelius in Chaucer's *Franklin's Tale* 'lerned gentillesse aright'?" In *Studies in Late Medieval and Early Renaissance Texts in Honour of John Scattergood*, edited by Anne Marie D'Arcy and Alan J. Fletcher, 181–200. Dublin: Four Courts Press, 2005.

– "The Mirror in the Marketplace: Januarie through the Looking Glass." *ChauR* 33, no. 2 (1998): 123–45.

Lynch, Kathryn L. *Chaucer's Philosophical Visions*. Cambridge: D.S. Brewer, 2000.

– "Despoiling Griselda: Chaucer's Walter and the Problem of Knowledge in the *Clerk's Tale*." *SAC* 10 (1988): 41–70.

– "'Diversitee bitwene hir bothe lawes'": Chaucer's Unlikely Alliance of a Lawyer and a Merchant." *ChauR* 46, nos. 1–2 (2011): 74–92.

– "Storytelling, Exchange, and Constancy: East and West in Chaucer's *Man of Law's Tale*." *ChauR* 33, no. 4 (1999): 409–22.

Macaulay, G.C., ed. *The Complete Works of John Gower*. Oxford: Clarendon Press, 1899–1902.

MacLaine, A.H. "Chaucer's Wine-Cast Image: Word Play in the *Reeve's Prologue*." *MÆ* 31, no. 2 (1962): 129–31.

Malo, Robyn. "The Pardoner's Relics (And Why They Matter Most)." *ChauR* 43, no. 1 (2008): 82–102.

Maltman, Nicholas. "The Divine Granary, or the End of the Prioress's 'Greyn.'" *ChauR* 17, no. 2 (1982): 163–70.

Mandel, Jerome. "Governance in the *Physician's Tale*." *ChauR* 10, no. 4 (1976): 316–32.

– "'Jewes Werk' in *Sir Thopas*." In *Chaucer and the Jews: Sources, Contexts, Meanings*, edited by Sheila Delany, 59–68. New York: Routledge, 2002.

Manly, John M. *Some New Light on Chaucer*. London: G. Bell, 1926.

Mann, Jill. *Chaucer and Medieval Estates Satire: The Literature of Social Classes and the* General Prologue *to the* Canterbury Tales. Cambridge: Cambridge University Press, 1973.

– *Feminizing Chaucer*. Cambridge: D.S. Brewer, 2002.

– *Geoffrey Chaucer, Feminist Readings*. Atlantic Highlands, NJ: Humanities Press International, 1991.

– "The *Speculum Stultorum* and the *Nun's Priest's Tale*." *ChauR* 9, no. 3 (1975): 262–82.

Manning, Stephen. "Fabular Jangling and Poetic Vision in the *Nun's Priest's Tale*." *South Atlantic Review* 52, no. 1 (1987): 3–16.

– "The Nun's Priest's Morality and the Medieval Attitude Toward Fables." *JEGP* 59, no. 3 (1960): 403–16.

Marenbon, John. *Boethius*. Oxford: Oxford University Press, 2003.

Marvin, Corey J. "'I Will Thee Not Forsake': The Kristevan Maternal Space in Chaucer's *Prioress's Tale* and John of Garland's *Stella maris*." *Exemplaria* 8, no. 1 (1996): 35–58.

Masi, Michael. "Boethius, the Wife of Bath, and the Dialectic of Paradox." *Carmina Philosophiae* 1 (1992): 65–78.

Mathewson, Effie Jean. "The Illusion of Morality in the *Franklin's Tale*." *MÆ* 52, no. 1 (1983): 27–37.

Maurer, Armand. *The Philosophy of William Ockham in the Light of Its Principles*. Toronto: Pontifical Institute of Medieval Studies, 1999.

McAlpine, Monica. "The Pardoner's Homosexuality and How It Matters." *PMLA* 95, no. 1 (1980): 8–22.

– "The Triumph of Fiction in the *Nun's Priest's Tale*." In *Art and Context in Late Medieval English Narrative: Essays in Honor of Robert Worth Frank, Jr.*, edited by Robert R. Edwards, 79–92. Cambridge: D.S. Brewer, 1994.

McCall, John P. "Chaucer and John of Legnano." *Speculum* 40, no. 3 (1965): 484–9.– "The *Clerk's Tale* and the Theme of Obedience." *MLQ* 27, no. 3 (1966): 260–9.

McCormack, Frances. *Chaucer and the Culture of Dissent the Lollard Context and Subtext of the* Parson's Tale. Dublin: Four Courts Press, 2007.

McEntire, Sandra J. "Illusions and Interpretation in the *Franklin's Tale.*" *ChauR* 31, no. 2 (1996): 145–63.

McGavin, John J. "How Nasty Is Phebus's Crow?" *ChauR* 21, no. 4 (1987): 444–58.

McGerr, Rosemarie P. *Chaucer's Open Books: Resistance to Closure in Medieval Discourse.* Gainesville: University Press of Florida, 1998.

McGowan, Joseph P. "Chaucer's Prioress: *Et Nos Cedamus Amori.*" *ChauR* 38, no. 2 (2003): 199–202.

McKenna, Stephen, trans. *Augustine: On the Trinity, Books 8–15*, edited by Gareth B. Matthews. Cambridge: Cambridge University Press, 2002.

McKinley, Kathryn L. "The Silenced Knight: Questions of Power and Reciprocity in the *Wife of Bath's Tale.*" *ChauR* 30, no. 4 (1996): 359–78.

McNamara, John. "Chaucer's Use of the Epistle of St. James in the *Clerk's Tale.*" *ChauR* 7, no. 3 (1973): 184–93.

McTaggart, Anne. *Shame and Guilt in Chaucer.* New York: Palgrave Macmillan, 2012.

Meyer, Robert J. "Chaucer's Tandem Romances: A Generic Approach to the *Wife of Bath's Tale* as Palinode." *ChauR* 18, no. 3 (1984): 221–38.

Meyer-Lee, Robert J. "Abandon the Fragments." *SAC* 35 (2013): 47–83.

– "Fragments IV and V of the *Canterbury Tales* Do Not Exist." *ChauR* 45, no. 1 (2010): 1–31.

– *Literary Value and Social Identity in the* Canterbury Tales. Cambridge: Cambridge University Press, 2019.

Meyers, Jeffrey Rayner. "Chaucer's Pardoner as Female Eunuch." *Studia Neophilologica* 72, no. 1 (2000): 54–62.

Middleton, Anne. "The Clerk and His Tale: Some Literary Contexts." *SAC* 2 (1980): 121–50.

– "The *Physician's Tale* and Love's Martyrs: 'Ensamples Mo than Ten' as a Method in the *Canterbury Tales.*" *ChauR* 8, no. 1 (1973): 9–32.

Miller, Clarence H., and Roberta Bux Bosse. "Chaucer's Pardoner and the Mass." *ChauR* 6, no. 3 (1972): 171–84.

Miller, Jacqueline T. *Poetic License: Authority and Authorship in Medieval and Renaissance Contexts.* Oxford: Oxford University Press, 1986.

Miller, Mark. *Philosophical Chaucer: Love, Sex and Agency in the* Canterbury Tales. Cambridge: Cambridge University Press, 2004.

Miller, Robert P. "Chaucer's Pardoner, the Scriptural Eunuch, and the *Pardoner's Tale.*" *Speculum* 30, no. 2 (1955): 180–99.

Minnis, Alastair J. *Chaucer and Pagan Antiquity.* Cambridge: D.S. Brewer, 1982.

– *Fallible Authors: Chaucer's Pardoner and Wife of Bath.* Philadelphia: University of Pennsylvania Press, 2008.

– *Medieval Theory of Authorship: Scholastic Literary Attitudes in the Later Middle Ages*, 2nd ed. Philadelphia: University of Pennsylvania Press, 2010.

– "Reclaiming the Pardoners." *JMEMS* 33, no. 2 (2003): 311–34.

Mitchell, J. Allan. "Chaucer's *Clerk's Tale* and the Question of Ethical Monstrosity." *SP* 102, no. 1 (2005): 1–26.

– *Ethics and Exemplary Narrative in Chaucer and Gower*. Cambridge: D.S. Brewer, 2004.

Montelaro, Janet T. "The Pardoner's Self-Reflexive *Peyne*: Textual Abuse of 'The First Epistle to Timothy.'" *South Central Review* 8, no. 4 (1991): 6–16.

Mooney, Linne R. "Chaucer's Scribe." *Speculum* 81, no. 1 (2006): 97–138.

– *Scribes and the City: London Guildhall Clerks and the Dissemination of Middle English Literature 1375–1423*. Woodbridge, UK: Boydell and Brewer, 2013.

Morgan, Gerald. "Boccaccio's *Filocolo* and the Moral Argument of the *Franklin's Tale*." *ChauR* 20, no. 4 (1986): 285–306.

– "The Self-Revealing Tendencies of Chaucer's Pardoner." *MLR* 71, no. 2 (1976): 241–55.

– "The Universality of the Portraits in the *General Prologue* to the *Canterbury Tales*." *ES* 58 (1977): 481–93.

– "The Worthiness of Chaucer's Worthy Knight." *ChauR* 44, no. 2 (2009): 115–58.

Morris, Thomas V. "The Metaphysics of God Incarnate." In *Oxford Readings in Philosophical Theology*, Vol. 1, edited by Michael Rea, 211–24. Oxford: Oxford University Press, 2009.

Morse, Charlotte C. "The Exemplary Griselda." *SAC* 7 (1985): 51–86.

Murton, Megan. "The *Prioress's Prologue*: Dante, Liturgy, and Ineffability." *ChauR* 52, no. 3 (2017): 318–40.

Muscatine, Charles. *Chaucer and the French Tradition: A Study in Style and Meaning*. Berkeley: University of California Press, 1964.

– *Poetry and Crisis in the Age of Chaucer*. Notre Dame, IN: University of Notre Dame Press, 1972.

Myles, Robert. *Chaucerian Realism*. Cambridge: D.S. Brewer, 1994.

Nakley, Susan. "'Rowned She a Pistel': National Institutions and Identities According to Chaucer's Wife of Bath." *JEGP* 114, no. 1 (2015): 61–87.

Narkiss, Doron. "The Fox, the Cock, and the Priest: Chaucer's Escape from Fable." *ChauR* 32, no. 1 (1997): 46–63.

Neuse, Richard. *Chaucer's Dante: Allegory and Epic Theatre in the Canterbury Tales*. Berkeley: University of California Press, 1991.

– "The Knight: The First Mover in Chaucer's Human Comedy." *UTQ* 31, no. 3 (1962): 299–315.

– "Marriage and the Question of Allegory in the *Merchant's Tale*." *ChauR* 24, no. 2 (1989): 115–31.

– "They Had Their World as in Their Time: The Monk's 'Little Narratives.'"
SAC 22 (2000): 415–23.

Neville, Marie. "The Function of the *Squire's Tale* in the Canterbury Scheme."
JEGP 50, no. 2 (1951): 167–79.

Newman, William. *Promethean Ambitions: Alchemy and the Quest to Perfect
Nature*. Chicago: University of Chicago Press, 2004.

Nichols, Robert E., Jr. "The Pardoner's Ale and Cake." *PMLA* 82, no. 7 (1967):
498–504.

Nicholson, Peter. *Love and Ethics in Gower's Confessio Amantis*. Ann Arbor:
University of Michigan Press, 2005.

– "The *Man of Law's Tale*: What Chaucer Really Owed to Gower." *ChauR* 26,
no. 2 (1991): 153–74.

– "The *Shipman's Tale* and the Fabliaux." *ELH* 45, no. 4 (1978): 583–96.

Nitecki, Alicia K. "The Convention of the Old Man's Lament in the *Pardoner's
Tale*." *ChauR* 16, no. 1 (1981): 76–84.

Nolan, Barbara. "Chaucer's Tales of Transcendence: Rhyme Royal and
Christian Prayer in the *Canterbury Tales*." In *Chaucer's Religious Tales*, edited
by C. David Benson and Elizabeth Robertson, 21–38. Cambridge: D.S.
Brewer, 1990.

– "'A Poet Ther Was': Chaucer's Voices in the *General Prologue* to the
Canterbury Tales." *PMLA* 101, no. 2 (1986): 154–69.

Nolan, Maura. "Medieval Sensation and Modern Aesthetics: Aquinas,
Adorno, Chaucer." *The Minnesota Review* 80 (2013): 145–58.

Normandin, Shawn. "'Non Intellegant': The Enigmas of the *Clerk's Tale*." *TSLL*
58, no. 2 (2016): 189–223.

– "The Wife of Bath's Urinary Imagination." *Exemplaria* 20, no. 3 (2008):
244–63.

O'Brien, Timothy D. "Fire and Blood: 'Queynte' Imaginings in Diana's
Temple." *ChauR* 33, no. 2 (1998): 157–67.

– "Seductive Violence and Three Chaucerian Women." *College Literature* 28,
no. 2 (2001): 178–96.

– "Troubling Waters: The Feminine and the Wife of Bath's Performance."
MLQ 53, no. 4 (1992): 377–91.

Oberman, Heiko. *The Harvest of Medieval Theology: Gabriel Biel and Late Medieval
Nominalism*. Cambridge, MA: Harvard University Press, 1963.

Obermeier, Anita. *The History and Anatomy of Auctorial Self-Criticism in the
European Middle Ages*. Leiden, Netherlands: Rodopi, 1999.

Ockham, William. *Summa Logicae, Opera Philosophica*, Vol. 1, edited by
Philotheus Boehner, Gedeon Gál, and Stephanus Brown. St. Bonaventure,
NY: The Franciscan Institute, 1974).

Oerlemans, Onno. "The Seriousness of the *Nun's Priest's Tale*." *ChauR* 26, no. 3
(1992): 317–28.

Oliver, Kathleen M. "Singing Bread, Manna, and the Clergeon's 'Greyn.'" *ChauR* 31, no. 4 (1997): 357–64.

Olmert, K. Michael. "The *Canon's Yeoman's Tale*: An Interpretation." *Annuale Mediaevale* 8 (1967): 70–94.

Olsen, Alexandra Hennessy. "'They shul desiren to dye, and deeth shal flee fro hem': A Reconsideration of the Pardoner's Old Man." *NM* 84, no. 3 (1983): 367–71.

Olson, Glending. "Chaucer, Dante, and the Structure of Fragment VIII (G) of the *Canterbury Tales*." *ChauR* 16, no. 3 (1981–2): 222–36.

– "A Reading of the Thopas-Melibee Link." *ChauR* 10, no. 2 (1975–6): 147–53.

– "Snub and White; Chaucer, Logic, and Strode." *JEGP* 117, no. 2 (2018): 185–211.

Olson, Paul A. "The *Reeve's Tale*: Chaucer's *Measure for Measure*." *SP* 59, no. 1 (1962): 1–17.

Olsson, Kurt. *John Gower and the Structures of Conversion: A Reading of the* Confessio Amantis. Cambridge: D.S. Brewer, 1992.

Orth, William. "The Problem of the Performative in Chaucer's Prioress Sequence." *ChauR* 42, no. 2 (2007): 196–210.

Osberg, Richard H. "A Voice for the Prioress: The Context of English Devotional Prose." *SAC* 18 (1996): 25–54.

Otten, Charlotte F. "Proserpine: Liberatrix Suae Gentis." *ChauR* 5, no. 4 (1971): 277–87.

Pakkala-Weckström, Mari. "Prudence and the Power of Persuasion: Language and Maistrie in the *Tale of Melibee*." *ChauR* 35, no. 4 (2001): 399–412.

Palmer, James M. "Your Malady is no 'Sodeyn Hap': Ophthalmology, Benvenutus Grassus, and January's Blindness." *ChauR* 41, no. 2 (2006): 197–205.

Palomo, Dolores. "The Fate of the Wife of Bath's 'Bad Husbands.'" *ChauR* 9, no. 4 (1975): 303–19.

– "What Chaucer Really Did to *Le Livre de Mellibee*." *PQ* 53, no. 3 (1974): 304–20.

Parsons, Ben. "Beaten for a Book: Domestic and Pedagogic Violence in the *Wife of Bath's Prologue*." *SAC* 37 (2015): 163–94.

Partridge, Stephen. "'The Makere of this Boke': Chaucer's *Retraction* and the Author as Scribe and Compiler." In *Author, Reader, Book: Medieval Authorship in Theory and Practice*, edited by Stephen Partridge and Erik Kwakkel, 106–53. Toronto: University of Toronto Press, 2012.

– "Minding the Gaps: Interpreting the Manuscript Evidence of the Cook's Tale and the Squire's Tale." In *The English Medieval Book: Studies in Memory of Jeremy Griffiths*, edited by A.S.G. Edwards, Alexandra Gillespie, and Ralph Hanna, 51–85. London: British Library, 2000.

Pasnau, Robert. "Form and Matter." In *The Cambridge History of Medieval Philosophy*, Vol. 2, edited by Robert Pasnau and Christina Van Dyke, 635–46. Cambridge: Cambridge University Press, 2010.

Patterson, Lee. *Chaucer and the Subject of History*. Madison: University of Wisconsin Press, 1991.

– "Chaucer's Pardoner on the Couch: Psyche and Clio in Medieval Literary Studies." *Speculum* 76, no. 3 (2001): 638–80.

– "'For the Wyves Love of Bathe': Feminine Rhetoric and Poetic Resolution in the *Roman de la Rose* and the *Canterbury Tales*." *Speculum* 58, no. 3 (1983): 656–95.

– "'The Living Witnesses of Our Redemption': Martyrdom and Imitation in Chaucer's *Prioress's Tale*." *JMEMS* 31, no. 3 (2001): 507–60.

– "The *Parson's Tale* and the Quitting of the *Canterbury Tales*." *Traditio* 34 (1978): 331–80.

– "Perpetual Motion: Alchemy and the Technology of the Self." *SAC* 15 (1993): 25–57.

– "'What Man Artow?': Authorial Self-Definition in the *Tale of Sir Thopas* and the *Tale of Melibee*." *SAC* 11 (1989): 117–75.

Pattison, Andrew John. "Ironic Imitations: Parody, Mockery, and Barnyard Chase in the *Nun's Priest's Tale*." *ChauR* 54, no. 2 (2019): 141–61.

Patton, Celeste A. "False 'Rekenynges': Sharp Practice and the Politics of Language in Chaucer's *Manciple's Tale*." *PQ* 71, no. 4 (1992): 399–414.

Payne, F. Anne. "Foreknowledge and Free Will: Three Theories in the *Nun's Priest's Tale*." *ChauR* 10, no. 3 (1976): 201–19.

Pearcy, Roy. "Chaucer's Amphibologies and 'the Old Man' in the *Pardoner's Tale*." *ELN* 41, no. 4 (2004): 1–10.

– "Does the *Manciple's Prologue* Contain a Reference to Hell Mouth?" *ELN* 11, no. 3 (1974): 167–75.

– "Épreuves d'amour and Chaucer's *Franklin's Tale*." *ChauR* 44, no. 2 (2009): 159–85.

Pearsall, Derek. *The Canterbury Tales*. New York: Routledge, 1985.

– "Chaucer's Pardoner: The Death of a Salesman." *ChauR* 17, no. 4 (1983): 358–65.

– "Chaucer's Religious Tales: A Question of Genre." In *Chaucer's Religious Tales*, edited by C. David Benson and Elizabeth Robertson, 11–19. Cambridge: D.S. Brewer, 1990.

– "Eleanor Prescott Hammond." *Medieval Feminist Forum* 31 (2001): 29–36.

– "The *Nun's Priest's Tale*." Part 9 of *A Variorum Edition of the Works of Geoffrey Chaucer*, Vol. 2, *The Canterbury Tales*. Norman: University of Oklahoma Press, 1984.

Peck, Russell A. "Chaucer and the Nominalist Questions." *Speculum* 53, no. 4 (1978): 745–60.

– "The Ideas of 'Entente' and Translation in Chaucer's *Second Nun's Tale*." *Annuale Mediaevale* 8 (1967): 17–37.

– ed. *John Gower:* Confessio Amantis. Kalamazoo, MI: Medieval Institute Publications, 2006.

– "Sovereignty and the Two Worlds of the *Franklin's Tale*." *ChauR* 1, no. 4 (1967): 253–71.

Pelen, Marc M. "Chaucer's *Cosyn to the dede*: Further Considerations." *Florilegium* 19 (2002): 91–107.

– "Chaucer's Wife of Midas Reconsidered: Oppositions and Poetic Judgment in the *Wife of Bath's Tale*." *Florilegium* 13 (1994): 141–60.

– "The Escape of Chaucer's Chauntecleer: A Brief Reevaluation." *ChauR* 36, no. 4 (2002): 329–35.

Peterson, John. *Aquinas: A New Introduction*. Lanham, MD: University Press of America, 2008.

Peterson, Joyce E. "The Finished Fragment: A Reassessment of the *Squire's Tale*." *ChauR* 5, no. 1 (1970–1): 62–74.

Petty, George R., Jr. "Power, Deceit, and Misinterpretation: Uncooperative Speech in the *Canterbury Tales*." *ChauR* 27, no. 4 (1993): 413–23.

Pigg, Daniel F. "Performing the Perverse: The Abuse of Masculine Power in the *Reeve's Tale*." In *Masculinities in Chaucer: Approaches to Maleness in The Canterbury Tales and Troilus and Criseyde*, edited by Peter Beidler, 53–62. Cambridge: D.S. Brewer, 1998.

– "Refiguring Martyrdom: Chaucer's Prioress and Her Tale." *ChauR* 29, no. 1 (1994): 65–73.

Pinti, Daniel. "The 'Comedy' of the *Monk's Tale*: Chaucer's Hugelyn and Early Commentary on Dante's Ugolino." *Comparative Literature Studies* 37, no. 3 (2000): 277–97.

Pironet, Fabienne. "William Heytesbury and the Treatment of *Insolubilia* in Fourteenth-Century England Followed by a Critical Edition of Three Anonymous Treatises *De insolubilibus* Inspired by Heytesbury." In *Unity, Truth, and the Liar: The Modern Relevance of Medieval Solutions to the Liar Paradox*, edited by Shahid Rahman, Tero Tulenheimo, and Emmanuel Genot, 255–334. New York: Springer, 2008.

Pitard, Derrick G. "Sowing Difficulty: The *Parson's Tale*, Vernacular Commentary, and the Nature of Chaucerian Dissent." *SAC* 26 (2004): 299–330.

Pitcher, John A. *Chaucer's Feminine Subjects: Figures of Desire in the* Canterbury Tales. New York: Palgrave Macmillan, 2012.

Pizzorno, Patrizia Grimaldi. "Chauntecleer's Bad Latin." *Exemplaria* 4, no. 2 (1992): 387–409.

Plummer, John F. "'Hooly Chirches Blood': Simony and Patrimony in Chaucer's *Reeve's Tale*." *ChauR* 18, no. 1 (1983): 49–60.

Portnoy, Phyllis. "Beyond the Gothic Cathedral: Post-Modern Reflections in the Canterbury Tales." *ChauR* 28, no. 3 (1994): 279–92.

Powell, Stephen D. "Game Over: Defragmenting the End of the *Canterbury Tales*." *ChauR* 37, no. 1 (2002): 40–58.

Pratt, Robert A. "Some Latin Sources of the *Nonnes Preest* on Dreams." *Speculum* 52, no. 3 (1977): 538–70.

Prendergast, Thomas A., and Jessica Rosenfeld, eds. *Chaucer and the Subversion of Form*. Cambridge: Cambridge University Press, 2018.

Price, Merrall Llewelyn. "Sadism and Sentimentality: Absorbing Antisemitism in Chaucer's *Prioress's Tale*." *ChauR* 43, no. 2 (2008): 197–214.

Price, Richard, and Michael Gaddis, trans. *The Acts of the Council of Chalcedon*, Translated Texts for Historians 45, 3 vols. Liverpool: Liverpool University Press, 2005.

Pugh, Tison. *Chaucer's (Anti-)Eroticisms and the Queer Middle Ages*. Columbus: Ohio State University Press, 2014.

– "'For to be Sworne Bretheren Til They Deye': Satirizing Queer Brotherhood in the Chaucerian Corpus." *ChauR* 43, no. 3 (2009): 282–310.

– "Gender, Vulgarity, and the Phantom Debates of Chaucer's *Merchant's Tale*." *SP* 114, no. 3 (2017): 473–96.

– "Mutual Masochism and the Hermaphroditic Courtly Lady in Chaucer's *Franklin's Tale*." *SAC* 33 (2011): 149–81.

– "Queering Genres, Battering Males: The Wife of Bath's Narrative Violence." *Journal of Narrative Theory* 33, no. 2 (2003): 115–42.

– "Queering Harry Bailly: Gendered Carnival, Social Ideologies, and Masculinity Under Duress in the *Canterbury Tales*." *ChauR* 41, no. 1 (2006): 39–69.

Pulsiano, Philip. "Redeemed Language and the Ending of *Troilus and Criseyde*." In *Sign, Sentence, Discourse: Language in Medieval Thought and Literature*, edited by Julian N. Wasserman and Lois Roney, 153–74. Syracuse, NY: Syracuse University Press, 1989.

Purdon, L.O. "The Pardoner's Old Man and the Second Death." *SP* 89, no. 3 (1992): 334–49.

Rack, Melissa J. "'I nam no divinistre': Heterodoxy and Disjunction in Chaucer's *Knight's Tale*." *Medieval Perspectives* 25 (2010): 89–102.

Rahman, Shahid, Tero Tulenheimo, and Emmanuel Genot, eds. *Unity, Truth, and the Liar: The Modern Relevance of Medieval Solutions to the Liar Paradox*. Logic, Epistemology, and the Unity of Science 8. New York: Springer, 2008.

Rajna, Pio. "L'Episodio delle questioni d'amore nel *Filocolo* del Boccaccio." *Romania* 31 (1902): 40–3.

– "Le Origini della novella narrata del 'Frankeleyn' nei Canterbury Tales del Chaucer." *Romania* 32 (1903): 204–67.

Ramazani, Jahan. "Chaucer's Monk: The Poetics of Abbreviation, Aggression, and Tragedy." *ChauR* 27, no. 3 (1993): 260–76.

Raybin, David. "Chaucer's Creation and Recreation of the 'Lyf of Seynt Cecile.'" *ChauR* 32, no. 2 (1997): 196–212.

– "The Death of a Silent Woman: Voice and Power and Chaucer's *Manciple's Tale*." *JEGP* 95, no. 1 (1996): 19–37.

– "'Manye Been the Weyes': The Flower, Its Roots, and the Ending of the *Canterbury Tales*." In *Closure in the* Canterbury Tales*: The Role of the Parson's Tale*, edited by David Raybin and Linda Tarte Holley, 11–43. Kalamazoo, MI: Medieval Institute Publications, 2000.

– "*Sir Thopas*: A Story for Small Children." *SAC* 39 (2017): 225–48.

– "'Wommen, of Kynde, Desiren Libertee': Rereading Dorigen, Rereading Marriage." *ChauR* 27, no. 1 (1992): 65–86.

Read, Stephen, and Catarina Dutilh Novaes. "*Insolubilia* and the Fallacy *Secundum Quid et Simpliciter*." *Vivarium* 46, no. 2 (2008): 175–91.

Reames, Sherry L. "Artistry, Decorum, and Purpose in Three Middle English Retellings of the Cecilia Legend." In *The Endless Knot: Essays on Old and Middle English in Honor of Marie Borroff*, edited by M. Teresa Tavormina and R.F. Yeager, 177–99. Cambridge: D.S. Brewer, 1995.

– "The Cecilia Legend as Chaucer Inherited It and Retold It: the Disappearance of an Augustinian Ideal." *Speculum* 55, no. 1 (1980): 38–57.

– "Mary, Sanctity and Prayers to Saints: Chaucer and Late-Medieval Piety." In *Chaucer and Religion*, edited by Helen Phillips, 81–96. Woodbridge, UK: D.S. Brewer, 2010.

– "A Recent Discovery Concerning the Sources of Chaucer's *Second Nun's Tale*." *MP* 87, no. 4 (1990): 337–61.

Reed, Thomas L., Jr. "Nebuchadnezzar and Chauntecleer: Chaucer's Fortunate Fowl." *NM* 89, no. 1 (1988): 44–56.

Reichl, Karl. "Chaucer's *Troilus*: Philosophy and Language." In *The European Tragedy of Troilus*, edited by Piero Boitani, 133–52. Oxford: Clarendon Press, 1989.

Reiss, Edmund. "The Final Irony of the *Pardoner's Tale*." *College English* 25, no. 4 (1964): 260–6.

Rex, Richard. *The Sins of Madame Eglentyne and Other Essays on Chaucer*. Newark: University of Delaware Press, 1995.

Rhodes, Jim. *Poetry Does Theology: Chaucer, Grosseteste, and the* Pearl-*poet*. Notre Dame, IN: University of Notre Dame Press, 2001.

Richardson, Janette. "The Façade of Bawdry: Image Patterns in Chaucer's *Shipman's Tale*." *ELH* 32, no. 3 (1965): 303–13.

Ridley, Florence. *The Prioress and the Critics*. Berkeley: University of California Press, 1965.

Rigby, Stephen H. "The Knight." In *Historians on Chaucer: The 'General Prologue' to the Canterbury Tales*, edited by Stephen H. Rigby, 42–62. Oxford: Oxford University Press, 2014.
– "The Wife of Bath, Christine de Pizan, and the Medieval Case for Women." *ChauR* 35, no. 2 (2000): 133–65.
– *Wisdom and Chivalry: Chaucer's Knight's Tale and Medieval Political Theory.* Leiden, Netherlands: Brill, 2009.
Riley, Deirdre. "Retraction and Re-Collection: Chaucer's Apocalyptic Self-Examination." *Mediaevalia* 36/37 (2015–16): 263–90.
Robertson, D.W., Jr. "The Physician's Comic Tale." *ChauR* 23, no. 2 (1988): 129–39.
– *A Preface to Chaucer: Studies in Medieval Perspectives.* Princeton, NJ: Princeton University Press, 1962.
– "The Wife of Bath and Midas." *SAC* 6 (1984): 1–20.
Robertson, Elizabeth. "Apprehending the Divine and Choosing to Believe: Voluntarist Free Will in Chaucer's *Second Nun's Tale*." *ChauR* 46, nos. 1–2 (2011): 111–30.
– "Aspects of Female Piety in the *Prioress's Tale*." In *Chaucer's Religious Tales*, edited by C. David Benson and Elizabeth Robertson, 145–60. Cambridge: D.S. Brewer, 1990.
– "Practicing Women: The Matter of Women in Medieval English Literature." *Literature Compass* 5, no. 3 (2008): 505–28.
Robertson, Kellie. "Medieval Materialism: A Manifesto." *Exemplaria* 22, no. 2 (2010): 99–118.
– *Nature Speaks: Medieval Literature and Aristotelian Philosophy.* Philadelphia: University of Pennsylvania Press, 2017.
Robinson, F.N., ed. *The Works of Geoffrey Chaucer*, 2nd ed. Oxford: Oxford University Press, 1957.
Robinson, Ian. *Chaucer and the English Tradition.* Cambridge: Cambridge University Press, 1972.
Rock, Catherine A. "Forsworn and Fordone: Arcite as Oath-Breaker in the *Knight's Tale*." *ChauR* 40, no. 4 (2006): 416–32.
Rogers, William E., and Paul Dower, "Thinking about Money in Chaucer's *Shipman's Tale*," In *New Readings of Chaucer's Poetry*, edited by Robert G. Benson and Susan J. Ridyard, 119–38. Cambridge: D.S. Brewer, 2003.
Rosenberg, Bruce A. "The Contrary Tales of the Second Nun and the Canon's Yeoman." *ChauR* 2, no. 4 (1967–8): 278–91.
– "Swindling Alchemist, Antichrist." *Centennial Review* 6, no. 4 (1962): 566–80.
Rosenfeld, Jessica. *Ethics and Enjoyment in Late Medieval Poetry: Love after Aristotle.* Cambridge: Cambridge University Press, 2011.
Rossi-Reder, Andrea. "Male Movement and Female Fixity in the *Franklin's Tale* and *Il Filocolo*." In *Masculinities in Chaucer: Approaches to Maleness in the*

Canterbury Tales and Troilus and Criseyde, edited by Peter G. Beidler, 105–16. Cambridge: D.S. Brewer, 1998.

Rowland, Beryl. "Chaucer's Blasphemous Churl: A New Interpretation of the *Miller's Tale*." In *Chaucer and Middle English Studies in Honor of Rossell Hope Robbins*, edited by Beryl Rowland, 43–55. London: Allen and Unwin, 1974.

Russell, Stephen J. *Chaucer and the Trivium: The Mindsong of the Canterbury Tales*. Gainesville: University of Florida Press, 1998.

– "Song and the Ineffable in the *Prioress's Tale*." *ChauR* 33, no. 2 (1998): 176–89.

Saiber, Arielle, and Aba Mbirika. "The three *giri* of *Paradiso* XXXIII." *Dante Studies* 131 (2013): 237–72.

Salter, Elizabeth. *Chaucer: The Knight's Tale and the Clerk's Tale*. London: E. Arnold, 1962.

Saraceni, Madeleine L. "Chaucer's Feminine Pretexts: Gendered Genres in Three Frame Moments." *ChauR* 51, no. 4 (2016): 403–35.

Sayce, Olive. "Chaucer's 'Retractions': The Conclusion of the *Canterbury Tales* and Its Place in Literary Tradition." *MÆ* 40, no. 3 (1971): 230–48.

Scala, Elizabeth. "Canacee and the Chaucer Canon: Incest and Other Unnarratables." *ChauR* 30, no. 1 (1995): 15–39.

– *Desire in the* Canterbury Tales. Columbus: Ohio State University Press, 2015.

– "Desire in the *Canterbury Tales*: Sovereignty and Mastery between the Wife and Clerk." *SAC* 31 (2009): 91–108.

– "Historicists and Their Discontents: Reading Psychoanalytically in Medieval Studies." *TSLL* 44, no. 1 (2000): 108–31.

– "The Women in Chaucer's 'Marriage Group.'" *Medieval Feminist Forum: A Journal of Gender and Sexuality* 45, no. 1 (2009): 50–6.

Scanlon, Larry. "The Authority of the Fable: Allegory and Irony in the *Nun's Priest's Tale*." *Exemplaria* 1, no. 1 (1989): 43–68.

– *Narrative, Authority, and Power: The Medieval Exemplum and the Chaucerian Tradition*. Cambridge: Cambridge University Press, 1994.

Scattergood, V.J. "Chaucer and the French War: *Sir Thopas* and *Melibee*." In *Court and Poet: Selected Proceedings of the Third Congress of the International Courtly Literature Society, Liverpool, 1980*, edited by Glyn S. Burgess et al., 287–96. Liverpool: Francis Cairns, 1981.

– "Chaucer in the Suburbs," in *Medieval Literature and Antiquities: Studies in Honour of Basil Cottle* (Cambridge: D.S. Brewer, 1987), 145–62.

– "The Manciple's Manner of Speaking." *Essays in Criticism* 24, no. 1 (1974): 124–46.

– "The Originality of the *Shipman's Tale*." *ChauR* 11, no. 3 (1977): 210–31.

Scheps, Walter. "Chaucer's Theseus and the *Knight's Tale*." *Leeds Studies in English* 9 (1977): 19–34.

Schibanoff, Susan. "Taking the Gold out of Egypt: The Art of Reading as a Woman." In *Gender and Reading: Essays on Readers, Texts and Contexts*, edited by Elizabeth Flynn and Patrocinio P. Schweickart, 83–110. Baltimore: Johns Hopkins University Press, 1986.

– "Worlds Apart: Orientalism, Feminism, and Heresy in Chaucer's *Man of Law's Tale*." *Exemplaria* 8, no. 1 (1996): 59–96.

Schlauch, Margaret. *Chaucer's Constance and Accused Queens*. New York: New York University Press, 1927.

Schneider, Paul Stephen. "'Taillynge Ynough': The Function of Money in the *Shipman's Tale*." *ChauR* 11, no. 3 (1977): 201–9.

Schrader, Richard J. "Chauntecleer, the Mermaid, and Daun Burnel." *ChauR* 4, no. 4 (1970): 284–90.

Schrock, Chad. "Neoplatonic Theodicy in Chaucer's 'Legend of Philomela.'" *SP* 108, no. 1 (2011): 27–43.

Schulenberg, Jane Tibbetts. "Saints' Lives as a Source for the History of Women, 500–1100." In *Medieval Women and the Sources of Medieval History*, edited by Joel T. Rosenthal, 300. Athens: University of Georgia Press, 1990.

Schwebel, Leah. "Redressing Griselda: Restoration through Translation in the *Clerk's Tale*." *ChauR* 47, no. 3 (2013): 274–99.

Schweitzer, Edward C. "Fate and Freedom in the *Knight's Tale*." *SAC* 3 (1981): 13–45.

Scott, William O. "Chaucer, Shakespeare, and the Paradoxes of Dream and Fable." *CEA Critic* 49, nos. 2/4 (1986–7): 25–32.

Seal, Samatha Katz. *Father Chaucer: Generating Authority in the* Canterbury Tales. Oxford: Oxford University Press, 2019.

– "Pregnant Desire: Eyes and Appetites in the *Merchant's Tale*." *ChauR* 48, no. 3 (2014): 284–306.

– "Reading Like a Jew: Chaucer's *Physician's Tale* and the Letter of the Law." *ChauR* 52, no. 3 (2017): 298–317.

Seaman, David M. "'The Wordes of the Frankelyn to the Squier': An Interruption?" *ELN* 24 (1986): 12–18.

Sebastian, John T. "Chaucer and the Theory Wars: Attack of the Historicists? The Psychoanalysts Strike Back? Or a New Hope?" *Literature Compass* 3, no.4 (2006): 767–77.

Sedgewick, G.G. "The Structure of the *Merchant's Tale*." *UTQ* 17, no. 4 (1948): 337–45.

Severs, Jonathan Burke. "Is the *Manciple's Tale* a Success?" *JEGP* 51, no. 1 (1952): 1–16.

– *The Literary Relationship of Chaucer's Clerkes Tale*. Yale Studies in English 96. New Haven, CT: Yale University Press, 1942.

Sharma, Manish. "Chaucer, Kant, and Continental Materialism." *diacritics* 45, no. 2 (2017): 54–83.

Sherman, Mark A. "The Politics of Discourse in the *Knight's Tale*." *Exemplaria* 6, no. 1 (1994): 87–114.

Shimomura, Sachi. "The Walking Dead in Chaucer's *Knight's Tale*." *ChauR* 48, no. 1 (2013): 1–37.

Shoaf, R. Allen. *Dante, Chaucer, and the Currency of the Word*. Norman, OK: Pilgrim, 1983.

Sidhu, Nicole Nolan. "'To Late for to Crie': Female Desire, Fabliau Politics, and Classical Legend in Chaucer's Reeve's Tale." *Exemplaria* 21, no. 1 (2009): 3–23.

Silverman, Albert H. "Sex and Money in Chaucer's *Shipman's Tale*." *PQ* 32, no. 3 (1953): 329–36.

Simmons-O'Neill, Elizabeth. "Love in Hell: The Role of Pluto and Proserpina in Chaucer's *Merchant's Tale*." *MLQ* 51, no. 3 (1990): 389–407.

Simons, Rita Dandridge. "The Prioress's Disobedience of the Benedictine Rule." *CLA Journal* 12, no. 1 (1968): 77–83.

Simpson, James. "Religious Forms and Institutions in *Piers Plowman*." In *The Cambridge Companion to Piers Plowman*, edited by Andrew Cole and Andrew Galloway, 97–114. Cambridge: Cambridge University Press, 2014.

– *Sciences and the Self in Medieval Poetry: Alan of Lille's* Anticlaudianus *and John Gower's* Confessio Amantis. Cambridge Studies in Medieval Literature 25. Cambridge: Cambridge University Press, 1995.

Sisk, Jennifer L. "Religion, Alchemy, and Nostalgic Idealism in Fragment VIII of the *Canterbury Tales*." *SAC* 32 (2010): 151–77.

Skeat, Walter W., ed. *The Complete Works of Geoffrey Chaucer*, 2nd ed., 7 vols. Oxford: Clarendon Press, 1899.

Sleeth, Charles R. "'My Dames Loore' in the *Canterbury Tales*." *NM* 89, no. 2 (1988): 174–84.

Smith, Charles R. "Chaucer's Reeve and St. Paul's Old Man." *ChauR* 30, no. 1 (1995): 101–6.

Smith, D. Vance. "Death and Texts: Finitude Before Form." *Minnesota Review* 80 (2013): 131–44.

– "Medieval Forma: The Logic of the Work." In *Reading for Form*, edited by Susan J. Wolfson and Marshall Brown, 66–79. Seattle: University of Washington Press, 2006.

– "Plague, Panic Space, and the Tragic Medieval Household." *South Atlantic Quarterly* 98, no. 3 (1999): 367–414.

Smith, Warren S. "The Wife of Bath Debates Jerome." *ChauR* 32, no. 2 (1997): 129–45.

Spade, Paul V., trans. *William of Ockham: De insolubilibus*. Creative Commons Attribution, 2002.

– "Five Early Theories in the Mediaeval *Insolubilia*-Literature." *Vivarium* 25, no. 1 (1987): 24–46.

– "*Insolubilia* and Bradwardine's Theory of Signification." *Medioevo: Revista di storia della filosofia medievale* 7 (1981): 115–34.

Spade, Paul V., and Stephen Read. "Insolubles." In *The Stanford Encyclopedia of Philosophy*. Fall 2018 ed., edited by Edward N. Zalta. Accessed 1 November 2021. https://plato.stanford.edu/archives/fall2018/entries/insolubles/.

Spearing, A.C. *The Franklin's Prologue and Tale*, 2nd ed. Cambridge: Cambridge University Press, 1994.

– *The Medieval Poet as Voyeur: Looking and Listening in Medieval Love-Narratives.* Cambridge: Cambridge University Press, 1993.

– *Medieval to Renaissance in English Poetry.* Cambridge: Cambridge University Press, 1985.

– "Narrative Voice: The Case of Chaucer's *Man of Law's Tale.*" *New Literary History* 32, no. 3 (2001): 715–46.

Spector, Stephen. "Enmity and Empathy in the *Prioress's Tale.*" In *The Olde Daunce: Love, Friendship, Sex, and Marriage in the Medieval World*, edited by Robert R. Edwards and Stephen Spector, 211–28. Albany: State University of New York Press, 1991.

Spies, Heinrich. "Chaucers Retractio." In *Festschrift Adolf Tobler*, 383–94. Braunschweig: Berliner Gesellschaft für das Studium Neueren Sprachen, 1905.

Staley, Lynn. "Gower, Richard II, Henry of Derby, and the Business of Making Culture." *Speculum* 75, no. 1 (2000): 68–96.

Stein, Robert M. "The Conquest of Femeneye: Desire, Power, and Narrative in Chaucer's *Knight's Tale.*" In *Desiring Discourse: The Literature of Love, Ovid Through Chaucer*, edited by James J. Paxson and Cynthia A. Gravlee, 188–205. London: Associated University Presses, 1998.

Steiner, Emily. "Authority." In *Middle English*, edited by Paul Strohm, 142–59. Oxford: Oxford University Press, 2007.

Steinmetz, David C. "Late Medieval Nominalism and the *Clerk's Tale.*" *ChauR* 12, no. 1 (1977): 38–54.

Stepsis, Robert. "*Potentia Absoluta* and the *Clerk's Tale.*" *ChauR* 10, no. 2 (1975): 129–46.

Stevens, Martin. "'And Venus Laugheth,': An Interpretation of the *Merchant's Tale.*" *ChauR* 7, no. 2 (1972): 118–31.

Stevens, Martin, and Kathleen Falvey. "Substance, Accident, and Transformations: A Reading of the *Pardoner's Tale.*" *ChauR* 17, no. 2 (1982): 142–58.

Stock, Brian. *Augustine the Reader: Meditation, Self-Knowledge, and the Ethics of Interpretation.* Cambridge, MA: Harvard University Press, 1996.

Stock, Lorraine Kochanske. "The Meaning of *Chevyssaunce*: Complicated Word Play in Chaucer's Shipman's Tale." *Studies in Short Fiction* 18, no. 3 (1981): 245–9.

Stockton, Will. "Cynicism and the Anal Erotics of Chaucer's Pardoner." *Exemplaria* 20, no. 2 (2008): 143–64.

Storm, Melvin. "The Pardoner's Invitation: Quaestor's Bag or Becket's Shrine?" *PMLA* 97, no. 5 (1982): 810–18.

– "Speech, Circumspection, and Orthodontics in the *Manciple's Tale* and the Wife of Bath's Portrait." *SP* 96, no. 2 (1999): 109–26.

Strange, William C. "The *Monk's Tale*: A Generous View." *ChauR* 1, no. 3 (1967): 167–80.

Straus, Barrie Ruth. "The Subversive Discourse of the Wife of Bath: Phallocentric Criticism and the Imprisonment of Criticism." *ELH* 55, no. 3 (1988): 527–54.

Stretter, Robert. "Rewriting Perfect Friendship in Chaucer's *Knight's Tale* and Lydgate's *Fabula Duorum Mercatorum*." *ChauR* 37, no. 3 (2003): 234–52.

Striar, Brian. "The *Manciple's Tale* and Chaucer's Apolline Poetics." *Criticism* 33, no. 2 (1991): 173–204.

Strohm, Paul. "Form and Social Statement in *Confessio Amantis* and the *Canterbury Tales*." *SAC* 1 (1979): 17–40.

– *Social Chaucer*. Cambridge, MA: Harvard University Press, 1989.

Stubbs, Estelle, and Linne R. Mooney. *Scribes and the City: London Guildhall Clerks and the Dissemination of Middle English Literature 1375–1423*. Woodbridge: Boydell and Brewer, 2013.

Stump, Eleanore. *Aquinas*. London and New York: Routledge, 2003.

Sturges, Robert S. *Chaucer's Pardoner and Gender Theory: Bodies of Discourse*. New York: St. Martin's Press, 2000.

Summit, Jennifer. "History as Topography: Petrarch, Chaucer, and the Making of Medieval Rome." *JMEMS* 30 (2000): 211–46.

Szittya, Penn R. "The Friar as False Apostle: Antifraternal Exegesis and the *Summoner's Tale*." *SP* 71, no. 1 (1974): 19–46.

Tatlock, J.S.P. "Chaucer's *Merchant's Tale*." *MP* 33, no. 4 (1936): 367–81.

Taylor, Gary. "'Greyn' and the Resuscitation of the Little Clergeon." *SFQ* 34 (1970): 82–9.

Taylor, Joseph. "Chaucer's Uncanny Regionalism: Rereading the North in the *Reeve's Tale*." *JEGP* 109, no. 4 (2010): 468–89.

Taylor, Karla. "Social Aesthetics and the Emergence of Civic Discourse from the *Shipman's Tale* to *Melibee*." *ChauR* 39, no. 3 (2005): 298–322.

Taylor, Paul Beekman. "Chaucer's *Cosyn to the Dede*." *Speculum* 57, no. 2 (1982): 315–27.

– "The Parson's Amyable Tongue." *ES* 64, no. 5 (1983): 401–9.

Ten Brink, Bernhard. *History of English Literature*. Translated by W.C. Robinson. New York: H. Holt, 1893.

Thom, Paul. *The Logic of the Trinity: Augustine to Ockham*, 19–41. New York: Fordham University Press, 2012.

Thomas, Susanne Sara. "The Problem of Defining *Sovereyneytee* in the *Wife of Bath's Tale*." *ChauR* 41, no. 1 (2006): 87–97.

Tinkle, Theresa. "Contested Authority: Jerome and the Wife of Bath on 1 Timothy 2." *ChauR* 44, no. 3 (2010): 268–93.

– "The Wife of Bath's Marginal Authority." *SAC* 32 (2010): 67–101.

Tolkien, J.R.R. "Chaucer as a Philologist: The Reeve's Tale." *Transactions of the Royal Philological Society* (1934): 1–70.

Tomasch, Sylvia. "Judecca, Dante's Satan, and the *Dis*-placed Jew." In *Text and Territory: Geographical Imagination in the European Middle Ages*, edited by Sylvia Tomasch and Sealy Gilles, 247–67. Philadelphia: University of Pennsylvania Press, 1998.

– "Postcolonial Chaucer and the Virtual Jew." In *The Postcolonial Middle Ages*, edited by Jeffrey Jerome Cohen, 243–60. New York: Palgrave, 2000.

Trask, Richard M. "The Manciple's Problem." *Studies in Short Fiction* 14, no. 2 (1977): 109–16.

Travis, Peter W. "Chaucer's Trivial Fox Chase and the Peasant's Revolt of 1381." *Journal of Medieval and Renaissance Studies* 18 (1988): 195–220.

– "Deconstructing Chaucer's *Retraction*." *Exemplaria* 3, no. 1 (1991): 135–58.

– *Disseminal Chaucer: Rereading the Nun's Priest's Tale*. Notre Dame, IN: Notre Dame University Press, 2010.

– "The Manciple's Phallic Matrix." *SAC* 25 (2003): 317–24.

Trigg, Stephanie. *Congenial Souls: Reading Chaucer from Medieval to Postmodern*. Minneapolis: University of Minnesota Press, 2002.

– "Friendship, Association, and Service in the *Manciple's Tale*." *SAC* 25 (2003): 325–30.

Tripp, Raymond P., Jr. "The Darker Side to Absolon's Dawn Visit." *ChauR* 20, no. 3 (1986): 207–12.

Turner, Joseph. "Rhetoric and Performing Anger: Proserpina's Gift and Chaucer's *Merchant's Tale*." *Rhetorica* 34, no. 4 (2016): 427–54.

– "Speaking 'Amys' in the *Franklin's Tale*: Rhetoric, Truth and the Poetria Nova." *ChauR* 52, no. 2 (2017): 217–36.

Turner, Marion. *Chaucerian Conflict: Languages of Antagonism in Late Fourteenth-Century London*. Oxford: Oxford University Press, 2007.

Twombly, Robert G. "The *Pardoner's Tale* and Dominican Meditation." *ChauR* 36, no. 3 (2002): 250–69.

Twu, Krista Sue-Lo. "Chaucer's Vision of the Tree of Life: Crossing the Road with the Rood in the *Parson's Tale*." *ChauR* 39, no. 4 (2005): 341–78.

Usk, Thomas. *The Testament of Love*. Edited by R. Allen Shoaf, TEAMS Middle English Texts Series. Kalamazoo, MI: Medieval Institute Publications, 1998.

Utz, Richard, ed. *Literary Nominalism and the Theory of Rereading Late Medieval Texts: A New Research Paradigm*. Lewiston, NY: Edwin Mellen Press, 1995.

Van, Thomas A. "False Texts and Disappearing Women in the *Wife of Bath's Prologue* and *Tale*." *ChauR* 29, no. 2 (1994): 179–93.

Van Dyke, Carolynn. "The Clerk's and the Franklin's Subjected Subjects," *SAC* 17 (1995): 45–68.

Vance, Eugene. "Chaucer's Pardoner: Relics, Discourse, and Frames of Propriety." *New Literary History* 20, no. 3 (1989): 723–45.

Vasta, Edward. "How Chaucer's Reeve Succeeds." *Criticism* 25, no. 1 (1983): 1–12.

Vaughan, Míceál F. "Personal Politics and Thomas Gascoigne's Account of the Chaucer's Death." *MÆ* 75, no. 1 (2006): 103–22.

Wallace, David. *Chaucerian Polity: Absolutist Lineages and Associational Forms in England and Italy*. Stanford, CA: Stanford University Press, 1997.

– "In Flaundres." *SAC* 19 (1997): 63–91.

Walling, Amanda. "Placebo Effects: Flattery and Antifeminism in the *Merchant's Tale* and the *Tale of Melibee*." *SP* 115, no. 1 (2018): 1–24.

Walls, Kathryn. "Absolon as Barber-Surgeon." *ChauR* 35, no. 4 (2001): 391–8.

Warner, Lawrence. *Chaucer's Scribes: London Textual Production, 1384–1432*. Cambridge: Cambridge University Press, 2018.

– "Woman is Man's Babylon: Chaucer's 'Nembrot' and the Tyranny of Enclosure in the *Nun's Priest's Tale*." *ChauR* 32, no. 1 (1997): 82–107.

Waterhouse, Ruth, and Gwen Griffiths. "'Sweete Wordes' of Non-Sense: The Deconstruction of the Moral *Melibee*." Part I in *ChauR* 23, no. 4 (1989): 338–61; Part II in *ChauR* 24, no. 1 (1989): 53–63.

Waters, Claire M. "Holy Duplicity: The Preacher's Two Faces." *SAC* 24 (2002): 75–113.

Watson, Nicholas. "Censorship and Cultural Change in Late-Medieval England: Vernacular Theology, the Oxford Translation Debate, and Arundel's *Constitutions* of 1409." *Speculum* 70, no. 4 (1995): 822–64.

– "Conceptions of the Word: The Mother Tongue and the Incarnation of God." In *New Medieval Literatures*, edited by Wendy Scase, Rita Copeland, and David Lawton, 85–124. Oxford: Clarendon, 1997.

Watt, Diane. *Amoral Gower: Language, Sex, and Politics*. Minneapolis: University of Minnesota Press, 2003.

Watts, William H. "Chaucer's Clerks and the Value of Philosophy." In *Nominalism and Literary Discourse*, edited by Hugo Keiper, Christoph Bode, and Richard J. Utz, 145–55. Amsterdam, Netherlands: Rodopi, 1997.

Weele, Michael Vander, and Deb Powell. "'Fruyt' and 'Chaf' Revisited, or What's Cooking in Chaucer's Kitchen?" *CEA Critic* 57, no. 3 (1995): 39–50.

Weisl, Angela Jane. *Conquering the Reign of Femenye: Gender and Genre in Chaucer's Romance*. Cambridge: D.S. Brewer, 1995.

Wentersdorf, Karl. "Imagery, Structure, and Theme in Chaucer's *Merchant's Tale*." In *Chaucer and the Craft of Fiction*, edited by Leigh A. Arrathoon, 35–62. Rochester, MI: Solaris Press, 1986.

– "Theme and Structure in the *Merchant's Tale*: The Function of the Pluto Episode." *PMLA* 80, no. 5 (1965): 522–7.

Wenzel, Siegfried. "Notes on the *Parson's Tale*." *ChauR* 16, no. 3 (1982): 237–56.

– "The *Parson's Tale* in Current Literary Studies." In *Closure in the* Canterbury Tales: *The Role of the* Parson's Tale, edited by David Raybin and Linda Tarte Holley, 1–10. Kalamazoo, MI: Medieval Institute Publications, 2000.

– "The Source for the 'Remedia' of the *Parson's Tale*." *Traditio* 27 (1971): 433–53.

– "The Source of Chaucer's Seven Deadly Sins." *Traditio* 30 (1974): 351–78.

Wetherbee, Winthrop. *Chaucer and the Poets: An Essay on* Troilus and Criseyde, 224–44. Ithaca, NY: Cornell University Press, 1984.

Wheeler, Bonnie. "Dante, Chaucer, and the Ending of *Troilus and Criseyde*." *PQ* 61, no. 2 (1982): 105–23.

– *Representations of the Feminine in the Middle Ages*. Dallas: Academia Press, 1993.

Whitney, Elspeth. "What's Wrong with the Pardoner? Complexion Theory, the Phlegmatic Man, and Effeminacy." *ChauR* 45, no. 4 (2011): 357–89.

Williams, David. "Radical Therapy in the *Miller's Tale*." *ChauR* 15, no. 3 (1981): 227–35.

Williams, Tara. "'T'assaye in thee thy wommanheede': Griselda Chosen, Translated, and Tried." *SAC* 27 (2005): 93–127.

Wilsbacher, Greg. "Lumiansky's Paradox: Ethics, Aesthetics and Chaucer's *Prioress's Tale*." *College Literature* 32, no. 4 (2005): 1–28.

Wimsatt, James I. "John Duns Scotus, Charles Sanders Peirce, and Chaucer's Portrayal of the Canterbury Pilgrims." *Speculum* 71, no. 3 (1996): 633–45.

Windeatt, Barry. *Troilus and Criseyde*. Oxford Guides to Chaucer. Oxford: Oxford University Press, 1995.

Winnick, R.H. "Luke 12 and Chaucer's *Shipman's Tale*." *ChauR* 30, no. 2 (1995): 164–90.

Winstead, Karen A. "Chaucer's *Parson's Tale* and the Contours of Orthodoxy." *ChauR* 43, no. 3 (2009): 239–59.

– *Virgin Martyrs: Legends of Sainthood in Late Medieval England*. Ithaca, NY: Cornell University Press, 1997.

Wogan-Brown, Jocelyn, Nicholas Watson, Andrew Taylor, and Ruth Evans, eds. *The Idea of the Vernacular*. University Park: Pennsylvania State University Press, 1999.

Wolfe, Matthew C. "Placing Chaucer's *Retraction* for a Reception of Closure." *ChauR* 33, no. 4 (1999): 427–31.

Woods, William F. "Private and Public Space in the *Miller's Tale*." *ChauR* 29, no. 2 (1994): 166–78.

Wurtele, Douglas. "Chaucer's Franklin and the Truth about 'Trouthe.'" *English Studies in Canada* 13 (1987): 359–74.

– "The Penitence of Geoffrey Chaucer." *Viator* 11 (1980): 335–60.

Yager, Susan. "'A Whit Thyng in Hir Ye': Perception and Error in the *Reeve's Tale*." *ChauR* 28, no. 4 (1994): 393–404.

Yamamoto, Dorothy. "Noon Oother Incubus but He: Lines 878–81 in the Wife of Bath's Tale." *ChauR* 28, no. 3 (1994): 275–78.

Yeager, R.F. "*Pax Poetica*: On the Pacifism of Chaucer and Gower." *SAC* 9 (1987): 97–121.

Yeager, Stephen. "Chaucer's Prudent Poetics: Allegory, the *Tale of Melibee*, and the Frame Narrative to the *Canterbury Tales*." *ChauR* 48, no. 3 (2014): 307–21.

Young, Karl. "The Maidenly Virtues of Chaucer's Virginia." *Speculum* 16, no. 3 (1941): 340–9.

Yunck, John A. "Religious Elements in Chaucer's *Man of Law's Tale*." *ELH* 27, no. 4 (1960): 249–61.

Zedolik, John. "'The Gardyn is Enclosed Al Aboute': The Inversion of Exclusivity in the *Merchant's Tale*." *SP* 112, no. 2 (2015): 490–503.

Zeeman, Nicolette. "The Gender of Song in Chaucer." *SAC* 29 (2007): 141–82.

Zieman, Katherine. "Chaucer's Voys." *Representations* 60 (1997): 70–91.

Ziolkowski, Jan M. "The Humour of Logic and the Logic of Humour in the Twelfth-Century Renaissance." *Journal of Medieval Latin* 3 (1993): 1–26.

Zitter, Emily Stark. "Anti-Semitism in Chaucer's *Prioress's Tale*." *ChauR* 25, no. 4 (1991): 277–84.

Index

God's divine, 55; judgment and,
12–14; logic of, 20, 29, 62, 98, 181,
264; marriage and, 60; maternal,
160; (non)-synthesis of formalism
and materialism, 17; as ordering
principle, 66–7; Theseus's formal
conception of, 68; undecidable,
60–1; war and, 69, 77
love as paradox, 3
Lowe, John Livingston, 195
Lucas, Angela, 53
Luke, 218
Lynch, Kathryn, 11, 12, 142

McCall, John, 145
McEntire, Sandra, 58
McGerr, Rosemarie P., 6
McKinley, Kathryn, 132
McNamara, John, 149
Macrobius, 6
Malyne, 93–8, 100, 102, 169, 288n66
The Manciple, 30, 225, 234,
240–53, 263
The Manciple's Prologue (Chaucer),
240, 243, 321n45
The Manciple's Tale (Chaucer), 235,
240, 242–8, 250–3, 255, 257, 271n19,
279n42, 321n43, 321n45, 322n54
Mandel, Jerome, 162, 212
Mann, Jill, 13, 119, 151
The Man of Law, 99, 100–17, 123,
126, 140–1, 148, 155, 169, 174, 194,
196, 266
The Man of Law's Introduction
(Chaucer), 100–5, 116, 127, 140;
theme of, 100–1
The Man of Law's Prologue (Chaucer),
104–5
The Man of Law's Tale (Chaucer),
102–10, 112–15, 149, 196, 229, 259,
290nn13–14, 291n33
Marenbon, John, 5

marital fidelity, illusion of, 59
marital love, formal conception of, 55
Mark, 218
marriage, 123–4, 126, 132; adultery,
192; Emelye and Palamon, 67; love
and, 60; marital sex, 186, 190–1;
Walter and Griselda, 144–5
Marriage at Cana, 133
Mars, 67, 68–9, 74, 120, 264; temple
of, 69; Venus and, 71–2
Martianus Capella, 155
martyr, 203–4, 207, 226, 232, 235
martyrdom, 201, 210–11, 227–30,
318n18
Mary, 115–16, 160, 196, 198–201,
206–11, 219, 226, 234, 244, 301n74,
310n53
masculine, 36, 86, 98, 113, 115, 118,
128, 223; *auctoritas*, 116; authority,
100, 111, 117, 121, 131, 152; desire,
84, 133; domination, 119; fashion,
59; final cause, 111; form, 63, 73,
75, 105, 109, 116, 150, 156, 179,
181, 245; formalism, 41; identity,
285n40; love, 63; order, 73, 75;
position, 120, 286n47; power,
116; prose, 235; purpose, 72;
purposefulness, 227
mastery, 17, 47, 58–60, 80, 87, 127–8,
130–2, 146, 163, 165, 195–6, 220,
246; absolute, 82, 196; abusive,
105; Christian doctrine, 233;
formal, 81, 83–4, 105; formalism,
144; judgmental, 262, 266; marital,
134; matrimonial, 126; physical,
82; problem of, 142; submission
and, 143; unilateral of God, 169;
vengeance and, 124, 134, 161
materialism, 41, 46, 51, 60;
anarchic, 253; author's control,
98; capitulation, 129; chance, 65;
churlish, 88; Cook's, 98; deceptive,

70, 75; rebellion against rational, 74–5; social, 72, 79; of things, 87; truth and, 27; universe, 26
Organon (Aristotle), 9
Orpheus, 155
Oswald, 29, 79, 90, 92, 94, 95
otherworld/otherworldly, 15, 209–10, 235
Ovid, 101, 103, 127–30, 163, 244, 252
Oxford, 6, 9–11, 41

pagan, 228–9, 232, 235, 316n103; authority, 227; characters, 109; illusion, 51, 52, 53, 55, 59, 62; lore, 51; teaching, 52; women, 101, 103
Palamon, 67–8, 75–6, 77, 82, 96
Paradiso (Dante), 29, 264–5, 266
paradox, 28, 112, 144, 264; of chivalry, 64; Liar, 9–12, 14, 16, 39, 88, 175, 184, 266; love as, 3, 14, 19, 60, 206, 216
The Pardoner, 14, 17, 20, 65, 119–20, 122, 161, 169–77, 179–84, 189, 194, 255
The Pardoner's Introduction (Chaucer), 169
The Pardoner's Prologue (Chaucer), 169–70, 172–4, 176, 305n60
The Pardoner's Tale (Chaucer), 168, 177, 181, 183–4, 189, 302n19
Paris, 155
The Parliament of Fowls (Chaucer), 103
The Parson, 30, 129, 158, 225, 235–6, 243, 253–63, 266
Parson's prologue, 225, 234–5, 253–9
The Parson's Tale (Chaucer), 149, 217, 253–8, 260–3, 323n59, 324n65, 324–5n67
participation, 23–4, 266
particular, 13, 23; material, 44
particularity, 4, 17, 19, 145

passion/*passio*, 76, 82, 214–15, 218, 224, 230, 265
paternal, 62, 110, 165, 180, 199–200
patriarchy/patriarchal, 110, 118, 121, 131, 133, 135, 292n38
Patterson, Lee, 64, 65, 76, 78, 89, 119, 128, 156–7, 166–7, 171, 187, 196, 199–200, 218, 229, 233, 243, 254, 307n7, 313n79
Paul, 172–6, 180, 255, 261, 263
Pauline doctrine, 202
Pearsall, Derek, 33, 176
peasant revolt, 34
Peasant's Revolt, 32
peccatorum miserere, 205
pedagogy, 231, 233, 238. See also teaching
Pelen, Marc M., 4
penance/penitential, 102, 110, 113, 178, 188, 241, 243, 256–7, 260, 262, 294n57, 324n65, 325n71
penitence, 253, 255–8, 260, 324n65, 325n67
Pennaforte, Raymund, 256, 260
Pentecost, 140
Peraldus, William, 256
Perkyn Revelour, 98
Pertelote, 36, 41–5
Petrarch, 140–51, 153, 174, 266, 297n33
phallic *jouissance*, 62, 63
Phebus, 52, 235, 243–52, 321n43, 321n45
philia, 21
Philology, 155
Philo of Alexandria, 5
philosopher's stone, 229, 236, 239
Philosophical Chaucer (Miller), 19
philosophy, 17, 141–2, 234, 236, 237, 239; alchemical, 30, 225, 231, 235, 236, 237–8, 240, 320n32; contemplation of, 18; formalist,

84; Kant, 274n64; of language,
10; law and, 141; Man of Law's,
109; materialist, 239; moral, 6;
naturalistic, 288n68; Plato, 46;
poetry and, 141; prose and, 225;
secular, 235, 238, 239, 251, 253;
unauthorized, 30, 225, 239–40, 243,
250. See also nominalism; realism

Phoebus, 52

The Physician, 161–9, 194, 196

The Physician's Tale (Chaucer), 20,
161–3, 165, 167–9, 196, 302n21

Physics (Aristotle), 17

Pierian Muses, 103

Pierides, 103–5, 113, 141

Piers Plowman (Langland), 15, 22, 23

pilgrimage, 19, 24, 80, 170,
254, 321n43, 324n65, 325n71;
Canterbury, 124, 133, 172, 194, 230,
241, 260; social hierarchy of, 79,
86, 90

Pinkhurst, Adam, 98

Plato, 4, 5, 6, 7, 46, 145, 235, 236, 237,
239, 247–51

Platonism, 4, 8, 251; Christianized, 23

play, 57–8, 121, 122; fantasy, 135;
playful, 182–3

pleasure, 30, 82–3, 128, 142, 209,
227, 235; carnal, 177; feminine,
46; husband and wife, 185–7, 191;
sexual, 96, 113

Plotinus, 5

Pluto, 104–5, 109, 116, 155–7, 159,
300n60

Poetria nova (Geoffrey of Vinsauf), 32

poetry, 4–6, 17, 196, 214, 220, 225,
234–6, 238–40, 248, 255, 263,
321n43, 325n45; authorized,
30; Chaucer's, 4, 11, 39, 46, 102,
276–7n23, 319–20n32, 325n71;
Christian, 234, 253, 321n45;
competition, 104; Dante's, 266;

hagiographical, 30; kinds of,
278–9n42; philosophy and, 141–2;
rejection of, 323n59; secular, 235,
238, 243–4, 251–3; unauthorized,
30, 240, 251, 257

political absolutism, 144

politics, 60, 70, 144

pollution, 197, 198, 226

polysemy, 34

potentia absoluta (absolute power),
8, 143

potentia ordinata (ordained power), 8

preaching, 90, 120, 172, 174–5,
287n53, 287n57

predestination, 36, 42, 54, 74–5, 84,
200, 202, 223–4, 265

predetermination/predetermined, 8,
35, 222, 256

Preface to Chaucer (Robertson), 18

prescience, 11, 35, 73, 77, 79

Price, Merrall Llewelyn, 196

primum mobile, 106, 110

principalis, 10

The Prioress, 16, 29, 44, 112, 185,
193–215, 220, 223–4, 228, 259,
264, 266

The Prioress's Prologue (Chaucer),
193, 209–10, 311n59

The Prioress's Tale (Chaucer), 185,
193–4, 196–7, 199–201, 203–9,
211–13, 215, 219–20, 258, 310n48,
312n68

The Prologue of Sir Thopas (Chaucer),
208, 209

Prologue to *The Monk's Tale*
(Chaucer), 220

Prose Lancelot, 40

Proserpina, 104–5, 109, 116, 155–7,
159–60, 300n60

prostitution, 188, 191

providence, 26, 55, 70, 76, 106, 108,
284n29, 290n13

Timaeus (Plato), 4
time keeping, 39
tragedy, 221, 265, 315n99, 316n103,
    316n107
transcendence, 14–15, 23–4, 78, 216,
    254, 261, 265
transcendental illusion, 20, 274n64
transcendent causality, 36
Travis, Peter, 31, 33, 34, 41, 252
treatise/*tretys*, 11, 15, 216–19, 224,
    230, 253, 256–62, 313n85, 314n89,
    324–5n67
Tree of Penance, 260
Trevet, Nicholas, 106, 111, 112,
    114, 115
trinity, 16, 177, 264–5, 326n81
Troilus and Criseyde (Chaucer), 11, 21,
    24, 102, 103, 264–5, 271–2n31
Troy, 32, 284n24; fall of, 32
truth, 10, 40, 50, 54, 59, 120;
    Christian, 51, 54, 59, 62; Christ's
    resurrection, 140; deception
    and, 59, 129, 135; divine, 4, 8, 62,
    227, 229; falsity and, 9, 11, 39,
    41, 130, 184; fiction and, 11–12,
    40, 51, 121, 243; formal, 54, 59,
    66, 250–1; intentional, 135; lying
    and, 11–12, 159–60; order and,
    27; Platonic, 248; play and, 97,
    121; poetry and, 11; spiritual, 19,
    34, 187
Turner, Joseph, 50
Tyrwhitt, Thomas, 230

unauthorized discourse, 257
unauthorized doctrine, 231, 238
unauthorized enjoyment, feminine
    jouissance, 63
unauthorized philosophy, 225,
    239–40, 243, 250
unauthorized poetry, 30, 239, 240,
    251, 257

undecidability, 12, 14, 20, 29, 46–7,
    51, 57, 77, 87–9, 146, 150–1, 182,
    195, 204, 278n38; of charity, 204;
    Chaucerian, 29, 46; conception of,
    278n38; of Knight's tale, 77, 87–8;
    of Liar paradox, 12; of love, 20, 29,
    146, 195; of *Reeve's Tale*, 89
undecidable, 17–18, 21, 24, 38, 41,
    44, 47, 49–51, 59–60, 62, 65, 76–7,
    81, 88, 104, 120, 126, 131–3, 140,
    142–3, 149–51, 153, 157, 173,
    175, 183, 190, 194, 201–2, 214,
    267, 278n38; logic of love, 181;
    structure, 218–19, 222, 260
unequivocal, 24, 51, 57–8, 255
unity, 21, 144, 230, 279n50
universal(s), 7, 23; form, 44, 266
universality, 13, 17, 145
univocal, 33–4, 39, 51, 57–8, 62, 120,
    147, 168, 221, 225
univocality, 33, 224, 248
Urban (Pope), 228–9, 231–2

Valerian, 227–9, 231–2, 238
Van, Thomas A., 119
vanity, 36, 43, 77, 321n43
vengeance, 68, 90–1, 95–6, 107, 115,
    123–6, 134, 137, 139–40, 161, 168,
    204, 214–15, 217–18, 220
Venus, 25, 26, 67–9, 71–2, 74, 120, 155
vernacular, 14–15, 24, 273n46, 285n33
vetus homo, 176, 177, 304n39
vice, 165–6, 242, 258, 325n70
Vinsauf, Geoffrey of, 32
Virgil, 195
Virginia, 162–9, 177, 196, 302nn19–20
virginity, 95, 117, 151, 203
Virginius, 162–9, 301n9, 302n18
Virgin Mary, 115, 116, 160, 196, 198,
    199, 200, 201, 206, 207, 209, 210,
    211, 226, 234, 244
Virgin Mother, 196